...TSTONE

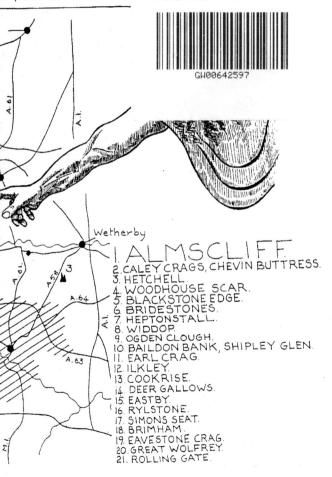

Wetherby

1. ALMSCLIFF.
2. CALEY CRAGS, CHEVIN BUTTRESS.
3. HETCHELL.
4. WOODHOUSE SCAR.
5. BLACKSTONE EDGE.
6. BRIDESTONES.
7. HEPTONSTALL.
8. WIDDOP.
9. OGDEN CLOUGH.
10. BAILDON BANK, SHIPLEY GLEN.
11. EARL CRAG.
12. ILKLEY.
13. COOKRISE.
14. DEER GALLOWS.
15. EASTBY.
16. RYLSTONE.
17. SIMONS SEAT.
18. BRIMHAM.
19. EAVESTONE CRAG.
20. GREAT WOLFREY.
21. ROLLING GATE.

YORKSHIRE GRITSTONE

The Millennium Edition

Compiled, Revised and Edited by

DAVE MUSGROVE

On behalf of the Yorkshire Mountaineering Club

Illustrations and Art Work by Nigel Baker

Other contributory assistance for this volume received from:

John Aylward
Tony Beard
Mike Bebbington
John Belbin
Steve Bostock
Pete Brown
Dave Burnett
Paul Clarke
Steve Coates
Robin Costello
John Dunne
Frank Fitzgerald
Paul Kitchingman

Derek Hargreaves
Bob Larkin
Tony Marr
Brian Middleton
David Musgrove Jnr.
Phillipe Osborne
Mark Radtke
Dave Sarkar
Brian Swales
Bill Todd
Ken Tilford
Chas Ward
Chris Wilson

GUIDEBOOK BIBLIOGRAPHY

1913 **Some Gritstone Climbs**   John Laycock

1923 **Recent Developments**   Fergus Graham

1951 **Kinder and Northern Areas**   Allan Allsopp

1957 **West Yorkshire Area**   Allan Allsopp and Brian Evans

1965 **New Climbs, West Yorkshire Area**   Allan Austin for Y.M.C.

1969 **Yorkshire Gritstone**   Mike Bebbington for the Y.M.C.
      A Rock Climber's Guide

1974 *Re-print with addenda*

1982 **Yorkshire Gritstone**   Eddie Lesniak for the Y.M.C.
      A Rock Climber's Guide

1987 **Yorkshire Limestone**   Graham Desroy for the Y.M.C.
      + Gritstone Supplement

1989 **Yorkshire Gritstone**   Graham Desroy for the Y.M.C.
      Abridged Version In Lycra

1993 **Bouldering on Yorkshire Gritstone**   Steve Rhodes

1994 **The Yorkshire Supplement**   Dave Musgrove for the Y.M.C.

1997 **Wild Bouldering in Yorkshire**   Tony Barley + Nigel Baker

1998 **Yorkshire Gritstone**   Dave Musgrove for the Y.M.C.
      The Millennium edition

Printed by Joseph Ward Colourprint Ltd, Churwell Vale, Shawcross
Business Park, Dewsbury, West Yorkshire WF12 7RD.

Distributed by Cordee, 3a, DeMontfort Street, Leicester LE1 7HD

ISBN 0 9515267 3 1

CONTENTS

PHOTOGRAPHS

Black & White photos

INTRODUCTION

Believe it or not it is now 9 years since the last Yorkshire Gritstone guide was published. That edition conceived, designed and edited by Graham Desroy set a standard for definitive British climbing guides that has been much copied, but never bettered, in the intervening years. There was so much good work and relevant information in that volume that this book set out to be simply a revision and an update. That was three years ago.

Once the work started it emerged that so many new climbs had been done, and were still being found as the publication deadline approached (despite the appalling summer of 1998), that some crags would need a complete re-write. In the end most have been thoroughly revised and re-checked, some by several parties, in an effort to track down and eradicate that elusive creature *Tykus Sandbagii*. It is hoped that the population is now in serious decline.

Six new crags have been added to the main section and 17 to the minor crags section which seems incredible when one considers that Gritstone climbing has flourished in Yorkshire for over one hundred years. Over 1200 new climbs have been documented since 1989. That the new climbs recorded are evenly spread across the grade range is also an indication that the area is far from stagnation and the prospects for further development are bright.

A few crags, such as Shipley Glen, remain much the same as the development there has all been directed towards pure bouldering, which is now catered for in minute detail in other publications. Some of the most significant new boulder problems, and some new bouldering crags not catered for elsewhere, have been included for the sake of completeness and more particularly because some climbers took the time to record their efforts. For those of you who didn't - and feel aggrieved - its tough!

For a long time I was sure that we would need to split the book into two volumes but after much discussion and scientific market research (on the crag, at the wall and down the pub!) the consensus from you was that one book was best. Well, you knew how heavy the last one was and I told you this would be even bigger. I just hope you've put in enough training to carry it to Simon's Seat and Rylstone! Don't say you weren't warned.

Dave Musgrove
October 1998

ACKNOWLEDGEMENTS

The main contributors to the production of this book are credited on the title page but a few, as always happens, brought extra enthusiasm to the task and made contributions that were so significant they deserve a special vote of thanks. Once again **Nigel Baker** has excelled with his drawing and virtually every diagram, map and plan is testimony to his artistic skill. **Tony Marr**, above all others has put in incredible efforts to re-write the whole of Brimham, Slipstones and Brown Beck Crags and assisted **Frank Fitzgerald** with Birk Gill and a revision of Rylstone. **Tony** and his team compiled and revised several graded lists and offered sensible advice on many general aspects of the guide. **John Belbin** revised and re-checked virtually every sub-extreme route on Robin Hood's Rocks, Eastby, Widdop and Earl Crag and provided the background research to enable a full write up of The Scout for the first time. **Brian Swales**, the guru of Crookrise, oversaw the scripts for all the Barden and Embsay Moor crags and **Mark Radtke** wrote up Hawkcliffe, and Sharhaw for the first time and revised Guisecliff and graded lists of the harder extremes at several other crags. At Caley **Paul Clarke** devised a new format for a tour of the crag taking in all the best boulders and classic micro-routes.

Several manuscripts for each crag were distributed to numerous parties of differing climbing abilities to try to get a more representative grading consensus as well as a general up-date and check on the relative positions of new routes. Of those who sent them back with significant amendments I would like to thank: **Pete Brown** and **Paul Kitchingman** (Almscliff), **Jon Aylward** (Chevin Buttress, Dovestone, Cat Crags), **Dave Burnett** (Brandrith), **Phillipe Osborne** (Brimham Outliers, Crookrise and grading corrections throughout), **Ken Tilford** (Eavestone), **Brian Middleton** (Heptonstall), **Dave Sarkar**, (Hetchell), **Mike Bebbington** (Horsehold Scout and Ilkley), **Tony Beard** (Mythem Steep), **Steve Coates** (Ogden Clough), **Steve Bostock** (Rolling Gate), **Bill Todd** and **Brian Swales** (Sharphaw), **Chris Wilson** (Woodhouse Scar), **Bob Larkin** (Lord's Seat), **Derek Hargreaves** (Earl and Scout Hut Crag), **Dave Musgrove Jnr.** (Great Wolfrey). **Chas Ward** Gilstead, **Philip Statham** (Honley Quarry), **Dave France** (Stainland), **Malcolm Townsley** (Blake Dean), **Daimon Beal** (Holmfirth). Don't blame the above alone however for any mistakes as lots of fingers got into the pie during the final phases and even I can't remember now who suggested many of the amendments.

Tony Barley and **Nigel Baker** allowed me a free hand to plagiarise and summarise their Wild Bouldering guide, to bring some new areas to a wider audience. **Nigel** and his wife **Stella**, **Andy Watts**, **Mike Bebbington**, **Graham Exley** and **Bernard Newman** undertook the bulk of the proof reading. My wife **Lyn** supported me in many ways during the production of this volume, not least as general secretary, proof reader, photo critic, but mostly by not complaining about my obsessive late night sessions on the word processor.

Robin Costello and **John Belbin**, as BMC area access officers deserve a special mention for their continuous efforts over many years in securing our continued use of many crags, in addition to checking and revising access notes within this manuscript.

I accrued a collection of several hundred photographs from dozens of photographers. Those whose pictures I used are credited in the captions. Those who let me have use of their collections but turned out unlucky, I'm sorry ......   I thank you all the same. Special thanks to **Adidas** for permission to use their professionally obtained shot of Savage Earth (Widdop Wall) on the front cover free of charge.

On the production side **Chris Wilson** represented the Y.M.C. Committee's interests and **Mike Bebbington** sorted out the financial administration with his usual expertise. Both gave me excellent support and encouragement. **Graham Exley** and his technical production team at Joseph Ward Colourprint, in particular **Roy Brunskill** and **Michael Woodhead**. once again proved they are the undisputed leaders in the guidebook printing industry and made my job a pleasure during the final stages.

Despite the extensive re-write, it must be acknowledged that the majority of the crag scripts are still based on material compiled by writers of earlier generations and I have tried to retain much of their humour, style and creative skill where it was possible. This book is a testament to all earlier contributors and editors stretching back to foundations laid ninety years ago when **John Laycock** produced the first guide chronicling events on Yorkshire crags.

Dave Musgrove
October 1998

ACCESS AND CONSERVATION
(PLEASE READ THIS BEFORE VISITING ANY CRAG!)

The crags documented within this guide are owned by a wide variety of interests. In some cases they are actually owned with a purpose of protecting public enjoyment of them, e.g. Ilkley (by Bradford City Council), or Brimham (by the National Trust).

In others, however, they are privately owned and climbing survives due to agreements reached after patient discussions with a sizeable helping of goodwill on both sides. While official access and/or management agreements do exist on some sites, the access arrangements operating at many locations are often unofficial or informal, and an aggrieved landowner could withdraw goodwill at any time.

As a general rule, it should be remembered that climbers do not have a God-given right to climb where they please, or behave however they like. The public do have a legal right to walk on public rights of way marked on OS maps, which often stretch along the top or bottom of crags but these do not include the climbs upon the crags themselves. If, therefore, an access agreement doesn't exist or the land is not owned by the National Trust, then technically speaking a climber may be trespassing. This used to be just a civil offence, with the landowner only having the power to evict but recent changes in legislation have complicated the issue somewhat and there may now be circumstances in which climbers could be deemed to be breaching the criminal law.

The oft mooted concept of 'The Right To Roam' is not yet a reality, and probably never will be in its widest sense, however things do seem to be improving and good relationships built up over many years of sensible compromise have paid dividends to the extent that we now have access to more crags than ever before.

Unlike the limestone area, only a small number of the crags in this Guide are within the Yorkshire Dales National Park boundary and therefore subject to the benefits of such protection.

The majority of the problems encountered over the years involve crags on grouse moors where the land owners fears about disturbance by excessive noise, dogs and, in particularly fire, are totally understandable. Grouse shooting is a legitimate and long established country pursuit and the land management to accommodate it is expensive. Careless disturbance during the nesting season can usually be avoided by following agreed approach routes and instructions regarding dogs must be heeded. On days designated for shooting access will inevitably be restricted for obvious reasons.

Several crags are also within areas designated as Sites of Special Scientific Interest (S.S.S.I.) and this status is sometimes quoted by gamekeepers as the reason why climbing is not permitted. English Nature monitor these areas and experience shows that disturbance by climbing is rarely a problem to them. Don't argue about this on the crag but report references clearly to the B.M.C.

Aggressive confrontation with gamekeepers and land owners in such areas can easily lead to long term problems but if you are challenged whilst climbing ask politely what the specific problems are and why your presence is causing offence. Do not get into arguments but report back accurately the details you have been given to the B.M.C. office at the address below. It will also be useful to obtain the name and position of the person asking you to leave.

British Mountaineering Council
177-179 Burton Road, Manchester, M20 2BB.
Tel 0161 445 4747 : Fax 0161 445 4500
e-mail: bmc_hq @cix.comulink.co.uk

Barden Moor and Barden Fell Access Area

This includes **Crookrise, Deer Gallows, Rylstone, Rolling Gate, Air Scar, Halton Heights** and the crags surrounding **Simon's Seat**.

Relationships with Duke of Devonshire's Estate which manages all this land are excellent and no permission to climb is required at present. Climbers must, however, obey the access by-laws that specifically apply to this area (principally, no dogs and no fires). Notices containing full by-laws are posted at each access point and these will indicate advance notice of closure dates for shooting or because of high fire risk in periods of drought.

Shooting may take place on up to 30 days each year, between August 12th and late December but never on Sundays. To check possible closure dates telephone the National Park Information Office 01756 752774 (7 days a week from Easter to 31st October) or the Devonshire Estate Office on 01756 710227 (office hours).

TECHNICAL AND ETHICAL NOTES

Adjectival Grading System

(VS's are just V.Diffs without ledges - Nat Allen, circa 1965)

M = Moderate, D = Difficult, VD = Very Difficult, S = Severe, VS = Very Severe, E = Extremely Severe. The prefixes M = Mild and H = Hard are used to supplement the basic grades up to Extreme but all Extremes are now indicated by a suffix number i.e. E1 - E9.

This is the long established traditional British grading system which, in theory, should give you a general idea of the overall standard of a climb. It allegedly takes into account technical difficulty, exposure, strenuosity, protection possibilities, looseness etc. In the olden days when climbers climbed for fun, usually nursing a hangover on a Sunday after a diet of beer and chips the night before, it seemed to work quite well and Nat Allen's old adage wasn't far from the truth. Now that some of you take the game seriously, train vigorously and regularly and, unbelievably, in some cases stay sober, a given grade can mean different things to different people. The grading system has therefore been refined to give a little more help (or confusion) to assist your choice of climb.

Technical Grades

Basically an open-ended system from 4 to 7 with suffixes a, b and c. Not to be confused with the continental system regularly used on bolted limestone routes and in many climbing walls. This system is supposed to give you an indication of the pure difficulty of the hardest move on a climb irrespective of all other factors (i.e. A 6a move just above the ground should be just as hard as a 6a move ten metres up with no protection. The former may merit E1 and the latter E6 - at least that's the theory.) The system is supposed to be objective but relies on the subjective judgement of individual climbers. Some are strong; some are better on slabs; some hate jamming and some revel in offwidth chimneys. Defining the parameters of a given grade that fits all these climbing styles is still open to wide debate.

P Grades

Introduced as an experiment in the last edition they have not caught on nationally but the majority of local climbers who expressed an opinion voted for their retention in this volume. P grades give added information about the seriousness of a climb and its protectability potential. They assume the climber has a full range of wired nuts and camming devices plus the experience and technical ability to use them effectively. They also, in general, assume that you have the strength to hang on long enough to place them. **P1 does not guarantee that a leader won't hit the ground if he falls**, and on shorter, unprotected 'micro-routes' the anticipation of a short fall onto relatively flat ground won't automatically generate a P3 rating. With the above in mind the following is a guide to the *possible* consequences of a leader fall.

P1= Generally well protected routes with falls likely to only damage egos.
P2 = Those bolder routes with sparse protection which may even be deck outs if the fall is relatively short onto a reasonable landing. Good gibber potential with plenty of air time. Could be painful.
P3 = Dire consequences. Do not fall of these nasty numbers because you're going to have to be lucky to walk away from a P3 lob. Get full life insurance now.

Note: The recent introduction of thickly padded bouldering mats and their use below some of the more serious P3 aretes and micro routes complicates the grading system even further. The gradings used throughout this book **do not** assume the use of such mats.

Star Quality

A guide to the first time or irregular visitor only. Please do not ignore routes without stars. Virtually every climb in this book has intrinsic quality when clean and in condition. Conversely, some of the 3 star routes may lose their appeal in less than perfect conditions or after periods of neglect.

Boulder Problems

The dramatic upsurge in power-bouldering in recent years has led to the production of several specialist bouldering guides which can only compliment the information in this book. The policy for inclusion of boulder problems in this guide was that they should be easily recognisable as climbing specific independent features without the constraints of holds that are 'out of bounds' or only from sitting starts etc. Many of the older classic problems included in previous editions such as those at the Bridestones, Shipley Glen, Caley and Slipstones have been retained on the premise that most fit this criteria and in fact many are now better classified as 'micro-routes' , i.e. short solos which require mental as well as physical commitment. The fact that individual crag writers have dealt with the descriptive and grading style differently may seem a little confusing at first sight but soon makes sense when you step off your mat and on to each particular crag. English technical grades have been used for all problems as opposed to Fonts or Vs or Bs which I feel would have created more confusion if mixed in with the route grades. These may not truly reflect the overall difficulty of modern power problems but the reality with most bouldering is that there are only two grades i.e. those you can do and those you can't!

ETHICS (Pegs, bolts, chipping and brushing)

The basic philosophy of gritstone climbing is well accepted and understood. Pegs are not accepted on natural grit, and only limited use as a last resort is tolerated on quarried rock. Bolts should not play any part in modern gritstone climbing, and apart from one obvious and rather embarrassing exception at Caley, have all but been eradicated and should never be re-placed.

Despite the popularity of some routes artificially created by chipping many years ago this practice has been outlawed now for over 50 years. It is morally indefensible and could be classed as a criminal offence.

Wire brushing to clean lichen from new routes or problems is acceptable if done thoughtfully and sensitively but if done to excess will irrevocably damage the rock. Despite its rough outer texture most gritstone is covered with a relatively thin outer skin which can easily be worn through to softer rock below. Once a climb or problem is established a stiff nylon or bristle brush should be all that is required to keep it in condition and the lichen at bay.

New Routes

All claims for new routes should be written up in the format used in this guide and sent to me.

Dave Musgrove,
1, Lindley Farm Cottages,
Cinder Lane,
Lindley Nr. Otley.
LS21 2QN.

EMERGENCY PROCEDURE and FIRST AID

In any accident requiring medical assistance or evacuation dial 999 and ask for the POLICE. They will summon the most appropriate response. They will require details of the nature of the injuries and the location of the incident. (Grid references are included in this guide for every crag, but on the the more extensive ones you will need to be more specific).

Walking wounded can receive treatment in the casualty departments of the following hospitals:

> St. James's, Leeds
> The General Infirmary, Leeds
> Harrogate General
> Wharfedale General, Otley
> Airedale General, Steeton, Keighley
> Bradford Royal
> Halifax General
> Huddersfield Royal

FIRST AID

1. IF SPINAL or HEAD INJURIES are suspected DO NOT MOVE THE PATIENT without skilled help, EXCEPT to maintain BREATHING.

2. IF BREATHING HAS STOPPED, clear the airways and commence artificial respiration. Do not stop until the victim breathes unaided or expert opinion diagnoses death.

3. STOP BLEEDING by applying direct pressure.

4. SUMMON HELP.

5. Keep the patient warm.

6. Don't Panic, offer reassurance, and stay calm .

CAR CRIME

Opportunist car thieves regularly tour country lanes and beauty-spot car parks on the look out for easy pickings. They are particularly interested in Cheque books and Credit Cards and as such clothing, hand bags and brief cases left on view are an obvious target. Other expensive items such as cameras watches and binoculars are also a temptation.

Most crag car parks have been targeted from time to time and the best advice is to ;

a) Leave nothing of value on view.

b) Leave nothing on view that may appear to contain anything of value.

c) Try to avoid very secluded parking places.

d) Take all valuables to the crag with you.

e) Lock your car by all means but remember a locked and alarmed car is not in itself any deterrent to a thief in a remote area. He will simply break a window or force your boot in seconds and drive away in his own vehicle.

f) Note the registration numbers of any suspicious vehicles hanging around car parks and notify the local police. 112 or 999 in all areas if you think an immediate response may prevent a crime or catch an offender. Or, in West Yorkshire 0860 6060606 - In North Yorkshire 01609 783131, to report a crime or suspicious incident.

SPECIAL NOTICE

Despite its glamour, and the improvements in protection equipment in recent years, climbing is still a potentially dangerous sport. This is particularly the case for those making the transition from basic experience on indoor walls to outdoor crags. Do not over-estimate your ability. The gradings on climbing walls bear no real resemblance to those outdoors and many of the features of gritstone and the necessary techniques to climb it cannot be replicated artificially. The writers and producers of this book have made every effort to ensure consistency in gradings and accuracy in descriptions, however no guarantees can be given and anomalies will, undoubtedly, be found. It is worth remembering that strong man's Severe may be a weakling's Extreme and a bold climber's P1 could be P3 to the timid or the inexperienced. The wearing of helmets is strongly recommended on all occasions!

Pricing and The Access Fund

Yorkshire Mountaineering Club guidebooks are produced by unpaid volunteers and any surplus income is re-invested for the financing of future editions and supplements. The pricing of Yorkshire guide-books in the past has been set solely on this basis. Despite the increase in information contained in this volume modern and more efficient production methods have enabled us to keep prices low and, for the first time, allocate a proportion of the income to the British Mountaineering Council Access Fund. The B.M.C. has, over the years, secured and maintained access to numerous crags in our area and is continuing to negotiate on our behalf for freedom to climb. We feel sure you will be happy to help in this way.

ALMSCLIFF CRAG

"Well, Almscliff may have become an obsession with us but at any rate it has placed in our possession a muscular efficiency that has stood us in good stead during our brief holidays amongst the fells and kept us fit when many are merely living on memories of departed prowess." - Claude Dean Frankland, c. 1923.

SITUATION AND CHARACTER   The crag is a conspicuous landmark sitting high on the northern ridge of Lower Wharfedale, about 1 mile north-west of the main Otley-Harrogate road near Huby and half a mile west of the village of North Rigton. It is about 5 miles south-west of Harrogate and 10 miles north of Leeds. As to its character, John Laycock said in 1912: *"Gritstone clings closely to the skin and to the affections.... and Almscliff is one of the best illustrations of this."*

The crag - *The* crag, in fact - consists of two tiers of rock, Low Man and High Man. High Man is separated into a south-west and north-west section by a level rift. The rock is clean, exceptionally sound, best-quality gritstone and, because it is a summit, it carries no drainage and thus dries quickly. All standards and types of climbs are here but the rocks are well rounded and so proficiency in hand-jamming is a useful asset. With modern camming devices there are few climbs that cannot be protected. The steepness of the rock and the brutishness of the climbing at "Arms" Cliff ensure that some climbs may seem undergraded. This is traditional. Be warned that *"The cliff is visited by climbers of exceptional skill and climbing of a somewhat desperate danger is indulged in"* (C. E. Benson 1906)

APPROACHES AND ACCESS   The best approach is by private transport, leaving the Otley-Harrogate road (A659) at either the North Rigton turn-off if approaching from Harrogate or the Gravelly Hill Lane or Huby turn-offs (look for signposts to Stainburn) if approaching from the Otley- Pool side. **Do Not park** outside the farm below the crag, but at a convenient corner lay-by below the western side of the crag on the Stainburn road. **Do not block gateways or access to fields**. Buses on the Bradford-Otley-Harrogate service stop at Huby from where the crag is about 30 minutes walk away (public footpath sign a few hundred metres down the main road towards Pool). Trains on the Leeds-Harrogate line stop at Weeton, just outside Huby, also about 30 minutes walk away.

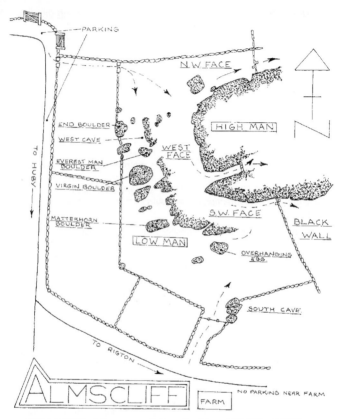

THE CLIMBS   These are all described from RIGHT to LEFT.

LOW MAN

The first climb starts well up the gully on the extreme right of the
Low Man.

1 Kiernan's Traverse and Rough Crack   10m HS P1 1931
4b A delicate tip-toe traverse left for 5 metres leads, by way of a
shallow corner, to a pleasant rounded crack. This can be reached
more easily from directly below giving a more balanced VD.

2 Roast Beef 5m E2 P2 1985
6a Climb straight up to and through Kiernan's Traverse using a small pocket in the top wall. Small Friends protect.

3 Yorkshire Pudding 7m E2 P3 1973
5c The prominent shallow corner crossed on Kiernan's Traverse is left boldly via a long reach to gain a large pocket up and right, and a still interesting finish.

Left of the direct start to Rough Crack and just right of the lower section of Stewpot is a slightly undercut blunt nose. Climbed direct without recourse to the holds on Stewpot this gives a bold aperitif to the previous routes known as **Something's Cooking** (E2 6b).

4 Stew Pot 11m HVD P2 Pre 1900   ★
Start at the foot of the flake that crosses the wall from bottom right to top left. Good holds lead up from this past a circular hole to an awkward move on to a ledge at 7 metres. Finish by the incipient crack or the slab on its right.

5 Low Man Easy Way 13m D P1 C1870   ★★
A classic beginner's route but with an awkward start, following the large flake running up to the left from the start of Stew Pot. From the ledge at the top take the easiest line up the short upper slab.

6 Pinnacle Direct 12m HVD P1 Pre 1997   ★
Pull onto the bulge between Easy Way and Pinnacle Flake and step right. Climb up the front of the flake, trending left, without recourse to the neighbouring routes, to the ledge at the top. Step right and climb the short upper slab.

7 Pinnacle Flake Climb 12m S P1 Pre 1912   ★
4a From a recess a couple of metres left of Low Man Easy Way an awkward step up and left is made on to a sloping ledge. Steep but easier climbing leads up the left edge of the flake to the top

8 Fluted Columns 14m VD P1 Pre 1900   ★★★
Known originally as Fluted Pillars this classic climb compares in quality to the best of grit V.Diffs The prominent flutings at half height are gained from directly below with occasional steps left and right to find the best holds. The precarious bulge above the flutings is climbed direct via a small pocket.

9 Fluted Crack 14m S P1 Pre 1900
4b The prominent chimney and crack immediately left was part of the original Fluted Pillars in the 1890s. It deserves its independence if only for the technically interesting lower section.

The obvious steep wall left of Fluted Crack is split by a ledge at one

Low Man

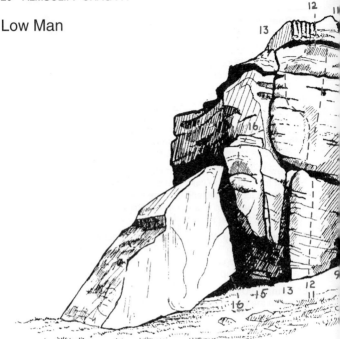

third height The central section of the wall can be ascended via three, almost independent, lines.

10   Wharfedale Wall   14m   E5   P2   1994
6c A microscopically independent line squeezed between Whisky Wall Direct and Fluted Crack. The lower section climbs the shallow scoop to a stiff mantelshelf onto the right-hand end of the ledge. The crux is contained in the central section via tiny pockets and small creases which lead to the rounded break and better holds in the eyes above. Easier climbing in the same line leads to the top. On the first ascent side runners were used in Fluted Crack, but the edge of the crack was not used for progress.

11   Whisky Wall Direct   14m   E4   P3   C1975
6a The centre of the wall provides a very bold line. From the big ledge, climb direct using the obvious pockets and a monster reach.

N. Baker

12 Whisky Wall 15m E3 P3 1973
5b The original line, nice moves but still quite bold. Gaining the first ledge is problematical, except for giants, then commit yourself, to gain two pockets in the centre of the wall before moving left to reach a horizontal break (almost in the crack). Climb up just right of the crack (Whisky Crack) then step back right to the centre of the wall and finish direct. Side runners maintain sanity, but reduce the grade.

13 Square Chimney & Whisky Crack
15m MVS P1 Pre 1912   ★★★
4b A superb combination. The obvious box-shaped cleft, often the scene of much cursing, can be climbed in classic back and foot style by those who've had the right apprenticeship. The steep jamming crack above the chimney is gained by a step right from the block, utilising good horizontals on the left to get established.

14 Spirit Level 17m E2 P2 1997
5b Gain Whisky Crack from any appropriate start and then traverse

right across the central section of Whisky Wall (hands in the
second break down from the top) to finish up Fluted Columns. The
protection is at the start of the traverse - the crux is at the end!

15   V Crack   8m   HVS   P1   1942
6a A climb that can turn you inside out! The narrow V-shaped crack
on the left wall of Square Chimney is difficult to gain direct. An
easier variation (5b) is to start from the ledge within the chimney.

16   Pigott's Stride   8m   VS   P2   Pre 1923   ★
4c The bulges to the left of Square Chimney are reached by
climbing the edge of the Matterhorn Boulder opposite until it is
possible to turn round and bridge (gulp) to the main crag. A
frightening pull across is followed by a step right and better holds.
Finish up Whisky Crack.

17   Torpedo   9m   E1   P2   1977
5c From the base of the gully between the Matterhorn Boulder and
the main crag rises the popular V Chimney. Climb this for 3 metres
and then make a traverse right to gain good holds leading round on
to the nose of Pigott's Stride.

18   Trident   8m   E3   P2   1994
5c The left side of the steep rib above the traverse of Torpedo. The
strenuousity, and dubious protection provide the deterrent!.

19   Depth Charger   8m   HVS   P2   1977
5b From the start of Torpedo's traverse continue straight up the
right wall of the chimney on good holds but long reaches.

20   Up Periscope   6m   E1   P1   C 1979
5b A logical conclusion to all the last three routes is the wall above
the ledge direct, about 2 metres left of Whisky Crack to surface on
the final moves of Pram Pusher's Paradise.

21   V Chimney and Traverse   15m   HVD   P1   Pre 1894   ★
Take two steps up, and one down, the glass-like chimney to a
delightful traverse left across the slab below the roof. Finish on top
with a semi-mantel.

22   V Chimney Direct   10m   VS   P1   1942
5a Follow the previous route and gain the start of the traverse. Now
over the roof by a precarious mantelshelf or the western roll.

23   A Step in The Right Direction   10m   HVS   P2   1992
5b The lower wall to the left of V Chimney is climbed via two small
pockets to reach the slab below the roof. Move right to where V
Chimney Direct provides a logical finish.

24 Pram Pusher's Paradise 14m VS P1 1972   ★★
5a Climb up to the slab under the roof from the gully bed a few
metres left of V Chimney and move across to its top right-hand
corner. A surprising swing right gains good holds and jams for a
spectacular horizontal traverse to the nose just left of Whisky Crack.
Climb straight up on flutings to finish. The line can be extended at
about the same standard above Whisky Wall, along the *'Top Shelf'*,
to Fluted Columns.

25 Angelic Upstart 7m HVS P2 1997
5b From the start of Pram Pusher's climb the rib just left of the thin
crack to a good hold then pull over via a pocket to an easier finish.

26 Envy Of Angels 7m E3 P3 1997
5c Start from the gully just left of Pram Pushers Paradise and climb
easily up to a ledge. Without using the left arete, make a committing
pull over the bulges above and finish direct. A side runner placed
round the corner reduces the grade to E1 but the original ascent
was a bold on-sight solo.

28 The Low Man Girdle 30m S P1
Follow the easiest line leftwards from the bottom of Rough Crack to
the traverse of V Chimney and Traverse. A belay below Whisky
Crack is logical. Many variations are possible.

HIGH MAN

The South Face
From Black Wall on the extreme right of the upper tier to the dry-
stone wall. Below Black Wall, is a hollow which, until a few years
ago invariably contained a large evil smelling pool. The first climb
starting in a short gully on right of Black Wall is a rather contrived
and escapable problem up the steep wall just right of the rib of
Black Wall. **Stepoffable** (5b)

28 Black Wall Direct 8m HVS P1 1980
5b Climb the right rib, left of the gully until the natural traverse of
the original line tempts you to move left. Ignore temptation (and
rational judgement) and press on straight up to a rounded sloping
finish. Fun - for the spectators!

29 Black Wall 10m VS P1 1941   ★
5a The original line and an old favourite which starts easily and
draws you on to a gymnastic finish. Climb the right edge over an
awkward bulge until a traverse left leads to a small resting ledge.
Now aim for the nick in the top edge. Easy when you know how!

30   Blackpool Promenade   20m   E1   P1   1975   ★
5b A diagonal traverse from the foot of Black Wall to the top of South Chimney. Start from the rib and swing left above the top of the flake on Black Wall Eliminate. Follow this route to the junction with Birdlime and reverse this until just below the bulge on South Wall Traverse. Pull up left and squirm along the rounded breaks until an escape is possible just right of the top of the chimney.

31   Black Wall Eliminate   15m   E2   P1   1966   ★★★
5c A tremendous climb. Steep and strenuous. Gain, with difficulty, a standing position on the large black flake by a fingery lay-away. Pull up and traverse left until below a thin vertical crack with two small pockets on its left. Use these to reach the next break and swing boldly round the nose on solid jams to an easy finishing crack.

32   Blackhead   10m   E4   P2   1990
6c The convex wall above the left side of the flake provides a less popular eliminate but requires a telescopic reach. Continue direct to finish just left of Black Wall. Originally done using an old bolt-hole which was subsequently filled in. The crux may now be impossible to all but giants! Using the start of BWE the line is worth E2 5c.

Five metres left is a tiny ramp leading leftwards and just left again is a small polished gangway slanting right. The next 6 routes all start from here.

33   'Arries 'Ook   13m   E4   P2   1975   ★★
6a A technical excursion with an unthinkable landing when the pool has formed. From the top of the polished gangway traverse right on undercuts until it is possible to stride across to an obvious large black foothold. Climb straight up from here to the break. Fix solid runners then make a monster reach up and right to gain the top break and an easier finish. **Direct Start** (6c)★★ Layback the steep little ramp to gain the large black foothold - a good problem in its own right.

34   Kitson Did It First   10m   E3   P1   1973
6b Climb the shallow scoop directly above the polished gangway about a metre right of the arete. Two pockets assist progress but the arete is off-limits. Traverse off from the break or continue straight up as for South Wall Direct.

35   Birdlime Traverse   19m   HVS   P1   1946   ★★★
5a A classic trip. Climb the polished gangway, traverse left to the arete and mantel on to the nose. Now up the right-hand side of the slab to a traverse line. Drop down, and move right under the overhangs to meet the thin vertical crack of Black Wall Eliminate. The pockets on its immediate left provide the key to move up and

Chris Hague – Whiskey Crack (MVS), Almscliff   photo: Jim Higgins

then right to finish as for Black Wall.

36 South Wall Traverse 13m VS P1 Pre 1923   ★★
4c Follow Birdlime to the step down at the top of the slab, whence a little crack and a blind move in an exposed position leads to good holds and a move right to the final crack of Black Wall Eliminate. Finishing direct is harder, less secure and less enjoyable.

37 South Wall Direct 11m E1 P1   1988
5b Follow Birdlime to the top of the slab. Now straight up as directly as possible over bulges to an elephantine finish. Contrived and not very satisfying.

38 South Face Climb 12m MVS P2 Pre 1912   ★
4c As for Birdlime, climb the awkward polished gangway and tip-toe left to a precarious mantel on to the nose and then cross the slab easily to climb the right-hand side of the chimney, over a bulge, direct to the top. The upper part is rather artificial.

39 South Chimney 11m D P1 C1870
The prominent chimney is something of a thrutch at the start.

Three classic problems near South Chimney are often used as variation starts to routes in the vicinity.

The Nose (6a) ★★ is just right of the chimney and is climbed direct.**The Wall** (5b) is immediately left of the chimney. **The Slab** (5c) ★★★ is a polished series of slopers just left again. All have micro variations too numerous and complicated to mention. The Black Wall can be traversed at low level all the way from South Chimney rightwards at 6c★★.

40 Yellow Wall 14m E2 P2 1966   ★
5c A bold, intimidating climb which traverses left from South Chimney under the large overhang to finish up a short crack. Hand holds are poor, footholds out of sight and protection difficult to place. But worthwhile for all that.

41 Yellow Peril 12m E4 P2 1980
6a Half way along the traverse of Yellow Wall is a finger hole in the roof. Use this, and a western roll, to surmount the overhang.

42 South Chimney Layback 15m S P1 Pre 1912
4b The prominent vertical crack to the left of South Chimney is climbed on jams (crux) to reach a niche. Step right and layback easily up the edge of the flake across the slab to reach, and finish up, the chimney.

43 Shuffle Crack 12m E1 P1 1958
5c The niche above the short vertical crack is climbed to the roof.

High Man –
The South Face

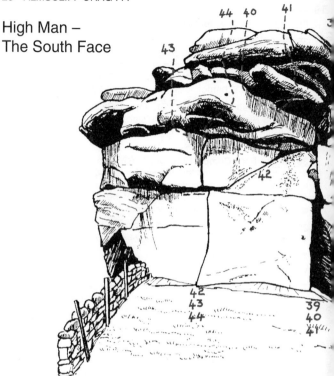

Traverse left with difficulty for a couple of metres to reach easy ground.

44   China Syndrome   12m   E5   P2   1980   ★★
7a The wall right of Shuffle Crack leads to the break and a large flake forming a lip in the prominent bulge. Reaching the hole up and right from here is technical and highly gymnastic. Finish direct with another tenuous move along the way.

A low-level excursion **The Dry Stone Traverse** (6b)★ along the smooth horizontal break from the dry-stone wall to South Chimney Layback provides an interesting problem and much amusement when the cattle have been grazing in the vicinity. **Off The Wall** (5b)★ is an easier version moving up right to the niche of Shuffle Crack.

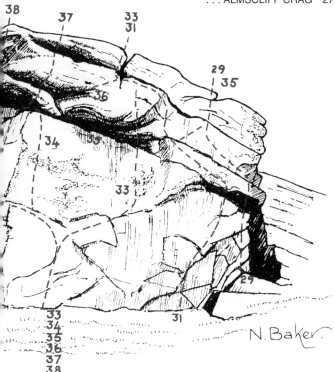

45 Fence Buttress 11m VS P2 Pre 1982
5b Step off the stone wall (now somewhat lower and therefore harder) and climb up left to step back right onto the small flake. Continue straight up with a bold little step onto the upper slab.

The South West Face is the area left of the wall to The Rift

An old 5c problem **The Ladder** climbs the well spaced holds just right of the next crack - in fact some think it is an easier alternative!

46 Stomach Traverse 12m VS P1 Pre 1894
4c Get physical and attack the hanging crack just left of the stone wall to a ledge where problems thankfully diminish. Step up right and maximise the enjoyment by climbing all the remaining bulges to the top. The climb got its name by originally starting in the crack to the left (not much easier) and squirming right along the ledge.

The South West Face

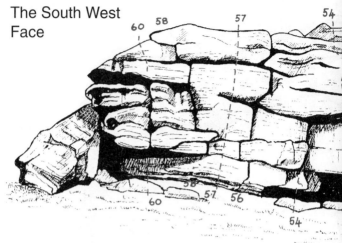

47   Jacob's Ladder   11m   HVS   P1   1940
5b   A worthwhile, but escapable, eliminate. The steep wall between the two cracks is climbed direct with a polished, problematic start to a substantial ledge. A short wall is followed to a delicate semi-mantelshelf to finish.

48   Central Crack   10m   HS   P1   Pre 1894   ★
4b   Grunt or glide up the wide smooth rounded crack. Step right and climb the short rib to effect an awkward entry into the final niche.

The undercut block to the left of Central Crack that ends on a substantial ledge - the Tennis Court of old articles - contains impeccable bouldering. **The Crucifix** (5c)★★★, one of Almscliff's most famous problems, is the inverted cross round the left-hand end. **Crucifix Arete** (6a)★★ just right is much harder if done twice without using the same hold twice (the break counts as one) or without the break at all. The Crucifix itself can be started from a sitting position using only the vertical crack, no jams and avoiding the horizontal (6c). It is also possible to hang from the break by your toes. Various traverses swing both ways but the pride of the problems is **Pebble Wall** (6b)★★★ which climbs the centre of the undercut block and is the start of:

49   Rectum Rift   10m   E3   P2   1972   ★
1. 4m   6b   Climb Pebble Wall to the ledge.
2. 6m   6a   Continue straight up and, using undercuts and a

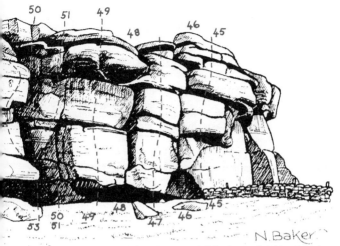

N.Baker

monster reach, ascend the obscene cleft in the roof. A Hex 9 makes it P1, have you got one?

50 Crack and Wall 12m HS P2 Pre 1912
4b Climb the corner left of The Crucifix to the ledge. Step up and left using flutes into the chimney. A finish out right at the top adds interest.

51 Acetabulum 11m E1 P1 1973
5c A difficult variation finish to the last climb, taking the short hanging crack in the left side of the roof to a rounded and insecure finish..

52 Three Chockstones Chimney 10m Easy Peasy P1
C1870
A good beginner's route; more often used as an easy way down.

Left of the chimney is an undercut wall which can be traversed at three levels (5a, 6a and 6c), the lowest being the hardest. Climbing out below the undercut just right of centre is the classic **Demon Roof** (6c/7a) ★★★ involving a heelhook on a molecule and minuscule holds to reach an obvious ear of rock up right (There are now several variations). **Stu's Roof** (7b)★★★ is the even harder roof just left again. Climbing the bulge just left of the chimney via a jump for the break and a rockover left to reach a small pocket is more reasonable (6a)★★ and provides an independent start for the next route.

53 Dolphinian 10m E1 P1 1976   ★

5b A neat little route up the right-hand side of the wall to the left of the chimney, normally started from the chimney. From the break, move over the bulge and then launch boldly up rightwards with a long reach for a rounded break then a good flute just left of the arete.

54 Demon Wall 10m HVS P1 1940   ★★★

5a One of Almscliff's more famous climbs. Starting to the left of the roof climb a crack for three metres and traverse delicately right to a short flake in the bulge. Climb the flake, step left, then straight up on rounded breaks to grope blindly for the finishing hold set well back on the ......! (Go and look if you're that un-adventurous).

55 Bird's Nest Variation 10m MVS P2 Pre 1940   ★

4c Climb the thin crack, as for Demon wall, using holds on the left to reach the horizontal. A high step and a long reach bring the next break within reach and a step left gains the prominent nose and an easier finish. It is possible to finish by an even more artificial variant straight up at E1 5b.

56 Bird's Nest Crack 10m HS P1 Pre 1900   ★★

4b The popular and polished central crack line is the old-fashioned classic of this face. Climb straight up until a step right gains the curious projection. Pull up and onto the projection and finish more easily.

57 Forgotten Wall 10m E5 P1 1980   ★

6c A direct line up the wall one and a half metres left of Bird's Nest Crack. Climb to the level of Thompson's Traverse using the vague diagonal groove and a long reach (a good problem in its own right 5c). Make intricate and technical moves on to the sloping shelf and a harder move still to gain a standing position and the next break. The upper wall is easier but maintains interest to the top.

58 The Traditional Climb 10m VS P1 Pre 1923   ★★

4c The next crack system to the left is distinctly awkward, although well protected.

59 Traditional Eliminate 10m HVS P2 C1973   ★

6a A must for the connoisseur. Climb the wall a metre or so left of the parent route. Using holds in the previous climb is cheating. The traditional start is by a jump to the handrail from the boulder a couple of metres out from the base of the crag. Ouch!

60 Pothole Direct 10m VS P1 1938   ★

5b The vertical crack system nearest to the left end of the South West Face. The crux is contained in the first 3 metres but the continuation on good holds is steep and delightful.

The lower wall immediately left of Pothole Direct can be climbed on tiny finger pulls moving left **Dots And Dabs** (6b), but the best problem hereabouts is **Jam Pot** the overhang just right of the cave via a high jam on the lip (5c/6a depending how low you start).

61 The Pothole 13m VD P1 Pre 1900
The original, but inferior, way of climbing the route starts up the slabby boulder on the left before traversing right on to the main face high up, avoiding all difficulties.

The whole of the South West Face can be traversed at every level and many combinations can be contrived. The following two, however, have long been regarded as routes and are both worthwhile. The proficient can combine them in bold solo circuits.

62 Thompson's Traverse 18m HVS P1 1934   ★
5b Start up Bird's Nest Variation and, at 4 metres, traverse left to Bird's Nest Crack. Traverse the sloping break on tiny finger holds to Traditional Climb (crux) and continue more easily but delightfully leftwards all the way to The Pothole.

63 High Level Traverse 18m VS P1 1957   ★
4c This is the top break from Traditional Climb to Bird's Nest Crack. It can be started from Pothole at the same grade, and extended into Demon Wall at 5a.

THE RIFT The wide rift that separates the South West Face from the North West Face contains a number of short routes on its north side.

64 Rift Crack 7m VS P1 Pre 1969   ★
5a A fun route. The bottomless curving crack 3 metres right of Tight Chimney has a long reach to good holds on the right to start and a useful pocket high on the left. From here grope blindly through the upper crack for a finishing hold that is set well back.

65 Constipation Crack 7m VS P1 Pre 1969
5a Often confused with Rift Crack but never previously recorded. The hanging crack 2 metres right of Tight Chimney is hard to enter and leads to a bulge and a step left to finish through the notch above Tight Chimney.

The undercut wall above a prominent boulder between Tight Chimney and Constipation Crack is **Suppository Wall** (5c) climbed without recourse to the edges either side. A short but serious problem, don't slip off or you'll quickly appreciate how the problem got its name.

66   Tight Chimney   7m   M   P1   C1870
The obvious narrow cleft is well supplied with holds.

67   Daisy Chain   7m   E3   P3   1985
6b   The small overhang and wrinkled wall a couple of metres left of
the chimney provides entertainment out of all proportion to its size.

68   Oubliette   8m   E2   P2   1969   ★
6a   The shallow vertical depression a little further left is gained from
the right and climbed precariously on small holds. Finish rightwards
along the break.

69   Clematis   10m   E2   P2   1969   ★
5c   A couple of metres left of the shallow depression good holds,
but long reaches, lead steeply to the wide horizontal break. Step up
right to gain the large pocket in the top bulge and span left from this
to gain better holds in a shallow scoop. Harder and more direct **The
Nelly Moser Finish** (E3 6a/b) climbs straight over the bulge
immediately above the pocket.

70   Hobgoblin   10m   E2   P1   1983
5c   From halfway up Clematis, traverse left to a tiny pocket and pull
up to gain the break just left of the nose. Strenuous.

The Rift Traverse (5b)★★ is an excellent low-level excursion from
the stile at the head of the gully moving left to finish in West Chimney.
The 2 crux sections being beneath Clematis and the Goblin.

THE WEST FACE   The corner of The Rift turns to the West Face
and is capped by a massive scooped overhang beneath which are
two circular holes, the Goblin's Eyes.

71   Orchrist   11m   E5   P2   1973   ★
6b   The Goblin's roof. Climb the breaks past the Goblin's Eyes to
the roof and swing out right into the niche on the lip. A long reach
and a tenuous slap left may bring success. The protection is worth
mentioning. A No. 8 hexentric is placed in the left side of the roof
and tied down. One rope goes through this while the other rope
passes through runners high in the opposite wall of The Rift.

72   The Goblin   11m   HS   P2   Pre 1894   ★★
4b   A varied and worthwhile exercise. Climb past the Goblin's Eyes
to a constricted move left on to a ledge. Climb the chimney above,
best on the outside, thankful that it is not as bad as it first appears.

73   Bancroft's Roof   9m   E2   P2   1973
6b   The bulges to the left of the bottom part of The Goblin are taken
at the widest point to pull onto the nose, finishing on flutes. The first

bulge is the crux - variations are possible on the more exciting upper section.

74   The Zig Zag   11m   Decidedly Difficult   P1   Pre 1912
The original grade (1912) is most appropriate for this polished horror, now technically at least 4b. Climb a recess 3 metres to the left of The Goblin until an obvious hand traverse left can be made to a hidden flake in the roof, which leads to 'jugs' and easy climbing.

75   Zig Zag Direct   11m   VS   P1   Pre 1912   ★
4c   A popular roof climb. Instead of taking the traverse left, approach the overhang with trepidation. Surprisingly, it goes with relative ease - if you can find the right combination of holds and jams!

76   Syrett's Roof   8m   E3   P2   1972   ★★
6b   The overhang left of Zig Zag provides a serious problem and involves a precarious rock-over, and hopeful slap up right. It sees many more failures than successes. A left-hand finish is also possible.

77   The Nose Direct   9m   HVS   P1   Pre 1912
5b   The thin, strenuous, crack splitting the overhang to the left. Painful but determined jamming is the key.

78   The Nose   9m   VS   P1   Pre 1912
4c   Another polished horror . The prominent projection to the left of The Zig Zag is won with difficulty - don't blow it! Breath easier above.

79   West Chimney Rib   6m   HVS   P2   1997
5b   The right-hand rib of the chimney is easy to start but with a crux moving right over the bulge at the top. A left hand finish is also possible at 4c, but artificial and hardly worthwhile.

80   West Chimney   11m   M   P1   C1870
A deep cleft, the depths of which are cemented up. It provides a convenient descent.

81   Jess's Roof   8m   E By Gum   1994
7a   The huge roof in the cave in the upper reaches of West Chimney is a desperate extended boulder problem for most of the way but a fall from the last section just after the crux could prove very painful. Large Friends, either mechanical or in the form of a human catching party, are highly desirable for the finish.

82   Retribution Rib   11m   E2   P3   1945
5b   Climb the left-bounding rib of West Chimney until it is possible to step across with difficulty on to the large block capping the chimney. Protection in the chimney is cheating.

83   Retribution Rib Direct   10m   E5   P3   1991   ★★
5c The rib is climbed direct by those who dare. No protection and
an unthinkable landing add spice to otherwise excellent moves. The
Wild West would have been a better name.

NORTH WEST FACE

This section of Almscliff contains the finest selection of climbs on
the crag and some of the best gritstone outings in the country. Left
of the Retribution Rib is a large corner capped by a roof.

84   Crack Of Doom   11m   VS   P1   1941   ★★
4c Intimidating from below, but protection is good and difficulties
short-lived. Climb the corner crack to the overhang. Confidence is
needed to launch out rightwards, but good finishing holds are soon
to hand.

85   Impending Doom   12m   E4   P1   1980   ★
6a From the top of the corner of Crack Of Doom climb out to a
small ledge on the lip of the overhang and make a lurch up and
right around the rib to escape.

The West Face

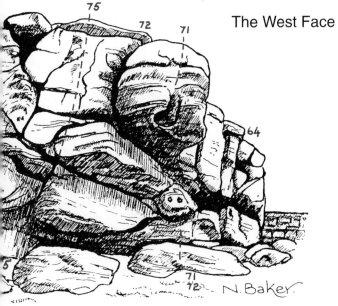

75
72
71
64
5
71
72
N. Baker.

86 Megadoom 12m E5 P2 1997 ★★
6b Goes where Impending Doom should have gone. Straight up from the lip on the left side of the rib with heart-stopping moves in an outrageous position. Fall off the top and you'll land at Caley!

87 Great Western 15m HVS P1 1943 ★★★★
5a The only four-star route in the book; a contender for the best climb on gritstone. Climb Crack Of Doom to the roof. Traverse elegantly leftwards in a magnificent position and make a strenuous pull to a resting place at a pinnacle in the niche. Finish direct or, for maximum exposure and the best jams on the crag, take **The Five Star Finish**. Swing out right to a short steep crack.

88 No Mans Land 20m E2 P1 1991 ★
5b A strenuous and rather more technical extension to the traverse of Great Western. From below the niche step left, across the crack of Western Front and climb up the wall to the left of the pedestal.

89 Grand Illusion 13m E4 P2 1979 ★★★
5c (6a for the short?) A bold and intimidating climb in an amazing position. Only 3 new moves but each one earns a star. Climb the corner as for Crack of Doom until stopped by the overhang. Reach

out left to gain a good slot, then another and eventually, with adrenaline pumping, the **Five Star** finish of Great Western.

90   Western Front   13m   E3   P1   1958   ★★★
5c   Another magnificent climb, offering a fierce and intimidating direct approach to the pinnacle of Great Western. Start just left of Crack of Doom. Bridge out of a small corner onto the sloping lip and swing left on better holds until it is possible to pull up to the inverted Y. Climb this (crux) to join and finish as for Great Western. If the finish of No Mans Land is taken the whole route is probably worth E4 -This combination is now known as **Over The Top**.

The next climb is of purely historical interest and starts down the crevasse below Western Front.

91   Leaf Climb   20m   VD   P1   Pre 1900
Climb the crack in the crevasse without bridging across and walk right to the foot of West Chimney. Climb the left side of the capstone if you can and follow the chimney until easy ledges lead out and left to juggy bulges above Crack of Doom.

The impressive yellow wall to the left contains **The Niche** ★★★ One of Almscliff's oldest known problems. 5b to 6b depending how many others are in at the time. Four would appear to be the limit.

92   Every Man Has His Niche   6m   E4   P3   1987
6b   A bold micro route or a contrived variation start to the next climb. Gain The Niche, then teeter horizontally out of its right side to reach sloping holds. A further move right gains an escape below the start of Western Front whilst a mantelshelf gains the start of the next climb.

93   The Ems Telegram   20m   E5   P2   1977   ★★
6b   A tip-toe left and a bold lurch from a letterbox gain good holds on Western Front and good Friends. Swing left to the nose and a perfect small runner in a horizontal break (unfortunately awkward to place). Another swing left and down (crux) leads to a good hand-hold below the base the curving crack. Pull up awkwardly into this, getting very tired by now, to join and finish up The Wall of Horrors.

The left side of the yellow wall is the setting for one of Almscliff's most famous climbs.

94   The Wall of Horrors   18m   E3   P1   1961   ★★★
6a   A big, sustained and classic expedition with an aura that still commands respect. Left of The Niche is a cup hold 4 metres above the ground, and gaining this is the technical crux. From the good hold climb a crack and a small roof to the horizontal break. Stand

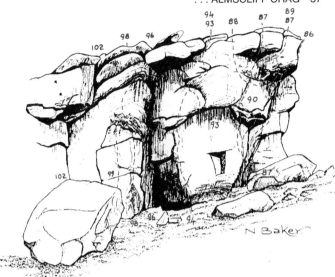

up (2nd crux) and climb right, then left, up the wall to the V-notch at the top. A variation on the left, **Horror of Walls** E4 6b is possible. Starting and finishing as for the parent route. It needs an independent start before being really worthwhile.

The technical crux of the next climb is also the start of The Wall of Horrors, but this may not seem so as its end is neared.

95 All Quiet 25m E4 P2 1974   ★★
6a A very fine but long and strenuous line that links Wall of Horrors to Crack of Doom. Climb Wall of Horrors to the horizontal break. Swing down and launch strenuously rightwards on a hand traverse above The Niche to, hopefully, join the hand rail of Western Front. Slam a last few jams into the diagonal crack that leads to the corner and finish as for Crack of Doom. Phew.

96 Long Chimney 18m HVD P1 1893   ★★★
Originally known as The Great Chimney, this prominent cleft left of The Wall of Horrors is now well polished but still a classic of its type. Best climbed facing left and finished by a short exposed traverse out to the left near the top. The inside finish is more secure but less satisfying.

A large detached pinnacle to the left about half the height of the crag is **The Pulpit**. It has four routes (now 5 – see 'Afterthoughts').

97 The Easy Way 8m M P1 Pre 1894
The chimney facing Long Chimney.

98 Pulpit Corner 18m E1 P2 1927/56   ★
5b The right arete of The Pulpit, gained from the left, provides a tricky problem. A prominent flake at half height is overcome with a move of some delicacy. From the top of The Pulpit step up left to the rounded break and follow it awkwardly to better holds on the right.

99 Al Says 6a 8m E4 P2 1988   ★
An exciting 'boulder problem' up the thin flake on the front of The Pulpit. A runner in the flake on the right is allowed - but will it stop you in time? - And, was Al right????

100 Fat Man's Misery 8m S P1 Pre 1894
The narrow cleft on the left-hand side of the pinnacle succumbs to brute force.

101 Merlin 14m E3 P3 1984
5c An artificial but bold eliminate starting up the green arete just left of the Pulpit. Climb straight up to a junction with Frankland's then move right along the horizontal to join Pulpit Corner. Attempt to finish slightly more directly than that route over the bulges. High side runners reduce the P (but also the E) grade .

102 Frankland's Green Crack 18m VS P1 1919   ★★★
4c A tremendous classic, quite high in the grade but constantly interesting, varied and sustained. Layback the green crack to a tiny ledge below the overhang. Make a delicate two-step right and pull up awkwardly into the constricted upper groove. The final overhang, perhaps best mastered by wide bridging, ensures interest is maintained to the end.

103 The Big Greeny 14m E3 P2 1973   ★★★
6a A route with a big feel about it and a bold finish up the wall left of Frankland's. Climb with some difficulty to the curving break. Pull out left and climb the steep wall using two obvious holes, and a little faith that there is something else over the top.

104 Fungus The Bogeyman 14m E4 P2 1980
6a Harder climbing but not as good as its neighbour, or its name! Instead of picking about in the holes of Big Greeny move left and climb the bold blunt nose right of the chimney. The start is artificially independent and just left of that of The Big Greeny.

105 Parsons' Chimney 17m HS P1 1900   ★★★
4b Another vintage classic. The cave belay is reached by bridging the overhanging corner direct, or more elegantly, from the flake of

Overhanging Groove. From the cave climb up and out with increasing exposure, turning round to finish on good holds on the left rib. Quite Exciting!

106 Toad's Nose 15m E4 P2 1995
6b Start up the rib between Parson's Chimney and Overhanging Groove to the ledge and then continue up the hanging rib above with a hard section at the start. Difficulties ease a little higher up but the climbing is bold.

107 Overhanging Groove 17m HVS P2 1941   ★★★
5a The fine groove on the left of Parsons' Chimney offers a climb as good as anything else on the crag. Climb the layback flake crack to the cave. The continuation crack soon becomes blind and a long stretch is needed to reach the security of the magnificent finishing jugs.

108 Central Climb 15m VS P1 Pre 1923   ★★
4c The easiest VS on this wall but still good value. Take the system of rounded vertical and horizontal cracks left of Overhanging Groove with a step left at half height.

109 WASC 15m E3 P2 1976
6a Follow Central Climb to the shallow triangular niche at half height. Now climb directly up the steep wall with great difficulty to a thin vertical crack near the top of the face. A direct start is possible up the hanging rib from the foot of Overhanging Groove.

110 Z Climb Eliminate 14m E1 P1 1946   ★★★
5b A very fine hybrid. The best and easiest E1 on the crag. Start to the left of Central Climb and gain the top of the jamming crack on Z Climb by way of a thin crack and precarious step left to a black flake. Follow a rounded crack slanting up to the right into Central Climb and follow this for a couple of metres. From just below the top step to the right to reach a thin flake in a shallow groove and climb this in superb position to finishing jugs.

111 Microscopic Wall 13m E3 P2   ★
6b Climb the superdirect start to Z Climb Eliminate, over the bulges to gain the black flake (E2 5c) and continue to finish up the right-hand side of the blunt arete above the top traverse of Z Climb. The start is hard but the crux is way up at the top.

112 Z Climb 15m VS P1 1940   ★★
4c The obvious Z-shaped crack system, starting from a recess 2 metres left of Central Climb provides a tough and varied exercise for the grade. Launch out on a swinging leftwards traverse to a big ledge. Step back awkwardly rightwards (crux) and climb on wrist-searing jams until it is possible to move left again to finish.

The North West Face

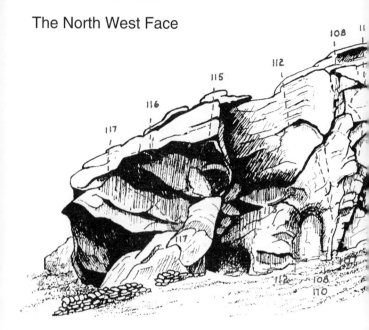

113 Why Climb 10m E3 P2 1976
6a From the first ledge of Z Climb attack the problematic bulge
above by a long lurch up and right to reach the final arm of the Z.

The wall just right of a cave in the corner provides several good
problems with many variations. The fine bottomless crack of
Teaspoon Variation (5c)★★★ is an old classic whilst the undercut
Gray's Wall (6a)★★ just right is a fingery gem.

114 Cup and Saucer 13m VD P1 1891   ★
A contortionist's delight with several variations. The obvious caves
can be climbed on the right or left, the latter being most interesting.
From the top of the huge capstone climb the wall on the left of the
gully.

Just left of Cup and Saucer a short wall provides more problems but
left again is a series of large overhangs, beneath which is a glacis
which rises from left to right. The next climbs start from the apex of
the glacis.

N. Baker.

115 First Night 10m E2 P1 1973
6a Climb up to a large flake, reach for the lip of the overhang and pull on to the left side of the rib with difficulty. A further swing right and ascent of the right hand side reduces the grade to 5c.

116 Encore 10m E2 P2 1973   ★
5c A bold excursion through the overhang. Follow First Night to the flake and traverse left to the break in the roof (hidden nut slot on the crux). Climb spectacularly over the bulge to the easy slab above.

117 Finale Slab 13m HVS P2 1957   ★★
5b The easiest climb hereabouts, but not without its moments. Start midway up the glacis. Climb to the overhang and traverse delicately leftwards (crux) across a steep slab to a short crack which provides an exciting way through the bulge.

118 Penny Pip 11m E4 P3 1995
6a From halfway up the glacis below Finale Slab move up left to a pocket and then climb diagonally left across the 'slab' on small sharp pockets to finish left of Finale Slab.

119   Exit Stage Left   11m   E4   P2   1988
6b From about halfway up the glacis traverse left on the lip of the
overhang until a wild swing gains a large hold. Swing up and left
and climb to easy ground.

120   All Our Yesterdays   16m   E5   P2   1982   ★★
6a A fine climb that follows the old peg traverse across some very
uncompromising ground. Start in the gully down and left of the
glacis. The traverse ends in the left side of a shallow cave. Climb
the rib above (crux). May need cleaning to guarantee its star quality.

121   The True Two Ton Sardine   10m   E3   P2   1979
6a Start in the dank quarried bay round to the left and ascend a
dirty overhanging flake to gain better holds in a traverse line.
Continue with more difficulty straight up.

122   Twelfth Night   15m   E2   P2   1973   ★
5c A rising left to right traverse line which follows a crack with old
wedges in it crossing the flake of Two Ton Sardine to reach a
sloping ledge. Finish up the slab above. A reasonable climb that
deserves more traffic despite its sombre aspect.

123   Fisher's Traverse   16m   HS   P3   1940   ★
4b A good climb that requires some cool, but is often forgotten.
Start about 30 metres beyond the dry-stone wall just short of the
entrance to North East Gully. A long and exposed traverse across a
steep slab above the overhangs leads to an awkward pull into a
scoop slanting right. Finish up easy slabs.

124   North West Girdle   65m   E1   P2   1944   ★★★
A truly classic expedition, nicely sustained and crossing the most
exciting sections of the crag.
1. 18m 5b Start up Z Climb and follow it until it breaks back left to
finish. Traverse delicately right into Central Climb. Step down to the
triangular niche and hand traverse into the cave of Parsons'
Chimney. Belay.
2. 12m 5b Another delicate section leads upwards on the right until it is
possible to swing round the corner for a hand traverse into Frankland's
Green Crack. Step down and across delicately to The Pulpit. Belay.
3. 15m 5b A very long stride or a hand traverse lead into Long
Chimney. Ascend the chimney to a possible belay adjacent to the
base of the bulge on the right wall. The next section is the crux and
gives plenty of food for thought, particularly for the last climber.
Step boldly across under the overhang and traverse airily above the
top of Wall of Horrors to the pinnacle of Great Western.
4. 10m 5a   Descend Great Western, traverse right and finish,
fittingly, up Crack of Doom.

Variation pitch 2: It is possible, and aesthetically more satisfying, to avoid the step down on to The Pulpit by following the obvious rounded break below Frankland's to join Pulpit Corner and follow it round to belay in Long Chimney. No change in grade but beware of rope drag.

It is possible to girdle the whole crag by linking traverses from Fisher's to Birdlime Traverse, with the reversal of Finale Slab being the most difficult section.

NORTH-EAST GULLY

The large rift just left of Fisher's Traverse contains numerous problems and micro routes which because of the aspect often look green and unappealing. Only the following have been formally recorded and named but the area is worth exploring by the true devotee on a warm dry summer evening,

125 Corner Crack 7m D P1
Near the head of the gully on the east wall. Beware of the block.

126 Green Wall 8m S P2
The wall on the left of Corner Crack. There is also a traverse to the left from near the top of this route (VS 4c).

127 Lichen Wall 7m S P2
The face on the right of Corner Crack.

128 Green Gully Wall 8m HVS P2 1967   ★
5a The steep wall and high arete on the left of the gully when looking up. Convenient pockets assist a step left to a rounded finish.

129 Green Gully Rib 7m VS 1997
4c The rib and wall above, to the left of Green Gully Wall.

Many other variations exist hereabouts.

130 The Final Finale 20m HVD 1997
5a The long narrow slab running the full length of the gully has one bold high step over the overlap above the crevasse. Assemble your team below you on the slab and go for it. Last one up buys the beer!

THE BOULDERS   (see diagram page 18 for orientation)

"The bouldering at Almscliff is second to none" - C.E. Benson 1906.

Almscliff has an almost inexhaustible supply of brilliant problems and usually soloed micro routes. The following is a collection of some of the timeless classics. Very often each problem has micro

variations which can make the standard of difficulty much greater. If in doubt, consult;
A definitive bouldering guide,
One of the many local gurus usually in-situ, or,
Use a sitting start, discount all obvious holds, use your imagination and get stuck in.
Locals and regular devotees will not need this, or any guide so please don't scoff at the attempt to incorporate some more information by way of stars and P grades etc. to old classics. This is simply an attempt to assist newcomers or irregular visitors to get started.

A   End Boulder
Morrell's Wall (6a) ★★★ A classic problem up the undercut east face. Many variations exist, the hardest utilising just one hold.

End Wall (5a) ★   An interesting rising traverse from the left across the north wall. Harder variation starts are possible by manteling in from further right 6c on the left, 5c on the right.

The High Step (5b) ★★ The centre of the field side of the wall via a high rock-over move. At least five other lines can be contrived up this face.

B   The Flying Aretes
The steep impending north wall can be climbed to its apex via:-

The Left Wing (6a) ★★★   The left arete from the edge of the path.

The Right Wing (6a) ★ The right arete from the adjacent boulder.

C   The Everest Man Boulder
A popular and well scratched block just above the path. The following, though usually soloed as problems, are all long enough to be treated as micro routes.

The South Col   7m HS P1   ★★
4b The polished holds lead up right to an awkward step onto the overhung glacis.

The South-West Face 6m E2 P3   ★★
5c A direct line via the high central pocket and a rounded scary finish.

The Lhotse Face 7m VS P2   ★★
4c A diagonal line from bottom right to top left.

The Hillary Step 6m HVS P2   ★
5b Start just right of the left rib and make an awkward step up to join the previous line to finish.

The North Ridge 6m E1 P2   ★
5c Climb around and up the front of the nose from a start on the left.

The East Face 5a Climb the back of the block trending left to effect a pull-over.

D The West Cave Group

A more continuous edge of problems and short routes at the extreme left end of the lower tier above the path. Starting from the right;

Pork Chop Slab (5c) ★ The steep and fingery slab at the right-hand end has a reachy crux at the top.

Three Swings Traverse (5b) ★★★ A classic excursion which traditionally starts low down just left of Pork Chop Slab and moves left, crossing the gully, to gain the polished ramp and the 'swings' beyond. Finish around the final rib, the third swing; or better, up the rib above it.

The undercut wall above the start of Three Swings can be ascended via a number of variants, all around 6a.

The Postman 7m MVS P1   ★★
4c Climbs the wall right of the gully past a slot to the ledge and then continues up to the highest point via juggy bulges.

The Blunt Edge 6m E1 P3   ★★
5b The gully side of the rib via pockets and a precarious and rounded lay-away finish.

The Chimney Flake 6m HVS P1   ★
5a The sharp edged crack up the gully wall leads over a bulge to an easier finish.

West Cave Wall 7m S P1   ★
4a Skate up the polished gangway left of the gully to a bulge and pull through to an easier upper slab.

Hammill's Rib 6m E4 P3
6b The hanging arete just right of the peg scarred groove is climbed on shallow pockets.

Barley Mow 6m E4 P2
6b The hanging, pegged-scarred, groove is hard but protectable. It is a serious solo.

The Ear 6m VS P2   ★★
5a The left arete crossing the final 'swing' of Three Swings Traverse.

E   The Virgin Boulder

This enormous tilted block is a crag in its own right. There are many problems, variations and low level traverses but most of those recorded below can be regarded as real climbs or micro routes and are described clockwise starting from the middle of the north face. Almost all have been soloed - but!!

North Face   7m   D   P1   C1900
A well-scratched descent route running diagonally up, or more usually down, the north face.

The Scoop   5m   HVS   P3   C1972   ★
5b   The shallow scoop just right of the arete above the bottom of the descent route.

North Top Corner   4b   The right-hand edge of the east face.

Thompson's Route and **Central Route,** both   4c   are the next two easy? lines to the left - there is a 6a start between them.

The Virgin Climb   8m   S   P2   C1900   ★★
From the middle of the east face take the easiest line around the south-east corner to the left and ascend on good pockets to the top.

Chastity   6m   E2   P3   C1979   ★
5c   The wall above the initial traverse of Virgin Climb, just right of the arete, often proves traumatic on first acquaintance. It can be started direct up the undercut rib at 6b.

Fisher's Stride   15m   VS   P2   C1940   ★
5a   A committing stride is made on to the south face of the Virgin from the adjacent slab followed by an upward traverse to the left to a sloping ledge. An exposed step round the corner is made and the traverse continued to another sloping ledge. From the bottom left-hand corner of the ledge a delicate ascent leads to the top. It is possible to start direct from the gully at 6b. It is also, allegedly, possible to jump onto the Virgin and then back again without touching the rock with your hands - *which is Virgin' on the ridiculous!*

Magnum Opus   12m   E5   P2   1988   ★★
6b   To the left of Fisher's Stride is an obvious ramp. Gain this from below and layback to its top. Swing left and follow the crack to finish up the crux of Opus. **The Direct Start** (7a) Climbs the hanging groove to the left from a pocket, via a side-pull and a slot to reach the break

Opus   10m   E4   P2   1977/79/97   ★★
6b   The large yellowish wall to the left contains a line of widely-spaced slots and holes. Climb these to a horizontal break and

protection below a small roof from where the original finish moves left; **Hocus Pocus** moves right to gain the slab; and the **Supo Direct Finish** climbs over the roof and up the short rib above. All are allegedly the same grade.

Gypus   10m   E3   P3   1982
6b From the foot of Opus a wild lay-away from a small flake enables the 'ledge' of Gypsy to be reached at its right side. Rock up left to finish.

The Gypsy   10m   E3   P3   1973   ★★★
6a A strenuous classic. Start at the bottom corner and climb the crack and rib until a swing right enables the "ledge" to be reached. Rock up leftwards to a worrying finish.

The Virgin   13m   E3   P2   1973   ★
6b A climb which does not often yield at the first attempt. Start at the left end of the overhanging west face. Pull into the horizontal crack and follow it rightwards until a small hole enables an obvious pinch to be reached. Pull over and finish easily. **Variations**;- It is possible to continue the traverse into The Gypsy and also to traverse with the break at foot level to gain the large pinch.

Jack on Fire   7m   E4   P2   1988   ★
6c The wall above the start of The Virgin has one tricky move, just right of the scoop. Protection is a Friend 4 in the large hole on the right.

The Lady   6m   E4   P2   1985
6c The cold and unyielding north-west arete.

The Bitch   5m   E4   P3   1990
6c The thin crack to the left of The Lady is short but with a nasty landing.

The Tramp   5m   E3   P2   1985
6b The wall midway between the thin crack and the arete on the north face.

F Behind the Virgin Boulder is a long low overhang with a series of popular roof problems.

G The undercut block right of the Virgin Boulder sports several traverses and numerous pumpy problems, many made longer with sitting starts. The boldest **Frightening Territory** (6b) ★ climbs pockets up right of the crack but the modern classic is **The Keel** (7a) ★★★ which starts way back under the nose and emerges on the right up onto the slab. It has recently been done without the 'chip on the lip'!

H   The Matterhorn Boulder Contains a number of easy lines
suitable for tiny tots and absolute beginners on the big slab. The
vertical south face is **Matterhorn Ridge** (5a) ★★ climbed with the
use of the crack on the right edge. The gully face is the start of
Piggott's Stride but can be continued to the top of the boulder at 4c
to create a good short route in its own right.

J   The Overhanging Egg   The bulging faces provide the best
sport, providing that sitting starts are used. The girdle is a minor
classic.

K   M.K. Wall

M.K. Original (5b) ★ A short problem on the right up shallow
pockets to a rounded finish.

M.K. Traverse 10m E3 P3   ★★
6a A series of 'bullet holes' below the top are traversed from right to
left with increasing seriousness. Reversal is also good value.

Aimless Wall 6m HVS P1
5b Straight up, just right of the rounded crack.

The split block (**The Trousers**) in the centre of the field below Low
Man is **OUT OF BOUNDS**. In order not to worsen the already
uneasy relationship with the farmer, please respect this ban.

L   North Boulder
This lies opposite the Pulpit and provides at least eight variations.
The best being **The Centre Of The Slab** (5b) ★★★ direct and
precarious.

The South Cave Group
These rocks are the first encountered if approaching on the path
directly above the farm. There are around ten problems here but
unfortunately some are now marred by the proximity of a barbed
wire fence.

ALMSCLIFF CRAG – GRADED LIST

E5
China Syndrome (7a)
Magnum Opus (6b)
Retribution Rib Direct (5c)
Forgotten Wall (6c)
Wharfedale Wall (6c)
Megadoom (6b)
All Our Yesterdays (6a)
Orchrist (6b)
The Ems Telegram (6b)

E4
All Quiet (6a)
Toads Nose (6b)
Opus (6b)
Orchrist (6b)
Exit Stage Left (6b)
Al Says 6a (6b)
Blackhead (6c)
Everyman Has His Niche (6b)
Penny Pip (6a)
Fungus The Bogeyman (6a)
Yellow Peril (6a)
Whisky Wall Direct (6a)
Horror Of Walls (6b)
Impending Doom (6a)
'Arries 'Ook (6a)
Grand Illusion (5c)
Over The Top (5c)

E3
Microscopic Wall (6b)
Kitson Did It First (6b)
The Big Greeny (6a)
Rectum Rift (6b)
The Wall of Horrors (6a)
Why Climb (6a)
The True Two Ton Sardine (6a)
WASC (6a)
Western Front (5c)
Merlin (5c)
Trident Finish (6a)
Whisky Wall (5b)

E2
Nelly Moser Finish (6a)
Bancroft's Roof (6a)
Encore (5c)
Roast Beef (6a)
Oubliette (6a)
First Night (6a)
Yellow Wall (5c)
Twelfth Night (5c)
Yorkshire Puddin' (5c)
Black Wall Eliminate (5c)
Clematis (5c)
Spirit Level (5b)
Retribution Rib (5b)
Hobgoblin (5c)

E1
Torpedo (5c)
Acetabulum (5c)
Shuffle Crack (5c)
North West Girdle (5b)
Pulpit Corner (5b)
Dolphinian (5b)
South Wall Direct (5b)
Z Climb Eliminate (5b)
Blackpool Promenade (5b)
Up Periscope (5b)

HVS
Depth Charger (5b)
Finale Slab (5b)
The Nose Direct (5b)
Birdlime Traverse (5a)
Great Western (5a)
Jacob's Ladder (5b)
Demon Wall (5a)
Overhanging Grooves (5a)
Green Gully Wall (5a)

VS
V Chimney Direct (5a)
Pothole Direct (5b)
Pram Pusher's Paradise (5a)
Fence Buttress (5b)
Rift Crack (5a)

Constipation Crack (5a)
Black Wall (5a)
Fisher's Stride (5a)
Frankland's Green Crack (4c)
Z Climb (4c)
Pigott's Stride (4c)
Green Gully Rib (4c)
South Wall Traverse (4c)
Zig Zag Direct (4c)
Crack Of Doom (4c)
Traditional Climb (4c)
High Level Traverse (4c)
Central Climb (4c)
West Chimney Rib (4c)
Stomach Traverse (4c)

MVS
South Face Climb (4c)
Bird's Nest Variation (4c)
Square Chimney & Whisky Crack (4b)

HS
Parsons' Chimney (4b)
The Goblin (4b)
South Chimney Layback (4c)
Central Crack (4b)
Kiernan's Traverse and Rough Crack (4b)
Bird's Nest Crack (4b)
Fisher's Traverse (4b)
Crack and Wall (4b)

S
The Zig Zag (4b)
Fluted Crack (4b)
Pinnacle Flake Climb
The Virgin Climb
Green Wall
Lichen Wall
Low Man Girdle
Fat Man's Misery

HVD
The Final Finale
Pinnacle Direct
Stew Pot
V Chimney and Traverse
Long Chimney

VD
Fluted Columns
Rough Crack Direct
The Pothole
Leaf Climb
Cup and Saucer

D
South Chimney
Corner Crack
Low Man Easy Way

M
Tight Chimney
Three Chockstones
Chimney

MICRO- ROUTES

Jess's Roof (7a)
Jack on Fire (6c)
The Bitch (6c)
The Lady (6c)
The Tramp (6b)
Hammill's Rib (6b)
Barley Mow (6b)
Daisy Chain (6b)
Something's Cooking (6b)
M.K. Traverse (6a)
The Virgin (6b)
Syrett's Roof (6b)

Gypus (6b)
The Gypsy (6a)
Chastity (5c)
Envy Of Angels (5c)
The South-West Face (5c)
The Blunt Edge (5b)
The North Ridge (5c)
Traditional Eliminate (6a)
V Crack (6a)
Thompson's Traverse (5b)
Angelic Upstart (5b)

The Scoop (5b)
Aimless Wall 5b
Stepoffable (5b)
The Chimney Flake (5a)
The Hillary Step (5b)
The Ear (5a)
The Nose (4c)
The Lhotse Face (4c)
The Postman (4c)
The South Col (4b)
West Cave Wall (4b)
North Face

PROBLEMS WITH NAMES

7b
Stu's Roof

7a
The Keel
Magnum Opus DS
Demon Roof

6c
Arries Ook DS
Black Wall Traverse

6b
Frightening Territory
Dots and Dabs
Fishers Stride DS
Pebble Wall
Dry Stone Traverse

6a
The Left Wing
Crucifix Arete
The Right Wing
Dolphinian DS
Morrell's Wall
Gray's Wall
The Nose

5c
Suppository Wall
Forgotten Wall DS
The Slab
Teaspoon Variation
Pork Chop Slab
The Ladder
The Crucifix
Jam Pot

5b
The Niche
The Wall
The Centre Of The Slab
Three Swings Traverse
The High Step
The Rift Traverse
MK Original
Off the Wall

5a
Matterhorn Ridge
The East Face
End Wall

4c
Thompson's Route
Central Route

4b
North Top Corner

ASH HEAD CRAG

N.G.R. SE 143754

SITUATION AND CHARACTER The crag is situated on top of Masham Moor between Lofthouse and Masham, approximately 3 miles north-east of Lofthouse, near Pateley Bridge. It comprises a compact collection of buttresses and large boulders well worth a visit on a summer's day. The aspect is generally north-west, fairly quick drying and the rock is well-weathered natural grit. However, its position is rather spoiled by the proximity of two shooting lodges slap-bang in front. Do not be deterred however, if only to tick the classic line of Thunder Crack and its Lightning variant. Though somewhat remote a visit here can easily be combined with the more extensive bouldering venue of Sypeland Crag a mile or so to the south.

APPROACHES AND ACCESS Ash Head is approached from the Lofthouse-Healey road across the top of Masham Moor. When approaching from Lofthouse follow the steep road to the top of the moor where an open rough road signposted 'unsuitable for motors' leads off to the right. This can be followed for 2 miles through two gates and past two turnings, always keeping left. The crag marked on the O.S.map as Combs Crags can now be seen on the left behind the two shooting lodges. A public footpath leads directly to the rocks from the main track. **Negotiations to ensure continued climbing access are ongoing and are highly dependent on considerate behaviour. The crag should be avoided during the shooting season. Permission to climb should be sought beforehand by ringing the estate office at Ripon (01765) 689224. Please, no dogs, no fires, no large parties and of prime concern no damage must be caused to the shooting lodges**.

THE CLIMBS These are described from left to right. From behind the middle of the left-hand building the first route is:-

1 The Horn 8m HVS P1
5a Start below and climb directly to the obvious line of knobs. Old-fashioned protection techniques help!

2 Barnstorm 9m HS P1
4b Start 3 metres right of The Horn below a thin crack. Climb up to the thin crack, traverse right for 3 metres and then finish up the corner above.

3 Flake Crack 6m S P1
Climb the obvious flake 3 metres right of the arete between the buildings.

4 Dust Off 11m E2 P2
5c On the wall behind the righthand building. Start 2 metres from the left-hand edge. Climb a short crack then straight up the blank wall above to the horizontal break. Move 3 metres right and finish direct.

5 Tip Off 9m VS P1
4c Start 2 metres to the left of the arete behind the middle of the righthand building. Climb direct past the break and up the wall to the top break and so join Windy Wall.

6 Windy Wall 10m S P1
Climb the arete behind the middle of the righthand building to the top break and then move 1 metre left and finish direct.

7 Headstand 10m HS P1
4a Climb the chimney behind the righthand building to the overhang and then move right to finish.

An easier but inferior variation combining parts of the last two climbs was originally recorded as **Fluted Rib** (VD).

8 Last Rites 9m VS P1
4c Climb the crack system in the wall to the right of Headstand to the top break. Move right under the overhang and finish direct.

9 Thunder Crack 12m VS P1   ★★★
4c Climb the arete behind the righthand end of the right-hand building to the break. Hand traverse right for 3 metres to the base of an overhanging curving crack. Climb this and move left under the overhangs and on to the slab to finish.

10 Lightning Variation 11m HVS P1   ★★
5c Start directly below the curving crack of the previous route. Climb the blunt rib to gain the crack and up this to the overhang. Move right and finish up the slab.

11 Up and Under 9m VS P1
4c Climb the arete 10 metres right of Thunder Crack to the grassy ledge. Move left then up the V-chimney to finish on the right.
The wall to the right provides several interesting problems and contains:-

12 Wanderlust 17m VD P1
Traverse the wide crack in the wall right of Up and Under from right to left.

Opposite the start of Wanderlust is a large detached boulder known as the **Rhombic Block**. This can be traversed in its entirety at about Severe but also provides eight more conventional climbs. The side facing Wanderlust contains:-

13   The Actress   8m   VS   P1
4c   Start 5 metres from the left arete and climb the green wall to finish up the short shallow corner.

14   Gangrene   8m   HS   P1
4b   Start 5 metres to the right of The Actress and climb the green wall to a shallow sloping groove which leads to the top.

15   The Result   8m   HS   P1
4b   On the west side of the Rhombic Block. Climb the diagonal crack, move left and finish up the slab above.

16   The Tea Party   8m   HVS   P1
5c   In the middle of the south face of the Rhombic Block. Climb the two bulging cracks. Tricky!

17   The True Knobbler   8m   E1   P2
6a   Climb the wall to the left of The Tea Party, the upper part proving very difficult.

18   Rhyme   7m   S   P1
The blunt south-east arete of the block.

19   Rhythm   8m   VD   P1
The cracked east face of the block.

20   Easy Ridge   7m   M   P1
The north-east arete of the block.

21   A Climb   6m   S   P1
Opposite Easy Ridge is an A-shaped crack system. Climb the left-hand crack.

BAILDON BANK

SITUATION AND CHARACTER Baildon Bank is a series of quarries high above the Aire Valley at Baildon, near Shipley. It faces south-east and consequently gets the morning sun. In places the rock transcends mortal experience and would-be aspirants are advised to carry a bucket and spade. Elsewhere magnificent quarried gritstone cracks and flared arches rise majestically to meet stout elm, oak and sycamore rivalling the very best this fair isle can offer. If routes are loose this is indicated in the description. If routes are extremely loose this is not indicated because they have probably fallen down. It would be unfair not to point out that over half the routes are good quality with excellent concrete post or tree belays and at least one fifth rate with the best and are spread throughout the grades. The Bank also holds interest for those interested in viniculture; copious nettles and blackberries are evident throughout the summer.

APPROACHES AND ACCESS Baildon Bank follows a contour from the Bay Horse Inn on the Baildon road westwards towards Shipley Glen. From the main Shipley to Otley road (A6038) bear left on to Baildon road one mile out of Shipley at the traffic lights. Follow this for almost 2 miles to the Bay Horse Inn. Turn left and the quarries soon appear high up on the right. Park below and walk up. The Bradford to Baildon bus 661 passes below the quarries. Train users on the Bradford-Ilkley line can alight at Baildon station and walk west along Station Road until the Baildon road and the Bay Horse Inn are reached after half a mile.

THE CLIMBS are described from RIGHT to LEFT starting to the left of the fence above Sandals Primary School. To the right of the fence are a number of good boulder problems. Numbers in brackets were painted below the routes that existed several years ago. Though fading, many are still visible and included after route names to assist location.

1 Stretch (1) 10m E1 P2
5b Start in the middle of the broken wall just left of a detached flake. Climb the crack and left side of the blank-looking head wall on small positive holds.

2 Stretcher (2) 8m E2 P3
5c Climb the centre of the short wall to the left. Gain the obvious break and continue on negative holds to an Amazonian finish.

To the left are various short problems.

3   Karen (3)   10m   S   P1
Fifty metres left of Stretcher is the next buttress. Karen climbs the short fine crack at the righthand end and finishes up ledges above. An alternative start up the right arete is 5a, followed by a 12-metre hand traverse leftwards (5b).

4   Grot (4)   10m   S   P2
Climb the grot in the centre of the buttress.

5   Gold Rings (5)   10m   VS   P1
4c The corner crack is laybacked to ledges on the left. Finish up the wall above.

6   Gold Rings Alternative   10m   E1   P2
5c Climb the fine sharp short arete left of the corner utilising a flake high up to join Gold Rings at the ledge.

7   La Cathedralle   15m   VS   P2
4c Behind a large boulder with an obvious drill line (4b) is a small bay. Climb the right corner crack, avoiding a "York Minster" if possible.

8   Pearly Gates (8)   15m   S   P1
Climb the chimney to a ledge and continue up a flake crack to a corner finish. An alternative finish (E1 5b) can be made by traversing right from half way up the flake on to the nose. Continue direct up the overhung arete on good holds.

9   Nude Groove (9)   15m   HVS   P2   ★
5a Find a way through the overhangs to a grassy ledge. Follow the eponymous groove left of the obscene wall. Finish up the mosaic to join the corner of Pearly Gates.

10   Toss Off (10)   15m   HVS   P2
5a Climb directly through roofs to reach the groove left of Nude Groove. Follow this and the wall above leftwards to a finish at a large tree.

11   Quietus   15m   E3   P2   ★
6b Climb the wall and gain a small ledge on the arete. Move back left on to the wall and climb direct to the flake on Hades. Usually protected by a side-runner in Hades (E5 without).

12   Hades (12)   20m   VS   P2   ★★★
4c Climb the corner to a sandy overhang. Traverse right to a flake crack and finish with sensational barndoor laybacking to a sloping ledge.

13 Olley 15m E3 P2
5c Climb the blunt arete right of Epitaph direct to the top. (Peg or side-runners required below the final wall).

14 Epitaph (13) 20m HS P1   ★★
4a Follow the obvious flake. Step left to below a V-groove. Continue left on to the arete and follow cracks leftwards to the top. Very good climbing but a devious line.

15 Epitaph Direct 18m VS P1   ★★
4b From the sloping ledge on Epitaph continue up the V-shaped corner and negotiate the bulge above.

16 Future Times (15) 18m E1 P2
5b Climb the sandy wall left of The Epitaph flake to an undercut at 3 metres. Move up to the sloping ledge of Epitaph and follow the discontinuous crack system up the scoop on the right.

17 Going for Oneness (17) 15m E1 P2
5b Climb the crack immediately left of Future Times moving right through undercut flakes to a small sentry box. Follow the arete on the left to the top.

18 Ram (18) 15m E1 P2   ★
5b Climb the crack through the sandy overhang to finish as for Epitaph.

To the left of Ram is a very thin peg crack. This is:–

19 The Sunday Lunch Mob 12m E4 P3
6b By an extraordinary mantelshelf, climb the wall just right of the thin crack to the overhang making a very difficult move to a large hold, then easily to the top.

20 Geeta Nob Out 12m VS P1
4b Climb the flake 1 metre left of the thin crack.

21 Pinnacle Flake 10m S P1
Follow the big flake crack to a grass ledge.

A low-level boulder problem exists in the form of a traverse from Pearly Gates to Pinnacle Flake (6b).

22 Bamboozle Bottom 50m VS P1
4c It is possible to do a high-level traverse along the sandy break rightwards to finish up Gold Rings.

23 Feel the Buzz 7m HVS P3
6b The small wall left of Pinnacle Flake. Follow the chipped holds until they disappear and miraculously gain a break. Move right and up to finish.

24 Chimney (21) 8m D P1
Climb the orifice in the cave-like constriction.

25 Theakstone Man 8m HS
4a Start 3 metres right of Dave's Crack. Climb the rightward
slanting flake to a small ledge then the thin slanting crack to the top.

26 Dave's Crack (22) 8m VS P1
4c Start behind the huge boulder. Climb the steep wall on its right
to the break. Move left and continue up the crack. A direct start up
the arete is E1 5c P2.

27 Rip (23) 15m S P1
Follow the diagonal flake and finish over the small roof above.

28 Van Winkle 15m E5 P3   ★
6b Start 1 metre left of Rip until a horizontal line of handholds is
reached (imagined). Traverse left at this level to the base of a thin
vertical crack. Climb up the hanging groove, move left, up right and
then up to the top. A direct start is available at 6c by starting from
just right of the left arete until the parent route is joined. A direct

finish is possible at 6b by trending up and rightwards from the top of the thin vertical crack.

29 Big Curver (24) 15m HVS P2 ★
5b A compelling line. Follow the huge curving flake crack utilising holds on the wall at half way. Finish up a rather unsavoury groove to a tree.

30 Leeway (25) 15m VS P2
4c Another flake for your delight and delectation begins at the base of Big Curver and trends left and up. Finish as for Big Curver.

31 Slit 15m HVS P2
5b To the left is an obvious overhung chimney flake. Layback the flake past a large chockstone at three-quarters height. Not a midget's gem!

32 The Vice (27) 17m A1
Follow the bolt holes up the overhanging side of the flake.

33 Solomon's Diedre (28)   15m   VS   P1
4c Climb the corner until forced right on the wall.

The next buttress, **Scar Buttress**, gives a selection of the best routes on the crag.

34 Moria (29)   15m   E2   P1   ★★
5c The steep crack with interesting manoeuvres in the last 5 metres. Strenuous.

35 Intrepid (30)   15m   E6   P3   ★★
6a Follow the line of bolt holes left of the arete of Moria.

36 The Flakes (31)   15m   E3   P3   ★
5c Climb the corner to a peg runner and follow the line of tenuously-attached flakes to the top. Any creaking counts as extra E points. The flakes have been climbed without recourse to them (E4 6a P3).

37 Scar (32)   15m   E2   P2   ★★★
5c The magnificent crack in the centre of the buttress. Follow this ecstatically to the break. Continue gleefully up the wall past a peg above, finishing rightwards. A more direct finish is slightly harder.

38 Scar Wall (33)   15m   E5   P3   ★
6b Follow a vague flake line left of Scar on small holds. Finish interestingly over the dinner plate roof. Not for the faint-hearted.

39 Scar Arete (34)   15m   E5   P3   ★★
6c Climb the arete. Not for dwarfs. (May be impossible since a vital hold came off at half height).

40 Fizzicle Fizzle   20m   E3   P2
5c A high-level girdle starting from the ledge on Scar Arete and traversing the break (bold after the flakes) to finish up Moria.

Round the corner from Scar Arete is an apparently-blank wall.

41 Gesticulation (35)   15m   E4   P3
6b Follow the small holds until a long reach gains a good ledge. Finish up Paddy's Route.

42 Paddy's Route (36)   15m   VS   P2
4b The wide crack becomes two smaller ones. Saharan finish.

43 No Pegs Please We're British   7m   E1
5b The wall to the right of Twin cracks moving right near the top.

44 Twin Cracks (37)   7m   S   P1
Left of Paddy's route. The cracks and chimneys above.

45 Rocking Chimney (38)   7m   VD   P1
The wide crack with a chockstone at the top.

46 Red Wall 6m HVS P3
5c The wall between Rocking Chimney and the thin crack of Promenade. Sadly chipped by the less able.

47 Promenade (39) 10m M P2
Ascend the crack to the obvious ledge. Foot traverse right and step across the yawning chasm of Rocking Chimney above the Twin Cracks. A technical masterpiece of its grade.

48 Layback Crack (40) 7m VD P1
Follow the crack to a hawthorn tree.

49 Adamski 6m MVS
4b Start as for Peapod and climb straight up using pockets and the right arete.

50 Pea Pod (41) 6m S P1
Climb up into the eponymously-named crack and then exit direct.

51 Whillan's Arete 7m VS P2   ★★
4c A route with a feeling of exposure totally out of proportion to its technical difficulty. With several hundred side runners placed in Pea Pod, climb the left arete. Great view of the box quarry which may be visited if the ascentionist attempts too violent a mantelshelf finish!

The large black hole beyond Whillan's Arete has a number of good routes but adventurous climbers, in addition to the normal rack of gear, will require a trowel, secateurs and a flame thrower. The routes are described for posterity. Some of them are actually still climbable. Those that are not have the following grade: HF = Horrendous Finish; HS = Horrendous Start; HM = Horrendous Middle.

The routes are described anti-clockwise starting from Whillan's Arete. (The 'B' numbers indicate Box Quarry routes only)

B1 Ian's Bolt Route 18m A1
Follow the line of rusty old bolts over the roof.

B2 Syrett's Crack 18m E2 P2
5c Follow the large crack. Move left on dubious holds and finish up the crack above.

The routes on the next wall can be reached with machete or helicopter.

B3 Push Off 10m VS HF P2
4c Climb the corner crack right of the arch.

B4 Depegomania 10m HVS HS, HF P2
5a The leftwards-trending crack left of Push Off.

B5 The Arch 10m HVS HS, HF P2
5a The crack on the left side of the arch.

B5 Time 12m HVS HS, HF P2
5a The crack system 5 metres left of The Arch.

B7 Wet Wall 15m HVS HF P2
5b Three metres left again is a ledge at one-third height. Gain this and the cracks above.

B8 Hidden Corner 15m S HF
Around the arete, climb the corner.

The back wall is disected by a large arete and corner.

B9 Sometime 15m VS HS, HM, HF
4c The extremely-vegetated crack on the righthand side of the back wall.

B10 Flake Wall 15m E1
To quote an old guide: "The very fragile flake cracks, the top probably needs recleaning"!!!

B11 Flake Corner 15m HVS P1
5b The corner.

B12 Green Arete 15m E4 P3
5c The obvious arete. Begin up the wall left of the corner passing an antique golo. Climbable.

B13 Timex 15m E5 P3
6a Climb the blank wall (hopefully!).

On the left wall of the box quarry is:–

B14 Overtime Wall 12m HVS HS, HM, HF P2
5b Climb the overgrown cracks to a ledge and wall. .

B15 Spider 15m HVS HF, HS P2
5a From the obvious paint splurge, climb the corner and wall above.

B16 Saw Off 15m HVS P2
5b Climb the crack left of the splurge.

B17 Drop Out 15m VS P2
4c Left of Saw Off is an obvious fallen block (unusual for Baildon Bank). Climb directly above the block.

B18 Cream Legs 15m VS P2
4b The next crack left.

B19   Ulley Right   15m   VS   P2
4c   The crack system leads to the lefthand end of the grass ledge.

B20   Ulley Left   15m   HVS   P2
5b   The crack to the left is hard to enter and follow. Continue up the
arete above.

B21   Closing Time   10m   E4   P2
6b   The thin crack system left of Ulley Left.

Hurray you're out of the quarry!

52   Cold Bum   8m   S   P1
The wide crack directly opposite Whillan's Arete, just outside the
Black Hole.

53   Hirst Wale   7m   VS   P3
5a   Climb the short wall left of Cold Bum via chipped holds. Then
reverse it!

54   Tiles   7m   S   P3
To the left is a broken wall (no, not the rest of Baildon Bank). Climb
this if you dare.

55   Lay Away (69)   18m   VS   P3
5a   Burn carbs up the obvious overhanging start then continue
delicately up the slabs above to finish left or right (a pint for anyone
who finishes direct).

56   Yellow Way (70)   18m   S   P3
Climb the corner immediately left and finish as for Lay Away Left Hand.

57   Cavern (71)   18m   VD   P2
Climb the corner left of Mellow Wall.

The wall to the left has been soloed as far as the third break but no
one has had the lobotomy required for the final wall.

58   Flake Crack (72)   12m   HS   P2
4a   The next buttress along sports a tree at half height. Below this is
a flake which is followed to a break and then climb more delicately
up the wall above.

59   Adam's Apple   14m   HS   P2
4b   Start as for Flake Crack over the bulge and then traverse left to
a mantelshelf finish a couple of metres left of the upper flake.

60   Sensational Exposure   15m   M   P2   ★★
Climb the blocky corner past a cave.

61   Eternal Peace (73)   15m   A1
Follow the peg crack left of the corner. Traverse left and finish up

the crack in the centre of the wall. (Oft considered as a free route, but still not done?).

62 Last Edge (74) 15m E5 P3   ★★★
6b Start up the left wall and move into the pod crack. Step up on to the arete with difficulty and move up to good holds right of the arete. A testament to Iain Edwards at his best.

63 Bramble Crack (75) 12m VS P1   ★★
4c The double cracks in the corner provide for a plethora of protection on this sustained route.

64 The Fin (76) 10m Traditional HVS!
5a The fin in the crack leads to a chimney. For devotees only.

65 Chipper (77) 12m E3 P3
5b The overhung and undercut buttress to the left of The Fin has chipped holds left of the roof. Follow these to the top. Unprotected.

66 Cool Trickster 15m E5 P3   ★★
5c If singing helps to calm the nerves, start now. Go over the roof as for Chipper then move right to the arete. A hard move brings either better holds or the ground. Either way, stop singing.

67 Sabre Crack (78) 10m MVS P1
4b To the left of the undercut buttress is a recessed slab with two corners. This is the righthand corner.

68 A Path For An Evil Soul 10m E6 P?
6b A slightly contrived line up the wall between Sabre Crack and Matey's Crack. Thin crimps and a hard mantel lead to good ledges on the slab. Enter the groove above (crux) and finish on a sandy ledge.

69 Matey's Crack (79) 10m VS P2
4c The lefthand corner.

70 Agame (80) 10m E5 P3
6a The wall and arete immediately left is climbed with great difficulty.

The slabs to the left hold many esoteric undercut problems. The corner 15 metres left of Agame has been climbed, but the number of rescues exceeds the number of ascents.

71 Steel Monkey 8m E1 P?
5b The right arete of Crucifix, avoiding the chipped holds.

72 Crucifix 8m HVS P3
4c The buttress to the left with a tarred crucifix is climbed in its centre to the midway break, followed by more natural holds to the top.

The next 30 metres contain excellent roof-and-wall problems which, if combined, can give routes of 8-10 metres up to 6a. Two poor routes (82) and (83) are reminiscent of Blackpool beach.

73   Agoa (84)   8m   VS   P3
5a To the left is an overgrown corner. This rarely-repeated gem takes the wall and hanging flake on the right.

74   Ego (85)   7m   VD   P1
The corner is climbed on good holds.

The next slab contains many excellent routes in the lower grades.

75   Born Free (86)   7m   S   P2
This route takes the right arete.

76   Black (87)   6m   VD   P2
The next crack along.

77   And (88)   6m   S   P1
The next crack is laybacked.

The wall to the left gives a 5a problem if taken in its centre.

78   Tan (89)   6m   VD   P1
The wide broken crack moving right at the top.

79   Doodle (90)   10m   VS   P1
5a The wall left is climbed direct to a thin crack. Tunnel vision helps.

80   Conch (91)   10m   HS   P1   ★★
4b The crack in the centre of the wall is a Baildon classic!

81   Ruf (92)   9m   VS   P3
5a The wall left of Conch and right of the small corner is climbed to a thin crack. Almost as myopic as Doodle.

82   Agnostic's Arete (93)   10m   S   P2   ★★
The obvious arete in the centre left of the slab. Traverse through choss left at the top to finish.

83   Missout   10m   E1   P3
5a Climb the wall 1 metre left of Agnostic's Arete via flakes to a pocket and the top.

84   To A Reckless Flash (95)   10m   E4   P3
6a Climbed in memory of a sadly-missed Friend. From the number (95) climb the wall direct with a very difficult move on to the top wall.

85   Half Crack (96)   9m   MVS   P1
4b Three metres right of the large corner is a curving crack at half height. Reach it and climb it.

86 Dan Dan the Fighting Man (96a) 6m VS P2
4c Climb the thin crack 2 metres left.

The corner can be climbed at Diff but the finish is four grades harder.

87 No Top (98) 8m VS P1
4c The very overhanging crack left of the corner.

88 Jammy (99) 7m S P1
4c The next crack is best climbed on the jugs. Finish up the arete.

89 HMS Amethyst (100) 12m S P1   ★★
4a This route takes the detached flake and arete to the right.

The corner formed by the flake is Severe.

90 Joanna (102) 15m VS P1   ★★★
5a The next feature, in a recessed lower bay, is a superb crack starting as a finger jam and ending somewhat higher and later as a chimney. After an awkward start difficulties ease but the quality remains constant.

91 Arufe 15m MVS P1   ★
4c In a similar vein, the hanging corner to the left is climbed to a wide crack.

92 Annudarufe 15m VS P2
4c One of the number of ways up the wall and overhang to cracks above. Now (sadly) overgrown.

93 Poison 13m S P1
Climb the crack system containing the sprouting tree stumps.

94 Last Day 12m HVS P2
5a To the left, a thin crack splits the overlap. Climb it.

95 Best Forgotten (108) 12m MVS P3
The rubble filled corner is ....!

96 Rawhide 6m E5 P2
6b Climb the arete to the left with a peg runner.

97 Jeanette 6m S P1
From the ledge, climb the wide crack. On the first ascent, Shipley Fire Brigade turned up in order to effect a rescue after worried residents below had seen falling blocks.

98 Turk In The Hole 8m HS
4a Start 3 metres right of Heave Too. Climb the left side of the 'diving board' and stand on it with difficulty. Follow the arete to the top.

The rock now falls away to a broken gully. The next climbing is 40 metres to the left.

99   Heave Too (110)   8m   E3   P1   ★
6b Climb up to a V-notch in the roof, clip the bolt and go for it.

100   Pullover (111)   8m   VS   P1
4c Climb to the parallel cracks and finish up these.

101   Jumper (112)   9m   HVS   P3
4c To the left is an arete. Climb this and the wall to the right. Sadly vandalised.

102   Jericho Wall (113)   9m   VD   P1
The corner crack. Broken.

103   Curving Cracks (114)   9m   HVS   P2
5b Climb the wall to a ledge and then leftwards up the corner cracks. Harder than it looks.

104   Pillar   9m   MVS   P2
4b Start as for Jumper but climb the pillar to the left.

105   Stubby Legs   9m   VS   P2
4c Climb the crack left of the pillar.

106   Ramp (116)   9m   HVS   P1
5a Follow the leftwards ramp from Stubby Legs into the corner.

107   Do Knot (117)   10m   HVS   P3
5a Climb the sandy crack to the top.

108   Green Wall (118)   10m   S   P2
Chimney, bridge and mantelshelf the green corner.

109   Smear Fear   9m   E5   P3   ★
6a Start below the sharp undercut arete. Climb up to the roof then spreadeagle yourself between a small hold and the arete. Follow the arete to finish.

110   Fingers   12m   E1   P2
5c Climb the corner on the left wall and, from the ledge, follow thin cracks rightwards to finish as for Do Knot.

111   Back Crack Corner (120)   10m   MVS   P1
4b Start as for Fingers but climb the back crack. The grade reflects the temporary nature of the grass ledge.

112   Rampart Arete (121)   15m   E2   P2   ★
5c As for Fingers to the ledge. Place numerous nuts in the crack, then traverse leftwards to the arete which, though bold, has big holds.

(Once graded V.S. – Very Stupid).

113 Swingover (122) 10m E3 P2   ★★★
5c Climb the hanging groove in the arete to a good nut placement (you'll need it) and cavort upwards. Excellent, if a little brave to start.
(Pl with Sliders to protect crack).

114 Armageddon (Outahere) 12m E6 P3   ★★★
6c From the start of Back Crack Corner swing left round the arete and climb the 'not as blank as it looks' wall to the break below the bolt. Clip the bolt, cry "salvation", and then work out how you are going to climb the blunt left arete. Try it, then work out another way. As hard as it looks.

115 Wombling Wall (123) 12m E4 P2   ★★★
6a Follow the crack in the centre of the buttress to a ledge. Make a hard move up to a peg (not in place) in a break. A mega rockover leads to better holds.

It is possible to climb the left arete on its left but its proximity to Swingover makes it rather too esoteric for a name and number.

116 Prairie Steps (124) 12m S P1   ★★
Follow the corner crack. Excellent.

117 Chimney Route (125) DO NOT CLIMB

118 Count Up (126) 12m VD
Climb the very broken arete to the left.

119 Potch Wall (127) 12m VS P3
If you must, climb the wall to the left direct to a corner.

120 Hotch Crack (128) 10m D P3
Climb the broken crack from the broken flake to the broken top. Broken. (You will be!).

121 Quaint Rock Wall (129) 10m S P2
At last! An improvement. Boulder the wall left of the flake and finish easily.

122 Banana Groove (130) 9m S P2
Up to the left is a short overhung groove. Climb this and the flake above.

123 Bee Sting (131) 10m HVS P2
4c Boulder up the wall left of Hotch Crack past a solution pocket which contained the bee (now deceased). Move up and right to a thin flake and the top. Boldish.

Several problems can be climbed to the left. The next buttress is 100 metres left, past steps with a guard rail.

124 Monkey Puzzle 10m VS P1
4c The right wall of the first corner contains a steep crack. Climb this and a pair of thin cracks in the head wall above. An easier (Hard Severe) left-hand version of this exists.

125 Split 'Em 10m HVS P2
5a The corner is capped by an overhang. Climb through this with difficulty to the top.

126 Up and Over 15m VS P3
4c Bravely climb to the sand castle overhang. Remove the grass tufts and climb the slab above. (Of botanical interest).

127 Africa 15m E1 P3
5b The undercut wall to the left is difficult. From the ledge above meander to the top.

128 Coronation Street 15m S P2
Follows a direct line up the shattered cracks.

129 All Fall Down 15m S P2
The shattered crack to the left is followed by the shattered crack above. Other starts are possible but broken.

130 Mash 6m S P1
To the first short crack of the lower buttress starting from a block.

131 South Wall 6m HVS P2
5c The wall left of the large block is undercut and has a large hold at half height. Reach this with ease (if you are 2 metres tall) or difficulty (if you are shorter) and continue.

132 Bygones 8m VD P1
The good crack with a small corner to start.

133 Balless Jess 8m MVS P2
4b The undercut wall left of Mash.

134 The Blob 10m D P1
The block-filled crack.

To the left is a shattered corner. Not recommended.

135 Broken Off 9m VD P1
To the left of the corner, this is the flake-filled crack.

136 Camera Shake 9m HVS
5b The centre of the smooth wall left of Broken Off.

137 Cracker 10m HS P1
4a The wide broken crack to the left past a bulge.

138 Knut 10m VS P2
4c The wall to the left has a crack at 3 metres. Climb this to a ledge. Move 2 metres left and reach over the bulge. Finish up the slabs.

139 Waredustitgo? 10m VS P3
The pile (laughingly referred to as rock) is climbed to a piece of natural grit, which is followed to the top.

There are a number of natural gritstone boulders to the left which provide some amusement, especially if someone falls off.

Two hundred metres left is a pile of choss which defies Newton' s 1st Law of Gravity. The following routes are recorded for posterity - But are not recommended!

140 Suityuself (148) VS
141 Directional Route (149) VS
142 Z Route (150) S
143 Bowlover (151 S
144 Slant Eyes (152) VS
145 Cavern Route (153)

146 Satire (154) 8m E2 P1   ★★★
5b This is the exception. Climb the hidden overhanging face by a widening crack. Excellent. Makes Higgar Tor look like a slab!

One hundred metres to the left overlooking the Cricketers' Arms is the bottom quarry. It is up to 20 metres high. Unfortunately, some climbs have poor finishes and a third rope belay tied to trees and hung over the side is a wise precaution for those of a delicate nature. Otherwise the climbing here is excellent and many routes are worth a try. Arrival at the base of some routes is controlled by the size of the nettle colony.

147 Descent Route 8m M P1
Climb the very broken cracks at the righthand side of the right buttress.

148 Blockhead (157) 9m VD P1
Climb the cracks to a tree (jungle warfare).

149 Green Border (158) 10m VS P2
4c The arete on the left. Difficulty depends on size.

150 Crab (159) 10m S P1
The chimney corner crack to a large tree.

151   Chat (160,161)   10m   S   P1
The next crack along, with a variation start up the slab to the right.

152   Diff (162)   10m   D   P1
The wide crack with a sycamore at 2 metres.

153   Arkansas   9m   S   P1
The corner crack to the right with yet another tree, this time at 3 metres.

154   Cleanstone Wall (163)   7m   E1   P3   ★
5c   At last a good climb. Climb directly up the centre of the short yellow wall to a small niche and flake crack.

155   Cleanstone Crack (164)   7m   VD   P1
The disappointing crack is climbed past an obvious hanging 50-ton block. There is a possibility of a route over the roof (tee hee!).

156   Coming Corner - is best avoided!

157   Fly Groove (166)   10m   E2   P3   ★
5c   From a perched flake enter the shallow groove with difficulty. Continue more easily to a crack and poor finish.

158   Iain's Swansong (167)   10m   E6   P3   ★★
6c   To the left a very thin crack leads to a blank wall and barn door flake. Good luck.

159   Lost Gold   10m   HVS   P2
5a   Climb broken cracks to a large open groove which provides the fun.

160   Anniversary Arete   11m   HVS   P2
5c   The flakes, wall and vague arete left of Lost Gold.

161   V Route   10m   S   P1
Climb the corner past choss to choss.

162   Viper   10m   VS   P1   ★
4c   To the right of the large cave is a leaning flake which forms a small corner. Climb this to a short slab and finish up the grooves and through the overhangs.

163   Adder Finish   E2   P2
5c   The arete to the right at the top. Runner in left crack advisable.

164   Scoop   10m   E3   P3   ★★
5b   Climb to the obvious dirty ledge right of the cave. Follow the scoop up and left to a niche below the overhang. Follow the crack system/corner to a 'V' in the final overhang.

165 Scythe Man 12m E5 P2
6a Climb the back wall of the pit. Now boldly out across the roof. Layback the corner and finish by traversing right under the final roof to the arete and finish on the lefthand side of roof at widest part.

The next series of routes start from a boulder which finishes 1.5 metres below an arete (172).

166 Mandy Fly Me 18m E2 P2   ★
5b Step on to the arete. Climb directly to a hanging groove and flake using the wall and arete. Finish as for the Scoop.

167 Triang 20m HVS P1   ★
5a Start as for Mandy Fly Me. Follow the series of triangular overhangs until 3 metres from the top. Either move left (5b) and finish at the bolt or move right to the arete to finish as for the Scoop.

168 Desperado 20m E3 P2   ★★
6a Start as for Mandy to the ledge. Traverse left along the lip of the overhang to the holds (which are there somewhere!) on the left of the arete. Traverse left and then up the groove finishing directly to the bolt.

169 Gentle Persuasion 18m E4 P2
6a Takes a bold line right of Ann of Cleaves. Climb up to the roof (peg) move right to join Desperado for 2 metres then finish direct.

170 Anne of Cleaves 18m E3 P2   ★★
5c Ascend the open groove in the centre of the quarry, turning the overhang on the right. Worth seeking out.

171 Lightning 18m HVS P2
5b From the ledge 4 metres up Anne of Cleaves climb the thin crack in the left wall to a ledge. Beware the loose block! Finish directly or more safely left.

172 Futurama 15m VS P2
4c Climb broken ledges to the corner flake just left of the centre of the quarry to a tree belay.

173 Hergest Ridge 18m E4 P3
5c From the base of the corner of Futurama traverse left to the arete and boldly follow this direct. Easier for the tall.

174 Carnival Carousel (179) 15m HVS P2
5a The quarry reduces in height slightly. The corner left of Hergest Ridge is climbed past a difficult move at half height.

The walls and cracks immediately left have been climbed but the finish requires blasting.

175   Bipod (180)   10m   MVS   P1
4c At the left end of the quarry are two buttresses. The righthand one is split by a vertical crack at half height. Climb this.

176   Hemispheres (181)   8m   HVS   P2
5b Start as for Bipod and traverse 1 metre left to a flake. Move up to a peg. Traverse left to another peg and finish direct. There is a direct start to the first peg.

177   Yob Society   9m   HVS   P2
5a Climb the right wall and arete of the next buttress.

178   Enterprise   9m   E2   P2
6a The front face of the pillar is climbed by an enterprising traverse from the left to reach the just-wrong-size jamming crack.

179   Playtex   70m   E5   P3
6a A girdle starting up Carnival Carousel and finishing as for Viper with a lot of bold climbing. From the ledge on Carnival Carousel traverse right to Hergest Ridge arete and on past Futurama to belay on the ledge of Anne of Cleves. Belay. Climb the wall on the right by hard moves to join Desperado past the difficulties. Go right past Triang. Traverse round the arete. Reverse the Scoop cracks and belay. Traverse right to finish as for Viper. A lot of hard climbing justifying the grade.

BAILDON BANK – GRADED LIST

E6
Iain's Swansong (6c)
Armageddon (6c)
A Path For An Evil
Soul (6b)
Intrepid (6a)

E5
Scar Arete (6c)
Timex (6a)
Cool Trickster (5c)
Smear Fear (6a)
Last Edge (6b)
Agame (6a)
Scythe Man (6a)
Scar Wall (6b)
Van Winkle (6b)
Rawhide (6a)
Playtex (6a)

E4
Gentle Persuasion (6a)
Hergest Ridge (5c)
Green Arete (5c)
To a Reckless Flash (6a)
Sunday Lunch Mob (6b)
Closing Time (6b)
Wombling Wall (6a)
Gesticulation (6b)

E3
Quietus (6b)
Heave Too (6a)
Olley (5c)
Scoop (5b)
Desperado (6a)
Anne of Cleves (5c)
Chipper (5b)
Swingover (5c)
The Flakes (5c)
Fizzicle Fizzle (5c)

E2
Enterprise (6a)
Rampant Arete (5c)
Syrett's Crack (5c)
Stretcher (5c)
Fly Groove (5c)
Moria (5c)
Scar (5c)
Satire (5b)
Mandy Fly Me (5b)

E1
Ram (5b)
Future Times (5b)
Going for Oneness (5b)
No Pegs Please... (5b)
Stretch (5b)
Steel Monkey (5b)
Fingers (5c)
Africa (5b)
Missout (5a)

Cleanstone Wall (5c)
Gold Rings Alt (5c)

HVS
The Fin (5a)
Feel the Buzz (6b)
Red Wall (5c)
Curving Cracks (5b)
Hemispheres (5b)
Wet Wall (5b)
Lightening (5b)

Overtime Wall (5b)
Saw Off (5b)
Ulley Left (5b)
Anniversary Arete (5c)
Ramp (5a)
South Wall (5c)
Camera Shake (5b)
Carnival Carousel (5a)
Big Curver (5b)
Nude Groove (5a)
Toss Off (5a)

The Arch (5a)
Time (5a)
Yob Society (5a)
Depegomania (5a)
Last Day (5a)
Spider (5a)
Triang (5a)
Split 'Em (5a)
Crucifix (4c)
Bee Sting (4c)

BIRK GILL CRAG, COLSTERDALE   NGR SE 136817

SITUATION AND CHARACTER The crag is situated on the north side of the ravine through which flows Birk Gill. Facing south, and much more sheltered than nearby Slipstones or Brown Beck, the crag makes an ideal winter venue.

APPROACHES AND ACCESS Approach as for Slipstones from the same parking place (see map on page 497). When the open moor is reached a faint path, running nearly due west through the heather, below the bull-dozed track is followed. As the path peters out continue in the same line for about ten minutes with a ravine down to the left and the rocks soon come into view. Near to the eastern end, a series of large boulders, one of which forms a cave, leads down the side of the ravine towards a steep undercut wall and a slab. **The crag lies within an SSSI and access is delicate. English Nature have no objections to climbing provided the approach described above is used and the gamekeeper, Tom Spencely 01677 460218 is notified before your visit. Dogs are not allowed.**

THE CLIMBS are described from right to left, starting further right than the line of boulders described above.

1 Bygones 5m VD
The short crack on the right side of the first buttress.

2 Cat Walk 9m HS
4b Start right of the arete. Gain the right-hand crack and follow it leftwards to exit up a short chimney.

3 Quantum Leap 8m E2
5c Climb the arete direct on its left side, starting at the lowest point. A thin finish!

4 Class Action 10m E2   ★★★
5b The big line of the crag climbing the corner throughout.

5 Class Action Left Hand 10m E1   ★
5b Start just right of Birk Gill Crack and cross the wall diagonally to join and climb the upper section of Class Action from mid-height.

6 Birk Gill Crack 8m HS   ★
4b The corner crack.

7 Heartbeat 8m S
4b The awkward chimney in the left wall of the corner.

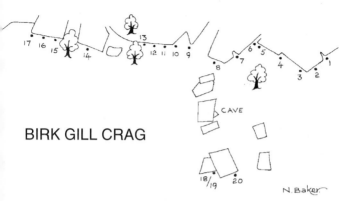

BIRK GILL CRAG

N. Baker

8 Downbeat 5m VD
The centre of the stepped wall round the blunt arete to the left.

9 Cutting Edge 5m HVS   ★
5c The steep arete across the gully

10 Facade 7m HVS
5a The next arete is gained from the right and finished direct.

11 Black Groove 7m HS   ★★
4b Climb directly into the groove.

12 Narrow Margin 8m HVS
5b Start from the lowest point below the arete, move up and right to
gain a slanting ledge and step up and left to finish up the arete.

13 Little Wonder 7m VS
4c Climb the wall by a series of flakes until a pull right gains a shelf.
Finish direct.

14 Sorrento 6m S   ★★
4b Climb the centre of the wall to an awkward exit.

15 Fast Track 6m HS
4b Direct up the wall left of the tree to finish up a square recess.

16 Party Piece 6m HS
4b The centre of the wall to an awkward exit.

17 Tough Enough 6m HVS
5b Follow the thin crack near the left edge of the wall throughout.

The next three climbs are on the undercut wall and the slab near the bottom of the line of boulders below the main line of the crag.

18 Mary Archer   8m   VD
The line between the overhang on the left and the slab on the right is followed direct.

19 Corvus   9m   HS   ★★
4b Follow Mary Archer and traverse left above the overhang to finish on the far corner.

20 Frank's Slab   9m   VD   ★★
Start at the right -hand corner, gain the slab and follow the easiest line.

BRANDRITH

SITUATION AND CHARACTER   The crag sits in splendid isolation on a ridge facing north across Redshaw Gill and Blubberhouses Moor giving distant views of Brimham rocks and Simon's Seat. Its northerly aspect is surprisingly sheltered, though some routes are slow to dry and tend to a green tinge after wet weather. During summer months the venue is superb. The rock is well-weathered and sound, often producing spectacular roofs and some amazing finishing jugs! Indeed, its appearance, with pinnacles and prows, bears a strong resemblance to Staffordshire's Ramshaw Rocks. The two main buttresses never attain a height of more than 12 metres and on most of the longer routes protection is abundant. A significant number of the climbs fall into the 'micro-route' category and provide excellent solos above generally good landings. At the end of the day there are few finer crags upon which to relax and enjoy the sunset in peaceful solitude.

APPROACHES AND ACCESS   The crag is best reached from the A59 Skipton-Harrogate road. At the Blubberhouses cross-roads (about 9 miles from Harrogate, 11 miles from Skipton and 8 miles from Otley), take the West End road north-westwards as if approaching Thruscross Reservoir. Follow this lane for exactly 1 mile to where the plantation joins the road and note the gate on the left. Park 400 metres further on in the lay-by at Redshaw Gill and walk back up the road to the gate. Follow a track from here, keeping to the wall-side, for 300 metres to another gate. Go through this, over a stile to another gate 50 metres further on. From here follow the 'sheep trod' westwards until the East Buttress becomes visible. Follow the track until above the rocks and then turn right to avoid submersion in bracken. 20 minutes car to crag.

IMPORTANT NOTICE   These crags are on private land and there is no public footpath. **Access should only be attempted by the route described above and not direct from Redshaw Gill.** Small groups are preferred and dogs are <u>not</u> allowed. Permission to climb must be obtained by phoning:
Mr. Walker, Bothams Farm, Blubberhouses 01943 880274.

THE CLIMBS
The East Buttress is best viewed on arrival from the large flat platform conveniently positioned in the sunshine right in front of the crag. Directly in front is the obvious Cave Crack, to the left is a

The East Buttress

sharp Prow, right is the Shark's Fin Pyramid and further right
another superb prow. The Climbs are described from left to right.

1 Sunset Staircase 5m D P1
Four metres left of the prow is an obvious 'staircase', a pleasant
introduction.

2 The Hoper 5m VD P1
Two metres left o the prow a scruffy corner improves near the top.

3 Left-hand Variant 9m VS P2
4c Start from The Hoper and hand traverse the 'healthy' crack on
the prow's left side to join Indian's Fin.

4 Indian's Fin 6m HS P3   ★
4b Start just right of the prow. Get established on the tiny ledge by
moving left dynamically or somewhat inelegantly. Finish on
heavenly holds.

N. Baker

5 Filthy Grovels 5m S P1
The 'yukky' corner in the bay just had to be climbed by someone. Now that it has you don't have to!

6 Battlecat 8m E3 P2 ★
6b Mince along the impressive roof crack. Fingerless gloves or a mobile transfusion service on-hand might reduce the subjective difficulties somewhat. Friends protect if you've got the strength to place them - or enough gather below to field!.

7 Evening Ambler 12m VS P2 ★★
4c The fine crack splitting the block below the topmost roof is gained by a short wall. The short-lived crack leads to a break with some fine hidden holds. Hand traverse the break leftwards round the corner (small thread) and finish up the mossy slab.

8 The Torso Twins 10m E2 ★
5c A more direct finish to Evening Ambler via the crack above the roof utilising small holds to the right to gain a juggy break. Bridging is tempting but not allowed.

9   Cave Crack   9m   MS   P1   ★★★
The classic of the crag. The cracked corner yields to bridging and a
fine open finish. Come back round and do it again!

10   Butterfingers   9m   E1   P2   ★★
6a   The fine roofed groove just right. A hard move to get established
in the groove (crux) leads to the bulge. Step right along the break
and go over on good holds. Alternatively, and slightly harder, from
the roof reach left to a small layback flake and finish up the fluted
groove.

11   Rocking Chockstone Chimney   8m   VD   P1
The unappealing broken crack is followed to the ledge. Finish up
the crack in the left wall above

12   The Cheat   10m   MVS   P2
4c   From the ledge on the last route hand traverse left onto the
upper face of Butterfingers and finish up this.

There is a moderate chimney just right and then,

13   Upset Crack   6m   HD   P1
The crack on the right hand side of the split buttress.

The pyramidal block on the right has a short dirty left arete **First
Route** (Diff)

14   Sharks Fin Crack   5m   HS   P1
4b   The crack splitting the 'finned' buttress. Keep to the fins all the
way and imagine you're on the Mittellegi ? Sad.

15   Pioneers Slab (Keep The Faith)   6m   D   P2   ★★
From the toe of the buttress ascend the beautiful slab.

Moving across to the right prow.

16   Diwaly   6m   VS   P3
5a   Start in the centre of the wall to the left of the prow and climb it
using the left arete to gain the upper lip. Pull over onto the ledge
and finish easily. Using the boulder is cheating - falling onto it is
painful.

17   Entertainment Traverse   10m   VD   P1   ★
Girdles the prow from left to right (and back again if you wish)
following the obvious break Start and finish on the ground! Fun,
and usually soloed to avoid inevitable rope drag.

18   Leader's Lament   9m   HS   P2   ★
4c   Start along Entertainment Traverse and then forsake it for the
greater excitement of the delicate moves straight up the arete. The
last guide said "Looks preposterous for Hard Severe". It is!

19 Leaders Lament Direct 8m   HVS   P2   ★★
5b The prow direct, surprisingly. Thought provoking, but very good.

20 The Flakes 6m   S   P1
4a The far right-hand prow has a flake crack on the right side.
Follow this to a 'beached whale' mantelshelf. Not as good as it
looks.

A few small easy boulder problems conclude this section before a
tramp through the heather leads in 300 metres to:-

The West Buttress
Approach past a rocking stone characterised (typically) by immense
stability. At the left-hand side of the main buttress is a boulder with
an undercut slab and a triangular face – the mantel on to the former
is **Ecofriction ★** (6b), while the arete on the steep side is **Problem
Child ★★** (5c). **Block Crack ★** (5a) is the short and awkward left-
leaning crack forming the right side of the 'triangle'.

To the right is a gully leading up into gloomy bay to the left of the
huge roof. On the right side of the bay is a small cave.

21 Rocky Slab 6m   S   P1
4a Start just left of the cave then up the slab and awkward ledges
to another 'rocking stone'.

22 The Haven 5m   HVD   P1
The cave and square cut chimney above.

Back out of the bay the next routes tackle the huge roofed blocks
just right:–

23 Going Bald 8m   HVS   P3   ★
5a Climb the short groove below and left of the roof to a ledge. The
easy-angled slabby rib above requires a committing first step - and
complete faith in sticky rubber! Unfortunately Brandrith seems to
have found a cure for baldness - 'hair' keeps re-growing on the
slab.

24 Sod's Law 12m   VD   P2
An interesting excursion. Start under the roof and wander left on to
the platform on the previous route. A constricted traverse right on
the ledge along the lip of the roof leads to an easier escape.

Providing a direct start to Sod's Law may prove an intriguing
challenge to those with an exceptional ape index. The short flake in
the roof on the right, **Edge Biter** (5a) will be enough of a reach for
most.

The West Buttress

25 Bag Of Snot 8m HS P1
4b Start on the grotty slab splitting the gully. Up and across this rightwards and then a high step over the bulge above.

26 Verdi Grease 8m Hard Very Radioactive P2
If climbing 75-degree snot is the bag you are into, then this is the route for you. It takes the slab and bulge direct at about VS 5a.

The next routes lie on the impressive Brandrith Buttress – a large slab with two shallow grooves rearing above deep-rounded breaks.

27 New Broom Sweeps Green 11m E1 P2 ★
6a A technical start is accomplished by climbing the small overhang low down on the left side of the buttress. The shallow groove above, just right of the left arete and left of Finger Dancer, gives a bold but much easier finish.

28 Finger Dancer 12m E1 P3 ★★★
5a A superb pitch. Climb a short crack just right of the overhang to a ledge on Discord, continue confidently straight up the shallow groove on superb finger holds to a slightly harder move over the bulge at the top. The original finish moved right just below the top and is perhaps slightly easier - but just as bold.

N. Baker.

29 Intruding Fool 12m HVS P2 ★
5b A climb on fingery ledges between Finger Dancer and Harmony, protected by a Friend in the latter. Slightly harder, technically, than its neighbours and somewhat myopic, but worthwhile.

30 Harmony 12m HVS P1 ★★
5a A prominent weakness in the large slab right of Finger Dancer's shallow groove gives an intermittent crack line. Amble up to a rounded horizontal crack and step up to an obvious hand-jam slot. Another awkward move gains the finishing continuation crack. A No. 3 Friend is useful.

31 Discord 10m MS P2
A series of diagonal breaks from right to left across the buttress lead to a small ledge. Move left round the corner and up into the short fluted groove to exit on good holds.

32 Slab And Crack 11m MVS P1 ★
4b A short narrow crack just right of Discord leads to a ledge below a big daddy of a crack in the upper arete. Big 'Bongs' protect. Originally graded VD!

33 Antlers Route 11m VS P2 ★
4c The amazing Antler formation just has to be climbed. From the mid-way platform (best reached by the right arete), layback the thin corner crack, finishing on the weird gargoyle.

34 Eastern Arete 11m VS P2   ★
4c Climb the arete of Antlers Route to the ledge then the continuation arete above finishing on the small 'antler' in a superb and highly
photogenic position.

35 Nameless Chimney 11m D P1
A Classic of the *genre*! Bridge elegantly ★★; Back and Foot with
style ★; or grovel up the back ●. The choice is yours - the grade's
the same.

36 Summertime Solo 8m HS   ★
4b Directly up the pillar to the right of the chimney, without recourse
to either of the adjacent routes. No, not even when it gets harder at
the top.

37 Western Crack 8m S P1
The wide crack right of the pillar with a bit of a thrutch at the top.

38 Western Bulge 8m HVS P2
5b Immediately right of Western Crack is a buttress with an
undercut bulge at half height. Climb the small slab beneath this and
pull over to good holds and a mantelshelf. Finish more easily.

39 The Opportunist 7m VD P2
To the right of the bulge take a crack to a ledge. Traverse right
along this to finish into the 'bucket' scoop above.

40 Crack And Wall 7m MS P2   ★
There is a small bay to the right. Follow a crack in the left wall to the
ledge of Opportunist and finish just left of the 'bucket'.

41 Flummox Arete 7m VS P1
5b The arete left to the right of a small gully provides a fine problem
start when clean.

42 Flummox Crack 7m VS P1   ★
4c The large crack succumbs to a splendid layback. Rather Nice.

43 Why Not ? (Do a Girdle) 20m S
4a Start from Bag Of Snot and follow the obvious breaks
rightwards, reversing most of Discord and negotiating all the aretes
and chimneys, to Flummox Crack - keeping low towards the end.
Finishing up Flummox Crack makes it 4c.

The two aretes on the extreme right look to provide some (rather
harder) fare. But have they been done yet?

BRANDRITH – GRADED LIST

E3
Battlecat (6b)

E2
The Torso Twins (5c)

E1
New Broom ... (6a)
Butterfingers (6a)
Finger Dancer (5a)

HVS
Problem Child (5c)
Western Bulge (5b)
Leader's Lament Direct (5b)
Intruding Fool (5b)
Going Bald (5a)
Harmony (5a)

VS
Block Crack (5b)
Flummox Arete (5b)
Diwaly (5a)
Edge Biter (5a)
Verdi Grease (5a)
Evening Ambler (4c)
Leaders Lament (4c)
Eastern Arete (4c)
Antlers Route (4c)
Left-hand Variant (4c)
Flummox Crack (4c)

MVS
The Cheat (4c)
Slab and Crack (4b)

HS
Summertime Solo (4b)
Indian's Fin (4b)
Shark's fin Crack (4b)

S
Filthy Grovels
The Flakes
Rocky Slab
Western Crack
Why Not (Do A Girdle)

MS
Cave Crack
Discord
Crack And Wall

HVD
The Haven

VD
The Hoper
Rocking Chockstone
Chimney
Entertainment Trav.
Sod's Law
The Opportunist

D
Upset Crack
Nameless Chimney
Sunset Staircase
First Route
Pioneers Slabs

BRIDESTONES

SITUATION AND CHARACTER   The Bridestones consist of a spasmodic confusion of small attractive boulders, buttresses and pinnacles that lie exposed high on the moors above Todmorden. This unique collection of rocks offers the climber an almost inexhaustible supply of quick drying boulder problems and micro-routes on clean, excellent, grit. Known locally as the "Kebs", the edge varies in height from four to eight metres and extends over an area of about one square mile. Good landings mean, for the most part, that "the move" can be pushed to the limit and ropes are rarely seen. But beware, there are some very serious problems here and success on these may require not only exceptional technical ability but a liberal sprinkling of good old-fashioned neck! As an experiment, for this edition, E and P grades have been added to some of the longer or more serious undertakings as an indicator to the first time or irregular visitor. As protection placements are rare the P grade should be taken to indicate the potential for injury from a slip or fall from the crux whilst soloing. Perhaps the only real route that is protectable is The Obscene Cleft, but only if your second is awake and a quick runner! Locals and regulars may well scoff and quibble but then they won't need this guide will they?

Since the last edition the pace of bouldering development has accelerated and become a total end in itself for some devotees. Local activists may well be able to identify 3 or 4 times as many problems than are described here but the intention of this guide is to record clearly identifiable lines up natural features. The Bridestones has numerous low-level traverses, sitting-starts, double dynos and one move wonders but to find them you will need to purchase a specialist bouldering guide or follow around one of the usually in-situ 'gurus'. This book will give you a taste of the best. Your favourite problem is here somewhere the only downside being the proximity to Lancashire - but even Lancastrians are fairly civilised and usually friendly when out on the crag.

APPROACHES AND ACCESS   The A646 Burnley-Sowerby Bridge road gives the easiest approach from east or west. From Burnley, turn left at Cornhole, up Shore Lane. This leads steeply north to join the Long Causeway after about a mile. Turning right at the junction will lead, in another half mile, to the isolated Sportsman's Inn on Keb Hill and parking facilities.

Approaching from Sowerby Bridge, a right turn to Mytholm, which is

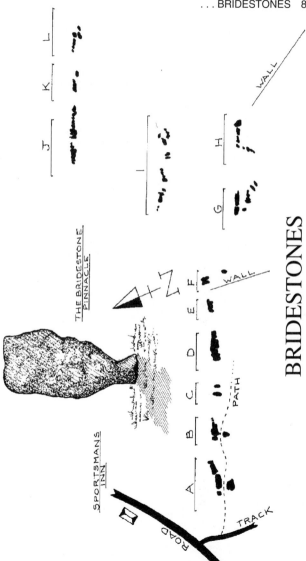

BRIDESTONES

just past Hebden Bridge, zig-zags up Badger Lane. This joins the
Long Causeway at Blackshaw Head. One and a half miles towards
Burnley is the Sportsman's Inn.

The Inn is the usual start and finish of an evening's activity on the
Bridestones. There seems to be no problem parking and leaving
cars near the inn. East of the inn, a public footpath will be found
after two hundred metres. This leads across the moor to a triangula-
tion point above the Small Smart Wall area. The more usual
approach is by a short fifty-metre walk downhill, towards Burnley,
and taking the farm track leading leftwards toward the Spy-Hole
Pinnacle area. This can easily be seen from the beginning of the
track.

Recent access to the Spy-Hole Pinnacle, Indian's Head and Big
Sister/Little Brother areas has been extremely delicate. These
sections are within sight and sound of the farmhouse below and on
occasions the occupant has asked climbers to move on. These
blocks can be avoided by taking the track above them, gained by a
stile next to the gate on the farm track. Visitors should therefore be
diplomatic if approached. Selfishness or poor behaviour could put
the Bridestones into serious jeopardy. Some of the best routes are
in these areas and it would be a tragedy if they were lost to all. If
you think closure couldn't happen then look across the road to
Hugencroft, once a popular bouldering area, now closed to
everyone.

THE CLIMBS

The climbs listed here are generally the most obvious lines
following easily recognised features some are clearly short classical
boulder problems whist a few are undoubtedly real micro-routes.
Many fall into a grey area somewhere between and often the
difference will only become apparent as you contemplate the option
of making a last slap for the top or contriving a retreat! Good Luck

A - SPY-HOLE PINNACLE AREA

The first area as one approaches along the farm track. A superb
venue with some very hard, committing problems.

1   The Mantelshelf 6m   E2   P3   ★★★
6b Taken direct or approached from the right. The most technical
problem in the area. Intricate and absorbing and, even though the
crux is low down, with a serious feel due to the landing.

2   Usually Green 6a The green wall behind and left of the
pinnacle.

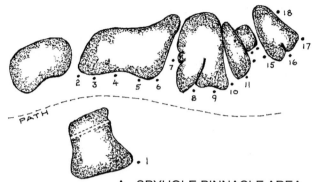

A - SPYHOLE PINNACLE AREA

3 The blunt rib just right gives hard, fingery climbing at 6a. No bridging!

4 Voyeur 7m E2 P2 ★
5c Up, then delicate moves right to join the next route.

5 Never Saw It Coming 6m E1 P1 ★
5c Use the sandy pocket and a delicate touch to climb the blunt rib.

6 Look Out 6a The rounded arete is taken direct.

7 Twin Cracks 4a These can be climbed separately if one has tunnel vision or nothing better to do.

8 Big Bulger 6m E1 P1
5b Climb the obvious feature, trying to loose as little skin as possible.

9 Cleo 6m E4 P3 ★★★
6c The rounded, bulging wall and arete is superb but desperate.

10 The right side of the arete is almost as difficult at 6b.

11 Face Ache 6m E3 P ★★★
6a/b The face just right of the arete on finger nicks and crimps is a classic.

12 Telescope 5m E1 P2 ★
6a The wall left of the corner.

13 Short Corner 4b Obvious and pleasant.

14 Short Sighted 5m HVS P2 ★
5c This takes the slabby wall right of the corner.

15 Just left of the arete is climbable at a more amenable 5c .

16 A nice 4c takes the feature to the right, but may feel a little bold to those of nervous disposition.

17 Out of Sight 6a A finger-ripping problem just round the corner.

18 Further round finds the centre of the wall a tenuous 6a.

B - INDIAN'S HEAD AREA
This area is well provided with climbs that have length and seriousness that gives some of them route status.

1 Cochise 6m E2 P2   ★★★
6a The arete of the pinnacle, moving right to finish.

2 Warpath 7m E1 P3   ★★
5b This is the easiest way to the top, but still quite gripping. Climb up then follow the obvious traverse rightwards to the nose and good finishing holds.

3 Tete De Chien 6m E2 P1   ★
6b A direct version of Warpath using an old peg hole to overcome the roof. Very dynamic. This route can be lengthened by reversing the traverse of Warpath and finishing up Cochise. A sustained effort!

4 Crucifixion 8m E3 P2   ★★
6c A totally-committing problem. Start from the arete and follow the traverse leftwards to finish up the Indian's nose. Try and forget about the ground dipping away!

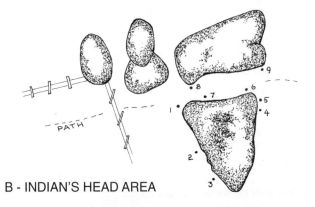

PATH

B - INDIAN'S HEAD AREA

5 Horror Arete 5m E3 P2   ★★★
6b A brilliant climb with a hard finish (the crux). The original way
scuttled round rightwards to finish.

6 A Bridge Too Far 5m E2 P2   ★
6b Once the crux is embarked upon it is impossible to escape.

7 Bridge to Safety 5m E1 P1   ★
6a A good wall climb which is escapable - guess how?

8 Long Knife 6m E2 P2 ★★
The superb arete of the back wall can be climbed on its left side at
6a and on its right-hand side at 5b.

9 The opposite end of the wall provides a stiff 5c.

A leap across the top provides the most challenging way off but it is
possible to bridge down from No 7.

C - BIG SISTER AND LITTLE BROTHER
A very pleasant pair of boulders, with quality problems and excellent
landings.

1 Big Sister The wall just left of the short crack is taken direct
(5c). The crack can be used as a slight variation start.

2 Sad Sister 5c Take the flaky crack, which ends just before the
top, which is the crux. The most serious problem on the block.

3 Sisters of Mercy 6a Left of the square recess is a short wall.

4 Soul Sister 5c Right of the recess.

5 The Hanging Flake provides a pleasant 4c.

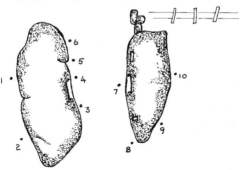

C - BIG SISTER / LITTLE BROTHER

6 The Sisterhood 5b Slightly to right is a small roof, providing a long reach from undercuts.

LITTLE BROTHER

7 Brotherly Love 5b The centre of wall is an obvious challenge.

8 Oh Brother! 5b Take the arete on its left-hand side.

9 Twin Brother 5c A much harder proposition is the arete on its right-hand side.

10 A Little Pain 5c The blunt edge to the right proves the name right.

Two girdles exist here. Starting from the blocks at the back of the boulder, a high traverse without using the top is 6a. The low traverse is harder and the difficulty is sustained round the arete to continue past Little Pain (6b).

D - THE CASTLE

1 Chink in the Armour ★★ 6a A superb wall climb following the obvious pockets.

2 Keep Crack ★★ 5a Obvious, a classic.

3 Initial Wall 5b This is taken direct and may prove frustrating trying to find the "chipped" initial, which is the finishing hold. (Purists will do without 5c).

4 Castle Crack 5a A short steep crack leads to easier ground.

5 Crenallation An alternative start, another strenuous 5a.

6 The Castle Flake 10m VD P1   ★
At last! A real climb, with real runner placements, that goes right to the top.

7 The stepped left wall of the gully without bridging provides a greasy 4c.

8 The Drawbridge 6m MS P1
Bridge across until it is possible to pull left onto the final moves of the last problem.

9 Boiling Oil 6m E2 P2   ★
5c The right wall of the gully moving left to finish.

10 Knight's Honour 6m E3 P2   ★
6a This arete provides a hard start and a scary finish.

D - THE CASTLE

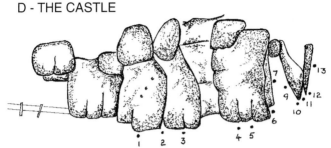

11 Knot to Knight 5a An easier proposition just left of the layback.

12 Enjoy It 4c Layback and . . . . . .

13 Wall To the right the wall provides two variation finishes: 5b to the right, 5c to the left.

A traverse, **The Moat**, can be made of the whole buttress. It can be made very sustained depending on where it is taken. The lower the traverse, the greater the difficulty.

E - SENTRY BOX AREA

1 Rifle Crack 5m S P1   ★
The obvious crack provides a pleasant layback .

2 Sentry Box 5m VD P1   ★
 Jam and squirm up into the box.

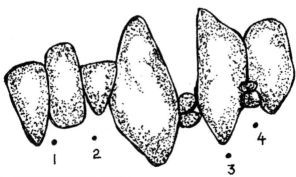

E - SENTRY BOX AREA

3   Taken direct the arete is a short but difficult 5c.

4   To the right is an equally short but hand-tearing crack 4c.

F - TILTED PINNACLE

1   The Groove   5a   Jam, thrutch or elegantly bridge the fissure - quite serious.

2   The slight cracks give a pleasant 4b.

3   Up the wall then traverse is 5a.

4   Lean and Mean   6a   A more direct version with a hard finish (don't they all!).

5   Ear'oule   5a   Use the flake to climb the rounded bulge.

6   An extremely short, frustrating mantelshelf that proves time-consuming and is ungradeable

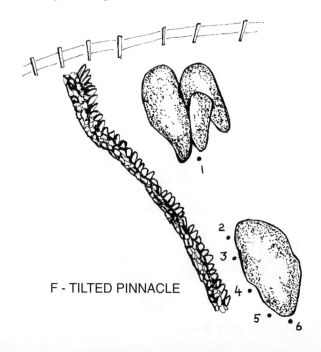

F - TILTED PINNACLE

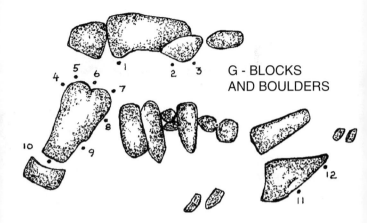

G - BLOCKS
AND BOULDERS

G - BLOCKS AND BOULDERS

1   Tea Break ★ 5a A big pull on the obvious.

2   Coffee 5b Over the roof on its left.

3   Hot Chocolate 5c The same roof on its right is more difficult.

4   Left of the chipped holds is a rounded arete 5b.

5   Another of those 5bs takes the wall to the right of the obvious
feature.

6   The Groove   5m   HS   P1   ★★
4b The obvious central line.

7   To the left of the groove is a rounded 5b.

8   Block Off   5m   E1   P2   ★
5b Quite a good wall climb with a little height.

9   Not Cadburys 5a This climbs the "flake" to the left.

10   Slide Off 5c The smooth funnel at the back of the block is
harder than it looks.

11   Duck 5b An old problem that climbs another funnel.

12   Dive 5c To the right, the wall gives a few stiff moves.

H - OBSCENE CLEFT AREA

H - OBSCENE CLEFT AREA

1 **The Hidden Green Wall** on its right-hand side 5b.

2 **Veins** on the left-hand side are also 5b.

3 **Bruiser** 5b Take the crack direct.

4 **Nice Try** ★★5b Climb the delectable arete.

5 **Touchdown** ★★ 4c An excellent route up the slight crack.

6 The face to the right is 5c.

7 **The Belt** 15m E1 P1   ★★
5b The main block gives a traverse at the obvious level and is quite sustained on the opposite side.

8 A short, demanding problem that ends at the break 6b.

9 **The Obscene Cleft** 6m E6 P2   ★★
6c Climb the grotesque orifice with some difficulty and a little trepidation.

10 **Black Cheek** ★ 6a Try and get to the break then traverse off.

11 **Beta Blocker** 6m E3 P2   ★
6a Another micro-route with the crux pulling into the funnel from the right. Quite a serious proposition.

I - WHILLAN'S JAM AREA

1   Scoop 4b ★★ An obvious feature, climbed inelegantly, on the left side of the large boulders.

2   Tom's Wall ★ 6a A delicate approach pays dividends.

3   Jerry's Arete ★★★ 6c The elegant arete is taken on its left side.

4   Big Body Squirm ★ 4a An old classic destined to ruin a pair a lycra bottoms!

5   Slap 5c The arete just right, the name refers to the last move.

6   Whillan's Jam ★★ 5b If you've never felt one before, here it is!

7   Another of those blunt aretes 5c.

8   Fish 4c-6a With or without the chips! Grade depending.

9   Fingers 5b Using small ledges move up to a finishing mantelshelf.

10   A similar problem to the left 5b.

11   Try and layback the rounded edge without using the convenient boulder (6a).

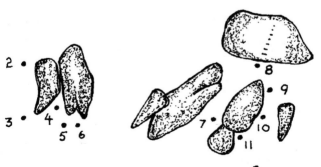

I - WHILLANS JAM AREA

J - SMALL SMART WALL AREA

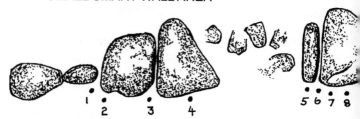

J - SMALL SMART WALL AREA

A delectable area that is the home of many superb classic problems with good landings.

1 Short And Sharp 5c The wall left of the arete is.

2 The Villain ★★ 5c This takes the slight cracks in the nose.

3 Damn And Be Jammed ★ 4a The crack.

4 Perfection ★ 5a-5b Good quality climbing up the slab. Various starts and finishes will dictate the grade.

5 Straight And Narrow ★ 5b Take the narrow face direct.

6 Its A Cracker 5m S P1   ★
The straight crack. One for yer dad!

7 Rampant 6m E2 P2   ★★★
5c The narrow ramp proves more difficult than it first appears.

8 Charlotte Rampling 5m E3 P2   ★★
6b A direct start to reach the top of the ramp.

9 Face Slap 5m VS P1   ★★
4c Follow the delightful layback flake line.

10 Small And Smart ★★★ 6a Climb the centre of the wall where there are holds. Excellent.

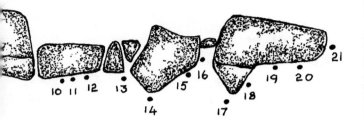

11 Smarter ★★ 6b Just to the right using the same finishing hold as Small and Smart.

12 Holdless ★ 6c Try and make progress up the very thin wall right of Smarter.

13 Just right of the gully is a short wall 4c.

14 Flake Out 6m E1 P1   ★★★
5b Gain the flake from the left.

15 Flake Off 5m E1 P1   ★★
5c Gain the flake from the right edge.

16 Green wall 6m E2 P3   ★★
6a The obvious wall taken direct. Bold.

17 Big Nose ★ 5b The arete direct.

18 The side wall gives a good 5b problem.

19 Slightly set back, the left side of the wall is 5c.

20 A similar problem on the right is also 5c.

21 Round the corner the neat face is 5b.

K - THE GROOM STONES

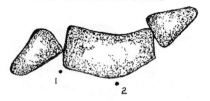

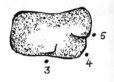

K - THE GROOM'S STONES

1 Buttonhole 6a The often green wall has a 'necky' feel.

2 Things to Come 5m E3 P2   ★★
5c A mantel start, then the wall direct. Harder than it looks.

3 The Best Man Wins ★ 6b A small hold helps access to the
slight flake. The finish, a mantelshelf, is the crux.

4 Bridesmaid ★★ 5b Nice moves up the right-hand side of the
arete.

5 Honour and Obey ★ 5a The pleasant groove to the right gives
a taste of real climbing!

L - THE BRIDESTONE AREA

The Bridestone itself is now said to be unstable and sways in the
wind. Fatties beware!

1 Last Love 5a Flakes provide the substance of the route.

2 Big Bash 6b Linking the two pockets proves frustrating, but
superb.

3 Solemn Promise 5b Classic Jamming.

4 The back of the boulder provides an interesting problem
providing either a direct route or, from the same place, a move left
to the obvious feature. Both variations are 5c.

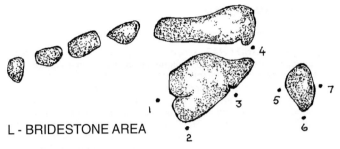

L - BRIDESTONE AREA

5 The Bridestone 5b The easiest way on to the top of this
unique pinnacle using the sandy pockets.

6 Egg 6b Taken direct, this is another very hard problem which
will find you slapping for the holds.

7 Ovoid 6c Difficult moves up will enable a slight traverse left to
join Egg at its finish. A real 'bolder' problem.

About ½ a mile to the west, at a lower elevation is another
collection of boulders with about 15 more problems, including an
excellent arete.

The best approach is via a feint track leading off below the Obscene
Cleft area.

BRIMHAM ROCKS

SITUATION AND CHARACTER The myriad boulders, buttresses and pinnacles that make up Brimham lie on the northern rim of Nidderdale about 5 kilometres east of Pateley Bridge and 3 kilometres north of Summerbridge. The weird and wonderful-shaped rocks that attract visitors and climbers alike were once thought to be the creation of Druids; legends like these remain in the names of the rocks – The Druid's Writing Desk, The Castle and the Druid's Idol. The National Trust, which now owns Brimham, has restored the house and built a refreshment kiosk and car parks.

The grit is as rough as any anywhere, erosion having left an uneven hardness full of coarse-grained sand and quartz pebbles. There is a wide variety of climbing; delicate slabs, bold walls, a profusion of steep, hand jamming cracks and a number of off-width cracks that have a strange siren-like quality. The rock is rounded in many places leaving difficult mantelshelf finishes on many routes. Large Friends are invaluable and the possession of a 'tube chock' makes routes like Gigglin' Crack, Bog Crack and Tube Break a lot safer. When the sun shines it is possible to bask in it all day, moving round the different faces. There is very little seepage on the boulders, making it possible to climb all year round. Brimham has a feel of adventure about it. Climbing here can be real fun.

APPROACHES AND ACCESS From the centre of Summerbridge, which sits astride the B6165 Knaresborough-Pateley Bridge road, a steep winding lane leads up to a cross-roads, beyond which lie Brimham Rocks and its car parks. The rocks are managed by the National Trust and there is a charge during the summer (£2.00 per car in 1998). The cross-roads is also used as a reference for locating Brimham's outlying crags.

THE CLIMBS To help you find the climbs, in what can be a confusing area, the rocks have been divided into three sections: 1. The Pinnacles; 2. Cubic Block and the Southern Edges; 3. Lover's Leap and the Northern Edges. Each area can be easily reached independently from the car park, or you can follow on from one to another.

THE PINNACLES

From the north end of the car parks, an unsurfaced track leads to Brimham House. For access to the pinnacles use this track as a

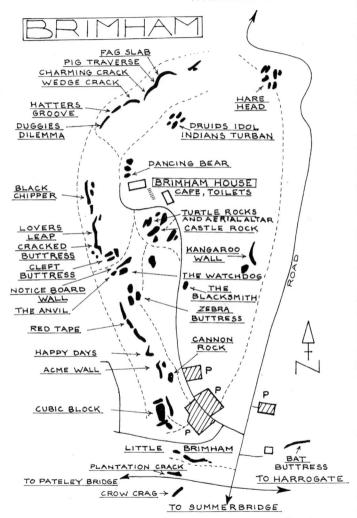

reference. On early visits the visitor may find himself returning often to the track. Although this may not be the quickest way round, it is the least confusing.

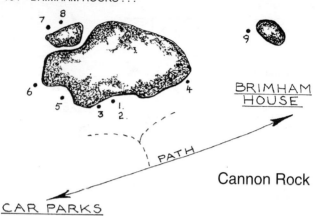

Cannon Rock

Cannon Rock

Follow the track leading north out of the car park for 75 metres until a small car park is reached on the right. Cannon Rock can be seen 50 metres to the left of the track and has the obvious twin cracks of Frensis up its centre.

1 Frensis 10m VS P1 1956   ★
5a Climb to the twin cracks and follow these to the overhang. Traverse right until it is possible (just) to mantel on to the ledge.

2 Frensis Direct 11m E1 P1 1957   ★★★
5b Follow Frensis to the overhang, step left and follow the rounded crack with difficulty. An excellent extension to the original route.

3 Goof Aydee and The Mango 10m E2 P2 1990
5c The pocketed wall 1 metre left of Frensis, finishing leftwards over the roof above Maloja via the arete.

4 Point Blank 6m HVS P1 1990
5b Start 4 metres right of Frensis below a jamming crack splitting the overhang. Pull over the awkward roof and follow the short crack to a mantelshelf finish.

5 Maloja 11m VS P1 Pre 1957   ★★
4c To the left of Frensis is a ledge. Climb on to this and up the crack above, use the flutings to reach better holds. Step left and climb past the cannon blast to the top.

6 Mons Meg 9m VS P2 1974
5a The series of bulges forming the nose to the left can be climbed on undercuts, pinches and pockets. All rather rounded.

7 Go Joe 9m HVS P1 1958
5a From a boulder below the large roof, a crack on the right can be gained – if you're lucky!

8 Cannon Route 9m D P1 Pre195 ★
Start from the same boulder as Go Joe but traverse left around the roof and climb past the other end of the cannon blast.

Walk down from the north end of Cannon Rock to a pinnacle with a boulder with a huge roof to its left.

9 Legover 6m HVS P2 1972
5a Climb the front of the pinnacle to an exciting finish that is easier than it looks.

Return to the main track, follow it north until 150 metres from the car park it bends round to the right. Zebra Buttress and Crown Rock are to the left of the track.

Crown Rock is the free-standing pinnacle nearest the track and has an obvious wide crack line.

10 Roadside Crack 8m E1 P2 Pre 1957
5b Climb the crack to the top. Much harder now since the demise of old chockstone.

11 Morose Mongoose 8m E4 P2 1988 ★
6b Climb the bulges between Roadside Crack and a small cave round to its left. Very hard to start, very hard to finish.

Inside Crown Rock is a hole known as the kissing chair, presumably because two people can sit in it comfortably. Six people is the record, but it is far from comfortable.

The next routes are on the southside of the large block to the left of Crown Rock.

12 Right-hand Bias 13m HVS P2 1972
4c Climb a rib to the right of a tree using a fluting to below the widest part of the roof, when its true dimensions are realised. Now stomach traverse rightwards.

13 Top Dead Centre 6m HS P1 1972
Twenty two metres to the left is a chimney which is climbed with difficulty.

14 Left-hand Bias 7m MVS P1 1972
4c Start on the nose to the left of Top Dead Centre at the entrance to the open gully. Trend left to a flake in a bulge (this can also be reached direct) and pull over to the top.

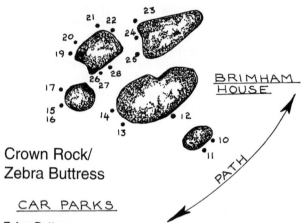

Crown Rock/ Zebra Buttress

CAR PARKS

Zebra Buttress

Across the gully are three large free-standing boulders close together. The first of these consists of three blocks stacked on top of each other with a slab below an overhang on its south-west side.

15   The Mantelshelf 12m HVS P1 1972   ★
5a Climb the right side of the slab to the overhang. Pull round the arete and traverse right until it is possible to mantel on to the ledge. Follow the scoop to finish.

16   Steady VS Arete 8m E3 P2 1988
6a Follow The Mantelshelf to the overhang and continue up the arete with long reaches and stiff pulls.

A good 5b traverse starts up a short wall right of The Mantelshelf, crossing Vam and descending to Jackabu. Continue along the break past Gwyneth to the ledge of Felicity.

17   Vam 8m E3 P2 1977
6b Climb the centre of the slab to the overhang (thread). Use a huge hold to jump for the top. To succeed you need to be exceptionally tall or have grasshopper blood.

18   Vamoose 8m D P1
The Chimney to the left provides good exercise for beginners and/ or veterans.

19   Jackabu 11m E1 P2 1988   ★
5b Start at a crack left of the chimney. Superb laybacking leads to a nasty little mantel on to a ledge. The wall above and slightly to the

left is gained using an undercut; the finish is bold with the last hold hard to find.

20 Peekabu 10m E2 P3 1988
6a A direct start to Jackabu. Climb the wall left of the crack to a horror mantelshelf. Finish as for Jackabu. A good problem.

21 Gwyneth 12m E4 P2 1977   ★
6a Round the corner is an overhang with a shallow scoop above. Surmount this with difficulty to gain the ledge. Climb up to reach a deep blank scoop and finish up this. An alternative start gains the ledge from the right then traverses left (5b) - but the finish is still the real crux!). Both lines have optional sitting starts at 6a/b.

22 Felicity 12m E2 P1 1962
5b This is the deep crack between Gwyneth and the gully to the left. The overhanging section at the top provides the entertainment.

23 House Points Tomorrow 8m E2 P2 1988
5c Start on a boulder to the left of the gully. Climb the bulges to reach a gently rising break, traverse right with difficulty to a good jam and pull over to finish.

Walk through the gully back towards Top Dead Centre.

24 Don't Step Back Crack 9m E1 P2 1988
5b Looking into the gully there is a crack in the left wall. Start at the bottom of this (not on the ledge). Climb the crack, without stepping back, then don't stop, till you're safely on top!

25 Lay Back And Think 6m E1 P2 1988
5c Continuing into the bay another crack is reached. Follow this to a sensational layback and a tricky finish.

Opposite the previous route is a chimney separating two blocks. The next two climbs take the crack to its right.

26 Closet Crack 8m VS P1   1959
4c Climb the crack past a hole to a deep horizontal break. Stomach traverse left or, more sensibly, step off.

27 Tube Break 8m E3 P2 pre 1980
6a Follow Closet Crack to the break, traverse right to below a wide crack and head jam to the top. The crack can be laybacked; it saves your ears but is 6b.

28 Tube Break Direct Start HVS P2 1993
5b From the boulder right of Closet Crack climb the shallow groove into the cave of Tube Break. Finish up this or sneak off right. A good problem.

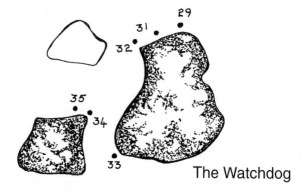

The Watchdog

The Watchdog
Thirty metres to the north of Zebra Buttress is a clump of boulders known as The Watchdog. The major boulder is severely undercut and has a prominent prow. The routes are described from left to right and begin at a crack just right of the prow.

29 Ratbag 8m HS P1 1959
4b Climb the crack to a ledge and pull over into a puddle (correction: natural rock basin).

30 Rattler 18m E1 P2 1988
5c A girdle of the buttress. Start up Ratbag and traverse into Rat Arsed, step up to the break and continue past Rat Trap to finish easily.

31 Rat Arsed 8m E4 P2 1988 ★★
6c The undercut wall 2 metres right of Ratbag is climbed with great difficulty to the cave. Move left and pull over the overhang on good holds.

32 Rat Trap 8m HVS P2 1972 ★
5a From the top of the boulder on the right step across and climb the rib in a fine position. Finish up the crack on the left. The rib can be reached from the ground at 5c.

33 Ratfink 9m E3 P2 1988
6a Climb to a pocket in the wall right of Rat Trap and follow the wall above. Not as easy as it looks.

Across the gully opposite Ratfink is a large boulder with two problems.

34 Rataonee 7m E2 P1 1988
5c Start just left of the arete and climb to a good break, then traverse left and up to a wide horizontal crack. An entertaining move to finish.

35 Ratatwoee 6m HVS P1 1988
5b Follow the arete direct.

The arete left of Ratatwoee is 6a. There is a hand traverse around Watchdog Buttress:– a pumpy 5c.

Looking down from The Watchdog, Cleft Buttress can be seen and further north is Brimham House. Right of the house is Castle Rock, Aerial Altar and Turtle Rocks.

The Blacksmith
To locate the next routes return to the track at Crown Rock. Across the track from Crown Rock is a narrow pinnacle with an old notice board just below the top. This is The Blacksmith.

36 Cocoa Club Board Meeting 8m E5 P2 1988
6b A novel climb. Take the boulder-problem groove below the notice board. Move up left to the notice board, use this for protection and a hand hold (don't pull too hard) to gain the top. A desperate, unnerving finish.

37 Bare Back Side 6m HVS P2 1988
5c Gain the top of The Blacksmith from behind, via a short crack and worrying mantelshelf.

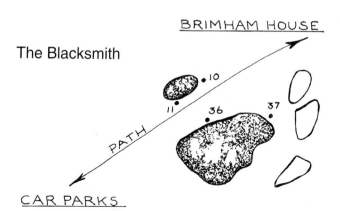

The Blacksmith

Kangaroo Wall

Immediately after The Blacksmith look right, eastwards, across open ground to a smooth wall with three perched boulders on top and a tall pinnacle 50 metres to its right. These are Kangaroo Wall and Black Tower.

38 Kangaroo Wall 6m VS P2 Pre 1970 ★

4c The right end of the wall is climbed stepping left to a deep hole. Mantel on to the ramp above and finish easily left, or better, up right via the arete.

39 Sir Les 6m E3 P2 1988

6b Climb the centre of the wall using two rounded layaways in a green scoop.

40 Botany Bay 6m E1 P2 1977 ★

5c Climb the left side of the main wall past a pocket. Stepping right enables a difficult mantelshelf to be made on to the ledge.

41 Dame Edna 6m E4 P3 1988

6b Start as for Botany Bay but swing left into the shallow groove for a precarious finish.

42 The Road Rage Experience 6m E6 P3 1994

6c From the obvious cave make a very long reach out above the roof to small sandy edges, then utilising the edge of the shallow groove, slap left to the jug on top of the nose.

43 Walleroo 7m E2 P2 1993

5c Start to the left of the cave in a shallow scoop. Climb up and slightly right, and then up to 2 'eye holes'. The finish may need a brush..

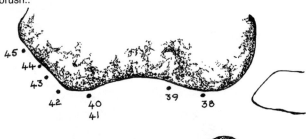

Kangaroo Wall

44 Crackaroo 6m MS P1 1995
The awkward wide crack 7 metres left of Botany Bay.

45 Concave Slab 6m VS P1 1995   ★
4c The slab left of Crackaroo, crossing rightwards to a small ledge.
Step up into a hole and finish over the final block.

46 Black Tower Face 10m HVS P2 1973
5a Opposite Kangaroo Wall is a pinnacle. Start at its northern
corner and trend left to a ledge (from where you can walk off). Climb
to an undercut flake, and use this to gain a good hold on top.

47 North West Arete 8m VD P1 1997
Start at the lowest point of the arete to the right of Black Tower
Face, and a couple of metres left of the descent route. Climb
straight up to the notch in the final bulge and pull over on the right.
A harder finish is possible to the left but out of character to the rest
of the route.

About 100 metres south of Kangeroo Wall is large slab. This gives
about a dozen fine problems and one worthwhile route:-

48 Bilberry Groove 10m HS P1 1993   ★
4b On the left side of the main face is an obvious corner/groove,
gain it and follow it to the upper slab. Harder and better than it
looks.

The left-hand wall of the boulder can be climbed pleasantly via the
diagonal ramp at Diff.

Castle Rock
Return to the main track. After 120 metres Castle Rock is reached
to the left of the track. This is a major buttress with fine climbing. It
has a grassy clearing below it.

Start at a tree below the wall nearest the track. The routes are
described from RIGHT to LEFT.

49 Rainy Day 14m HVS P2 1971   ★
5c Climb the wall behind the now rather intrusive tree (which may
have gone by the time you read this) with difficulty to reach better
holds. Move left to the ledge on Cakewalk and finish straight up the
tower above.

50 Cakewalk 10m VS P1 1956
5a Left of the tree is a short crack. Tackle this and the difficult wall
above to a hole. Move up to a ledge and traverse rightwards to walk
off on a larger ledge to finish.

The next climbs are on the larger buttress to the left **-Castle Rock**.

Starting just left of the gully splitting the blocks is:-

51   Kneewrecker   12m   E1   P1   1995
5b Climb a short wall to a recess. Gain a short hanging crack and follow it to a large ledge. the leaning, undercut crack (crux) is climbed to the top. Escapable but worthwhile.

52   Picnic Alternative Start   12m   E3   P2   1974
6b Start one metre right of a thin crack in the lower wall and climb up past a large pocket to gain a ledge. Move left to a hole and finish straight up, as for Picnic.

53   Picnic   12m   E2   P1   1973   ★★
5c The thin crack bisects a ledge and becomes a short hanging corner rising to half height. Follow this to its top, step right and climb to a deep hole. Pulling out of this on to the fluted top is awkward.

54   Picnic Variation   12m   HVS   P1   1956   ★
5a Follow Picnic to the top of the hanging corner where a short, but awkward traverse left brings the sanctuary of Jabberwok's easy finishing chimney into reach.

55   Jabberwok   12m   MVS   P2   C1950   ★★
4b Below the chimney in the centre of the buttress is a short slanting crack. Climb the wall 2 metres left of the base of the crack on good but widely-spaced holds. Step right round the overhang to finish up the chimney. The slanting crack can be climbed as an equally good and better protected, but slightly harder, variation start (VS 4c).

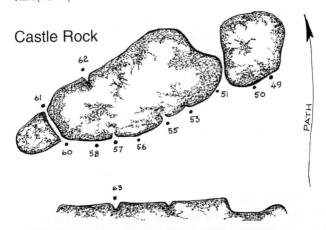

Castle Rock

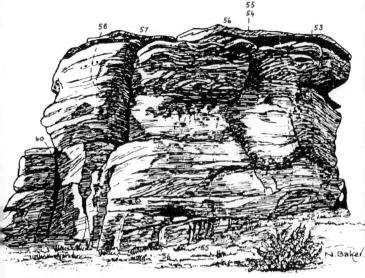

56 Swan Arcade   12m E4 P2 1976   ★
5c The wall to the right of Desperation Crack can be climbed with
technical moves on small holds. Traverse right to below the widest
part of the roof and climb out carefully on broken flakes to a spike
on the lip, and good pro at last! Now finish with a difficult pull-over
just left of Jabberwok's chimney.

57 Desperation Crack   12m HVS P2 Pre 1957   ★★
5b The fine, compelling off-set crack line is climbed easily at first to
a real grunt of a finish. (Large Friends help – one above pulling and
one below pushing are best).

58 Michael Michael Superman   12m E3 P2 1988   ★
5c Takes a line up the buttress left of Desperation Crack. Climb up
and out of the niche, trend right and pull over the bulge (just left of
the crack). Climb the steep slab above. Quite hard for the grade.

59 Hawk Traverse   21m HS P2 1959
4b Climb the corner at the left end of the buttress for 4 metres until
it is possible to traverse right into Desperation Crack. Climb this
until the traverse can be continued under the roof to finish up the
chimney of Jabberwok.

60 Castle Corner   6m D P1 1997   ★
The enjoyable corner crack used as the start to Hawk Traverse.

Climb the corner, pull onto the ledge on the left and scramble over boulders to finish. A good beginners route.

61 Squeeze Crack 6m HS P2 1997
4b The obvious crack around the corner about 5 metres left of Castle Corner. The grade depends on your girth - don't get stuck!

62 Castle Crack 6m HS 1995
4b The obvious crack 3 metres left of Squeeze Crack.

The low level traverse of the buttress is 5b either way. The elephant's bum to left of Castle Corner is a 6a traverse.

There is a prominent crack in the buttress opposite Desperation Crack. This is:–

63 Bog Crack 9m E1 P2 1963
5b Follow the crack past a 5-metre thread runner to a bold and hard finish.

To the left of Bog Crack is an overhanging niche containing several excellent and popular boulder problems all 6a or above.

Aerial Altar and Turtle Rocks
Behind Castle Rock and facing Brimham House is the large tower called Aerial Altar and a group of boulders split by a chimney culminating in a weird-shaped rock with a thread and two perched boulders on top: Turtle Rocks.

The next two routes are on the Aerial Altar on the side facing the house. Descent is down the track side and is awkward.

64 Mumbojumbo 13m E1 P2 1971
5b Above marshy ground is a flared crack. Follow this to a ledge on

Turtle Rock

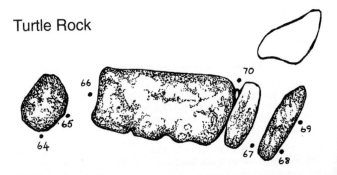

the right. An undercut in the bulge above and a long reach gains a
pocket and thus a ledge. Climb to a pocket on the lip on the right
and pull over (or bottle out).

65   Back Breaker 13m VS P2 1972
5a Five metres right of Mumbojumbo is this twisting broken crack-
line rising from a ledge.

66   Excursion 18m VD P1 1971
Climb on to a ledge opposite Back Breaker, traverse left and climb a
short, desperate crack. Traverse back right and up a mossy wall to
finish.

67   The Turtle Rocks Chimney 9m VD P1   ★
Climb the chimney between Turtle Rocks and the boulders on the
left, step on to a ledge on the right then up to the perched rocks.
Abseil or climb down.

68   Cantilever Pinnacle 9m VS P2 1965
5a Start at the front face of the boulder and climb leftwards to the
obvious thread. Pass this to the ledge, and climb the groove to the
top.

69   Halcyon Daze 9m E2 P2 1988   ★
5c Climb the wall below the two perched boulders.

70   Keystone Chimney 8m HS P1 1996   ★
4b To the right of the rear exit to Turtle Rocks Chimney is a
narrower chimney blocked by a chockstone. From inside the south
end of the chimney climb up into the ceiling to place protection.
Step down and work outwards to bridge up beneath the 'keystone'.
Pull around it to finish. An excellent route reminiscent of Parson's at
Almscliff, but shorter.

Dancing Bear
The next route lies on The Dancing Bear and can be reached by
following the track past the left side of the house to the obvious
shaped boulder.

71   Dancing Bear 7m HVD P2   ★
Follow the polish up the west face of The Dancing Bear. Descent is
by following the polish back down.

72   Dancing Bear variant 7m HVD P1 1996
The short crack and shallow corner round to the right of the ordinary
route proves interesting.

The next three routes take aretes on the tall boulder north of
Dancing Bear. The longest and steepest is:-

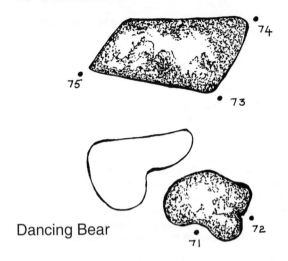

Dancing Bear

73 Tender Homecoming 9m E8 P3 1990   ★★
7a The desperate rounded arete. Start on the left till a move right
gains the arete and a 'less than positive' finish. The fall is survivable
but could well involve hospitalisation!

74 Eyes Right 6m HVS P2 1988
5c The arete to the right of Tender Homecoming.

75 Eyes Left 6m HVS P2 1988
5b The arete right of the descent, and left of Tender Homecoming.

Indian's Turban
Follow the path for 120 metres past the Druid's Writing Desk (where
you can drop down to halfway along the northern edge) to the
Druid's Idol, a large boulder on a 30-centimetre plinth. Indian's
Turban Rocks are 20 metres to the right. The routes are described
clockwise from the chimney on the west face.

76 West Indian's Turban Route 8m S P2 1996
Climb the chimney crack between the pinnacles on the west side.
(easier than the original way on the eastern side but large chocks
are needed for protection).

77 Indian's Turban West 8m MVS P2 Pre 1957   ★
4b On the west face is a series of scoops. Follow these.

78 Indian's Arete 8m S P2 1962
4b Climb the northern arete. The initial bulge being the crux.

79 Zero Option 7m VS P1 1996   ★
5a Take the centre of the steep east wall direct. Gain the small
black hole in the break below the top and step up to finish on a
small flake.

80 Indian's Turban Route 8m HS P2 Pre 1957
4a The chimney-cum-crack between the boulders.

81 Board To Tears 8m E3? P2 1988
5c? Left of the chimney was a notice board which provided a
crucial hand-hold, now, alas, all that remains are the bolt heads.
These can still be reached and used for protection but whether the
climb has been repeated without pulling on the board is not clear, it
certainly looks harder than its original grade .

82 Harry's Crack 6m MVS P1 1970
4b The overhanging crack at the south end of the boulders
provides a desperate finish.

The pocketed wall to the right is a 6b problem.

83 Jibber 6m VS P2 1996
5a Climb the awkward wall left of Harry's Crack via short cracks
and a pocket to the hole.

84 Argy Bargy 5m MS P1 1996
The pleasant crack in the left end of the wall.

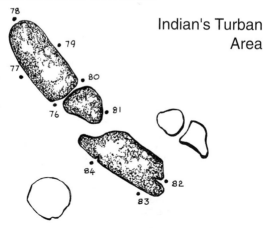

Indian's Turban
Area

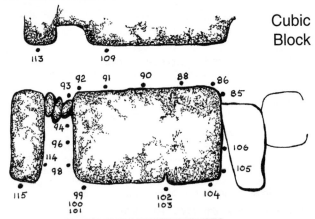

Cubic
Block

CUBIC BLOCK AND THE SOUTHERN EDGES
The Cubic Block and the beginning of the Southern Edges is best
approached from the left-hand (western) car park. From the top left
corner of the car park follow a path over a small rise and down to
the Cubic Block. The east face is the first reached and provides the
easiest climbs. The overhanging face provides immaculate
bouldering and low level traverses.

85 Ugly 11m HVS P1 1980
5c To the left of the east face is a small cave with a diagonal crack
leading rightwards to the arete. It is possible, but only just, to follow
this and gain the arete which leads easily to the top.

86 Old Corner 9m HVD P1 Pre 1957   ★
Follow the left arete of the east face to a short crack. Climb this and
the ledges above. Take lots of big runners.

87 Shorty's Dilemma 9m S P1 1988
A worthwhile variation starting just right of Old Corner at a shallow
hole. Use the hole to gain a sloping shelf and pull over the overlap.
Finish direct.

88 Heather Wall 11m S P1 Pre 1957   ★
Start below a ledge at 3 metres at the left side of the face. Gain this
and follow the crack rightwards to the top.

89 Heather Wall Variant 10m HS P2 1976
4b Start directly beneath the final crack on Heather Wall and climb
straight up the wall towards it via a bulge. Step right, avoiding the
crack, and climb to the top.

90   Great Slab   11m   HVD   P1   Pre 1957   ★
To the right of the ledge on the previous route is a cave. Climb up to this and follow it to the base of a crack on the right that leads to the top.

91   Square Root   11m   HS   P2   1964   ★
4b   Start just right of a pointed boulder and take a direct line up the slab using small holds and breaks.

92   Cubic Corner   11m   MVS   P2   Pre 1937   ★★
4b   A very fine and popular climb that gets progressively harder up the right arete. Friends provide adequate protection

93   Thin Line   11m   HVS   P2   1963   ★
5a   Around the corner is a pile of boulders. From the top of these climb the slab just right of the arete. A little bit sustained, and quite bold, but never technically too taxing.

94   Stone Wall   12m   E1   P2   1974   ★★
5b   Start to the right of the boulders just left of a thin crack. Climb up to horizontal breaks and move right until you are standing just left of an arched overlap. Climb boldly up the slab to an exhilarating and satisfying finish.

95   Rough Stuff   13m   HVS   P2   1989   ★
5b   From the short vertical crack climb direct to the short curving corner which marks the left end of the overlap between Stone Wall and Rough Wall. Climb the overlap direct just right of the curving corner.

96   Rough Wall   13m   VS   P1   1957   ★★★
5a   Excellent throughout. Start below thin cracks in the upper wall. Climb up to the first, and step left to a second crack above the overlap. A difficult move over this concludes a splendid route.

97   Rough Neck   12m   VS   P1   1989   ★
5a   To the right of the finish of Rough Wall is a short corner below the overlap. Climb direct to this, reach right over the overlap to a twin pocket, and finish up the wall.

98   Moss Side   13m   VS   P1   Pre 1958   ★★
4c   Start just right of Rough Wall and trend rightwards to a sloping ledge high on the right arete. Move left, good jams, and make a precarious step up to gain the top.

Round the arete is a steep overhanging wall with a fierce crack in its centre and the difficult Joker's Wall routes to the left. The next three routes are variations on a theme and all start in the same place. Be warned – none are easy.

99   Joker's Wall Arete   14m   E3   P2   1974   ★
6a   A few long, imaginative moves up the pocketed overhanging wall right of the arete bring a sloping ledge into reach. Use a good undercut pocket to gain the ledge and cracks above. Finish direct.

100   Joker's Wall   14m   E4   P2   1971   ★★
6a   From the first significant break at 4 metres make a strenuous traverse right to a larger ledge. Step up and left to the next break and follow this strenuously back to the sloping ledge on the arete. If you can gain a standing position on it, move up right to finish.

101   Joker's Wall Crack   12m   E4   P2   C1975   ★
6b   From the larger ledge, step up and climb the flared bottomless crack above. Looks easy, doesn't it? An independent start can be made up the wall just left of Minion's Way.

102   Minion's Way   11m   HVS   P1   1957   ★★★
5b   A Brimham classic!. The horrific crack in the centre of the wall has a nasty habit of making a mess of unsuspecting hands. The layback crack above is much easier.

103   Wisecrack   15m   HVS   P1   1993   ★★
5b   Climb Minion's Way to near the top and then swing left and traverse a high horizontal break to the top of Joker's Wall Crack. Step up and continue left. The high traverse is pleasant - the crux is still the start of Minions Way.

Joker's Traverse ★★ at low level from Joker's Wall to Minion's Way is 6b. A direct line to the ledge right of Joker's Wall is **No Joke★** (6b) even with a long reach. **Minion's Close (**6a) is the wall on 'dinkies' just left of crack of Minion's Way - some think its an easier alternative! **The Overhanging Flake** to gain the ledge right of Minion's Way is yet another 6b.

104   The Bottom Line   12m   E7   P2   1989
6c   A strenuous and appalling looking line through the sloping shelves and overhanging 'bottom' between Minions Way and Beatnik. It is however, one of the best protected E7s on grit. The start is from the flake on the right.

105   Beatnik   12m   E3   P2   1963   ★
5c   The yellow wall inside the cave has a hanging crack. From this, gain a thinner crack and pull over the bulges to rounded ledges. Traverse left to a sloping ledge from where you can scramble off up the easier upper slabs. An old test piece but quite low in this grade.

106   Cave Chimney   11m   HVD   P1   Pre 1970   ★
Bridge up the chimney in the back of the cave, or start up the diagonal cracks. A much better climb than it looks.

The **Cubic Slabs** to the right of Cave Chimney are particularly suited to beginners. The easiest variant is a Moderate. Try the right edge with no hands!

Opposite the east face of the Cubic Block is a jumble of small walls with many variations, the best of which are:-

107   Problem Wall Arete   6m   VS   P1   Pre 1997   ★
5a   Climb the slanting crack and the tricky arete.

108   Problem Wall Direct   8m   HS   P1   Pre 1997
4c   Mantelshelf onto the incut ledge of the normal route (crux) and then step up right to finish using the short vertical right-hand crack.

109   Problem Wall   8m   HD   P1   Pre1957
A foot traverse that starts behind the tree and leads right until it is possible to escape up the ramp onto the right-hand corner.

110   Green Crack   6m   VD   P2   Pre 1997
Start behind the tree of Problem Wall and climb straight up to gain the short vertical crack and ledge. Finish up either the crack on the left, or the awkward overlap behind the holly.

111   Little Corner   5m   D   P1   Pre 1997
The corner and crack just right of Idle Slabs is ideal for beginners.

112   Idle Slabs Arete   5m   MS   P1   1980
The arete left of Little Corner with an awkward step past the hole.

113   Idle Slabs   6m   M   P1   Pre 1997
The easy-angled slab that leans against the left end of Problem Wall.

The next two routes lie on a larger boulder opposite the north face of (Rough Wall) the Cubic Block.

114   Moss Lane   9m   HS   P2   1964   ★
4a   Step off a boulder opposite Moss Side next to the fence. Climb the large flake and follow the diagonal faults rightwards, using the top edge as and when necessary.

115   Moss Alley   8m   VS   P2   1964   ★
5a   Round to the left of Moss Lane and over a fence is a slabby boulder with a flake at 2.5 metres. A difficult pull gains this. Trend left to finish.

From Cubic Block the edge can be followed northwards through the woods. The following buttresses are dotted along the edge and can be hard to find.

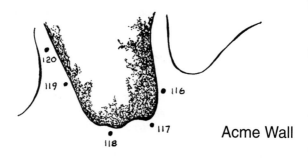

Acme Wall

Acme Wall Area is found by following the lower path north for 75 metres. It consists of a steep slab with a wide blunt undercut arete at its right end.

116 Forever Man 6m HVS P2 1985
5a To the right of the arete is a small wall. Climb this without recourse to the arete if you can see the point.

117 Peerless 6m HS P2 1965   ★
4a From a flat boulder climb the arete direct.

118 Appiewand 6m HS P2 Pre 1970   ★
4b Left of the arete is a short crack; use this to gain a ledge at two-thirds height and mantelshelf to finish. A route that is both hard to start and finish. An alternative start up the wall to the left is 5a.

119 Acme Wall 7m E3 P2 1980   ★
6a The main wall has a small pocket. Climb up to this and do the best you can with it to reach the break.

120 Acme End 5m VS 1994
5a From the left end of the wall, below and left of the tree, climb diagonally rightwards using a good pocket to finish right of the tree.

121 Acme Wall Traverse 18m HVS P2 1980
5a From the extreme left end of the wall follow the upper break rightwards, cleaning as you go.

122 Acme Wall Lower Traverse 12m VS P2 Pre 1997   ★
5a Start at the extreme left end of the wall. Cross the delicate wall using the obvious hole to finish up the right arete. Excellent climbing.

Happy Days Area
Forty metres leftwards is a buttress split by a horizontal crack at half height with a holly tree to the left and a sharp undercut prow.

123 Layback Crack 7m HVD P2 1965
To the right of the prow is a wide crack.

124 Bilge Crack 7m E2 P1 1980
6a A mysterious route, its repulsive nature being strangely attractive. It takes the hanging crack.

125 Bilge Pump 7m E3 P2 C1988   ★
6b Step on to the prow with difficulty and follow it with even more difficulty. Starting from the ground is 6c.

126 Happy Days 7m E3 P1 1978   ★
6b Left of the prow is a niche at chest height which is gained by desperate moves. The bulging wall and pocket above also prove perplexing. Really average climbers may have to traverse in from the left.

127 The Belfry 13m S P1 1970   ★★
4a Various techniques can be used to climb the chimney which becomes progressively more overhanging and exhilarating. At the top of the chimney traverse right to a large dubious-looking thread. Finish past this.

128 R.P.T. 13m S P2 1965/89   ★
4a The leaning left arete originally finishing via the traverse of the Belfry. Best extended by moving left at the top of the arete over bulges to the top. (HS 4b).

129 H.K.T. 7m S P1 1965
4a In the wall left of the arete is a diagonal crack. Follow this to a prickly finish.

130 Stretching Hekate 8m VS   1994
5a Climb the crack of HKT to the top and then make a delicate move up to the next break. From here 3 mantels lead to the top.

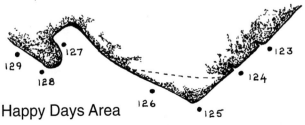

Happy Days Area

The traverse round the Happy Days buttress is 5c. From the start of
The Belfry it is possible to traverse right under the roof and out onto
Happy Days at 6c.

Red Tape Area
Eighteen metres to the left is a small buttress with a deep chimney
containing three chockstones. With great imagination this is called
Chockstone Chimney. The walls on either side contain a number of
problems and micro routes the best of which are :-

131   Unfinished Crack   5m   HVS   P2
5a   The short wall and flake crack under the roof a few metres right
of the chimney.

132   Hanging Arete   5m   E2   P2
6a   The arete right of the chimney to an awkward escape.

133   Hanging Crack   5m   E1   P1   ★
5c   Climb the crack in the wall just right of the chimney. An
interesting problem.

134   Chockstone Chimney   8m   D   P1   Pre 1957   ★
Climb the flake in the chimney until a standing position on the
chockstone can be achieved. Progress to the top.

135   Merle   8m   S   P2   C1965
4a   A series of rounded ledges lead up the rib left of the chimney,
the start being the most awkward.

136   No-problem Wall   5m   HVS   P2
5c   Straight past the undercut in the break to a difficult finish.

Continuing left for 20 metres Red Tape Buttress is reached. This is
a steep wall undercut on its right side. Down on the path is a
wedge-shaped boulder which may help location.

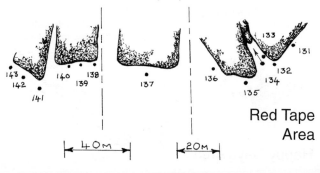

Red Tape
Area

├── 40M ──┤   ├─ 20M ─┤

137   Red Tape   11m   E2   P1   1971   ★★
5b A fine open climb direct up the centre of the wall with a long reach at mid height and a mantelshelf finish. It is possible to traverse right to the arete. This is less difficult, less protected but less sensible.

It is possible to traverse Red Tape Buttress at various levels. There is a horrendous 6c, rock over to the right of the start of Red Tape.

Continuing north for 40 metres are two small buttresses. The left-hand one has a steep arete and across the gully to the right is a slabby wall and the following climbs.

138   Slab Arete   6m   VD   P1   Pre 1997   ★
4a An enjoyable climb up the stepped right arete.

139   Centre Point   6m   D   P1   Pre 1997
The slab is ideal for beginners and has a number of variations.

140   Cyclops   6m   MS   P1   Pre 1997
4a Up the wall to the hole then to the top.

141   Gordon's Proffer   6m   HVS   P2   1981   ★
4c Follow the steep arete on the left-hand buttress to the overhang, then either traverse left and up or, if feeling brave, push straight on (5a).

142   Acme Error   6m   HVS   P2   1981   ★
5a Climb the wall left of the arete past a pocket to a delicate finish.

143   Long John's Rib   6m   HS   P2   Pre 1989
4b The left arete is an old, but previously un-recorded, problem deserving of independence.

Continuing leftwards a large area of open land is reached with Cleft Buttress and Notice Board Wall prominent in the centre. This is the start of the Lovers Leap and Northern Edges section.

Lover's Leap and the Northern Edges
This section starts at Cleft Buttress and Notice Board Wall and runs along the edge to Brimham's most northerly tip. Cleft Buttress and Notice Board Wall lie in open ground that can be found by walking along the southern edge or by dropping down through the boulders below Brimham House.

Notice Board Wall
The most obvious features on Notice Board Wall are the crack and the two old bolt heads – all that remains of an old notice that banned climbing.

144   Notice Board Wall   8m   E2   P2   1981   ★
5b The left-hand crack stops halfway up. At this point step left to climb boldly into and out of the scoop above.

145   Take No Notice   9m   E4   P2   1988   ★
6b Takes the wall directly past the old bolts. This is pleasant; reaching the pocket on top is not.

146   Notice Board Crack   9m   VS   P2   Pre 1937   ★★
4b A classic gritstone crack – claimed to be Brimham's oldest VS. Squirm up the rounded crack to the right of the old notice board bolts.

147   Buena Ventura   10m   E2   P2   1980
6a Climbs the bulges just right of the crack. A desperate boulder problem start soon leads to easier climbing.

148   Gluon   10m   E2   P2   1995   ★
5b Start in the gully to the right of Notice Board Crack. Step from a sharp boulder onto the wall and gain a slot. Step leftwards and then pull out onto a big ledge. A mantel then leads to the exit up a shallow fault in the final bulge.

The Anvil To the right of, and slightly below, Notice Board Wall is a large two tier block.

149   Mild Steel   6m   S   P2   1997
From the foot of the gully to the left gain a rounded ledge and move right for two metres until it is possible to step up and mantelshelf onto the big ledge. Traverse off easily to the right or step left to climb the short flake in the blunt arete (**Tensile Strength** E1 5b).

150   Spring Steal   10m   E1   P2   1992   ★
5c Starts on the right-hand side of the lower tier. Climb the awkward slanting depression in the slab to a ledge. A delicate move is then required to surmount the top block just left of centre.

Moving round the back of the block to the right is:-

151   The Flue   6m   VD   1995   ★
The Corner chimney in the recess at the rear of the Anvil.

152   Boc No Hero   5m   E2   P2   1995
5c A steep pocketed wall just left of The Flue with long reaches to a rounded finish. No Bridging.

Cleft Buttress
Opposite Notice Board Wall is the rather complex Cleft Buttress which comprises of three gullies between three large boulders. One boulder, the Cleft Pinnacle, is free-standing, while the other two are connected

Cleft Buttress

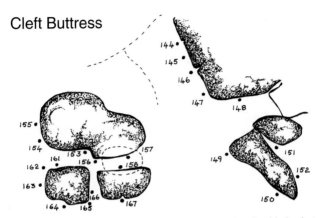

by a large rock bridge. The central gully offers excellent bouldering but beware, descent can be perplexing from all three blocks!

153 Lancet Crack   12m VS P1 1958   ★★
5a Follow the thin crack at the centre of the gullies up and over the roof in a fine position.

154 Syrett's Rib   12m E1 P2 1976★
5b The blunt and rounded arete left of Lancet Crack is followed in its entirety.

155 Gordon's Wall   12m E1 P1 1976
6a Climb the rounded bulges 2 metres left of Syrett's Rib with a very long reach for the most appallingly sloping holds.

156 Stone Age Reveller   12m E4 P1 1997   ★★
6b The rib to the right of Lancet Crack is climbed precariously on the right to good holds. A contorted pirouette onto the projecting nose may then just enable slopers to be reached at the top of the scoop above. Finish up right as for Druids Reality.

157 Druid's Reality   16m HVS P1 1987   ★
5b The steep wall to the right of Lancet Crack and below the rock bridge is climbed to the roof. Traverse left in a ludicrous position to a short groove. Finish easily.

158 Cleft Buttress   12m D P1 Pre 1957
Start opposite Druid's Reality and follow polished holds to a ledge to the right of the roof. Pull on to the big ledge and either climb elegantly up a short wall or squirm up a sloping ramp to the top. Then wonder how to get down?

159 High Steppa 6m HVS P2
5c The short slabby wall around the corner to the right of Cleft Buttress has a pocket above a boulder. Gain the pocket and climb to the ledge. Finish up or down Cleft Buttress.

The remaining routes are on the free-standing pinnacle. Start at the innermost corner (opposite Lancet Crack) and move round anti-clockwise. Descend down Cleft Pinnacle.

160 Cleft Pinnacle 12m HVD P2 Pre 1957
Using the arete and a couple of high steps climb the left edge of the green slab to a ledge. Trend left to finish.

161 Max Crax 10m S P2 Pre 1997
4a Climb the two metre crack in the centre of the wall and make a thin step up to good holds. Finish more easily up a short crack in the top bulge on the left.

162 Cleft Arete 10m VS P1 1976
5a The arete right of Cleft Pinnacle climbed on the left. The outside edge gives a good 5c problem.

163 Womb With A View 11m E1 P1 1988
5c Take the short crack in the wall right of Cleft Arete and behind a tree, then the wall to another short crack leading over the bulges.

164 Murky Crack 10m MVS P1 1958
4c The overhanging crack is followed until it is possible to traverse right.

Carrying on into the gully:

165 Murky Rib 7m HVS P1
Can be climbed on either side. The left is 6a the right 5b.

166 Mantelshelf Blues 6m E1 P1 1982
6a Climb the wall 2 metres right of the arete using a thin pull and a high step up. Wrongly named High Steppa in the last guide.

167 Perverted Crack 6m VS P1 C1958   ★
5a The rounded bulging crack on the front face of the right-hand block. A good old fashioned test-piece, now partially obscured by a tree.

THE NORTHERN EDGES

Cracked Buttress
This buttress with its many cracks, lies to the north west and is the start of the Northern Edges proper.

N. Baker

168 Cracked Corner 9m VD P1 Pre1957 ★
The right-hand corner of the buttress soon eases after an awkward start.

169 Frost In The Shadows 12m E2 P2 1989
6a An interesting eliminate between Cracked Corner and Right Hand Crack. The start and finish both require long reaches

170 Right-Hand Crack 12m VS P1 C1950 ★★★
4b The right-hand crack in the wall is followed to a ledge. Finish up the wider crack. A superb climb.

171 Grit Attack 12m HVS P1 1988 ★
5b The series of horizontal breaks between Right-hand Crack and Central Crack finishing up either of the adjacent routes from the last ledge.

172 Central Crack 12m VS P1 Pre1957 ★★
5a The central crack is followed past a small overhang to a good crack which widens to give an insecure finish. An escape left or right below the final crack reduces the grade to 4b.

173 Parallel Cracks 11m VS P1 1956 ★
4c The twin cracks with another hard finish. Each crack can also be climbed independently at the same grade. The left-hand one has an interesting finish trying to locate a 'secret' hold.

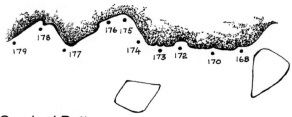

Cracked Buttress

174   Chox Away   10m   E3   P2   1988
5c   The arete and rounded breaks behind the tree left of Parallel
Cracks give a bold climb with the main difficulties in the middle
region.

175   In Retrospect   10m   HVS   P1   1972
5a   Between the wall and the chimney is a hanging crack which is
reached by climbing the wall just right of the chimney. The crack
can be reached direct by using a rounded layaway (5c).

176   Druid's Chimney   9m   MS   P1   Pre1970   ★
The chimney is climbed with respect to the flake in the left wall at
the top.

To the left of the chimney is a groove with a birch tree.

177   Double Back   8m   MS   P1   1971   ★
Climb the slabby right wall of the groove. Step right under the
overlap allowing a good crack to be reached.

178   Birch Climb   9m   HS   P1   Pre 1957
Climb the crack at the back of the groove and step left to the birch
tree. Scramble up the tree until you can launch yourself into the
offwidth crack above. Getting harder as the tree loses more
branches.

On top of the crag, above Birch Climb is a balanced boulder called
the **Boat Rocking Stone**. To get your VS tick climb on to it and
traverse right to the end (a lot quicker to reverse).

179   Crossover   9m   VS   P1   1957
4c   As the name implies a climb that crosses Birch Climb. The
overhanging crack left of Birch Climb leads to the tree. Now step
right to gain a crack.

180   Alcove Chimney   5m   HD   P1
The obvious chimney left of Crossover and right of Lichen Slab.

The next route takes the detached slab to the left.

181   Lichen Slab   8m   VD   P3   Pre 1957   ★
Looking out for a steady stream of abseilers, climb the centre of the slab. A good route for beginners to second but protection is sparse for the leader.

182   Left Edge   10m   HS   P2
4b Contrived but interesting. Climb to the large depression in Lichen Slab then, using holds under the roof and a flake on the left, traverse delicately across to the gully bed. Step back right and climb up the thin crack to a ledge. Finish up the top slab or crawl off right.

Lover's Leap Area
To the left of Lichen Slab the crag increases in height and has a series of chimneys, the biggest of which is Lover's Leap Chimney with its huge perched boulders at the top. Lover's Leap is legendary, the scene of the end of Edwin and Julia's elopement after they were chased there by her father and his vassals. To the right of Lover's Leap Chimney is the wide crack of Nameless Chimney and right again is the chimney of President's Progress.

183   Lost Corner   6m   D   P1   1997
Climb the pleasant right hand corner in the hidden bay up and left of Lichen Slab.

184   Secret Crack   6m   VD   P1   1997
The wide crack in the left-hand corner.

The next climb starts at a lower level, and just right of the chimney of President's Progress.

185   Love Bite   10m   E2   P2   1997
Contrived, but with some interesting climbing.
1 4m 4a Climb the corner beneath the prow of rock to the top of the block on the right, or,

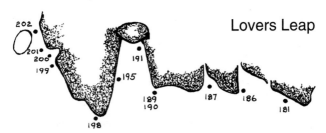

Lovers Leap

1a 4m 5b Take the hanging crack just left of the corner to gain the block.

2 6m 5c From the top of the block pull up into a cave via flutings and move out left to the nose to escape.

186 President's Progress 12m HVD P1 1955   ★
Scramble up from the right to a ledge at half height and bridge the recessed cracks in the wide chimney above. A harder but purer start is direct up the short chimney below the big ledge.

187 Nameless Chimney 14m HS P2 1957   ★
4b The much larger chimney to the left leads to a ledge. The finishing crack proves awkward.

188 Stepped Buttress 14m E1 P2 1996
6a A contrived but worthwhile extension to a popular boulder

problem. Start from the foot of Nameless Chimney and climb the centre of the steep slab on the right to a big ledge. Climb the front, or more easily the right arete, of the blocks above and then tackle the 'interesting' final bulge (crux) by way of the flake on the rounded top.

The next climbs take the walls of Lover's Leap Chimney.

189 Bilberry Jam   15m   E3   P1   1988
6a A linked series of problems on the Right Wall starting up the right arete to the ledge and then the right-hand of the two short hanging cracks finish up the easier groove and pull out right of the overhang

190 Right Wall   14m   VS   P1   1957   ★★
4c The right wall of the chimney. Climb the short crack a few metres left of the arete to a ledge, step up and move left to climb the left-hand hanging crack above a hole. Follow the groove above finishing right of the overhang.

191 Ambidexter   12m   HVS   P1   1973
5a A contrived route that visits most of the crag. Climb the right

side of the boulder at the back of the chimney and make a delicate traverse to the crack on Right Wall. Move up to the roof and traverse left to a belay (essential to reduce rope drag). Crawl up, out between the boulders and traverse left to the top of the climbs on the left wall. An unusual, exposed and spectacular finish.

192 Leap Frog 12m E5 P3 1976
6a The left arete of the right wall. Climb the wall past a pocket to a ledge. The arete on the left provides serious technical climbing. Finish over the boulders above.

The next five routes start up the crack in the left wall.

193 Lover's Leap Chimney 14m S P1 Pre1937   ★★
Rumoured to be Brimham's oldest climb and certainly one of great character. Climb the now well polished crack (4b) until it is possible to stride across into the cave on the right. A belay can be arranged here and then a choice is made either to climb the left-hand chimney at V.Diff or, better but harder, the wide right-hand chimney at hard severe.

194 Resurrection 15m E6 P2 1989   ★
6b Start from the cave of Lovers Leap Chimney and follow twisting cracks up the wall leftwards to join and finish as for the final move of Left Wall.

195 Left Wall 15m E5 P2 1977   ★★
6a A compelling line with just adequate protection. After the initial crack step left to follow the thinner crack. Move up and right to good holds on which to summon courage for the final push to the top.

196 Love Bug 15m HVS P2 1970/1994   ★
5a As for Left Wall, but at the top of the first crack traverse left to the arete which is followed all the way on good holds.
Variation Start 5a Start as for Love Bug but leave the crack almost immediately for a delicate traverse left to the arete at a lower level.
Direct Start 5b The right-hand side of the arete, between the starts of Birch Tree Wall and Love Bug, to join the parent route where it traverses in from the right.

197 Left-Wall Girdle 20m HVS P2 1981
5a Follow Love Bug to the arete and take the easiest line left across Birch Tree Wall to finish up Black Bob.

198 Birch Tree Wall 15m VS P1 Pre 1957/78   ★★★
4c A classic Brimham outing offering fine open climbing, technically low in the grade. Start just to the left of the arete of Lover's Leap. Climb the wall and step on to the arete. A thin traverse left allows a scoop to be climbed. Follow the gangway leftwards to the top or

step right to a rib and an awkward mantelshelf finish.
Direct Start (6b) ★ The wall below the scoop via an obvious pocket. Imagination helps.

199 Enigma 12m E1 P2 1971/2 ★★
5b Start below an overhang at mid-height to the left of Birch Tree Wall. Climb up to this then right to a block, now up the wall above stepping left on to a ledge. The shallow groove above feels insecure.
Enigma Variation (5b)★ Attain the ledge below the groove by a long reach for a jam crack.

200 Difficult Crack 7m VD P1 Pre1957
The crack to the left of Enigma is climbed past a jammed block.

201 Black Bob 9m VS P2 1981
4c Climb the flakes left of Difficult Crack, making a rightwards rising traverse into that route. Finish leftwards up the slab.

202 Who Needs Friends 9m E3 P2 1980/95 ★
5c Start just right of the boulder (on to which it is possible to jump from the crux!). Climb to the first horizontal break and push on to the second. Now step left to a short jam crack.
Arete Finish (5c) Slightly harder. At the second break step right and climb direct to finish on the blunt arete.

203 Friends And Enemies 10m E4 P2 1994
5c From the top of the pedestal to the left of Who Needs Friends move directly up the wall to the rounded break. Step right to finish up the final cleft of Who Needs Friends.

There are several good problems on smaller rocks to the left followed by a short wall with a large pinnacle above it.

204 George II 12m HVS P2 1963
1. 6m 4c Climb the wall using flakes to a dodgy pull on to the ledge using a hollow hold.
2. 6m 5a Walk left to below a short, usually dirty, crack. A heel hook provides the key to gain the top. Abseil descent, either from the boulder or, more entertainingly, one at each end of the rope.

A further 10 metres left again is a narrow wall partially hidden by boulders with a capping roof at the top.

205 White Rose Flake 7m VS P1 C1958 ★
5a Climb the centre of the wall using a flake to the roof. Exit rightwards.

206 White Flag 6m VS P2 1990
5a The rib to the left of White Rose Flake.

Black Chipper Area

Thirty metres north is an area of boulders recognisable by a number of aretes and a dog-legged crack.

On the right is a boulder with two aretes and to the right of these is an alcove with cracks in both corners. On the right wall of this alcove is

207   Flaky Wall   5m   VS   P2   1966
5a   The hanging wall on flaky ledges.

208   Straddle   5m   MVS   P1   1966
4b   Bridge up the right-hand corner.

209   Alcove Wall   6m   VS   P2   1966   ★
4c   The awkward wall, just right of the start of Combination Cracks, trending right to escape at the top.

210   Combination Cracks   14m   VS   P1   Pre 1989   ★
1. 7m   4c   The crack in the left-hand corner of the alcove, that narrows at two-thirds height.
2. 7m   5a   Walk up and left on to the ledge above Dogleg Crack. The overhanging crack to the right of the second pitch of Dogleg succumbs to a variety of methods.

211   A Sign for the Dynosaurs   6m   E2   P1   1988
6b   Climb the overhanging crack and groove above the first pitch of Combination Cracks.

212   Successor State   7m   E4   P2   1986   ★
6b   The right-hand of the two aretes is tackled with extreme difficulty.

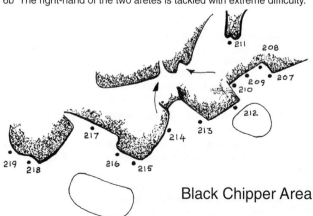

Black Chipper Area

213 Ritornal 6m E1 P2 C1980   ★★
5b The left arete offers good climbing with a few delicate moves at
the top.

214 Dogleg Crack 12m E1 P1 C1960   ★
1. 7m 5a The very obvious dogleg crack in the bay.
2. 5m 5c The wide continuation crack provides much amusement.

215 Rotifer 8m E3 P3 1977   ★★
6a The arete left of Dogleg Crack. Interesting moves lead to a
nose; above the interest is multiplied by an alarming lack of holds.

216 For Crying Out Loud 7m E2 P2 1982   ★
6b On the wall left of the arete is a prominent arch. Start at its right
end and move up to pockets. Trying moves lead up the wall. If at
first you don't succeed, keep trying.

217 The Arch 7m E2 P2 1974   ★
6a The narrow ledge below the arch is gained by a tricky
mantelshelf. Step right to the crown of the arch and pull over.
Apparently it is possible to use combined tactics to climb the slab
above; this seems a bit silly.

To the left is a leaning pinnacle with a large holly bush at its base. It
has two routes.

218 The Black Chipper 12m E2 P2 1966   ★★★
5b The infamous . . . Starting at two large pockets, the wall left of
the arete is climbed to a ledge. Scoops above lead to a vital, but
small, thread runner. Move right to a naughty chipped hold on the
top. It is argued which is the hardest – finding it or using it. If you
wish to avoid this dilemma, do it without.

219 Natural Grit 12m E3 P2 1975   ★
5c The wall above the holly bush is climbed to reach the left end of
the ledge (No. 4 Friend up on the left). Make your way right to the
thread on Black Chipper from where bold and precise climbing
leads left up the scoop.

Duggie's Dilemma Area
The edge disappears for 200 metres and reappears below The
Druid's Writing Desk. This can also be reached by following the
path north from Brimham House.

220 Tight Chimney 6m D P1 Pre 1957   ★
The obvious chimney at the right end of the buttress.

221 Spare Rib 6m E2 P2 1977
5c The arete to the left of the chimney.

222 Duggie's Dilemma 6m MVS P2 1955   ★
4c Climb the wall and ledges left of the arete, an awkward
mantelshelf at mid-height providing the main obstacle.

223 No Doubt 6m HVD P1 Pre 1989
To the left of the ledge on Duggie's Dilemma is an overhang. Climb
up to its left side and continue to the top. Harder direct

224 Gully Arete 7m HS P2 1972   ★
4b The arete across the gully gives a nice climb with degree of
boldness.

Moving left round the corner is the groove of Grit Corner.

225 Lunatic Rib 8m VS P1 1981
4c Climb the short overhanging groove to the right of Grit Corner.
Pull round the roof on to the green slab. Finish anywhere you want.

Duggie's Dilemma Area

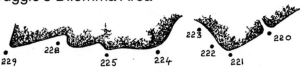

226 Pebbledash 8m E2 P2 1990
5c Start right of Lunatic Rib in the V chimney. Avoiding the block forming the chimney climb the delicate wall to a thin crack splitting the overlap. Surmount the overlap and finish up the crack and corner above. Good thin moves.

227 Grit Bit 8m HVS P2 1966
5c Start as for Lunatic Rib but swing up right to a fist-sized hold and use this to gain the arete. Easier ground leads to the top.

228 Grit Corner 10m VD P1 Pre 1957
Follow the groove to a capping boulder and finish right. A much better finish takes the steep wall to the left and merits a star.

229 Gnome's Arete 10m HVS P2 Pre 1970 ★
5a The wall and arete left of Grit Corner. A good route albeit on chipped holds. Interest is sustained.

Hatter's Groove Area
The next area contains Hatter's Groove, an obvious deep-cut groove 75 metres further along the path. This area is often out of the wind but being north-west facing suffers from lichen and takes longer to dry out than many parts of the crag. During the summer months however it provides some fine climbs

230 Lichen Chimney VD P1 1955
The large crack round to the right of Hatter's Groove.

231 Right Hand Arete 8m HVS P2 1981
5a Follow the arete until forced right.

232 Hatter's Groove 12m VS P1 1955   ★★★
5a A classic VS when dry, and much better than it looks. At the top of the corner move left (crux) and pull into the smooth upper groove. A good thread protects.

233 Hard Hat 13m E1 1990
5c A high right-hand finish to Hatter's Groove, around the final capstone to a difficult mantelshelf escape

Hatter's Groove Area

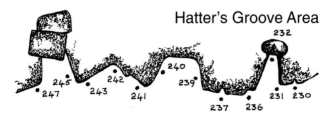

234 Easy Exit   10m   VS   P1   Pre 1982
4c Climb Hatter's Groove until a couple of metres below the top it is possible to traverse on to Right-hand Arete. Not a lot easier than the original finish!.

235 Grit Escape   13m   HVS   P1   1993
5b Start as for Hatter's Groove then follow the thin crack across the right wall to the notch in the arete. Step left and climb the short wall, using the arete, to join 'Easy Exit'. Finish up the chimney on the right.

236 Grit Expectations   12m   E4   P2   1975   ★★★
6a Begin to the left of Hatter's Groove at two pockets at head height. Attain the groove and a high wire placement. Using the groove and holds on the right gain the break (crux). A pocket above enables the top to be reached. Step right into Hatter's Groove.

237 Slippery Crack 12m MVS P1 1955   ★
4b The crack in the wall to the left of Grit Expectations. It is worth
persevering past the dirty start.

238 Serendipity 12m E3 P2 1995
5c Start just left of Slippery Crack and climb a short scruffy crack
into The Pulpit. Gain the wall on the right, cross the notch and make
a difficult move to reach the top of the sloping nose. Further
difficulties lead leftwards to an escape right beneath the capstone.
Better, and harder, than it looks.

The crag drops back to form a recessed ledge; **The Pulpit**.

239   Graft Crack 6m VS P1 1955
4c Starting in The Pulpit, the right-hand crack.

240   Brief Crack 6m MVS P1 1955
4b The left-hand crack.

241   Cracked Rib 8m VS P2 1957
5a Swing on to the rib from the left side of The Pulpit and follow the
crack. The rib can be gained direct from the ground at 5c.

242   Last Crack 8m HS P1 1955
The corner crack.

243   Close To The Hedge 8m E4 P2 1977   ★
6a A fine, scary, technical climb up the imposing arete. Climb the
wall right of the arete to a hole (good small wire thread). Step left on
to the arete and make for the top.

244   Hedgeup 7m E4 P2 1997   ★
6a The direct finish to Close to The Hedge. Same grade and
almost as scary, though a hand placed peg and a poor nut in
pockets above the thread provided some solace.

245   Running On Red 7m E2 P2 1988   ★
6a The wall left of the arete provides good climbing when clean. A
difficult start leads left to a hole then steep but easier climbing to the
top.

In the back of the gully are several cracks and chimney problems.

246   The Hattery Arete 9m VS P2 1973   ★★
4c Across from Close To The Hedge is another fine arete. Climb
this to a horizontal break, step up and follow the continuation arete
to the top.

247   The Hattery 9m HVS P2 1966   ★★
5a Climb the arete to the break, step left and climb the bold wall
above on pockets and layaways.

Wedge Crack Area
The next half a dozen routes lie between The Hattery and a huge
undercut prow. All the routes are usually repulsively lichenous but
are graded for ascents in such conditions; They will only appeal to
the true connoisseur

248   Mad Hatter 8m E1 P1 1972
5b Recommended for the novelty factor. Start below a rounded
prow at head height. Step up right and then back left to gain the

Wedge Crack Area

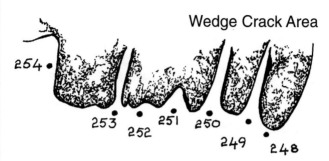

base of the evergreen slab above the bulge. Grovel up this and trend right to finish.

249 Wedge Crack 8m E1 P2 C1965
5b The narrow chimney requires a high expenditure of energy. Udging and grunting seem to help but this is not a route to attempt in your best lycra, shorts or tee-shirts.

250 Choked Chimney 9m VD P1 1960
Follow the easy corner past a chockstone.

251 Viper 8m HS P1 1971
4b The V-groove to the left. Passing the chockstone is the worst move in the world.

252 Boa Cracks 11m HVS P1 1962
5b Start below an undercut jam crack in the arete. Undercut the arete and jam the crack, or is it the other way around? The groove to the right is similar and probably slightly more pleasant.

253 Constrictor Chimney 12m S P2 1955
The chimney right of the large prow. A right-hand exit at the top gives a bottle-out option.

254 Charlie's Dilemma 9m E5 1981 ★
6a Climbs the groove left of the prow. Chimney up to the first of two pockets. Climb to the second and step right on to a rounded ledge. Now direct to a difficult finish.

Green Prioress Area
Across the wide gully from the large prow is a wall with its lower section in a cave. The next three routes are here:

255 Here Be Dragons 9m VS P1 1994
5a The arete and crack right of Corner Crack, over the overhang

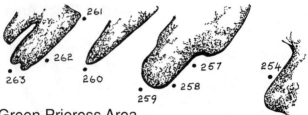

Green Prioress Area

and then a hard move to finish in Corner Crack. Not much new climbing.

256 Games with the Nephfesch   9m   E1   P1   1994
5c The same arete from the other side, to a break then a long reach to rounded holds and the top.

257 Corner Crack   9m   S   P1   1955   ★
4a Follow the crack out of the cave passing an overhang at mid-height.

258 Lichen Wall   6m   E3   P2   1982
5c From a ledge up and left of Corner Crack climb the wall trending left to a horror mantelshelf. A nasty little climb. Originally graded HVS 5b!

259 Classic Bagger   6m   E1   P2   1974
5b Climbs the left side of the arete. Follow the three holes to the arete. Alternatively the top can be reached from the second hole (this only warrants two-thirds of a tick).

Left again is a buttress split by a crack in its lower half.

260 Green Prioress   9m   E1   P2   1978   ★
5b Climb the crack in the front of the buttress to a large pocket on the right. Possible thread runner (10-metre sling!). Move up left to a ledge and finish up the arete.

Charming Crack Area
The next buttress is a steep slab with the overhanging Charming Crack at its left end.

261 Mantelshelf Corner   8m   S   P2   1957
The right-hand arete of the steep slab is climbed by alternating between the arete and the ledges.

262 White Wash   9m   E3   P3   1976   ★
5c The steep slab right of Charming Crack past a pocket to a break

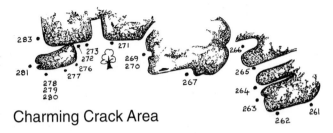

Charming Crack Area

(last runners). Pull up on pebbles. The final move requires a long reach and neck.

263 Charming Crack 9m E1 P1 1956 ★★
5c A Joe Brown classic. The severely-overhanging crack succumbs – just!

264 Brutaliser 9m E3 P1 1970 ★
5c The wider overhanging crack is a classic of its genre. Determination is essential.

265 Charming Chimney 8m HVS P2 1972
4c The wide chimney; start inside and work outwards.

266 Hanging Flake 6m HVS P2 Pre 1970
5a In the left wall of the next chimney (up the gully) a flake with a vegetated finish.

Pig Traverse Area
Opposite Hanging Flake is a small diff chimney and a bold problem arete. Down to the left is a groove.

267 Hanging Groove 7m E1 P2 1976 ★
5b Climb the groove to a break, step left to the top.

268 Mohole Direct 7m E3 P2 1992
6b A very difficult entry can be made into the Mohole via a series of tiny edges leading up and left. Finish direct.

Around the corner is an offwidth crack. This is the start of the next two routes.

269 Mohole 9m VS P2 1963 ★
4c Climb the crack until it is possible to hand traverse right to the arete. Swing round this and then up to the mohole. Finish direct.

270 Three Trees Crack 7m VS P2 1957 ★
4c Layback the crack.

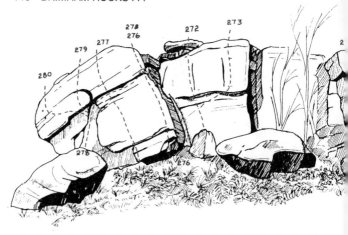

271 Jelly Baby Wall 6m E4 P2 1989

6a Start 4 metres left of Three Trees Crack and just right of a narrow gully. Wobble up the wall via a faint crack and step right to a good break to finish. Don't bite off more than you can chew.

To the left of the trees, a dry-stone wall meets a slab with a recessed wall to its right.

272 Pathos 8m E3 P1 1980 ★★

6a Start below the right-hand crack in the recessed wall. Step across the void and climb the wall to the break. Follow the left-hand crack.

273 Lithos 9m HVS P1 1976 ★

5b Follow Pathos to the break, traverse right to below the right-hand crack and use this and the arete to finish.

274 Lithos Direct Start 8m E1 P1 C1976

6b Desperately-thin climbing leads to the bottom of the crack.

275 Long Funnel 10m VD P2 1956 ★

The tapering chimney at the start of Pathos. The top is not as hard as it looks.

The wide crack to the left is not as easy as it looks, particularly when trying to come down it.

276 Pig's Ear 9m HVS P2 1988

5b The right arete of the slab.

277 Pig Slip Cow Punk 9m E6 P2 1990
6b The slab and wall between Pig's Ear and Pig Traverse, crossing
Pig Traverse to finish just right of Sow's That.

The next three routes start at the base of the slab.

278 Pig Traverse 12m HS P1 1956   ★★
4b Climb the cracks to the overhang. A tricky move allows a
traverse right to the arete.

279 Sow's That 9m E5 P2 1988   ★★
6b Follow Pig Traverse to the overhang and step up left to a finger
pocket in the overlap above. Keeping cool, climb thinly rightwards to
the top.

280 Reach For The Sty 9m E5 P2 1988   ★
6b Follow Sow's That to the pocket. Reach left to a larger pocket
(crucial 1 slider, placed blind). Step left and up.

281 Gigglin' Crack 10m E6 P2 1976   ★★★
6c The ferocious overhanging offwidth crack can be climbed in
style if you are good. If you're average, it's a struggle to get in – and
very easy to get spat out higher up.

282 The Snuffer 11m HVS P1 1961
5b The deep chimney to the left. Start well inside and back-and-
foot out to gain a jam and ledge on the left. Good value.

283 True Grit 11m E4 1970   ★★
6b The thin bulging crack to the left of the chimney chews fingers. If
you can reach the ledge follow the wider crack on the left.

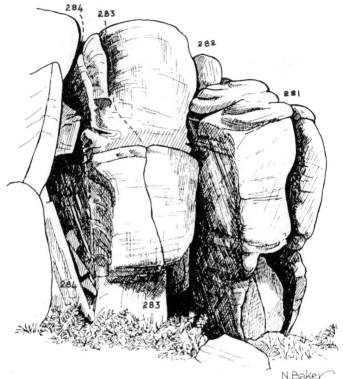

N.Baker.

284 Narrowing Chimney 8m VD P1 Pre 1970
The block-filled chimney is climbed to a really tight squeeze.

285 The Shootist 6m E3 P2 1978
6a Scramble over boulders on the left until below a green slimy
wall. Pull up to a small overlap (1½ Friend) step over this and
commit yourself.

Fag Slab Area
The next buttress consisting of clean slabs and grooves is a popular
spot.

286 Filter Tip 7m E2 P2 1981
5c The right arete offers a bold micro route. Start from the ledge in
the gully and make a couple of tricky moves at the start.

287 Senior Service 8m E3 P3 1997 ★
5c Good climbing with a bold start but not high in the grade. Step
up left from the foot of the arete and climb slopers to below the
overhanging top block. Surmount this by use of a pocket.

288 Fag End 8m S P2 1959 ★
4a Start at a recess and follow the crack and chipped holds above.

289 Smoke Ring 27m HVS P2 1975
5a A bit of a drag!. Climb Fag End to the break which can be
traversed left into Fag Slab Variant. Step through Fag Slab and
make a difficult move into Little Funnel, continue into Allan's Crack
and follow this into the top of Hourglass Chimney.

290 Silkcut 8m E3 P3 1984 ★
6c Start at the foot of Fag Slab Variant. Make a very hard move up
right, over the overlap, to stand in a break. Step left and smear up
to a higher break, then pockets, to a sapling.

291 Fag Slab Variant 8m VS P2 1955 ★★
4c The leftward-leaning groove is interesting and popular.

292 Woodbine 8m HVS P1 1980 ★
5b A technical eliminate between Fag Slab and its variant.

293 Fag Slab 8m S P2 ★★
4a Climb the innocuous-looking groove at the extreme left end of
the slab.

Allan's Crack Area

On the south side of the gully/recess at the rear of Fag Slab are two shallow corner cracks.

294   Finders Keepers   7m   VS   P1   1994
5a   This is the left-hand crack with an awkward step at mid height.

295   Hyde And Seek   8m   VS   P1   1994
4c   The right hand corner crack in the same recess.

296   Little Funnel   8m   VS   P1   1955   ★
5a   The overhanging, narrowing chimney crack to the left of Fag Slab provides good exercise in bridging and jamming .

297   Allan's Crack Right-hand.   12m   VS   P2   ★
5a   Climb Allan's Crack to the overhang, pull right around the apex of the roof to join Little Funnel. Step up and left onto the lip of the roof then trend right to finish at the top right corner of the final wall.

298   Allan's Crack   12m   VS   P1   1955   ★★★
4c   A climb of the highest calibre. Take the layback on the slab left of Little Funnel. Move left round the overhang at half height and then step up right to finish on the wall.

299   Allan's Crack Direct   11m   HVS   P2   ★
5b   Climb the slab left of Allan's Crack. Move up to a foothold on the left arete and climb direct.

300   Bellyporker's Progress   10m   E7   P2   1980
6c   The overhanging side of the left arete of Allan's Crack.

301   Hourglass Chimney   11m   VS   P2   1956
5a   The first chimney left of the hanging rib.

302   Mae West's Rib   10m   E4   P1   1988
6b   The rib and crack to the left gives an interesting problem with good protection. Gain the ledge on the right of the gully and pull up on to the next ledge using the crack, the rib, the crack, the rib etc. Finish easily.

The chimney at the back can be climbed at about HVS if you're daft enough.

303 Hoover 9m S P1 1964
4a The thin flake in the left wall.

304 Vax 8m VD P1 Pre 1997
The flake and groove to the left of Hoover.

305 Dyson 7m VD P1 Pre 1997
The awkward wide crack in the arete.

306 Tilt 5m HVS P2 Pre 1997   ★
5c The hanging groove.

307 Wilt 5m VS P1 Pre 1997   ★
5a The crack splitting the overhang.

Playout Area
Across the wide gully is a steep slab leading left to grooves and
chimneys.

308 For Pete's Sake 7m E2 P2 Pre 1980
6a Climb the slab behind the tree past a flake to a deep pocket. An
apt name.

Round to the left is a bay with a tree in it. The next route takes the
right arete of the bay.

309 Fat Belly Gut Bucket 6m HVS P1 1988
5c A direct line through Chicane. Climb the arete left of the prow to
the break, step left and climb direct to the top.

310 Chicane 12m E3 P3 1972
6a Climb the short corner in the right side of the bay to reach a
handrail. Follow this right under the prow into a scoop and finish
with a very nasty mantelshelf.

311 Deep Chimney 6m S P2 1972
The chimney at the back of the bay, starting at a small pointed
boulder.

312 Lilo 10m HVS P3 1957
5a Climb the broken cracks below the capping roof left of Deep
Chimney. Traverse left under the overhang. Awkward, strenuous,
dirty, protectionless and frightening - well worth searching out!

Playout Area

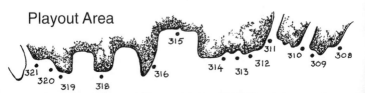

313 Half Crown Corner 6m   VS   P2   1961   ★
5a The groove to the left of Lilo is supplied with enough holds to provide a good boulder-problem-cum-route.

314 Flake Out 6m   VS   P1   1965
4c Climb the flakes to the left to a small ledge finishing up the cracks above.

A deep gully to the left has a crack in the back.

315 Wayout 9m   MVS   P1   1972
4c Layback or chimney towards a good thread below the overhanging block. Traverse left around the block to finish on top of it.

Two cracks in the hidden bay behind Wayout are severes.

316 Fallout 7m   VS   P2   1965
4c The scoopy slabs left of Wayout are climbed on rounded holds to a long pull at the top. This climb is more often than not in poor condition.

317 Playout 9m   XXX   P1   1972
Gains the award for Brimham's dirtiest climb and is graded accordingly – triple X for unadulterated filth. The grade relates directly to the depth of lichen. Gain the easy-angled prow from the left with difficulty. Climb to a thread runner and impossible mantelshelf. Originally the top required combined tactics.

318 Blind's Crack 6m   E2   P2   1965
5b The crack across left from the prow of Playout is climbed to a nasty exit.

The two chimneys in the bay to the left have been climbed (perhaps they shouldn't have been).

319 Britt 9m   E1   P2   1963   ★
5b Climb the rib on the left of the narrow buttress until a knob can be reached. Use this to gain the groove. A good, bold route.

320 Chinese Crack 8m   VS   P2   1958
4c The corner crack is climbed finishing on the right

321 Brown's Crack 7m   VS   P1   1982
4c If only it was just brown! The jamming crack in the upper half of the wall left of Chinese Crack provides an insignificant climb.

Keeper Crack Area
In order to climb the last four routes it is necessary to find them. The buttress can be reached by crossing the stonewall left of Britt and following the path down and round for 360 metres.

Keeper Crack

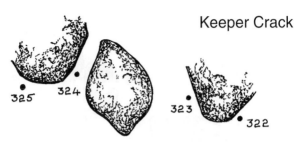

325 324 323 322

322 Dennis The Menace 7m E2 P2 1982
6a Climb the crack that starts halfway up the right end of the right-hand buttress. Difficult to reach and difficult to leave - and not easy to protect.

323 Keeper Crack 8m VS P1 1956
4c The obvious crack with the chockstone.

324 Fook Nose 8m E3 P2 1982
5c After a scrappy start, climb the crack that leads into a groove. The crack stops 1 metre from the top – you shouldn't (but I bet you do).

325 Detour 14m VD P1 Pre 1970
Climb the short crack in the front of the buttress, move left along the terrace below a corner/chimney/crack. Finish up this.

Hares Head Area
This area, never previously described, is in the North East Corner of the estate not far from the road. It can be approached from the car-parks by following the path past Kangeroo Wall and continuing for about 300 metres to an isolated collection of boulders and small pinnacles. The first climb is on a the west face of a block capped by an overhang. There is scope for more development here but only for micro-routes and yet more boulder problems.

326 Zakely Syndrome 7m VS P1 1994
4c The central groove leads to, and through the crack in the roof.

327 Zakely Right-hand 6m S P1 1994
The crack on the right of Zakely Syndrome, escaping right under the top block.

Twenty Metres south of the last route is a block containing four climbs. All require a roped descent or the capability to reverse severe.

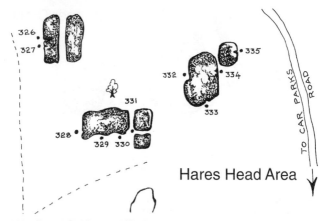

Hares Head Area

328 Stone Cold 7m VS P1 1994
5a A shallow corner on the west face leading to an interesting exit.

329 Knobbly Wall 6m VS P1 1994
4b Climb the centre of the south wall on Knobbly edges.

330 Little Wonder 6m VS P1 1994
4c The wall just left of the chimney on the south face. Gain the sloping ledge direct and continue via the diagonal crack.

331 Inside Out 5m S P2 1994
Ascend the chimney mainly on the outside.

A larger block 25 metres north east of the last climb provides:

332 Emerald Eye 8m S P1 1994
Climb directly into, and out of, the obvious hole in the west face of the block.

333 Forced Entry 8m HVS P1 1994
6b Start below and to the left of a hanging crack by a cave. Pull up and hand traverse into the crack (crux). finish more easily up the crack.

334 Hare's Head Crack 8m VS P2 1994
5a The obvious hanging crack in the wall just left of the corner on the east side of the block. Start using the crack and corner to a ledge. Step back left and finish direct.

335 Homefront 6m E1 P2 1994
5c The bulging crack in the east face of the subsidiary block.

BRIMHAM ROCKS – GRADED LIST

E8
Tender Homecoming (7a)

E7
The Bottom Line (6c)
Bellyporker's
   Progress (6c)

E6
Pig Slip Cow Punk (6b)
Resurrection (6b)
Road Rage
   Experience (6c)
Gigglin' Crack (6c)

E5
Sow's That (6b)
Reach for the Stye (6b)
Cocoa Club Board
   Meeting (6b)
Leap Frog (6a)
Left Wall (6a)
Charlie's Dilemma (6a)

E4
Rat Arsed (6c)
True Grit (6b)
Mae West's Rib (6b)
Joker's Wall Crack (6b)
Take No Notice (6b)
Morose Mongoose (6b)
Close to the Hedge (6a)
Grit Expectations (6a)
Jelly Baby Wall (6a)
Hedge Up (6a)
Dame Edna (6b)
Successor State (6b)
Stone Age Reveller (6b)
Joker's Wall (6a)
Friends And
   Enemies (5c)
Gwyneth (6a)
Swan Arcade (5c)

E3
Alternative Start to
   Picnic (6b)
Bilge Pump (6b)

Happy Days (6b)
Vam (6b)
Mohole Direct (6b)
Silk Cut (6b)
Chicane (6a)
Joker's Wall Arete (6a)
The Shootist (6a)
Tube Break (6a)
Michael Michael
   Superman (5c)
Ratfink (6a)
Sir Les (6b)
Rotifer (6a)
Bilberry Jam (6a)
Pathos (6a)
Steady VS Arete (6a)
Lichen Wall (5c)
White Wash (5c)
Serendipity (5c)
Acme Wall (5c)
Who Needs Friends (5c)
Who Needs Friends
   Arete (5c)
Natural Grit (5c)
Brutiliser (5c)
Beatnik (5c)
Senior Service (5c)
Fook Nose (5c)
Chox Away (5c)

E2
A Sign for the
   Dynosaurs (6b)
For Crying Out Loud (6b)
Peekabu (6a)
Buena Ventura (6a)
Birch Tree Wall
   Direct (6b)
Bilge Crack (6a)
Running on Red (6a)
Pebbledash (5c)
Frost In The
   Shadows (6a)
Hanging Arete (6a)
Dennis The Menace (6a)
For Pete's Sake (6a)
The Arch (6a)
Filter Tip (5c)

Rataonee (5c)
Halcyon Daze (6a)
Boc No Hero (5c)
Picnic (5c)
Love Bite (5c)
Walleroo (5c)
House Points
   Tomorrow (5c)
Spare Rib (5c)
Gluon (5b)
Goof Aydee And
   Mango (5c)
Black Chipper (5b)
Felicity (5b)
Notice Board Wall (5b)
Red Tape (5b)
Blind's Crack (5b)

E1
Lithos Direct (5b)
Stepped Buttress (6a)
Gordon's Wall (6a)
Mantelshelf Blues (6a)
Spring Steal (5c)
Botany Bay (5c)
Rattler (5c)
Womb with a View (5c)
Hard Hat (5c)
Home Front (5c)
Games With The
   Nephrash (5c)
Hanging Crack (5c)
Charming Crack (5c)
Layback and Think (5c)
Syrett's Rib (5b)
Britt (5b)
Classic Bagger (5b)
Frensis Direct (5b)
Wedge Crack (5b)
Bog Crack (5b)
Roadside Crack (5b)
Dogleg Crack (5a, 5b)
Stone Wall (5b)
Green Prioress (5b)
Mumbojumbo (5b)
Kneewrecker (5b)
Mad Hatter (5b)
Ritornal (5b)

Jackabu (5b)
Enigma (5b)
Enigma Variation (5b)
Hanging Groove (5b)
Tensile Strength (5b)
Mad Hatter (5b)
Don't Step Back
    Crack (5b)

HVS
Forced Entry (6b)
Murky Rib L.H. (6a)
Bare Back Side (5c)
Ugly (5c)
Rainy Day (5c)
Unfinished Crack (5c)
Tilt (5c)
Fat Belly Gut
    Bucket (5c)
Grit Bit (5c)
High Steppa (5c)
Druid's Reality (5b)
Eyes Right (5c)
Desperation Crack (5b)
Grit Escape (5b)
Pig's Ear (5b)
Boa Cracks (5b)
Allan's Crack Direct (5b)
Tube Break Direct (5b)
Point Blank (5b)
Ratatwoee (5b)
Rough Stuff (5b)
Lithos (5b)
The Snuffer (5b)
Left Arete (5b)
Eyes Left (5b)
Grit Attack (5b)
Druid's Reality (5b)
Woodbine (5b)
Murky Rib R.H. (5b)
Lilo (5a)
George II (4c, 5a)
Lovebug (5a)
Left Wall Girdle (5a)
Love Bug Variant (5a)
In Retrospect (5a)
Blind's Crack (5a)
The Hattery (5a)
Rat Trap (5a)
Black Tower Face (5a)

Go Joe (5a)
Picnic Variation (5a)
Minion's Way (5b)
Legover (5a)
The Mantelshelf (5a)
Gnome's Arete (5a)
Acme Error (5a)
Right-hand Arete (5a)
Forever Man (5a)
Acme Wall Traverse (5a)
Smoke Ring (5a)
Charming Chimney (4c)
Hanging Flake (5a)
Ambidexter (5a)
Gordon's Proffer (4c)
Right-hand Bias (4c)
Thin Line (5a)

VS
Hourglass Chimney
Cracked Rib
Hatter's Groove
Stone Cold
Frensis
Hares Head Crack
Zero Option
Central Crack
Lancet Crack
Moss Alley
Rough Neck
Cantilever Pinnacle
Jibber
Back Breaker
Cake Walk
Mons Meg
Rough Wall
Little Funnel
White Rose Flake
White Flag
Finder's Keepers
Half Crown Corner
Acme End
Stretching Hekate
Acme Wall Low Trav.
Perverted Crack
Here Be Dragons
Allen's Crack Right-hand
Wilt
Combination Cracks
Easy Exit

Allen's Crack
Hattery Arete
Jabberwok
Chinese Crack
Jabberwok Variant
Kangaroo Wall
Closet Crack
Mohole
Three Trees Crack
Fag Slab Variant
Hyde And Seek
Graft Crack
Alcove Wall
Flaky Wall
Parallel Cracks
Crossover
Right Wall
Keeper Crack
Flake Out
Fallout
Birch Tree Wall
Problem Wall Arete
Black Bob
Brown's Crack
Little Wonder
Zakely Syndrome
Knobbly Wall
Moss Side
Maloja
Concave Slab
Notice Board Crack
Right-hand Crack
Lunatic Rib
Cleft Arete

MVS
Harry's Crack
Murky Crack
Left-hand Bias
Indian's Turban West
Duggie's Dilemma
Wayout
Cubic Corner
Jabberwok
Slippery Crack
Straddle
Brief Crack

HS
Problem Wall Direct

Hawk Traverse
Pig Traverse
Fag Slab
Viper
Indian's Turban Route
Keystone Chimney
Squeeze Crack
Birch Climb
Castle Crack
Square Root
Heather Wall Variant
Bilberry Groove
Ratbag
Top Dead Centre
Appiewand
Gully Arete
Nameless Chimney
Left Edge
Moss Lane
Peerless
Last Crack
Long John's Rib

S
Indian's Arete
Merle
Indian's Turban West
Max Crax
Mild Steel
Heather Wall
The Belfrey
Constrictor Chimney
Corner Crack
Mantelshelf Corner

Fag End
Lover's Leap Chimney
Zakely Right-hand
Inside Out
Hoover
Deep Chimney
Emerald Eye
R.P.T.
H.K.T.

MS
Argy Bargy
Shorty's Dilemma
Druid's Chimney
Crackaroo
Double Back
Cyclops
Idle Slabs Arete

HVD
Cleft Pinnacle
Cave Chimney
Great Slab
No Doubt
President's Progress
Cleft Pinnacle
Old Corner
Dancing Bear Variant
Layback Crack
Dancing Bear

VD
Long Funnel
Slab Arete

Cracked Corner
Difficult Crack
Green Crack
Left Edge
Lichen Slab
The Flue
Grit Corner
Narrowing Chimney
Vax
Dyson
Detour
North West Arete
Secret Crack
Choked Chimney
Lichen Chimney
Turtle Rock's Chimney
Excursion

D
Problem Wall
Chockstone Chimney
Alcove Chimney
Cannon Route
Castle Corner
Lost corner
Vamoose
Cleft Buttress
Tight Chimney
Little Corner
Centre Point

M
Idle Slabs
Cubic Slab

BRIMHAM OUTLYING CRAGS

SITUATION AND CHARACTER   There are four outlying crags to Brimham Rocks. Bat Buttress (NGR 211639) is the obvious crag seen on the right from the road when approaching Brimham Rocks from Summerbridge. It faces south and on the whole dries quickly. The rock is generally clean and solid but a little sandy in places.

The Plantation Crack area is situated in the woods to the north of the Wilsill road (NGR 206638). The main buttress is clean although some of the other routes need a regular brushing. The crag stays damp after rain due to its proximity to the woods which also block out much of the sunlight in mid-summer.

Crow Crag lies in Braisty Woods which are to the south of the Wilsill road over a field. The main buttress (NGR 205636) is reasonably clean and faces west but again, the buttresses in the trees are somewhat 'evergreen'. Worth a visit however.

Little Brimham is a recently revealed collection of rocks in the woods to the left of the approach road and stretch from a point about 200 metres north west of Kimberly House Farm to a point about 200 metres south of the Cubic Block. Mainly micro-routes and problems but sheltered in the winter and spring and reasonably quick drying.

APPROACHES AND ACCESS All the crags are on private land, outside the National Trust Boundary. They are all approached as for Brimham to the last cross-roads at NGR 209637. If approaching from Summerbridge or Harrogate Bat Buttress is the first crag seen behind Kimberley House Farm 200 metres on the right.

For Bat Buttress approach through the farm yard and **always ask permission of the farmer Mr Barker.** Climbing is invariably permitted subject to there being no dogs, and relatively small parties. **Under no circumstances should you approach from the Nidderdale Way path.**

For Plantation Crack turn left at the cross-roads (if approaching from Summerbridge) down the Wilsill road. Park 50 metres down this road. Another 50 metres beyond is a wall on the right running along the top of the woods. Follow this (on the wooded side) until a boulder abuts the wall. Descend to the bottom of the edge and continue along to a clean buttress split by a wide crack. This is Plantation Crack.

Parking for Crow Crag is by the second gate on the left down the
Wilsill road (approx. 300 metres from the cross-roads). Go through
the gate and cross the field to its top right-hand corner. Cross the
wall and follow a vague path up a bracken field and then along its
top by another wall. Thirty metres beyond this is a descent down the
right-hand side of the crag which leads to the top tier.

Little Brimham is best approached from the short track on the left
just after passing the entrance to Kimberly House Farm. A footpath
leads rightwards below the woods, the rocks are up to the right
amongst the trees. **These rocks should not be approached
across the fields from the car parks near Cubic Block.**

BAT BUTTRESS   The routes are described from left to right. Eight
metres left of the main buttress is a broken wall.

1   Escape Route   14m   MVS   P2   ★
4b Gain a shallow groove on the right-hand side of the lower wall
and climb to a heathery ledge. Climb up under the overhang and
swing right to a narrow ledge finishing up the top wall on slopers
and the edge of a shallow crack.

At the left side of the main buttress is a short ramp leading to a
narrow ledge. This provides the start of :-

2   Yo-Yo   12m   VS   P2   ★
4c Follow the ramp and move right along the ledge to cracks which
allow an exit onto the large ledge above. Finish up the scoop in the
upper wall.

A more direct version climbs the flake in the scoop above the start
to a rounded pull onto the large ledge. (5a/b) The narrow ledge can
also be gained in a couple of places further right by 5c boulder
problems

3   Fiddlesticks   9m   HVS   P2   ★
5c Climb the boulder-problem arete on its left-hand side, finishing
up the sandy overhanging, pocketed wall round to the left or better
the upper scoop on Yo-Yo. The arete can also be climbed on the
right at E1 6a

4   Trio Wall   11m   HVS   P1   ★★
5a A superb little route. Layback up the flakes at the left end of the
front face. Finish up the scoop above.

5   Batman   14m   E3   P2
5c The evil-looking overhanging offwidth is gained by a very
strenuous traverse from the right using holds both under and over
the overlap. A more attractive, and less strenuous, start can be

made up the lower wall just right of Trio Wall.

To the right is a gully with a slab at its base.

6 Caped Crack 7m HVS P1
5b From inside the gully move left on the east facing wall to gain the obvious hanging crack. Struggle up it.

7 Grotto Wall 7m E1 P2
5c Gain the west wall of the gully from the back of the crag and use a pocket to the left of a thin blind crack to move up with difficulty to a higher pocket. Climb to a thread and move left to the arete. Tip-toe up this to the top.

8 Bat Buttress 20m D P1 ★
Climb the slab to the overhang. Traverse right and finish up the slabs to the right of the nose. Pleasant.

9 The Riddler 20m E3 P1 ★★
6a Climb the right side of the arete, just right of the start of Bat Buttress, to a ledge under the nose. Climb the sharp arete and move left to 'nostril' of the nose and arrange protection. Use pockets to pull up and right then compose yourself for the final moves to good finishing holds.

10 Bat Buttress Direct 14m E1 P1 ★
5c Start 2 metres right of the slab and make a desperate rock-over to a ledge using a spike. Continue up the flake and wall or traverse right to a crack which leads to the ledge.

11 Dragnet 15m HVS P1 ★
5b Start 3 metres left of the right-hand side of the buttress and gain a break. Climb the flake and wall above to a ledge. Finish up the easy wide crack beyond.

Three hundred metres to the right is Oak Tree Wall.

12 A-Corner 6m S P1
Start just left of the left arete. Go up and round on to the front face and traverse into Oak Tree Crack to finish.

13 Heart of Oak 6m HS P1
4b Start just left of the central crack. Climb to a thin crack and aim for the arete up which the route finishes.

14 Sparrow Wall 6m E1
6a A short, sharp problem squeezed in between Heart Of Oak and Oak Tree Crack. Finish through the breaks.

15 Oak Tree Crack 6m VD P1
Climb the crack in the centre of the wall passing through an oak tree.

16 Easy Way 6m D P1
Climb the right-hand end of the wall passing a tree on either side.

PLANTATION CRACK AREA
The routes are described from RIGHT to LEFT. Fifty metres right of
Plantation Crack is a long, low moss-covered buttress. Near its
right-hand end is a hanging flake. This is:–

1 Evergreen Cracks 8m S P1
Bridge the wide crack and finish up the cleaner crack above.

2 Abrasion 12m E3 P2   ★
5c Climb the dirty stepped arete on the right of a bay 6 metres left.
The wide crack crossing the headwall provides a short, sharp and
desperate finish.

3 Yankie Beau 10m E3 P2
5c Start 4 metres right of Plantation Crack and traverse left to the
arete. Layback this to a small break and protection on the left in
Plantation Crack. Move back right to a final break and thence the
top.

4 Plantation Crack 10m HVS P1   ★★
5a A surprisingly good route (there's got to be one good route on
every crag). Traverse into and ascend the wide crack splitting the
buttress. Finish direct for optimum enjoyment.

5 Side Track 16m HVS P2
5a From the base of the wide crack continue traversing to a ledge
of the left of the arete. Move up and round to finish up the arete and
slab above.

6 Southern Belle 10m E3   ★
6a Start 2 metres right of Greenfingers beneath a blind flake. Use
the flake to gain a horizontal break and take the thin crack on the
right to reach another break and the top.

7 State of the Union 12m E2
5c Follow Southern Belle to the top break then traverse right to
Plantation Crack. Move up and right again to finish as for Yankie
Beau.

8 Greenfingers 9m VS P1
4c Essentially a direct start to Side Track (or is that an indirect
start?). Climb the cracks below the arete to the ledge on Side Track
which is followed to the top (sometimes).

Fifty-five metres left of Plantation Crack buttress is a small clean
face with a wide crack above the tree.

9 Salubrious Navaho Indians 10m E1 P2
5c Climb the wall right of Easter Egg Crack starting just right of the tree where a long reach gains the big break. Use slopers above to reach the notch in the left arete and climb it to the top.

10 Easter Egg Crack 6m HS P1
4b Climb the crack to a sapling, step right and up to finish. The wise will climb the tree until a move on rock gains the sapling which can be used to reach the security (?) of the heather above.

11 Easter Egg Ridge 7m E2 P2
5c The arete to the left provides a hard problem. A long reach may gain the ledge above the arete. The slab above is not much easier and the ground is even further away!

Five metres left across the gully is a broken slabby buttress.

12 Left-hand Arete 9m S P1
The right arete unfortunately has a dirty lower half followed by a better finish.

13 Overhung Buttress 6m HVS P1
5a The left arete of the buttress is climbed on its left side.

Thirty metres left and slightly lower is a dirty prow.

14 The Prow 8m S P2
4b Climb the crack on the left-hand side of the arete to a hard step on to a small ledge. Finish up the slabs more easily.

15 Deception 7m S P1
Opposite The Prow is a crack below an overhang. Climb the crack, step left and over the overlap to the slab above.

16 Bracken Crack 7m HS P1
4b A micro variation on the previous route (both of which are absolute rubbish). Instead of bottling out left, face the massive challenge of overcoming the huge roof crack!

CROW CRAG

Worth a visit or two. Peaceful and idyllic, but bring a brush. The routes are described from Left to Right starting at the left-hand side of the lowest tier which is the first part of the crag encountered following faint paths.

1 Holly Tree Climb 8m HS P2
4b Not a good start, this route has the dubious distinction of being the worst on the crag. If you must, climb the groove below the large holly tree at the left-hand end of the crag.

2 Strongbow 10m VS P1

5b Hard moves gain the green gangway on the wall to the left. A traverse left leads to a bow-shaped crack which is climbed to the tree. Care is required on the short moss-covered crack above, if you de'cider' to do it. Not bad - after a brush up.

3 Owl Chimney 12m VS P2   ★

5a The wide corner chimney is ascended to the overhang. Step left and finish up the twin cracks.

The next three routes share a common start on the arete to the right.

4 Virtual Reality 12m E4 P1   ★

6b Pull onto the arete as for Vomer and follow the arete until it is possible to hand traverse left along a good break onto the over-hanging wall. Thin moves up a blind crack lead to good holds and a finish up the groove on the left as for Vomer. Good climbing and clean rock until the finishing groove.

5 Vomer 13m E2 P2

5c The original route but, unfortunately, very dirty in its upper section. The front face of the slab is gained by a hard move round the arete (crux). Continue to the sapling, surmount the overhang and boldly climb the wall to the ledge. Finish up the filthy groove on the left.

6 Vomit 16m E2 P1   ★

5c The name describes the climber's response to, and the state of the wall, ledge and finishing groove of Vomer. This is a cleaner, longer, harder - but better protected alternative. Climb the crux of Vomer but continue up the arete to the final break and good Friends. Harder but exquisite moves follow up the overhanging section before an urgent hand traverse left gains the good holds on Virtual Reality. Catch your breath and then continue the traverse boldly to finish up the twin cracks of Owl Chimney.

7 Grasshopper 13m VS P1

4c Climb the corner on the right-hand side of the recessed slab. Move right and climb the grass-filled crack to a ledge above which the short wall is climbed to the terrace. Not recommended without a thorough clean.

At the left end of the upper tier is -

8 Salieri 13m E3 P3   ★

5c Climb over blocks to the left of the large tree at the foot of the chimney and gain the wall just right of the arete. Climb boldly, straight up on small holds. A poor No1 wire protect the final moves and it would be wise to check and clean the top edge before an ascent.

9   View From The Hill   8m   VD   P3   ★
The slabby right arete of a buttress with a tree growing from its base.

10   Amadeus   13m E4   P2   ★★
6a Gain the wall just right of the chimney and move up to a horizontal break. Traverse left on finger pockets to the arete and dodgy pro in a pocket. Layback up the arete to good holds and a ledge. Pull around the bulge above direct to finish. Low in the grade but the crux is interesting, and delicate.

11   Curious Motion   10m   HVS   P1
5b To the right of Amadeus is a slabby buttress with a slanting crack in it, starting in a small shallow cave, left of a projecting belay tree. Climb the crack to a ledge and on via layback to another ledge. Move left to a platform and then crawl right to a mantel onto the final block. Alternatively, from the platform move left onto a steep slab with an exposed mantel to finish.

12   Sameness   8m   S   P2
4b A crack, left and slightly down from the top pitch of Corkscrew is climbed to a heathery finish

The upper tier now blends into the upper section of the more complex Corkscrew Buttress and the next route starts lower down on the left side of this.

13   Crack And Chimney   13m   VD   P2
On the left of the lower buttress is a green crack behind a tree. Climb this to a traverse up a grass gangway. (The sane will go right to the half way ledge and chance the jump!). Climb the diabolical chimney above the gangway to finish.

14   Nonawin   13m   HVS   P2
5a Climb a scoop in the lower wall with difficulty to gain a short slab leading to the half way ledge. Finish up a dirty shallow corner just right of the trees or better the groove of Summer Dreams.

15   Corkscrew   15m   E2   P1   ★
1. 10m   5c A climb for the connoisseur of enigmatic routes only! The fierce crack in the front of the buttress is climbed until a traverse can be made to the wider crack. Climb/ascend/grovel up this to a belay on the broad ledge above. Strenuous but very good if its clean.
2. 5m   5a Unless you are extremely tall, jump for a hold below the sapling on the left-hand edge of the slab. Finish up the crack above.

16 Corkage 14m E3 P2
6a Climb the wall just right of Corkscrew to reach the break of
Spoiler, and below a small bulge with blind cracks, (good wire) a
hard pull enables the grass ledge to be gained. Move right and
climb the arete to the right of End Slab.

17 Spoiler 12m VS P2
4b Not a good route. Start at the right-hand end of the front face
and climb to a break. This is followed across the buttress to a large
grass ledge. Finish up the top pitch of Corkscrew or End Slab (both
harder) alternatively a traverse can be made into Crack and
Chimney.

18 Summer Dreams 6m VS P3
5b A delicate and rather tenuous groove behind the tree on the half
way ledge .

19 End Slab 5m HVS P3   ★
5b Hard moves lead up the scoops at the right-hand end of the
slab on the half way ledge. Good but short.

Half way up the right-hand side of Corkscrew Buttress is a wide
crack above a small cave 3 metres left of a holly tree.

20 Lost Crack 6m VS P2   ★
4c Climb the crack which is hardest at the start and lacks protection.

21 Intreegued 7m VS P1
5a A hard move left from Lost Crack gains the flake which is
followed through the tree to the top. Worth a peep.

22 Armed, Dangerous And Off Medication
10m   Grade 11...P2   ★
A fun route. Go through the cave and squeeze up through a hole
into a smooth protectionless chimney. This is climbed direct using
the frog technique (not of the red point variety) to an exit between
boulders. Different!

Two hundred metres right of the upper tier is a tall narrow buttress
called, strangely - Narrow Buttress.

23 Staircase Chimney 9m VD P1
The block-filled chimney on the left of the buttress is reasonably
pleasant.

24 Narrow Buttress Chimney 11m VS P1
4c Start at the foot of the buttress and climb to a ledge on the right.
Continue up the chimney above exiting from the back. Probably the
only route in the guide which can be climbed facing any direction.

25 Six Inch Stare 13m E2 P3
5c On the right of Narrow buttress is a thin crack that ends just
before the top. Climb the short wall to the crack and continue up it
using the left arete to a difficult finish. Needs Brushing.

26 Passing Strangers 11m E2 P3
5c Further right is a cone shaped block split by a flared crack. This
route takes the once cleaned slab left of the crack. Bold and thin
above the break but sadly prone to regeneration of lichen.

27 Horizontal Memories 11m E2 P2
5c Climb the flared crack with an awkward balancey move leaving
the halfway ledge. A Friend might hold!

LITTLE BRIMHAM

A whole host of problems and micro routes 3 to 6 metres high
jealously guarded and developed spasmodically over the last 30
years by Tony Barley. The rock is generally very good, typical of
Brimham's best, but landings are variable. All the climbs have been
soloed but a rope may be sensible on first acquaintance with some
of the longer lines. Seventy Five problems have been claimed and
named here and full details can be found in Tony's guide - Wild
Bouldering In Yorkshire. The following sample should be enough to
whet your appetite.

From the limited parking area at the end of the short track, on the
left after passing Kimberly Farm, take the path through the right-
hand gate and the first two problems **Thunderball** (5a) and
Licence To Kill (5c) leaping from the boulder, are immediately
apparent on a small prow on the right. Moving left into the trees
more esoteric problems can be contrived but the first feature of real
significance is a prominent, sharp and bulging, narrow fin.

1 Shaken Not Stirred ★★ (5b) You might be if you fluff the
sequence up the right-hand side of the arete.

2 For Queen And Country ★★★ (5a)   The fin direct. Worth
fighting for?

3 On Her Majesty's Secret Service ★★ (5a)   Nice moves on the
left side of the prow.

To the left again and slightly lower is another even sharper arete.

4 Back In The U.S.S.R. (5c) The blunt rib just right of the arete.

5 Boris Or Bust ★★★ (6b) The right edge of the prow. A harder
but smaller High Noon!

6 Natasha's Just Desserts ★ (5c) Climbs the left side of the prow but without really using the edge.

7 The Spy Who Loved Me ★ (4c) The scoop and pocket on the left wall.

8 License To Thrill ★★★ (5c) The big clean wall to the left is a superb micro-route with a reachy finish. An on-sight solo is worth E3.

9 Pussy Galore ★★ (5c) The rib from the right - rockover left.

10 Bold Finger ★ (5c) The rib from the left - rockover right.

Ten metres left is a block with a scoop near the top.

11 Whitehall (5b) Gain the scoop without recourse to the chimney..

Thirty metres left a series of slabs and cracks offer easier lines but across a wide gully is a large undercut block.

12 Supreme Soviet (5b) A precarious pull up and left onto the right rib of the block.

13 Western Alliance ★★ (5b) Ingenious moves gain the groove above the roof.

14 Kruschev's Chimney (3b) Classic stuff.

To the left is the major feature of this part of Brimham, a superb looking hanging arete and an immaculate steep wall. Both are unclimbed but should provide tempting fare for some young worthy contender?

15 Cuban Blockade (5b) the shallow groove on the left of the unclimbed wall looks better than it is.

16 First Strike (5b) is the rib to the left, the last route on the lower tier.

The higher tier of rocks above the last few routes is known as **The Aiguille De Premier Alert.** It is actually a series of detached pinnacles with some excellent and quite exposed lines on the main block.

17 Eastern Block (5a) The square, left end of the block.

18 Missile Crisis ★ (5a) The left side of the front face.

19 Bomber Command ★★ (5b) Climb a short wall to a ledge and then the upper wall just left of centre. Superb!

20 Heat Seeker ★ (5a) Another good exposed line, just right of centre from the same start.

21 Red Alert ★ (5b) A contrived start up the awkward undercut groove gives access to the headwall on the left before moving right to the edge of the rib.

22 Missile Attack ★★★ (5a) The overhanging prow direct, above a big drop. Good holds seem to materialise from nowhere as do runner placements for those with a rope. A steady HVS lead.

There are several easier problems on the slabby blocks to the right.

150 metres to the north across some open ground is the next section known as **Bovine Buttress.** This area is slightly more open and with generally better landings. The first 8 problems from the right are fairly insignificant but things soon improve when the main bulging prow is reached.

23 Cowboy Daze ★★★ (6b) A borderline E3. The most prominent undercut arete can be protected, but the landing is soft and the solo much more satisfying.

24 The Watering Hole ★★ (5b) On the left of the rib is a scoop and obvious pocket. Gain the ledge and upper break via this and finish boldly right to the 'watering hole' on top, or, less boldly but still with interest, up left.

25 Chewing The Cud (5a) The flake crack on right at the back of gully.

26 Side Saddle ★ (4b) The most prominent flake on the left side of the gully.

27 Cleft Hoof (5b) The next one to the left is more undercut.

28 Trailblazer ★ (5b) The left-hand groove is the cleanest line.

29 Saddle Sore ★ (5b) Just left of arete a hard start gains good holds.

30 Beef Crisis ★★ (6a) From base of faint ramp move up right to highest point.

31 Riding Bareback ★★ (6b) Very hard start up ramp leftwards to good finish.

32 Just Grazing ★ (4b) Hole to breaks at left side of this wall.

33 Hang Low ★ (6b) A left to right low-level traverse finishing up Saddle Sore.

34 Home On The Range ★ (5a) Steep wall on good holds to left of easy corner.

35 Rawhide (5c) The big rounded prow to the left leads to a scary finish.

The last two problems here are directly down below Cowboy Daze.

36 Wielding The Branding Iron ★★ (5b) Climb the thin crack above the right side of the roof.

37 Tan Your Hide ★ (5b) The wall right of the crack and the upper arete.

BROWN BECK CRAG

SITUATION AND CHARACTER Although the rocks are well known as Brown Beck they are actually marked as Lobley Crags on 1:25000 series O.S maps. The true Brown Beck Crag is situated several hundred metres to the East, and midway between Slipstones and Lobley Crags, and comprises a jumble of clearly visible boulders. Situated 1.5 kilometres up the valley from Slipstones, the crag faces south, south west and is quick drying. It extends for approximately 150 metres comprising walls and free standing blocks which rarely exceed six metres in height. The rock is soft gritstone which can be lichenous in places. Boulders beneath the crag provide some interesting problems.

APPROACHES AND ACCESS Follow the approach described for Slipstones but continue along the main track up onto the moor, cross the head of the stream and continue up the valley over rough moorland (no continuous path) for about 1 kilometre to where the rocks will be seen to the left. Car to crag - 40 mins.

THE CLIMBS These are described from RIGHT to LEFT.

Buttress 1 - The Watch Tower
This is the isolated block at the extreme right end of the crag.

1 The Watchman 5m D P1 1997
Start at the left side of the front (south) face. Surmount the overlap and climb the short wall.

Buttress 2 - Tilting Buttress
Situated 15 metres to the left (west) of the Watch Tower.

2 Little Wall 4m D P1 1997
Climb the centre of the East wall.

3 Tyto 6m S P1 1997 ★
Climb the stepped arete to an awkward exit around the top block.

4 Cheap Trick 6m S P1 1997 ★
Gain the sloping ledge by a variety of ways. The strenuous hanging crack provides the exit.

The buttress drops in height and forms an angled corner. The next climbs ascend the short wall just left of the corner.

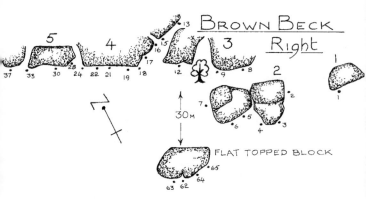

5 Gideon Up 3m VS P1 1997
5a Climb the bulge just right of the thin vertical crack.

6 Off Beat 3m D P1 1984   ★
The pleasant curving flake crack.

7 Rugrats 4m VS P1 1997
5a Ascend the steep wall passing a recess in the break. Awkward.

BUTTRESS 3 - HOLLY BUTTRESS
Situated behind Buttress 2, it forms the right end of the main edge.

8 Staircase 5m HD P1 1997
Start a few metres right of the Holly Tree. Step from a boulder onto
a stepped wall, trend leftwards to finish on the top block.

9 Big Boss 5m MVS P1 1983
4b Climb the rib and bulge right of the Holly.

10 Top Man 5m S P1 1983
4b Climb the arete left of the Holly on its right side.

11 Holly Hover 5m VS P1 1988
4b Start just left of the arete, move up to the break, and traverse
left to finish up a short flake.

12 Wichita Linesman 6m HVS P1 1983   ★★
5b Start in the crevasse and climb the hanging corner crack. Not
too hard if a positive approach is adopted.

Buttress 4 - Main Wall
The next climb starts near the top of the wide gully on the left wall.

13 Gully Wall 3m S P2 1997
Climb the slabby scoop in the wall.

14 Talespin 4m VS P2 1997
4b The wall past a shallow pocket to an awkward exit.

15 Dab Hand 4m VS P2 1997
4c Climbs the right arete of the narrow chimney. Start in the chimney but pull out right to finish. Bridging is not allowed.

16 Cutting Edge 4m E1 P2 1989   ★
6a The tricky arete just left of the narrow chimney is climbed mainly on the front face.

17 Escape 7m VS P2 1983   ★★
5a Gain the ledge via the short wall. The hanging flake proves awkward to reach but slightly easier to leave.

18 Ingham's Route 7m E2 P3 1984
5c The short arete is climbed onto the ledge. Continue up the bold overhanging arete.

19 Transcendence 6m E1 P2 1983   ★
5c Climb the flake just left of the arete to pass the overhang. Finish up the ramp.

20 Phenomenology 6m E2 P2 1983
6a Climb the wall just right of the left facing groove of Pella.

21 Pella 6m VS P1 1983   ★★★
4c Gain the superb left facing groove to exit up the capped corner.

22 Nuttall's Mintoe 6m HVS P1 1988
5a Climb the wall between the hanging crack and the groove direct, finish up a leaning scoop.

23 Let the Children Play 6m VS P1 1983
4c Climb direct to, and up, the hanging crack.

24 Child's Play 6m HVS P1 1983
5c Climb the wall just right of the hanging ledge.

25 Cadbury's Flake 6m HVS P2 1988
5a Ascend the wall just left of the hanging ledge via a suspect flake. Gain the ledge and finish up the awkward wall.

26 Mouth To Mouth 5m VS P1 1988
5a Climb the wall 2 metres left of the hanging ledge.

27 Browned Off 17m VS P1 1988
5a A traverse of the Main Wall. Start from Mouth to Mouth and follow the break rightwards to finish up Escape.

Buttress 5 - Letterbox Wall

28 Dealer 6m VS P1 1983
4c Climb the narrow wall at the entrance to the gully.

29 Bahia 6m HVS P2 1983   ★
5b Start just left of the arete. Climb the wall passing a rock scar.

30 The Wobbler 6m E1 P2 1988   ★
5b Start a metre right of the niche and climb the delicate wall
rightwards to the break. Finish direct.

31 Brown Boots 6m HVS P1 1983   ★
5b Climb the wall via the Letterbox slot.

32 Big Boots 5m VS P1 1983
4c Climb the wall just right of the left arete.

33 Dawn 4m S P1 1983★
4a The left arete of the wall.

34 The Other Arete 10m VS P1 1988
4c Climb the left arete (Dawn) to the break, follow the break to the
right arete and finish.

35 Curving Chimney 4m D P1 1984
The short chimney. The blunt arete on the left is **Bryan's Rib** (D)

36 Chimney Wall 4m MS P1 1988   ★
4a Climb the wall 2 metres left of the chimney using a pocket hold.

37 Clean Sweep 4m MS P1 1988
4a Ascend the stepped wall 4 metres left of the chimney. Enjoyable climbing.

Buttress 6 - Narrow Buttress
Situated 15 metres to the left of Buttress 5.

38 Den 5m VS P2 1984
5a Climb the right arete on its left side.

39 Eric 5m HVS P2 1983
5b Climb the centre of the front wall starting from the left.

40 Cave Chimney 5m D P1 1997
This is the short capped chimney separating the buttresses. Climb
the left arete of the chimney.

Buttress 7 - Owl Buttress

41 Square Corner 4m VD P1 1997
The short, awkward corner behind the block.

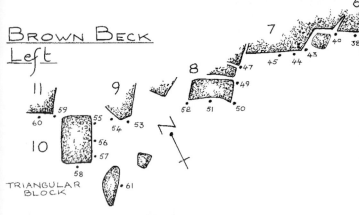

BROWN BECK Left

42 Owl Wall 5m HS P2 1988
4b Step off the block and climb the wall on flat holds.

43 Pussy Cat 7m VS P1 1988
5a Start right of the arete. Two breaks lead to a small slot, step left then back right to finish.

44 High Adventure 8m HVS P2 1983   ★
5a Start under the jutting roof. Climb up into the chimney then hand traverse the lip of the overhang to the arete and finish direct.

45 Go Within 7m VS P2 1983
4c Climb the wall 1 metre left of the roof.

46 Owl Corner 3m D P1 1997
The short corner.

47 Heartbeat 4m VD P1 1997
Climb the wide crack just left of the corner.

48 Fire Brigade 5m VD P2 1997
The obvious wide chimney.

Forming the left side of the chimney is the massive block of Buttress 8.

Buttress 8 - Leaning Buttress

49 Next of Kin 5m E2 P2 1989
6a Climb the left arete of the chimney.

50 L'unacy 5m E2 P2 1984   ★
5c The overhanging arete of the block with a nasty finish.

51 Last Gasp 4m E2 P2 1984
5c Climb the centre of the leaning wall to another 'interesting' exit.

52 Clueless 3m VS P1 1984
5a Climb the left arete on its right side.

A few metres further left is a small buttress with a slabby arete, this is:-

Buttress 9 - Little Buttress

53 Butt End 4m D P1 1997   ★
Pleasant climbing up the slabby arete.

54 Butt Head 3m D P1 1997   ★
Climb the wall just left of the arete.

Buttress 10 - Sunken Buttress

This is the large slabby block slanting down the hillside.

55 Undun 4m VS P1 1984
5a Start 1 metre from the right edge of the slab. Climb the slab direct.

56 Slant 4m HVS P1 1984   ★
5b Climb diagonally leftwards up the centre of the slab. Enjoyable moves.

57 Big Easy 4m HVS P1 1989   ★
5b Start just right of the left edge and climb the wall/slab direct.

58 Drop Zone 4m E1 P2 1989
5c Climb the overhanging wall on sloping breaks to a difficult finish.

Buttress 11 - Last Buttress

59 Bedlam 4m VS P2 1984
4b The steep arete direct.

60 Ledge End 3m D P1 1997
Climb the stepped wall direct.

THE BOULDERS
There are many good boulder problems to be discovered below the main edge but only those climbs currently reported are described here.

TRIANGULAR BLOCK
Situated a few metres below Buttress 10.

61   South Face Route   4m   HVS   P1   1984
5b   Climb the centre of the face via a slanting fault.

FLAT TOPPED BLOCK

Situated 30 metres below Buttress 2. The climbs are described left to right and start at the obvious hanging crack on the south side of the block.

62   Hanging Crack   4m   HVS   P1   1988
5c   Climb the distinctly awkward crack.

63   Problemina   4m   HVS   P1   1989
6b   For those climbers possessing rubber legs and a 2.5m reach, here's one for you! Ascend the roof just left of Hanging Crack.

64   Bandido   4m   HVS   P1   1988
5b   Start just right of the crack. Gain the ledge and obvious pocket direct.

65   Hombre   4m   HVS   P1   1988
5b   The arete to the right.

A further 30 metres lower is another free standing boulder, this is Easy Block. Several short, easy climbs can be made on this block, but non warrant descriptions. For those wanting further exercise, there is another small crag about 15 minutes walk up the valley. The face is quarried and about 5 metres high. Three easy climbs are recorded, the right trending crack, a small corner and the wall to the left.

BROWN BECK CRAG – GRADED LIST

E2
Phenomenonlogy (6a)
Ingham's Route (5c)
Next of Kin (6a)
L'unacy (5c)
Last Gasp (5c)

E1
Cutting Edge (6a)
Transcendence (5c)
Drop Zone (5c)
The Wobbler (5b)

HVS
Child's Play (5c)
Bahia (5b)
Eric (5b)
Brown Boots (5b)
Wichita Linesman (5b)
High Adventure (5a)
Cadbury's Flake (5a)
Nuttall's Mintoe (5a)
Problemina (6b)
Hanging Crack (5c)
Slant (5b)
Big Easy (5b)
South Face Route (5b)
Hombre (5b)
Bandido (5b)

VS
Escape (5a)
Den (5a)
Mouth to Mouth (5a)
Browned Off (5a)
Pussy Cat (5a)
Pella (4c)
Let the Children Play (4c)
Dealer (4c)
Big Boots (4c)
Rugrats (5a)
Dab Hand(4c)
Clueless(5a)
The Other Arete(4c)
Go Within(4c)
Undun(5a)
Holly Hover(4b)
Bedlam(4b)
Talespin(4b)
Big Boss(4b)
Gideon Up(5a)

S
Owl Wall(4b)
Top Man(4b)
Tyto
Cheap Trick
Dawn
Gully Wall
Chimney Wall
Clean Sweep

VD
Fire Brigade
Heartbeat
Square Corner

D
Staircase
Butt End
Curving Chimney
Butt Head
The Watchman
Ledge End
Cave Chimney
Off Beat
Little Wall
Owl Corner

CALEY CRAGS

SITUATION AND CHARACTER   The rocks are located 2 miles east of Otley in the Chevin Forest Park facing north and overlooking Otley and the Wharfe Valley. The crag consists of two sections: Roadside Buttress, marked on the map as "Rocking Stone", and situated just to the left of the Caley Gate, and the Main Buttress, approximately 600 metres to the west.

The rock is perfect natural gritstone attaining a height of 15 metres on the Main Buttress where several classics across a range of grades can be found.. The routes in the Roadside area reach a height of 9 metres but seem longer; many are in the harder grades and even the easier ones tend to be serious. The bouldering at Caley is of high quality with bold slab problems being a speciality. During the winter months the crag puts on a green coat and is best avoided. However from around mid March to late October the rocks dry out quickly and summer evenings here can be superb.

APPROACHES AND ACCESS   The best approach is from the main Leeds-Otley road (A660). When approaching from Leeds, pass straight through the Dyneley Arms cross-roads (junction with the A658), round the S bend at the top of the Chevin until roadside parking is reached on the left by the Caley Gate. **Park close to the wall and beware of fast moving traffic when opening your car door!** A regular bus service runs between Leeds and Otley, with a stop just below the crag.

THE CLIMBS
Roadside Boulders (right-hand section)
These are reached by a short walk leftwards from Caley Gate. The first feature to notice is a short steep offset crack, usually impregnated with chalk. This is Lightening Crack but to get your bearings on a first visit walk down below this to gear up on a flat block just round to the left. The crack in the slab above is Morris Crack but the largest boulders above and left, separated by the deep, open corner of Little Cenotaph, contain some of Caley's most famous test pieces. Are they routes, micro-routes or boulder problems? Once you've tried a few you'll be as confused as us - but however you classify them I'm sure you'll agree they are amongst gritstone's finest.

The climbs start on the buttress forming the left side of this corner and are described from left to right. Follow The Tour!

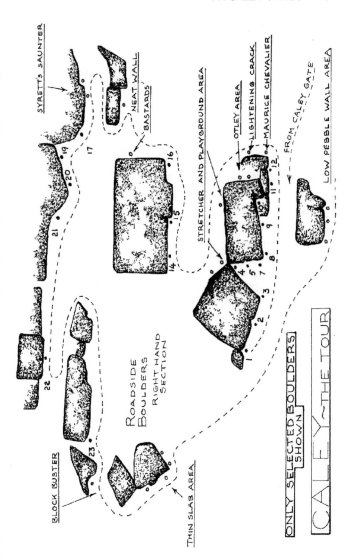

SYRETT'S SAUNTER

NEAT WALL

BASTARDS

OTLEY AREA

LIGHTENING CRACK

MAURICE CHEVALIER

FROM CALEY GATE

LOW PEBBLE WALL AREA

STRETCHER AND PLAYGROUND AREA

ROADSIDE
BOULDERS
RIGHT HAND
SECTION

THIN SLAB AREA

BLOCK BUSTER

ONLY SELECTED BOULDERS
SHOWN

CALEY ~ THE TOUR

1 Psycho   8m E5 P3   ★★★
6b A classic 'problem' of the `70s. Step off the big boulder adjoining the slab. Hard moves right gain the chicken heads. Careful use of these may gain the top. The landing is good - but a long way down!
The Direct Start (6c) From the base of the crack climb diagonally leftwards to reach the chicken heads.

2 Adrenaline Rush   9m E5 P2   ★★★
6b Climb the crack up the middle of the slab to its termination, whence a struggle using small pockets and deft footwork might enable the top to be attained. Well placed protection and a fast belayer should prevent the fall from the top resulting in broken bones, but not a loss of skin.

3 Marrow Bone Jelly   9m E7 P3   ★★★
6c Technical and sustained slab climbing up the right arete of the slab provides Caley's boldest line. Either start direct or round to the right; both are hard. A thumb press high up provides something to aim for and momentary respite.

4 Little Cenotaph   8m VS P1   ★
5a The wide corner is easier and better than it looks.

5 Unfinished Crack   8m VS P1   ★★
4c The right wall of the corner contains an unfinished crack. The route follows it to its end. Thereafter shallow holes and trepidation lead to the top.

6 Ephedrine   8m E4 P2   ★
6a The wall just right of Unfinished Crack, climbed on perturbing pockets and a degree of faith. The only runners available are in the crack, use them if you must - but can you reach them!

7 Permutation Rib   8m E1 P3   ★★★
5c Unprotected but really satisfying. Climb the right arete of the corner by a cunning traverse in from just right of Unfinished Crack (crux), moving up and around the arete to better holds. Much easier, though still awkward, climbing leads boldly to the top. A 6a start avoids the initial traverse but If you are tall or a good jumper, climb direct up the undercut front from the boulder. (5b to 6c depending on your reach!)

8 Waite   7m E5 P1   ★★
7a The shallow, undercut groove between Permutation Rib and Rabbit's Paw Wall. Desperately hard to start but with a reasonable landing. The E grade is probably irrelevant.

Those with a vivid imagination may identify the imprint of a gigantic rabbits paw on the steep green wall to the right.

9 Rabbit's Paw Wall 8m HVS P2 ★★★
5b Right of the rib is an undercut wall containing a number of large shallow pockets. Trend leftwards up the wall on good holds if you can master the initial difficult moves.

10 Hanging Groove 6m E3 P3 ★
5b The nasty little leftward-facing hanging corner at the right-hand side of the wall above the gangway provides an intimidating route with a seriousness out of all proportion to its length. The slab below provides only temporary deceleration before a trip to Wharfedale General becomes imminent. Once graded VS - and some argue it still is. You choose!

Around to the right on the west face is **Chips** (4b) an old problem up chiselled holds. Traversing right into the centre of this wall to gain a short hanging crack, is the superb **Otley Wall** (6a)★★★. The crack can also be gained from below and slightly to the right **Otley Direct** (6b)★★★ which is even more satisfying and avoids all chipped holds. **Courser Edge** (5a)★ is the arete on the right. The shorter slabby south face, **The Playground** has numerous variants and traverses but right again, starting from a boulder above an ankle snapping hole is **The Stretcher** (6a) ★★ (you may need one if you slip) - the crux is really the first long move between shallow pockets after getting established but retreat is not really an option! Right again is the much safer **Chicken Heads** (5c)★ short and satisfying - 6a for some but only 5b once you've mastered it!. Stepping in from the right doesn't count.

The tier starting below and just right of Rabbit's Paw Wall contains

11 Morris Minor 6m MS P2
The slab to the left of the crack using shallow chipped holds. There are harder variants each side without the chips.

12 Morris Crack 6m HS P1 ★
4b The steepening wide crack; laybacking the top half provides the crux.

13 Morris Dance 6m HVS P2 ★
5b Climb the wall left of the arete and immediately right of the wide crack. The top proves to be the crux and many 'Foxtrot Oscar' back down again or 'waltz' out into the crack.

The arete to the right, and on its right side, **Maurice Chevalier** (6b)★ is very nearly a route with a scary crux but a reasonable landing. **Lightning Crack** (6a) ★★ The thin offset crack is a classic boulder problem which is technical and often frustrating, an optional finish hand-traverses the top edge left to the apex.

The roadside face of the boulder below contains four good problems. On the right is **New Jerusalem** (6c)★★ the deceptively steep, crimpy wall to slopers. **The Cruel Crack** (5a) the short, undercut crack on the right does not forgive sloppy jammers. **Low Pebble Wall** (6a) ★★ the slab just left was once a superb 6b problem. Sadly now chipped. **No Pebble Wall** (7a) is the slab just to the right of the left arete. Getting established is hard - staying with it high up is serious. Using the arete is said to be cheating but still worth hard 6c!

Directly behind the Little Cenotaph area is a huge boulder easily recognised by the flake which splits the centre of the leaning north face.

14 Andy's Route 6m E4 P2   ★
6c The undercut wall from the flat block to the left of the flake has but one line of weakness and a hard landing,

15 The Great Flake 8m E6 P2   ★★★
6b Climb gracefully up the flake, hopefully reaching the top before gravity takes control. A cunning secret runner placement is alleged to bring it down to E5?

Pass the brilliant looking and well brushed last great problem and try:

16 Nothing's Safe 6m E5 P2   ★
6c Climb the arete right of the flake using a combination of jams, small holds and technique. Difficult for many, impossible for most.

The right wall of this block is undercut and has a sloping lip which may tempt mantel fiends. **Bob's Bastard 1** (5c) pulls across and mantels using a shallow pocket 2 metres left of the right side of the lip. **Bob's Bastard 2** (6b) swings along and hauls over to the very shallow runnels just to the left.

A traverse along the lip to the grass crack has been rumoured though no one now remembers by whom or when. A smaller boulder just opposite these problems has a neat little wall - **The Neat Wall** (5b)★.

Just above begins a mini escarpment of problems and micro-routes which leads leftwards along the crest of the hillside. The first feature on the right is a short shallow groove containing the initials MBKC, hence **MBKC Groove** (5b). Just left is the brilliant problem **Syrett's Saunter** (6c)★★★ frustrating, attractive and a classic of its kind. A.k.a. Pebble Wall and Impossible Wall.

On the same piece of rock but starting from the left edge is:-

17 Harry's Heap 6m E1 P2   ★★
5c Known by many as The Knobbler a technical start from an embedded block enables a precarious move to be made via a small pocket across right to the knobbles. An interesting step up leads to an easier finish up the blunt central rib.

18 The Knobbler Traverse 8m E2 P2   ★★
6a From the knobbles on the previous route continue via a tenuous hand traverse around the rib across Syrett's Saunter to the top of MBKC Groove.

Moving across and left, at a slightly higher level directly behind the Great Flake block is a larger and steeper wall which begins as a green slab fringed with heather.

19 Rising More Slowly 6m E2 P2
5b A bold rising traverse from right to left across the usually green slab. Difficulties ease when the horizontal break is reached but the heathery fringe requires careful handling.

20 Terry 6m E4 P2   ★★
6c The wall direct. Climb up and left, starting 4 metres right of the blunt rib, on pebbles and rockovers.

Up and around left is a shallow scooped groove, an old and classic boulder problem - or is it a route?

21 The Gripping Groove (5c) ★★★   Gain the scoop from the left and bridge delicately to the top bearing in mind that the ground drops away alarmingly below and to the right. Even the bounciest Bouldering mat won't help if you slip here!

The last feature in this upper section is a short steep wall topped by a perched block.

22 The Rocking Stone Roof 6m VS P1   ★
5b A problematic start below the centre of the roof gains a good ledge and the break below the bulge. Lean out and grope blindly over the precariously perched roof - don't pull it off - to find good holds on top!

Slightly below the general line of the edge, (down and just left of the RS Roof) above a well pruned tree is one of Caley's very best mini solos.

23 Ron's Reach 7m E3 P2   ★★★
6a The superb left to right rising traverse line leads tentatively to a precarious move onto the right rib of a shallow scoop. Step up boldly but with less difficulty to the top. Also known as Ripper Traverse.

Thin, steep and highly tenuous, **Ben's Groove** (7a)★★ is the line just right of the traverse, whilst to the left, in a small bay, is the frustrating **Block Buster** (7a)★ which usually requires the ability to jump, or to build a pile of stones, to reach a vague arete and a flake.

Below, amongst a jumble of many other fine blocks in this vicinity will be seen two boulders, one on top of the other. These provide several excellent problems on the triangular, front face of the lower slab and the steeper west wall including; **Left Hand Groove** (4a), **The Slab** (4c) just to the right of the arete. **Curver** (4b) The curving line, up and over the overlap trending to the right. **The Thin Slab** (5c) ★★ The slab just left of the leaning right arete, trending left to safety half way; or **Thin Slab Direct** E3? (6a) ★★ follow the arete all the way - a mini Marrowbone? **The Arete** (6c) Layback boldly up the arete on its right side. **Right Wall** (6a) The wall right of the arete to the short crack (5b with a swing from the right)

Roadside Boulders (left-hand section)
Leftwards across the hillside, on the skyline and 20m past the overhead power lines, is an impressive set of boulders with a roof at the right-hand end. This area gives several serious problems and a couple of hard routes. The obvious right to left **Roof Traverse** (6c) is both hard and strenuous. **Rib Tickler** (5b)★ is the arete to the left, climbed on the right. The wall with flakes just to the left is **Martins Muff** (6a) ★★, or 6b if climbed direct. A prominent hanging flake to the right of the big blunt arete gives the line of **Webster's Whinge** (6b)★★

24   To Be Is Not To Bolt   7m   E6   P3   ★★
6c Another Manson masterpiece up the big arete. A sustained and insecure sequence leads to the first pocket and continues with little respite to the top. To avoid serious back injury it is recommended that falls from the upper slab are avoided and the sharp boulder behind is well padded.

25   The True Pebble Wall   7m   E5   P3   ★★
6c The original line on this boulder takes the blunt arete a little further left. A very hard start leads to an easier but worrying finish onto the mossy upper slab. The landing is safer than To Be... but!

On the very left of this wall is a faint hanging flake crack.

26   Death Drop 2000   6m   E4   P2   ★
6b Step off the boulder or, harder, direct off the ground, and climb the faint crack, you'll wish you hadn't – but carry on up the hanging flake because the landing's poor. Marginal wires might give some encouragement.

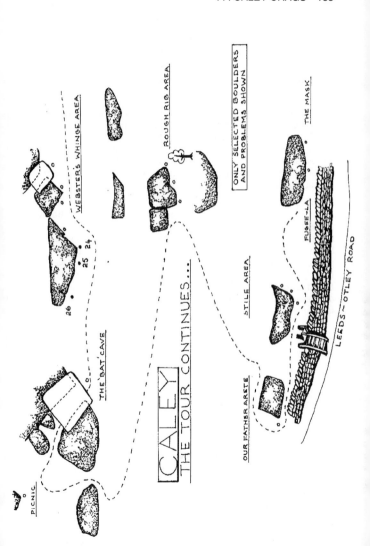

ROUGH RIB AREA

WEBSTERS WHINGE AREA

ONLY SELECTED BOULDERS
AND PROBLEMS SHOWN

THE MASK

24
25
26

FUGGE-LA

THE BAT CAVE

STILE AREA

CALEY
THE TOUR CONTINUES...

LEEDS ~ OTLEY ROAD

PICNIC

OUR FATHER ARETE

There are many lesser boulders to the left and below this area all with several problems each. The furthest left, high up, is the tall slim Picnic Table block with **Picnic** (5c)★ climbing the main arete direct. Twenty metres down the hill from this is a long low truncated slab with numerous mantelshelf problems between 5b and 6c. Up and right of this is a crevasse-cum cave with an unusual roof crossing on the inside. **The Bat** (6a) hanging from jams and pockets.

Half way down the boulder field below, just underneath a boulder with a clean-cut face facing the road is a nice block with a square face again facing the road, and a short corner to its left. There are about a dozen problems here the best being; **Rough Rib** (5b)★★ the left arete direct or gained by the groove on the right and a short traverse; **The Face** (6a)★ The centre of the face is bold and thin at the top; **Layback Arete** (4c) The right arete.

Down by the wall near the road are three excellent boulders. The first, furthest east and behind the bus stop contains **Our Father's Arete** (6a)★★ a short but precarious square cut arete, and a pumpy traverse, **The Halo** (5b) around the top edge. The second, just behind the stile has several problems including three 5 metre solos up the right hand side; **Stile-istic** (4c)★★ pads up the right wall, **Free Stile** (5b)★ smears up the slab just right of the arete and **Not My Stile** (6b)★ is the left side of the same arete. The third, 40metres further right, contains **Fugee-la** (6a) up the middle of the face and **The Mask** (6b) on the left side of the right arete.

THE MAIN CRAG
This is reached by following the main path up and right of Caley Gate for 500 metres. This area comprises a number of boulders and a more substantial edge set back on the hillside.

Two large boulders greet the approaching climber. The one on the right is known as the **Sugar Loaf** and contains a number of very popular mini-routes and problems. These are described in an anti-clockwise direction from the east face. Numerous variations exist but the following are the best and most independent. The whole block can be girdled at various levels and the easy angled south face can be climbed anywhere (in various places without hands).

27 Angel's Wall 7m HVS P1   ★★★
5a A Caley Classic. Climb the centre of the east wall starting with a fingery swing from just right of the obvious layback flake. Reachy moves on heavenly buckets lead to an entertaining finale over the apex of the roof on big holds. The direct start is 5c and other variants move in from the right at different heights The best and

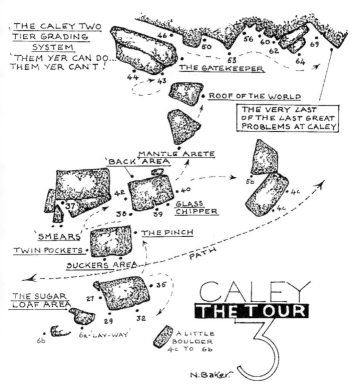

most independent is:

28 Angel's Wing 8m E2 P3
5c Start at the lowest point of the east wall just left of the arete and climb up parallel to it, without recourse to it, to gain the final move of Angel's Wall.

29 Plantation Ridge 9m VS P1   ★
4c The arete forming the junction of the east and north faces is climbed mainly on the right but is usually started by a swing round from the left.

30 Plantation Wall 9m HVS P2   ★★
5a A satisfying technical exercise in slab climbing taking a direct line about a metre right of the arete without recourse to it at any point.

31   The Can 9m E2 P2   ★
5c Climb the wall three metres right of the left arete, stepping precariously right above the high overlap.

32   Central Route 8m VS P2   ★★
5a The shallow cracks just right of centre lead to an awkward move left and a thin step right to finish.

33   Sweet Tooth 7m HVS P2   ★
5a The right-hand rib of the north wall. Start on the boulder and from the halfway break make a precarious step-up left onto the upper slab and use a shallow pocket to gain the top.   A tricky direct start just left of the rib provides a good problem in its own right **The Cavity** (6a).

34   Route 3 7m HS P2   ★
4b Start just left of centre on the vertical west wall and climb to the rising break. Gain the top by use of a hidden pocket just round the edge of the left arete.

35   Route 2 7m VS P2   ★★
4c Climb directly up the centre of the west wall.

36   Route 1 6m HVS P1
5a The prominent short crack running up rightwards.

A good solo circuit is to ascend and descend Routes 1,2 &3 without touching the ground or stepping onto the top. The low-level traverse of the block is also worthwhile with the crux on the section to the right of Route 1 (6a/b).

There are many smaller boulders lower down on this side of the track on which excellent short problems abound.

By the other side of the track is an obvious square boulder. Many of the lines and traverses are testaments to generations of chippers, a number of whom, unfortunately, still exist. There are however around 20 problems on this block, and even a few with no chips at all. The face above the path is 5 metres high.

Starting on the left side of the wall above the path, just right of a smaller block, is; **Scary Canary** (6c)★ which climbs the right side of the vague arete on diminishing holds. Right of here the wall has two heavily chipped lines **Suckers Rib** (5a)★ follows the blunt rib in the centre of the wall and is almost as easy without the chips, and **Suckers Wall** (4c) which isn't! Around the arete the right wall has a tiny ledge; **The Pinch** (6b)★ Reach the ledge from the right and (try) gain the top with the aid of a pinch.

At the back of the block is a crack , a low level traverse rightwards from this to the arete is **Low Traverse** (7a)★. Several vertical problems can be found on the wall to the right and around the arete, some chipped and some not so. The best, on the right side of the chipped east wall, is probably **Twin Pockets** (5c)★ Step off the boulder, gain the twin pockets and move up right to a hole. The **Front Traverse** (6c)★★★ is an excellent low traverse from the last problem around the arete onto the front face.

Behind the Suckers Wall block is a steeply-overhanging boulder which lies on top of a low angle slab. It has a smaller block below it on the left and an intimidating layback crack on its left-hand side. The slabs have several problem starts but the best two are **Smear Arete Right** (5a)★, the right rib of the smaller block and **Smear Arete Left** (5c)★, The left side of the same arete.

37 Roof Layback 6m VS P2
4b The undercut and intimidating layback. Don't linger as you fight your way to an exciting finish on holds which are thankfully large. Clean your boots first.

Adjacent and to the right of the layback crack boulder is a huge square block split by a prominent wide crack. The arete to the left of the crack gives:-

38 Black Jumper 8m E1 P2   ★
5b Climbing or jumping (don't miss!) from an adjacent boulder gains a good hold on the arete. Some continue up the arete to finish; the less fortunate break bones on the jagged rocks below. The arete has also been gained from the right, **The Indirect Start** from just left of Boot crack at 6c.

39 Boot Crack 8m VS P1   ★★
4b The wide crack. The timid will jam and thrutch, and find the climb hard whilst the bold will layback and reach the top with elegant ease. Its a classic!

Just right of the crack is a roof problem **The Glass Chipper** (6a) ★★ A reachy undercut move is required to gain a standing position on the slab below the rib. Continue up this, climb down easily right, or, for maximum adventure, follow **The Soft Shoe Shuffle** (5c) ★★ a bold high level traverse with hands in nicks in a faint horizontal crack just below the top until a step down leads round the arete onto the back wall. Traverse right across this and swing round to finish up the wall just right of the south-east arete.

40 Shoe Shine 8m MVS P3   ★
4b The arete to the right of Boot Crack is started from the slab on the right and climbed boldly on small chipped holds in a superb position.

41 Sneakers 7m HVS P3   ★
5b The wall just right of the arete is climbed with interesting moves above the shallow groove to good holds near the top.

A couple of harder (and P3) variations can be contrived up the centre of the right wall but the lines are serious and rather indistinct. Moving up and left from the right edge of this wall is easier and less scary **The Green Streak** (5a) ★. Around the corner the back wall provides problems but the best are at the right hand end. **Back Wall** (6b) The wall just to the left of the arete without using it. **Back Edge** (6a) The left side of the arete. Around the corner is **Back Side** (6a)★, a cheeky little number, the wall around the arete via a pocket on the right. Quite bold.

42 Rick's Rock 7m E4 P2   ★
6b The centre of the wall is climbed past 2 old bolt heads to a scary finish.

Further up the hillside are a couple of very worthwhile boulders. The lower one is undercut on its left side giving excellent, interchangeable 5b/c problems with wet bum starts plus a 6c low rightward traverse finishing up **Mantle Arete** (5b/c). The upper of the two has a distinct angled roof on its right side. This is known as **The Roof Of The World** ★★★. Many variations exist from 5b to 6c some allow jumping, some don't.

The left-hand end of the main crag is easily recognisable just up the hillside where a huge boulder forms a crevasse in front of it. This provides a convenient descent path and some short slab problems (4b to 5c) on its inner face. The arete at the foot of the crevasse is **The Gatekeeper** (5b). On the outer face of the boulder are several escapable mantel-shelf problems (5a to 6a) but if continued up the (usually green) headwall they feel more like real routes:

43 The Crenellated Ridge 7m HVS P3   ★
5a A step up left from a short ramp gains the right-hand side of the slab. Step boldly up right to small ledges and eventually the security of the crenellations on top.

44 Hot Green Chillies 8m E3 P3   ★
5c A problematic start below the centre of the slab is followed by a step right to below the centre of the headwall. Climb boldly, straight up, with a long blind reach for the top.

45 Fried Green Tomatoes 6m VS P2
4c From below the heather ledge on the left end of the slab swing up and right to gain a foot-ledge below a slight corner, and a small nut in a horizontal slot if you're leading. Good handholds then allow

a long reach for the top. Worthwhile.

The right to left traverse across the **Green Glacis** is only 4a but is thought provoking to the timid!

The climbs on the main edge are described from left to right starting in the crevasse.

46 Fingerknacker Crack 8m E3 P1 ★
6a The right end of the crevasse contains a very steep overhanging crack which is usually climbed with frustration, difficulty and much cursing. Once graded HVS 5b - which led to much more cursing!

47 The Sentry Box 8m HVS P2 ★
5b A connoisseur's classic. Just right is a shallow leftward-facing corner crack. Use this to gain entry into the niche (highly problematic on first acquaintance). The finish is fun too!

48 Redundancy Rib 8m E1 P1
5c The right side of the niche forms a hanging rib; climbing it provides the route and possibly hours of entertainment.

49 Storm In A Teacup 9m HVS P2
5b Moving rightwards again is a large scoop with a holly tree at the bottom. Start left of the holly and climb direct to the hanging slab right of Redundancy Rib. From the right of the slab make a long reach to obvious holds high up to the left. The vertically challenged may find it harder - much harder!

50 Holly Tree Scoop 11m D P1 ★
Climb past the tree and ascend the scoop. The wide crack on the left provides an alternative finish.

51 Frank Miller 11m E2 P1
5b Right of the holly is a steep wall which runs into a slab. Climb the wall and faint crack in the slab. The climb unfortunately collects dirt and needs a regular brushing; if its clean its worth doing.

Just to the right a blatantly undercut arete has a shallow depression/corner halfway up on its left side.

52 Noonday Ridge 15m E1 P2 ★★★
5b Climb the right side of the arete until it is possible to move left round the arete to gain the shallow depression and good runners. Continue up the slab to exit on the right.

53 High Noon 14m E4 P2 ★★★
6a ♪ Do not forsake the arete that awaits you; or die a coward, a craven coward......♪ From the shallow depression of Noonday Ridge swing round to the right and go for it. Tradition dictates at least one

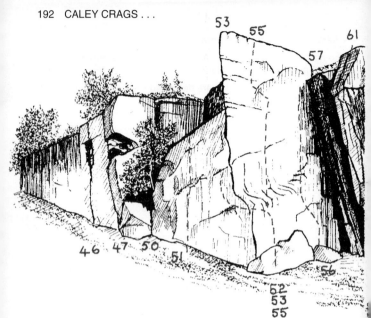

fall from near the top. Make sure your second is paying attention!

54 Gary Cooper   15m   E3   P2
6a No whimp of a route - the original line on the wall. Climb direct
to just below the shallow depression of Noonday Ridge, swing
round the rib and make a rising traverse rightwards moving up to
clip the old bolt and finish at the top of the large corner.

55 Fred Zinnerman   14m   E4   P2   ★★
6b A later and better production directly up the wall. Climb the
centre of the wall on the right side of the arete to the rusty old bolt
(sell-by date?) which is by-passed on the left. Easier for the tall,
risky for the heavy!

56 Welcome To The Neighbourhood   14m   E1   P2   ★
5c Surprisingly independent, the slab just left of Lads Corner. Start
at a short crack and finish into the corner only at the very top. A
Friend and a wire in slots in the slab are adequate to protect the
crux. Side runners in Lads Corner reduce the overall grade.

57 Lad's Corner   14m   VS   P1   ★★
4c The crag drops back to form a large corner, which is easier than
it looks. Slightly! The finish often gets dirty after heavy rain.

58 Block Chimney 14m VS P1

4c The impending chimney just right of the corner starts steeply but easily, the upper section, however, only succumbs to those who have undergone a classical gritstone apprenticeship. Indoor wall students need not apply!

59 Amazing Grace 14m E6 P2

6c A 'physi-kelly' demanding climb up the rib to the right of, and starting in, Block Chimney. The large chockstone in the chimney provides much-needed protection for the difficult moves across and up rightwards. Finish up the much easier thin upper crack.

60 Compulsion Crack 15m VS P1 ★

5a The second wide crack right of the corner leads through a shallow chimney on to a slab and an easier finish.

61 Compulsive Viewing 16m HVS P2 ★★

5a Climb Compulsion Crack for 6 metres to just below its crux and then trend left up the scoop to a good horizontal break. Step up left again to a thin finishing crack in a superb position on top of the rib.

62 Forecourt Crawler 15m E4 P1 ★

6b The final feature of the corner is a shallow flared crack. Climb it to the roof and continue up the steep wall to the large jug so tantalisingly close. The original route moved left under the roof to finish with less difficulty up Compulsion Crack.

A through cave lurks to the right.

63 Indecent Postures 16m E2 P1

5c A series of problems and variants linked together to give an amusing combination. Back and foot up the entrance to the cave and exit with difficulty to gain a ledge and junction with Pedestal Wall. Step up and swing out left to gain the good jug on the direct finish to Forecourt Crawler and finish up this.

64 Pedestal Wall 18m S P2 ★★

A large block now leans against the crag. Climb steps up the left front of this to reach a ledge and squirm up the short chimney. Step left and climb the short steep wall above. Finish up the sharp arete.

There are many problems in the vicinity of the through cave and the slabs which front it. Several linked variants have been claimed as routes over recent years but to include all permutations would be most confusing and this area has been soloed over by all the local stars for at least the last 50 years. The following two hybrids however seem to fill a gap between Pedestal Wall and Rib And Slab and may help reduce the number of future claims.

N. Baker

65 Triple 'A' 16m E1 P3
5c Climb the right-hand edge of the initial slab of Pedestal Wall by smearing up the front (or, at 6a, laybacking the edge from the right) to the ledge and then climb boldly up the left front edge of the pedestal itself to the top. Step across and climb straight up the top slab through the diagonal break to the top.

66 Cave and Slab 14m MVS P2
4b The right arete of the central opening of the through cave is climbed to the apex. Scramble up a short chimney and climb straight up the top slab to the left of the obviously chipped holds.

67 Rib and Slab 14m VS P2 ★
4c Climb the steep slabby arete which forms the edge of Square Chimney, awkwardly to a ledge. Continue up the right-hand side of the upper slab on chipped holds.

68 Square Chimney 14m HVD P1 ★
The recess provides a traditional back-and-foot exercise. Climb to the ledge and layback up the narrowing corner above.

69 Tippling Crack 12m E1 P1
5b The right side of the recess contains a steep widening crack which should be climbed without bridging across the gap.

70 Dypso 11m E2 P2
5c Climb Tippling Crack to the horizontal break, hand-traverse right almost to the arete and climb the short head-wall to gain the slab above. The crux section can also be approached from the routes to the right - less strenuous but less satisfying.

The lower arete right of Tippling Crack is perhaps the next 'last great problem' at Caley?. To the right is a steep two tier slab above an eroded bank.

71 Tipster 10m HVS P2   ★
5a Gain the lower slab from the right and move across to the first block in the horizontal break. Pick your way up the blunt nose and slab above.

72 Tip Off 9m E2 P3   ★
5b From the start of Tipster step up and stand in the break then, using small finger pockets on the upper section, move up and delicately left to gain the easier rib.

73 Rip Off 7m E3 P3
6a Once again climb the slab just left of the wide crack to the horizontal break. This time do battle with the right arete above to finish. Alternatively, jump into the wide crack to escape.

74 Flue Crack 8m D P1
The unimpressive wide crack is climbed to its muddy conclusion.

75 I Can't Believe It's A Girdle, Girdle 36m E2 P2
5c The easiest line is described here. Start up Flue Crack and follow the level of the horizontal break round to Square Chimney, a good pitch. Easily across the Pedestal. Traverse above the Forecourt Crawler groove, up Compulsion Crack and across the scoop to near the top of Block Chimney. Descend this then across to finish up Noonday Ridge. Take stances and packed lunch as necessary.

The crag now opens into a wide bay which provides a slippery means of descent. On the right of the bay is the next buttress.

76 V Chimney 9m VD P1
Climb the obvious V chimney left of the arete. It is guarded by a large chockstone at its base.

77 Quark Walk 20m HVS P1   ★
5b Start up the V chimney until it is possible to traverse rightwards round the arete and along the horizontal break to the obvious stance. Continue straight up over the bulge to finish.

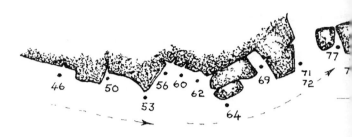

CALEY THE FINAL CONFLICT

78 Quark 15m E4 P2   ★★★
6a A particularly good route - hard, sustained and with a thrilling
finish. Worth E5 for an on-sight flash - but these are very rare. Climb
the thin crack until a spin around the arete and back again leads to
the break. Finish boldly up the wall above about a metre or so right of
the arete (or, as is more usual, slink off right to join the Scoop).

79 Charm 15m E6 P2   ★★
6c The wall right of the peg-scarred crack, with a runner in the
crack for protection. The faint left-trending ramp provides the line.

80 Strangeness 14 m E7 P3   ★
6c The right-hand of the trio of hard routes up the wall. Climb the
blank wall on pockets, smidgens and non-existent holds. There is
rarely a queue!

The short scruffy corner on the right provides the start of the next
two routes.

81 The Scoop 15m VS P2   ★★
4c Climb the awkward corner to the grass ledge. Follow the crack
up and leftwards to a ledge. The exposed open scoop is then
climbed delicately leftwards to the top - an excellent finale.

82 Zig-Zag 15m S P1   ★
A popular route. Climb the corner to the grass ledge. Follow the
crack leftwards then back rightwards on good jams to finish.

83 I Can't Remember 6m HVS P2
5a From the grass ledge right of Zig-Zag climb the wall and shallow
scoop direct to reach the finish of Zig Zag.

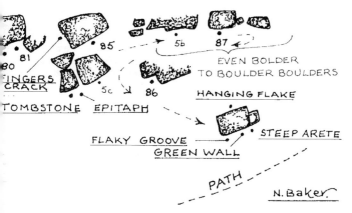

FINGERS CRACK

81
80

TOMBSTONE   EPITAPH

85

5c   86

5b   87

EVEN BOLDER
TO BOULDER BOULDERS

HANGING FLAKE

FLAKY GROOVE
GREEN WALL

STEEP ARETE

PATH

N. Baker

The edge now deteriorates and becomes more fragmented. Twenty-five metres right, where the boulders start, is an obvious two pitch broken ridge. The obvious peg scarred crack high on it's left side is **Fingers Crack** (5c)★, whilst the centre of the lower, rectangular left-hand slab is **The Tombstone** (4c) ★ and **The Epitaph** (5a)★ is the right arete.

84   Double Ridge   15m   S   P2   ★
The main ridge can be conveniently split into two pitches. Take the easiest line up the crest.

The slabs to the right of both sections have a number of popular variations. (5a to 5c). One of the best (i.e. editor's favourite) is:-

85   Dusk   6m   HVS   P2   ★
5b   The centre of the steep slab right of the upper section of Double Ridge is climbed delicately on tiny nicks to a break. The bulge above provides an airy finish on good holds.

86   The Highly Scary Groove   7m   HVS   P2
5a   The clean cut groove in the left rib of a steep slabby boulder ten metres down and to the right. Bridge neatly to the top and then gibber onto the slab on the right to finish. Its not really that scary!

87   One Man and His Dogmas   6m   E5   P3   ★
6b   On a tall obloid block up and to the right is a micro-route for brave souls. Start up the wall to the right of the arete and move left along the 'break'. Follow the arete to the top.

Nearly finished now but before you go to pub check out the last large block down below. It contains several nice problems that often get forgotten. The best are described starting from the left arete of the lower wall; **Flaky Groove** (5b)★★ The groove, trending slightly right of the arete. **Green Wall** (6b)★ The centre of the green wall. **Steep Arete** (6a) The left side of the right arete. **Above The Slab** (5c) The right side of the same arete above the sloping shelf. **The Hanging Flake** (6b) is the best of several shorter problems on the back wall.

Go on then - as long as you started at the beginning and finished here you deserve a pint , or three!
See you in The Junction.

CALEY CRAGS – GRADED LIST OF CLIMBS

E7
Marrow Bone Jelly (6c)
Strangeness (6c)

E6
To Be Is Not To Bolt (6c)
Amazing Grace (6c)
The Great Flake (6b)
Charm (6c)

E5
One Man & His Dogmas (6b)
Nothing's Safe (6c)
The Real Pebble Wall (6c)
Psycho Direct (6c)
Psycho (6b)
Adrenaline Rush (6b)

E4
Quark (6a)
Forecourt Crawler (6b)
High Noon (6a)
Andy's Route (6c)
Terry (6c)
Fred Zinnerman (6b)
Rick's Rock (6b)
Death Drop 2000 (6b)
Ephedrine (6a)

E3
Gary Cooper (6a)
Fingerknacker Crack (6a)
Rip Off (6a)
Ron's Reach (6a)
Hot Green Chillies (5c)
Hanging Groove (5b)

E2
The Knobbler Traverse (6a)
Frank Miller (5b)
I Can't Believe It's A Girdle, Girdle (5c)
Angel's Wing (5c)
Indecent Postures (5c)
The Can (5b)
Dypso (5c)
Rising More Slowly (5b)
Tip Off (5b)

E1
Black Jumper (5b)
Redundancy Rib (5c)
Welcome To The Neighbourhood (5c)
Triple 'A' (5c)
Tippling Crack (5b)
Noonday Ridge (5b)
Permutation Rib (5c)
Harry's Heap (5c)

HVS
Morris Dance (5b)
Rabbit's Paw Wall (5b)
Sneakers (5b)
Quark Walk (5b)
Storm In A Tea Cup (5b)
I Can't Remember (5a)
The Sentry Box (5b)
Rocking Stone Roof (5b)
Highly Scary Groove (5a)
Route 1 (5b)
Tipster (5a)
Dusk (5b)
Angel's Wall (5a)
Compulsive Viewing (5a)
Crenellated Ridge (5a)
Sweet Tooth (5a)
Plantation Wall (5a)

VS
Block Chimney (4c)
The Scoop (4c)
Compulsion Crack (5a)
Lads Corner (4c)
Little Cenotaph (5a)
Fried Green Tomatoes (4c)
Unfinished Crack (4c)
Central Route (4c)
Route 2 (4c)
Boot Crack (4c)
Rib And Slab (4c)
Plantation Ridge (4c)
Roof Layback (4b)

MVS
Shoe Shine (4b)
Cave And Slab (4b)

HS
Morris Crack (4b)
Route 3 (4b)

S
Zig-Zag
Pedestal wall
Double Ridge
Morris Minor

HVD
Square Chimney

VD
V Chimney

D
Flue Crack
Holly Tree Scoop

THE CALEY CLASSICS – PROBLEM LIST

7a
Ben's Groove
Waite
The Low Traverse
Block Buster
No Pebble Wall

6c
Roof Traverse
The Arete
Scary Canary
Front Traverse
New Jerusalem
Syrett's Saunter

6b
Bob's Bastard 2
Maurice Chevalier
Not My Stile
Green Wall
Hanging Flake
Webster's Whinge
Back Wall
The Pinch
Otley Direct

6a
Our Father's Arete
The Face
Martin's Muff
Thin Slab Direct
Back Side
The Stretcher
Low Pebble Wall
Otley Wall
The Cavity
Steep Arete
Lightning Crack
Back Edge
The Bat
Right Wall

5c
Bob's Bastard 1
Soft Shoe Shuffle
Fingers Crack
Smear Arete Left
Glass Chipper
Twin Pockets
Above The Slab
Gripping Groove
Picnic
Chicken Heads
Thin Slab

5b
Mantel Arete
The Halo
Rib Tickler
Rough Rib
Free Stile
Roof Of The World
The Neat Wall
The Gatekeeper
MBKC Groove
Flaky Groove

5a
The Green Streak
Suckers Rib
Courser Edge
Smear Arete Right
The Epitaph
The Cruel Crack

4c
Stilistic
Layback Arete
Sucker's Wall
The Tombstone
The Slab

4b
Chips
Curver

4a
The Green Glacis
Left-hand Groove

CAT CRAGS

SITUATION AND CHARACTER   Cat Crags is a south facing collection of large boulders situated above the A59 Harrogate-Skipton road. The crag is split in to two sections each comprising several blocks The right hand section of rocks are located above a small plantation partly obscured from the road but the more open left-hand section is clearly visible about 100 metres left of the trees. The rock is compact, clean gritstone and nowhere exceeds seven metres in height, although when mantleshelfing at the top of some routes it feels significantly higher. The landings are variable, runners are usually superfluous, but can often be arranged on the harder routes. The crag is quick drying and provides a worthwhile bouldering and 'micro-routing' venue.

APPROACH AND ACCESS   Approaching from the Harrogate direction the crag can be seen on the right of the road, a mile or so beyond Blubberhouses and half a mile short of the more obvious buttress of Dovestone, with which a visit can be combined. **The crag is on private land and there is no automatic right of access, people climbing here do so entirely at their own risk. Permission to visit the crags may be obtained from:- Mr P. Walker, Bothams Farm, Blubberhouses 01943 880274. Dogs are not allowed.** There is a parking space for three cars below the plantation at the right-hand end of the crag. Approach by walking up the road for approximately 120 metres, to where a bridge crosses the stream and a grassy track leads diagonally across the hillside between the two buttresses. (Beware the man-eating bracken in mid-summer.)

THE ROUTES Those detailed below are considered worthwhile, many shorter problems exist but are more suited to specialised bouldering guides. The left hand section of the crag comprises a steep clean free-standing buttress with a steep boat-like prow at the left side of its main face, this is the main buttress. Behind this is a buttress, severely undercut at its left side. To the left of the main buttress is a small free-standing block. Routes are described from left to right and start on the left wall of the undercut buttress. The first three are very short but provide a useful warm-up.

1 Route One 4m VD
Climb the open crack splitting the short wall left of the undercut buttress.

2   Route Two   4m   HS
4c Climb the fingery wall immediately right of the open crack to good finishing holds.

3   Route Three   4m   VS   ★
4c Just left of the undercut arete is a shallow groove, undercut at its base. Pull over and climb the groove direct.

4   Route Four   5m   E1
5c Start just right of the undercut arete. With difficulty gain a standing position on the lip, reach the top.

5   Route Five   6m   VS
5a Start under the roof as low as you can get. Climb across the roof and up onto the wall via a crack and hollow sounding flake system.

6   Getting Groovy   6m   VS
4c Right of the undercut is a short vertical crack, climb this and stretch left to flakes which give access to the shallow finishing groove.

7   The Red Wall   5m   HVS
5b From the top of the short crack move up to the overlap and step precariously up right to finish.

The wall to the right provides various problems.

The next routes are on **THE MAIN BUTTRESS.**

8   There Is No Route Seven   6m   S
Climb the slabby arete at the rear of the buttress to a ledge. Finish by springing off the caterpillar to a classic mantelshelf at the top.

9   The Yaks Progress   7m   HS
4b A variation which links the start of the last route to the finishing crack of the next.

10   Caterpillar Crack   6m   HVS
5a Mantelshelf onto the ledge 2.5 metres left of the prow-like arete. A second mantelshelf leads over the dirty undercut ledge to the bilberry caterpillar below a short crack. Climb the crack to finish.

11   Ginger Tom   6m   E3
6a Mantelshelf onto the ledge directly below the prow. Gain the undercut arete with an amazing amount of difficulty. Continue up the left side of the arete to finish.

12   Cat Baloo   6m   E3   ★★
6b Climb the centre of the main wall first using horizontal breaks and then pockets, (not so much a pocket more a hope). Move left

and up to the top.

13 Cats Eyes 6m E3   ★
6a Start just left of the obvious shallow corner. Using vague flakes
attain a standing position in the break. Move left to the suspect
block, continue straight up the wall to finish in a rightwards tending
crack.

14 Bonington's Made It 6m E2   ★★
6a The obvious shallow, stepped corner which splits the main face.

15 Catastrophe 6m E3   ★
6a Start just right of the shallow corner, climb the steep wall using
horizontal breaks to the roof. A jump may then enable the top of the
crag to be gained.

PINNACLE:
The free standing block to the left of the main buttress has several
problems. The front face is **Pussy** (5b) The overhang at the back
when climbed direct is **Pussy Galore** (6a). The block can be
circumnavigated using horizontal breaks **Felix** (5b). The slabby side
is useful as a descent unless you are a Diff. leader in which case
you have to jump off the end.

Other pump-outs include a R to L traverse of the rear buttress
(exiting round the nose) and a high and low traverse on the road
side of the main buttress.

PLANTATION ROCKS
A short walk along the edge takes you to the right-hand crag. The
main areas of interest are the buttress behind the plantation and a
smaller buttress about 10 metres left. The small buttress on the left
has four vertical problems on its front face and the obligatory
traverse, plus a 5a problem on its right wall between the arete and
the sapling.

A narrow gully runs behind the right hand buttress and 2 metres
inside on the back wall is **The Rack** (5b) A good problem with a
l o n g stretch for the top.

16 Prow 5m S
Climb the blunt arete passing two spikes.

17 Fine Time 5m VS
4c Climb the 'spiky' arete from the right with a reachy start.

18 Jet Propulsion 6m E2
6b Start 2 metres right of the arete. Climb directly up the wall using

all the propulsion you can get to gain the small hole. Easier climbing leads to the top.

19 Double Stretch 6m   HVS   ★★
5a Climb the flake system in the centre of the buttress. Excellent.

20 Longer Stretch 6m   E1   ★
5c Climb the wall between the flake system and the undercut arete which bounds the right hand end of the buttress.

21 The Shelf 6m   HVS
5b Climb the undercut arete, somewhat dynamically if starting direct.

22 God 6m   HVS
5b Two metres right of the arete the wall is still undercut. Move up the wall using good horizontal flakes, to a poor ramp, move right to finish.

23 Faith 5m   E1
5c Three metres right of the arete is a perch 3 metres above the ground. Mantelshelf onto the perch and teeter into a standing position, reach the top.

24 Friction 5m   VS
4c Round the corner from the perch is a narrow wall. Climb it using horizontal breaks and long reaches.

CAT CRAGS – GRADED LIST

E3
Cat Baloo (6b)
Cats Eyes (6a)
Ginger Tom (6a)
Catastrophe (6a)

E2
Jet Propulsion (6b)
Bonington's Made It (6a)

E1
Longer Stretch (5c)
Route Four (5c)
Faith (5c)

HVS
The Shelf (5b)
God (5b)
Red Wall (5b)
Double Stretch (5a)
Caterpillar Crack (5a)

VS
Route Five (5a)
Getting Groovy (4c)
Fine Time (4c)
Route Three (4c)
Friction (4c)

HS
Route Two (4c)
The Yak's Progress (4b)

S
There Is No Rt Seven
Prow

VD
Route One

CHEVIN BUTTRESS AREA   N.G.R. SE 213445

SITUATION AND CHARACTER The quarry and adjoining natural edge are situated on top of Otley Chevin above the East Chevin Road, giving a variety of climbs in a fine position. The buttress area consists of seven natural outcrops. The largest is 18 metres high and gives a small collection of high quality climb on fine natural grit. The smaller outcrops provide a variety of boulder problems and short routes.

The climbs in the quarry are very different. The routes are longer and the rock much more friable. Overall they have a more serious feel. The rock dries quickly in the summer but gets little sun and stays greasy for most of the winter. The area contains some very good routes but a few in the quarry are best avoided (at all costs!).

APPROACHES AND ACCESS Approaching from Otley - from the bottom of Leeds Road - take the East Chevin Road up the steep hill. Near the top on the right is the East Chevin car park. Park here or, if you have walked, collapse. A track leads from the car park first to the quarry, then on to the buttress.
NOTE: This car park is a favourite haunt of 'beauty spot' car thieves. Don't leave clothes or valuables on display.

THE CLIMBS
These are described from left to right.

THE QUARRY

The first route, an isolated arete, is found by following the path from the car park for 100 metres and then striking up through the scrub to the line of the edge.

1 Magic Rabbit 6m   E4   P3
6a Boldly climb the left side of the clean and pronounced arete.

There are other short, scrappy buttresses hereabouts but the next named climbs are 100 metres right on the rocks nearest the main path at the start of the quarry proper.

2 Pooh Sticks 9m   HVS   P2
5b A scrappy climb starting from a spike at the foot of a ramp to the left of the prominent gully. Climb the front face of the pinnacle moving left up a diagonal break to ledges. Step up and trend right to the arete and the top.

3 Solo Slab 8m HS P3
4b Climb the left edge of the slab forming the left side of the wide gully.

4 Deception 9m HVS P1
5a Climb the crack on the right wall of the gully.

Round to the front on the right is a dirty chimney with a cleaner, undercut wall on its left.

5 Last Regret 10m E2 P2
5c Start at the foot of the chimney and gain the left wall. Follow this moving further left near the top.

6 Sand Crab 10m VD P1
The dirty, sandy chimney, climbed direct.

Across broken rock to the right begins the impressive Freestyle Wall. The first climb, described only as a variation in the previous guide, takes the steep thin crack to the left of the longer main wall.

7 The Thin Crack 10m HVS P2
5b Climb directly up the thin crack to easier ground near the top.

8 Freestyle 20m HVS P1   ★
5a Start at the lowest point of the quarry and climb the impressive undercut crack line over the initial bulge and then leftwards to broken rock at half height from where a number of variation finishes are possible. The best is straight up, trending right at the top. Easier is the more broken line just left, which can be combined with an easier left-hand start to form an independent, but inferior, route in its own right. A harder and bolder variation, a traverse, has also been made rightward from half height into the upper reaches of the next route.

9 Cool For Cats 20m E5 P2
6b Start up Freestyle to below the overhangs. Move up right to a pocket then directly up the wall placing a runner in Freestyle at half height.

10 Jenny Tulls 20m E5 P2
6b The hardest and most challenging line on the Chevin. Start below the centre of the wall and climb the roof with great difficulty to dubious flakes above. Continue direct up the much more amenable thin, peg-scarred, crack.

11 Revision Revolt 23m E3 P2
6a Climb the broken gully on the right for 6 metres until a move left allows a ledge on the wall to be gained. Finish up the middle of the wall, passing a large slot. A direct start would turn this into a better route.

The next routes start at a higher level in the bay to the right.

12 Graunch 11m Dreadful.
Start up the short, overhanging corner at the left end of the bay and
continue up a mixture of loose rock and grass.

13 Max Wall 12m MVS P1
4b Jam up the short overhanging crack to the grass ledge and
follow the continuation cracks direct to the top.

14 Bellow 14m VS P1
4c Climb the rightward-slanting, thin crack line just left of the
shallow corner.

15 Ladder Climb 14m HS P1
4b A shallow corner is climbed, utilising ledges first on the right and
then the left, spaced at regular intervals.

16 Ladder Climb Direct 14m HVS P1
5b A direct start up the crack on the right joining the parent route at
half height.

17 Weasel 15m HVS P1   ★★
5b The open, but most pronounced, corner in the centre of this bay
provides a good sustained exercise in bridging.

18 Lindsay, Lindsey 15m E1 P2
5c A variation start to Rampant Hippo which takes the wall to the
right of Weasel on small broken holds to a break. Move across into
Rampant Hippo and follow this to the top.

19 Rampant Hippo 15m VS P1   ★
4c A good line providing steep jamming in an unfortunately sandy
crack. The finish requires care.

20 No Prisoners 15m E1 P1   ★★
5b One of the best lines in the quarry. Start up Rampant Hippo and
swing right to gain the thin crack just right of the arete. Follow this to
the top.

21 Layback Corner 16m HVS P2
4c Climb the diagonal crack rightwards to gain the next corner and
a finish up the loose dry-stone wall at the top.

22 The Inmate 14m E2 P2
5c Climbs the short blank corner on the right to finish up the
previous climb.

23 Smokey Joe's Last Freakout 12m Vile P2
The horrific chimney in the right-hand corner of the bay.

The right wall of the bay contains three short cracks of roughly similar standard of difficulty. The central one is the cleanest and best, and worth doing despite its name.

24 Porno Crack 6m HVS P1
5c The peg-scarred crack is 'flashed' direct.

CHEVIN BUTTRESS

To the right, the buttresses form a natural edge beginning with some boulders and short walls. The first problem of note is **Straight Crack ★** (5b) The obvious vertical crack.

The next block is undercut and known as Pygmy Buttress. It has four distinct problems - all are harder than they look.

Little People (6b) The overhang and left arete; **Pygmy Traverse ★** (6a) The overhang followed by a traverse right; **Porky** (6a) The right-hand side of the wall to join the finish of the traverse and; **Obstinacy** (5c) A left to right traverse below the roof finishing at the foot of Porky.

1 Twin Cracks 6m HVS P1
5b The rightward-slanting crack line up to the right of a heathery gully gets a more appropriate grade this time than the miserly HS 4b in the last guide!

Ten metres further right is the Main Buttress which, for its size, contains a high proportion of top-quality climbs as good as any in the area.

2 Rear Entry 6m E1 P2
5c Start below a bulge well up the bank on the left side of the buttress. Climb the overhang and wall above to the top.

3 Leech's Wall 8m VS P2   ★
4c Climb boldly up a faint scoop in the middle of the left wall to a break. Step right to avoid the roof and finish up a short corner. It is possible to finish direct over the bulge at 5a.

4 Visual Deception 12m E2 P3
5b An eliminate squeezed between Leech's Wall and Chevin Buttress. Start from the short green slab just left of the deep crack and gain the wall above, climbing direct just left of the crack. Side runners are not allowed at this grade, but escape is always possible to the right.

5 Chevin Buttress 16m VS P1   ★★★
4c A fine and classic climb with an exposed finish. Start just left of

N. Baker

the arete and climb the steep crack until it fades out. Move right to the arete and then to the top. A direct finish is only slightly harder and equally as good.

6 Gronff Left Hand 16m E4 P1 ★

6a The arete is climbed from the overhanging crack. The crux is the move up from the crack to the next horizontal via a very long reach (jump?), but this can be avoided by a step right, which reduces the grade to E3 5c.

7 Gronff 16m E2 P2 ★★★

5c An exhilarating climb taking the wall just right of the arete. Gain a diagonal sloping ledge and then, using undercuts, make a long reach up left to better holds. Continue up the middle of the wall to the top.

8 The Waster 15m E1 P1 ★★★

5b A compelling and technically-interesting line. Climb the awkward groove and flake direct, finishing over the bulge on to a short slab.

9 Vampire's Ledge 18m VS P2 ★

4c A meandering route starting up the rightward-slanting cracks leading to the deep groove of Central Climb. Move up and out left on to the upper slab and cross it leftwards to finish by a pleasantly delicate series of moves.

10 Central Route 15m S P1   ★
Pleasant climbing and the easiest route on the crag. Takes the deep
central groove leading up left beneath the overhangs. Move into the
higher niche and exit via cracks above.

11 Central Route Direct 14m VS P1   ★★
4b The prominent crack is gained over the first bulge reached from
Central Route. Good jamming and protection lead to the top.

12 Slide In 14m E1 P3
5b Climb the wall right of Central Route just left of a small
overhang. Independence from the next route is difficult to maintain.

13 Slide Back 14m HVS P2
5b Climb a short corner to an overhang and pass this on the left via
some bold reachy moves to gain the easier upper wall.

14 The Backslider 13m E2 P1   ★
5c Climb the short shallow corner, as for Slide Back, to the
overhang. Climb the steep groove on the right via a hard move to
reach a break. Finish up the wall above.

15 Growler 12m VS P1
5a A poor climb on the slab right of Backslider. Move right to a
crack, (tree belay if required) and climb it to finish direct up the
arete or better move left climb the blunt arete in the middle of the
upper slab.

16 The Girdle Traverse 36m VS P1   ★★
An excellent trip marred only by the rope drag which invariably
affects pitch two.
1. 18m 4c Start behind a large tree on a terrace at the right-hand
side of the crag and climb to a horizontal break. Hand traverse left
and descend across a delicate slab to gain the jamming crack.
Swing down this under the bulge to belay on ledges further left.
2. 18m 5a Swing left again and follow an exposed hand traverse
across The Waster to reach the arete and continue round the corner
at the same level before moving up to join Leech's Wall below the
bulge. Follow the rounded crack beneath the bulge to the end of the
buttress.

To the right of the main crag, a series of smaller buttresses provide
numerous short climbs and problems. Only the first and last three
buttresses attain the requisite route length of six metres. The rest,
however, all have serious landings above a steep uneven slope. If
in doubt, employ a rope or a competent catching team.

17 Blunt Nose 6m HS P2
4b 'Pick' your way up the left arete of the first buttress.

Groovy (4c) is the groove in the centre of the buttress via a blind flake and the right arete. Whilst **Two Foot Tumbler** (5b) is the thin blind crack just right of the central groove.

Fifty metres right is the Split Buttress containing, **Split Ends** (5c). Mantelshelf on to the narrow ledge to reach a side pull and move up left to a flat ledge and the top.

Forty metres further right is a cleaner, compact buttress containing **Sweet and Sour** (5c) the short crack in the left wall and **Done But Not Dusted** (5b) the left arete. Just right of a small oak is **Slape** (5a), gain the left-hand ramp and continue direct. **Short and Sweet** (4c) climbs the right-hand ramp whilst in the centre of the buttress is the shallow **Fossil Groove** (5a). The centre of the slabby wall right of Fossil Groove is **Done and Dusted** (5c) and the short crack on the right is **Nine Foot Crack** (4c).

Some 100 metres right is the last buttress, a small dirty quarry.

18 Another Deception 6m HVS P1
5b Climb the thin vertical crack in the cleanest wall.

19 Layaway 7m E1 P2
5c Follow the thin crack to the break then traverse right to the arete.

20 Give-away 8m E4 P3
6b Climb the arete direct with great difficulty.

If you've still not had enough take a walk through the woods westwards and, with luck, after about a kilometre you may come across the West Chevin Boulders which provide more amusing problems among the trees. These rocks have been known to devotees of green gritstone for many years and provide reasonable problems in years of drought. The following' micro-classics' are the only three known to have been recorded.

21 Raynman 7m E1 P2
6a Climb the centre of the largest boulder easily to the break. Undercut right and pull into the shallow groove. Reachy!

22 Time After Time 7m HVS P3
6a The brushed left arete. From a couple of pockets make a massive slap up the arete and gain a break. Sneak off round left to finish.

23 Perfect Jam 7m HS P1
4b One hundred metres lower down the path below the last routes is a small buttress with an obvious crack. Climb it.

After that, and only when you've done everything else on Yorkshire gritstone, go in search of the following last two skeletons. From the car park go up the road for fifty metres and enter the woods through a disused gateway. Thrash around for a while until you come upon the following.

24 Dennis the Dilapidated Pensioner 6m HVS P1
5b Climb the wall on the right of the imposing (?) buttress.

25 Midget Digit 6m E1 P1
6a Climb the thin crack in the middle of the wall past an old bolt.

CHEVIN QUARRY AND BUTTRESS – GRADED LIST

E5
Jenny Tulls (6b)
Cool For Cats (6b)

E4
Give-away (6b)
Magic Rabbit (6a)
Gronff Left Hand (direct) (6a)

E3
Revision Revolt (6a)
Gronff Left Hand (easier var.) (5c)

E2
Backslider (5c)
Gronff (5c)
Last Regret (5c)
Visual Deception (5b)
The Inmate (5c)

E1
Midget Digit (6a)
Raynman (6a)
Slide In (5b)
Layaway (5c)
Rear Entry (5c)
No Prisoners (5b)
The Waster (5b)

HVS
Time After Time (6a)
Porno Crack (5c)
Weasel (5b)
Slide Back (5b)
Dennis the Dilapidated Pensioner (5b)
The Thin Crack (5b)
Freestyle (5a)
Deception (5a)
Another Deception (5b)
Ladder Climb Direct (5b)
Pooh Sticks (5b)
Twin Cracks (5b)
Layback Corner (4c)

CROOKRISE

N.G.R. SD 987557

SITUATION AND CHARACTER Crookrise may well be a high moorland crag and apparently a long (by modern cragging stands) walk from the road, but it's a short-sighted climber who lets this put him off from the feast of quality routes and inexhaustible supply of boulder problems in a wonderful and generally sunny setting. The crag lies at the south-west corner of Barden Moor overlooking Skipton and the Vale of Craven. It is composed of clean solid gritstone varying in height on the main crag from 10 to 20 metres. Slab and technical wall climbing are the specialities here. The crag is somewhat exposed in bad weather, but in summer it retains the sun into the evening making it perfect for mid-week bouldering. Even in winter on those crisp, dry, sunny afternoons the quick drying and sheltered nature of many of the bays make it a truly all year round venue.

APPROACHES AND ACCESS. The best approach is from Embsay village which lies 2 miles north of Skipton just off the Skipton-Harrogate road (A59). From the Elm Tree Inn in the centre of the village, turn left taking the road (Pasture Road) towards the reservoir until the sailing club car park is reached. Stop here. To continue by car will seriously annoy the farmer and may well jeopardise the access to the crag. Walking is the only alternative – don't give up, it will all be worth it in the end. Follow the gravel track along the S.W. side of the reservoir and cross the stile on the right into the Access Area. Follow the track north-west to meet the wall running up on the left of the moor. Follow this up the hill for a few hundred metres until the first section of the crag can be seen over the wall. This is Woodside Buttress (not the best buttress for a first visit) The main crag can be reached by continuing along the right-hand side of the wall, passing some boulders (Moorside Boulders) to the top of the moor and then crossing over the stile. The path from the stile to the edge of the crag brings you to End Slab (routes 11 onwards). **There are no restrictions on climbing but the approach cuts through the Barden Moor Access area. See special notes on page 10.**

THE CLIMBS
These are described from RIGHT to LEFT.

WOODSIDE BUTTRESS Cross the wall just past the copse of pines where it is interrupted by a cluster of flat-topped boulders. The first prominent 'flying buttress' is, in fact, a large boulder topped by another which contains a number of entertaining problems ranging from 4a to 5a and may well provide more sport than the main buttress.

The first climb starts on the arete of the next buttress across the grassy gully.

1   Embsay Buttress   10m   VS   P2   1956
4c Follow the arete of the buttress using a selection of flakes to an awkward and rather bold finish up the head wall.

2   Fat Man's Agony   8m   VD   P1   1956
The obvious chimney to the left of Embsay Buttress provides amusement, especially if you happen to get stuck in the final tight squeeze.

3   Fern Crack   VD   P1   1956   ★
This takes the twin-crack line just left of Fat Man's Agony finishing up the right-hand crack.

4   Grassy Gully   8m   M   P1   1956
The grassy, rock-strewn gully which separates the two main buttresses. Often used as a descent.

5   Woodside Wall   11m   S   P2   1956
Start on the small detached block at the foot of the left-hand buttress. Move up from the right-hand end of the block to a vague ledge at 3 metres then trend right on to a heathery ledge. Finish with care over the overhanging ledges at the top.

6   Woodside Buttress   12m   VS   P1   1956   ★
4b Start from the detached block at the foot of the buttress and attack the arete direct, moving firstly on to the left wall and then back right at half height.

7   Seres   12m   VS   P2   1966
5a Start as for Woodside Buttress but move strenuously across the steep left wall by way of a hole until a V-notch in the overhanging ledges allows the top to be reached. Sustained.

8   Wallflower   10m   VS   P1   1966
4b This starts about half way up the grassy bank, at the foot of the left wall of the buttress. As the name suggests it is steep, green and often damp. Climb the wall to the V-notch of Seres.

The edge now becomes broken although a multitude of boulders provides entertainment on the way to the main crag. The next routes lie on an isolated wall about 200 metres left of Woodside Buttress and behind the large 'Everest' boulder.

9 Pitou   7m   E3   P2   1974
6b Climb the wall at its centre passing an obvious pocket near the top.

10 Fitou   7m   E2   P1   1988
6a Climb the left edge of the buttress moving right to a prominent flake and the top.

Left along the boulder field for 150 metres to reach the main edge.

END SLAB

This area is at the extreme right end of the main edge and is easily recognised by the undercut slab and cave gully above. The routes are described from right to left along the slab and then in a clockwise direction through the gully finishing back above the right-hand edge of the slab.

11 Edge   7m   HS   P2   Pre 1957   ★
4a Start at the right side of the slab and move up delicately to the half-way ledge. Continue up the right arete of the slab via a large pocket.

12 Route 1   18m   VD   P2   Pre 1900
Start as for Edge to the half-way ledge. Foot traverse leftwards for 5 metres to reach and follow the diagonal crack to the top of the slab. An extension can be made up the buttress on the left.

13 Route 2   7m   VS   P2   1930   ★★
5a Start at the least undercut part of the slab about 2 metres left of Route 1 and climb delicately on polished holds to the mid-height ledge. A thin crack takes you to the crux and leaves you wishing it hadn't!

14 Route 2.5   7m   HVS   P2   Pre 1949   ★
5a Start 2 metres left of Route 2 and take a direct line up the slab. An escape can be made from the final moves by reaching left into the crack of Route 1.

15 Route 4   10m   HVS   P1   1966   ★
5c Start between Routes 2.5 and 3 (by the initials LJ) and make a hard pull (crux) on small holds to reach the half-way ledge. Move left, crossing the diagonal crack, and finish up the wall by way of two large pockets.

16 Route 3   8m   S   P1   Pre 1949
Start in the undercut V groove and climb this to the half-way ledge, finishing up the rightward slanting crack of Route 1 above.

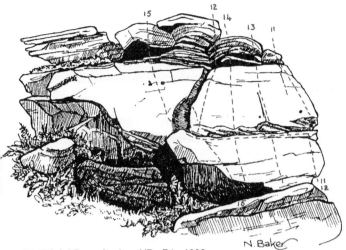

N. Baker

17 Trivial Pursuit 6m VD P1 1998
Start 4 metres left of Route 3 and gain the right-hand end of the
Broad Shelf. Follow the diagonal crack pleasantly rightwards to
finish.

18 Dirty Tackle 5m S P1 1998
The ramp to the left of Trivial Pursuit is climbed to the shelf. Finish
up the short flake crack.

The lower entrance to the cave gully is the next feature. This can be
followed round to the top of End Slab. The gully contains several
sporting problems, a strenuous finger traverse known as **The
Twilight Zone** (6a) and now, several short routes of questionable
quality and independence.

19 Dewhurst Mill 8m VS P2 1994 ★
4c Climb the wall and hanging crack at the right (entrance) side of
Cave Gully, to the ledge. (Opposite Lonesome Pine). Step left onto
the gully wall and climb boldly to the top.

20 Overhead Projection 8m VS P1 1991
4c Start at the foot of the rib inside the gully and climb rightwards
up the overhanging wall to the first break. Traverse right to join and
finish as for Dewhurst Mill

21 Gibb's Rib 7m E2 P2 1994
6a The blunt rib above the traverse in Cave Gully - without touching
the backwall.

22 Facade 5m S P1 1998
Step from the boulder onto the wall using the hole and trend left to the final slab. The start without the boulder is 4c.

It is possible to climb out of the gully at around Diff at several points but back at the eastern end is a buttress on the left (looking out) with a large nose.

23 A Vicious Slice Of Mango 6m VS P1 1991
4c Start under the nose and move up to finish on the left of it.

24 A Malicious Cut Of Grapefruit 6m HVS P1 1991
5a Climb up to and over the nose described in the last route, as directly as possible.

Directly below End Slab is a small buttress which is split by a crack.

25 Cave Crack 7m VD P1 1974
Climb the crack direct to exit on to the path below the slab.

26 Midget Morsel 7m MS P1 1988
Climb diagonally left from the foot of Cave Crack to the top of Shelter Stone.

27 Shelter Stone 9m S P2 1976
Climb the wall and bulge left of Cave Crack, starting from the lowest point.

Returning to the upper level, left of End Slab;

28 Lonesome Pine 6m E3 P2 1984
6a Start on the rib immediately left of the gully and climb direct passing an obvious flake at 4 metres to a tricksome finish .

29 Twin Cracks 9m VS P1 Pre 1923   ★
4c Directly behind the large fir tree are two parallel cracks. Climb these passing a large thread to an awkward exit on the right. The tree provides some security and a means of escape for those who want to go no 'fir'ther.

30 Ledge Buttress 9m VS P2 1960
4c The wall and ledges left of Parallel Cracks provide a wandering route. Start at the lowest part of the wall and move rightwards to a difficult move on to the ledge. Move left and finish direct.

31 Leaning Wall 8m VS P2 1978
5a Start just left of Ledge Buttress, at the left corner of the main wall and climb direct up the rib to the ledge. Pull over the bulge using a pocket.

32 Side Salad 9m VS P2 1991
5a Start 2 metres left of Ledge Buttress by a sidepull. Up the short walls above to pull out via another huge sidepull.

33 Tiger Rag 8m HS P2 1951 ★
4c On the left arete of this buttress is an undercut ledge. Start from the boulders at the bottom of the gully and make a strenuous pull on to the ledge. Finish up the wall on the left. A variation start up the groove to the right of the usual line is 5b.

34 Traverse and Crack 8m VD P1 Pre 1949 ★
Start halfway up the gully and make a difficult rightwards traverse to gain and follow the obvious crack in the headwall.

35 Basic Training 7m S 1994
Start as for Traverse And Crack but then climb the wall direct.

36 Ryan's Folly 7m D P1 Pre 1923
On the left wall of the gully is an obvious deep chimney. It provides an excellent way of adding credible tattiness to over smart 'craggies'.

37 Diet-Pepsi 6m HVS P2 C 1970
6a A short tough micro-route up the fingery wall left of Ryan's Folly. Starting life as a mere 5c boulder problem, this minor classic demonstrates the benefits of an aggressive marketing campaign.

38 Chockstone Crack 7m D P1 Pre 1900 ★
From the boulder on the left of the gully make an initial high kick to gain and follow the crack on the front of the buttress.

39 Bilberry Crack 7m VS P2 C1930 ★
4c Left of Chockstone Crack is an obvious crack with an undercut start. Struggle over the bulge and follow the left arete of the buttress to a committing finish.

40 Bilberry Wall 7m VS P2 1977
5a Starting just left of the jammed boulder? Climb the wall round to the left of Bilberry Crack, finishing at the same point.

41 Hidden Wall 5m VS P2 1994
4c In a bay behind the large boulder on the same buttress as Bilberry Wall. Start 2 metres right of the corner and climb direct to rounded finish.

42 Friction Slab 7m MVS 1994
4b Start at the bottom of the smooth slab in the back of the bay. Climb the slab direct to a ledge and continue, veering leftwards above the gully. A direct finish is slightly harder.

CRAVEN BUTTRESS

This large area of rock consists of two main buttresses, at right angles to each other, producing a step in the line of the crag. On the right – and on the left of the previous routes – is a large boulder which provides interesting problems up both the slabby and overhanging sides. The next route starts where this boulder meets the steep overhanging buttress.

43   Slab and Nose   9m   S   P1   Pre 1923   ★
Skate up the initial slab and then move right to follow a series of ledges to the top.

44   Slab & Nose Alternative   10m   HVS   P2   1956   ★
5a   A harder start laybacks up the valley face of the slab and then moves up left from the top of the slab in a more exposed position.

The left arete of this buttress provides the start of one of the crag's finest routes, The Sole. The next 2 routes start as for this route but break out right .

45   Mother's Little Helper   9m   E2   P1   1976   ★
5c   Climb the initial crack in the arete and traverse right above the first overhang. From the middle of this, climb direct to the top using long reaches.

46   Family Matters   8m   HVS   P1   1977   ★★
5b   A good line at a consistent standard. Continue delicately up the arete from where The Sole starts to move left.

47   The Sole   10m   HVS   P1   1956   ★★★
5b   Climb the difficult initial crack by a series of awkward layback moves until the fine leftward-sloping crack on the left wall can be reached. Follow the crack to finish at the square-cut nick.

48   Streaky Re-Sole   ungradeable   1988
The Sole can be gained at half height by a ludicrous jump from the grassy ledge on the left of the normal start.

49   Sole Direct   8m   E3   P2   1981
6c   The top of the diagonal cracks can be gained by improvising directly up the apparently blank wall below them.

50   Malcolm's Route   7m   VS   1989   ★
4c   Five metres left of the start of The Sole climb the wall just right of a blunt rib utilising two pockets.

51   West Wall Climb   7m   MVS   P2   1937   ★
4b   A pleasant wall climb, usually soloed, climbing the blunt rib in the centre of the wall by a series of positive finger slots.

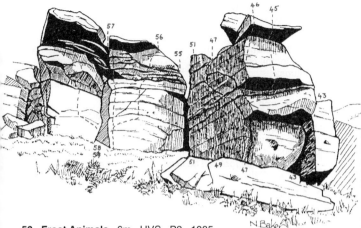

N Baker

52 Frost Animals 6m HVS P2 1985
5b More fingery moves up the wall left of West Wall Climb, close to the gully entrance.

Left of this route is a deep black gully which provides an easy way up or a means of descent.

53 Jug Wall 5m HS 1981
4b The Juggy wall in the back of the gully to a steep finish.

54 Nasty 7m VS P1 1997
Climb the left wall of the gully a metre to the right of Craven Crack to an un-nerving finish.

The next route starts at the left of the entrance to the gully.

55 Craven Crack 10m MVS P1 C1930   ★
4c An old severe recently up-graded by popular request. Climb the crack using a variety of techniques until a ledge is reached just below the overhangs. Follow this round rightwards to a more sensible finish.

56 Walker's Wall 10m HVS 1952   ★
5a Start 3 metres left of Craven Crack at an obvious rib. Climb this for 3 metres until a traverse can be made into the centre of the wall. This is climbed direct to the overhang which is taken just right of centre by a long reach for a hidden hold. The **Footloose Finish** is just left of centre at 5c and this can be combined with a boulder problem start on the lower wall to provide an independent eliminate.

57   Chimney Variation   10m   VS   P1   pre 1957
5a As for Walker's Wall but continue up the left edge of the slab
moving into the chimney at the top.

58   Griffith's Chimney   10m   HS   P1   Pre 1923   ★★
4a One for the connoisseurs! Climb the chimney in the centre of
the buttress using a range of contortions originally depicted in the
Karma Sutra. The final section is best tackled on the left wall.

59   Longlurch   12m   E2   P2   1974   ★
5c Start just left of Griffith's Chimney by hand traversing into the
centre of the wall. A series of strenuous moves leads to good holds
on the lip where a long grope rightwards will hopefully find the
elusive pocket. Most mortals will then finish up and left. It has been
alleged that the top roof can be climbed direct - you are welcome to
try but its not E2!

60   A Reach Too Far   E3   P2   1997
6a The easy slab left of Longlurch is climbed until it is possible to
move right to a large hole and protection. Move straight up from
here via a long reach to a sloper.

61   Moulson's Climb   10m   S   P1   Pre 1923
At the left edge of this buttress is a leaning slab. Follow this and the
crack above to reach the rocky chimney and easy ground.

To the left, the crag becomes broken for 15 metres until **EASTER
GULLY**, a large square-cut recess, is reached. The next route of
any note starts just right of the gully.

62   Problem Buttress   10m   HS   P1   Pre 1923
4a Make a boulder-problem start up the initial wall to a ledge and
then follow easier ground to the top.

The back of the gully provides three worthwhile crack climbs.

63   Crookrise Crack   8m   S   P1   Pre 1949   ★
Follow the right-hand crack by way of a steep start.

64   Easter Crack   8m   VD   P1   Pre 1949
The central crack provides an interesting if somewhat painful
exercise in jamming.

65   Crack Climb   8m   S   P1   Pre 1923
Layback and jam the left-hand crack.

Starting below and left of Easter Gully at the left-hand end of an
undercut block is **Indirect Little Crack** (6b)★ No need to rope up
for this one – it never gets more than 2 metres off the ground!. Hand
traverse the crack and ledges leftwards to finish on a broad ledge.

66   Face, Arete and Wall Climb   10m   VD   P3   Pre 1923   ★
Nice climbing in three short stages but not easy to protect. Start up the front of a block which guards the entrance to Grovelhog Gully and gain a broad ledge. Move right on to the arete and follow it to another ledge. Climb the back wall to the top. Starting directly below the arete by a painful jamming crack is a 4c variation.

67   Grovelhog   6m   VD   P2   1994
Start on the back of the broad ledge at the entrance to Grovelhog Gully, right of the obloid block below the prow/overhang. Climb the wall to a ledge below the prow, step left up the slab to finish. A more direct finish over the prow is VS 4c.

68   Perplexity   8m   HVS   P1   1997
6a Ascend the right edge of the tall obloid block to the left Grovelhog Gully by a step from the ledge on the right. Make complex moves up a shallow overhanging corner to a good flake and an easier slab finish.

Left again is a gully which provides a useful descent route though climbing up it to the second wedged boulder followed by an ascent of the slab on the right is a pleasant Diff, **Induction** (P1).

CENTRAL SLAB

To its left of the descent gully is a large area of slabby rock. The first section of this slab between the gully and Diagonal Crack can be climbed almost anywhere, providing popular short solo problems in their own right. Numerous claims for routes in this area have proved extremely confusing for guide writers. The following selection is an attempt to clarify legitimate lines.

69   Octopus Direct   10m   VS   P2   ★
4c Start up the slab one metre left of the gully and climb direct passing an overhang at the top.

70   Octopus   14m   S   P2   Pre 1957
4a Start in the middle of this section of slab and climb up to the ledges. Traverse right for about 3 metres, moving up, and crossing the direct to finish over the easier bulge just left of the descent gully. A left-hand finish joining Diagonal Crack is more satisfying and slightly easier.

71   East Of The River   11m   VS   P2   1992
5a Somewhat artificial. The slab one metre right of Diagonal Crack, is climbed to the break. Move left across the crack- line and climb the easier upper section of Winter Rain.

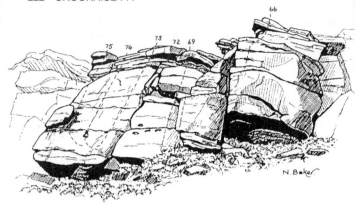

72 Diagonal Crack 12m VD P1 Pre 1923 ★★
This takes the large rightwards-trending crack up the middle of the slab. The difficulty is mainly at the start, which bears the scars of scores of frantically-flailing boots.

The next three routes start from the foot of Diagonal Crack.

73 Winter Rain 11m E2 P2 1987
5c The slab one metre left of Diagonal Crack. Start directly over the bulge by gymnastic pulls on small pebbles. Step right and continue, initially with difficulty, easing gradually. Side runners are not allowed at this grade but escape is easy between moves.

74 Old Lace 10m VS P3 1952 ★★
5a From 2 metres up Diagonal Crack traverse left along the obvious break for 2 metres until a move up can be made to an obvious large pocket from where delicate moves, easing gradually, lead directly to the top of the slab.

75 Arsenic Slab 10m S P2 1950 ★★
Follow the traverse of Old Lace and continue in the same line until directly below a jutting flake. A committing pull on the edge of this leads to easier but unprotected padding up the blunt rib.

The Direct start to Arsenic Slab makes a good problem at 6a. And a low-level traverse **Long Lace** from the obloid block to the next route is fun at 5a.

76 The Jolly Pleasant Scramble 10m Mod
The gully to the left of the slab can be climbed until a step right leads up a jolly pleasant slab. It can also be used as a descent.

SHELF BUTTRESS
On the left of the gully lies a large impressive sweep of rock containing some of the best and longest climbs at Crookrise.

77 Cat's Whiskers 13m VS P2 1952   ★★
4c Start 2 metres left of the gully and climb direct to a ledge at 6 metres. Make an airy step left on to the slab above and climb this to the overhang. Traverse left under this by what used to be called a 'stomach traverse' (hands and feet recommended) until a break in the wall allows the top to be reached.

78 Lyndhurst 11m E1 P2 1994   ★★
5b Start 1 metre right of Long Climb. Either make a couple of moves up the crack to the wide ledge or, more easily, start from the ledge. Climb the obvious groove above and pull onto the slab to gain the traverse of Cat's Whiskers. Make the 'airy' move left on this climb and then continue through the overhang on good holds.

79 Long Climb 12m MVS P1 Pre 1923   ★★★
4b Left of Cat's Whiskers is an obvious crack splitting the buttress. Climb to this and follow it to the overhang from where the 'stomach traverse' left leads to the top.

80 Elm Tree Wall 10m E3 P2 1974   ★
6a Climb direct up the wall immediately left of Long Climb until a difficult finish can be made over the bulge and rounded breaks. The right edge is used by most for the final moves.

81 The Shelf 10m E2 P2 1956   ★★★
5b A classic of the district which should not be underestimated. At the left side of the buttress a series of cracks leads up to an obvious pocket at 6 metres. Climb these and from the pocket reach straight up for a sloping shelf. An exhilarating airy mantel then brings the top of the crag within reach.

82 The Forager 11m VS P1 1994   ★
4c Climb the Shelf for 4 metres until a rising traverse can be made out left on good jams to a ledge in the chimney. Climb the wall on the right of the chimney, just left of the arete, to a ledge and finish over the final overlap.

83 Open Chimney 10m VD P1 Pre 1923
The wide chimney tests a variety of techniques, but be careful when pulling on some of the chockstones.

84 Buster 12m S P1 Pre 1957   ★★
Climb the first 4 metres of Open Chimney until a teetering traverse left, feet in the diagonal crack, leads to the left arete. Climb up this to a jug then move right in a great position to pull onto the sloping

N. Baker

top with the aid of a good flake.

85 Buster Direct 10m HVS P1 1977 ★
5b Start 2 metres left of Open Chimney and climb the problematic wall with a l-o-n-g reach to a leftward-slanting crack which may enable you to join the parent route.

86 Chockstone Chimney 12m VD P1 Pre 1923
Climb the twin cracks left of Buster to a ledge. A flake and a chimney lead to the top.

At this point the crag becomes broken by a heathery ledge with rocky tiers above and below it. At its left-hand end the upper tier forms an impressive buttress containing the obvious rising ramp line of Slip 'n' Slide.

87 Narrow Crack 8m MS P1 Pre 1923
Follow the heathery ledge leftwards for about 7 metres until a crack is reached. The main difficulties are concentrated in the first 3 metres.

To the left, heathery ledges lead to a gully and deep chimney.

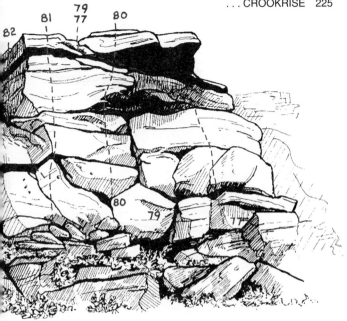

88 Bull's Horns 9m VS P2 1954 ★
4c Start on the arete right of the gully and make a hard move to grab the obvious horn. Keep tight hold to tame the beast and then lead it more easily up the crack and ledges to the top.

89 Bull's Eye 11m VS 1995 ★
4c A variation start to Bull's Horns starting up a corner crack 3 metres right of the parent route. Step up onto the lip of the slab and traverse left using the 'eye' to join and finish as for Bull's Horns.

90 Matador 7m HVS P2 1997
5a Start as for Bull's Eye but climb straight up to the break from the eye. Continue to the top using the right arete to a rounded finish.

91 Crooked Chimney 8m VD P1 Pre 1923
The deep chimney will prevent sunstroke, but lotion may still be needed for the gritstone rash.

92 Sunstroke 9m HVS P2 1966 ★
5a Start just left of Crooked Chimney and make a perplexing rising traverse across the wall to join the left-hand crack. Climb this and move left on to the slab to finish.

93 Sunstroke Direct 8m HVS P1 1966 ★
5b The crack of Sunstroke can be gained directly by some cryptic bridging.

94 Slip 'n' Slide 8m E6 P3 1976 ★★★
6a The obvious ramp line leads to a hard exit. Sticky rubber may help the feet but can you control your head?

95 Duck 'n' Dive 7m E5 P3 1990 ★
6b The technical and scary groove one metre right of Green

N. Baker.

Crack. The technical crux is low down and it just may be
possible to contrive protection higher up, but?

96 Green Crack 8m VS P1 pre 1923
4b Bounding the buttress on the left are two parallel cracks. Climb
the left-hand of these moving right below the top.

97 Knuckleduster 8m VS P1 1955
4c Sprightly moves up the wall left of Green Crack allow a
rightwards traverse to be made into that route at the top. A direct
finish over the block overhang is also good value at 5a.

98 Knuckle Crack 8m VS P1 1955 ★
4c Start at the end of the heathery ledge. Move up boldly, don't look back, that's the secret to Knuckle Crack.

The continuation of the ledge traverses below the infamous **'Secretary Nose'** the jutting block at the top of Straight Crack and Leaf Crack. First recorded in 1923, it is worth the detour! The rocky band directly below Slip 'n' Slide is not really worth losing any skin over, but further left it becomes cleaner and more compact providing some interesting climbing. The first route takes the prominent crack below and to the left of Knuckle Crack.

99 Straight Crack 15m HS P1 Pre 1949
4a Climb the crack until it finally deposits you on the ledge at half-height. Follow the easier slabs to the top.

100 Leaf Crack and Slab 15m VS P1 Pre1949 ★
4c This takes the prominent crack with a large thin flake protruding from it at half height. Climb the crack, awkwardly at first, until moves right round the bulge lead to easier slabs and the top.

101 Magic Tricks 7m E2 P2 1985
6a Using sleight of hand move right from the foot of Long Day to climb the overhanging wall left of Leaf Crack and Slab.

102 Long Day 14m HVS P1 1963 ★
5a Start at the right-hand rib of the deep gully. Climb into and up the scoop on the arete until the halfway ledge is reached. The continuation arete above is awkward to start but leads to much easier ground.

FAREWELL SLAB

Above the left end of the lower tier is a compact slab extending over the deep gully at its right and undercut at its left. The next routes start from the heather ledge between the tiers usually gained from the left. Most of the routes are described with reference to the obvious central line of Walkers Farewell.

103 Winter Traverse 10m E1 P3 1958 ★
5a The right-hand end of the ledge drops away to form a grassy gully. Start about 2.5 metres right of Walkers Farewell with an awkward step onto a small hold. Traverse boldly rightwards on the wall above the void until a delicate move up brings the top edge of the slab within reach.

104 Ice Fall 9m E2 P3 1992 ★
5b Start as for Winter Traverse until halfway along, step up onto a foot break and climb the centre of the slab on selected pockets. The hardest moves are at the top!

105 Wonderloaf 8m E2 P2 1962/71   ★
5b Step onto the slab just left of Winter Traverse, and climb the
wall direct to a narrow ledge. Follow the short flake crack at its right-
hand side until the overhang is reached. Take this, with some
difficulty, direct. An introductory pitch can be climbed just left of the
lower right-hand arete, but is usually dirty and avoided.

106 Pen Sketches 8m E2 P3 1987
6a Climb to the left end of the narrow ledge and move directly up
the slab to the break in the overlap to finish.

107 Walker's Farewell 18m HVS P2 1952   ★★
5b This climb takes the obvious gangway on the lower tier to reach
the heather ledge. Now make a very difficult step onto the upper
slab below the obvious central pocket and climb awkwardly straight
up the slab to finish via the obvious crack in the bulge.

108 A Lifetime's Dream 8m E4 P3 1986   ★
6b Climb the wall direct, 3 metres left of Walker's Farewell, using a
series of pebbles and small pockets.

109 Walkover 10m E3 P3 1977   ★★
6a Climb the curving, left edge of the slab. Certainly no walkover!
Although the hard part of the route is only just above the ledge, the
lack of reasonable belays make it a somewhat daunting lead.

110 Gambling With Crystals 8m E5 P3 1992
6b A direct line through Walkover. Start 3 metres left of Walkover at
the extreme left edge of the narrow ledge. Using undercuts in
pockets pull onto the traverse of Walkover and continue direct via
further pockets and pebbles. (True independence from A Lifetime's
Dream is questionable)

111 Quashqui 8m HVS P2 1994   ★
5b The gully wall left of Walkover and just to the right of the
hanging wedged boulder is climbed to a rounded finish. Strenuous.

112 High Step Climb 7m D P1 Pre 1923
The gully to the left of the Walker's Farewell slab provides some
bridging followed by a wall and slab on the right.

113 Born Again 6m D 1994
Start in the back of the gully that runs parallel with the crag behind
the hanging, wedged boulder. Climb the wall and emerge through
the slot with difficulty - not suitable for those with large frames!

114 Stepping Out 6m VD 1994
Start at the junction of the 2 gullies beyond the wedged hanging
boulder. Climb the gully wall by the corner and step out right to
finish above the boulder.

HEATHER WALL

The wall to the left of the gully has a small overlap at half height and provides three pleasant routes, all good value for their grades!

115   Right Hand Route   7m   VS   P1   1955

4c   Start right of the shallow central groove of the wall moving slightly right at the overlap. Cross this and continue up the right edge of the wall above.

116   Central Route   7m   MVS   P1   Pre 1957

4b   Start from the boulder, left of the shallow groove, and climb directly to the top, crossing the overlap.

117   Left Hand Route   7m   VS   P1   Pre 1957

4c   Start as for Central Route but move left at the overlap. Cross this and follow the left edge of the wall to the top.

SLINGSBY'S PINNACLE

To the left of Heather Wall is a large buttress with a detached flake lying against the right-hand side. This has, in the past, been described as a pinnacle, apparent when viewed from the top, but not from the bottom! The next 5 routes all vie for independence on the clean right wall.

118   Moonshadow   9m   HVS   P2   1994   ★

5b   From just left of the short corner climb to the middle of the flake and then via a series of small horizontal breaks continue without deviation to the top slightly right of centre.

119   The Flake   8m   S   P1   Pre 1923

The obvious rightward-trending flake crack. Climb this and, with feet on it, traverse across to the easy ground at the edge of the wall.

120   Spellbinder   9m   HVS   P3   1985   ★★

5a   Climb onto the first section of the flake and move up to the rounded break and runners on the left. Continue moving first slightly right and then left to finish direct.

121   Flake Wall   10m   MVS   P2   1951   ★

4b   Follow the flake for 3 metres and step up onto the wall to a rounded break. Traverse left to a ledge on the rib which is followed to the top.

122   Mother's Milk   8m   VS   P3   1992

4c   A direct start to Flake Wall from the top of the Hovis boulder.

123   Hovis   10m   E1   P2   1958   ★★★

5c   Excellent climbing up the shallow groove on the right-hand side of the front face of the buttress. Start from the large detached flake (or direct from the ground just left at 6a) and traverse leftwards with difficulty until an awkward move up right allows balance to be regained in the shallow slabby groove. Elegant moves of decreasing difficulty follow, but protection is always elusive.

124 Wholemeal 9m E3 P2 1997   ★
6a Start direct from the ground just left of the Hovis flake and gain the arete. Climb straight up right of Hovis to a gradually easing finish. May be harder for the short.

125 Mighty White 10m E4 P3 1997   ★★
6b Climb the old, but highly problematical, superdirect start to Hovis to gain a standing position in the twin pockets below the small flake. Move up directly to more pockets using the flake and pebbles then a very bold move up to better holds and protection before a slopey finish. Starting further right and moving right to place a Friend in Hovis before the bold move reduces the grade to E3 6a

126 Small Brown 9m E4 P3 1958   ★★★
6b A bold technical classic climbing the steep arete at the left of the front face. The arete can be started direct or from the left (the original way). Neither is easy with the crux gaining a standing position on a sloper at the foot of a vague groove at half height. The difficulties fortunately decrease higher up.

127 Massive Attack 9m E5 P3 1996   ★★
6b A more direct and sustained version of Small Brown. Keep to the left of the arete - and 'keep on' to the top.

128 Slingsby's Chimney 10m HVD P1 Pre 1900   ★★
4a An excellent example of the traditional gritstone chimney. Climb the awkward and polished start until moves can be made deeper into the darkness. Bridge, or back and foot, up the centre of the upper chimney to the top.

129 Fear No Evil 12m E2 P3 1996   ★
5c Climb to the ledges halfway up Slingsby's Chimney and venture into the darkness. Step off the end of the block and climb the steep slab direct on marginal slopers to finish just left a small roof. Bridging is not allowed.

130 Premium White 10m E1 P2 1997   ★
5b Climb Slingsby's Chimney for 3 metres and continue up the rib to the ledge at 5 metres. Climb straight up the blunt arete to the top.

131 Chimney Buttress 12m HS P2 Pre 1923   ★
4b Climb the first 3 metres of Slingsby's Chimney and then move on to the left-hand rib. Traverse left into the centre of the buttress and climb to the top trending left to find the biggest holds.

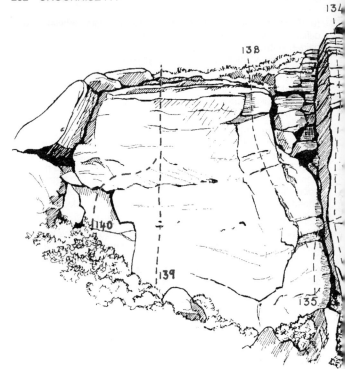

132 The Fly 6m E3 P2 1979 ★
6c Levitate up the wall to the left of Slingsby's Chimney using 2 shallow pockets, minuscule pebbles and lots of faith in friction. From the break half-way choose any finish or traverse off, you've earned the tick!

133 Crease Direct 9m E1 P2 1957 ★★
6a A superb exercise in technical bridging up the prominent shallow groove to good pockets. From the halfway breaks a steep but much easier wall leads direct to the top.

134 Crease Arete 9m E2 P2 1997
6a Moving left from the foot of the groove follow the arete throughout. The upper half climbed on the right is still 5c but reasonably protected by a Friend.

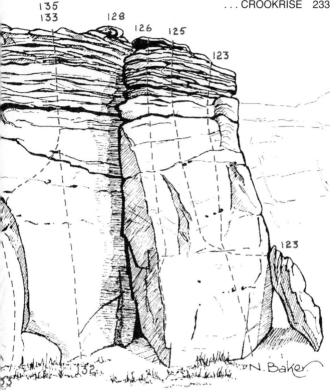

N. Baker

135 Crease 11m VS P2 1952 ★
5a Start in the block-filled gully at the left end of the buttress and climb up and then hand traverse rightwards around the arete using prominent pockets. From the last pocket move on to the main face and take the easiest line up the wall to finish.

136 Pebble-dash Yer Toilet 7m E2 P2 1992
5c The upper part of the Crease Arete climbed, with the aid of a flake, on the left side.

137 Slingsby's Girdle 20m HVS P2 1961
5a Girdles the entire buttress from right to left. Start by reversing Flake to join and follow Flake Wall to the rib. Cross Hovis and Small Brown just below the top, move round into Slingsby's Chimney and then follow the traverse of Chimney Buttress. Phew!

138 Rushlight 7m S P2 1966
The short slab across the gully is climbed in the centre to a steepening finish. The left rib provides a variant at MVS 4b.

139 Streaklet 7m E3 P2 1988
6b Start directly above the rock step and make desperate moves to gain the break. Finish direct.

140 Breaking Out 6m E2 P2 1985
5c Start at the left of the buttress and break out right to mantle onto a ledge before an awkward finish.

A traverse of the buttress at half height from Rushlight to Breaking Out is a good bold solo at 5c/6a

The edge now runs into a jumble of small boulders interspersed with a few larger buttresses and some interesting routes. About 60 metres to the left is the overhanging **SADCOCS** boulder (see below), and between this and the more prominent Scoop Buttress is a smaller block upon which **Wallace** (5a) Climbs the overhanging front face, moving to the right edge at the top. Whilst **Gromit** (4c) starts at the bottom left-hand side and climbs just left of the arete to a difficult finishing move.

SCOOP BUTTRESS
This buttress lies 150 metres left of the end of the main edge.

141 Scoop Wall 7m MVS P2 Pre 1989
4a Climb the south-facing wall of the buttress at its right-hand end to reach a scoop and leftward-trending gangway.

142 Mindbender 9m E1 P3 1996   ★
5b Start below a shallow groove on the South Face of the buttress 3 metres left of Scoop Wall. Climb up the groove, step right and make a difficult move to gain the pocket in the middle of the wall. Move up and rock onto the sloping gangway to finish.

143 All In The Mind 9m E3 P3 1996   ★★
5c Start at the foot of the south face 2 metres left of Mindbender. Climb up to the wide ledge and make a series of bold and tenuous moves up the right side of the arete.

144 Mindless 9m HVS P3 1996   ★
5a Start at the foot of the buttress on the valley side and climb past two large pockets to a crack and move left to gain the ledge. Climb the thin slab right of Scoop using the arete.

145 The Scoop 7m HS P3 1960
4b Round the corner to the left, above two pine trees, is an obvious scoop. Nice line, pity about the green rock.

GREEN BUTTRESS

This buttress lies at the same level and 150 metres left of Scoop Buttress, about 30 metres into the wood. The buttress contains a prominent undercut arete with a large fir tree conveniently placed for emergency retreats. The routes are worthwhile but prone to gather woodland detritus.

146 Green Velvet 8m E2 P1 1988   ★
5c Strenuous but worth the effort. Climb the obvious finger crack with some difficulty until an exit can be made on to a ledge. Easier ground leads to a heathery finish.

147 Greenland. P. 8m E3 P2 1988
6b The undercut arete is followed direct after a difficult start.

148 Agag 8m E2 P2 1966
5c The leftward-facing wall is climbed just left of the arete to an awkward finish. Don't stray too far left!

149 Wailing Wall 7m HVS P1 1988
5a The wall is climbed at its left-hand end to a short crack and an easier finish.

EVASION BUTTRESS

Lying about 50 metres further left and containing an obvious capped corner.

150 Evasion 6m VS P1 1988   ★
5a Good Value. Climb directly up the wall right of the corner, step right below the roof and finish with a long reach for the flake crack.

151 Avoidance 6m S P1 1986
Climb the corner until a move right round the overhang leads to the top.

THE BOULDERS Crookrise is a boulderer's paradise providing hundreds of problems of all types. There are far too many to describe in this guide but the following selection, on the most prominent blocks, should get you hooked. Beware however, not all of the landings are perfect, and many of the problems are really routes in disguise - Its a long and painful hobble back to the car park!

MOORSIDE BOULDERS

These boulders lie on the main path to the crag, just after Woodside Buttress, and provide several short problems. The obvious arete and the friction slab provide the most fun.

EVEREST BOULDER

This boulder lies about 100 metres left of Woodside Buttress. It is easily identifiable by its enormous size and also by the diamond-shaped slab on its southern side. The steep slab provides four excellent and quite serious micro-routes. **The Left Arete** (5c); **Left Centre** (6a); **Right Centre** (6b), and the **Right Arete** (3c), which is also the usual descent. The west face provides two classic jamming problems: **Right-hand Crack** (4b), is straightforward but **Ron's Crack (I)** (6b) is rather different! Tape up to climb the left-hand crack direct. The north face features a rightwards-sloping ramp which, if started direct above the bone-crunching boulders, gives: **Rampant Bilberry** (6b) - you may also think E3!

HOT POT BOULDER

The Boulder with an Ash Tree on top below Easter Gully. **Hot Pot** (E2 P2 6a) Climb the leaning wall to an awkward mantel-shelf. The left-hand variant is 5b.

RUFFIAN BOULDER

This huge boulder lies about 50 metres directly below Long Day (Route 74). Its outward face contains two excellent real routes along with various pumpy boulder problems, variation starts and low level traverses.

152 The Urchin 10m VS P2 1966   ★
4c At the right-hand end of the face is a short, bulging wall topped by a slab. Make awkward moves on to the slab and then traverse leftwards passing a small overlap to reach the top.

153 The Ruffian 11m HVS P2 1960   ★★
5a A big climb for a boulder but well worth seeking out! The steep crack in the centre of the wall is climbed strenuously until a juggy traverse leftwards leads onto the slab. Climb this airily on the left to the top.

154 Artful Dodger 10m HVS P2 1988
5b Climb the steep, and often dirty, north face of the Ruffian boulder finishing at the apex.

FOOTPRINT BOULDER This is the large, pointed boulder above and to the left of the Ruffian boulder. The slab facing the crag has an obvious 'footprint' pocket just above its undercut face.

155 Footprint Slab 6m MVS P2 1988
4b Pull on to the undercut slab just right of the footprint and follow it direct.

156 Footprint Arete Right-hand 6m MVS P2 1988
4b Layback up the left arete of footprint slab.

157 Footprint Arete Left-hand 6m HVS P2 1987
5a/b Layback up the south face of the arete.

158 Elephant Trods 7m HVS P2 1988
5a A bold traverse right-to-left across the south face over an ever-increasing drop.

MATTERHORN BOULDER

This is the pointed boulder 15 metres left of Footprint Boulder and directly below the Hovis area.

159 Horny Matter 6m HVS P2 1981
5c Climb the steepening crack on the valley face to an awkward finish.

160 Layback Crack 6m VS P1 1981
4c Climb the layback crack on the right face of the boulder, moving right at the top.

GENTIAN BOULDER

This is the large boulder about 25 metres down the hillside from the Matterhorn Boulder. It has a large, obvious diamond-shaped slab which is undercut at its left-hand end.

161 Sunshine Slab Right-hand 6m MVS P2 C1970 ★
4a Climb the right-hand flake of the slab passing two rounded pockets to a steep finish.

162 Thin Air 7m HVS P3 1960 ★
5a Take the slab direct passing a thin mantel to reach the obvious flake.

163 Sunshine Slab Left-hand 7m VS P2 C1970 ★
4c Pull on to the undercut ledge and move up and left to the arete. Follow the slab to the top.

164 The Gentian 8m S P2 Pre 1969
Often green rather than violet but worthwhile. Start at the left-hand side of the undercut end of the boulder and make an athletic move to gain the base of the slab. Move up and right to the top. It is also possible to start 3 metres right of the original by a hard pull over the overhang to gain the slab.

The undercut base of this boulder is home to **Jason's Roof** (7a)★★★, a long and powerful problem traversing out from the back to emerge around the lip. One of the best and hardest challenges of its type on gritstone.

END BOULDER
This boulder lies at the end of the main edge, below and just left of Breaking Out. It is identified by an impending overhanging crack.

165 Ron's Crack (II)   6m   E3   P1   C1974   ★
6b   Climb the overhang on good holds until an awkward series of finger jams brings the top into sight. Protection is good but hard to place otherwise its a bold and serious solo. The front face of this boulder also provides a couple of more pleasant micro-routes at HVS 5a.

SADCOCS BOULDER
This boulder lies just below the wall which runs along the top of the crag and about 60 metres left of the end of the main edge. The face overlooking the valley is overhanging and provides many problems including **Right-hand End** (4c): **The Offwidth Crack** (4c); **Central Roof** (6b) Direct, using shallow pockets on the lip; **Hanging Flake** (6a); **Left-hand Rib** (5a). Hand traversing the boulder, with or without feet, provides a good pump at the end of the day.

FAIRY'S CHEST
This area is situated about 350 metres left of the Sadcocs Boulder and can be reached by following the wall leftwards towards the wood. Pass the trig point, cross over a stile and then continue along the wall until two large boulders are reached. This is the Fairy's Chest. The boulders contain several interesting problems (some long enough to be called routes) including an obvious, peg-scarred crack.

CROOKRISE – GRADED LIST

E6
Slip 'n' Slide (6a)

E5
Duck and Dive (6b)
Massive Attack (6b)
Gambling With Crystals (6b)

E4
A Lifetime's Dream (6b)
Mighty White (6b)
Small Brown (6b)

E3
Fly (6c)
Pitou (6b)
Ron's Crack (II) (6b)
Greenland.P. (6b)
Walkover (6a)
Sole Direct (6c)
Streaklet (6b)
Lonesome Pine (6a)
Elm Tree Wall (6a)
Wholemeal (6a)
A Reach Too Far (6a)
All In The Mind (5c)

E2
Magic Tricks (6a)
Fitou (6a)
Pen Sketches (6a)
Gibb's Rib (6a)
Fear No Evil (5c)
Green Velvet (5c)
Longlurch (5c)
Mother's Little Helper (5c)
Winter Rain (5c)
Pebble-dash Yer Toilet (5c)
The Shelf (5b)
Agag (5c)
Wonderloaf (5b)
Ice Fall (5b)
Breaking Out (5b)

E1
Premium White (5b)
Crease Direct (6a)
Hovis (5c)
Lyndhurst (5b)
Mindbender (5b)
Winter Traverse (5a)

HVS
Perplexity (6a)
Diet-Pepsi (6a)
Route 4 (5c)
Horny Matter (5c)
Buster Direct (5b)
Spellbinder (5a)
Family Matters (5b)
The Sole (5b)
Frost Animals (5b)
Walker's Farewell (5b)
Quashqui (5b)
Moon Shadow (5b)
Sunstroke Direct (5b)
Footprint Arete Left-hand (5a)
Route 2.5 (5a)
Mindless (5a)
The Ruffian (5a)
Long Day (5a)
Wailing Wall (5a)
Elephant Trods (5a)
Slingsby's Girdle (5a)
Artful Dodger (5a)
Thin Air (5a)
Spellbinder (5a)
Sunstroke (5a)
Walker's Wall (5a)
Matador (5a)
Slab & Nose Alternative (5a)

CROW'S NEST WOOD QUARRY   N.G.R. SD 996266

SITUATION AND CHARACTER   The quarry is on the south side of the Calder Valley, almost above Hebden Bridge railway station. It is well hidden in the wood that gives the quarry its name. It is tree lined and very sheltered and is thus at its best for climbing in late autumn, winter and early spring for it is then more open to light. The three separate sections of the quarry give a good selection of climbs in the middle to upper grades. The rock is a fine grained grit and usually solid but prone to vegetation and the build up of woodland detritus on the ledges. The stars were allocated when the climbs where in their newly cleaned state.

APPROACHES AND ACCESS   There are no access restrictions. The quarry is approached from the railway station; a road leads left under a bridge, followed by a right-hand hairpin bend. Two tracks lead off from the bend. Park near here and follow the second track behind a livestock factory, then cross a field to a junction. Go left here, follow the path, cross a stream and turn right into the quarry. Ten minutes from the road.

THE CLIMBS
The climbs are described from left to right commencing with the face some 35 metres left of the main face.

1 Mantelpiece 11m HVS
5b Climb the crack above the 'fireplace', then the wall above. A grass slope leads to tree belays.

2 Afterthought 12m S
Climb a wide crack in a slab, trend right then left to a small corner. Go up this and left to a mantel finish. Tree belays above.

3 Crache 11m VS
4c Climb the crack of Afterthought then continue up and gain a niche. The crack above leads to the grassy slope and tree belays.

4 Nic's Route 12m VS
4c Start 6 metres right, at an elder bush. Climb the wall trending left to a large ledge. A thin crack leads past a stump to finish.

5 Diagonal 15m VS
5a Start left of the 'fireplace'. Move up and follow the horizontal groove rightwards to a slanting crack. Follow this to the niche of Crache then step right into Nic's Route (hard for the short). Continue along a horizontal crack to gain a crack with a sapling,

finish awkwardly up this.

A broken area on the right is bounded by a stream, a wall right of this yields an obvious crack.

6 Himalayan Balsam 20m E3   ★
5c Climb the crack to ledges. An overhanging niche above leads to an awkward finish. A strenuous route which may be split at the ledges.

MAIN FACE
The long wall from the arete on the right gives some good climbing.

7 Reversed Image 20m HS   ★
4b The obvious crack in the arete leads to a flake. Climb this on the left, or, straight up (harder - 4c).

8 Wet Wednesday 20m HVS
5b Climb the narrow crack right of Reversed Image to ledges. Continue up the wall to a thin crack finish. If damp at the top, a 5a traverse is possible to gain Reversed Image.

9 BG and His Brush 20m E3
6a The wall right of Wet Wednesday is climbed past two pockets to an overlap (PR in situ). Go over this to ledges and finish as for Wet Wednesday.

10 The Big Wind Up 20m E2
5c Follow a scoop, crack and arete right of BG and His Brush.

11 Icy Start 20m VS   ★
4c A corner crack leads through an overhang to a niche, and a slabby corner above to an awkward finish (sometimes dirty). An alternative finish is to traverse left (5a) to join Reversed Image.

12 The Bow 23m E2   ★
5c Climb a boat-shaped prow to an undercut, then move right to a niche. Traverse left and up to a small hole. Go straight up to ledges which lead right to a bay. A groove on the left leads to a finish.

13 Crow's Nest Wall 20m HVS   ★
5a Climb cracks and a groove on the right to square-cut overhangs right of a niche. Pull over the overhang and continue up the groove to a slabby bay, finishing up the groove on the left. Care with protection.

14 Floss 15m E2   ★
5b Ten metres right is an overhanging groove which leads to a wall split by cracks. A strenuous move leads over a bulge to a wall and ledge. Move up to a cracked groove and the top.

15   Travelling Right   43m   E2   ★
1 23m 5c Climb Himalayan Balsam to the ledges. Follow a line to
Reversed Image and move down then right to the niche on Icy
Start. Nut belays. The ledges of Himalayan Balsam can also be
reached by abseil, though this reduces the grade of this pitch to 4c.
2 20m 5b Gain a line of holds leading across to the obvious bay.
Go down from a sapling to just above the overhang, then move
delicately right to join Floss. Finish up this. Alternatively, from the
belay, climb down to gain the traverse line of The Bow. Go right to a
niche and cross Crow's Nest Wall to regain the original route at the
delicate traverse right.

Opposite the Main Wall is a buttress with an overhanging face.

16   Hot Temper   15m   HVS
5c The left side of the arete left of Calcis Crack to a large ledge.
Finish up a flake/crack above.

17   Calcis Crack   15m   VS
4c Climb the crack to a large ledge. Finish to the left or as above.
The arete can also be reached via the arete starting on its right, 5b.

18   Stainless Steel Screw   15m   HVS
5b Climb Calcis Crack for 5 metres then go up right to gain a
leftward-leaning crack leading up to a break. A crack on the left
leads to an ungainly finish, strenuous.

19   Birch Wall Fritters   14m   VS
4c Climb a corner, cracks and block to a birch tree. The cleft on the
right and a crack on the left culminate in an awkward finish.

20   Ringpull   12m   VS
5a The converging cracks on the wall right of Birch Wall Fritters
form a wider one at the confluence. Climb these cracks to a large
ledge and finish up the arete, escapable.

DARBY DELPH

SITUATION AND CHARACTER The crag lies on the north side of Booth Dean Clough. It is immediately below the A672 midway between junction 22 (M62) and Ripponden. It is clearly visible from the motorway. The main wall faces south over Booth Dean reservoir. The quarry is, for the most part, composed of solid gritstone. The long main face is steep with unusual holds due to the strata of the rock. At the west end is a wall at right angles to the main wall. This is more like normal quarried grit. The climbs have a bold, overhanging feel to them. "HVS in E1 situations" said one visitor. It is a sheltered spot, faces the sun and is often in condition when other crags are not.

APPROACHES AND ACCESS The owners are thought to be the local council. Whilst no access problems arose in the years after the original development, since 1988 a pair of peregrines have used part of the main wall as a nesting site. The R.S.P.B. monitor the site and **climbing is discouraged during the nesting season (March to July).** Small lay-bys at the western (uphill) end provide parking as does the gate area east of the quarry (don't block the gate). A walk down the grass slope at the west end leads to a track which goes up into the quarry.

THE CLIMBS
The quarry has two walls, one set back from the other at its west end. These are at right angles to the main wall. The main wall has few natural landmarks of any size. So, routes tend to follow a succession of minor features. The routes are described from left to right.

WEST WALLS
The left wall has a ditch beneath it thus the starts are all steep. Belay stakes (not obvious) are in place at the tip of the grass slope. The first route is just right of a short arete.

1 Watch It 6m HS
4b Gain a little corner, follow a crack left to a niche and the top.

2 Catch It 7m VS
4c Start as for Watch It. Trend right and climb the wall.

3 Crack It 9m VS
4b Twin cracks lead to a wider one. Continue to a leftward finish.

4 Munch It   9m   VS
4c A few metres or so right. Pull on cracked blocks, gain a flake line and go up until a step left leads to Crack It.

5 Longer   9m   HVS
5a Right again is a little corner at 4 metres. Gain the corner and continue with long reaches to a ledge and the top. Hard for the short.

6 Shaky Start   9m   VS
4b Climb to a prominent flake at 5 metres. Continue with a leftward finish.

The right-hand section of the west wall averages 20 metres in height. Good block belays. Just right of the left arete is:–

7 Caractacus   20m   VS
4c Ledges lead right to a corner which leads to a ledge. The thin crack may be taken direct, 5a, or by a detour left then right. The upper wide crack is gained and a finish made left of a large block.

8 Just in Time   20m   HVS
5a Right is a corner. Climb to a ledge. Step left and go up a crack to the overhang. Go over with difficulty to a wide crack and follow it to finish.

9 Completion   18m   HVS   ★
5b Start 4 metres right. Follow a thin crack to a large ledge. Go up past a horizontal niche and gain twin cracks. A thin crack leads to the top.

10 Correction   16m   HVS   ★
5b Start 3 metres left of the main wall corner. Follow a thin crack system to a wider crack finish.

THE MAIN WALL
Twelve metres right of the corner is a thin crack, left of this is:–

11 Moon Tiger   16m   VS
4b Climb the wall to a little reddish corner which leads to the top.

12 Gnatty   16m   VS
4c The thin crack leads to a leftward finish.

13 Chironomid   16m   VS   ★
5a The wall 2 metres right leads to a 'cave'. The overhanging corner above is gained with effort. The top is near.

14 Bloodsucker   17m   HVS
5a The next crack line leads to a sandy belt and a steep precarious finish.

15 Illusion 20m HVS   ★
5a Start at a mini slab. Climb up to a flake, pass a niche above then go steeply up to the sugar loot. Traverse right and up to finish.

16 Wusac 17m HVS
5a A line up the right hand end of the large ledge passing a short crack. Trend right then up to the large ledge and the finish of Illusion.

Thirty metres right are two 'eyes' at 7 metres. Left of these is:–

17 Deliverance 20m VS   ★
5a Climb the wall to the sloping fault. Go over a bulge and up a wall to a groove. Climb the left side of this to finish.

Further right is an overhang with parallel cracks above.

18 Windy 20m VS   ★
4c Climb the wall left of the thistley field. Go up left on to a projection. Now move right to a blocky groove which leads to the top.

Pool Wall is to the right. The routes can be gained by traversing if the stepping stones are covered. The wall is bounded on its left by a very loose groove/corner. Four metres right is:–

19 White Streak 20m HVS   ★★
5b Climb the wall left of the streak to a flake. Go up to a slanting crack them a corner crack above. Go over a bulge and left then, up to finish. Sustained.

20 White Green 20m HVS   ★
5a Right of the streak. Climb the black wall to an obvious crack in the overhang. This leads to a square niche. Left then right to finish.

21 Green Streak 20m HVS   ★
5a Follow the grey/green wall to a thin crack at 6 metres. Go up and right to a small 'cave' beneath the overhang. Go over this, step left, finish direct.

22 Pool Wall 20m HVS   ★
5a Climb the black/grey wall past shot holes to a short stepped crack. Go up to a little black corner. Step right and go left above the overhang. Finish direct.

23 Flank Attack 25m VS   ★
5a Gain a sloping ledge at the right side of the wall. Go up left then right to ledges on the arete. A large ledge above leads to a long traverse right to the top of White Tower. (A perilous grassy finish from the ledge is also available).

An obvious wide corner crack is on the right. The left wall gives:–

24   Question Mark   25m   HS
4b Climb the wall to the corner. Traverse left to the arete. Finish as for Flank Attack.

25   Digger   17m   HVD
The wall leads to the corner crack. Its top leads to a finish right to the White Tower.

The White Tower is an obvious feature.

26   Left Arete   16m   MVS
4b Climb the wall below the arete then this to the top. Escapable.

27   White Tower   16m   VS   ★★
4c Climb the wall up the centre of the tower.

28   Right Arete   16m   HS
4b Climb the wall then go up the arete to finish. Escapable.

29   Plugged   17m   VD   ★
Go easily up to the concave wall then diagonally to White Tower.

30   Grey Man   16m   HS
4b Easily to the slanting weakness which leads to the top.

A shored up tunnel entrance is further right.

31   Cave Wall   16m   MVS
4b Climb the wall below and left of the tunnel. Follow the slanting line left to finish.

Right of the cave is:–

32   Masgor   16m   HS
4b Climb up to a large ledge. Awkwardly gain a flake/blocky corner and the top.

33   Sloper   17m   HVD   ★
Climb the corner to the overhang. Traverse right to finish up Booth Dean Arete. Variations. At the roof traverse left to Masgor, VS 4c or, step left and pull straight up VS 5a.

34   Booth Dean Arete   16m   HVD   ★★
Climb the blunt arete to sharper ledges. Step right then up left to finish.

The orange/pink wall may be climbed almost anywhere at HVD/S standard.

35   Organe   16m   VD
Go up to a thin crack, 2 metres right of Booth Dean Arete. Then

diagonally left to Booth Dean Arete.

36 Rogane 16m HVD
Go directly up to the right-hand end of overhanging black blocks.
Avoid those on the right.

37 Nogare 16m MS
4a The wall a metre or so right of Rogane.

38 Garone 16m MS
4a The wall further right leads to a short crack at the top.

39 Angore 16m HVD
The wall between Garone and the deep V groove.

Right of the V groove is a clean wall.

40 Half Done 12m HVD
Climb to a corner, gain the little arete and go up a wall to a grassy
finish.

To the right is some white rock then a belt of black rock below
overhangs.

41 Little One 10m VD
Climb the wall to the shallow cave. Swing up and out left. Finish
direct.

42 Swapped 10m VS
5a As for Little One but pull with difficulty, rightwards and up to the
top.

DEER GALLOWS

SITUATION AND CHARACTER   Deer Gallows is the obvious crag in the middle of the moor directly above Embsay Moor Reservoir, between Crookrise Crag on the left and the prominent hill of Embsay Crag on the right. The crag takes the form of a main wall 40 metres long and 12 metres high. Separated from this by an unusual wide rift is the Pinnacle, of similar height. Below the Pinnacle, on the downhill side, is a large, easy-angled block with a pleasant sunbathing spot at its base. It is a friendly place with good landings, being well suited to soloing. The rock is mainly clean, windswept and quick drying. There is much on offer to the middle-grade climber for a crag of its modest size and even one or two problems to test the hard men.

APPROACHES AND ACCESS   The crag lies within the Barden Moor Access Area so see special notes on page 10.   Approach as for Crookrise until the stile into the access area is crossed. Follow the path eastwards for a few metres or so then bear left (north) up a vague track up the hillside leading to a point west of the crag. When level with the rocks traverse across to reach the crag (20 minutes from the car park). A more direct approach lures you into an extremely succulent bog!

THE CLIMBS   These are described from left to right along the Main Wall. The first problem being an old chiselled V. Diff on the extreme left.

1   Rift Arete   8m   VS   P2
5b   Make hard initial moves up the left arete of the main edge. Not serious as it is possible to step off at half height. Harder if climbed from the right.

2   The Pocket   11m   HVS   P2   ★★
5c   Climb desperately up to the large pocket on the pebbly wall. Finish using two rock eyes in the wall above.

A harder variation on the lower wall is **Pebble Promenade** (6a) just to the right reaching the smaller pocket by some mega-thin pebble tweaks and harder still, **Pochette Surprise** (6b) is the wall just right again with a very long reach for the obvious small pocket. Both finish at the heather ledge.

3 Fist Crack 11m VS P1   ★
5a Jam the obvious crack to a ledge, then attack the hanging flake with vigour. Harder than it looks.

4 Balance 12m VS P1   ★
5a Start a few feet right of the previous climb. Mantelshelf precariously on to the smiling footledge. A crozzley orifice aids access to a stance above, from where the route swings out right to finish direct.

5 The Nose 12m VS P1
4c Right again, a crack starts about 3 metres off the ground. Climb up to this and ascend it until below an obvious jutting shelf (The Nose). Make an awkward move to stand on this (crux) and finish straight up.

6 Cave Crack 12m VS P1   ★★
4c The route of the crag, to the right of Balance. Climb easy rock into the cave and then exit awkwardly leftwards round the roof. Nicely old fashioned.

7 Cave Crack Alternative 12m VS P1   ★
5a This route climbs the blind flake into the left-hand side of the cave. Now pull up using the high finger crack and step right to finish up the wide crack.

8 Rock Bottom 12m E3 P2
5c Climb easily into the cave, then not so easily out of it over the roof, utilising a good undercling. Telescopic arms are useful. Rather strenuous and falling off the crux is not recommended.

9 Brown Dancer 12m E1 P2
5b An eliminate and contrived line just to the left of Hangman's Wall. Start below the right-hand side of the cave and climb the bulges and wall directly, making some awkward moves on dirty breaks. Wandering rightwards into the next route is not allowed.

10 Hangman's Wall 12m E1 P2   ★★
5b A gem of a route which climbs directly up the fine wall via several horizontal breaks. Start just left of the foot of the obvious chimney (Deer Gallows Chimney) below a short crack. Climb straight up to an insecure finish.

11 Deer Gallows Chimney 12m VD P1
Surprisingly pleasant if climbed on the outside.

12 Deer Gallows Wall 12m HVS P2   ★
5a Up the wall just right of the chimney, the crux being the attainment of a ledge just below the top. Similar in character to, but

easier than, Hangman's Wall.

13   Wreath 10m VS P1
4c Step off a boulder and string together two disjointed cracks right of Deer Gallows Wall. Above these make a thin move to reach easier ground. The stone basin at the top gives a stagnant finish to a rather contrived route.

14   The Skinner 40m VS P1
The inevitable girdle of the Main Wall, but worthwhile.
1. 20m 5a Climb the easy chimney at the left-hand end of the Main Wall and hand traverse the horizontal crack to a hard step into Fist Crack. Continue rightwards past Balance and swing around The Nose to belay in the cave.
2. 20m 4c Step down a little and traverse on jams across to the crack of Hangman's Wall. Step across the chimney on to Deer Gallows Wall and keep traversing right to finish up Wreath. A desperately-constricted traverse can be taken out of the cave (suitable for dwarfs only) to begin pitch 2, but this increases the standard dramatically.

The Pinnacle The easiest descent is by reversing Deer Gallows Original.

15   Deer Gallows Original 8m D P1
Situated on the east face of the pinnacle, an obvious rising traverse leads diagonally leftwards to a wide exit crack.

The **Rift Wall** of the Pinnacle gives the following routes.

16   Staircase Rib 9m VD P1
The left-hand rib. Climb easily up a series of small ledges until forced to step right. Move up and back left to finish up a short slab. A nice little route.

17   The Cringe 13m HVS P1
5b Climb up a wide crack to the through cave (possible belay). A rather unusual body position enables the short hanging crack above to be gained. Use this and anything else which comes to hand to get a footing on the flakes under the roof. Now quickly grab the top and congratulate yourself. A beckoning and strenuous route which cannot be denied. Harder for the short.

18   Pinnacle Wall Left-hand 10m S P2
Start in the middle of the wall below a shallow scoop. Climb past this then trend leftwards up a flaky crack to a tricky mantelshelf. Finish at a peeping boulder. An easier start is the wide crack to the left.

19 Pinnacle Wall Right-hand 9m S P1
Start as for the left-hand route, then climb directly past the two short cracks to the top.

20 Layman's Arete 9m D P1
Climbs the right-hand rib of pinnacle rift wall. Start up an inviting ferret-sized crack and then climb the arete on jugs.

Round the corner from Layman's Arete, on the wall facing Crookrise, is an easy-sloping gangway. Here is:-

21 Zig Zag 12m MVS P1
4b Go leftwards up the easy ramp to the first short crack. Climb this and zig awkwardly right to a small ledge. Move up and zag, even more awkwardly left, to another small ledge. Now straight up!

22 Nozeds 10m VS P2
5a From the top of the first crack the Zigs and Zags can be eliminated by climbing staight up.

23 Knows 10m HVS P1   ★
5b Climb the hanging crack right of Zig Zag (hard to reach) on to a comfortable ledge. Pull up using another short crack then swing strenuously rightwards on small flutes to finish direct.

Other problems, some very hard, can be worked out near Zig Zag and Deer Gallows Original, but most have unappealing landings. The extensive, easy-angled block on the downhill side of the Pinnacle provides several nice routes. On the side facing Crookrise is:-

24 Gallows Pole 8m VS P2
5a From the bottom right-hand corner, climb on to the block using poor holds and a long reach. Traverse leftwards to an obvious toe hole in the lichenous slab and then mantelshelf neatly to finish (or perform an ungainly belly roll).

25 Left-hand Route 12m VD P1
Start at the very toe of the buttress and move diagonally rightwards on big holds past a large pocket. Climb up and layback around the left side of the detached flake.

26 Right-hand Route 12m VD P1   ★
Another route with an inspiring name! This little beauty starts at the very pocketed wall some 6 metres right of the buttress toe. Climb the wall to the ledge and then move round the right side of the flake.

The two-tiered slab right of the last climbs is split at half height by a ledge. The following routes all give excellent climbing.

27 Slip 9m HVS P2   ★
5c Climb easily up to the ledge just right of Right-hand Route. The move on to the upper slab might take some working out. Once stood on the lip, smear up the left side of the slab to finish.

28 Slither 9m E1 P2   ★
6a Step on to the tongue of rock from the left and finish scarily via a slight runnel in the slab above

29 Slide 9m HVS P2   ★
5b Classic faith-and-friction climbing. Gain the right side of the upper slab via the protruding tongue of rock, approaching it from the right.

About 50 metres right of the main crag is a group of lichen-covered boulders which present a varied selection of problems. Further possibilities exist here but the enthusiast will need a wire brush.

DEER GALLOWS – GRADED LIST

E3
Rock Bottom (5c)

E1
Slither (6a)
Brown Dancer (5b)
Hangman's Wall (5b)

HVS
The Pocket (5c)
The Cringe (5b)
Slip (5c)
Slide (5b)
Deer Gallows Wall (5a)

DOVESTONE (Previously known as Ravens Peak)
N.G.R. SE 141554

SITUATION AND CHARACTER The crag is prominent on the north side of the A59 1½ miles west of Blubberhouses. The rock is generally clean cut but weathered and friable at the top and climbs tend to be strenuous. The open south easterly aspect gives superb views down the valley and with the added bonus of catching the sun for much of the day it is worth a visit, perhaps combined with a bouldering session at nearby Cat Crags.

APPROACHES AND ACCESS Cars can be parked on the hard shoulder at the top of the hill. Approach by walking along a level grass track, which leads off from the end of the roadside barrier and takes one direct to the top of the crag. **Dovestone is situated on private land and there is no official right of access to the crag. Permission to visit the crag must be obtained from Mr P. Walker, Bothams Farm, Telephone: 01943 880274.** This is invariably given provided shooting is not in progress, but dogs are not allowed.

THE CLIMBS The first two climbs are on the right hand side of lesser crag 150 metres up-stream of the main buttress.

1 Waltzing Matilda 7m VD P2
Start 4 metres from the right of the buttress below a small roof. Climb up to and over this on good holds to the terrace then up the right arete to the top.

2 Class Warrior 6m VD P1
Climb the right edge of the wall to the top.

Routes on the main buttress are described from left to right starting on the left wall.

3 Winter Wall 6m S P1
4a Climb the centre of the short wall left of a wide crack.

4 Summer Crack 6m HS P1
4b Climb the wide crack splitting the left wall of the buttress.

5 Rave On Wall 8m VS P1
4c Climb the wall right of the Summer Crack utilising a thin crack.

6 A Coin For A Beggar 8m E1 P2
6a Climb the left arete of the buttress on its left side. (a.k.a August Arete)

7 Frogging Wall 8m E2 P2
6b Takes the wall between the left arete of the buttress and Fog
Crack starting just left of Fog Crack. Gain a standing position in the
wide break with difficulty, rock over leftwards with even more
difficulty and finally jump to reach a good hold and easier climbing.

The centre of the lower front face is split by two vertical cracks, the
left crack is :-

8 The Fogger/Fog Crack 8m VS P1   ★
4c Climb the left hand crack.

9 Mist Crack/Autumn Fog 8m HVS P2
5c Climb the wall between the two vertical cracks using a rock
over, small holds and a blind pocket.

10 Autumn Crack 8m VS P1   ★
5a Climb the right hand crack.

To the right is an impressive face with a shallow corner on its right,
and the wall containing Autumn Crack forming a chimney on the
left. The next three routes start from the ledge at the top of the
chimney.

11 Ravens Peak Wall 16m VS P1
4b Start three metres left of the top of the chimney below a small
overhang. Step across the void and gain the ledge below the small
overhang. Hand traverse the ledge to reach a crack on the right,

move up and diagonally right to the top. Finishing straight over the roof at the top increases the grade to 4c, but is still not worthwhile. (Beware of loose blocks)

12   Faithful Wall   12m   HVS   P2   ★
5b Start at the top of the chimney. Once more into the breech or as it were across the void to make a difficult move up the thin crack and gain a good hold. Continue more easily up breaks and ledges to the top.

13   The Great Santini   12m   E4   P2   ★
6a A good route. Step over the gap as for Faithful Wall and traverse right into the centre of the face, climb the wall with difficulty on sloping holds.

14   Pellet Climb   15m   S   P1   ★★
4b To coin a phrase the 'classic of the crag', taking the rightward facing corner which bounds the right hand side of the main wall. Climb the corner and short wall above to reach the overhang. Move left and gain the top via another corner.

15   Eliminate B   12m   HVS   P1
5b Start on the pedestal at the bottom of Pellet Climb. Leave the ground with difficulty and climb directly up the wall on sharp flakes and flat holds.

16   Fingers   12m   VS   P1
4c Climb the crack right of the shallow corner to a wide break. Move more easily left and back right to finish on a ledge.

17   Eliminate A   10m   VS   P1
5a Climbs the right arete of the buttress on its left side. Utilising the arete surmount the undercut face and gain a standing position on the wall. Move up until level with the top of the crack of Fingers, step left onto the face proper and up to a horizontal break, an awkward move enables the top to be gained.

18   Finale   6m   S   P1
4a A short route up the right wall of the buttress.

19   Led Zeppelin   35m   HVS   P1
1. 5b Start up Summer Crack move right at three metres, continue round the arete and across the sloping ramp to reach Fog Crack, continue into Autumn Crack and up onto the ledge. Belay.
2. 4c Follow Ravens Peak Wall then traverse right to the hole on Faithful Wall and continue rightwards round the arete passing a natural thread into Pellet Climb. Descend a few feet and continue traversing to the right arete. Move round the corner to finish as for Finale.

EARL CRAG

SITUATION AND CHARACTER The crag is really prominent on the south-eastern skyline above the village of Cowling on the A6068 Colne-Keighley road and is easily recognised by the two monuments at either end. About a kilometre in length, the edge consists of a series of broken buttresses with a north-westerly aspect. At the far left end there is a dangerously loose quarry which until recently was generally avoided by those who valued their lives. The crag can be cold and unfriendly on dull days and is at its best on a late afternoon or summer's evening when it catches the sun. It is also an ideal bouldering venue. In winter the crag sees little sunlight but, due to its exposed position, tends to dry out relatively quickly with only sheltered sections and those prone to seepage going green. One or two esoteric gems are invariably vegetated and rarely climbed, they are included only for the sake of the historical record.

APPROACHES AND ACCESS Immediately on entering the village of Cowling from Crosshills turn left on a minor road to Oakworth which runs over the moor and passes below the crag. Limited parking exists at the quarry end of the crag where a footpath leads through the quarry and along the top of the edge. Alternatively, continue along the road to cross-roads and turn right (signposted to Colne). The road runs parallel to the crag and, after about 1 kilometre, there is a car park on the right. A footpath then takes you down to the monument at the right-hand end.
NOTE: Please do not approach across the fields below the crag as the farmer does not take kindly to this kind of activity.

THE CLIMBS The climbs are described from left to right starting from the quarried bay.

1 Sicca 7m E3 P3
6b A vague groove, the right-hand of two, and wall above it 10 metres to the left of the overhanging arete at the left end of the quarry.

2 Riddance 8m E4 P3 ★
6a The well brushed overhanging arete climbed boldly on its left side

Towards the left-hand end of the crag proper there is a large fiercely undercut hanging groove, (Mind Bomb) followed by a vegetated terrace complete with trees at 3 metres. The routes, and also a small area of good boulder problems, begin 25 metres left of this groove.

3 Pitch at Will 7m E1 P2 ★

5b The first real feature on the edge is a steep undercut arete. Start up a thin crack on the left and traverse right under the arete until a move up and left can be made. Make a long reach for the arete and climb to the top.

Just to the left of Pitch at Will up the centre of a smooth wall is the classic **Problem Wall** (6a), with a harder arete to its left. 7 metres right is a slab with a couple more hard problems.

4 Old Timothy 8m VS P1

4b The fern filled groove left of the fiercely undercut arete is not really recommended.

5 Tick Tock Man 7m VS P2

4c A poor and contrived traverse. From the top of Old Timothy hand traverse right across the top of Mind Bomb and Early Riser. Continue rightwards to finish.

The Pendulum Traverse is a low-level swinging hand traverse round the buttress right of Old Timothy. Strenuous but technically ungradeable.

6 Mind Bomb 8m E7 P3 ★

6c Gain and climb the hanging groove in the arete left of Early Riser. A Friend low down prevents a roll down the hillside but little else.

7 Early Riser 8m E5 P3 ★★

6a The obvious gangway on the wall left of the grassy terrace. A superb and technical bridging/smearing exercise. Low in the grade, but …Dare you make the last move? - And where will you land if you slip?

8 Rowan Tree Corner 9m D P1

The green chimney crack at the left-hand side of the terrace.

9 Pee Pod 7m VS P3

4c Bridge up the overhanging green groove a few feet right.

10 Jump to the Beat 8m E4 P3 ★

6b Climb the arete just left of Hatchet Crack starting from the grassy terrace.

11 Hatchet Crack 10m E3 P3

5c Climb the dirty, offwidth crack just right of the grassy terrace. A strenuous 'chop' route.

12 The Scent Of A Woman 12m E4 P3

5c Follow wafer like flakes to the right of Hatchet Crack to gain Fishladder then layback the reverse side of Kipper's arete.

13 Fishladder 10m E1 P2 ★
5b Just right of the upper part of Hatchet Crack is a slim gangway.
Start from the large ledge on the right and make a difficult step up
and round to gain the gangway - climbing up it is then much easier.

14 The Kipper 17m E4 P3 ★★
6a The bulge below Fishladder is climbed strenuously to the large
ledge (numerous variations). Now climb the fine arete above the
start of Fishladder on its right-hand side past a large hole near the
top.

15 Edge of Darkness 9m E4 P3 ★
6c Gain the crack to the right of The Kipper with great difficulty and
then move left to reach a large pocket just below the top. Use this
with imagination to gain easier ground.

N.Baker

16 Erasor Slab 10m HVS P1   ★★
5b A route with a reputation for stopping VS leaders (and the
short). Start at the right-hand side of the slab to the right of The
Kipper and climb to the break. Move 3 metres left to below a good
hold. Make a long reach for this to finish on the large ledge. When
combined with Fishladder it gives a superb, and possibly 3 star
outing. A 5c variation start can be made from Kipper, moving right.

17 Erasor Slab Direct 8m E2 P2   ★
6a From the break climb straight up with an even longer reach near
the top.

18 The Twister 6m E3 P3
6a Traverse the wall right of Erasor Slab from left to right, with a
hard move to finish up the rib.

19 Problem Rib 7m E1 P3 ★
5b Take the arete above Erasor Slab, just left of a deep chimney. Good value.

20 White Wall 7m E2 P2
6b The wall just to the right of the deep chimney is climbed with hard on-off moves to obvious pockets and the break above.

21 Grey Wall 7m HS P3 ★
4c A difficult initial move up the wall just right of White Wall leads via good pockets to the break. An easier finish is made right along the break. A direct finish via slopers is 5b - and serious.

22 Mantelshelf Slab 7m HS P2 ★
4b About 7 metres right and below Grey Wall is a slab with several large pockets. Climb the slab first left then right to a break. Reach up to a good flat hold and mantelshelf for the top.

23 Run A Mock 7m E2
5b A bold left-hand finish to Mantelshelf Slab finishing up pockets and flakes.

Numerous boulder problems can be found in this area.

A few metres right, and at the same level as Erasor Slab, is a prominent undercut rib with a pedestal below its left wall.

24 Pedestal Wall 7m E2 P2 ★
6a Step off the pedestal and climb the wall above moving diagonally left to a small scoop below the top.

25 Pedestal Rib 8m HVS P3
4c From the top of the pedestal, climb right on pockets and traverse round the rib and straight up. Or, slightly easier, via a sloping ledge to the top.

26 Pedestal Rib Direct 9m HVS P3
5b Easier for the tall. The wall just right of Pedestal Rib is climbed with a long reach to a shallow hole just below the sloping ledge on the previous route. Finish up Pedestal Rib.

Three metres right, a pointed boulder projects over the top of the crag. A moderate chimney runs up its left-hand side.

27 Overhanging Wall 8m S P2 ★
A short fun route. Traverse from the right of the chimney over a perched block to make a long reach to jugs taking you over the bulge to finish up and to the left. Taken in reverse, starting up the rib is even better, but 4b.

N. Baker

28 Overhanging Wall Direct Finish 8m E4 P3
6a Where overhanging Wall moves left go straight up pulling round the pointed boulder. Previously HVS 5b - another classic Yorkshire Sandbag!

29 Awkward Crack 8m S P1
4b The thin, dirty, corner crack to the right. The awkward start can be avoided up the wall to the right but the grade's the same.

30 Cave Traverse 12m HVS P3   ★
5a Start between Awkward Crack and Cave Wall at a shallow groove. Make a hard move up the groove to gain the traverse line and follow this right just above the cave to the arete. Finish up the left side of the arete.

31 Cave Wall 10m MVS P2
4b Start at the back of the shallow cave and swing out left on good holds on to the main face. Gain the traverse line and finish 1 metre right of Awkward Crack. Good, but the finish can be dirty.

32 Cave Direct 8m VS P2
5a Climb the centre of the face, above the traverse line via a good pocket.

33 Deep Chimney 10m D P1
The chimney just right of the cave. This can also be gained starting in the cave and moving right at about MVS.

34 Little Greeny 10m E2 P2   ★★
5c Climb the wall just right of Deep Chimney using the obvious poor pocket on the difficult upper section. Good climbing but quite serious.

N. Baker

Just right are twin cracks both about V Diff. and the wall just right offers a couple of short harder problems. Across the gully on the right there is an overhanging nose of rock known as **The Indicator**.

35 Flake Crack 10m VS P1   ★
5a The overhanging crack left of The Indicator is climbed strenuously on good jams to easier ground.

36 Indicator Crack 10m S P2
4a The crack on the right of The Indicator can be climbed from the cave, by a traverse in from the right or direct up the nose. Good fun!

37 Lower Indicator 10m MVS P2
4b The prow of rock below The Indicator is climbed to the ledge. Finish up the wall just right of the crack.

There is a moderate chimney to the right and then:-.

38 Cosmic Baby 10m E1 P2
5b Climb the undercut rib left of Time To Go gaining the flat hold above the nose direct, or from the right. Continue straight up with a delicate move near the top. The edge of the chimney is out of bounds.

39 Time To Go 10m HVS P2   ★
5a Five metres right of the last route is an overhung corner with a large chockstone at two-thirds height. Climb the bulging wall just left of the corner.

Above and to the right of routes 21 to 34 and at the same level as Grey Wall are many superb boulder problems. On the lower tier broken rocks intervene for 10 metres with one or two boulder problems until a fine slab is reached.

40 Slab Corner 8m VD P2   ★
A well-polished route up the right-hand edge of the slab which offers
good climbing.

There are more short problems to the right until, after about 80
metres a boundary wall with a stile runs across the edge. Halfway
between the wall and the last route are two large blocks.

41 Block and Chimney 8m VD P2
Climb the left-hand corner of the lower block to an overhung ledge.
Move right and finish up the chimney splitting the upper block. A
direct start (4b) can be made up the wall below the chimney.

The next routes are situated to the right of the boundary wall. The next
obvious feature is a steep corner crack with an arete on either side.

42 The Ribber 8m E3 P3
6a Climb the wall left of Green Rib using the small cleaned holds.

43   Green Rib   9m   E1   P2   ★
5c   The arete to the left of the corner. Technically very interesting - some think 6a!

44   Green Rib Right-hand   10m   E2   P3
6b   An even harder problem start. Gain the arete by traversing in from the right.

45   Butterfly Crack   12m   VS   P1
4c   Climb the dirty, offwidth corner crack using layaways and jams. Good, but strenuous.

46   Butterfly Wall   9m   E2   P3
6b   Climb the wall right of Butterfly Crack using the old bolt holes. Finger-ripping stuff.

The next feature is a route with many variations which are constantly being claimed, and re-claimed, as new routes. In an attempt to avoid further correspondence the four most popular are described below. If you believe you've found another way check with Dennis Gray - he's sure to have seen the Bradford Lads do it 50 years ago! Each variant is probably P2 or 3, somewhere around VS (depending who you believe), between 4b and 5a and around 2 stars - sort 'em out for yourselves - I'm totally confused!

47   Shothole Ridge (Left)
Climb Butterfly Crack until a finger traverse can be made to the arete. Move round this and up via a large ledge.

Shothole Ridge (The Rib)
Go straight up the rib from the left end of the platform via three slanting ledges.

Shothole Ridge (Original?)   ★
From the right edge of the platform gain the slab and move delicately left towards the corner. Step round onto the rib and finish straight up as before.

Shothole Ridge (Straight Shot)
Start as for Shothole Ridge, (the original I think) but climb straight through the scoop and roof above.

48   Mantel Maniac   9m   E3   P2
6b   The wall to the right of Shothole Ridge. Gain the horizontal break and make a mantelshelf off the break for the top. Or traverse the break right and climb the wall further right at about 6a.

49   Blade   9m   VS   P2
5a   Just right of the last route is an obvious jutting prow of rock. Start on the right and finish up the prow.

50 Little Demon 6m MS P2
The well scratched slab a few metres right of the prow has 3
variants: the left arete is 4c; manteling up from the right and then
the right edge is 4b; with the mantel and directly up the centre being
totally dependent on your height! Not bad for Mild Severe ?

About 70 metres further right is another block with an obvious V-
cleft in it above a cave.

51 Cave Crack 6m MS P2
Enter the obvious V cleft by an awkward move from the left. Go up
on the left to finish with difficulty. A jug on the arete may help. A
direct start is a little more strenuous.

52 A Stretcher Case 9m E1 P2
5c From the direct start to Cave Crack move up to a good break
using the right arete and two eyes on the face. Move left along the
break and make both strenuous and delicate moves up the arete to
gain adequate holds and a rounded finish.

53 YAB Chimney 10m VD P1
The chimney splitting the next block. Dirty!

Further right is the impressive Main Buttress but just to its left is -
Little Buttress.

54 Trifle 8m HVS P2
5b The shallow groove and crack in the buttress 6 metres left of
Little Buttress.

55 Little Buttress 10m D P1
Start on the left of the small buttress and move up and rightwards
over ledges.

56 Moonlight Saunter 7m HVS P2
5b Delicate bridging up the obvious shallow groove just right of the
start of Little Buttress quickly leads to an easy finish.

MAIN BUTTRESS AREA
This fine buttress is the largest and most impressive on the edge
and has some of the best routes in the area. The first two start on
the left wall.

57 Distant Early Warning 18m E6 P2   ★
6c Very thin climbing up the hairline cracks left of Desert Island
Arete. An excellent line up a long standing problem. Gear is very
limited although lesser mortals may find more on abseil.

58 Abstract Attitude 18m E5 P2   ★★
6b The shallow groove in the wall left of Desert Island Arete is

gained by breaking right from the start of Distant Early Warning via a slot and pocket. Hard moves up and then right gain the first break before the situation eases near the top.

59 Desert Island Arete 20m E6 P2 ★★★
6c A magnificent climb up the left arete and wall of the Main Buttress. Gain the first break by a very technical problem start. Move up to the next break and climb the front of the buttress direct a metre or so right of the arete. The second crux, high up, is well above the gear - be prepared to fly.

60 Viscount's Route 18m HVS P1 ★★
A gritstone classic which attacks the front of the Main Buttress via the obvious hanging crack.
1. 9m 5b The hanging crack is strenuous and reached either direct or by a hand traverse from the right.
2. 9m 4c From the ledge continue up the corner crack to a rounded finish.

61 Perch Wall 20m HVS P3 ★★
5b Start as for Viscount's route, but traverse right from below the

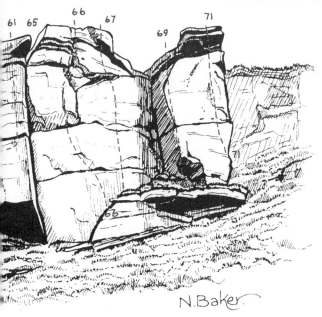

N. Baker

hanging crack along the break and out into a very exposed position on the right arete. A few awkward and poorly-protected moves up the wall left of the arete lead to the ledge. Easy climbing to the top. Fine value.

62 Valentine's Frog 18m E1 P2
5b From the second pitch of Viscount's Route traverse the upper section of the buttress leftwards to the arete and finish up this.

63 Flight 17m E1 P2
5b Climbs the wall and overhanging groove right of the start of Perch Wall. Follow Perch Wall until below the groove. Climb the groove to finish up Perch Wall.

64 Liz's Wall 9m E3 P2
6b Climb the centre of the wall left of Earl Crack, starting up that route. The technical grade reduces the later you leave the corner.

65 Earl Crack 17m VS P1   ★★★
4c Another classic. The compelling corner crack to the right of Viscount's Route.

66   Earl Buttress   16m   E2   P1   ★★★
5b   Very fine climbing up the thin cracks and bulges in the centre of the wall right of Earl Crack. Sustained and quite strenuous but without a discernible technical crux.

67   Captain Gap   9m   E2   P3
6a   The blank-looking wall 3 metres right of Earl Buttress. A long reach may be useful.

68   Main Buttress Girdle   28m   VS   P2
4c   Starts at the left side of the buttress and follows the obvious half-height break to the ledge of Viscount's Route (VD so far). Go right through a hole to Earl Crack, descend 9 metres and hand traverse to finish on grassy ledges.

Just right is a large buttress with a smooth front face with an undercut arete on its left side.

69   Evasion   9m   HVS   P2   ★
5a   Climb the left arete, with difficulty at the start, using the shallow vertical flake as a layback hold. An easier start can be made by traversing in from the left.

70   Stall   10m   E3   P3
6a   Climb the centre of the wall between Evasion and Trite Rib by traversing in from the left along the break.

71   Trite Rib   10m   E3   P3   ★★
5c   Poorly-protected but excellent climbing up the right-hand arete of the buttress. Start just right of the arete and swing left on to the front. Climb a shallow groove to a good hold and finish more easily. A direct start can be made at 6c.

72   Alien's Stole My Bolt Kit   12m   E5   P3
6b   Climb the wall right of Trite Rib, starting at the same point.

73   Chockstone Crack   7m   S   P1   ★
4a   The obvious crack right and above the last route.

Right again is a great prow of rock, Prow Buttress. Between this and the last route are a few short climbs and problems.

74   Prow Chimney   7m   D   P1
A pleasant route up the chimney at the left end of the prow.

75   Prow Buttress   14m   MS   P2   ★
Start in the centre of the buttress right of Prow Chimney. Ascend slabs until it is possible to traverse left to the rib of the chimney. Finish up this, trending right towards the top. A direct start can be made at a similar grade.

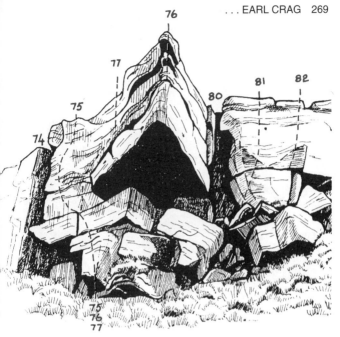

76 Tiger Wall 14m MVS P2   ★★★
4b A superb little route finishing up the arete of the prow. Follow
Prow Buttress until a few hard moves enable a traverse right to the
arete. Finish up this in a fine exposed situation. A variant (VS 4b)
stepping up and traversing higher is no harder but less protected.

77 Jock Jones 10m VS P3   ★
4c Follow Tiger Wall to the start of the traverse but then step up
and climb direct to the top on good holds.

78 Tiger Traverse, Routes 1 and 2
7m VS P2 and HVS P3   ★★
The right wall of the prow has two horizontal breaks which can be
traversed from right to left. The upper is VS (4c) and the lower is
HVS (5a). They are both good, though poorly protected, and finish
up the arete of the prow.

79 The Prowler 7m HVS P3
5b A direct line up the wall of the Tiger Traverses. Start on the
lower traverse line until the middle of the buttress can be climbed.

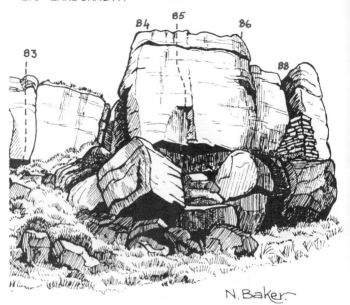

N. Baker

80 The Extinguisher 6m M P1
Climb the chimney on the right of the prow. Climbing the outside of
the chimney is better and Diff.

81 Mousehole Slab 8m VS P3   ★
4b From the foot of Extinguisher move right on to a ledge. Above is
the Mousehole – straight up the slab via this to finish.

82 Rat Juggling 8m E1 P3
5a From the right-hand end of the last ledge of Mousehole Slab
climb the blunt rib on poor holds.

Just right are a couple of problems, a sharp arete, a layback crack
and:–

83 Rat Au Vin 6m E1 P3   ★
6a Just to the left of the layback crack is a sharp arete. Climb this
with difficulty.

84 Sweet Apples 8m E4 P3   ★★
6b Climb the next arete just left of Sour Grapes. Very bold and
unprotected.

85 Sour Grapes 8m E3 P2   ★★
6a A wall runs up to the crag and just left of this is a niche and crack. Strenuously pull into the niche and reach for a poor hold at the top of the thin crack. Finish moving slightly left on small pockets. Hard for the short.

86 Boundary Wall 6m HVS P3
5b Now misnamed as the wall has been replaced with a fence (hence the up-grade). Gain and climb the wall directly above the fence. Don't fall off!

87 Grape Nut 6m E2 P2
6b Just right of the boundary fence is a chimney. Climb the left arete of the chimney by a leap from an adjacent boulder to a good hold.

88 Wall Chimney 6m D P1
The deep clean-cut chimney right of the boundary wall.

There are many good problems in this area and around the monument – aretes, walls and slabs of all grades which can provide hours of excellent bouldering. Just follow the chalk – and your nose.

89 Hand Traverse 6m VD P2
Follow the obvious upward-sloping break on the lower tier below the monument.

90 Cut Throat 6m E2 P2   ★
6b Towards the left-hand end of the Hand Traverse is a shallow groove (a good 5c problem in its own right), climb the slab to the left of this. Good value - some say Derbyshire E5!

91 Ledge Climb 7m HS P2
4a At the right-hand end of the lower tier is a large undercut square block with a ledge at 3 metres. Climb to the ledge from the right (or direct at 5a) and finish up the arete.

92 Solo Slab 11m VD P3
About 300 metres further right is a large slab. The right-hand arete gives a good little route.

EARL CRAG – GRADED LIST

E7
Mind Bomb (6c)

E6
Desert Island Arete (6c)
Distant Early Warning
(6c)

E5
Alien's Stole My Bolt Kit
(6b)
Abstract Attitude (6b)
Early Riser (6a)

E4
Edge of Darkness (6c)
Sweet Apples (6b)
Jump To The Beat (6b)
The Kipper (6a)
Riddance (6a)
The Scent Of A Woman
(5c)
Overhanging Wall Direct
(6a)

E3
Trite Rib Direct Start (6c)
Mantel Maniac (6b)
Sicca (6b)
Liz's Wall (6b)
Sour Grapes (6a)
Hatchet Crack (5c)
The Twister (6a)
The Ribber (6a)
Trite Rib (5c)
Stall (6a)

E2
Green Rib Right-hand
(6b)
Butterfly Wall (6b)
Cut Throat (6b)
White Wall (6b)
Pedestal Wall (6a)
Captain Gap (6a)
Grape Nut (6b)

Erasor Slab Direct (6a)
Little Greeny (5c)
Earl Buttress (5b)
Run A Mock (5b)

E1
Rat Au Vin (6a)
A Stretcher Case (5c)
Green Rib (5c)
Cosmic Baby (5b)
Flight (5b)
Problem Rib (5b)
Fishladder (5b)
Valentine's Frog (5b)
Pitch at Will (5b)
Rat Juggling (5a)

HVS
Perch Wall (5b)
Trifle (5b)
Moonlight Saunter (5b)
Pedestal Rib Direct (5b)
Boundary Wall (5b)
Erasor Slab (5b)
The Prowler (5b)
Viscount's Route (5b)
Flight (5a)
Evasion (5a)
Time to Go (5a)
Cave Traverse (5a)
Straight Shot (5a)
Tiger Traverse Rt. 2 (5a)

VS
Tick Tock Man
Flake Crack
Pee Pod
Blade
Cave Direct
Butterfly Crack
Earl Crack
Main Buttress Girdle
Jock Jones
Tiger Traverse Rt. 1
Pedestal Rib
Mousehole slab

MVS
Lower Indicator
Tiger Wall
Cave Wall

HS
Grey Wall
Ledge Climb
Mantelshelf Slab

S
Awkward Crack
Chockstone Crack
Indicator Crack
Overhanging Wall

MS
Little Demon
Prow Buttress
Cave Crack

VD
Hand Traverse
Slab Corner
YAB Chimney
Block & Chimney
Solo Slab

D
Rowan Tree Corner
Deep Chimney
Wall Chimney
Prow Chimney
The Extinguisher
Little Buttress

EASTBY CRAG

SITUATION AND CHARACTER Eastby Crag is the most southerly of the series of gritstone outcrops which encircle Embsay Moor. It is 3 miles to the north-east of Skipton, on the fellside above the village of Eastby. Its southerly aspect, combined with its lack of major drainage lines, means that it dries rapidly and enjoys the sunshine (if you get lucky!) for most of the day. The crag stretches for about 200 metres along the hillside and attains a height of 20 metres. It appears from the road to blend into the vegetation somewhat but it is much better than appearances suggest. Most of the climbing is on compact buttresses and steep, delicate slabs. For those who prefer something a little more thuggish there are sufficient steeper climbs on which to 'work out'. This is a particularly good winter crag when the absence of the bracken makes many of the easier slabs appear cleaner and more appealing than they are in mid-summer.

APPROACHES AND ACCESS When approaching by car the villages of Eastby and Embsay are well signposted off the A59 Skipton by-pass. From Embsay follow the road signposted Barden Towers and Pateley Bridge until just beyond the village of Eastby the road climbs steeply and parking is available for 4-5 cars just before the S bend. (Don't block the big lay-by however as this is used as a turning point for the local bus). For those using public transport Skipton has good links with nearby conurbations with a regular bus service to nearby Embsay. Approach the crag through the gate with the estate notice 'No Climbing Without Permission'. **Access difficulties do occasionally recur here. The crag lies on the Bolton Abbey Estate, but outside the access area and permission to climb should be obtained from the Estate Office at Bolton Abbey 01756 710227. Dogs are not permitted and you are very much in full view of the agricultural tenant who works the land below. Please close all gates, leave no litter, be respectful and help keep relations cordial.**

THE CLIMBS are described from left to right and for ease of identification, and in order to provide sensible consistency, some of the starts have been interchanged or descriptions amended from those described in previous guides. Eastby Buttress, the slim 20-metre-high continuous prow containing the classic Pillar Front towards the left-hand side of the crag is the most obvious feature. On approaching this feature up the hillside a couple of subsidiary blocks below the general level of the edge are the first to be encountered. The right-hand and lowest offers a couple of short solo warm-ups.

1 Aperitif Right 6m VD P2
Start at the lowest point of slab and climb the blunt rib trending right then straight up.

2 Aperitif Left 6m S P2
Climb flakes up the left-hand side of the blunt rib.

To the left is a steep 5 metre pebbly slab offering several problems. The most central, and hardest, with a fall potential twice its actual length is **A Pair Of Teeth** (6a)★, possibly worth E3 on sight.

Moving up to the level of the main edge the first real route can be located high up by reference to twin trees growing out of the slabs about 15 metres up the crag. The start is best gained by scrambling up rightwards between two 2 large hollies.

3 Blue Max 13m HVS P2
5a From a groove below the twin trees step right and climb a short steep slab to gain a ledge just right of the right-hand tree (an oak). Surmount an overhang above the oak (crux) and continue more easily to the top of the pinnacle. If the overhang is taken on the left the grade is reduced to severe.

There are some short easy angled slabs to the left but the next named routes are described with reference to a small oak on the path thirty metres left of Eastby Buttress.

4 Mr Grumpy 10m HS P2
4b Start 2 metres left of the oak at an undercut slab. Pull over the bulge from the left and move right to climb the arete until it is possible to step across right to finish up a short steep wall. A direct start over the nose is 5a.

5 After Hours 10m D P2   ★
Start behind the oak. Pull onto the slab and up to a small overhang. Pull over and climb the pleasant arete on the right. The subsidiary arete to the left is a V.Diff variant. At the top traverse 20 metres right to reach the descent path.

6 Opening Time 10m D P1
Start at the lowest point of the slabs 5 metres left of the descent path and climb up to the small overlap. Pull over and continue up the steepening pocketed slab.

7 Jaywalk 7m MVS P3   ★
4b An entertaining left to right, diagonal traverse of the undercut,

upper slab above the descent path. An excellent continuation to Mr Grumpy.

8 Last Orders 14m VS P2
4c Start just left of the base of the descent path. Climb the slab for 5 metres to a ledge and step across right to a pocketed slab. Climb this (unprotected but not too hard) to a ledge below the bulge. Arrange small wires then pull through onto the upper slab and climb direct to the top.

The next three routes start just to the left of Eastby Buttress providing slab and groove pitches much better than their appearances suggest.

9 Mantelshelves 18m HVD P3
Start at the lowest part of the slabs, just to the left of a short corner capped by a small overhang. After the initial steep bulge easy-angled, though sparsely protected, slabs lead up just left of a vague rib to a ledge. Step right and 'mantel' into the scoop in the upper slab.

10 Heather Flake 21m MVS P2   ★
4c A series of old variants linked to create a fine direct line. Two short corners form alternate starts to the next climb but the hanging nose between them provides an interesting preamble to this line. Difficulties soon ease but delightful slab climbing follows the easiest line up clean rock a metre or so left of Eastby Groove to a ledge near the top. Step across right and climb the sharp edged flake in fine position to magnificent finishing holds.

11 Eastby Groove 20m S P1
This is the wide groove separating Eastby Buttress from the easy-angled slabs on its left. Climb the first corner, move right and then the groove direct passing a niche at half height. Holds and protection often hide shyly under the vegetation.

12 Swastika 35m HVS P2   ★★
A diagonal traverse across the main buttress. The quality of the climbing and magnificent situations more than compensate for the lack of a clearly defined line.
1. 16m 5b Climb the second corner and follow Eastby Groove to the halfway niche. Arrange protection and step down right with difficulty onto the slab. Traverse the gangway of Pillar Front, crossing Pillar Rib, to belay on Eastby Buttress.
2. 19m 5a Traverse right as for The Padder and continue traversing above the large overhang to gain Whaup Edge. Follow this to the top. A slightly easier version traverses the higher break at 4c.

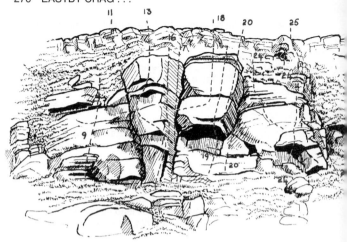

13 Pillar Front   20m   E2   P3   ★★★
5b   A magnificent route up the front of the imposing buttress. Not
technically high in the grade, but bold and quite reachy. Start
directly below the centre of the Buttress at the lowest point and
make rather problematic moves up the blunt rib. Climb to the
overlap where an awkward step up gains the main slab above.
Head confidently leftwards up a shallow gangway to a small ledge
on the left arete. Stay calm and make a bold step up right to a
better ledge below a bulging roof (devious thread or large Friends).
Go through the break to the upper ledge and move right then back
left onto the fine finishing slab.

14   Blinkered Variation   18m   E3   P3   ★
5c   A bold superdirect version of Pillar Front climbing the wall
directly between the first and second overhangs. As the name
suggests total independence from Pillar Front is difficult to maintain.

15   Mistaken Identity   E1   P2   ★
5b   A slightly harder, though artificial, variation on the next route,
Pillar Rib, is to climb it entirely on its left-hand side.

16   Pillar Rib   20m   VS   P1   ★★★
4c   Another fine climb. Start just right of Pillar Front and gain the top
of the first block more easily Step over the bulge on the right with
difficulty and continue up the rib mainly on its right-hand side,
finishing leftwards up the last few moves of Pillar Front.

N. Baker

17 Eastby Buttress 20m VD P1   ★★★
One of the best V.Diffs in Yorkshire providing excellent climbing up the wall and cracks to the right of Pillar Rib. Ascend slabs beneath the left side of the very undercut Padder Slab. Step left on to the wall and ascend a series of wrist-locking jamming cracks to the top. An alternative finish can be made directly up the crack between the normal route and The Padder (VS 4c).

18 The Padder 18m E1 P2   ★★
5b Climb the first 10 metres of Eastby Buttress until it is possible to traverse rightwards above the large overhang. Climb the centre of the slab via a 'friendly' pocket and welcome runners in the horizontal break. Pad up the slab via a shallow groove finishing between the two blocks above. A direct start over the left edge of the roof is possible, but only for those not 'vertically challenged' (6a).

19 Action Traction 18m E4 P3
6a Start under the right hand side of the large overhang. Pull through the roof using a small pocket and/or a very long reach to flat holds and a committing crux mantle. Continue directly up the delicate and poorly-protected slab between The Padder and Whaup Edge.

20 Whaup Edge 18m VS P2   ★★
4b An old classic. Climb up to the right of the overhang and step left above it to reach the rib. Continue boldly up this to the top. The difficulties, which are never technically excessive, gradually diminish with height.

21 The Mason's Arms 18m E1 P3
5b A rather blinkered variant on Whaup Edge. Instead of stepping
left climb the right-hand face of the edge using pebbles and the rib,
finishing over the top block.

22 The Cavendish 18m VS P2
4c Start as for Whaup Edge/Waterfall Chimney until 2 metres past
the move left of Whaup Edge. Climb the shallow groove on the left
to the break, step right and climb the prominent crack, finish direct,
or, probably better, move left to finish as the previous route.

23 Waterfall Chimney 18m D P1
Really only of any interest to dedicated botanists. Ascend the
vegetated corner to the right of Whaup Edge. Great care must be
taken not to fall down any of the rabbit holes.

To the right of Waterfall Chimney is a clean concave slab and below
and slightly right of this is a short wall topped by a small roof.

24 The Struggler 12m VS P1
5a The short initial wall leads to a crack in the roof formed by a
perched block. Climb the crack with ease or a struggle dependent
on your arm strength. (If you fail a HS cop-out leads right below the
roof). Wander off easily above, or take one of several variants up
the concave slab above and left;
● **The Chipper** (S 4b P3) The desecrated scoop left of the faint
overlap leads to a ledge below a bulging wall. Traverse right across
the top of the slab to easy ground.
● **The Direct Finish** (E3 5c P3) Follows the faint overlap up and
leftwards with a delicate move to reach the horizontal break. Step
slightly left and climb the short bulging wall above on large pebbles.
● **Crossing The Line** (E3 5c P2) Don blinkers and tip-toe up the
right hand side of the slab without recourse to the right arete. A
small Friend in a pocket near the start should ensure survival.
● **The Logical Finish** (VS 4c P2) The right edge of the slab
provides the most sensible finish to the parent route.

25 Broken Arete 30m M P1
Although artificial, a good introductory route for beginners. It
ascends a series of ribs and slabs separated by grassy ledges 3
metres to the right of The Struggler. Finish at the highest point of
the crag just below a dry-stone wall.

To the right of Broken Arete is a bay containing a bulging wall
beneath a large roof and a couple of short but worthwhile problems.
Impetus (5b)★ Climb the right arete of the steep wall on the left-hand
side of the bay via a series of ledges. **Aretus** (5c)★ Follow the more
serious curving arete of the slab on the right-hand side of the bay.

Right again, and at a slightly lower level, is a smooth slab below a large block split by a boot-width crack. This is **Knuckle Slab**.

26   Scoop and Crack   12m   S   P1   ★
4a   Climb the short groove left of Knuckle Slab to just beneath the roof. Step right to climb the boot-width crack to finish at a small birch tree.

27   Knuckle Slab Arete   12m   HVS   P2   ★
5b   Gain the arete right of Scoop and Crack by crossing the left wall, laybacking the edge and moving round to finish as for Knuckle Slab. A 6a direct start via a small pocket above the overlap giving access to the arete for the left hand is called **Knees Up Mother Brown. -** You'll see why when you try it.

28   Index Variation   10m   VS   P2   ★★
5a   Start just right of the direct start where the overlap narrows and climb the centre of the slab, crossing the traverse line of Knuckle Slab, to a shallow groove. Bridge delicately up this finishing up a short slab on the right.

29   Knuckle Slab   12m   VS   P2   ★
4c   Start at the right-hand side of the slab and either hand or foot traverse the horizontal crack above the overhang to a shelf on the left arete. Move up boldly to below the roof. Step left and finish up the slab above or better up the big crack.

30   Birch Tree Crack   25m   VD   P1
A poor climb starting up the crack on the right-hand side of Knuckle Slab to a small ledge. Continue up the curving crack to the right of the steep head wall to a large terrace and thread belay. Finish up the short ridge above.

31   Early Doors   9m   MS   P2
Start 1 metre right of Birch Tree Crack. Climb the slab direct to a thin finish (common with Index Variation)

Across a narrow gully is the prominent **Nose buttress**.

32   Lobe   9m   HVS   P3
5b   Start half way up the gully on the left-hand side of the buttress. Confidently ascend the blunt rib past rounded ledges and a scoop to the top. Bold, but not as hard as it looks.

33   Thumper Direct   15m   E5   P3
6a   Bolder and harder than the original but with little in terms of quality to justify the extra danger. From the start of the horizontal traverse climb the obvious thin vertical seam via pockets then swing right to attain a standing point on the slab under the small triangular overhang. Finish up and left.

34 Thumper 15m E4 P3   ★★★
5c A bold but excellent climb. Traverse rightwards as for Nose
Climb until a prominent slot (2¹/₂ Friend) marks the line up the wall
to a pull up on to a shallow pocket in the steep slab. Rock over right
and then step precariously back left. The final moves are slightly
easier but the lack of protection maintains excitement to the top.

35 Nose Climb 15m S P2   ★★★
4a A good one to 'pick'. Start at the left side of the buttress.
Traverse the obvious horizontal breaks to the arete. Up the small
slab to attain a short jamming crack and hence the top.

36 Nose Climb Original 11m S P2   ★
4a Good value. Climb the steep right-hand wall of the buttress on
small ledges to reach the arete. A short traverse left allows a pull on
to the arete. Finish up this and the jamming crack above.

37 Rock and Roll 10m HVS P2
5a Climb the wall to the right of Nose Climb Original then move left,
crossing the slab, to climb the upper slab just left of the crack.

38 Recess Crack 9m MS P1
Climb the horrid wide crack formed by an arrowhead-shaped slab
and the 'nose' buttress.

39 Lucy 8m E1 P2
5b The Arrow-head shaped slab just right of Recess Crack is
climbed direct without recourse to the edges of the slab. Touching
either arete reduces the grade to 5a.

For the next 25 metres the crag becomes a jumble of large
overhanging blocks and small buttresses containing a few short
problems which, unfortunately, are very vegetated. To the right of
this broken ground is an easy-angled slab below two very large
perched blocks.

40 Mist Slab 20m MVS P2
4b Climb a short crack formed by a block at the foot of the slab.
Follow the left-hand arete until stopped by an overhang. Make an
awkward step left and then traverse delicately rightwards above the
lip of the roof. Finish up the right arete. Good climbing but an
unsatisfactory line.

41 Mist Slab Direct 20m HVS P2   ★
5b A better line with a definite crux. Pull through the overhang
using a short flake on to the upper slab. Finish up the arete.

42 Slab and Chimney 20m VD P1
Start below the centre of the slab at a short wall. Surmount the block

using a short crack (strenuous) and climb the centre of the slab to the wide chimney. Climb the chimney until it is possible to break out rightwards on to the short slab up which the climb finishes.

43 Cheshire Cat 7m E4 P3   ★
6b Attacks the large roof right of Mist Slab. A long reach and prehensile tail would appear to be useful assets for the short struggle. Start at the top of the easy-angled slab at the foot of the wide chimney. Hand traverse the lip of the roof rightwards to attain an obvious flake which is used to gain the slab above. Protection is rather imaginary (best to arrange for your second to catch you).

Immediately right of Mist Slab is **Block Buttress**, a large block with an undercut base and short crack splitting its right-hand arete. The left-hand arete has been cleaned but still awaits a 'clean' ascent.

44 Genuflex 8m E3 P2   ★
6a Start at the obvious large undercut 2 metres left of the crack in the right arete. Climb directly up the front via the horizontal break. Initially thuggish, then delicate; a good little eliminate.

45 Hangs 10m E4 P3   ★
6a Start up the crack in the right arete to the small ledge. Climb leftwards and move up with increasing difficulty to reach the rounded upper left edge of the buttress which is followed to the top.

46 Block Buttress 8m HVS P1   ★
5a Short but fierce. Start at the right-hand arete. Climb a short hanging crack strenuously to gain a small ledge and continue more easily up the right edge.

47 Thrutch 9m S P2
A dirty chimney immediately right of Block Buttress. Move left at the top and finish up Block Buttress. Not recommended.

48 The Hatchback Forager 6m HVS P2
5a The centre of the narrow pinnacle via a short groove with a long reach to a small ledge.

Below and right is a short slab with an undercut left arete.

49 Pullover 9m VS P2
4c A hard pull directly through the small overhang on to the centre of the slab and then straight up.

50 Stepover 9m MVS P1
4b Step on to the edge of the slab from the right and follow this delicately to the top.

The next two climbs are on the small buttress with a dry-stone wall at its base.

51 Corner Crack 6m S P1
The steep overhanging crack in the corner 3 metres left of the stone wall.

52 Corner Groove 6m S P1
The shallow groove 2 metres left of the stone wall.

Above the last four routes two large blocks give problem finishes at about 5a with a Diff between the two. Directly beneath the dry-stone wall is a buttress with an obvious hanging crack on its right arete.

53 Easy Touch 6m E3 P3
5c The 'granular' rounded left arete is short but serious. The adjacent nose is out of bounds.

54 Defective Too Early 9m E4 P2   ★★
6b Start in the middle of the buttress. An awkward move enables a standing position to be attained in the horizontal break. Delicate moves rightwards allow the hanging crack to be gained. Continue up the rounded arete to the top.

55 Defective Direct 9m E4 P2   ★★
6b Start directly beneath the hanging crack and climb the arete to gain the hanging crack from the right. Finish up the right-hand arete.

Moving back up to the dry stone wall above Defective Buttress is:-

56 The Boldness Of Youth 8m E2 P3
5c A line just right of the dry stone wall. Start just over the wall and climb up generally just on the left of the slabby arete. Finish on good jugs.

Ten metres right of the dry stone wall is small steep buttress believed to be the home of the next route?

57 Accidental Baby 6m E1 P3
5c The green arete on the right side of the block might be easier after a good brush.

Thirty metres to the right of the stone wall is a small quarried section only included for the sake of completeness its 4 routes are overgrown and unappealing.

58 The Flake 10m S
Climb the wall below the obvious flake passing it on the left. Finish over the small bulge above.

59 Original Route 12m D
The obvious slanting groove containing a tree at 3 metres.

60 Waterfall's Crack 12m S
Start awkwardly up a wide shallow groove to gain the foot of the

fine crack on the arete. Climb this to the top.

61   Hollybush Groove   12m   S
The more distinct groove in the centre now contains a birch - the
holly is long gone.

Fifty metres right of the dry stone wall is fine and prominent
undercut arete. A lesser rib to its left is:-

62   Baby, Baby   5m   VD   P1
A clean and pleasant solo.

63   Dead Babies   7m   E5   P3   ★★
6b Start in a corner on the right and traverse in above the roof to
gain the rounded arete which is climbed on pockets and pebbles. A
direct start gains the pockets at 6c.

EASTBY CRAG – GRADED LIST

E5
Dead Babies (6b)
Thumper Direct (6a)

E4
Cheshire Cat (6b)
Defective Direct (6b)
Defective Too Early (6b)
Action Traction (6a)
Hangs (6a)
Thumper (5c)

E3
Genuflex (6a)
Blinkered Variation (5c)
A Pair Of Teeth (6a)
Struggler Direct Finish (5a)
Crossing The Line (5c)

E2
Easy Touch (5c)
Pillar Front (5b)
The Boldness Of Youth (5c)

E1
Accidental Baby (5c)
Mistaken Identity (5b)
The Mason's Arms (5b)
Padder (5b)
Lucy (5b)

HVS
Swastika (5b)
Mist Slab Direct (5b)
Block Buttress (5a)
Knuckle Slab Arete (5a)
The Lobe (5b)
The Hatchback Forager (5a)
Rock & Roll (5a)
The Blue Max (5a)

VS
The Struggler (5a)
Index Variation (5a)
Pillar Rib (4c)
Pullover (4c)
Knuckle Slab (4c)
The Cavendish (4c)
Last Orders (4c)
Heather Flake (4c)
Whaup Edge (4b)

MVS
Jaywalk (4b)
Stepover (4b)
Mist Slab (4b)

HS
Mr Grumpy (4b)

S
The Chipper
Scoop & Crack
Eastby Grooves
Corner Crack
Nose Climb
Nose Climb Original
Thrutch

MS
Early Doors

HVD
Mantelshelves

VD
Eastby Buttress
Slab & Chimney
After Hours Variant
Aperitif Left
Apéritif Right
Birch Tree Crack
Baby, Baby

D
Opening Time
After Hours
Waterfall Chimney
Broken Arete

EAVESTONE CRAG

SITUATION AND CHARACTER *"Ea'ston Beck murmurs through a charming woodland gorge, here branches curve gracefully forming cool and shady bowers. The woodland path passes through an immense rock of sandstone, split in two and some sixty feet height":* Edmund Bogg described the valley thus in 1870 in his book 'From Eden Vale to the Plains of York' Little has changed but some of the former woodland path is overgrown by rhododendrons.. This extensive crag offers a unique climbing experience in a 'land that time forgot' setting.

The crag has 18 separate buttresses all with distinctly different characteristics. The best time for a first visit is the Spring, just before the trees come into full leaf but many of the areas are climbable throughout the year. The Buttresses on the northern side of the lake get winter sunshine and several have short routes and fine bouldering. The Eavestone, Wedge and Tin Pan Alley offer the best of the longer hard routes but are rarely in condition in the shade of winter. For a first visit at any time try The Fort for a range of quality routes from Severe to E3. In the Spring and Summer The Eavestone and Wedge offer routes of a similar quality to those on the Cubic Block at Brimham.

The whole valley is a wildlife haven, sheltered from strong winds and in spring and summer all the rocks dry quickly. The vegetation is invasive in some areas but all the starred routes are relatively clean and should stay so given regular traffic.

The Mystery Buttress and The Little Sails are the least attractive and not recommended for a first visit.

APPROACHES AND ACCESS. The crags lie halfway between Pateley Bridge and Ripon; half a mile north of the B6265 from which Eavestone is signposted down a gated road. Follow the road to the farm and bear right. Park in a lay-by on the hill adjacent to the woods. Follow the signed footpath into the wood and downhill to the end of the upper lake. The Drawbridge and Fort buttresses can be seen at the waters edge. Prior to visiting the other buttresses a walk down the main path to below Little Sails is worthwhile in order to view and locate the Galleon towers and the Eavestone from across the lower lake. No access problems have been encountered but fishing and shooting syndicates do pay for their sport in these woods. It would be unwise to antagonise these groups by noisy or anti-social behaviour.

1. FORT BUTTRESS/CASTLE WALLS 2. LITTLE SAILS
3. WALL ON MIRRORED WATER 4. SUNNYSIDE BUTTRESS
AND THE GEMSTONES 5. BOATHOUSE BLUFF
6. THE CREVASSE AREA X. MYSTERY BUTTRESS
7. THE DRAWBRIDGE 8. KLOOF CRAG 9. JIB SAIL
10. GALLEON TOWER 11. THE EAVESTONE 12. THE WEDGE
13. THE PROW 14. ALLEY PALLEY WALL 15. TIN PAN ALLEY.

THE CLIMBS

THE FORT BUTTRESS

This is the first buttress seen after entering the wood from the lay-by, standing proud from the north side of the small upper lake. It is invariably clean and quick drying. The first climb is approached through the tunnel and from water level at the left side of the pinnacle (when looking from across the lake). Descent from the Fort is via an exciting tree bridge and a gully which leads back to the foot of Castellan.

1 Apache 9m E1 P2 1990 ★
5c Climb a flake on the left of the buttress and step right to gain a short crack on the front. Step up and left from this to gain the shelf on the arete before a final move right gains a precarious mantelshelf finish.

2 Wet Landing 10m S P1 1965
4b A poor climb, now superseded by Portcullis. Start at water level below the left arete and traverse right on crumbly rock to a crack which is climbed to reach the block filled chimney above. Up this to finish.

The next three climbs all start from the water level below the right arete of the buttress when viewed from across the lake.

3 Portcullis 16m S P1 1989 ★★
4a An expedition with a sea cliff atmosphere which wanders across the front face of the Fort. Start with a water-level traverse to reach a corner. Climb this to a ledge and traverse left (crux) to an optional belay at the foot of the chimney. Up the chimney until cracks on the right provide an exposed finish to the top.

4 Excalibur 17m E2 P2 1989 ★
5c As for the last climb, traverse left at water level but climb a flake just short of the corner. Traverse left from the break to reach the steep slanting crack and climb this to the top. Make a spectacular and difficult hand traverse back right to finish just left of the blunt arete. (The original finish avoided the hand traverse and simply stepped left into the chimney from the top of the flake, this is still worthwhile but only HVS 5a.)

5 The Alamo 14m E2 P1 1989 ★★★
5b Climb the easy crack line from water level to the break below the hanging crack in the bulge. Jam up this then step left and climb the right side of the slabby rib via a pocket to the top. A superb and photogenic climb which is invariably clean and quick to dry.

6 Oubliette 13m E2 P1 1967 ★★
5b Another good climb starting higher up the bank just left of the entrance to the tunnel. Climb the pocketed wall to below the roof and then move left round the corner to gain the short crack common with Alamo. Step up right from this to gain a series of short dislocated cracks which lead to the top.

7 Hallmark 11m E3 P2 1967 ★
5c The groove in the arete just left of the entrance to the tunnel provides a steep and demanding line.

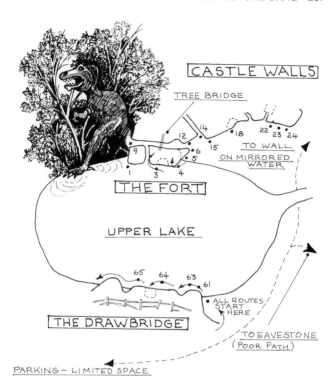

8 Rearguard 10m MVS P1 1990
4b Start in the centre of the tunnel and bridge up until ledges on the back of the pinnacle can be reached. Make an awkward move onto these to finish at the tree bridge.

Further through the tunnel a short chimney is passed it can be ascended at around V.Diff but is usually reserved for descent. The left arete on leaving the tunnel is:-

9 Scalp 6m HVS P2 1990
5c Climb the wall to a horizontal, swing right to the arete and finish up the crack to the block. Short, but interesting and worth seeking out.

The next climbs are on the edge behind the pinnacle starting at the end of the tunnel opposite Scalp. The first four are short and best treated as boulder problems. **Portal Rib** (5b) The rib opposite Scalp climbed via a scoop and bulge on its left. **Sangatte** (4b) The wall just left of Portal Rib. **See the Light** (5a) Climb the same rib keeping to the right. **French Connection** (4c) Climb a short wall just right of the rib to finish up a good jamming crack.

10 Whistling in the Dark 10m HS P1 1991
4b Start inside the tunnel, right of the jammed boulder, below the left-hand groove in the back wall. Climb the flake in the groove and a short steep crack. Traverse right and finish up the centre of the wall. It is possible to bridge across the cleft for much of this route and finish more directly on the left. Doing this reduces the grade to V.Diff.

11 The Keep 9m S P2 1965
4a A second shallow groove leads up the dark slabby wall from the centre of the tunnel. Take this, trending right on rather friable rock.

12 The Gatekeeper 8m E3 P3 1991   ★
6b The blunt rib with two small prominent flakes immediately right of the entrance to the tunnel is climbed direct.

13 For Keepsake 9m HVS P3 1990   ★
5b A slight but interesting climb with a bold crux. Start as for Gatekeeper at the foot of the rounded rib. Gain two small flakes and step right to a ledge then up the right arete with a long reach to finish.

To the right is the main descent gully and right of this begin:-

THE CASTLE WALLS

14 Castellan 9m VS P1 1971   ★
4c A prominent slanting crack line at the upper limit of its grade. Start just right of the gully and ascend the crack passing the overlap with difficulty.

15 Battlement 9m E3 P2 1990   ★★
6a The fine slabby rib is now climbed direct. Small flexible Friends on the left protect the crux - just.

16 The Dirty Rascal 10m E1 P2 1989
5c Climb to a hole in the centre of the slab and step up to the overlap. Move left and climb a short scoop just right of the blunt arete.

17 The King of the Castle 9m E2 P2 1989   ★★
5c A direct line up the centre of the slab past the hole with a thin pull on small holds to surmount the overlap.

18 Rampart 10m HVS P2 1989   ★
5b Start below the right rib of the slab and pull up awkwardly to gain a standing position, and a hold below the overlap. Trend right and swing round the rib on hidden holds to finish direct.

19 Ditch 8m HVS P2 1990
5c A technical scoop just right of the rib gives a direct start to the previous climb.

20 Casement Crack 8m VD P1 1990
The obvious off-width crack leading to a holly tree.

21 Dungeon 9m S P1 1989
4a In the recess is a dirty crack leading to a cave. Climb this and finish up the chimney.

22 Stockade 9m VS P1 1989
4c Utilising the right edge of the crack of Dungeon make a tricky start then climb pleasantly to the break, moving right to finish.

23 Merlon 8m E1 P1 1990   ★
6a A technical start via layaways on the wall about two metres right of the crack leads to the horizontal break and an easier, but still interesting, direct finish.

24 Crenellation 8m E1 P1 1989   ★
5c Climb the centre of the steep wall to the break and then make a long reach from an undercut to gain a good hold and a finish at a leftward pointing horizontal spike and blocks.

25 Machicolation 7m VS P1 1989
4c The overhanging rib is climbed trending rightwards with a long reach at the top.

26 Arrow Slit 6m HS P1 1989
4b The cracks to the right of the rib provide a slight but interesting finale to this section of the crag.

THE LITTLE SAILS

This buttress is the first encountered, high above the main path, on the north side of the lower lake. It is perhaps the least appealing of all the crags at Eavestone with some loose rock and unpleasant landings, however if you must:-

27 The Plunge 6m S P2 1997
Start at the extreme left end of the walls behind a holly tree. Mantel onto the first ledge and then, taking care with dubious rock make easier mantelshelf and bridging moves to the top.

28 Sea Dog 7m VS P2 1997
4c Start at the lowest part of the wall below a curving flake and make easy moves to a ledge. From here, follow the dangerously loose flake until fingery moves are required to overcome the top.

29 Upper Sail 7m VS P2 1989
5a Climb the upper wall from a small protruding flake direct to a bold and worrying finish.

30 Lower Sail 7m VS P2 1989
5a Climb past a sandy pocket in the lower wall, move left and finish direct. A traverse right is possible for the faint hearted.

31 Shiver Me Timbers 9m VS P2 1990
5a Start just left of the overhang of the prow, gain a ledge and continue up and left to reach a steep upper wall which is climbed by the right rib.

The remaining climbs are relatively short problems on the ribs to the right. **Cannon Fodder** (5c) Climbs the left rib of the overhanging prow; **Ready for Action** (5b) The overhang and right rib of the prow; **Armada** (5a) On the narrow buttress 5 metres right is a short sharp arete, climb this then the left wall; **Finish the Bowls** (5a) Climbs the steep front of the narrow buttress via a sharp crack to a bold direct finish.

WALL ON MIRRORED WATER

Fifty metres further on an excellent little buttress overhangs the path at the waters edge. It is only about 5 metres high and the lines generally treated as boulder problems however they are almost all strenuous with the crux's at or near the top!

Still Water (4b) The left arete.

Rough Water ★ (5c) The scoop just right of the arete leads to a step right onto the shelf and a precarious direct finish.

Reflections ★ (6a) Start immediately left of the right arete and continue via a tiny pocket and monster reach to gain the top edge. Step left to effect the pull over.

Thin Ice ★★ (5b) Climbs the right arete first on the left then the right with an awkward high step up left to finish.

Troubled Water ★ (5c) Climbs the wall immediately right of the rib to the finish of Thin Ice.

Canada Dry (6b) Just right of Troubled water is an overhanging scooped wall. Climb the right side of this from a layaway pocket.

WALL ON MIRRORED WATER

a. STILL WATER ~ 4b
b. ROUGH WATER ~ 5c
c OVER THE LOOKING GLASS ~ 6b
d. REFLECTIONS ~ 6a
e. THIN ICE ~ 5b
f. TROUBLED WATER ~ 5c
g. CANADA DRY ~ 6b
h. MIRKY WATER ~ 5a

Murky Water (5a) The sandy bulge to the right is climbed trending right with a long reach to gain the top break.

Over the Looking Glass ★★ (6b) The inevitable traverse from the 'eyes' in the bulge near the start of Rough Water to the finishing moves of Canada Dry.

SUNNYSIDE BUTTRESS

Forty metres right is a taller buttress higher up the slope. It contains a prominent flake and is topped by a large tree.

32 Sundown 6m D P1 1989   ★
The left arete and blocks above.

a. BAUBLE (5a) b. LITTLE GEM (6a)
c. TOO MUCH TOO YOUNG (6b) d. THE FLAW (5b)
e. FLAWLESS (5b) f. ROUGHCUT (5c)
g. LITTLE SPARKLER I (6a) h. PYRITES (4c)

SUNNYSIDE BUTTRESS

GEMSTONES

LAKESIDE PATH

← WALL ON MIRRORED WATER ~ 40 METRES

TO BOATHOUSE BLUFF →

33 Sundial 7m HVD P1 1989 ★
The scooped wall just right of the arete.

34 Sunstroke 7m VD P1 1989 ★
The V crack to a chimney finish.

35 Winter Sunshine 7m MVS P1 1989
4b Climb the blunt rib right of the V crack to a dirty ledge, finishing easily on the left or, for more fun, up right to the tree .

36 Sun-Up 8m VS P1 1989 ★★
4c The flake crack is climbed to the top and an awkward step left is then made to gain a ledge and a finish on the nose on the right to the tree. A direct finish from the flake is 5a.

37 Sun Bird 8m HVS P1 1989 ★
5b Climb the wall right of the flake and continue direct over two bulges to finish right of the tree, escaping right after the first bulge is easier but not allowed.

38 Sun Bingo 8m VD P1 1994
The right arete of Sunnyside Buttress. Start on the left, move right from the break and finish direct to the tree.

The next blocks to the right contain some immaculate boulder problems and are known as:-

THE GEMSTONES.

Bauble (5a) An insubstantial little trifle up the scoop in the left wall of the first block; **Little Gem** ★★★ (6a) The left arete of the first block provides the best problem at the crag, with the crux at the top!

Too Much Too Young ★ (6b) The wall between the arete and the wide crack; **The Flaw** ★ (5b) The obvious off-width crack, a must for connoisseurs. **Flawless** (5b) The right arete of first block, climbed on the right.

Rough Cut ★ (5c) Climb the front face of the right-hand block finishing up the left arete with a precarious slap; **Little Sparkler** ★★ (6a) The front face direct moving right from the flake to a difficult finish; **Pyrites** (5a) Not as good as it seems. The wall and scoop just right.

Beech Peach (5c) The isolated overhanging block about 60 metres further right is climbed at its highest point, just left of the beech tree growing from the side of the block, whilst **Oakey Kokey** (5b) is the shorter wall on the left below the oak tree.

Continuing on the northern bank of the lake the next landmark is a wooden boathouse, immediately above this, and almost hidden by trees in summer, is :-

BOATHOUSE BLUFF

Approached from the left the first feature is an undercut flake which doesn't quite reach the top, it provides:-

39 Strange Attractor 6m E3 P2 1990   ★★
6a Gaining the flake is not easy and leaving it to reach a high side-pull feels committing. The rounded finishing ledges are usually sufficient to finish on.

40 Pebbledash 9m E4 P3 1990   ★
6c A highly problematic start, one metre right of the flake involves a tendon ripping pull on pebbles before the horizontal is reached. Traverse right with less difficulty to make a precarious mantel onto the nose to finish.

41   Heave Ho   10m   E2   P2   1990
5c Start just left of the prow and stretch from the pocket for the handrail. Muscle off round the corner until it is possible to attain a standing position on the wall. Climb the centre of the wall direct, passing a 'friendly' pocket to a rounded finish. Strenuous.

42   Pushing the Boat Out   10m   E3   P2   1990
5c Climb the awkward wide crack for three metres and then traverse left past the 'friendly' pocket to reach the nose. A very precarious mantelshelf move gains the top.

43   Starboard Crack   6m   S   P1   1989
4b Climb the wide (usually bramble filled) crack on the right, if you really must.

A fight through the undergrowth to the right for a few metres reveals more clean and climbable rock known as:-

THE CREVASSE AREA

Check out the finishes before climbing here, the vegetated fringe needs regular trimming, but all the climbs are good. The first feature is a short corner known as Sharp Corner, more useful as a way down.

44   Good Friday   8m   E3   P2   1990   ★
5c Begin below a pocket and groove near the right arete, and gymnastically gain a standing position above the roof. Traverse left with difficulty to reach a pocket in the headwall from which it is possible to power up left to finish.

45   Leaving The Bergschrund   6m   HVS   P2   1989   ★
5c Start, with difficulty, as for the previous route but continue up the groove and over the bulge to an easier, slabby finish.

46   Glacier Apron   6m   VS   P2   1989   ★
5a A deep crevasse cuts into the crag and its left wall is smooth and steep. A difficult pull gains this wall at the left-hand end and then leads pleasantly up slabby breaks to the top.

47   Touching The Void   7m   E2   P2   1990   ★★
6a From a small pocket in the middle of the crevasse wall climb technically to reach the dimples at mid-height. (Tree runner, but hands off!). Make a couple of moves left then finish just right of another tree. Sustained and intricate climbing.

Right of the Crevasse is a large block known as The Serac The climbs are described from left to right and the first four all start from a short chimney left of the blunt central arete.

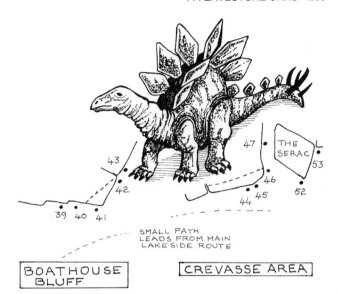

SMALL PATH
LEADS FROM MAIN
LAKE SIDE ROUTE

| BOATHOUSE BLUFF | | CREVASSE AREA |

48 Glissade 10m Diff P1 1991
Climb the chimney, move left along the ledge and around the rib to
a slabby finish. A finish right of the rib is 5a.

49 Ice Dance 7m HVS P2 1991
5b From the top of the chimney step left and climb the wall in line
with the left end of a small overhang, to a bold finish.

50 Cracked Ice 6m HVS P1 1991
5a The bulging crack moving right from above the chimney.

51 Iced Diamond 7m E1 P2 1991
5b Start up the crack but continue right to the arete.

52 Cream 7m E2 P2 1991   ★★
6a The blunt central arete is climbed direct from the prominent
pocket

53 Hanging Serac 6m E1 P2 1990   ★
5b The right arete is climbed via pockets and a shallow ramp on its
left to an awkward finish.

MYSTERY BUTTRESS

This buttress, although perhaps the largest at Eavestone, is the most rambling, overgrown, and least attractive. The area is best viewed and approached by crossing the dam at the foot of the lower lake and following a well marked path down the valley for about 150 metres to a viewpoint. A scramble down the bank, across the stream and up the other side will then bring you to the foot of your chosen route.

54 Narrow Slab 8m VD P1 1962
The cracked slab on the left of the buttress.

55 Mystery Man 12m VS P1 1988
5a Start below the chimney wide break in the top wall. Ascend direct slightly right of this break and then move awkwardly left to finish up the chimney.

56 Central Chimney 18m VD P1 1962
Start 5 metres left of the cave and climb rightwards to a chimney corner. Finish up this. A dirty route but not without its charms.

57 Tiptoe 20m VD P2 1962
Climb up to the right of the cave and overhang to bridge against a large detached block. Tiptoe left over some doubtful blocks, and continue left to gain and finish up Central Chimney.

58 Checkmate 12m HS P1 1965
4b The crack in the right wall.

To the left of Mystery Buttress on an indistinct path which leads through some boggy ground back towards the lower lake you will pass a small block with E8 chiselled on its right side.

59 Microchip 6m VS (4b) is the obvious and pleasant arete.

Mystery Buttress concludes the climbing on the Northern side of the lakes and for ease of location and description it is now best to return to the Upper Lake to begin the tour of the Southern banks. Although more shady this side provides a large number of climbs of quality and difficulty most of which are of greater stature than those on the sunny side.

THE DRAWBRIDGE

This is the closest crag to the lay-by. The top is approached easily by crossing the broken fence seen on the left on entering the woods from the car. Reaching the common start to all the climbs involves a steep scramble down well to the right, looking out. (See diagram on page 287).

60 Chainmail 7m VS P2 1990
4b The dirty left rib of the buttress passing a block to start.

61 Sea Of Tranquillity 8m HVS P1 1990
5b The first crack system on the left side of the buttress is gained from the right with the crux being reserved for a bulge at 6 metres

62 Dance On White Horses 9m E2 P2 1990 ★
5c The steep rippled wall above the bulge is climbed direct from a huge undercut. Strenuous moves lead to jugs on the protruding nose.

63 Ripples 9m HVS P2 1965 ★
5a Start with a difficult pull over the initial bulge as for the last route but once established step right to gain the crack which provides an easier finish.

64 Watery Grave 14m E3 P2 1965
5c An intimidating route taking the hanging crack above the niche in the centre of the crag. Start below the crack of Ripples and traverse right above the lake to a lonely position in the niche. Gaining the crack above is the crux and a finish out left concludes the climb.

65 Don't Pay The Ferryman 33m HVS P1 1990
A challenging low level traverse across the buttress from left to right. Start below Ripples.
1 18m 5a traverse right into the niche of Watery Grave and leave it at a low level to continue around a blunt rib to gain a corner and tree belay.
2 15m 5a Move right along higher ledges and then step down to a difficult low level finish onto the beach.

KLOOF CRAG

A subsidiary path leading from the bottom end of the upper lake down the right-hand side of the stream is followed for only a few metres before a small steep buttress can be seen on the right.

66 African Skies 6m S P1 1990
4a Climb the gully wall just left of the arete direct.

67 Mhlabatini 7m HVS P1 1990
5c Start below the bulging prow and use the undercut left arete to reach a hold. Climb the bulge direct (crux) and continue with slightly less difficulty to finish on the left.

68 Tonquani 8m VS P1 1990 ★
5b Start at the lowest point of the wall just right of the arete and surmount the difficult bulge. The upper wall is climbed direct on good holds.

69 Umkomeni   8m   MVS   P1   1990   ★
4c Start below an obvious letter-box slot and climb the wall direct
on widely spaced but positive breaks.

70 Sekorora   7m   HS   P1   1990
4b Gain a rectangular recess in the wall, climb past it and finish
adjacent to the rightward slanting ramp.

Following the stream for about 150 metres fallen trees block the
lakeside path. Trend up right to reach the first of two large towers,
this one is known as:-

JIB SAIL

71   Jib Sail   6m   D   P1   1989
This is the easiest route to the summit of the tower taking the short
back rib. Though it looks improbable from above it is also the
normal line of descent. It is easier than it looks.

72   Spinnaker   18m   S   P1   1989   ★★★
4a A superb climb in an exposed position. Start on the left side of
the wide undercut face of the tower and traverse right, round the
corner to a ledge above the overhangs. Make a long reach up and
step right to gain another ledge and a shallow corner which is
climbed on positive holds to the top.

73   Bowsprit   12m   VS   P1   1989   ★
5a Climbs the left arete from a start below the bulge. Pull up with
difficulty to gain the ledge of Spinnaker. Move up and left and follow
the edge as closely as possible.

74   Atlantic Voyager   13m   E2   P2   1990
5c Start from a shallow recess below the main overhang half way
along the face. Climb the bulges to the lip and pull up strenuously to
the left into the scoop and finish direct.

75   Yardarm   9m   VD   P1   1989
A diagonal line up the back of the tower from the foot of the descent
route.

THE GALLEON TOWER

The next tower is in two distinct tiers with an area of softer yellow
rock at mid height. Because of the recently fallen trees it is now
more usual to approach the right-hand side of the upper tier first,
descending to the lower tier via the steep earthy bank or by
crossing the central terrace to a cleaner descent on the other side.
The routes on the lower tier all offer worthwhile moves on sound

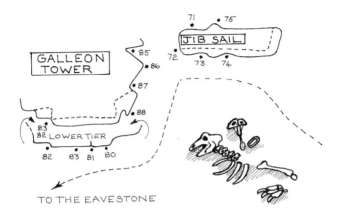

rock but unfortunately this buttress is not easy to keep clean and the vegetation is fighting back. The routes are described from right to left starting with two problems beginning from near the foot of the bank

Director (5a) The scooped wall just right of the right rib of the lower tier gives a slight but steep problem. **Savage** ★ (5c) Climb the right rib direct using a small finger flake and finish on the front face.

76 Brave New World 8m VS P2 1991   ★
4c Climb the short flake to a ledge and continue above moving right to finish.

77 The Pirates Ear 8m E1 P2 1991   ★
5b Climb the wall just right of the large chockstone to reach the 'ear' in the undercut wall above. Use this and a pocket to gain small holds and a bold direct finish.

78 Banana Boat 9m HVS P2 1991
5b Climb the blunt rib and scoop left of the easy groove and continue over ledges finishing up the rightward curving groove.

79 Long John Sliver 9m VS P2 1991
5a Climb the short problematic wall just left of the blunt rib at the base of the buttress to wide ledges. Move up and right from the top ledge to good finishing holds.

80 Jolly Roger 13m VS P2 1990
4b From the lowest point of the buttress a rounded ramp system diagonally right and then back left provides the line and some

awkward, thought provoking moves. Good value but collects detritus and needs an annual spring-clean.

81   Treasure Island   11m   E2   P2   1990   ★★
5b A good pitch which climbs the prominent vertical crack to the horizontal break, steps left and then finishes straight up the centre of the wall. Worth re-brushing

82   Spanish Main   30m   E1   P2   1989
Starts below the left rib of the lower tier at a tiny shallow corner.
1 10m 5b Climb the corner then the rib and wall to the right on small but positive breaks to the terrace just left of the stump. A bold pitch
2 20m 5a Move up to a capped corner at the left end of the upper tier. Swing right and pull up with difficulty onto the slab. Move right again to a steep crack which provides an awkward finish to the tree.

83 Galleon Tower   32m   HVS   P2   1990
An easier version of the previous route climbing both tiers.
1 10m 5a Gain the starting corner below the left rib of the lower tier and climb it exiting left up the blunt rib on good holds to reach the terrace. (A contrived but interesting extended start to this pitch can be made via the crack of Treasure Island and a leftwards hand traverse to gain the corner).
2 22m 5a Climb up to the capped corner and swing right to gain the slab. Cross this easily but in fine position to reach the top on the right hand side.

84   Captain Pugwash   21m   HVD   P1   1990
A poor climb up the left side of both tiers utilises a short crack system in the lower left wall and then precarious juggy blocks to climb the upper wall just left of the capped corner of the previous climbs.

The following routes all climb only the upper tier. They are de-scribed right to left starting high up the right wall.

85   Bilgewater   6m   VD   P1   1989
The short sharp corner high up towards the back of the tower has a dirty finish.

86   Gangplank   13m   S   P1   1989
4a Start to the right of a cave. Gain and cross a slab leftwards on suspect rock and finish up a chimney.

87   Keelhaul   18m   HVS   P1   1989
5b A sharp undercut layback crack springs from a cave in the right wall. Make a strenuous move to establish in the corner then climb up and left, across the wall to gain a wide ledge which is traversed

to the exposed buttress front and a direct ascent to the top.

88 Trapeze 16m HVS P1 1989   ★

5a Spectacular positions make up for a scruffy start. Climb the left
rib of the yellow sandy chimney to gain a niche just right of the
upper arete. Swing boldly round the nose and pull up into the short
bottomless corner which provides good holds to the top.

89 Roses of Picardy 12m E4 P2 1992

5c The flake in the roof on the right hand side of the front face of
the upper tier. Creaky!

90 Swashbuckler 10m HVS P1 1991

5a A steep pitch up the front of the Upper Tier starting above the
tree on the terrace. Climb the yellow wall to the roof just right of the
capped corner and pull over onto the upper slab. Continue direct to
finish just left of the Oak.

THE EAVESTONE

The best concentration of difficult quality climbs at the crag are to
be found on this huge multi-faceted block encountered on crossing
the stream to the left of the Galleon Tower. On arrival one is greeted
by the imposing sight of an overhanging wall containing two
bottomless cracks. The climbs are described in a clockwise
direction from these cracks, the first and hardest of which is :-

91 Genesis 15m E5 P2 1990   ★★★

6b The right-hand crack. Gain the sloping shelf from the right and
step up to attain a standing position on the second narrow shelf.
Move left to a flake from where the crux sequence begins. Move up
and right to gain the base of the crack and climb it with difficulty to
eventually reach the security of good jams but a still strenuous
finish.

92 Eavestone Crack 14m E4 P1 1989   ★★★

6a The short bulging crack above the left end of the shelf Gain the
shelf by an awkward mantelshelf on the left and climb the wall to
gain a good hold below the bulge. Reach left and start jamming,
finishing strenuously and painfully before moving right to easier
ground and tree belays.

93 Eavestone Wall 16m E3 P2 1990   ★★★

6b The big wall to the left contains this superb climb which has a
definite and problematic, but well protected, crux. The start is quite
bold however and climbs directly up the centre of the wall on
rounded breaks to a ledge just right of a hollow flake. The thin crack

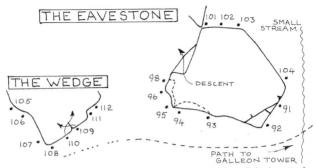

THE EAVESTONE

101 102 103 SMALL STREAM

DESCENT

104

98

96

95 94 93 91

92

THE WEDGE

105

112

106 111

109

107 110

108

PATH TO GALLEON TOWER

line up and right is the next objective but seems tantalisingly out of reach. Improvisation or telescopic arms seem to help but the upper section contains good holds leading to a rightwards finish.

94 Crazy Paver 16m E2 P2 1989   ★★
5c Start just right of the left arete and gain a hand traverse line leading right to ledges just left of the central, hollow flake. Step up and left to gain well spaced holds above the overlap, just right of the thin crack.

95 Eavesdropper 10m HVS P1 1967   ★★
5a An excellent pitch up the right-hand edge of the slabby rib on the north-east corner of the block.

96 Evenso 10m HVS P3 1967   ★
5a A bold and reachy line up the subsidiary rib one metre left of the previous climb. Positive holds are available for the steepening finish.

97 The Garden of Eden 14m HS P1 1991
4b From the foot of Evenso move left across a groove and up and left via pockets to a slabby corner. Up this to exit direct to the tree.

98 Under the Eaves 11m E2 P3 1990
5b Begin from marshy ground at the back of the Eavestone two metres left of the rib of Evenso. Pull over the first overlap to reach two pockets. Move up and then right on to the slab under the overhang and use small holds and a long reach to gain the ledge above and easy ground. Bold.

99 Eavestone Eliminate 12m E1 P2 1991
5c Start from a stump below the largest bulge on the back wall and move up right to cross the roof with difficulty to gain the slabby groove. Step out right onto the hanging rib and stretch for the top before the 'barn door' opens.

100 Forbidden Fruit   12m VS P2 1991
4c Start from the stump below the bulge and move up left to a flake in the roof. Pull over and climb the slab direct to ledges just below the top. Hand traverse left to finish on the rib.

The descent route from the Eavestone begins at the top of Evenso and takes a diagonal line across ledges to the foot of the next climb.

101 Stonerag   10m S P1 1967
4a The south-east arete, it is best approached from the right hand side of the Genesis wall at the foot of a short gully. Climb the wall just left of the rib and gain a short crack. Up this to the top of a pedestal and finish left.

102 Stonechat   10m HVS P2 1989   ★
5b A pleasant line climbing directly up the wall just right of a slight ramp. Start at the foot of the ramp, about two metres left of the gully. The technical grade depends much on the length of you arms.

103 Stonechat Ramp   11m E1 P3
5b A slightly more technical version staying closer to the line of the ramp to avoid some of the long reaches of the original line.

104 Life Begins At Forty   22m E6 P2 1991   ★★★
6c The big clean overhanging wall to the right of Genesis is climbed from left to right. Start up the crack in the hanging rib and move right, across the bulge to a flake. Continue the traverse until a smaller flake above the bulge provides the key to upward progress and a still steep finish.

THE WEDGE

This buttress, identified by its sharp clean arete is situated 50 metres behind the Eavestone. Its routes are described from left to right.

105 Wedge Iron   9m HVS P1 1989
5a The left wall direct, just left of the cutaway scoop. Often needs a brush.

106 Gorilla   12m VS P1 1966
4c Start in the centre of the left wall and climb the cutaway scoop to gain a handrail. Traverse right until it is possible to stand on the ledge and climb the cracks and blocks above moving left.

107 The Thin End   10m HVS P2 1965   ★
5a The main arete climbed on the left is easier than it looks with the crux probably being found on the final moves escaping directly over the perched blocks to finish on the nose at the very top.

108   Fat Chance   11m   E3   P2   1990   ★
5c The main arete climbed on the right-hand side by a precarious series of layaways. From the ledge at six metres step left and climb the blocks just left of the arete, or finish more easily up the crack of The Taper on the right.

109   The Taper   12m   HS   P1   1967   ★
4b Start up the steep crack 3metres right of the arete and climb it to a ramp on the left. Traverse this delicately and gain the cracks just right of the arete with difficulty or a little cunning. Finish steeply but more easily.

110   Wedgwood   12m   HVS   P1   1965   ★★★
5a The best climb of this grade on the crag. Start just left of the first crack of Taper and about two metres right of the arete. Climb the wall to gain the ramp, step right and continue using the two thinner cracks in the upper wall to a thought provoking, but well protected finish. Sustained.

111   The Heel   10m   S   P1   1965   ★★
4a Climb leftwards out of the overhung bay to gain the main right-hand crack-line and climb it direct by bridging.

112   Bunkered   9m   E2   P2   1989   ★
6a Start in an overhung bay and make a problematic series of moves to gain to gain a corner above. Step left out of this and climb the rib to the tree.

To the right of 'Bunkered' past the tree filled gully is a shorter wall containing two problems. **Rib Tickler** (5b) The short stepped rib is climbed from the right. **Treebeard** (5c) The steep wall just left of the rib needs a long reach to start.

Right again a thin crack in a corner gives :-

113   Wellington Crack II   8m   S   P1   1991
4b Climb the thin crack with a long reach up left for good holds; often dirty.

114   Secret Obsession   10m   HVS   P2   1991
5a An impending groove in the centre of the wall is climbed from cleaned ledges 3 metres right and down from the corner. Good if its clean.

115   Purely Esoteric   9m   VS   P2   1991
5a The wall one metre right of the groove leads to the beech tree on top.

Down further right from here an evil mossy off-width crack emerges from a black pool to give:-

116 The Fissure Barley 9m HS 1991
4b 'Slime' your way up the crack in traditional Guisecliff style.

To locate the next buttress follow a narrow path from the foot of the wedge descending eventually to the lakeside again. Continue, passing a large square block until a pointed boulder can be seen up to the right. Scramble up past this to reach the impressive Prow above a small valley.

THE PROW

117 Hurricane 10m E1 P2 1990
5b A direct line up the cleaned (it was once) slabby wall on the left of the main buttress.

118 Prowler 14m HVS P2 1989   ★
5b Climb the left rib to the roof, pull round left and via a long reach gain the ledge above the bulge. Continue more easily on cleaned breaks to the top.

119 Prow Crack 11m S P1 1990
4b The obvious oblique crack leading up right of the overhang is awkward at the start. It is easier to traverse in from the right (4a).

120 Swinging Free 18m E2 P2 1965   ★★★
5b An intimidating lead. Take the crack line to the right of the overhangs and then swing free for a long way left to effect a landing on a narrow ledge round the corner. Easier climbing then leads to the top just right of the tree.

121 Spitfire 12m VS P1 1990
5a Climb the long crack past the traverse line of Swinging Free to a ledge. A short horizontal hand traverse left then brings a ledge on the arete above the main overhang to reach and thence a slabby finish.

ALLEY-PALLEY WALL

This is a continuation of the Prow area slightly higher and up to the right.

122 Chiminalley 7m S P1 1989
4a The obvious chimney line with an awkward dirty finish.

123 Officer Dibble 9m E1 P1 1991
5c The bulging wall between Chiminalley and Alleycat is climbed direct.

124 Alleycat 9m HVS P1 1989
5b The steep wide crack line with a difficult move right to finish.

125 Alleycracker 9m HVS P1 1989   ★
5b The right hand, thinner crack line, sustained.

126 Going Catatonic 9m E1 P1 1991   ★
5c Climb the wall 2 metres right of Alley cracker with a problematic start and green but easier finish.

127 Backalley 8m S P1 1989
4b The front of the right arete, moving over or round the big block.

128 The Ginnel 7m HS P1 1991
4b The side-wall just right of the arete is climbed with a step right at half height to finish at a slim Ash tree.

Across a descent gully is a steep wall with a prominent horizontal crack at three quarters height. This gives:-

129 Top Cat 12m HVS P2 1991
5a Climb the mossy left rib to the top and swing across a shallow scoop to gain the hand rail. Follow it rightwards until a step up can be made to ledges to finish.

130 Alligator 8m E4 P2 1997   ★
6b Start at a two finger pocket just left of a short corner and climb the wall to a projecting nose of rock. Finish left, or move right to the finish of Crocodile.

131 Crocodile 9m E5 P2 1997   ★★
6b Climb the short corner to a flake and the overlap. Pull right to a good flat hold and slap up to the break. Finish more easily, direct.

TIN PAN ALLEY

Walk left from the foot of the Prow for about 50 metres passing below smaller outcrops then scramble up the hill to another large but severely undercut buttress. The climbs are described from left to right the first three starting in a bay from which a prominent traverse along a large smooth flake leads out right.

132 Jumping Jack 8m HVS P2 1991
5b A direct line up the overhanging scoop left of the flake with a very long reach or a jump for an obvious hold.

133 Dragonfly 11m HVS P2 1991
5a Traverse right along the big flake until just before the end and make a long reach up to reach a higher handrail leading back left. Follow this to a superb jug and climb straight up to finish at the tree.

134 Ride The Magic Dragon 10m HVS P2 1991
5b Traverse right along the top of the flake to reach a good ledge. A

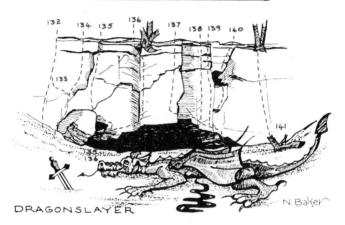

DRAGONSLAYER   N.Baker

precarious step up from here brings good holds and an easier finish.

135 Puff 11m E1 P1 1991
5b A strenuous crack leads from the cave on the left side of the crag. climb this and the wall above just right of the curving overlap.

136 Dragonslayer 14m E5 P3 1991   ★★★
6a A good climb with a devious, technical, and rather bold start, leading to the prominent slim groove below the central oak. From the cave bridge up and swing right to a traverse line above the overhang. Difficult moves gain the groove and good protection in the horizontal break at half height. Small holds above the break lead to a dubious block and a strenuous finish to the left of the tree

The next four climbs all start from an overhung niche near the centre of the crag.

137 The Meaning of Life 13m E2 P2 1991   ★★
5c The Prominent rib in the upper half of the crag. Start in the niche and pull out left, traversing with feet just above the roof to a thin crack. Use this to gain the square ledge above and continue past a crucial pocket to the top.

138 Here There Be Dragons 12m E3 P3 1991   ★★
5b A compelling line with great climbing but sparse protection. The

open groove in the centre of the crag is gained from the niche and climbed with long reaches between mainly positive holds.

The next two climbs are the easiest hereabouts but require regular traffic to keep them clean.

139 Tin 11m VS P1 1967
4c The left hand of the twin cracks emerging from the top of the niche.

140 Pan 11m VS P1 1967
5a The right hand twin crack.

141 Don't Worry, I'm a Nurse 10m E4 P2 1991   ★
6a A thin crack in the wall right of Pan leads to slots and a step left to a ledge. Finish back right to the roots of the tree.

EAVESTONE - GRADED LIST

E6
Life Begins At Forty (6c)

E5
Genesis (6b)
Crocodile (6b)
Dragonslayer (6a)

E4
Pebbledash (6c)
Alligator (6b)
Don't Worry I'm A Nurse (6a)
Roses Of Picardy (5c)
Eavestone Crack (6a)

E3
Gatekeeper (6b)
Eavestone Wall (6b)
Pushing The Boat Out (5c)
Battlement (6a)
Strange Attractor (6a)
Watery Grave (5c)
Hallmark (5c)
Good Friday (5c)
Fat Chance (5c)
Here There Be Dragons (5b)

E2
Cream (6a)
Touching The Void (6a)
Bunkered (6a)
Atlantic Voyager (5c)
Heave Ho (5c)
Excalibur (5c)
The Meaning Of Life (5c)
Crazy Paver (5c)
Under The Eaves (5b)
Treasure Island (5b)
The Alamo (5b)
King Of The Castle (5c)
Dance On White Horses (5c)
Swinging Free (5b)
Oubliette (5b)

E1
Eavestone Eliminate (5c)
Officer Dibble (5c)
Going Catatonic (5c)
The Dirty Rascal (5c)
Spanish Main (5b)
Merlon (6a)
The Pirates Ear (5b)
Apache (5c)
Crenellation (5c)
Iced Diamond (5b)
Puff (5b)

Stonechat Ramp (5b)
Hanging Serac (5b)
Hurricane (5b)

HVS
Mhlabatini (5c)
Jumping Jack (5b)
Ditch (5c)
Prowler (5b)
Scalp (5b)
For Keepsake (5b)
Alleycracker (5b)
Ride The Magic Dragon (5b)
Banana Boat (5b)
Wedgewood (5a)
Stonechat (5b)
Keelhaul (5b)
Alley Cat (5b)
Rampart (5b)
Galleon Tower (5a)
Wedge Iron (5a)
The Thin End (5a)
Leaving The Bergschrund (5c)
Sea Of Tranquillity (5b)
Ripples (5a)
Dragonfly (5a)
Ice Dance (5b)
Trapeze (5a)

Eavesdropper (5a)
Cracked Ice (5a)
Don't Pay The Ferryman (5a)
Top Cat (5a)
Swashbuckler (5a)
Secret Obsession (5a)
Evenso (5a)
Sun Bird (5a)

VS
Pan (5a)
Tonquani (5b)
Lower Sail (5a)
Upper Sail (5a)
Spitfire (5a)
Shiver Me Timbers (5a)
Brave New World (4c)
Castellan (4c)
Tin (4c)
Long John Sliver (5a)
The Microchip (4c)
Mystery Man (5a)
Bowsprit (5a)
Gorilla (4c)
Stockade (4c)

Forbidden Fruit (4c)
Purely Esoteric (4c)
Sea Dog (4c)
Glacier Apron (5a)
Machicolation (4c)
Sun-up (4c)
Jolly Roger (4b)
Chain Mail (4b)

MVS
Rearguard (4b)
Winter Sunshine (4b)
Umkomeni (4b)

HS
The Taper (4b)
The Fissure Barley (4b)
Whistling In The Dark (4b)
Sekorora (4b)
Checkmate (4b)
The Garden Of Eden (4b)
The Ginnel (4b)
Arrow Slit (4b)

S
The Heel (4a)
Spinnaker (4a)
Portcullis (4a)
Backalley (4b)
The Keep (4a)
Wellington Crack II (4b)
The Plunge (4a)
African Skies (4a)
Dungeon (4a)
Wet Landing (4b)
Chiminalley (4a)
Starboard Crack (4b)
Gangplank (4a)
Stonerag (4a)
Prow Crack (4b)

VD
Captain Pugwash
Sundial
Casement Crack
Sunstroke
Bilgewater
Yardarm
Sun Bingo

D
Jib Sail
Glissade
Sundown

GILSTEAD

SITUATION AND CHARACTER Known to the locals as Rod's rocks, this one small steep buttress and collection of boulders look almost like escapees from Shipley Glen. The outlook, across the Aire valley, is imposing rather than picturesque but worth a visit on an evening or a sunny winter's afternoon. The crag is south -west facing and the landings below the problems are generally good.

APPROACHES AND ACCESS The rocks are situated on the edge of a small stretch of moor between Bingley and Eldwick. When approaching from Bradford along the A650 turn right just before the Bradford and Bingley Building Society up Ferncliffe Road. After about 1 kilometre turn left into Pendle Road and follow it to a parking area at the end of a cul-de-sac. The main rocks are about 400 metres from here overlooking the valley. Other isolated boulders and small quarried walls litter the moor beyond providing endless possibilities for true devotees!

THE CLIMBS These are described from left to right. Only a dozen or so are long enough to qualify as real routes but most of the others are micro-routes usually treated as short solos. On the extreme left, at the top of the slope is a short problem **Horizon** (5a), which climbs the blank wall via a shot-hole. Between the shot-hole and the right arete is **Telescopic Alms** (6a), which may be easier for the tall.

1 Pocket Wall 5m E1 P3 ★
5c Climb the left side of the main face to, and over, the overlap using the well spaced chipped holds above. Short but with a serious feel.

2 Ski Jump 8m VS P2
5a Climb the wall to good holds and then make an awkward reach for the thin diagonal finger crack above the bulge. Follow the wider crack leftwards to finish.

3 Sickle Cell 8m S P1 ★
4b Start just right and follow the crack system leading up left to join and finish as for the previous route.

4 Joshua Tree 8m VS P2
4c Climb the wall just right again without recourse to the cracks on either side. Slightly artificial but the upper section, to gain a thin diagonal crack, is interesting and worthwhile.

5 Sacrilege 8m HS P1   ★
4b The steep crack just left of the chimney.

6 Celt 7m VD P1
The obvious chimney entered from the right, or slightly harder,
directly up the lower slab.

7 First Blood 8m S P1   ★
4b The crack line just right of Celt contains a massive jug. Climb to
this and surmount the bulge above. Continue steeply on good holds
to the top.

Between the two prominent cracks is a steep but narrow wall. Vying
for independence upon this are two technical exercises;

8 Moment Of Inertia 8m HVS P2
5c Power up to the thin crack and break on two incut holds (one on
the arete) then continue boldly up the wall above on ledges..

9 Headbanger's Hunger HVS P2
5c The rightward facing rib using chiselled holds and the small
ledge to the break. Straight up the wall above on small dubious
flakes, - now singular!

10 Knobbler 8m S P1   ★
4a A good line up the steep continuous crack splitting the right-
hand section of the main face. Finish to the left.

11 Ninja Darkness 8m E3
6b The hanging arete, right of Knobbler, on its left side, leads
through the roof.

12 Cream Dream 8m E2   ★
5c To the right of the arete ascend the blank looking wall by a
strong undercut to poor ledges. Finish direct on a rightward facing
rib, or, step left to the arete to an excellent finish up the right-hand
side (6b).

To the right and at a higher level, a series of shorter walls provide
excellent bouldering. The following are a sample of the better
known problems:-

13 The Needle 4b A thin crack in the slab on the first wall to the
right of the main buttress.

14 Rod's Rocks Traverse 6a★ This is a long left to right traverse
which begins at the base of The Needle and makes its way to a
welcome rest below More Pluck Than Luck and then continues to
finish up Santa On The Slates.

15   Photo Finish 6c★ Just right of the Needle, this technical test-piece climbs the blunt arete on its right-hand side via a small hanging flake and 'upside-down' holds.

16   Thingymybob 5c★ The wall just left of the sharp arete to a chipped pocket. Much harder than it once was since the demise of a flake.

17   No More Mr Nice Guy 5c The sharp arete taken on its left.

18   Friable Flake 4a A flake in the wall right of the arete.

19   Caveman 4a Climb over the chockstone above the deep cave.

20   More Pluck Than Luck 6b★ A contrived problem up the arete right of the cave. Gain thin single-finger holds from the arete and go for the top before the 'barn door' opens.

21   Knockin' Off The Pounds 6a From a short ramp climb to the quarry hole and a good crimp. A long reach gains the ledge above (harder for the short but an easier cop-out escapes right).

22   The Bomb 5b★ The wall left of the narrow chimney to the good ledge. Move left near the top to finish up the middle of the wall.

23   Direct Hit 5a As for the bomb but finish straight up.

24   Scruncher 3c The short chimney.

25   Wall Of The Endometrium 5c Start 2 metres right of the chimney and climb up and leftward to the first large pocket. Continue via the second large pocket to the top.

26   The Great Grit Neck Winding Machine 6a★ Straight up the centre of the wall.

27   Precinct 4b★★ The excellent slightly scooped wall just left of the large overhang.

28   Precinct Variation 4c Start as for Precinct but tip-toe right wards above the roof moving airily up via the curving crack one metre left of the arete.

29   Euphoria 6b Just left of the overhang, span out right to climb the undercut wall direct, joining Precinct Variation to finish.

30   Hitting The Roof 5c★ From the left wall, underneath the overhang, reach up for a good hold in the break and up again using a layaway to a flat topped projection on the left. Good holds to the top.

31 Grazer 5b A L-R hand traverse along the horizontal crack below the roof. A harder, but less corrosive, version uses poor holds on the lip, reaching into the crack at the extreme right. Both can be done footless!

32 Icarus 6a★ Climb the roof direct, somewhat gymnastically.

33 Hit and Run 5b The roof on its right side, moving left.

34 Santa On The Slates 4a The obvious chimney and the slab moving left.

Eight metres right an obvious and undercut acute arete provides interest.

35 Slap-addict-omy 6c Starting from the low break, attack the left arete with a slap and rock desperately up onto the apex.

Further right past some mini problems is a larger wall at right angles to the edge, near a wire fence.

36 Rachel's Traverse 3a Obvious broken cracks are followed rightwards to just below the top. Traverse horizontally right to a corner to finish.

37 Belly Button 4c Traverse at low level rightwards from Rachel's traverse to the right arete. Make a long move up and continue to the top.

38 Paddler 5c The blunt arete in the centre of the wall is climbed on the right.

39 Ouch 5c The middle of the wall via a long reach.

40 Addict 4b The right arete is awkward to start but worthwhile.

GILSTEAD – GRADED LIST

6c
Photo Finish
Slap-addict-omy

6b
Ninja Darkness
Cream Dream (left)
Euphoria
More Pluck Than Luck

6a
Telescopic Alms
Rod's Rocks Traverse

Icarus
Great Grit Neck .....
Knocking Off The
Pounds

5c
Hitting The Roof
Paddler
Thingymybob
Ouch
This Beer Tastes....
Wall Of Endometrium
Moment Of Inertia

No More Mr Nice Guy
Headbanger's Hunger
Cream Dream
Pocket Wall

5b
Hit And Run
The Bomb
Grazer

GREAT WOLFREY

SITUATION AND CHARACTER Sited in splendid isolation in the heart of Appletreewick Moor, about six kilometres from nowhere. A superb lonely setting giving one the feel of being a real pioneer. Due to its inaccessibility Great Wolfrey is not the place to have an accident, unless thoughtfully done after the Glorious Twelfth when, for a small fee, one of the passing 'sportsmen' may assist you by doing the decent thing.

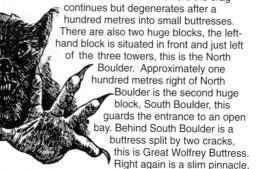

The crag varies in height from six to fifteen metres. The major features are three central towers, the right hand one is free standing and known as North Pinnacle. To the left of the Towers the crag continues but degenerates after a hundred metres into small buttresses. There are also two huge blocks, the left-hand block is situated in front and just left of the three towers, this is the North Boulder. Approximately one hundred metres right of North Boulder is the second huge block, South Boulder, this guards the entrance to an open bay. Behind South Boulder is a buttress split by two cracks, this is Great Wolfrey Buttress. Right again is a slim pinnacle, South Pinnacle, which is attached to the main crag by a jammed boulder that forms a natural arch.

The rock is good quality gritstone with only a light sprinkling of lichen. Despite its lack of a regular clientele the routes stay remarkably clean and only a few of the harder ones would need to be cleaned prior to an ascent, notably Little Red Riding Hood and A Company of Wolves. Some of the routes are bold to start which of course adds to the feeling of isolation on the moor. Werewolf, in particular, gives one of the best 'lonely solos' in Yorkshire. Gear can be found on most of the routes however and belays abound at the top of the crag for those with a less puritanical approach.

APPROACHES AND ACCESS The crag is undoubtedly on private land as the number of locked gates and helpful signs testify. All attempts to negotiate an official access agreement have failed. Nothing in this guide should be taken as implying

**a right of access but the routes are included for the sake of
completeness and in the hope that restrictions will be relaxed
in the near future.** Ample parking, for a small fee, is available at
the Grimwith Water Nature Reserve car park.

From the car park approach by walking across the dam and follow a
good permitted path round the lake until crossing the second bridge
over Gate Up Gill. From this point an inclined track can be seen
following the hillside about 100 metres above the stream. The track
leads to old quarry workings, passing the old water wheel foundations and the 'four second' shaft. Continue, contouring the hillside,
following the now redundant dike and pass through a narrow gate.
From the end of the dike continue up the side of the wall for about
800 metres, climb out of the shallow valley on the right and the crag
can be seen across the moor. The approach is a good hours walk
(if you run) and is not unpleasant for the 'wellyquipped'.

THE CLIMBS Routes are described from left to right, the first four
being located on a small buttress approximately one hundred and
fifty metres left of North Boulder. The main feature of the buttress is
the striking layback crack on its front face.

1 Autumn Gold 6m VS P1   ★
4c Climb the layback crack.

2 Auternative Arete 6m VS P1   ★
5a Climb the right arete of the front face.

3 Leapfrogger 6m VD P1
4a In the right wall of the buttress is a widening crack complete
with chockstones. Climb the crack, the main difficulty being
leapfrogging over the chockstone at half height.

4 Grove Time 5m D P1
Climb the shallow groove in the right wall before the buttress is
absorbed by the hillside.

The next climbs are on the steep arete between the previous
buttress and the rocking-stone.

5 Tea-cake Wall 5m VS P2
5a The wall to the left of Winter Of Discontent.

6 Winter Of Discontent 6m VS P2
4c Climb the steep arete utilising flakes on its left side.

7 Summer Of 76 6m VS P2
5b The wall immediately right of Winter Of Discontent. Start on the
right and trend left to finish just left of the arete on a thin flake.

The next two routes are below the rocking-stone which is the next obvious feature to the right.

8 Rock 'n' Roll 6m M P1
Climb the corner below and left of the rocking-stone.

9 The Duke 6m HVS P2
5b The arete directly below the rocking stone.

The routes described below are on the crag proper and start at a small pinnacle approximately sixty metres left of North Boulder and just right of the rocking stone. Behind the pinnacle is a wide gully with a chockstone filled crack in its right wall, this is Chockstone Crack.

10 Pedestal Arete 5m VS P1
5a Stand on the pedestal two metres above the ground. Climb up and left to the arete before reaching the top.

11 Alternative Arete 6m S P1   ★
4a Climb the right arete of the buttress.

The open gully is a useful means of descent.

12 Chockstone Crack 5m M P1
The crack, chockfull of stones in the right wall of the gully.

13 Chockstone Wall 6m VS P1
4b The narrow wall left of the chimney.

14 North Chimney 7m D P1
Climb the obvious chimney just left of the buttress with a band of small roofs.

15 Bone People 7m E2 P2
5c Climb the right arete of North Chimney on the right side throughout.

16 North South Divide 15m HVS P2   ★★
5b Climb North Chimney for about four metres. Move rightwards round the arete onto the face, follow the break for about three metres and pull over the small roof using good holds, continue up the shallow corner to the top.

17 Crock Around The Block 7m E2 P2
5c Start about one and a half metres right of the arete formed by North Chimney. Climb the wall with difficulty to reach the hand rail and a runner. Continue straight up to the top.

In the corner is an open chimney, stepped on the right. Climb the steps and exit through the cave to the right or squeeze up the narrow chimney to the left.

18 Wolfschmidt 9m E3 P2   ★★
6a An intimidating route up the first big face on the crag. Start below the steps forming the right edge of the chimney above, leave the ground with difficulty and move up and right to gain poor breaks. Continue up to a shallow 'V' and then move easily to the top.

19 Werewolf 9m E4 P3   ★★★
5c Bold and beautiful, a superb arete climb. Start at the flake right of the arete as for Wolf At The Door. Move up and left to the arete, go left round the arete and up the wall. Move back right to gain the arete below an obvious fin. Layback up the fin to finish. A direct start on the left of the arete is 6b.

20 Wolf At The Door 9m E4 P3   ★★
6a This routes climbs the wall and roof above the start of Werewolf via one powerful move. Start up the flake just right of the arete and continue up to the roof and a crucial, though hard to place, runner. Pull round the roof (crux) on sloping holds to reach the top.

21 Huff-Puff Chimney 8m M P1
The Chimney immediately right of Wolf at the Door.

22 Hangover Crack 9m S P1
The crack in the corner, strenuous for its grade.

23 Hangover Chimney 9m M P1
One metre right is another chimney/wide crack

To the right of Hangover Chimney is a pale green wall.

24 Shades Of Green 9m E3 P2
6a Start by climbing the thin crack just right of the arete formed by the previous route. The use of the crack and some dirty holds enables the ledge to be gained. Move right and finish up the wide crack.

25 Walter's Rib 9m E2 P2   ★★
5c Sometimes known as Brown's Rib, climb the superb arete left of the plaque.

26 In Memorium 9m E4 P2   ★
6a Start about two metres right of the plaque. Climb the centre of the wall using ledges and layaways (in that order) to gain the wide horizontal break at six metres. Runners are now available but, as you've done all the hard climbing, somewhat irrelevant. Finish in the crack on the left.

27 Arvel Chimney 9m D P1
Climb over the jammed blocks into the chimney. Thrutch you way up and over the chockstones.

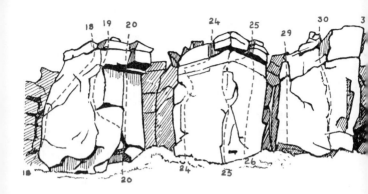

28 Grand Defiance 12m E2 P2
5b The narrow groove just right of Arvel Chimney. Sustained and quite serious.

To the right of the buttress with the plaque is a huge detached block, The North Pinnacle. The corner at the junction of the gullies provides the easiest way off the top. Alternatively the centre of the back wall can be descended at V. Diff.

29 Cowell's Rib 9m E3 P2   ★★
5c Climb the left arete of the front face of the pinnacle moving right at the top to gain the obvious flake.

30 Little Red Riding Hood 9m E4 P2   ★
6b Takes the ever-so-thin crack just left of the ever-so-green streak. Crawl up the face using the thin crack and the right arete to gain a flat hold. A small Berzin's style leap allows the break to be gained. Finish more easily through the niche on the right.

31 A Company Of Wolves 9m E4 P2   ★★
6b Climb the overhanging arete at the right hand end of the face, as difficult as it looks and somewhat gymnastic.

32 Bad Company 9m E1 P1   ★★
5b Start on the block at the entrance to the wide gully behind North Buttress. Climb the arete on its left side using large and small edges to gain the horizontal break, up again to another horizontal break and finish up the short vertical crack splitting the top centre of the block.

N. Baker

33 Limited Company 9m VS P2
4c The right arete of Bad Company is climbed on green ripples.

34 Good Friends 8m HVS P1   ★
5b The thin crack direct opposite Bad Company at the back of the
bay. A pleasant and safe route.

To the right of North Pinnacle is a small buttress with a crack
splitting the centre.

35 Lipstick Wall 10m HVS P1   ★
5c Take the wall left of Deception direct via a stone 'mouth' and
exit up the middle crack.

36 Deception 6m VS P1
4c Climb the wall to a ledge on the left. From the ledge climb the
left hand of three cracks to finish.

37 Loyalty Crack 8m S P1
4b Climb the crack in the centre of the buttress.

38 Sheep's Clothing 8m E2 P1
6a Climbs the wall left? of Loyalty Crack. Levitate up the wall on
mediocre holds to gain a small recess at four metres. Move up and
right to a blind crack, mantelshelf to finish.

The next 4 routes are in the left wall of the large bay behind South
Boulder.

39 Recess Arete 7m S P2
4b Obvious arete ending in a scoop in the bay to the right of, and
behind, Sheep's Clothing buttress.

40 Flow Arete 6m VS P2
5c Blunt arete just left of Foxy. Start using 2 sidepulls (no standing on the boulder) and follow the arete to the niche.

41 Foxy 6m S P1
Climb the thin crack left of Got It In One then step right to a ledge to finish.

42 Got It In One 6m VS P2
4c Climb the wall awkwardly using a poor horizontal break to gain a good break. Continue up blind vertical cracks to finish.

43 Wolfrey Crack Indirect 10m S P1
Climb the parallel cracks in the wall behind South Boulder. Follow the right hand crack until a short traverse leads into the left hand crack. Climb this to the top.

44 Great Wolfrey Buttress 9m VS P1
4c Start just right of the parallel cracks in the gully. Pull up into the horizontal break or handrail and move up the vertical crack. Move across the slab rightwards to mantelshelf onto the ledge. Finish up the crack in the wall above.

45 Holly Tree Hover 9m VS P1
5a Climb the blunt arete direct to the ledge on Great Wolfrey Buttress, finish as for that route.

46 Holly Bush Crack 7m D P1
Climb the crack with the holly bush growing near its base.

47 Heather Groove 7m D P1
Just right of Holly Bush Crack is a shallow groove, climb the groove then step over the void and climb the slabby wall using some flakes to finish.

To the right of Great Wolfrey Buttress is South Pinnacle. The Pinnacle is attached to the main crag by a jammed boulder forming an arch.

48 Slapstick Slab 7m HVS P2
5b The centre of the slab on the east face of the South Pinnacle.

49 West Face 6m S P1   ★
4a Climb the narrow west face of the buttress, easily at first, using horizontal breaks. A difficult move left at the top allows good finishing holds to be gained. Climbing the right arete throughout gives a grade of VS 4c.

50 Corner And Traverse 6m D P1
4a Climb the eastern arete of the pinnacle for a few feet. Move left and climb the groove to the top.

GUISECLIFF

SITUATION AND CHARACTER   Guisecliff lies on the northerly edge of Heyshaw Moor overlooking the Nidd Valley and Glasshouses near Pateley Bridge. The crag is north facing and extends as a high escarpment for a kilometre along the 300 metre contour line. In places the rock reaches a height of almost 30 metres making Guisecliff Yorkshire's largest gritstone crag. The nature and quality of rock varies, generally good and sound natural grit, but in parts it is softer and some areas have been quarried.

Certain sections of the crag could almost be described as individual craglets in their own right. As a result, a selective approach to the choice of buttress is best adopted on a first visit and for this purpose a recommended 'first timers hit list' has been provided. Whilst this cannot guarantee that everyone following these recommendations will be totally satisfied, it may avoid parties leaving the crag disappointed and empty handed, after hours of slipping and sliding around in the *Conan Doyle-esque* landscape that can be encountered along the base of the crag.

The majority of routes have been gardened at some time or other and the wooded aspect dictates that many of the less steep lines collect a new layer of arboreal detritus each year. The less frequented routes, therefore, have in many cases been reclaimed by nature and may require re-cleaning. Grades shown in brackets have not been individually checked in recent years and may not be accurate for on-sight ascents. Many of the steeper walls and aretes, on the other hand, stay clean and in good condition. For those keen to satisfy their pioneering urges further exploration of this extensive outcrop is sure to reveal new possibilities across the grades.

The crag is best visited after dry spells over the summer months. When warm and sweaty conditions make some of the neighbouring gritstone outcrops unpleasant, Guisecliff can make an attractive alternative. Approached in the right frame of mind, those seeking solitude away from the climbing masses, and prepared to put up with the possibility of some re-cleaning, will not be disappointed.

APPROACHES AND ACCESS   From the A59 Skipton-Harrogate road at Blubberhouses turn north at the sign for Stump Cross Caverns. Follow this road for 2 miles until the Stone House Inn is reached (good watering hole on the return journey). At the inn turn right and then left at the Heyshaw signpost after half a mile. Continue on this road with Z bends towards Pateley Bridge until

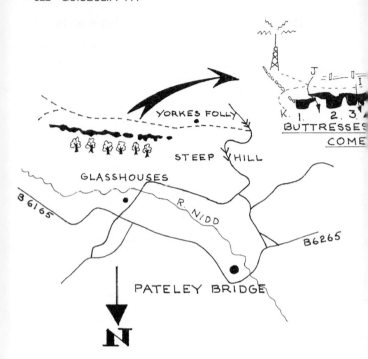

Yorke's Folly (the two masonry columns) can be seen on the right. Park by the wall leading to the folly.

From Harrogate and the north approach through Pateley Bridge, cross the River Nidd and turn left on the Otley road, go through Bewerley and, as the road climbs steeply up the escarpment, the west end of the crag will be seen to the left. (An interesting cubic boulder with problems lies on the left of the road below the escarpment.) Park the car by the wall leading to the folly.

From the parking spot take the path past the folly and cross the wall at the stile, passing boulders on the left. The path now climbs slightly and after a few hundred metres joins and then follows a wall. From where the path reaches this wall it runs along the top of the entire crag for about half a mile to the TV mast which is located above the eastern end and No.1 Buttress.

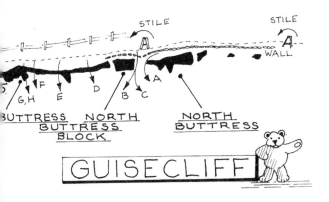

ACCESS TO SELECTED BUTTRESSES. A FIRST TIMERS HIT LIST.

(Described from west to east as approached from the parking spot the following four buttresses are highly recommended)

THE NORTH BUTTRESS A natural gritstone crag attaining a height of 24m. Excellent rock and striking lines with a 'Big Feel' particularly in the S - HVS range. Easy access and pleasant aspect at its base.

A hundred metres or so past the boulders the dry stone wall on the left forms a right angled corner. Cross the wall at the corner and follow the path down through the woods for a few hundred metres until a path contouring to the east brings you to below this large natural gritstone outcrop. (5 mins from the main path).

THE NORTH BUTTRESS BLOCK A natural gritstone outcrop sporting some gymnastic roof climbing. Excellent clean and quick drying routes in the Diff - E4 range. Easy access, user friendly and pleasant aspect.

From the boulders follow the path until it meets the wall, continue for several hundred metres until a further stile over a fence is crossed. A vague path now branches off down to the left. Follow this for thirty metres contouring to the right to reach the Block, a compact natural gritstone outcrop characterised by a large capping roof at its right-hand end.

COMET BUTTRESS An impressive natural outcrop attaining a height of 25m. Easily viewed from the top of the crag. The lower section is prone to seepage after wet conditions but access is easy and there are a number of excellent, long and memorable routes. VS - E5

From the stile at the North Buttress Block, continue along the top of the crag for about 250 metres until a large rock platform with an iron stake is reached. This is Comet buttress. The striking arete of The Scryking and the finishing wall of Mastermind can easily be viewed. Access is either by abseil or equally as easy by returning back up the path for about 20m where a descent down a short easy chimney can be found.

NOTE. When travelling along the top of the crag from the stile after about 100m keep a look out for a thin prominent flat topped block that projects out from the crag. This gives an easy access to Slot Buttress and vantage point to view the classic Warriors of Hunaman.

NUMBER TWO BUTTRESS
An intimidating quarried buttress offering a number of hard extremes E2 - E6. Easy access, relatively quick drying but some of the routes may need re-cleaning.

Situated at the far eastern end of the crag roughly below the TV mast. Approach along the cliff top and follow the path past the TV mast, the path doubles back on itself below the crag. Pass a number of quarried areas to eventually arrive at the obvious 'open book' corner of Number two buttress.

A detailed summary of descent routes is found in the text.

NOT TO BE MISSED		Buttress
North Buttress Crack	S	NB
North Wall Eliminate	HVS	CB
Comet Wall	HVS	CB
Campanile	HVS	NB
Double Top	HVS	NBB
The Creation	E2 5c	No.2
Shindig	E2 6a	NB
Aftermath	E3 5c	No.2
Dingbat	E3 6a	No.2
Cutting the Cord	E4 5c	NBB
Mastermind	E4 5c	CB
The Scryking	E5 6a	CB
The Warriors of Hunaman	E5 6b	SB
On the Edge	E6 6b	No.2

SUMMARY OF DESCENTS

A)   From the top of the North Buttress go east and scramble down a slope or abseil from
good trees.

B)   From the second stile on the main path, a path goes down to the left (N) to the overhung North Buttress Block (routes 91-94), which is immediately on the right.

C)   By the same path, continue 150 metres down leftwards (NW) to the North Buttress.
(routes 95+).

D)   Some 100 metres from the stile where the path falls slightly an easy gully leads back to the left (NW). This provides access through the cave to the back of the Aiguille de
Mouton (route 87).

E)   Some 170 metres from the stile and where the path is at its lowest level (120 metres NW of the rock platform) a flat-topped block (1m x 5m) protrudes over the crag towards the tarn. A descent left with a 'balance step' leads down to the Slot Buttress (providing access to routes 73 to 85).

F)   Forty metres NW of the rock platform a wide gully and a long step lead down to a short chimney. This is at the beginning of the long wall (between routes 70 and 71 providing access to routes 43 to 72).

G)   From the rock platform abseil down Comet Buttress (routes 58 - 65).

H)   From the same rock platform climb down the steep corner chimney of Scissors. (route 64 providing access to routes 43 to 72).

I)   Between Buttress Three and Four, down the west side of the protruding Number Three Buttress past trees.

J)   Between Buttresses One and Two behind the crevassed area, 20 metres west of the stone wall.

K)   At the restart of the wall (100 metres west of the TV aerial) go North down a boulder slope to the base of Buttress Number One.

THE CLIMBS
The routes are described from left to right.

NUMBER ONE BUTTRESS   A fairly compact buttress about 25 metres wide. The most notable features are the upright leaf of rock of The Pulpit and two short chimney-like recesses in the upper left-hand section.

1 The Verger   14m   E1   P1   1966
5b The left-hand end of Number One Buttress presents a steep narrow buttress with a thin rightward-facing corner in its upper section. Start 1 metre right of the left edge of the buttress. Climb a thin twisting crack and pull over the overhang to gain the small ledge at the foot of the corner. Climb the unhelpful corner (crux).

2 Lectern Chimney   15m   (MS)   1964
The left-hand of the two chimneys which are visible in the upper portion of the crag. Start 2 metres right of the left edge of the buttress. Follow broken rocks into the easy-angled chimney and continue to a recess below the steeper section. Face left and follow the chimney to heathery scrambling and the top.

3 The Belfry   16m   (HVS)   1966
4c The right-hand of the two chimney-like recesses, with a large tree at the top. Five metres right of the left edge of the buttress is a shattered crack. Climb this, passing a flake, into the recess. Leave the recess via the overhanging crack on the left; easier than it looks.

4 Curate's Crack   18m   (S)   1966
Starts 2 metres right of The Belfry at a chimney-crack in a corner. Climb up inside the crack and exit on to a large ledge. Now take the corner crack on the left started by a layback, to gain holds on the left wall. Continue more easily to the top.

5 Pulpit Steps   16m   (VD)   1966
Immediately left of The Pulpit is a large crack. Climb over a series of ledges to the top of The Pulpit. Up a short crack on the right then traverse off right along an unpleasant sandy ledge. Not recommended.

6 Pulpit Chimney   16m   (VD)   Pre 1954
The obvious square chimney at the right-hand side of The Pulpit. Up the impressive chimney to The Pulpit. Either of the two cracks above and a loose gully leads to the top.

7 Magnificat   14m   HVS   P1   1964   ★★
5a Takes a direct line up the steep buttress just right of Pulpit Chimney. Start below a large yellow flake which can be seen 5 metres up. Climb to the flake and up the left side of it. Pull over the overhang strenuously and finish directly up the twin cracks above. Alternatively, after the overhang step right and follow a slanting funnel to the top. A good clean route. Next comes a fan of vegetation and broken rock, then Number Two Buttress begins above the left of the two mine entrances.

NUMBER TWO BUTTRESS

Towards the left-hand end of this buttress is a smooth wall (**Post Office Wall**) split by two obvious cracks. Further right the crag becomes higher and takes the form of a corner. Right again a buttress stands forward and presents an imposing front with a barrier of overhangs at 8 metres. The best descent is to the left of Post Office Wall. Starting at the left-hand end we have:

8 Letterbox Climb 20m (D) pre 1950
A worthwhile route. Post Office Wall is bounded on its left by a corner and 1 metre left of this is a chimney. Climb the chimney to a ledge and pedestal belay below a cave. Bridge up the outside of the cave and exit left on to a large bilberry ledge. Climb the recess behind a tall tree and go through the letterbox slot to the moor.

9 Microcrack 14m HVS P1 1966
5a The obvious thin crack in the left-hand side of Post Office Wall. Climb with difficulty until the crack widens, then more easily to the top.

10 Postman's Crack 13m (VS) Pre 1957
4c A few metres right is a boot-wide crack climbed mainly by wedging. Strenuous.

11 Bold John 15m HVS P2 1966
5a Post Office Wall is bounded on the right by a blunt arete. Two metres left of this and lower down is a thin crack. Climb this until a horizontal break leads rightwards to a good ledge. Follow the improbable-looking arete above using layaways. A runner may be arranged in a small pocket on the right wall.

12 Sprog 14m (VS) 1960
4c In the right corner of the recess, right of Bold John, is a steep jamming crack. Climb this and the groove above exiting left at the overhang. Just right of the recess containing Sprog is a steep chimney leading to a large block roof full of doubtful blocks. right of the chimney we have:

13 Cretin's Crack 14m (VS) 1960
5a The crack behind the tall tree is easy to start , but strenuous wedging develops higher up leading to an awkward exit on to a grass ledge. Traverse left and up the corner to finish.

14 Drum Crack 22m (VS) 1963
4c A sandy flake crack just to the right. Climb the friable flake to a grass ledge. Traverse right in an exposed position and up a loose corner to the moor. To the right the crag becomes much more impressive and takes the form of a huge corner, with a mine entrance at its foot.

15 The Creation   23m   E2   P1   1965   ★★★
5c In the middle of the left wall is an obvious fierce crack, with a
large square block at half height. Climb the crack to a block, enter
the upper section by a precarious pull on fist jams and continue
strenuously to the grass ledge. The loose corner above leads to the
moor. A No. 4 Friend is useful on this excellent route.

16 Barleycorn   23m   E3   P2   1973   ★
5b The formidable-looking overhanging chimney in the angle to the
right of The Creation. Start from a ledge on the right and ascend the
neck of the chimney until it narrows to a chimney crack. Climb this
strenuously to a capstone, then easily up the ramp above. It is
possible to arrange protection for the upper chimney by climbing up
the back beneath the capstone.

17 On The Edge   23m   E6   1990   ★★★
6b The arete just left of the chimney of Illusion, protected by poor
friends low down but good pegs near the top.

18 Illusion   22m   HS   P1   1960
Ascend the block filled cleft passing behind the first obstruction and
finishing by an awkward move either left or right, over the bulging
chockstone near the top. Scramble up the easy gully to a cave. The
square flue at the back leads to the top.

19 Aftermath   23m   E3   P2   1973   ★★
5c A fine route with some bold climbing up the wall to the right of
Illusion. Start immediately right of Illusion and ascend to the
chockstone. Step right with difficulty into a shallow scoop. Traverse
delicately right to the rib and reach round to a peg runner. Move up
just left of the rib (crux). A hand traverse left and a mantelshelf lead
to a ramp which is climbed to a short, steep corner. Climb this to the
top. It is also possible to continue directly up the rib and left into the
steep corner. Route may need cleaning.

20 Hook Route   16m   E1   P1   Pre 1957   ★
5b In the prominent nose of the buttress is a square-cut
chimney set in overhangs. Ascend to the chimney proper and an
iron hook on the left. Climb to the roof of the chimney and pass
on good hand jams in the crack on the right. Finish up the wall
on the left.

21 Dingbat   20m   E3   P1   1966   ★★
6a On the right wall of Number Two Buttress is an impressive,
clean-cut, overhanging, corner. Climb this, sustained and very
strenuous. Move left to the prow and then straight up the steep front
of the buttress. Route may need cleaning.

22 Holly Grooves 14m (MVS) 1960
Starts a few metres right of Dingbat below broken grooves with a
holly at the top. Pull into an awkward niche, then up left into a
groove containing a small holly. The crack behind leads to another
holly, then left into a grassy groove with an awkward exit.

NUMBER THREE BUTTRESS   The left-hand and central parts of
this buttress are broken and mossy; the right wall is very steep and
mostly clean. The best descent is to the right (W). On the extreme
left of Number Three and near the top of the grass slope is a
smooth lichenous wall:

23 Right-hand Wall 10m VS P3 pre 1954
4c Start on good holds which dwindle and mantelshelf on to a small
ledge. Traverse left for 2 metres and climb the wall, directly at first,
then rightwards to a pocket. Make an awkward move up to the top
from here.

24 Short Chimney 14m S P1
Just down to the right from the last route. Climb the chimney for 8
metres to the trees. Step left and up twin cracks to the top.

25 Mantelshelfman 18m HVS P1 1974
5c Not much of a route to look at, but with some technical interest.
From the bottom of Short Chimney move right and up into an oak
tree. Ascend the thin crack behind the tree until a hard mantelshelf
gains either the narrow ledge above or the tree below. Climb the
slab, move right and up the wall and shallow groove using the
arete, to the overhang. Step left and up the arete to finish.

26 Tree Cracks 22m S P1 Pre1957
Starts 8 metres up left from the base of Number Three Buttress.
Follow the cracks first straight up then trending right towards an
oak. Over this and belay in the recess behind. Up to the overhang
above and make an awkward move over it to gain the grassy ledge.
Step right, then more easily to the moor.

27 Buttress Route 24m VD P1 Pre 1954   ★
A good route taking a direct line up the centre of the Buttress. Start
at tree stumps just above the base of the buttress and climb to a
grass ledge below and left of the pinnacle. Climb the pinnacle and
step off the top into the crack on the left. Follow this and the
chimneys above, finishing over a tree. An expedition for all seasons!

28 Clodhopper 24m (HS) 1974
Starts at the lowest point of the buttress. Ascend the left-hand crack
to reach the right side of the pinnacle. Step right and move up into
an overhung bay. Climb the overhang moving rightwards and

continue to the top.

29 Footpatter   24m   HS   P1   1964   ★
4b Takes a line up the arete overlooking the steep right wall of the buttress. Start at the lowest point of the arete and climb the wall followed by a crack to a small ledge. Continue to another grass ledge and thread belay low down. Climb the crack until a fine traverse right below the overhang leads to a delicate and exposed crack. Up this to a small ledge, then continue to the top. Needs cleaning. The right wall of Number Three overhangs and is split by cracks and grooves:

30 Pendulum   20m   E1   1964
5b Climb the groove just left of the most prominent crack to a loose block at 8 metres. Make a difficult swing left on to the arete and follow this (Footpatter) to finish. Strenuous moves on dubious holds call for strong nerves on this route.

31 Foreign Bodies   15m   E2   1989
5c Climb Pendulum to the loose block at 8 metres and layback into an awkward hanging groove above (peg runner). Climb the groove to the top.

32 Stretcher   20m   E1   P1   1964
5b The prominent crack right of Pendulum is ascended with some difficulty to a small cave. Pull round the overhang into the chimney-crack and make a long reach for a good hold. Continue steeply from here.

33 Ruminant   14m   (S)   1961
Further right is a shallow chimney-groove. After an awkward start easier climbing leads to a small tree and grass ledge on the left. Climb another groove above using tree roots to surmount the final overhang.

NUMBER FOUR BUTTRESS   Identified by a fine clean-cut chimney splitting the nose of the buttress. The left wall is tree-covered and at the extreme left end is the first route:

34 Overhanging Groove   14m   (VS)   1962
The double-tiered groove just left of the large oak tree. Climb the lower V groove to an awkward landing on an earthy ledge. Wide bridging moves are required to start the upper groove but it is then followed more easily to a pull out right.

35 Nippem   16m   (S)   1960
Takes the line of a deep V groove with a crack in the back just right of the large tree. A chockstone is visible against the skyline at the

top of the climb. Move up to the tree then climb the groove using the left rib to a ledge on the right. Good chock belay in the crack. Bridge up the corner then finish either under or over the summit chockstone.

36 Rootless Crack 18m (S) 1960
A few metres right of the large oak is a broken jamming crack. Climb this to a small ledge, step right and up the wall above to a larger ledge and tree belay. Traverse left and finish up the final corner of Nippem. A more difficult finish is to mantelshelf on to the tree on the right and follow a thin crack to an awkward pull-over on to the moor.

37 Chockstone Chimney 8m (M)
The obvious chimney just to the right leading to large ledges.

38 Kandahar Groove 20m (S) 1961
Right of Chockstone Chimney are two tall hollys. The open groove directly above the lower one provides the route. Step round on to a holly from a niche on the left and over vegetation. Trend rightwards over blocks to a ledge and oak-tree belay. Traverse left to a tree, move up to the thin bulging crack above, then round the corner. Scramble leftwards to finish.

39 Roc's Nest Chimney 24m HS P1 1937   ★★
4b Situated prominently in the nose of the buttress to the right. One of the classics of the crag and very worthwhile. Enter the chimney from the right by an awkward move. Climb strenuously up inside the chimney and exit right at the top. Up the gully then over blocks on the right wall. Scrambling remains.

40 Dhobi 22m (MVS) 1960
4b Follow the deep V-groove a few metres right of Roc's Nest Chimney. Climb past a cave, then over a bulge and up to a large chockstone. Pull over this with care, then move left to a tree. Up the gully as for Roc's Nest Chimney.

41 Stigma 23m (VS 1960
4c Starts in the right wall of the V-groove and takes a series of shallow grooves running up the steep wall. Ascend a narrow groove for 3 metres, then step right to a larger groove which is followed with increasing difficulty to a ledge and tree belay. The crack behind is well supplied with holds and leads to the final overhang. Traverse left to finish.

42 Ruscator 27m E1 P1 1966   ★
5b Climbs the nose of the high buttress right of Roc's Nest Chimney. A good route. A short square-cut chimney is set in the

overhangs at 7 metres. Gain this from the arete on the right and ascend it into a groove. Follow this back to the arete and climb to a long narrow ledge on the right below an impressive arched wall. Belay. Surmount the blank wall using a shoulder and a sling thrown round the tree above - an exciting manoeuvre. Those less suicidally- minded will probably prefer to traverse right to a crack with a heathery finish. A deep gully to the right marks the end of Number Four Buttress but is not a suitable descent.

NUMBER FIVE BUTTRESS   A very large expanse of rock extending 150 metres or so. The left-hand section is a high and rather vegetated wall with some large overhangs just right of a dirty gully (Shoulder Gully). After 80 metres is the lowest point of the buttress and the crag becomes broken by chimneys and gullies. The best descent is by abseil, by descending Scissors or by 'Long Step', 40 metres right of Scissors. Commencing at the extreme left-hand end of the left wall of Number Five is the steep gully separating it from Number Four. Right of this is the first climb of note:

43 Hawk Slab   17m   S   P1   1960   ★
A climb of considerable quality, one of the best of its grade on the crag. Start from a terrace just above the base of the crag and climb a steep cracked wall to a tree belay below a large corner. Move right along the base of the slab which forms the right-hand side of the corner. Delicately up the slab until a pull up can be made into a small cave. Traverse left and up a short overhanging corner. Route may need gardening. Four other routes have been done hereabouts but are heavily vegetated. Fifteen metres right of Hawk Slab is a gully:

44 Shoulder Gully   26m   VD   P1   Pre 1954
A very dirty and poor climb. Start a few metres right of the gully and climb a short wall below large overhangs to a terrace. Walk left to the foot of a chimney (sometimes a waterfall). The chimney leads to a ledge on the left, then around a block to a bilberry ledge. Move back to a tree belay above the chimney. The V chimney above leads to the top, the final move being the crux. Just right of Shoulder Gully is an area of large overhangs:

45 Nice 'n' Sleazy   24m   E3   P1   1978
5c Finds its way through the left-hand side of the overhangs. Start as for Shoulder Gully and ascend to a holly stump. Traverse carefully left to belay on a large shelf below the roof. The obvious roof crack and short chimney above lead to another ledge and tree belay. Finish up a gangway slanting up left, the last pitch of the girdle (Jaywalk).

46 Agrippa 30m E1 P2 1964   ★
5b An intimidating route, finding its way through the right-hand side
of the large overhangs. Start as for Shoulder Gully. Climb to the
terrace, then up to the roof just right of a tree stump. Traverse right
to a niche. Climb the slab on the right (peg) and move up until
doubtful flakes allow a traverse back left to a narrow ledge above
the main overhang. Climb the wall above to a ledge and belay.
Move right to a slanting groove which is awkward to start. Follow
the groove to the top. May need cleaning.

47 Agrippina 30m (HVS) 1971
5a Similar in character to Agrippa, but finishing up the wall further
right. Start as for Agrippa and follow it to the niche. Climb the slab
on the right (peg) then traverse with difficulty across the top of the
slab and up right to a large vegetated ledge. From the right end of
the ledge pull up and reach over the overhang. Traverse awkwardly
left to a large sloping foothold. Climb a crack using the right wall
and gain a scoop to finish.

48 Daniel 28m (VS) 1960
4c An interesting route finishing up the deep V groove between
Shoulder Gully and the nose of the buttress to the right. Start
several metres right of the gully and to the left of a large twisted oak
stump growing 6 metres up. Climb a steep clean wall and move
right to the oak. Go boldly over the overhang then move right round
the rib. Continue up through trees to a holly and ledge below the
overhang. Traverse right into the groove and climb it for 6 metres.
From here the groove may be finished direct over the dubious
chockstone, usually wet. Alternatively, make a rope move on to the
right rib, then ascend this to the top.

49 Tombstone 18m E1 P1 1970
5b Follows a steep and strenuous crack line 10 metres right of
Daniel and finishing right of the jutting prow. Scramble up into a
heathery bay below an obvious roof. Move left and up into a short V
groove capped by a triangular overhang. A rather grim struggle
gains the crack on the right, which leads via a niche to a ledge.
Step left to belay. Back right and up with difficulty into an overhanging groove. Up this and exit left.

50 Coyote Wall 12m (HS) 1965
Starts 4 metres right of Tombstone along the ledge. Climb to an oak at
3 metres, then the steep cracks behind. The middle section is the most
difficult. The next route starts from the lowest point of the buttress.

51 Jezebel 36m S P1 1961   ★★
An interesting climb with a fine, airy finish. Start at a corner capped

by overhangs. Climb the steepening corner until a traverse to the left arete can be made. Traverse left to a tree belay. Step up and right into a fist-wide crack. This leads to a heathery ledge, then traverse right to a good stance below a square chimney. Up the chimney to the overhang, then step out right in a splendid position onto the rib. Moderate rocks to the top. The **Arboreal Exit** is slightly easier but moves left to a ledge and then up via a tree.

52   By-Pass   VD P1 1961   ★
Start as for Jezebel. Climb the corner for 3 metres to a ledge then go diagonally right across the slab passing tree stumps to finish in Boundary Chimney. Very pleasant. Scramble off rightwards across ledges. Just round to the right is a small bay with a chimney on the right and a crack in the left corner. The latter marks the start of the next climb:

53   Autobahn   24m VS P1 1966   ★
4c A direct way up this part of the crag providing interesting climbing. Climb the layback crack, then up the groove moving left at the overhang. Traverse right beneath the prow to a large ledge and belay. Ascend to the large overhangs immediately right of the undercut nose. Swing left across the smooth wall (peg in place) to reach the nose, then easily to the top. An exposed and impressive pitch.

54   Boundary Chimney   12m HVD Pre1954
The obvious chimney on the right of the bay. Climb the chimney passing a large block with care, to ledges and a tree belay on the right. Either scramble off to the right, or take the **Direct Finish** (HS) up the large V groove above, with some loose rock on the way. At the foot of the crag, and rightwards, are 20 metres of broken rocks and then a black chimney-gully with a tree growing downwards at half-height.

55   Apparition   18m VD Pre 1954
An interesting climb of its type, dark and damp. Climb the chimney to the tree and over this to a ledge. Continue to the overhang, then either escape to the left or move right and finish direct.

56   KOYLI   20m (VS) 1955
Immediately left of Apparition is a steep slab split by two deep cracks partly obscured by a fallen tree. Ascend to an overhang at 3 metres and move awkwardly into the cracks above. Follow these to a belay on Apparition. In the arete to the left is a hanging crack. Step left and ascend this to the top. **Variation Start** (HVS 5b) a thin curving finger crack, 2 metres left of the normal start undercut at the bottom and rejoining the normal route after 8 metres.

57   The Kraken   17m   (VS)   1962
4c Follows a deep undercut groove reached by scrambling left
along ledges from the foot of Apparition. Enter the groove with
difficulty and climb past a holly until a traverse right to a narrow
ledge can be made. Above is a wall split by a thin crack which
provides a difficult finish. To the right of the back gully of Apparition
is a deep chimney capped by large overhangs. Just left of the
chimney is a knife-edged arete:

58   Phillipa's Ridge   23m   (HS)   1954
Start 3 metres right of the arete at the foot of the chimney. Climb
this to an oak at 9 metres. Left to the arete, follow this to an earthy
ledge and tree belay below a chimney-crack. The chimney above
leads to the top.

59   Brian's Climb   23m   (VS   1954
The deep chimney direct. Ascend the shallow Chimney into the
deeper one and continue up mostly on the right wall until a step left
on to a block can be made. Belay. Climb up the roof and, using
good jams, move out right on to the rib. Up this to finish.

COMET BUTTRESS   Right of Brian's Climb the buttress stands
forward presenting an imposing front and some of the best routes
on the crag. These are below the 'rock platform' described under
'access and descent'. Access by abseil down the routes is easy and
allows some cleaning and inspection. Alternatively descend
Scissors or 'Long Step'.

60   North Wall Eliminate   23m   HVS   P2   1963   ★★★
5a Climbs the fiercely-undercut rib split by a crack. Ascend the
chimney of Brian's Climb for 8 metres then traverse right out to the rib.
Follow this, in a very exposed position, to the top. Superb climbing.

61   Skyjacker   21m   E1   P1   1970   ★
5c To the right of the huge overhanging bay is a blunt rib, start at a
niche in the right wall. From the niche gain the front of the buttress.
Move left and follow the crack to a stance and belay on Comet Wall.
Make an awkward traverse left, then climb the exposed front of the
buttress using thin cracks. The lower pitch is frequently out of
condition but may be ascended using the two original aid pegs or
may be ascended with aid direct from the overhung bay or may be
avoided. The worthwhile exposed top pitch alone may be climbed
from Comet Wall stance (5b).

62   Mastermind   26m   E4   P2   1975   ★★★
5c A tremendous climb which ascends the lower rib of the buttress,
crosses the roof of the cave and finishes up the steep right wall. To

the right of the huge overhung bay is a blunt rib. Start at a niche in the right wall. From the niche gain the front of the buttress and climb the difficult blunt rib to the small stance on Comet Wall. Move up right to gain a horizontal crack above the block forming the roof of the cave. A short sensational traverse right leads to a hanging groove (runner). Climb the wall moving slightly right on widely-spaced flat holds. Bold climbing requiring careful rope work. The lower pitch (often damp) can be avoided and the route can be climbed direct from the ground by traversing the left wall of the cave.

63   The Scryking   20m   E5   P2   1997   ★★★
6a A superb route. A little contrived in its lower section but the upper arete is exciting exposed and committing. Start at the niche as for Mastermind, but rather than moving left immediately and gaining the front of the rib make an awkward move up to clip a peg in the wall. Make a balancey move left onto the arete, clip the peg in Mastermind and climb to the ledge with difficulty. Follow the traverse right as for Mastermind, but rather than continuing into the hanging groove place some good friends in the break and blast straight up the arete, making a committing move to gain the good break just below the top.

64   Comet Wall   20m   HVS   P1   1957   ★★★
5a Starts on the right-hand side of the face at a slimy corner below a roof. A fine climb with plenty of atmosphere. Climb the corner past a projecting block to a cave, then cross the vertical left wall to a small stance on the front of the buttress. Move into a flake crack on the right and climb this, and the very steep groove above, to the top. The **Left-hand Finish** HVS (5a) From the stance bridge up and climb the left-hand crack on wide jams. Slightly harder than the original. The slimy corner start can be avoided by scrambling up to the cave and traversing left across the wall.

65   Side-show   20m   HVS   P2   1970
5a Just right of Comet Wall and a few metres left of the gully is a crack and groove. Climb this to the top of a pedestal. Move up to a good horizontal break and semi-hand traverse left to a good foothold. Bold moves up left now to finish.

66   Synchromesh   35m   HVS   P1   1971
5a A diagonal route across the buttress commanding some exposed positions. Start immediately right of Apparition in a shallow corner. Climb up a crack in the right wall, round the rib and up the chimney. Traverse right to gain the rib, move right and up the steep face on layaways to gain the face of Skyjacker. Descend a little to swing across and up to the stance. Climb Comet Wall to the top of the crack then move right up the arete moving rightwards.

67 Scissors 12m M P1 Pre 1954
The gully on the right marks the end of Number Five Buttress. A
useful means of descent.

68 Jaywalk 122m HVS P2 1971
A high-level girdle of Number Five Buttress which covers some
interesting ground. Pitches (2) and (8) are the most difficult.
1. 12m 4b Scramble up to the cave of Comet Wall and traverse
steeply left to a stance and belay on the front.
2. 17m 5a An off-balance traverse left to a peg runner is followed
by a descent of 4 metres via awkward layback cracks. Left to the
arete and traverse to a tree.
3. 9m 4a Move left, up the rib then left into Apparition.
4. 14m 4c Cross the steep open corner on the left to reach a
narrow grass ledge on the front. Continue over saplings to a ledge
overlooking the direct finish to Boundary Chimney.
5. 12m 4b Traverse into the chimney, ascend it for a metre or so
then delicately left to a ledge.
6. 14m 4a Descend ledges, cross a square chimney, then a
descending traverse across a slab to a grass ledge. Scramble past
a tree and descend slightly to a tree belay.
7. 23m 4c Mantelshelf up left to gain a niche, traverse left and
swing round into the deep groove of Daniel. Continue for 9 metres
to belays on a large vegetated ledge.
8. 14m 5a Move down left and traverse the top of the slab using
dubious flakes above. Pull up left to gain a narrow ledge above the
main overhang, and climb the wall above to a belay on the left.
9. 7m 4c Climb on to the rib above and finish up the slab on the left.

THE LONG WALL   The wall which commences right of Scissors
consists of about 250 metres of more-or-less continuous rocks
varying in height from 8 to 18 metres. Much of it is heavily vegetated: but several good buttresses are found. Routes are best
identified in relation to descent routes D, E, F and H starting at
Scissors and working rightwards:

69 Millroy's Climb 12m (VD) Pre 1954
The obvious V groove just right of Scissors, usually very slimy.
Finishes in the middle of the path above.

70 Savage Sentence 15m E1 P1 1985
5b Six metres right of Scissors is a clean-cut green corner with a
projecting spike. From the base of the wall below the corner step
left off a slab across a deep hole on to a foothold below a short
groove. Climb the groove and continue up a leaning wall past the
spike. Finish up the open corner above. Ten metres right of

Scissors is a square bay between two undercut and overhanging aretes. The fine hanging flake on the left wall provides a hard route.

71   Guillotine   14m   E3   P1   1973   ★
6a   An aptly-named climb awaiting the chop! The flake crack requires a horizontal approach with strenuous and determined climbing to achieve the vertical section. Finish more easily.

72   Angle Crack   10m   HS   P1   Pre 1969
In the left corner of the bay is a crack. Start up to the right until one can step back left into the crack where it widens. Up the crack to the top.   Next comes a black tree-covered wall which ends after 30 metres at a projecting buttress with a huge oak 3 metres up.

73   Humus   15m   E3   P2   1988
5c   Climb the shallow groove just left of the oak, moving right through the overhang to a nasty pull out on the moor. May need re-cleaning.   To the right of Humus, some 40 metres right of Comet Buttress, is an easy ascent/descent route in the form of a short chimney with ledges on the left ('Long Step') and an easy-angled gully at the top.   The steep little buttress on the right provides two interesting climbs.

74   Ryvoan Crack   9m   MS   P2   1961
An imposing chimney-crack, the first 3 metres being the most difficult.

75   Haberdashery   14m   E2   P2   1974   ★
6a   Climbs the wall immediately left of Ryvoan Crack. A fine little route of considerable technical difficulty. A hidden gem, but only if pre-cleaned and dry. A thin layback crack leads to a standing position on a sloping ledge. Move up and make a hard move or long reach to gain holds beneath the overhang. A short steep traverse right to the arete leads to easier climbing.   Thirty metres down to the right is a buttress with a prominent overhang. Lower down to the right is a heavily-overgrown buttress, rounding the foot of this and ascending 10 metres we come to a chimney:

76   Forgotten Chimney   9m   (VD)   1954
Easily to the last metre or so then a short back-and-knees section. to finish.   At the top of the slope is the easy ascent/descent 'Balance Step' identified by the protruding block with the flat top. To the right is the Slot Buttress.

77   Careful Crack   10m   (VS)   1965
In the left wall is an obvious crack. Climb the cracked wall trending rightwards to below the crack proper. Pull over friable rock to enter it, then on to the top.

78 The Warriors of Hunaman   15m   E5   P2   1997   ★★★
6b The striking flying left-hand arete of slot buttress. A gymnastic climb with a well protected crux. Climb the initial arete passing a good peg to the large ledge below the roof. Stretch up and clip two further pegs then make a series of wild gymnastic moves through the roof and up the wall using the flying arete on the right. Superb.

On the right-hand side of the buttress are three breaks:

79 The Slot   13m   S   P1   Pre 1957
The left-hand line. Climb the chimney, passing behind the chockstone (or less securely over it), and climb to the overhang. Possible belay. Step right and follow the 'slot' above to finish.

80 Little Something   12m   VS   P1   Pre 1957
4c Start 3 metres right of The Slot at a small cave. Surmount the initial overhang with difficulty and up to a groove which leads to a tree. Then take the left ledge of the slab above, moving left at the overhang.

81 Winklepicker   12m   HVS   P1   1966   ★
5a The right-hand break is a thin crack line which cuts through the overhang at the top. Not especially difficult, but sustained. Move awkwardly up to a small pinnacle at 3 metres, then continue with difficulty to a niche below a final overhanging layback. On the right is a mossy slab and round the corner is a cracked wall capped by a large roof. A bilberry-topped boulder stands predominantly nearby.

82 Barracuda   14m   (VS)   1960
4c A blunt arete just right of an oak at the left end of the wall is climbed by balance moves to an earthy ledge and belay. A short wide crack above is awkward to start and strenuous to finish.

83 Shelter Climb   16m   D   P1   Pre 1950   ★
Follows a traverse line beneath the roof on the right. Up the left side of the cracked wall to a ledge under the overhang. Traverse right round the corner, using large holds on a shelf, to a small ledge. A gully leads to the moor.

84 Energy   18m   (HVS)   1966
5a A few metres right of Shelter is a deep hollow and springing from this is an obvious fiercely-overhanging crack. Pull over the initial overhang and then strenuously up the crack until the slab above can be gained. Easily to the top. Needs gardening.

85 Rhino   16m   (VS)   1960
4c At the right side of the hollow is a prominent rightward-facing corner, providing very interesting climbing. Climb the groove, easily at first, but with increasing difficulty until below a short overhanging

section. An awkward move brings jammed blocks within reach below the final overhang. Move on to the left rib, step round to a good foothold, then straight up.

NEEDLE'S HIGH BUTTRESS   Twenty metres on from the hollow a huge bilberry-topped boulder stands against the crag forming the Needle's Eye. Starting from the eye is a steep undercut cracked groove.

86   Offspring   13m   HS   P1   1989
4b   Climb the groove, gained from the left, and the wall above, passing the tree and finishing up the jam crack. Interesting.

87   Arbor Crack (Cordite Start)   13m   VS   P2   1961
5a   Just round the front from the eye is a steep wide undercut crack with a tree. Climb the difficult rib to gain the chimney crack, continue strenuously past the tree and finish up the chimney above. The chimney crack can still be reached from left despite the departure of Birtwistle's sapling at 3 metres.

88   Ledge and Crack   14m   (D)   1937
The steep cracked gangway a few metres right of the last climb. Climb on good holds to a ledge on the left, then up the crack finishing over a bulging block.

89   Oak Wall   10m   (HS)   Pre 1957
Climbs the steep wall a few metres right of the gangway of Ledge and Crack, and left of a dirty corner. Start towards the right of the wall and pull up to a thin tree. Traverse left and up to an oak. Belay. A slightly impending wall above is climbed on good holds to a rather awkward finish.

90   Wafer Crack   12m   (VS)   1966
Just right of the dirty corner is a straight narrow crack starting at half-height. Climb easily to the crack then by strenuous jams to the top. Twenty metres to the right, around the foot of a vegetated buttress, is a cave. High above this on the right is a pinnacle - the Aiguille des Moutons.

91   Intestine   12m   (M)   pre 1954
This is the cave. Climb the loose subterranean chimney and emerge through a hole on the right on to a grass ledge. The gully on the right leads to a large ledge behind the pinnacle.

92   Aiguille Des Moutons   5m   (VD)   Pre 1954
Starts from the finishing point of the previous route, which may also be gained by scrambling up a leftward-slanting grass rake 20 metres right of Intestine. Ascend directly to the top. Reverse to descend,

which may be awkward if wet. Easy access to or from the moor is available from behind the Aiguille des Moutons through the cave.

93 Take Five 9m (VS) 1961
5a A more direct way of reaching the Aiguille, starting up the right-hand side of the slab right of Intestine. Hardish climbing up the slab and groove on the right an up to the summit block by a tree. Round right to finish. Overgrown. To the right of the Aiguille is a high wall. The first feature is a steep vegetated crack containing a stout oak:

94 Crack Of Roots 18m (VS) 1965
Climb a shallow groove, then the crack on good jams to the tree. Continue more easily to the overhangs. The chimney above is awkward to enter and leave but holds seem safe. Several routes have been made up the next section of wall but are heavily vegetated. Rounding the foot of the buttress and ascending a short way there is a cutaway, and a few metres higher up is the end of the Long Wall. The last feature is a cave which narrows to a crack 5 metres up:

95 Bottleneck 9m VS P1
4c Worthwhile little route on typical rounded grit. Climb the cave until the walls converge, then pull out round the overhang into a short crack above. This gives out on to a heathery ledge. Continue up the short awkward crack, then under the summit boulder to finish through the cave.

Bottleneck is the last route on Long Wall, the next climbs are found by traversing 50 metres along the hillside to an isolated buttress of rounded gritstone. This is:

THE NORTH BUTTRESS BLOCK

96 The Chimney D P1
The obvious fissure at the left end of the block. Entry is awkward, but easier climbing follows.

97 Hotrod 13m VS P1 1966
4c Starts 6 metres right of The Chimney below a thin crack splitting the initial overhang. Climb this and move right to a bulging crack which leads to a small ledge. Traverse left for a metre then make a direct ascent up the wall by delicate balance moves.

98 Speedway 13m VS P1 1965
4c Three metres right of Hotrod is a thin crack in the bulge, and 3 metres right again is another thin crack leading to an overhang at 4 metres. Ascend either crack followed by the bulging crack above. Move left and finish up the awkward bulging green crack to the top.

99 Cutting the Cord 15m E4 P2 1997   ★★
5c Take the right-hand start to Speedway move slightly left and
then climb direct through the bulging pocketed wall to the roof.
Make a long reach round the roof to gain a horizontal break in the
lip, (medium friends). Ape excitingly rightwards for 4 metres until an
awkward move enables a standing position to be attained above the
roof . Pumpy.

100 Double Top 10m HVS P1 1958   ★★
5a An impressive line up the steep clean wall at the right-hand end
of the Block. There is a barrier of overhangs at the top. Ascend to
the ceiling, then move out left along a crack. After a metre or so a
short incipient crack in the bulge above provides a break. Surmount
the bulge strenuously, the final move being the most difficult.

101 Over the Top 10m E4 P3 1997   ★★
6a A committing lead directly through the roof above Double Top.
Follow Double Top to the ceiling. Arrange gear and gain good holds
just below the lip of the roof. Take a deep breath and in a positive
and unfaltering frame of mind turn the roof using slopers and a right
heel hook. The block can be girdled left to right finishing up Double
Top (**Ringway** 43m VS).

For the next climbs, traverse horizontally rightwards from the North
Buttress Block until a good path appears. Follow the path down to
the right for 150 metres until a high buttress can be seen (or follow
the path upward on to the moor at the stile).

NORTH BUTTRESS A fine crag about 25 metres high at its
maximum, the main feature being a great corner just left of centre.
At the left end is a subsidiary buttress which is, in fact, a pinnacle.
The front of this left-hand section is split by an easy-angled chimney
and a wide clean-cut crack:

102 Pinnacle Face 12m (VS) 1963
4c Starts 3 metres left of the wide crack. Ascend an awkward crack
to an overhang. Traverse right for 2 metres then up to the foot of a
slab. Climb this, and the blocks above, to the top of the pinnacle.

103 Thin Man's Delight 12m S P1 1937
The clean wide crack just to the right, which overhangs at the start.
A bulge at 3 metres provides some difficulty, the easier-angled
crack above leads to a ledge and block. Surmount the block and
gain the upper crack, up this to the overhang. Traverse right then on
to the top of the pinnacle.

104 Pinnacle Ordinary Route 12m D P1 1958
The grassy chimney 2 metres right of the previous route. Start at

the right edge of a mossy slab, make a high step up then left into the chimney. This leads to a cave. A crack in the left wall leads to the top. Fifteen metres to the right is the large corner of North Buttress Crack. Seven metres left of this is a prominent rib with an overhang at 2 metres, which marks the start of:

105 Midsummer Night's Dream 36m HVS P1 1972   ★
5b Finds its way up the buttress to the left of North Buttress Crack. Rather devious, but fine, clean climbing of much technical interest. Climb the rib by difficult layback moves for 4 metres then move easily to the overhang. With hands above this make a sensational hand traverse right to the blunt arete, and continue at this level to a belay in the corner. Move delicately left on top of the flake to reach a good flat hold. A difficult pull up gains a good ledge, then directly up the blunt rib to the top.

106 Caveman's Corner 14m (S) C1958
Starts 2 metres left of North Buttress Crack. Step left on to a wide sloping rock ledge 3 metres above the base of the buttress. Move left until it is possible to move up and gain a line of good holds for the hands. Make a semi-hand traverse left on to the rib of Midsummer Night's Dream, up this for a metre then follow an awkward heathery break leftwards on to bilberry ledges.

107 North Buttress Crack 17m S P1 1958   ★★
The great corner and crack on the left of the main buttress. A very fine climb. Ascend the crack for 5 metres to a good spike runner. Layback up the wide crack (often green) to a good hold on the left rib. Pull round a jammed block into a recess, then go through a constriction on to easier-angled rock. Follow this then scramble 6 metres left to a tree belay.

108 North Buttress Ordinary 20m S P1 1958   ★
This is a convenient means of avoiding the crux of North Buttress Crack but still provides worthwhile climbing. Start as for the previous route. Ascend to the spike runner, then traverse right and mantelshelf on to a small ledge below an obvious flake crack. Follow the flake up to the left then pull over on to the ledge above. Tree belay. Traverse left into the crack and finish up this as for the previous climb.

109 North Buttress Direct 24m HVS P1 1961   ★
5a Follows the obvious crack line 5 metres right of North Buttress Crack and finishes up the edge of the final tower. Ascend the pea-pod-shaped crack to the overhang, pull over this (crux) and continue to a tree belay. The short steep corner above leads to large terraces. Gain a narrow ledge at 2 metres and traverse out left

under the overhang to an exposed situation on the nose of the buttress. Move up and rightwards to the top.

110 Spring Fever 30m VS P2 1972
4b Start as for North Buttress Direct and, at the overhang, traverse right across the face. Mantelshelf up right and continue to the arete. Gain the ledge and walk left to the tree belay. Climb the short steep corner to the terrace. Pull up into a short slanting crack, move up right then leftward to finish.

111 Campanile 28m HVS P2 1972/87   ★★
5a An excellent pitch. Ten metres right of North Buttress Crack is a deep V groove. Start at the foot of the left rib. Climb the rib and slab trending slightly leftwards. Continue up the centre to the ledge. Move left and climb the short steep corner to the terrace (Belay). Move left under the roof and traverse the exposed tower face to reach a good pocket. Climb directly up the cracked face to the top. Alternatively traverse the ledge below the face into the corner of North Buttress Crack to belay. Move up and climb the face on the right to gain the pocket and on to the top.

112 The Cleavage 7m S P1 1972
The deep V groove 10 metres right of North Buttress Crack.

113 The Right Rib 9m VS P1 1972
4b Layback up the sharp crack in the right wall of The Cleavage and up right to gain the front face. Finish awkwardly up the arete moving left (often damp).

114 Gossamer 12m HVS P2 1972
5a Start near the base of the buttress just right of the gully of The Cleavage. Climb the slab to the horizontal break. Reaching the small overhang above is difficult and delicate, go rightwards into the centre of the face. Climb the cracks finishing right.

115 Albatross 12m HVS P2 1987
5b Start as for Gossamer but at the small overhang move left and climb adjacent to the arete finishing on the right rib. Ten metres right of The Cleavage is another deep cleft - The Catacomb. There are twin niches set in the overhangs both left and right of this.

116 Nobutjust 17m HVS P2 1972   ★
5b Start below the short undercut niche on the left of the cleft. Traverse left to a blunt nose and mantelshelf up on to the horizontal rail. Move right and delicately into the groove. Bridge up this to a good ledge. Traverse left and climb the cracks finishing rightwards. A direct start is also possible by climbing the overhang on the left and pulling right into the base of the groove.

117   Crystal Dance   13m   E1   P1   1987
5c   Start as for Nobutjust to gain the horizontal rail. Climb the slab above next to the thin curved crack (runner) using a small crystal hold. Move left to finish up the cracks.

118   The Catacomb   12m   (VD)   1972
The deep cleft starts steeply and has a loose subterranean exit.

119   Shindig   18m   E2   P1   1971   ★★
6a   The niche in the overhangs just right of The Catacomb. Start left of a holly and ascend to the roof. Gain the groove above with difficulty, then up left to an awkward exit. Ascend the wall and arete above to finish. A very good route.

120   The Fairway   12m   (MVS)   1972
4b   Start to the right and above the holly, at the right-hand side of an undercut slab. Gain the shelf on the left, then straight up to the wide horizontal crack. Traverse left, then rightwards to finish up a short crack. A girdle traverse (**Voortrek**, VS 4c) of the North Buttress area has been made starting across the hand traverse of Midsummer Night's Dream, then following a horizontal course at about 9 metres, finishing across the slab of the Fairway.

121   The Peeler   12m   VS   P2   1963
4c   This climb lies on an isolated buttress 20 metres to the right of the holly below Shindig. There is a thin bulging crack in the centre. Climb direct to the crack and up it until, at the top, it is possible to traverse right and mantelshelf to finish. A good route and a fitting finale to the escarpment.

Further right there are problems but no routes of any length. There is also a fine square block close to the road at the extreme end of the edge.

GUISECLIFF – GRADED LIST

E6
On the Edge (6b)

E5
The Warriors of
Hunaman (6b)
The Scryking (6a)

E4
Over the Top (6a)
Mastermind (5c)
Cutting the Cord (5c)

E3
Aftermath (5c)
Guillotine (6a)
Dingbat (6a)
Nice 'n' Sleazy (5c)
Humus (5c)
Barleycorn (5b)

E2
Shindig (6a)
Haberdashery (6a)
The Creation (5c)
Foreign Bodies (5c)

E1
Skyjacker (5c)
Crystal Dance (5c)
Savage Sentence (5b)
The Verger (5b)
Agrippa (5a)
Hook Route (5b)
Pendulum (5b)
Tombstone (5b)
Ruscator (5b)
Stretcher (5b)

HVS
Side-show (5a)
Mantelshelfman (5c)
Aggrippina (5a)
Midsummer Night's
Dream (5b)
Magnificat (5a)
Albatross (5b)
Nobutjust (5b)
North Buttress Direct (5a)
Double Top (5a)
Campanile (5a)
Crossover (5a)
Comet Wall (5a)
Gossamer (5a)
Energy (5a)
Synchromesh (5a)
Bold John (5a)
Winklepicker (5a)
Jaywalker (5a)
North Wall Eliminate (5a)
Microcrack (5a)
Belfry (4c)

HALTON HEIGHTS

SITUATION AND CHARACTER   Situated above the Halton Moor road near Eastby village, the crag consists of a number of quarried bays and some natural bouldering areas. It faces south-east and is slightly more sheltered than the natural edges hereabouts. The rock is quarried gritstone in the classic mould and gives rise to the usual array of walls, corners and aretes. The rock is good in places, poor in others. Where it is clean, some worthwhile routes exist. The quarry is pleasant and the summit viewpoint well worth a visit. More traffic would substantially improve the quality of some of the climbs, which follow good natural lines.

APPROACHES AND ACCESS   From Skipton take the Harrogate road (A59) and soon turn left signposted for Embsay. Through Embsay to Eastby and then follow the Halton Moor road past Eastby crag and up the S bend. After passing a vegetated crag and a cattle grid a parking space will be seen on the right. Below the road and a little further on are numerous small boulders with a few interesting problems whilst above the road an obvious path follows the fell wall up leftwards into the left-hand end of the quarries. An obvious needle of natural grit lies to the right of the first quarry. Two hundred metres up the road is a track into the right-hand quarry and 200 metres further on is a larger parking space on the right. The approach takes only minutes. **The crag is within the Barden Moor Access area so see special notes on page 10 for conditions.**

THE CLIMBS

THE LOWER QUARRY
The climbs are described from left to right. The short wall on the extreme left contains two thin cracks.

1   Left Crack   7m   VS   P2
5a   After a problem start the deficient crack is followed to a dirty and serious finish. Skulking in from the right is easier.

2   Right Crack   7m   MVS   P1
4c   The more definite right-hand crack.

3   The Arete   9m   VS   P2   ★
5a   A pleasant slabby arete which limits the left end of the next wall has a very tricky start.

Stake belays above this and the next few routes to the right.

The slab to the right contains two crack lines which provide useful reference points. Much chipping has taken place lower down and, though even in a quarry such as this the practice is to be deplored, it does give a problematic traverse line and the starting holds for the next seven routes, which all, unfortunately, have rather serious finishes.

4   Both Ends Burning   9m   HVS   P2
5c Directly up the slab just right of the arete to a small overlap. Step right to a shallow triangular niche then, with care, take the easiest line up to the top.

5   Coma Toes   9m   E2   P2   ★
6a Straight up into the triangular niche then climb the slab above direct via a rather bold mantelshelf. Perhaps the best route on the slab.

6   Crack Line One   9m   VS   P2
4c The ex-pegged and verdant crack.

7   In The Flat Field   9m   HVS   P2
5b The slab between the two cracks. Trend left or, if tired of life, go straight up.

8   Fission Chips   9m   HVS   P2
5c The boulder-problem wall and rib on the left of the next crack line. Move left to the poor finish of the previous route or the cleaner top section of the next route may be more appropriate.

9   Crack Line Two   10m   HVS   P2
5b The right-hand crack line leads into a cleaned brown niche, which may still be a little friable but looks infinitely safer than the 'damoclean' flakes which previously perched there.

10   Chip Chop   10m   E2   P3
5c The last route on the slab is difficult to start. Move up and right to gain holds and then a ledge. The vegetated slab above needs a good clean. A traverse into the heathery groove on the right is safer but no more pleasant.

11   Wombling Upwards   12m   MVS   P1
4b This route climbed the obvious corner to the right of the slab in its entirety. It has unfortunately reverted to nature and needs re-cleaning.

12   Empires and Dance   12m   E1   P2   ★
5b The arete to the right of the slabs is tricky at first and feels serious.

13 Urizen 15m E1 P3   ★
5b The obvious rib, short slab and hanging groove to the left of the impressive, (once) well scrubbed corner.

14 The Invisible Worm 15m E2 P2   ★★
5c The 'unclimbed groove' mentioned in the last guide became, for a while, the 'well scrubbed corner' mentioned above. It provides continually interesting and sustained climbing but in 1998 was overdue for another scrub.

To the right of the arete the crag is steep and vegetated, but contains an obvious smooth and, as yet, unclimbed groove. About 15 metres right of this groove is a broken overgrown line starting below and just right of two short, vertical shotholes about a third of the way up the cliff.

15 Censored 15m VS P1
4c Climb up and swing left above the shotholes to the base of a shield-shaped slab. Climb this and exit right to a good ledge. The heathery corner above was originally climbed on pegs, but looks feasible free if cleaned first.

Another old route, The Fingerstone, climbed an arete in this vicinity at Hard Severe but its exact whereabouts is in some doubt. The next named routes are some distance further right in two deep V-shaped bays known as the Twin Bays.

16 The Wild, Wild Goose Chase 11m HVS P2
5c A hard start up, then off, the shallow ramp on the left wall of the first bay leads to holds and an easier groove.

17 The Pretenders 11m E1 P1   ★
5b The thin crack just right.

The steep corner is unrecorded and the next route is:-

18 Get Nervous 8m HVS P1
5a Shake, rattle and roll up the cracks in the opposite wall of the bay.

The next route is the V-shaped slab on the right arete of the second bay. Other crumbling routes have been done in between but are left for the desperate to rediscover.

19 In Your Mind 6m HVS P2
5b The arete soon becomes slabby in a distinct V-shape.

The crag degenerates again to the right until the next obvious feature is a silver birch growing from the wall a few metres up the crag. To the right of the tree is a short corner and then a larger, more obvious one. To the left of this is:-

20 Small Wall 6m MVS P1
4b Climb thin cracks in the steep wall 2 metres left of the corner.

21 Tobermory 7m HS P1
4b The obvious corner, hardest at the top.

22 Black Wall Arete 7m HS P2
The left arete of the next slabby wall.

The Black Wall itself can be climbed almost anywhere at up to 5a
but the two easiest lines wander up at about Severe. To the right of
here is a steeper section capped by an overhang.

23 Greenham Cruisers 9m E4 P2   ★
6b The arete capped by the overhang needs some long-reaching
negotiations and care with fission products.

24 The Ugsome Thing 9m VS P1
4c The obvious groove line right of Greenham Cruisers

Above the quarry is a line of boulders which provide good problems
especially the slab at the right-hand end. The right rib of this is:-

25 Nuclear Winter 8m MVS P1
4c Pebble dash the rib. The slab direct is possibly 5a.

Over to the right is the pinnacle.

26 Easter Island 9m VD P1   ★★
Climb the long side starting from the lowest point. Descend by the
same line or, much better, jump across the gap as:-

27 The Quantum Leap 2m J1
One small step! The opposite sides are 4c and 5a.

Right of here are small outcrops and boulders but 300 metres right
is:

THE UPPER QUARRY
This contains four aretes and a wall on the right. These are obvious,
short and vary between 4c and 5b, the best being:-

28 Nick's Arete 8m HVS P2
5b The right-hand and longest arete.

29 Shortcake 8m HVS P1
5a The once-pegged crack round the corner, an historic route.

HAWKCLIFFE

SITUATION AND CHARACTER. Hawkcliffe crag is situated in a wood just above the B6265 between Keighley and Steeton. Although hidden from the road the location of the crag can easily be identified by Victoria Tower which sits above the crag. The crag contours the hillside for about 300 metres and attains a height of about 25 metres. The rock varies along the edge and buttresses of fine textured natural grit are to be found alongside smooth quarried faces. In general the routes tend to follow steep cracks or aretes and the climbing is usually strenuous and technical. The crag faces North East and the abundance of trees overshadowing certain buttresses can lead to the build up of lichen on certain routes. The leaf litter and uneven ground at the base of the crag may necessitate a little bushwhacking to get from buttress to buttress, but a persistent approach will give some rewarding adventure. The crag environment also provides a unique suburban ecosystem for a diverse range of wildlife and despite the close proximity of busy roads and towns Deer and Foxes can be regularly seen.

APPROACHES AND ACCESS The crag is on private land with no public right of way, however, in 1997 an access agreement for climbers was negotiated by the BMC by kind permission of the landowner, Lady Rozelle Raynes. The local agent is Mr Thompson of Hawkcliffe Farm who also manages the shooting rights to the estate.

The access agreement only relates to approaches from below. DO NOT ATTEMPT TO APPROACH FROM THE LANE ON TOP.

The crag is easily approached by road or rail. From the traffic lights in the centre of Steeton travel along the B6265 towards Keighley until, after about half a mile, Hawkcliffe wood can be seen on the right. There is a regular bus service between Keighley and Skipton that travels along the B6265 and the crag can be reached on foot from Steeton Railway station in about thirty minutes. Parking is a problem here but there is room for 4 cars on the verge near the lay-by on the south side of the B6265 between Hawkcliffe Wood and Hawkcliffe Farm at NGR 043441- please ensure sufficient space left for bus to pull in. Walk NW along the roadside for 40 metres to go through a gate on the left into the wood. (there is a fine stone archway just beyond this point). Follow the main track up through the wood to the crag, 5-10 minutes, passing a BMC access notice. After a few hundred metres the track levels out and branches. Follow the uphill right-hand branch, which eventually opens out into

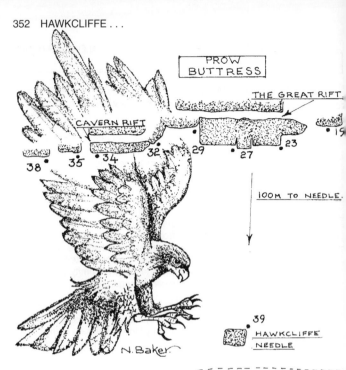

PROW BUTTRESS

THE GREAT RIFT.

CAVERN RIFT

100M TO NEEDLE.

N. Baker

39

HAWKCLIFFE NEEDLE

the 'Amphitheatre' (small ruin on the left). The obvious smooth slabby wall of Emerald Buttress should now be clearly visible directly in front of you with Amphitheatre Wall up to the far right and Prow Buttress is hidden 150metres off to the left. Whilst the crag continues rightwards beyond Amphitheatre Wall it is somewhat broken and overgrown **Note: Dogs are not allowed. Create a minimum of disturbance to wildlife, and keep gardening to a minimum. Leave no litter.**

THE CLIMBS are described from right to left when facing the crag starting with the right-hand arete of the Amphitheatre Wall. (A few metres to the right of Right-hand arete is an easy scramble to the top of the crag at Diff)

Amphitheatre Wall A fairly clean compact wall of natural grit.

1 Right-hand arete 18m VS P1
4c Takes the broken right-hand arete of the wall.

EMERALD BUTTRESS   TOWER BUTTRESS   AMPHITHEATRE WALL

HAWKCLIFFE

TO LOGGING AREA

TRACK

TO THE B6265 ~ 50M.

2 Syrett's Slit 18m E1 P1 ★

5b Follows the obvious offwidth crack just left of the arete.
Awkward at first to the large blocks (handle with care!) but easing
higher up.

3 The Crack of Dawn 20m E3 P2 ★★

5c An exciting and slippery little number. Follow Syrett's Slit to the
break. Traverse awkwardly left to the peg. Ah!. move strenuously
left to finish up the leftwards slanting crack.

The next route tackles the innocuous incipient crack system 4 metres left of Syrett's Slit.

4   Stepmother Jag   18m   E4   P1   ★★★
6b An excellent and technical climb with good but hard earned protection. Climb into the vague scoop (runners). It is possible to place an RP in the thin crack above from here and, whilst being awkward, this does provide better protection for the problematical crux. Make difficult moves to gain rounded holds in the niche above. Clip the peg and then move strenuously left to gain the good crack which is followed to the top.

5   Babes in the Boneyard   18m   E3   P2   ★
6a Start 5metres left of Stepmother Jag at the obvious corner which is climbed for a few metres to the break. Finger traverse rightwards along the break until a difficult move gains the finishing crack of Crack of Dawn. A committing lead.

6   Brian's Crack   12m   S   P1   ★★
4a The obvious corner crack provides a clean, well protected and enjoyable route.

7   Emmi's Orror   12m   D   P1
The dirty crack just left again.

Immediately to the left the crag becomes broken and stepped with two large overhangs, it is split by various cracks and chimneys and numerous possibilities exist for easier routes and variations.

8   What No Boc No   14m   HVS   P2
5b Takes the obvious, overhanging, prowy rib.

Tower Buttress Area
After about 15metres the crag rises again to form an impressive and prominent buttress with an overhang at half height. The overhang sports two pegs close together which protect the crux of Birdsong. The next route climbs the crack in the front of the buttress.

9   Freedom   20m   E2   P2   ★
5c Climb the initial crack to the right-hand side of the roof and then follow the hanging crack above.

10   Birdsong   20m   E7   P2   ★★★
6c Climb easily up the broken crack to a ledge below the niche. Clip the pegs and make powerful moves to gain an obvious undercut (crux). Continue with difficulty to gain good holds and a rest on the arete. Climb the arete above moving back onto the front face of the buttress near the top. Superb climbing in an excellent position.

The next climb starts 15 metres further left and just left of the corner.

11 Creaking Joints 12m E4 P2   ★
6a Scramble up to the large ledge. Climb the steep crack just left of the tree with awkward moves to finish.

To the left is a clean buttress with a series of horizontal breaks and a slabby arete on its left-hand side. The next route climbs the wall and then follows the left arete.

12 Zyo Kruk Klik 14m E5 P1   ★★
6b A technical but well protected route. Climb the centre of the wall to the top break. Traverse left to the peg and then make a high rock-over and a series of intricate foot changes to gain a standing position on the slab. Using the arete make a committing move to gain good holds. Peg belay/lower-off on the right.

Emerald Buttress is formed by a compact shield of quarried grit. Unfortunately it is overhung by trees and often sports a bright green coat of algae. Despite this its routes, when clean, are of excellent quality.

13 The Blood On The Shamrock 18m E6 P3   ★★★
6a Climbs the obvious, sharp right-hand arete of the buttress. Technical and committing.
Start just left of the gully below the arete. Climb easily up the arete and arrange friends in the break. Take a deep breath and make a series of superb and technical moves up the arete to eventually gain good holds. Superb - on completion!

14 Ginny Greenteeth 18m E5 P2   ★★★
6a A bold outing up the middle of the wall. Start up and to the left of The Blood on the Shamrock at an obvious notch. Pull onto the wall and make committing moves to gain a thin ramp. Move up to some small horizontal cracks which take some small, but good runners. Move up and left to gain a footledge and rest below the crux. Using some reasonable holds make a bold move to gain slopers just below the top. Keeping it together move slightly right and mantle the top. (probably advisable to clean the finishing holds prior to a lead)

15 Woodland Ecology 20m E5 P2   ★★
6a The original route on the wall, taking a more devious line and now superseded by the more direct Ginny Greenteeth, but still providing fine bold climbing. Start from the foot of Ginny Greenteeth but move right at half height to the finish of Blood On the Shamrock.

16 RIP 18m E1 P1   ★
5b Takes the thin finger crack up the slabby wall 8 metres left of Ginny Greenteeth.

17 Another one of Emmi's? 14m HVD P1
The wide crack in the corner just left of RIP

The crag now deteriorates for about 100 metres or so until it regains height. Central Wall is about 10 metres high and is split by numerous cracks in the Diff to Severe range. It has a large boulder abutting its base. The only recorded route in this area is;

18 First Steps 10m VD P1   ★
Climb onto the large vegetated boulder. Ascend the twin cracks to an overhanging corner and make a high step to finish this pleasant climb.

Great Rift Area
Further left the crag takes on grand proportions with the imposing Prow Buttress forming the front wall of The Great Rift. Here a geological fault has produced a huge chasm, which despite offering numerous challenging possibilities has a rather dank and sombre atmosphere. In contrast to this however the front face forms the impressive Prow Buttress which hosts some steep and striking lines.; Guarding the entrance to The Great Rift on the right is a fine slabby arete.

19 Abandon Hope 10m E3 P2   ★
6a From the lowest point of the rib climb up precariously with a long reach to the obvious break at 5 metres, and welcome nut runners. Another difficult pull gains better holds for the steepening finish.

A number of easy climbs were recorded inside the rift in the sixties, these included

20 Gully Exit 7m D
Described in 1965 as 'The only exit on the left of the Great rift'

21 Crack and Flutings 10m VD
A crack and wall climb via a bilberry ledge with a sensational finish. The obvious stepped crack to the left provides an alternative start.

Numerous possibilities exist for further routes in this inner sanctum but the only recent addition is -

22 Babylon 10m VS P1   ★
5a Takes an obvious hand-jam crack and arete just left of a steep groove in the vegetated narrow rift between the two main climbing areas. A very good line but one which will require regular traffic to keep it clean.

Prow Buttress
The front face gives some of the longest gritstone routes in
Yorkshire.

23 Flame Arete 20m E5 P2 ★★
6b Takes the right-hand arete of the main front face. Climb the
crack to a flake in the arete. Move up to a thin horizontal break
(runners) and then make difficult and technical moves up the fine
square-cut arete to gain better holds.

24 Gully Crack One 20m S P1
Start a couple of metres to the left of Flame Arete and climb the
obvious crack which eventually eases into a gully.

25 Gully Crack Two 20m S P1
Climb the Crack Immediately left of Gully Crack One.

26 Walk By 21m E3 P2 ★
5c A good climb that starts two metres to the left of Gully Crack
Two. Climb the thin crack in the vague chimney and then directly up
the right hand arete above. Strenuous.

27 Squirrel Crack 22 m E1 P1 ★★★
5b The steep, curving crack that runs up the right-hand side of the
overhanging prow provides an impressive and daunting route. The
green flaky groove provides an excellent introduction to the struggle
that ensues to exit the leaning pod for the perfect jamming crack
above.

The next climb starts round to the left of the prow at an obvious
chimney below a large observation boulder.

28 Blull Gumm Sloggitt 20m E2 P1 ★
6a A good, well protected, route up the slabby wall right of the
chimney. Bridge up the chimney to good Friend placements and
then traverse right to a peg. Make difficult moves up and right to
better holds and more 'Friendly' slots. Climb more easily to the top.

29 Constriction Chimney 20m HVS P1 ★
5b The chimney and crack direct. A classic, but this time enjoyable,
product of its era.

30 Driveby 20m E6 P2 ★★★
6b Gain the chimney and bridge up it until level with a peg on the
left. Place runners in the chimney and then move left and clip the
peg. Make difficult moves up the wall on small holds passing a
good small rock placement. Move up and slightly left to gain the
rounded top, take a deep breath and make an awkward mantle and
so gain the summit.

The wall immediately to the left contains three pegs which were placed by an optimistic Mick Ryan. The route has yet to be climbed.

31   Skylight Chimney   10m   D   P1   ★
A caving expedition up the obvious chimney on the left. Climb above the chockstone and emerge at the top of the crag via a 'skylight'.

32   Black Forest Gateaux   12m   E1   P2   ★★
5b The appealing vertical wall to the left of the chimney is climbed from the cutaway in the left arete. Make a precarious move right past a small niche to good holds and then move up to regain the unprotected, but much easier, upper arete.

The scrappy looking cracks and corners left again provide **Preference** and **Gyro** both 10 metre Severes. Left again is an attractive wall of natural grit with a hanging shield in its centre and obvious cracks at its right and left sides.

33   Birch Tree Crack   10m   HVD   P1
Climb the right-hand crack passing the large birch.

34   Cavern Rift Crack   8m   S   P1
Climb the left-hand crack direct.

Just to the left an easy access to both the top of the crag and the back of the rift can be found, and just left of this is a short clean wall of natural grit.

35   Lauren's Wall   8m   E1   P1
5c A smidget of a problem that would normally be a solo if it wasn't for the landing. Climb the wall moving left to the arete at two thirds height. A 1.5 'flexy' Friend protects the crux.

Dropping down a short gully leads round into a bay with a smooth impending back wall. To the right of the overhanging wall is a fine square arete.

36   Bubba   12m   E3   P1   ★★
6a From a good horizontal crack rock up onto the ledge on the nose and gain a slanting break on the left. Another difficult move gains a good hold on the front and easier moves on the right lead to a ledge below a sapling. Climb straight up just right of the crack to the top.

37   Back To Basics   12m   HVS   P2   ★
5a The overhanging corner crack is climbed from the tree via a couple of layback moves to a ledge below the wider upper section. Arm bars, thigh locks and holds on the right help to gain good holds on top.

38   The Call Of The Curlew   14m   E4   P2   ★★
6a The arete to the left of the bay provides a fine series of moves mainly on its left side on good clean, natural grit. A broken flake leads to a good Friend slot then a committing move gains a good hold and small wires. Use the arete to assist an awkward move onto a good foothold and then a thin finish can be protected using a Friend zero.

Hawkcliffe Needle
About a 100 metres or so below Prow Buttress is a free-standing pinnacle. This is best reached by continuing along the level track rather then taking the uphill right-hand branch when initially approaching the crag. The needle plays host to one classic problem which, unfortunately, appears to be particularly attractive to moss and lichen.

39   The Dawning   12m   E4   ★★★
6b The steep right-hand arete provides a three star route when brushed. Climb to the break and arrange good runners. Make difficult and committing moves to gain a good hold just below the top. Gibber to the summit. A fast moving belayer may provide some confidence.

40   Last of the Moustaches   12m   VS   ★
4c A pleasant climb up the left arete.

An easy ascent/descent can be found up chipped holds up the back side of the needle.

HAWKCLIFFE – GRADED LIST

E7
Birdsong (6c)

E6
The Blood On The
 Shamrock (6a)
Driveby (6b)

E5
Ginny Greenteeth (6a)
Flame Arete (6b)
Woodland Ecology (6a)
Zyo Kruk Klik (6b)

E4
Stepmother Jag (6b)
The Dawning (6b)
Call Of The Curlew (6a)
Creaking Joints (6a)

E3
Babes in the Boneyard
 (6a)
Walk By (5c)
The Crack of Dawn (5c)
Bubba (6a)
Abandon Hope (6a)

E2
Blull Gumm Sloggitt (6a)
Freedom (5c)

E1
Lauren's Wall (5c)
Black Forest Gateaux
 (5b)
Squirrel Crack (5b)
Syrett's Slit (5b)
RIP (5a)

HVS
Constriction Chimney
 (5b)
Back To Basics (5a)

HEBDEN GILL

SITUATION AND CHARACTER   Prominent on the hillside behind Hebden near Grassington, this crag, which is both quarried and natural, has a variety of routes, including some of length and quality. Some areas, however, are dirty due to lack of traffic and some of the quarried finishes are loose. It is a generally quick drying and sunny spot but the jumbled boulder slope below much of the crag is a detracting feature. The main buttress is steep and up to 18 metres high. Up and right is another smaller bay about 8 metres high. This runs rightwards along a quarried wall into The Crevasse - a very steep and impressive wall. Subsidiary buttresses and craglets litter the hillside for a further 400 metres or so up the valley and some potential for new routes still remains.

APPROACHES AND ACCESS   Hebden lies on the B6265 Grassington-Pateley Bridge road, 2 miles east of Grassington. From the main cross-roads in the village follow a gated road north for about 1 half a mile. Park in a small car park on the left by some cottages. Follow the track through the gate and over the river. Immediately turn right and follow the path to a boulder slope dropping from the crag. Meander up this or the neighbouring hillside to the crag. Roof Buttress and Copper Nob Buttress lie further up the valley and are best reached by continuing along the initial track until directly below them.

THE CLIMBS are described from left to right.

THE MAIN CRAG
This is the area above the main boulder slope starting on the left side of tallest buttress. In the first bay there is a short, cracked slab below a split block. This is :

1   Jerry and Ben   10m   HVS   P2
5a   Climb the crack in the slab. Move right and struggle up the 'traditional' crack. Desperate!

2   Tigga, The Bagpipe Dog   17m   S   P1
Climb the slab to the right of the initial crack of Jerry and Ben to a steep grassy area. Climb across to the wall on the right and up this to a large sloping ledge. Step around to the left to some fine finishing mantelshelves.

3   Wall And Nose   20m   HVD   P1
Climb the right wall of the overgrown corner to a tree. Finish up the

corner above or, more spectacularly, traverse right to the nose.

4 The Mutant Midge 20m HVS P2   ★
5a Essentially the old variation start to The Way. Start up the steep crack 1 metre right of Wall and Nose. Climb the wall above on the right to a short curving crack and triangular overhang. Move up and right to finish easily.

5 The Way 21m E1 P2   ★
5b From a rock platform below the blunt nose of the buttress, climb a groove to the overhang and step left to a small ledge. Move up and right to a thin crack. Finish left of the prow with less difficulty.

6 Midway 18m E3 P2   ★★
6a Takes the wall left of the corner via some brilliant moves. Start up twin cracks in a slab to the first overhang. Reach over this to a small flake and then the horizontal break. Step left up the wall to finish up a short chimney right of the prow.

7 Prosecutor 16m HVS P1   ★
5a Climb the obvious overhanging corner which is much better than it looks. Peg runner on the left.

8 Right of Way 18m VS P1   ★
4c The original route of the crag and a good one. Start as for Prosecutor then climb the thin cracks on the right to an overlap. Traverse right, pull on to a ledge and finish up a detached flake.

The next climbs are round to the right, up a steep grass slope.

9 Dan Dare 16m HVS P2
5b Start 5 metres up and right from Prosecutor, below a thin crack. Climb this and pull over the overhang. Finish leftwards up the slab.

Right again are two obvious right-angled corners.

10 Fat Crack 9m D P2
The obvious chimney on the left is not very good.

11 Thin Crack 9m VS P1
4b The crack in the centre of the wall is much better.

12 Tree Climb 9m HS P1
4b The corner on the right containing a tree has a strenuous start.

13 French Fancy 6m E1 P2   ★
5c The right arete of Tree Climb has some good moves. Step left at the top.

14 The Layback 9m VS P2
4c The next corner on the right has some loose blocks and is not recommended.

15 Innominate   9m   HVS   P1
5b Climb the crack in the wall right of the corner. Step right at the top.

Further right on the left end of the wall leading towards the Crevasse is:-

16 Fun with Friends   7m   VS   P1
4b The left-hand wide crack is quite strenuous.

17 Friendly Fun   8m   HVS   P1   ★
5a Climb the diagonal crack just to the right, joining Fun with Friends at the top.

The wall between Fun with Friends and Friendly Fun is a 6a boulder problem called Funny Friends.

18 Twin Cracks   10m   VS   P1
4c Climb the right-hand twin crack, finishing up the left-hand one.

19 The Buneater   12m   E1   P2   ★
5b Down and right from Twin Cracks is a hollow. From the bottom of this climb to a break. Step right into a shallow groove and climb this until a thin crack can be followed leftwards. Finish up the wall above.

20 Wacko Saco   13m   E3   P2
5b Climb the Buneater to the break. Now move right to the arete which is climbed on both sides.

The next routes are on the impressive Crevasse Wall. Belays are a long way back. On the extreme left of Crevasse Wall is an ugly corner with a Damoclean block at the top.

21 The Crag, The Climber, His Girl and her Dog
13m   HVS   P2
5a Start in the 'ugly corner'. Gain a large block and then use the corner crack to reach holds under the loose projecting block. Traverse left for a few feet and mantel up carefully amongst much avalanche potential!

22 Comeuppance   26m   E2   P1
5b A left to right traverse of the Main Crevasse Wall, following a rising break between the overhangs of the upper wall. The crux involves a well protected move on a pocket just after a halfway resting ledge.

23 Crevasse Wall   18m   E2   P3   ★
5b A bold and exciting route. Climb a short groove line to a horizontal break. Hand traverse right for a couple of metres and move up rightwards on good ledges. Step left to finish.

24 Climbing By Runners 20m E1 P2
5b Start in the centre of the wall, below and just right of an impressive overhang and directly underneath a suspicious-looking block overhang. Climb up cracks to this overhang. Step left and, holding your breath, pull over to continue up the capped chimneys to the top. Definitely suicidal.

25 Magnificrack 20m E3 P2   ★★
6a Hebden's best route gains the impressive hanging crack right of Climbing by Runners. Start below the hanging crack in the upper wall. Climb the initial wall (crux) to gain a thin, leftward-slanting crack. Up this to two pockets which are used to gain the overhanging crack. Finish up this.

The climbs now continue from right to left along the hillside around to the left of The Main Crag.

FAT MAN'S SLAB
A clean attractive slab about 30 metres round to the left of Jerry And Ben.

26 Do or Diet 6m HVS P2
5a The right-hand line, stepping off the boulder and using the right arete near the top.

27 Diethard, Slim With Avengence 6m E4 P3   ★
6a A bold direct line up the centre of the triangular slab from the embedded block. Deviation from the purest line may reduce the grade and the anxiety!

28 Fat Man's Slab 6m E3 P3   ★
5c The left-hand line of undercut flakes is climbed delightfully to a crux above the tiny overlap at the top.

29 Lardies Route 6m S P1
The left-hand rib should suit climbers of any stature.

COPPER NOB BUTTRESS
This is the big buttress about 400 metres left of the Main Buttress. It consists of a slabby wall with some vegetation at half height and a steep cracked wall round an arete on the left.

30 Bisexual Bratwurst 10m VD P2
The blunt right arete of the slabby wall is climbed on flakes and horizontal breaks.

31 Hieronymouse 10m HS P2
4b The central line of the wall is not very good with some bush-whacking in the middle.

32 Tall Man in the Bidet 10m VS P2
5a The left arete is climbed on the right-hand side, with a hard move low down.

33 Dead Man's Crankshaft 11m E2 P2   ★
6a Round the corner to the left is a cracked wall. Make a difficult start to gain a horizontal break and continue up the incipient crack and breaks above. A route that requires a stiff pull.

34 Shed Ahoy! 10m HS P1
4b Climb the corner left of Dead Man's Crankshaft. Step right on to a ledge and up to the top.

ROOF BUTTRESS
This is the buttress just left of Copper Nob Buttress. It can't be mistaken because of its prominent overhangs.

35 What!!! 9m HVS P2
5a Start near the right edge of the buttress. Climb the middle of the slab to gain the crack which runs round the roof at its right-hand end. Pull over on good holds to finish on vertical grass.

36 The Unpaid Chauffeur 9m E1 P2   ★
5a This takes the obvious corner on the left of the roof. Pull wildly over this on good holds.·

37 Adamant 10m HS P1
4b Climb the previous route to the roof. Traverse left to ledges and then the top.

38 Saunter 10m HS
4b At the left end of Roof Buttress a short ramp leads to a ledge. Continue up the wall above crossing an easy overlap to a second ledge and finish up a short crack.

HEBDEN GHYLL – GRADED LIST

HEPTONSTALL

SITUATION AND CHARACTER Heptonstall Quarry lies just below Heptonstall village and above the popular tourist town of Hebden Bridge (lots of good cafes!). The rock is very fine sandstone, generally solid, and averaging 20 metres in height. Belays at the top sometimes require imagination and a little faith. Heptonstall provides, perhaps, the most varied selection of quarried crack climbs in the district at all grades and requiring the full range of crack techniques, from wedged backsides and arm bars through to thin fingertip jams and, for added interest, barndoor laybacks. The routes are generally well protected but care must be taken on some of the finishes. On either side of the quarry and in the quarry itself there are smaller natural gritstone outcrops and boulders which are worthwhile in their own right.

The quarry faces south-west and is a sun trap, although the high precipitation experienced in the Calder valley may sometimes hinder the most enthusiastic of climbers.

APPROACHES AND ACCESS From Hebden Bridge follow the Heptonstall road which, depending on your approach along the A646, may necessitate the use of the turning circle at the west of the town. Take the first left turn to Heptonstall village. Just before entering the village take a left turn through a housing estate to the Heptonstall Social and Bowls Club where there is ample parking. From here walk down the walled path, past some new houses, on to the moor. Straight over the abyss and down to a path. Turn left, passing a natural outcrop, to the quarry.

THE CLIMBS These are described from left to right.

The Embankment
Once in the quarry the first routes are at the left-hand end on the smaller face at right angles to a large red wall.

1 Interlude 12m HS P1
4a The left edge of the Embankment starting round the corner from the Luddite-worn steps.

2 Curving Crack 16m VS P1 ★
4c The curving fist crack to the right of Interlude.

3 Main Line 16m VS P2
4c Two metres down and right. Contrive an entry over the small

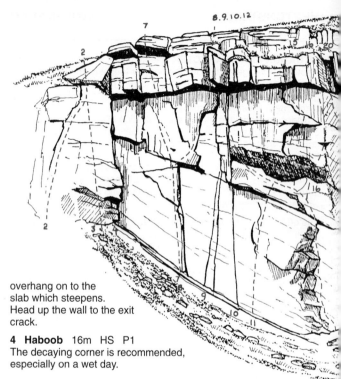

overhang on to the
slab which steepens.
Head up the wall to the exit
crack.

4 Haboob 16m HS P1
The decaying corner is recommended,
especially on a wet day.

The Red Wall
The rusty coloured wall of the upper quarry provides exciting peg-
scarred crack climbs from VS to E7.

5 Climb and Tick Conditions 18m E3
6a From three quarters of the way up Haboob swing right onto Red
wall and climb through the roof to the top. Good climbing requiring
long reaches.

6 Vertical Speed 20 m E7 P2   ★★
6c Start up the corner of Haboob to the tree and step boldly
rightwards making hard moves to the peg. Climb straight up the wall
past a newer peg, and more hard moves, to gain an obvious boss
and good holds. Now make the crux moves to gain the final crack of
Hard Line which is used as a finish..

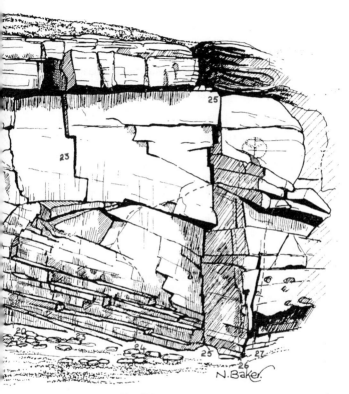

7 Hard Line 20m E5 P1 ★

6b Start up the first crack 4 metres right of the corner as for Thin Red Line to the first break. Then the left-hand crack and flake to the top break. Finish over the roof. Those desperate for new footage will also be able to climb a direct variation finish from the break at the same grade.

8 Thin Red Line 20m E2 P1 ★★★

5b A quarry classic. Steep and strenuous but protectable if you're strong enough to hang on long enough. Start up the first crack 4 metres right of the corner and follow it leftwards to the horizontal break. Step right and follow the right-curving flake to finish up the awkward exit chimney.

9 Demerara 20m E4 P1 ★★
6a Climb the very sustained double cracks 1 metre right of Thin Red Line to join that route below the curving flake..

10 Brown Sugar 20m E2 P1 ★
5c The crack 1 metre right of Demerara can be climbed direct up to the small roof or more usually by a detour to the right. Pull gymnastically over the roof and up the wide crack to finish up the exit chimney.

11 Badlands 12m E4 P2
6b The thin wall right of Brown Sugar passing a small roof on its left. Finish up or down Pulpit Route.

12 Pulpit Route 25m HVS P2 ★★
5a Start just left of the arete and traverse cracked ledges across the wall from right to left. Finish up the exit chimney of Thin Red Line. Precarious.

13 Pulpit Route Direct 8m E1 P1
5c Climb the wall 3 metres right of Badlands, passing the small roof on its right.

14 The Blue Bus 30m E6 P2 ★
6b A thrilling trip, traversing the technical and sustained finger break from pulpit route across A Step In The Light Green to finish up Orange Crush.

15 A Step in the Light Green 25m E6 P2 ★★★
6b Attacks the headwall above the middle ledge of Pulpit Route. Climb Pulpit Route to the ledge. Stretch over the leaning wall (peg) up to the right curving undercling. Over this to finish up the leftward-sloping ramp.

16 Orange Crush 25m E6 P2 ★★
6b The impressive arete to the right of A Step in the Light Green. From the ledge on Pulpit Route climb the bulging wall on good holds, clip the pegs and move right to the arete. Make exciting moves up this to a 'thank god' hold at the top.

17 Cream 25m E4 P3 ★
6a The short but bold arete right of Pulpit Route. Finish up any of the fissures above.

The Yellow Wall
This steep yellow wall bounded on its left by the pleasant corner climbs of Trepidation and Fairy Steps and on the right by the more awkward Bull's Crack has at its centre the well-known local landmark of Forked Lightning Crack, a testament to the grit,

fortitude and alcoholic capacity of local pioneer Don Whillans (not forgetting a couple of Woodbines).

18 Trepidation 20m VS P1
4c The corner crack is climbed for nearly 6 metres to a thin break where a shuffle left gains an obvious flake crack which is followed to the top.

19 Fairy Steps Direct 20m VS P1   ★★
4c Follow the corner as for Trepidation but at 6 metres carry on up the corner passing an awkward bulge to a ledge. Move left to the arete and finish in an exposed position on good holds.

20 Fairy Steps 24m HS P1   ★★
A worthwhile outing.
1. 18m 4b Scramble up the wall 2 metres right of the corner graffiti to reach a cave. Up the crack to more ledges and step left to a belay ledge.
2. 6m 4b Traverse left to the arete and finish up this on good holds.

21 Strange Brew 25m E2 P2
5b The corner crack that bounds the smooth yellow wall. As for Fairy Steps to the cave. Ascend the crack above direct to the dusty break. Traverse right past the wide exit chimney to the next crack system. Finish up this.

22 Skullduggery 22m E3 P1
6a As for Strange Brew to the dusty break. Move right for 1 metre than attack the cracked roof above. As Ray Jardine found out, Friends are useful.

23 Forked Lightning Crack 24m E3 P1   ★★★
5c The off-width crack in the centre of the wall requires ample nuts and large Friends. Leave the RPs behind. To layback or jam, the choice is yours; then flash to the top for 'thunderous' applause.

24 Midnight Lightning 24m E5 P2
6b Start right of Forked Lightning Crack. Up ledges to thin cracks. Climb with difficulty and an in-situ protection nut? to the small break, then head off right to the sanctuary of Bull's Crack, joining it above the triangular overhang.

25 Bull's Crack 25m HVS P1   ★★★
5a The superb corner crack up the right side of the yellow wall. Climb the crack, with some difficulty over the bulge, eventually landing on the Rabbit Ledge (possibly belay). Hop off the ledge and squirm up the pleasant chimney on the left.

26 Senility   12m   HVS   P1   ★★
5b Strenuous and sustained. The steep cracked wall to the right of
the corner provides excellent moves all the way to the Rabbit
Ledge. A (6b) variation exists to the left of Senility. Difficulty and
protection dependant on the size of the blinkers you are wearing.

27 Grindley's Grunt   15m   HVS   P1
5b Start right of the arete. Climb up the wall to the gap in the
overhang. Surmount this (perplexing crux) and finish up the sloping
ledges.

28 Boo Boo's Roof   15m   E2   P1
6b The less-defined and more difficult roof right of the Grunt.

29 Monkey Puzzle   12m   HVS   P2
5a Provides a finish for the last four routes from the rabbit ledge.
Climb past the rabbit and the peace symbol to the break. Traverse
right until holds provide an escape upwards.

30 Sunstroke Slab   18m   HS   P1   ★
Start at the right edge of the rabbit ledge.
1. 12m 4b Traverse across the slab rightwards following the
horizontal crack to a belay at the end of it.
2. 6m 4b Follow the groove to the top.

31 Heatwave   18m   E2   P1   ★★
5b A mega-pump, but safe and great fun. It takes the horizontal
crack line above Sunstroke Slab. Start on the right-hand end of the
rabbit ledge and climb the corner of Triplex Direct to the start of the
break. Traverse quickly right, slotting in Friends as appropriate, to
the tree. If arm strength allows continue to the arete and attempt to
gain the ledge with grace and dignity. Belay back above the corner
of Triplex.

Lower Quarry
Down to the right lies the slabby wall, cut by a band of overhangs,
of the lower quarry.

32 Triplex Direct   30m   E1   P2   ★
Start at the base of the lower quarry just right of the chossy corner.
1. 20m 5b Climb the wall to the first small overhang (pegs).
Traverse left on to the sandy wall over the small overlap and up to a
small sapling. Pass this on to the slab and the belay of Sunstroke
Slab on the rabbit ledge.
2. 10m 5a Climb the corner crack above to the top. A good
sustained pitch.

33 Big Ben   12m   E3   P1
5c A variation finish from the top crack of Triplex Direct breaking

out left up the cracked scoop to the top.

34 Poundstretcher 26m E3 P2
5c Start as for Triplex Direct up the initial slab but climb the large overhang directly above. Move immediately left above the overhang up a sandy pocketed wall to a small triangular overlap. Over this, up the slab and finish up the final crack of Triplex Direct.

35 Out On A Limb 24m E3   ★★
1. 12m Start as for Poundstretcher but where that route goes left to the sandy pockets move right (crux), into a scoop (PR) then up onto the right end of Sunstroke Slab. Climb the slab to belay at the vertical crack.
2. 12m Climb straight up the wall above, via a finger pocket, to tree in the break. Finish up the hanging groove behind the tree - the name of the route provides a clue as to how!

36 Triplex 40m E1 P1
A wandering line that is best climbed in three pitches.
1. 18m 5b As for Triplex Direct to the roof but break out right through the roof to a dirty corner which is climbed to a grassy belay ledge.
2. 12m 5b Traverse left across the sandy wall to a clean scoop. Up this to reverse the crack of Sunstroke Slab to the rabbit ledge.
3. 10m 5a Climb the crack above to the top (wooden wedge).

37 Man of God 34m HVS P2
1. 14m 5b Climb the slab and larger overhang right of Triplex, moving left slightly along the lip, to finish up the dirty corner and grassy belay ledge.
2. 8m 4c Up the groove on the left to another belay ledge.
3. 12m 5a Move rightwards up a series of ledges and walls to the top.

38 Cup and Lip 30m E3 P1
6a Three metres to the right climb the slab to the roof and, utilising a flake and pegged hold, climb the roof. When established escape right to ledges and eventually to the top.

39 Sue 30m VS P1
1. 12m 4c Climb the obvious flake crack trending left to flakes under the roof. Lunge over the roof on good ledges to a belay.
2. 18m Move right and follow your nose to the top.

40 Earthshrinker 12m E2 P1
5c The thin cracked roof right of Sue.

41 Scorpion 34m S P2
1. 17m Start just right at some chipped holds. Climb these if your

conscience allows to a traverse ledge which is followed right, then up a clean wall.

2. 17m Move left to a V-shaped depression. Climb this and scramble to the top. A harder, direct connection is reported.

The Black Wall Area
Beyond Scorpion, past the smooth unclimbed wall, up into the trees, lies the steep and blocky Black Wall.

42 Wasp Wall 18m MVS P1
4b The corner crack on the left of the grassy terrace. A bramble start leads to the crack. Up the crack, move left over the block and finish easily up left.

43 Sacrifice 18m HVS P2
1. 9m 5a Start a metre right of the corner. Climb the wall passing the flake to the tree.
2. 9m 5b The cracks above the tree provide a difficult finish.

44 Drainpipe Groove 18m HVS P1
5a The broken groove to a grassy ledge. Finish up the cracks above.

45 Trespasser 25m E2 P1   ★
The best route on the wall. Start left of the left corner crack.
1. 10m 5c Climb over the bulge into the thin peg-scarred crack, passing a large protrusion of metal to a grassy belay ledge.
2. 15m 5c Up the corner crack on the left to a traverse line right. Follow this and finish up the scooped wall to the top.

The bay to the right of Black Wall contains two worthwhile routes especially in high summer after a heavy shower when the vegetation is at its most luxuriant.

46 Hesperus 16m S or maybe even worse Pee green
The dirty right-hand corner in the bay.

47 Trespass Not 16m Hardly Severe P1
Climb the right wall of the bay.

Back to solid clean rock.

48 Fraternity 14m S P1
The crack and arete right of the botanical bay.

49 Fallout 11m HVS P1
5a Right of the arete, climb the depression to finish up Fraternity.

50 The Girdle Traverse 64m E3 P2
1. 18m 5c Starting from the top of Haboob traverse across the top break of the Red Wall to belay on Pulpit Route.

2. 14m 5a Reverse the traverse of Pulpit Route round the arete of Cream to belay on Fairy Steps.
3. 20m 5c Move right to a hand traverse. Step down and move across to join Bull's Crack. Traverse right and ascend Senility.
4. 12m 4c From the rabbit ledge climb Monkey Puzzle to finish or, more in keeping with the overall standard, finish as for Heatwave (5b).

The Left Hand Outcrop
This is the first of a series of broken buttresses of more natural rock leading left from the main quarry. It can be seen, and easily approached, by a stepped path leading off north from the main quarry descent and gives clean pleasant climbs well worth trying.

The routes are described from left to right.

51 Kassi 12m MVS P1
4b Start up a green wall just left of the deep chimney and climb direct to a high corner crack. The route originally moved into the chimney for a few moves at half height, the direct version is better and only slightly harder.

52 Nameless 14m VD P1 ★
The prominent chimney is a good one of its type providing an exercise in bridging and a constricted finish.

53 Windsong 15m VS P2
4c Climb the chimney to half height and make an awkward hand traverse out right to the arete which gives an airy but easier finish.

54 Columbus 28m VS P1
A wandering voyage – perhaps attempting to discover a New World!
1. 20m 4a Climb the groove just right of the chimney to below the prow. Traverse right across the buttress, taking care with some potentially-dubious flakes, to belay below the overhanging crack near the right edge.
2. 8m 4c Climb the bulging crack to the top.

55 Lumber Vertebrae 14m VS P1 ★★
4c The best line on the outcrop taking the short thin crack in the centre of the main face. Start just right of the lowest point of the crag and climb up to the thin crack, continuing direct to the top.

56 Short Back And Sides 12m E2 P2 ★
5c The hardest route on this buttress and one which may prove highly problematical for the short. Start above a heathery ramp at a short vertical crack. Climb this to a ledge and then ascend the wall above via a monster reach to a break. Continue over the bulge and up the slab using the shallow blind flake.

The outcrops and boulders further left provide numerous shorter routes and problems which are worth seeking out.

The Right Hand Outcrop
Two hundred metres right of the main quarry is another series of buttresses starting at the left with two small bays, the first one obviously quarried.

57   Nutian Jamb   6m   HVD   P1
The left arete of the first corner is climbed for 2 metres then move round to the left and follow a short crack.

58   The Corner   6m   HVD   P1
A rather unattractive line in the angle of the first bay.

59   Sentinel Crack   6m   VD   P1
A straight crack just right of the corner.

60   Sentinel Wall   6m   HVS   P2
5b   The steep right wall of the first bay provides an attractive, fingery problem.

61   Peepod   6m   D   P1
The scooped chimney crack just left of the arete.

62   The Left Arete   7m   HS   P2   ★
4b   The slabby left arete of the second bay is climbed, mostly on sloping holds, and requires a thoughtful approach. Good value.

63   Mille Feuille   7m   MVS   P2
4c   The many-layered wall just right of the first arete is climbed direct to the blunt nose in the centre where the difficulties ease somewhat for the final moves.

64   The Mitre   6m   S   P1
The crack just left of the corner chimney.

65   Descent Chimney   6m   M
As its name implies, in the corner of the second bay.

66   Afro With A Chin Strap   7m   HVS
5c   The Wall to the left of The Chimney. Start at the prominent flake and make a long reach for a pocket, then climb the wall direct.

67   The Chimney   7m   VD   P1
Mis-named. This is the steep crack line 1 metre right of the corner chimney.

68   Miss Rags -Tantric Mistress Of Mazland   10m   E4
6b A direct line up the wall below the left hand finish to a Dog With Two Tails.

69 Dog With Two Tails 13m HVS P2   ★
5a The prominent overhanging crack just right of the left arete of
the main buttress is climbed until a decision has to be made to step
up left or right to good ledges. If left, continue round the corner and
climb the steep wall to a small finishing notch. If right, climb
shelving ledges above. Both are worthwhile.

70 Pocket Wall 12m MVS P1   ★
4b In the centre of the main face are four neat round pockets.
Climb up to these and gain a ledge above on the right. Step back
left and climb the rib to the top.

Several new routes were climbed in this area as the guide went to
print. See page 687 for details.

71 Scarab 10m S P2
The right arete of the main face gained from a shallow diagonal
crack gives a pleasant line.

72 Coat of Arms Chimney 8m D P1
The chimney containing the perched shield is most awkward at the
start.

73 Badge Climb 9m VD P1
The steep cracked slabs just right of the chimney.

74 Main Buttress 11m HD P1
Grossly miss-named. This innocuous little climb is, however,
pleasant enough and starts up a shallow corner crack just right of
an easy-angled narrow buttress beyond the grassy gully. Step left at
the top of the crack to finish up easy rocks.

Other shorter routes and problems have been done among the
jumble of rocks further right, including the wild overhang known as
the Hunchback high up at the extreme right-hand end.

The Cubic Block
Returning to the main quarry, if you're still not ready for the cafe, the
prominent isolated block is worthy of attention for innumerable
problems and traverses on the overhanging face and pleasant slabs
and grooves on the valley side. Every inch has been climbed and
the variations are endless. Have fun.

HEPTONSTALL – GRADED LIST

E7
Vertical Speed (6c)

E6
The Blue Bus (6b)
A Step in the Light Green (6b)
Orange Crush (6b)

E5
Midnight Lightning (6b)
Hard Line (6b)

E4
Crearn (6a)
Miss Rags, Tantric Mistress
  Of Mazland (6b)
Badlands (6b)
Demerara (6a)

E3
Skullduggery (6a)
Cup and Lip (6a)
Climb &Tick Conditions (6a)
The Girdle (5c)
Poundstretcher (5c)
Big Ben (5c)
Forked Lightning Crack (5c)

E2
Boo Boo's Roof (6b)
Short Back & Sides (5c)
Trespasser (5c)
Earthshrinker (5c)
Strange Brew (5b)
Heatwave (5b)
Brown Sugar (5c)
Thin Red Line (5b)

E1
Pulpit Route Direct (5c)
Triplex (5b)
Triplex Direct (5b)

HVS
Affro With A Chin Strap (5c)
Man of God (5b)
Grindley's Grunt (5b)
Sacrifice (5b)
Senility (5b)
Fallout (5a)
Drainpipe Groove (5a)
Sentinel Wall (5b)
Bull's Crack (5a)
Dog With Two Tails (5a)

HETCHELL CRAG (or POMPEY CALEY) N.G.R. SE 376424

SITUATION AND CHARACTER The crag sits in delightful wooded seclusion in the heart of the Hetchell Wood nature reserve near Bardsey, close to the main A58 Leeds-Wetherby road, some 10 miles north-east of Leeds and 3 miles south-west of Wetherby.

The main wall is 100 metres in length with a maximum height of 11 metres. The unusual and serious nature of the rock compensates for any lack of stature. The rock is in fact unique in this guide, being more akin to sandstone, and offering pockets and protruding nodules along with flutings and rounded breaks. Only on the generally easy crack and chimney lines can reliable protection be arranged and soloing has long been the norm by the regulars. The generally good landings are a redeeming factor, though belays for top ropes can be engineered amongst the trees well back from the edge.

The crag's sunny westerly aspect is partially offset by its wooded situation, but once the leaves have fallen in autumn the crag receives the full benefit of any sunlight, making an afternoon visit particularly rewarding. Some routes suffer from sandy sediment being washed over them after heavy rain but this can be removed easily with a soft brush or rag.

Caution Because of the nature of the rock, holds do occasionally break without warning. Be wary on first acquaintance with the longer wall climbs. On no account should wire brushing be employed here and the top edge of the crag must be protected if top ropes are used.

APPROACHES AND ACCESS The crag is best approached from the A58 Leeds-Wetherby road. By bus from Leeds it is best to alight at Rowley Grange, a complex of derelict farm buildings on the right just beyond the New Inn at Scarcroft. From here a public bridleway leads eastwards direct to stepping stones across the beck and the main crag is then 100 metres up to the left. Beckside Buttress is a similar distance upstream to the right. Limited parking space is available at the start of the bridleway (room for three or four cars). The walking time is 10 minutes from here.

Further car parking can be found in a small lay-by on the right about half a mile further along the A58 towards Wetherby. From this spot a path leads up to and along the disused railway track to join the previous route 100 metres short of the stepping stones. This approach takes about 15 minutes but don't try to short cut across the fields and stream as soon as the crag is sighted. Irate farmers don't approve and you need to be an assault course specialist anyway. The shortest walk-in for drivers is from the lay-bys on the Thorner-Bardsey lane to the east of the crag (about 5 minutes) but this area is a favourite haunt of car thieves so make sure your insurance is paid up before risking this approach.

There are no restrictions on access but please respect the flora and fauna of the area and do not light fires.

THE CLIMBS
These are described from RIGHT to LEFT starting with the four technical boulder problems at the extreme right-hand end.

The First Crack (4c) A short crack on the right wall.
The Right Wall (5b) The wall just right of the arete.
The Right Arete (5c) ★ Fingery, with an ankle-twisting landing.
Jim's Wall (5b) ★ Takes the flake and pinches above the horizontal of Zig-Zag.

1 Zig-Zag 7m VD P1
Links the two wide cracks via a leftwards traverse.

2 Cassius Direct 10m VS P2 ★
4c Climb the scoop on huge holds to an awkward move into a scalloped depression. Continue direct by way of an airy mantel to reach chipped holds over the top. Quite bold.

3 Cassius Crawl 15m VS P2 ★★
4b Follow the direct to the move below the final mantelshelf and then make a delightful traverse left for 7 metres to reach a short crack up which the climb finishes. The best middle-grade climb on the crag.

The low-level bulge to the left has numerous rounded sprag holds on the lip and at least 5 separate problems between 6a and 6c to overcome it. The following two routes use a couple of these problems to start and then continue above.

4 Arc En Ceil 10m E2 P2
6b Climb over the roof just to the right of Rainbow (crux) and finish up the shallow scoops between Rainbow and Cassius Crawl.

5 Rainbow 10m E1 P2
6a Climb the roof towards the left side and step right to below the short vertical funnel in the second bulge. Climb this to reach easier ground and a finish on flutings slightly to the left.

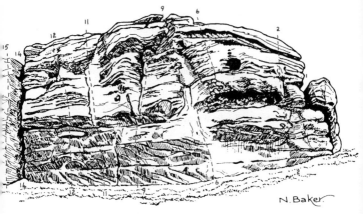

N. Baker

6 Crutch 11m HVS P2   ★★
5b A clean and satisfying climb, which appears rather intimidating
on first acquaintance. Climb the obvious shallow groove until it
bulges and then swing right to jugs. Stop posing and pull over
spectacularly to finish direct on flutings.

7 Crutch Direct 10m E1 P2   ★
5b Harder and strangely not quite as satisfying as the original. A
crucial hold often becomes engulfed in the ivy but reasonable
protection can be arranged.

8 Hunchback 10m E4 P2
6b The wall left of the groove contains an obvious depression
shaped like an inverted urinal. Don rubber gloves and undercling
this tenaciously to reach the break above. Continue by way of a
rounded boss to the top. The absence of craters below the crux
attests to the use of runners in adjacent routes, level with the
undercut and this grade assumes it. Blinkers are required to avoid
holds on other routes.

9 Bell 11m E3 P1   ★★
5c A very good line which is unfortunately marred for much of the
time by sediment which washes down from the niche. Climb the
wall steeply and gain the thin vertical crack in the centre from a two-
finger pocket below the bulge. Continue with difficulty into the niche
above, finishing up cracks to the right. A much harder direct finish is
possible up the tower above and left of the niche.

10 Bell Left Hand 13m E1 P1
5c An inferior line which escapes diagonally left from below the

crux of the parent route. The difficulties are less sustained but not without interest. Finish easily leftwards towards Pompeii Chimney on good ledges.

11 Bell End   11m   E2   P2   ★★
5c Prominent pockets in a shallow groove just left mark the start of this climb and lead via a rock-over or stiff pull using small crimps to gain the protruding nodules. The finishing depression above is awkward, reachy and quite serious but protection can be arranged in the holes below the final moves.

12 Lurcio's Lip   10m   E3   P2   ★
6c The large drooping tongue and an assortment of adjacent poor holds sometimes allow a standing position to be attained. Gaining the ledge above is 'way gnarly' but once on it the route finishes easily.

13 Up Pompeii   10m   E2   P2
6a The steep wall between the lip and the chimney sports a frustrating eliminate up the sloping plates.

14 Pompeii Chimney   10m   VD   P1   ★★
The obvious chimney in the angle of the crag. A popular classic with elegant bridging. A good beginner's route.

15 Ripple Arete   9m   VS   P2
5a The rounded, fluted arete gives a steep yet delicate exercise. Unfortunately it is often dirty.

16 Centurion   8m   S   P1   ★★
The steep crack left of the arete contains perfect jams and has added jugs on each side for good measure.

17 When In Rome   9m   E3   P3   ★
5b An interesting eliminate with an exciting finish. Climb the flange immediately left of Centurion and continue boldly up the front of the rounded upper rib just right of Dead Angst.

18 Dead Angst   10m   E4   P3   ★★
5c Boulder out the initial wall between the cracks (the technical crux), moving up to a bucket and a good rest. Deep breath. Move diagonally left up the bulging headwall to a sharp handrail. Look left for the crucial hold and make a long span up right off this to finish. Serious but very satisfying!

19 The Fall of the Roman Empire   10m   E4   P3
6a Start below a thin crack towards the right-hand side of the steep main wall. Climb the short vertical crack to the horizontal and pull up direct to the next traverse line and a green hole. Step up slightly

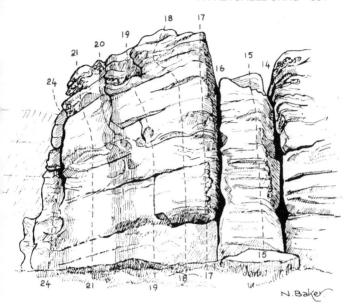

N. Baker

left and then finish through sandy bulges in the shallow overhanging groove.

20 Tiberius 11m E3 P2 ★

5c A good route, open, steep and invariably dry. Start as for the previous climb and follow it to the second traverse line. Move left for two metres to climb up the shallow leftward-facing corner with care.

21 Wailing Wall 10m HVS P2 ★★★

5a A fine direct line to the finishing corner of Tiberius. Start 3 metres right of a crack (Roman Crack) and make reachy moves up the steep wall to a small resting ledge in the middle. Continue up the corner or, better, the wall immediately to its left.

22 Tarquin's Terrace 13m VS P3 ★

4c A devious excursion on to the main wall starting and finishing just right of Roman Crack. Traverse right and pull up to gain the resting ledge on Wailing Wall. Climb back diagonally left from here to finish up the rounded arete immediately right of the top of the crack. All on large, but fragile-looking holds. Three points of contact advised at all times!

23 Caligula 10m E1 P3   ★
5b A very direct line between Roman crack and Wailing Wall crossing through Tarquin's Terrace twice.

24 Roman Crack 8m S P1   ★
The obvious enjoyable crack bounding the left edge of the main wall.

25 Veni Veci Oblivisci 8m HS P2
4b The rib between Roman Crack and Narrow Chimney, climbed mainly on the left.

26 Narrow Chimney 7m VD P1
The rift where the buttress drops back, bridging all the way.

27 The Empire Strikes Back 10m E2 P2   ★
6a Climb the wall between Narrow Chimney and Grease to a finger pocket. Make a difficult move up and left to gain the rounded holds just below the top. Traverse left without touching the top to finish above Augustus.

28 Grease 7m E4 P3
6c The tendon destroying, rounded slab 2.5 metres left of the chimney. Launch on, and slither to, a good pocket and the top - or watch commitment evaporate and wait for the rescue/ambulance.

29 Newton John 7m E3 P2   ★
6a Use an undercut slot to leave the foot-ledge two metres right of the runnel in the slab. Once over, leg it for the top direct.

30 Livia 8m E2 P2   ★★
5c The runnel is gained by an exciting rock-over. Follow momentum and good small edges and pockets slightly left to finish. Very rewarding.

31 Hadrian's Wall 8m E4 P3
6b The surprisingly-independent bulge and wall between the weaknesses.

32 Augustus 7m E1 P2   ★
5c A wild micro-route! From an obvious rounded undercut in the large roof reach enormous holds. Fabulous simian swings and heel hooks conquer the headwall.

The wide boulder choke just left gives a constricted squirm. Endless fun for the under-fives.

33 Et Tu Brute 6m E1 P1
5c The bulge immediately left of the chimney is worth a stab. A sloth-like start via the chockstone under the roof gains good holds in the break. Make a long reach to a rounded finish.

34 Daniel's Den 6m HVS P2
5c Left again is another way over the cave roof. Reach, pull and slap with not a lot of help from your feet.

The crag now loses height around the descent gully, but provides some sporting boulder problems. They all have micro variations but the main ones are:-

Dave's Wall (5a) ★ The short undercut wall from the ledge just right of the arete.
The Arete (5c) ★ Via an obvious pinch and long reach.
The Undercut (5c) ★★ The right wall of the gully - brilliant!
Gully Wall Traverse (6b) The left wall of the gully moving left just below the top and down round the arete to finish across End Wall. Touch the top and you're disqualified.
Layback Rib (5b) ★ The gully's left arete.
End Wall (4c) ★ The short front wall from bottom right.
End Wall Direct (5c) The left edge of this wall, avoiding twin cracks

35 Twin Cracks 5m VD P1
The short double crack system a few metres left of the wide gully.

36 Oak Scoop 5m HS P1
The scoop is gained from the left. The 'oak' tree - which died of Dutch Elm Disease? - has now totally departed the scoop making the route much harder.

37 Dutch Elm 6m VS P2
5a Climbs the wall between Oak Scoop and The Corbel. Trying to avoid both its neighbours at the start is one of the main difficulties. Once established, trend slightly right via a small deep pocket to the top.

38 The Corbel 7m VS P2   ★★
5a Gain the large protrusions and make an enigmatic move using both to reach small holds on the upper wall. Finish straight up.

39 Corbel Variation 7m E3 P2
6b Mantel directly on to the left projection (dislocating hip joints as appropriate). Move precariously up the sprags to finish direct.

40 Reach for a Peach 8m E4 P3   ★
6c A climb to 'cream' up! A technical exercise in the art of levitation, climbing the centre of the wall direct from poor undercuts to tiny dimples. But where do you put your feet?

41 Mitchell's Wall 8m HVS P2   ★
5b A steep and sequencey route climbing the wall just right of (and independent of) the chimney. Holds become elusive near the top

where a move right is required to reach the finishing break. A desperate problem start, **Lunging For Melons** (6c) moves up leftwards from the foot of Reach for a Peach.

42 Hanging Chimney 7m S P1
An obvious line towards the left end of the wall. Harder than it looks.

43 Smokeless Zone 6m VS P2
5a The wall and rib immediately left of Hanging Chimney.

44 The (Green) Wall 6m HS P2
4b The last route on the main edge spends the winter looking like an accident in a nuclear power station. It reputedly glows in the dark! Slither direct to the by now well decayed tree roots via pockets, and thence to the launderette.

Twenty metres to the left of the main crag a jungle bash reveals the majestic Turd Buttress. Those with a strong stomach may wish to try:-

45 S for B 6m E2 P2
6b A difficult start gains a series of undercuts and pockets leading up to, and round, the left of the big roof. The finish is rather overgrown.

46 Turd 8m E1 P2
5c The name can still just be seen scratched on the rock just right of the gully. Climb up on large holds until a difficult traverse right leads to an exit above the left end of the big roof. The name over-glamorises the route somewhat.

47 Turd Direct 6m E1 P2
5b Climb straight up to a worrying exit using a shallow blank pocket and overgrown slopers. Rumour has it that there are some good finishing holds somewhere further back but gardening gloves are required to get in under the brambles. An easier but rather pointless exit can be made round the corner on the left.

Across the gully on the occasionally slightly cleaner wall near the hawthorn is:-

48 Adamant 6m E2 P2
6b The steep central wall. Move up to finger pockets and step right using these to finish direct. Long reaches and dubious rock.

49 Tear Across the Dotted Line 6m E1 P2
6a Climb the wall left of centre using obvious pockets and a long reach to a committing finish swinging rightwards on dubious, but positive, holds.

50 Bronco 6m E3 P2
5c Climb the short left arete and make a difficult finish on the left side.

THE TRAVERSES
One of the characteristics of Hetchell is its tendency to interesting traverse lines. The lower lines are superb and strenuous being good for solo training all year round, often staying dry in the rain. The main girdle, however, is a conventional climb with two of the best pitches on the cliff.

51 The Main Wall Girdle 36m HVS P2   ★★★
1. 20m 4c Follow Cassius's Crawl to its final crack and step down into the niche on Bell. Make exposed moves left, past a dubious and curious thread, to reach easier ledges leading left to the platform above Ripple Arete.
2. 16m 5a Descend Centurion for a couple of metres until the traverse line at half height can be followed leftwards across the steep wall. A difficult step gains the green hole and a further stretch left (crux) gains the resting position on Wailing Wall. Finish diagonally left to exit on the arete just right of Roman Crack.

The Bell Wall Training Traverse
The wall between Pompeii Chimney and the right-hand end of the crag has been crossed at four levels all within bouldering height. Independence on certain sections is difficult to maintain but the persistent and pedantic should have lots of fun (and/or frustration) trying.

The Standard Traverse (5c) ★★★ Usually from left to right with hands generally at the level of Lurcio's Lip. Swing across the Rainbow bulge and finish up any of the problems on the extreme right. Can be extended by starting at ground level below Wailing Wall.

The High Level Traverse (6a) Feet generally at the level of Lurcio's Lip. Quite scary!

The Low Level Traverse (6b) ★★ Best from right to left with hands below the line of the standard traverse and continue below Lurcio's Lip to finish on the first slopers of Up Pompeii. Step across the corner (don't rest too long), press on around the arete, and keep low all the way to Caligula. Finish up this or (if still not pumped) return along Bob's Traverse and the Standard Traverse to where you started from!

The Super Low Level (6c) The lowest line possible with nothing above one and a half metres allowed. Silly!

52   Bob's Traverse   15m   VS   P2   ★
5b   A left-to-right traverse starting at the foot of Roman Crack along
the horizontal break. The final moves to gain Centurion suddenly
feel exposed as the ground drops away. Finish up the crack or
move down round Ripple Arete to link up with one of the Bell Wall
training traverses.

53   Lend Me Your Ears   15m   E3   P2
6a   Climb The Corbel to just below the top and then traverse left on
reasonable hand, but poor footholds, across the "Peach" Wall to
finish in Hanging Chimney.

Low Peach Traverse   (7a)   From the foot of The Corbel to the foot
of Hanging Chimney.

54   Superturd Traverse   6m   E bah gum   P2
6b   Follow the thin crack along the lip of the roof round to the left,
whence a depression allows an escape through a grass cornice.

Preparation H   (7a)★★   Start at the undercuts on S for B then
traverse right using a 'skyhook' chip under the roof to finish at the
right end. Move up and swing back left along Superturd if you've got
the umph!

Beckside Buttress
An isolated, undercut buttress about 250 metres upstream from the
main crag. A number of problems and variations are possible but
the best are:-

55   Beckside Buttress   6m   HS   P2
4b   Climb straight up the scooped and undercut main wall.
Pleasant.

56   Tadpole Traverse   10m   VS   P1
4c   Start at the toe of the buttress and pull up with difficulty below
the prominent roof. Traverse diagonally right from here to finish at
the top right-hand corner.

Tide Mark   (6b) ★ is a good low level traverse all the way round this
buttress

HETCHELL CRAG – Graded List

E4
Grease (6c)
Reach for a Peach (6c)
Hunchback (6b)
Hadrian's Wall (6b)
Fall of the Roman Empire
(6a)
Dead Angst (5c)

E3
Lurcio's Lip (6c)
Corbel Variation (6b)
When In Rome (5b)
Bronco (5c)
Newton John (6a)
Lend Me Your Ears (6a)
Bell (5c)

E2
Up Pompeii (6b)
Arc en Ceil (6b)
S for B (6b)
The Empire Strikes Back
(6a)
Tiberius (5c)
Bell End (5c)
Livia (5c)

E1
Tear Across the Dotted
  Line (6a)
Rainbow (6a)
Bell Left Hand (5c)
Turd (5c)
Augustus (5c)
Caligula (5b)
Et Tu Brute (5c)
Crutch Direct (5b)
Turd Direct (5b)

HVS
Daniel's Den (5c)
Crutch (5b)
Mitchell's Wall (5b)
Main Wall Girdle (5a)
Wailing Wall (5a)

VS
Bob's Traverse (5b)
Dutch Elm (5a)
The Corbel (5a)
Smokeless Zone (5a)
Ripple Arete (5a)
Cassius Direct (4c)
Tadpole Traverse (4c)
Tarquin's Terrace (4b)
Cassius Crawl (4b)

HS
The Green Wall (4b)
Veni Veci Oblivisci (4b)
Beckside Buttress (4b)
Oak Scoop (4a)

S
Hanging Chimney
Centurion
Roman Crack

VD
Pompeii Chimney
Narrow Chimney
Twin Cracks
Zig-Zag

HORSEHOLD SCOUT

SITUATION AND CHARACTER The buttresses, edges and outcrops facing north above Hebden Bridge are collectively known as Horsehold Scout. Steep slopes beneath the crags give a sense of exposure to these sadly neglected climbs. The buttresses give routes that often feel hard for the grade. As they face north, they have a covering of algae that gives them an off-putting green appearance.

APPROACHES AND ACCESS No access problems have been encountered. Approach from the west end of Hebden Bridge at Hebble End Bridge, beside a supermarket car park. This leads to Horsehold Road which climbs steeply to the right. The road leads under a buttress (nothing recorded) and up to limited parking where the road levels off. From here a gated path leads off to the right and runs well above the buttresses.

THE CLIMBS These are described from left to right.

The Scout.
This is the first buttress and is situated below a the seat that is 30 metres along the path from the road. On the left of this buttress there is a semi-detached pinnacle with an easy route up a flake on its left side. Right of this is a grassy area, then a large buttress with cracks in the centre leading to an alcove with overhangs above. Three metres left of this is a wide crack with a tree at the base.

1 Kestrel 17m HS P3 ★
Climb the crack to a ledge with a block belay. Move left across the wall behind the ledge and finish up the buttress.

2 Guano Grooves 20m VS P1
4c To the right are two parallel cracks. Climb these to the same ledge as the last route. Gain a niche below the overhang and move right to the finishing crack.

3 Birthday Crack 16m HS P2 ★★
4b Climb the jamming crack that starts three metres right to a ledge. Then follow the thin curving crack on the right on finger jams.

4 Trio 17m VD P1
Climb the corner on the right to join Birthday Crack, then move left and up an obvious flake crack.

5 Birthday Wall 16m VS P3
4c Start as for Trio, but continue up the wall above a metre from the arete.

The Buttress.
This is reached by continuing along the path until about 200m from the road a grassy spur leads down to the top of the buttress. This is the largest, and the best of the bunch. On the left and at right angles to the main face is a short, steep wall above a glacis, with an overhang along the top. Around the arete to the right is a prominent wide crack above a corner (Original Route), then a series of steep slabs. Right of these and set back, the rock continues, gradually decreasing in height and eventually merging into the hillside. The first route starts at the extreme left at a corner on the left edge of the glacis.

6 Pigeon Loft 9m D P2
Climb the corner until a leftwards traverse on a slab leads beneath overhangs to an exit. A poor route.

7 Homer's Flight 10m VS P2
4c Climb the same corner as Pigeon Loft, then traverse right across a vertical wall to a resting place. Continue up the corner above and finish by a crack in the roof or, more easily, by traversing left (S).

To the right, on the edge of the buttress, is an obvious corner leading up the glacis.

8 Odyssey 24m VS P1
5a Ascend a short wall then the corner to the glacis. Belay. Using a short crack, gain the perch in the centre of the wall and hand traverse right on to the front of the buttress. Finish up the crack.

9 The Bit 19m VS P2
4c Climb the short corner two metres right to a ledge, then follow the steep scooped wall above to an overhung ledge. This is just right of the main overhang. Continue up the wide crack of Odyssey.

10 Charleston Wall 16m VS P2 ★★
4c Mantel on to the first small ledge on the steep wall on the right and then on to the second small ledge. Follow a rib on the left and finish up the wide crack of the last route.

11 Original Route 16m S P1 ★
4a Climb the corner crack on the right to a ledge and belay. Gain the niche above and climb the difficult crack to the top.

12 The Long Climb 25m S P2
Start 2 metres right and follow a rib, then traverse to the ledge on Original Route. Traverse left again on to a small nose and up the groove to the top of the crag.

13 Greensleeves 18m S P3   ★★★
Climb the slabs on the right to a small bush. Ascend the groove on the left, moving left high up to finish at the top of Original Route.

14 Tap Dance 13m S P2
Up the crack and go diagonally right to the arete. Move up to the overhang and avoid this on the left to reach a ledge. Finish up a short wall.

15 Long Corner 13m VD P1
The obvious corner on the right and higher up the banking.

16 The Pod 10m S P2   ★
The flake crack 6 metres right to a ledge, then the steep wall above.

17 The Groove 8m VD P1
The groove on the right.

18 Overhanging Corner 8m VS P1
4c The short, dirty and green overhanging corner on the right, then easy ledges above.

19 Pocked Groove 8m VD P1
The groove directly behind the tree. Awkward to start.

20 Pocked Wall 7m S P2
The centre of the wall on the right.

The Cub
To reach this buttress follow the path until about 400 metres from the road where there is a grassy clearing and evidence of bonfires etc. The buttress is just below on the nose of the spur. The first route here is a thin crack leading to a jamming crack just left of the left arete of the buttress.

21 Gracelands 10m HVS P1
5a Hard to start, but relents after midway.

22 The Sizzler 11m VS P1   ★★
4b Climb the corner in the centre of the buttress and the left-slanting fault above.

23 Harriet 11m HVS P1
5a A direct start to The Sizzler up a thin crack just to the left.

24   Firelighter   13m VS   P3
4b Start just right of the toe of the buttress and take a direct line to the top. A long reach is an advantage.

25   Bigfoot   10m   VD   P1
The chimney/groove on the right.

26   Tumbril   10m   VS   P3
5a To the right is an overhang. Go over this on the arete and follow it to the top.

27   Phil's Route   8m   VD   P1
The groove on the right of the overhang.

28   Hartley's   7m   HS   P2
The jamming crack on the right.

Forty metres *left* there is a steep slab. This contains the following two climbs.

29   Portrait   8m   VS   P2
4c The left side of the slab.

30   Blue Watch   8m   VS   P2
5a The right side of the slab.

ILKLEY

SITUATION AND CHARACTER The Cow and Calf group dominates the skyline above Ben Rhydding on the edge of Ilkley moor. It lies alongside the Ilkley-Hawksworth road. The Rocky Valley, shown on some maps as Ilkley Crags, lies about 1 kilometre west of the Cow and Calf. It can be seen from the centre of Ilkley on the moor up and left of the old Roman Baths, White Wells.

Ilkley has always been the most important climbing area in Yorkshire (howls of protest from Almscliff devotees) and has plenty to suit all tastes. Its appeal is multi-faceted with both quarried and natural gritstone offering quality routes from the very easiest to the super desperates - and with ease of access to boot! The beginner will find Ilkley more amenable, perhaps, than any other Yorkshire crag. The moorland setting - weekend tourists apart - is pleasant with panoramic views over the Wharfe valley. You can pose for the crowds around the Cow and Calf and the Quarry or if peace and sanity be your scene, walk 'over the back' to Rocky Valley and get away from it all.

APPROACHES AND ACCESS The Cow and Calf has one of the shortest, easiest approaches of any crag anywhere. The car park is 100 metres from the rocks and can be approached along the moor road from Ilkley or from Burley-in-Wharfedale in the other direction. A path leads across to Rocky Valley about a kilometre away. Rocky Valley can also be approached direct from Ilkley by taking the path out of the top of the town centre to White Wells. There are bus and train services to Ilkley from Leeds, Bradford, Keighley and Skipton. There are no restrictions on climbing.

THE CLIMBS These are described from left to right, starting on the large rounded buttress to the left, when approaching from the car park. Some bouldering can be had on smaller blocks just left again.

Doris Buttress

1 Sinister Cracks 12m VD P1 1951
Step off the boulder at the left-hand end of the buttress and climb out right to a ledge and twin cracks leading to an obvious niche. Continue up the top slab just right of the arete.

2 Vital Spark 10m S P2 1994
An awkward start via a wide layback gains the ledge below the twin

cracks. Move left to the first ledge on the arete and climb it, passing two 'jugs', to the top

3 Sinister Rib 15m E3 P3 1959   ★★
5b Step off the lower boulder on to the chipped arete and climb directly to a horizontal break. The un-chipped upper arete is taken direct with a worrying step near the top.

4 Blackball 15m E3 P3 1978   ★
5c Start as for Sinister Rib and climb to the horizontal break. Step right, don blinkers, and climb the bold slab above. Marginal protection can be arranged in the break.

5 Doris 17m S P3 Pre 1958   ★
A popular top-rope route for beginners. The grade is for an on-sight lead. Step off the boulder and climb to the arete then traverse right on chipped holds to a mid-height break. Now straight up the slab on large polished holds.

6 Bald Pate 18m E1 P3 1943
5a Start as for Sinister Cracks. Step right on to a small footledge and traverse right on the horizontal break to the mid-height ledge of Doris. Traverse right for 2 metres then climb the awkward slab above to an easier finish.

A desperate modern problem is **Doris Direct** ★★ (7a) which climbs out from beneath the roof and up left to the chipped holds on Doris.

7 Bald Pate Superdirect 11m E6 P3 1980   ★
6c Climb the rounded undercut right hand arete of the buttress on its left-hand side. Hard moves to attain a standing position on the arete are followed by a nasty friction sequence to gain the sanctuary of the mid-height ledge. Finish up Bald Pate.

8 Bald Pate Direct Start 11m E2 P3 1957   ★★
5b Start on the right wall above a short corner and make a short delicate traverse left. Move up and round left to gain the ledge of Bald Pate. Finish boldly up this.

9 Deathwatch 11m E7 P3 1986   ★
6b The right wall of Doris Buttress directly above the start of the traverse on the last route. Climb direct on small holds.

10 Little Kaiser 9m HS P1 Pre 1951
4b A steep little route just left of the upper gully climbed on good, positive holds.

11 Grand As Owt 8m E3 P2 1997   ★
6a Climb the arete to the right of the gully in its entirety on the right-hand side. Small wires provide marginal protection in the break.

12   Where Blue Tits Dare   11m   E4   P2   1989
6b Start 2 metres right of the gully, as for Serendipity, then rock up left to a break. Step left and climb the wall on tiny knobbles .

13   Serendipity   10m   E2   P1   1974   ★
5b Start 2 metres right of the gully. Climb a short wall to a gain a thin (and often vegetated) crack system which is followed to the top. Very good when its clean.

14   Piton Wall   12m   HVS   P3   1956   ★★
5a Start a few metres right of Serendipity and climb the rightward-trending ramp, boldly, to gain good holds. Continue until a move right gains a layaway on a sloping ramp. Step up to a good hold at the top of the ramp and climb directly to easier ground.

15   Transparent Wall   13m   HVS   P2   1957   ★★★
5a Start up the peg-scarred cracks right of the previous route. At 4 metres step left to join another crack, move up and left to gain a large pocket. A tricky move past the pocket gains an easy finish up the slab above.

An excellent problem, **The Transparent Traverse** (5c) ★★ links the ramp of Piton Wall to the obvious 'eyes' just left of Transparent Wall.

16   Sticky Fingers   13m   E2   P1   1975   ★
5c The crack on the right-hand edge of the buttress is climbed direct to a large sloping hold at about one third height. Make a step left to gain the crack to the left then move up and step right to rejoin the original crack. Follow this to the top. The crack is sometimes climbed direct at a good 6a.

17   Magic Pie   8m   HS   P2   1997
4b Start 2 metres right of Sticky Fingers. Climb the short chimney then up the arete and wall above to a tricky but well protected finish.

N. Baker

THE QUARRY

The next routes start at the entrance to the quarry.

18 Desperate Dredd 6m E4 P3 1986
6a Climb the rounded arete up and left of the entrance to the quarry. It is taken on its left-hand side and requires a certain faith in friction. The centre of the slab just left, without recourse to the arete is slightly easier (E3 5c)

19 Highfield Corner 15m HVS P2 1941
5a Climb the wide cracks on the left at the entrance to the quarry and swing left to a ledge below a scoop. Step right and climb the wall on small holds to a rounded finish.

20 Nailbite 15m VD P1 Pre-1951   ★
Start at the same wide cracks and trend up and rightwards to gain a wide chimney.

21 Central Wall 14m E1 P2 1946
5b The overhanging wall right of Nailbite is difficult to start. Continue up the wall then move right to gain the hanging rib. Make an awkward move on to the rib and follow it to the top.

22 Sand Chimney 14m D P1 Pre-1951
Climb a short crack just right of the overhanging wall. Now follow the nasty chimney to the top.

23 Central Rib 15m HVS P2 1946
5a An artificial route. Start at the overhanging wall on the immediate left of the crack section of Sand Chimney. Up the rib and move across right into Wellington Chimney and climb the left wall to a spike on the left arete. Use this to swing round and then climb straight up.

N Baker

24 Wellington Chimney 15m D P2 Pre 1951   ★
The right-hand of the three chimneys is climbed into a cave. Back -
and-foot precariously to the top.

25 Overhanging Blocks 4m HVS P2 1943
5a From the top of Wellington Chimney attack the large perched
block above. Climb it just left of the nose with a difficult move to
finish.

26 The Stomach Traverse 10m HS P2 Pre1951
4a From the top of Wellington Chimney traverse up and right to
beneath the large perched block. Traverse right round the corner
and squirm off rightwards.

27 Wellington Crack 16m E4 P1 1973   ★★★
5c The striking thin crack line gives a superb, strenuous climb
starting with a short layback. Protection is excellent.

28 Loaded 18m E8 P2 1997   ★
7a Climb Wellington Crack for 9 metres and then traverse right to
the blunt arete. Climb this to the top. Very hard but relatively safe -
for an E8!

29 Snap Decision 16m E7 P3 1986   ★★
6c One of very few E7s to have been 'on-sighted'. The obvious
hanging groove in the wall right of Wellington Crack. An easy start
leads to a ledge. Launch on to the flake with serious climbing to

gain a peg runner. Hard moves up the groove gain another peg and even more desperate moves to finish! (Be warned, the pegs were poor to start with and have been rusting away slowly for well over 10 years!).

30 Shadowlands 10m MS P2 Pre 1992
The right-hand side of the arete just left of Curving Cracks. Traverse right at the top to belay and then scramble off.

31 Jiggery Not Pokery 10m HVS P3 1989
5b The wall between Curving Cracks and the arete to the left.

32 Curving Cracks 18m VS P1 1947   ★
5a The thin crack just right of the previous route is followed rightwards past loose blocks to a large ledge. Move right and climb the twin cracks to finish.

33 Gibbon's Wall 11m VS P3 Pre 1951
4c Climb a line of small incut holds up the wall to the large ledge.

34 High Street 10m E3 P3 1956   ★★
5c Bold and committing. From the ledge on Curving Cracks traverse up and left to gain a steep ramp. Follow it with increasing difficulty and rock-up right to good holds. Step left to gain the top.

35 Curving Corner 9m HVS P1 1947   ★
5b From the same ledge climb directly up the rib with interest.

36 Letter Box Crack 9m MVS P2 Pre 1951
4b The obvious wide crack in the lower wall is awkward to stay with. Knees have a habit of getting stuck!

37 Peg Wall 7m E1 P2 1976
6a The fingery wall right of the crack is climbed via the letterbox hold.

38 Peg Crack 7m HVS P1 1962   ★
5a The thin crack is taken on good fingerlocks to the ledge above.

39 Corner and Scoop 15m HS P2 1962
4a Just to the right, a short crack leads to the ledge. Move up into a short corner and climb the wall and short scoop to the top.

The next route is situated in the back of the quarry at the fine arete. Just to the left are several scrambles which are used for easy descents.

40 Guillotine 13m E6 P3 1975   ★★
6b Climb the square-cut arete on its left-hand side, moving round to the right at half height. Now direct up the arete to finish. Getting harder as it loses holds!

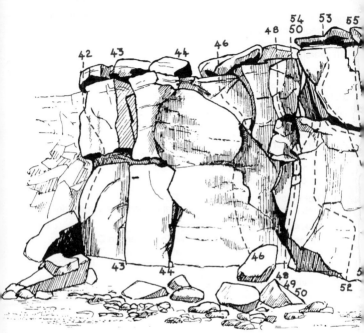

41 Big Buels 12m E6 P3 1997
6c The wall to the right of Guillotine. Climb the groove 4 metres right of the arete, move left to a somewhat dubious peg and climb direct to the top.

Twenty metres to the right is a pile of huge boulders, the result of a rockfall. In the process, several routes were demolished, including Friable Overhang and Thomson's Crack. Both still await re-assembly.

42 Propeller Wall 15m E5 P3   1972
5c The rib to the right of the rockfall. Start behind the large boulder. A problem start leads to a sandy break. Climb the hanging rib above with increasing difficulty. Bold and scary.

43 Old Crack 15m MVS P1 Pre 1951   ★
4b The prominent lower crack provides a pleasant interlude for those who can jam. Climb past the letterbox to a standing position. The top crack is either laybacked or jammed, both are awkward.

44 S Crack 15m VS P1 1939   ★★★
4c A very fine climb following the S-shaped crack on positive holds
and edges after an awkward start.

45 Fairy Wall 15m E2 P2 1979
5c The wall just right of S Crack is climbed via a hard mantelshelf
to the ledges. Continue on small but positive holds.

46 Fairy Steps 15m VD P2 1935   ★
The easier wall to the right is ascended on large but polished holds.
Stepping right into the scoop below the ramp at half height is the
easiest variant. The direct is mild severe.

47 V Chimney 15m VS P1 Pre 1951
4c Easy climbing up the gully leads to a desperate thrutch to finish.

48 Cherry Valley Rib 15m HVS P2 1944   ★
5a Climb the rib right of V chimney starting up Josephine Direct.
Move out left above the first roof and climb directly up the front face
of the rib. The rib below the first roof and the wall on the left can

both be climbed at about 5b.

49 Josephine Superdirect 15m MVS P1 1941   ★★
4b Start at the undercut twin cracks and follow these to the niche.
Solid finger-jams provide the key to the bulge in the shallow groove
above. A satisfying route.

50 Josephine Direct 16m HS P1 1931   ★
4b Good climbing but not really very direct. Follow the Superdirect
to the niche and swing right to a small foot ledge. Climb awkwardly
into the sentry box above and exit leftwards.

51 Little John 15m E1 P2 1951   ★
5b Teeter delicately across the undercut slab right of the start of
Josephine Direct to gain the arete of Short Circuit. Step up and then
left to a pocket and move across, then up, into the sentry box.
Finish as for Josephine Direct.

52 Short Circuit 16m E2 P3 1952   ★
5c Start at the chipped holds to the right. Gain a standing position
on the small ledge with extreme difficulty. Step left and finish boldly
up the arete to gain pockets below the Sentry Box. Use these
carefully but confidently to gain the 'Box' and the sanctury of
Josephine Direct's finish.

53 Hipgnosis 15m E3 P2 1975
6b Climb the thin wall right of Short Circuit to the big ledge. Step
left along this below an obvious hold in the wall above. finish direct
right of the Sentry Box.

54 Josephine 18m HS P1 1931   ★★★
4b A quarry classic. Climb the main crack system with an awkward
step left at 2 metres to the prominent ledges and a good stance and
belay if required. Traverse left and teeter delicately round the corner
(don't breath in!) into the Sentry Box. Finish out left.

55 Napoleon 15m VS P1 1938   ★★
4c The jamming crack above the Josephine belay provides an
excellent direct finish, well protected but good value at the grade.

56 Blucher 15m VS P1 1938   ★
4c The shallow, fingery corner to the right of Napoleon, also gained
from the Josephine ledge, is perhaps slightly easier.

57 Tufted Crack 15m E1 P1 1970   ★★
5c Start as for Josephine, but keep to the right to gain the thin
vertical crack in the headwall. Climb this with sustained interest on
tenuous jams.

58 Waterloo 15m E2 P2 1973
6a Start 3 metres right of Josephine and climb direct to the horizontal break. Finish up the wall above, joining and crossing the traverse of Walewska to finish precariously to its right.

Spider Wall 6a ★★★ The lower wall below the traverse of Josephine and just left of the rib via the well polished holds is a classic problem. The rib on the right is **Earwig Rib** (6a) There are a number of variations on both up to 6c.

59 Walewska 15m VS P1 1938   ★★★
4c The definitive gritstone VS! Start 5 metres right of Josephine at a short corner and gain the ledge on the left above Spider Wall. Step back right and layback up the crack above to the horizontal break and either hand traverse this leftwards to the final cracks. Or mantel onto the ledge halfway and step left to the cracks. A direct start joins the flake by a layback crack on the right at 5a.

60 Josephine Traverse 22m HS P1 1931   ★
1. 15m 4b Start as for Walewska to the ledge but continue traversing left below Tufted Crack and Blucher to a belay below Napoleon.
2. 7m 4b Finish as for Josephine.

Right again is a steep, slightly undercut wall split by an off-width crack. This is Botterill's Crack.

61 Not Tonight Josephine 15m E3 P2 1981
6a Start up Botterill's Crack until a traverse leftwards can be made on reasonable holds to a flaky crack. Climb this and step into Walewska. Move back right and climb the wall above.

62 Botterill's Crack 10m HVS P2 Pre 1931   ★★
5a The obvious wide crack provides a notorious offwidth exercise. Its really quite easy when you find the right sequence.

63 Flake Crack 10m HS P1 Pre 1951   ★
4a The flake crack just right provides an excellent short climb. Move right at the top.

64 Flake Crack Direct 10m E1 P1 Pre 1982
5c From the top of Flake Crack attack the wall above with confidence.

The whole area between The Quarry and The Cow provides numerous immaculate problems and micro routes. A handful of the longer slabs have traditionally been regarded as routes for many years but many more, both old and new are just as serious but have never before been formally named. The following selection can be located about fifty metres right of the quarry entrance where a large and shapely block forming the lowest tier of boulders can be identified by a blunt central rib bordered on the left by a slab and the right a steep wall. A classic low-level traverse across this block from right to left is **Ron's Traverse** (6b), but climbing either side of the central arete are:-

65 Old Spice 6m E2 P3 C 1965 ★
5b The right arete of the slab provides precarious 'padding' above a landing that needs well padding.

66 Baby Spice 6m E5 P3 1997 ★
6c The same arete climbed on the steep side.

67 Ladybird 15m HVD P2 Pre 1951
The three tiered series of well scratched and chipped broken slabs starting just left of the small birch tree is not as easy as it looks. There are several variations to the central section which all lead to a wide crack near the top but the most direct are all around 4b/c. The original V.Diff version is probably furthest left with an interesting finish up the final arete or a step right to the wide upper crack.

The next four climbs start on a wide ledge above **Dusky** (4c), a five metre, steep and narrow, chipped, introductory slab. They are all very bold and feel longer than they are, however, despite the P grades they have long been regarded as popular solos.

68 Eastern Night 7m MS P3 1960s
The left-hand face of the block is climbed pleasantly via a large pocket near the top.

69 Nightshade 7m HS P3 1960s ★
4b Climb directly up the left side of the slab finishing via a small fluting on the upper arete.

70 Dead Of Night 7m HVS P3 Pre 1989
5a The centre of the slab provides a nasty sloping finish.

71 Evening Wall 8m VS P3 1945 ★★
4c Climb the right-hand side of the slab to an exposed but well positioned upper arete.

Immediately left of The Cow is:

72 Cold Chisel 7m HS P3 Pre 1965
4b The left edge of the slab right of the descent gully is climbed on positive chips.

73 Chiseller 10m S P3 Pre 1951 ★
4a Follow the chipped slab all the way. Excellent for beginners (roped, of course).

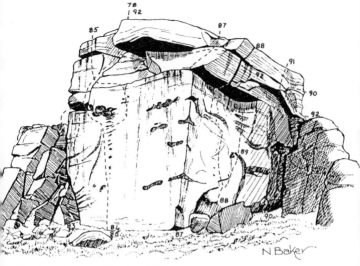

74 Gaz 6m S P2 Pre 1965
4b A good continuation to either of the last two routes up the short 'eponymous' slab to the small overhang, finishing awkwardly up the crack on the left.

THE COW

Is the huge square fronted buttress. The upper left wall contains several problems and three short routes towards the right-hand end.

75 Cow Crack 6m VD P1 Pre 1951   ★
Another popular finish to Chiseller. Climb the short crack high on the westward-facing wall of the Cow above and right of Chiseller, starting from a large boulder.

76 Cow Flap 6m VS P1 1992
5a Start from the right edge of the boulder below Cow Crack and climb direct, passing a small groove in the top half.

77 Cow Rib 7m HVS P3 1941   ★★
5a The exposed rib right of Cow Crack gives an intimidating problem. It can be approached by traversing the horizontal crack or from the ledge above Desperate Dan.

78 'A' Climb 25m S P1 Pre 1902   ★★★
An excellent route, popular for over 100 years.

1. 10m Climb Chiseller and belay on top. (The original route followed the gully on the right).
2. 10m Traverse right round the nose onto the main face to below a corner. Climb this to a large flake (runners) and step rightwards onto a ledge and exposed belay.
3. 5m 4b Climb directly above the belay into the awkward and polished wide crack.

79 Alternative Finish   15m   HVS   P1   1956   ★
5b From the belay, traverse out leftwards above the void to finish up Cow Rib.

80 Ferdinand   15m   HS   P2   1939   ★★
4a From the final belay on 'A' Climb, continue the traverse round the exposed corner to an airy chipped slab which leads to an easy finish out right.

81 Ferdinand Hand Traverse   15m   VS   P2   Pre 1969
4c From the belay, climb to the roof and hand traverse right to finish up the groove and overhang to the left.

82 Voyage To The Outer Limits   10m   E6   P2   1980
6b The large roof to the right of 'A' Climb's second belay is crossed to good holds. The wall above is hard and awkward. Pre-placed wires over old bolts provided protection on early ascents but the bolts were very old then!

83 Desperate Dan   10m   E7   P3   1979   ★★
6b The left-hand arete of the Cow is gained by stepping from the boulder on the left. Bold, technical and serious.

84 Cow Udder   10m   E1   P3   Pre 1958   ★
5a The line of chipped holds up the front of the Cow moving left joining 'A' Climb. The crux is low down but its along way to the first runner!

85 Mad Dogs   20m   E3   P3   1977   ★
1. 10m 5c Climb Cow Udder to just below the top. Traverse right on rounded holds to below the belay of 'A' Climb. Climb directly up to this.
2. 10m 5c Reverse 'A' Climb to above the corner. Climb the crack above to the break. A long reach leads to the top.

86 The Black And White Days   20m   E5   1992   ★
6b An extension to the traverse of pitch 1 of Mad Dogs to finish up the final moves of New Statesman.

87 The New Statesman   20m   E8   P3   1987   ★★★
7a Climb the improbable right-hand arete of the Cow directly to the top of Ferdinand. Bold and technical and without respite.

88   Milky Way   18m   E6   P2   1978   ★★★
6b   The thin overhanging crack and roof on the right side of the Cow provide one of Ilkley's pumpiest routes.

89   Galaxy   21m   E6   P3   1987   ★
6b   The scoop right of Milky Way is gained from 5 metres up that climb. Continue to the roof and finish up Milky Way.

90   The Marine Who Slept In   15m   E5   P2   1987   ★★
6a   Starts up the gully from Milky Way. Climb across left into the short groove to good holds and a good nut slot. Climb the easier but bold wall above to runners in Hand Jive and exit rightwards.

91   Fast Forward   18m   E6   P2   1998   ★★★
6c   A very hard continuation to The Marine Who Slept In via the shallow groove to an 'Elephant's Bum' finish.

92   Hand Jive   20m   E2   P1   ★
5c   The horizontal crack close to the top of the east face of the Cow. Climb from right to left to the belay of 'A' Climb or finish at Ferdinand. A good route to build the forearms.

Just right of the Cow is a small buttress. This is **The Sentinel**. There are several obvious variations. The well polished central line just right of the groove is the easiest and most popular (VD). The green wall just left of the groove is now alleged to 'go' at 6c!

Seventy metres to the right of the Cow is a group of steep walls facing Ilkley with an obvious overhanging groove in the middle. Before these are reached however are several boulders, all with numerous short routes masquerading as problems. The largest boulder, however, is now home to two 'real' routes, by anyone's standards.

93   In A Pickle   8m   E6   P3   1998
6b   The scary undercut slab up the left side of the large pinnacle boulder between The Sentinel and Lost Boots is climbed from pockets to pebbles to slopers.

94   Captain B.O.'s Kiss Of Death   8m   E3   P2   1990
6b   Climb the overhang and crack on the same boulder. Start from a flat block below the right-hand overhang and gain a small slot in the fork of the crack above the bulge. Crank up for the rib and use this and the crack to gain flutings which lead to the top.

To the right, and at a higher level, is a steep wall with a horizontal break running below the top.

95   Butch Crack   6m   HVS   P1   Pre 1970
5b   Using a horizontal slot gain a standing position on a green ledge

and make long stretch for the main break just right of the vertical crack. Pull up awkwardly into the unhelpful top crack to finish.

96   Cassidy's Crawl   7m   VS   P1   Pre 1970   ★
5a   Traverse the upper break leftwards from a start up the gully on the right. At the end pull up on good holds just right of the final arete.

The more defined short edge 20 metres right provides:-

97   Lost Boots   8m   VS   P2   Pre 1958
4c   Climb the chipped holds at the left-hand end of the walls to a small cave. Finish direct.

98   Patience   8m   HVS   P1   Pre 1951   ★
5b   To the right is a short ramp and leftward-leaning crack. After an awkward start, trend rightwards on improving holds to finish.

99   Waiting Room   8m   E1   P2   Pre 1989
5b   Start immediately right of Patience and climb to an obvious cave at 6 metres. Move slightly left to finish.

100   Little Hole   8m   E2   P2   C 1989
6a   Gain the obvious hole to the right. Reach up and right to a tiny ramp. Use this to gain the large ledge and safety.

101   Big Hole   8m   E1   P1   C1989
5c   Use the large orifice to reach a chipped hold. The large ledge is gained using two further chipped holds. Finish direct.

102   Doing the Business   8m   E3   P2   1984   ★
6b   Climb the bulging wall immediately left of the main groove using small pockets.

103   Green Chimney   8m   HVS   P1   1960s
5a   The overhanging groove is best climbed facing right. Finish awkwardly up left. Worms and wimps can wriggle off right.

104   First Arete   7m   E3   P2   C1989
6b   The overhanging arete is hard.

105   Three Mantels   6m   S   P1   Pre 1989
Start just left of the next obvious arete and mantel your way to the top. The first mantel is considerably harder than the next two - some suggest 5c!

106   Second Arete   5m   VD   P1   Pre 1989
Climb the arete, initially on its right. The arete direct is 5a.

A further 100 metres to the right, through a small fir wood, is a small isolated buttress which is undercut along its entire length.

107 Olicana Crack 7m VS P1 Pre 1951
5a The blunt cracked arete in the centre of the bottom lip provides
an awkward start. Finish more easily up the short layback crack. A
totally independent line, but less significant, can be climbed 2
metres to the left at the same grade.

108 Romans Rib 7m E5 P3 1998
6c The blunt hanging arete in the centre of the buttress.

109 Carrie 6m E3 P3 1977
6a The large roof to the right is gained from the slab. Make a long
stretch for a good hold. A telescopic reach helps.

The **Olicana Traverse** (5b) is a worthwhile problem crossing the
buttress at half-height from right to left.

Set a little further back is quarry containing rock of a poorer quality
to most of Ilkley's crags. It does however provide limited scope for
further problems if you've done everything else. Some 200 metres
right of Olicana Crack, beyond the quarry is a little buttress on the
end of spur overlooking a ravine.

110 Forgotten Buttress 7m S P1 Pre 1960
4a Start awkwardly below thin cracks and climb leftwards to finish
over bulging blocks.

111 Double Crack 7m VD P1 Pre 1960
The obvious twin cracks are followed to wider cracks and the final
block.

112 Mantelshelf Arete 7m S Pre 1960   ★
4a From the toe of the buttress move up onto the right side of the
arete which is followed pleasantly to a steep mantelshelf. Finish
over the prow of the capping block.

THE CALF   The large boulder below the Cow provides some short,
fierce routes and the hardest bouldering at Ilkley. Only the most
obvious of the problems are described.

Just to the right of the chipped steps is the Triple Pocket Problem
known as **Facet Wall** (6b) ★ and then the obvious, but desperate,
hanging crack of **Super Set** (7a) ★. **Car Park Crack** (5c) ★★ is an
old classic problem up the insecure jamming crack facing the car
park. **Bonington's Book Problem** (5b) ★★ is another old favourite
which climbs the undercut nose on well spaced buckets.

The overhanging back side of the Calf has three short routes and
many problems.

Three More Reps 6m E4 1987   ★
7a Climb the pegged crack slanting rightwards on the left side of
the face. Gain the obvious flake to a tricky finish.

Bernie the Bolt 6m E4 1985   ★★
6c The centre of the wall is climbed leftwards to the flake of Three
More Reps.

Gnome 6m E2 P1 1952   ★
6a The overhanging groove right of Bernie the Bolt.

Pebble Groove 7m HVS P2 1943   ★★★
5b The north face of the Calf is a big slab. Pebble Groove is the
runnel on its left side. It is about the same grade whether your body
is to the left (more strenuous) or to the right (delicate) both methods
are brilliant and worthwhile.

The slab to the right has been top roped at 7a. Can it be led?

Late Fever 10m E5 P3 1986
6c From the obvious groove to the right of Pebble Groove climb the
slab above using a pebble and a shallow pocket. An easier variation
The Early Starter (E2 6a)★ swings right from the top of the groove
using another small pocket to gain the upper groove above The
Ring.

The Ring (5c) ★★ is the undercut nose with the large thread
leading to a much easier upper groove. **Under The Stairs** (5b)
pulls over the overlap right of the arete of The Ring to join the steps
on the tourist route

ROCKY VALLEY

A prominent escarpment set above a shallow subsidiary valley half
a mile from the Cow And Calf. It faces generally north but each
buttress stands out and the routes on the flanks get some sunshine,
particularly in the evenings. The buttresses, one to six, are
numbered from left to right and the climbs are described in that
order.

Number One Buttress A fine compact buttress with a prominent
cave at its base.

1 Cooper's Slab 8m D P3 1931   ★
The obvious slab above the cave is approached from the left and
can be climbed up the centre or the right-hand edge. Easy but
worrying!

2 Beeline 11m HVS P1 1947 ★★★
5a A miniature classic. Start just to the right of the cave. Tricky moves lead to a fine hand crack which is followed to the top. Not a soft touch at this grade.

3 Beyond The Fringe 12m E5 P2 1975 ★
6a Start 3 metres right of Beeline. Climb the short wall to the horizontal break, arrange protection, and climb directly up the groove above. A bold proposition without recourse to side runners in Beeline, which reduce the grade.

4 Little 'A' Climb 10m S P1 Pre 1911
A pleasant route on the right-hand side of the buttress. Climb the short awkward crack and move left to a ledge. Finish up the short overhanging crack.

5 Herbaceous Border Variation 10m VS P1 1943
4c Start as for Little 'A' Climb but instead of stepping left to the ledge climb the dirty crack direct.

6 Dot's Cracks 9m S P1 Pre 1958
The short steep crack on the right of the previous route.

Number Two Buttress Fifty metres to the right are two clean-cut buttresses split by a large gully.

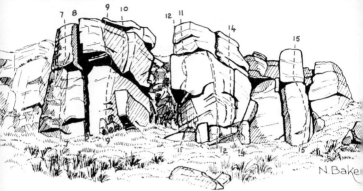

7 Stiction 9m VS P2 Pre 1911
4c An eliminate line, just left of the obvious chimney is climbed direct on small, polished holds.

8 Stiction Chimney 9m VD P1 Pre 1911   ★
Climb the wide chimney. A fine traditional struggle.

9 Nordwand 10m E2 P2 1957   ★
5b Climb the wall just right of the chimney to the horizontal break. Gain the rib and climb to the top on positive holds.

10 Scoop and Hole 10m HVS P2 Pre 1958   ★★
5a Start as for Nordwand to the horizontal break. A short traverse right leads to the hanging scoop. A difficult entry leads to an easier finish.

11 Superb Too Right 10m E6 P3 1986   ★★
6c Climb the blank-looking wall just right of the gully by means of a hanging seam. Finish direct up the steep wall above.

12 Berserker 14m E2 P2 1975   ★★
5b Climb the obvious arete on the right. A tricky move gains the horizontal break. Traverse left above the previous route then climb the short left arete. An excellent route .

13 Am I Brown 10m E1 1996
5b A blinkered line between Berserker and the Strid with a zero wallnut for protection. Side runners in The Strid are not allowed.

14 The Strid 10m HS P1 Pre 1911
4b The short slab in the corner is climbed until the crack in the left wall can be gained. Climb to the ledge then up the short slab above. Alternatively the crack can be climbed direct at VS 4c.

N. Baker

Flypaper (4c) ★★ Is the polished wall to the right of The Strid, it provides some amusement, but not as much as its neighbour **V Groove** (5b) ★ did when it was described as the same grade in the last guide. They were both Severe in the '82 edition!

15 Ivor the Engine 7m HVS P2 Pre 1989
5c The right arete of the small prow. A boulder-problem start leads to an enjoyable finish.

Number Three Buttress The next buttress has a prominent 3-tiered slab flanked by easy chimneys.

16 Black Chimney 7m D P1 Pre 1911 ★
A narrow strenuous chimney in the wall on the left of the large slab.

17 Minigrip 10m E2 P2 1978
5b Climb the prow left and above Three Slabs Route.

18 Three Slabs Route 11m MS P1 Pre 1911 ★★
The left-hand side of the slabs starting from the left. A direct start is Harder.

The large ledge can be gained by a polished performance on the wall below and to the right of Three Slabs Route **Bogey Wall** (5a) **HH**. The left-hand arete provides **Sod It** (5c) **H**, a fine problem.

19   Hades 10m   HVS   P2 1949   ★
5b   From the large ledge above Bogey Wall, climb delicately up the left edge of the slab above. After a touch-and-go start, holds rapidly improve. The right-hand side can be climbed and is even more delicate.

20   Peach Melba 10m   E6   P3   1986
6b   Climbs the steep green wall right of Bogey Wall.

21   The Flake Climb 15m   S   P1   Pre 1906   ★★★
One of the best climbs in the Valley. Start just right of Bogey Wall and climb easy rocks to a cave. A long stride leftwards leads to a ledge containing the large flake. Climb the flake and short wall to finish.

22   Gremlin's Wall 7m   E4   P3   1953
6b   The deceptively steep wall right of the upper section of The Flake Climb is climbed on small edges with only token protection.

23   Oak Tree Slab 10m   MS   P1   Pre 1911
Start right of Flake Climb. After the initial slab it is possible to climb the overhang on either side.

24   Oak Tree Crack 9m   HS   P1   Pre 1951
4b   The thin layback in the square corner below the obvious diminishing oak tree. Finish up the short chimney above.

25   Crack And Wall 9m   VS   P2   Pre 1958
4c   Start in the corner just to the right of Oak Tree Crack. Climb the crack to a ledge and finish up the left wall with difficulty.

26   Spiral 17m   S   P1   1962   ★
A pleasant girdle traverse of the buttress.
Start with an awkward swing up from the right on to Oak Tree Slab which is crossed to the large ledge and flake. Continue across Three Slabs Route and finish up Black Chimney. It can be done in two pitches if desired with a belay on the ledge on Oak Tree Slab.

Number Four Buttress   The buttress immediately right of the large grassy gully.

27   Sentry Box 10m   S   P1   Pre 1911   ★
Follow the left-hand crack until a short traverse right leads to a niche. Finish direct, or traverse left to a corner. The thin crack below the niche provides a direct start.

N.Baker

28 Kestrel 11m VS P1 Pre 1911 ★
4c A more strenuous route to the sentry box offering exciting
climbing up the wide chimney on its right. Finish as for Sentry Box.

29 Shock Horror 14m E6 P3 1977 ★★
6b Start as for Kestrel and move right at 4 metres to gain a
hanging rib. Climb direct up the blunt arete on small pockets.

The arete right of Shock Horror has been led, but only with pre-
placed protection. Named **Rodney Mullen** and graded F8a by the
first ascentionist, it still awaits a leader who can place the gear 'mid-
dyno' and keep going. The true grade could be close to E10!

30 Slide Zone 10m E4 P3 1977 ★
6a Start below the vague groove line round the corner on the right.
Technical moves lead to a good flake hold, then easier climbing to
the top.

31 Throstle's Nest Climb 10m HS P1 Pre 1911
4b The corner is climbed direct to a difficult exit.

32 Twin Cracks 9m MVS P1 Pre 1911 ★
4b The cracks are climbed using one or both until you're in a tangle.

33 Somersault 9m VS P1 1947   ★★
4c The thin crack provides superb strenuous jamming. Grit at its best!

34 Long Chimney 13m D P1 Pre 1911   ★★★
The chimney in the centre of the buttress is climbed direct and offers a perfect introduction for beginners. Climbing the awkward scoop to the right and traversing left to the chimney increases the grade to VD.

35 The Link 15m S P1 Pre 1958
A delicate traverse linking Long chimney with Sound Box. Climb the scoop of Long Chimney and traverse right across the slab to the crack of Sound Box. Finish up this.

36 Walker's Hangover 17m HVS P1 1952   ★★
5a Climb The Link to the steep thin crack and move up to a ledge with difficulty. Move left on to the corner and then direct to the top.

37 Sound Box 13m MVS P1 1936
4b Easy scrambling leads to an overhanging recess, climb this to a ledge and finish up the crack above.

38 The Tremor Wall Finish 5m HVS P1 1955
5b A hard problem. From the ledge on Sound Box climb the wall on the left. Can be dirty.

39 Tombstone Crack 14m MVS P1 Pre 1958   ★
4b The crack just right of Sound Box. Climb the groove to the crack and gain the ledge of Sound Box. Follow the nose on the right to finish.

Number Five Buttress   The smallest and most compact of the six buttresses.

40 Dale's Delight 9m MS P1 Pre 1958
A short climb on the left wall of the obvious gully. Start below a prominent block and climb direct.

41 Blasphemy Crack 9m HS P1 Pre 1906   ★
4b A boot-wide crack climbed by laybacking, jamming and much cursing.

42 The Chute 10m S P1 Pre 1911
The short narrow polished slab has an awkward start which will spit you out if you are not careful.

43 Gym Crack 9m HVS P1 1956   ★
5b Only a short route but quite demanding for the grade. The thin

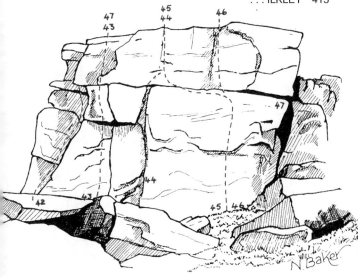

crack just to the right is followed to a larger hand crack. This is followed with difficulty to the top.

44 Sylvia 9m E3 P2 1973   ★
5c Climb the strenuous crack right of Gym Crack, finishing up Sylveste.

45 Sylveste 10m E2 P2 1956   ★★
5b A superb climb which starts at the lowest part on the right-hand side of the wall. Make a tricky mantelshelf and traverse left to the blunt nose. Finish up this with difficulty in a bold position.

46 Veste 9m E1 P1 1972
5b Climb Sylveste to the horizontal break and follow the shallow groove above to the top. A long reach is an asset.

47 String Vest 12m HVS P2 1996   ★
5a The very obvious traverse starting from the right and finishing up Gym Crack.

48 Little B Route 9m S P1 1948
Start across the shallow gully. Climb the thin crack to a wider finishing crack.

49 Beetroot 9m HVS P1 1961
5b Just right of Little B Route. Climb up and right to a small ledge.

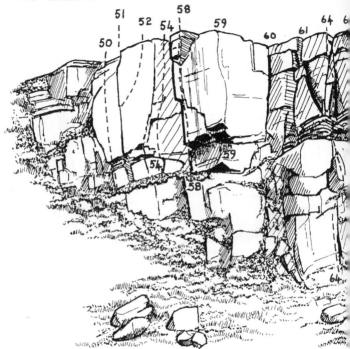

Use a vertical flake to reach a ledge on the right. A tricky move leads to the top.

Number Six Buttress   This is by far the most extensive buttress and consists of some fine walls, but is slow drying.

50   Fear Of A Failed Race   9m   E5   P3   1983
6a   This intimidating climb takes the smooth slab on the furthest buttress left. Climb on small edges to a nasty finish. (Side runners are cheating).

51   Catapult Crack   9m   VS   P2   1950   ★
4c   The wide off-width crack is climbed direct with the major difficulties at the start.

52   Blue Meanies Tea Party   9m   E3   P2   1984
5c   Climb Catapult Crack for 3 metres then move right and climb the arete right of the crack to the top.

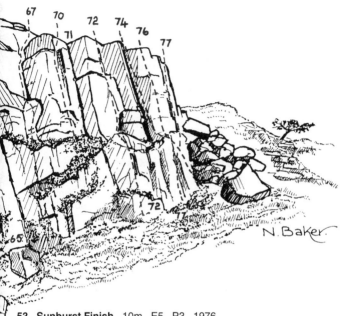

53 Sunburst Finish 10m E5 P3 1976
6a Start at the right-hand arete of the small buttress. From the
large ledge, jump or dyno to attain a large hold. Move left to a small
ledge and follow the right-hand arete to the top.

54 Ruby Parrot 10m E3 P3 1977   ★
5c Just right of Sunburst Finish is a vague groove line. Step out of
the corner and climb the groove on small edges.

55 Gutsie 10m VS P1 Pre 1911
4c Climb the left-hand of the twin cracks in the corner. Decidedly
awkward.

56 Stump Chimney 10m VS P1 Pre 1911
4b The right-hand corner crack is climbed until it forms a chimney.
Follow this to the top.

57 Diamond Dogs 11m E3 P2 1976   ★
5c The steep wall to the right of Stump chimney is climbed with
difficulty until a move can be made on to the right-hand arete. Finish
direct.

58 Blind Valley 13m E3 P1 1973   ★★★
5c The old peg route, Thor's Wall, on the front of the buttress, is
climbed direct to a tricky move at the top. Very satisfying.

59 Countdown to Disaster 14m E8 P3 1986   ★★★
6b Just to the right of Blind Valley is an obvious large blunt arete.
This is climbed direct on very small edges to a crux move at the top.
Although 14 metres long, there is a further 15 metres below the first
move. Do or die!

60 Brush Crack S 10m P1 Pre 1951   ★
The corner up and right from Countdown to Disaster.

61 Arrowhead S 10m P1 Pre 1911   ★
The diagonal crack to the right of Brush Crack.

62 Lady Mabel Route VD 12m P1 Pre 1911
Start up a broken slab to the left-hand diagonal crack. Climb this
until a hand traverse right is possible. Finish straight up.

63 Taj Mahal VD 12m P1 Pre 1958
Climb the broken arete immediately right of Lady Mabel Route.
Follow the left-hand of the twin cracks.

64 Windy Buttress VS 10m P1 Pre 1951
5a At the toe of the buttress is a steep little wall. Climb this to a
ledge below an inverted V crack. Follow this to the cave and finish
up the crack.

65 S Route VD 10m P1 Pre 1958
Climb the broken rocks right of Windy Buttress passing the inverted
V crack to a small ledge. Follow the right-hand crack to a wall at the
top.

66 The Ogre 12m VS P1 Pre 1951   ★★
4c Start at broken rocks below a conspicuous overhang. Climb the
indefinite crack to the overhang. Entering the final crack provides a
fine climax.

67 Matchbox 13m HS P1 Pre 1911
4b The crack a metre or so right of Ogre's top crack. Gaining the
crack is the major difficulty.

68 Smog Monster 12m E3 P3 1985
6b The arete right of Matchbox.

69 Smog Wall 7m HS P2 1954
4b Follow Matchbox until a step left above the roof can be made
into a thin crack. Up this to the top.

70 Overhanging Chockstone Crack 7m D P1 Pre 1911
Round the corner from Matchbox is a crack that can be used for a descent.

71 Double Chockstone Crack 15m S P1 Pre 1911
The straight crack right of the previous route is pleasant enough.

72 Holly Tree Route 15m D P1 Pre 1911
Climb the broken walls up the centre of the buttress. Another beginner's delight.

73 Spreading the Disease 10m E3 P3 1984   ★
6b Gain the arete right of Holly Tree Route from halfway up.

74 Spread-eagle 15m HS P1 Pre 1911   ★★
4b A good gymnastic struggle. Climb up the right-hand side of the obvious flake on polished holds. Hand traverse left to a square block and make an awkward move to gain the scoop. Various finishes are possible from here; the scoop direct being traditional.

75 Bird Of Prey 10m E1 P2 1980
5b The arete left of the scoop in the upper section of Spread-eagle

76 Bald Eagle 10m E3 P2 1974   ★★
5c From the block of Spread-eagle climb the arete to the right, on its right, via the slot.

77 Illegitimate Crack 15m VS P1 1935   ★★★
4c A fine climb, well protected and not too strenuous. The shallow chimney is gained via the flake and thin crack. Continue up the crack above.

78 Tricyclist 10m E2 P2 1978
6a The thin slab to the right is climbed on its left side.

The slab to the right has been ascended in a couple of places offering the same type of climbing as Tricyclist. One route has been named:-

79 Cyclist 10m E4 P2 1985
6a Climb the centre of the slab.

80 Rag Slab 10m HVD P2 Pre 1969
The slab on the end of the buttress proves tricky.

81 Too Far S P1 1960s
A girdle of Number Six Buttress. A lot of effort for little worthy climbing, and sure to make you popular with anyone else on the buttress.
1 From Rag Slab to Spread-eagle.
2 Hand traverse into Double Chockstone Crack, then to Overhanging Chockstone Crack.

3 Traverse at the same level to Matchbox.
4 Descend Matchbox and traverse to The Ogre.
5 At the same level traverse to Brush Crack.
6 Traverse to the ledge in Stump Chimney and finish up this.

ILKLEY – GRADED LIST

E8
Countdown to Disaster (6b)
New Statesman (7a)
Loaded (7a)

E7
Snap Decision (6c)
Death Watch (6b)
Desperate Dan (6b)

E6
Superb Too Right (6c)
Shock Horror (6b)
Fast Forward (6c)
Big Buels (6b)
Voyage To The Outer
 Limits (6b)
Peach Melba (6b)
Galaxy (6b)
Milky Way (6b)
In A Pickle (6b)
Bald Pate Super Direct
(6c)
Guillotine (6b)

E5
Sunburst Finish (6a)
Fear Of A Failed Race
(6a)
Marine Who Slept In (6a)
Late Fever (6c)
Romans Rib (6c)
Baby Spice (6c)
Black And White Days
(6b)
Beyond The Fringe (6a)
Propeller Wall (5c)

E4
Slide Zone (6a)
Cyclist (6a)

Bernie The Bolt (6c)
Three More Reps (7a)
Where Blue Tits Dare
(6b)
Wellington Crack (5c)
Gremlins Wall (6b)
Desperate Dread (6a)

E3
Captain BO's Kiss Of
Death (6b)
Smog Monster (6b)
First Arete (6b)
Bald Eagle (5c)
High Street (5c)
Blue Meanies Tea Party
(5c)
Diamond Dogs (5c)
Grand As Owt (6a)
Doing The Business (6b)
Carrie (6a)
Not Tonight Josephine
(6a)
Sinister Rib (5b)
Ruby Parrot (5c)
Sylvia (5c)

E2
Tricyclist (6a)
Short Circuit (5c)
Waterloo (6a)
Fairy Wall (5c)
Little Hole (6a)
Hand Jive (5c)
The Early Starter (6a)
Minigrip (5b)
Sylveste (5b)
Stickyfingers (5c)
Berserker (5b)
Norwand (5b)
Bald Pate Direct Start
(5b)

Old Spice (5b)
Serendipity (5b)

E1
Bald Pate (5a)
Peg Wall (6a)
Tufted Crack (5c)
Central Wall (5b)
Little John (5b)
Veste (5b)
Big Hole (5c)
Flake Crack Direct (5c)
Bird Of Prey (5b)
Am I Brown (5b)
Waiting Room (5b)

HVS
Ivor The Engine (5c)
Hades (5b)
Pebble Groove (5b)
Gnome (5c)
Curving Corner (5b)
Jiggery Not Pokery (5b)
Cow Udder (5a)
Highfield Corner (5a)
Central Rib (5a)
Overhanging Blocks (5a)
Scoop and Hole (5a)
Gym Crack (5b)
Tremor Wall Finish (5b)
Patience (5b)
Beetroot (5b)
Piton Wall (5a)
Transparent Wall (5a)
Cow Rib (4c)
'A' Climb Alt Finish (5a)
Dead Of Night (5a)
Beeline (5a)
String Vest (5a)
Butch Crack (5b)
Green Chimney (5a)
Walker's Hangover (5a)
Botterill's Crack (5a)

VS
Curving Cracks (5a)
Cow Flap (5a)
Olicana Crack (5a)
Windy Buttress (5a)
Kestrel (4c)
Gutsie (4c)
Stiction (4c)
Catapult Crack (4c)
Napoleon (4c)
Blucher (4c)
Crack And Wall (4c)
Walewska (4c)
Somersault (4c)
The Ogre (4c)
Stump Chimney (4c)
S Crack (4c)
Cassidy's Crawl (5a)
Bogey Wall (5a)
Ferdinand Hand
Traverse (4c)
Evening Wall (4c)
Illegitimate Crack (4c)
Lost Boots (4c)
V Chimney (4c)
Gibbon's Wall (4c)

MVS
Twin Cracks (4b)
Old Crack (4b)
Letter Box Crack (4b)
Josephine Superdirect
(4b)
Ladybird Direct (4b)

HS
Flypaper (4c)
Smog Wall (4b)
Josephine (4b)
Throstle's Nest Climb
(4b)
Josephine Traverse (4b)
Little Kaiser (4b)
Tombstone Crack (4b)
Matchbox (4b)
Oak Tree Crack (4b)
Spread-eagle (4b)
Sound Box (4b)
Blasphemy Crack (4b)
Cold Chisel (4b)
Nightshade (4b)
Josephine Direct (4a)
Ferdinand (4a)
Flake Crack (4a)
Corner And Scoop (4a)
Magic Pie (4a)

S
Three Mantels
Too Far
Little A Climb
Brush Crack
Arrowhead
Spiral
Sentry Box
The Flake Climb
Forgotten Buttress
Dot's Crack
Doris
Mantelshelf Arete
Little B Route
A Climb
Gaz
Double Chockstone
Crack
Vital Spark
Chiseller
The Chute

MS
Fairy Steps
Oak Tree Slab
Shadowlands
Three Slabs Route
Dale's Delight

HVD
Ladybird
Eastern Night
Rag Slab

VD
Lady Mabel Route
Taj Mahal
Nailbite
S Route
Stiction Chimney
Sinister Cracks
Double Cracks
Cow Crack
Second Arete

D
Wellington Chimney
Black Chimney
Overhanging Chockstone
Crack
Sentinel
Sand Chimney
Cooper's Slab
Holly Tree Route

OGDEN CLOUGH

NGR SE 055318

SITUATION AND CHARACTER The rocks are situated on Ogden Moor just west of where the Pennine Way crosses Ogden Beck. Facing west-south-west they catch all the afternoon and evening sun and are reasonably sheltered. The rock is rough and sound, taking little drainage, though after rain some areas can remain slimy. The rocks consist of two square-cut bays at each end of the crag with a V-shaped bay in the centre. At the right end is a subsidiary buttress.

APPROACHES AND ACCESS The easiest approach is from the Ogden Water car park which is reached by turning off the A629 Keighley - Halifax road along Ogden Lane which runs down the side of the Whole Hog Inn. From the car park (**see notice board at the entrance for closing times**) follow the bridle path along side the north side of Ogden Water onto the open moor high above Ogden Beck until the Pennine Way is reached at a small dam in the valley. The rocks are on the right bank above the dam.

THE CLIMBS
The first three routes are on a small quarried face up and to the right of the subsidiary buttress. Climbing the face direct just left of the wide crack on the right gives **Peanuts** (4b); the central line through the small overhang is **Charlie Brown** (4b); while the left arete **Woodstock** goes at (4a).

The subsidiary buttress on the right of the main crag has a steep little wall facing downstream. The reachy problem straight up the centre of the face finishing just right of the top block is **Garfield** (5b); while the left arete is **Marmaduke,** a good problem at about (5a). On the front face the central line is **Tom** (5b); whilst the innocent-looking left arete **Jerry** (4b), has a 5a finish if the step around left is avoided.

Separating the subsidiary buttress from the main edge is a deep shallow gully and running out leftwards from the top of the gully on to the main face is a wide roof. Several problems take the roof and the face above (all at about 5b/c) though care is needed with some of the "dinner plates" in the ceiling.

The blunt nose of the buttress marks the start of the routes, which are described from RIGHT to LEFT.

1 Snoopy 7m E1 P1
5b The right arete with a hard finish.

2 Linus 7m E3 P1   ★★
5c Takes the centre of the blunt arete, again the hardest moves are at the top.

3 Joe Cool 7m E2 P1   ★★★
5c The right arete of the first square bay is a bold proposition with several long reaches. Size 3 Friends are useful.

4 Steve's Stroll 7m E2 P1   ★★
6a Two metres left of the arete are two small finger slots. Climb straight up, with more long reaches and a rounded finish.

5 The Reach 7m E2 P1   ★★
6a In the centre of the right-hand wall of the bay is an obvious letterbox. Climb past this and bear rightwards to the rounded finish of Steve's Stroll.

6 Mike's Meander 7m E2 P1   ★★
6a Climb straight up above the letterbox to a rounded finish.

7 Gollyberry 6m VS P1   ★★
4c The right-hand crack at the back of the bay is a classic jamming and bridging problem.

8 Central Wall 6m E1 P2
5b The centre of the back wall is steep and more difficult than it looks, especially at the top. Protection or holds in the side cracks are cheating!

9 Damp Crack 5m MVS P1
4b The left-hand crack usually is!

10 Erosion 5m HVS P1
5a Climb the centre of the left wall of the square cut bay.

11 The Steps 6m VD P1
Start as the previous route and follow 'the steps' leftwards to the arete, moving right to finish over the obvious overhang.

Moving left out of the square-cut bay reveals the easy-angled slabs of the V-bay. These are broken into four buttresses, by a chimney on the left and two deep, steep cracks on the right. The hanging right arete, **High Step Arete** (5a) is a good problem if taken direct with no recourse to the crack on the left.

12 Dexter 6m VD P1
Climbs the right-hand crack starting in a small chimney.

13 Evening Wall 6m S P1   ★
The face between the two cracks to an awkward finish.

14 Robertson's 7m VD P1   ★
The central crack gives a classic hand and fist-jamming problem.

15 Twilight 7m HS P2   ★★
4b The slab between the left of the two cracks and the chimney is
another good route with an interesting finish.

16 Sinister 5m D P1
Back-and-foot the chimney then finish either right or left round the
capstone.

17 Visage 6m MVS P2   ★
4c The face left of the chimney is harder than it looks. Protection or
holds on either arete are cheating at this grade.

The left wall of the V-bay has a very feint arete at the entrance to
the deep gully at the back.

18 Fingers 4m E1 P2
6a Climb the overhanging face right of the blunt arete on small
incuts above a nasty landing.

19 First Impression 5m HVS P1   ★
5a Start just left of the blunt arete and climb straight up to the short
vertical crack at the top.

20 Jitterbug 6m HVS P1   ★
5b The middle horizontal crack has an obvious mouth in the middle
of the wall. Climb through this to a good hold at the top.

21 Lasting Impression 6m E1 P1   ★
5b Left of the previous route is a slot in the lower break, use this
and climb the wall direct to a rounded top or, move left to a slightly
easier finish.

An eliminate, **Surplomb,** at 5c struggles for independence on the
wall between Lasting Impression and Hammill's Horror.

22 Hammill's Horror 6m E1 P2   ★
5b The left arete on its right-hand side. Rather scary with a rotten
landing.

23 Scorpion 7m HVS P2   ★
5a The right arete of the front face has an awkward but protectable
finish. Using the chipped hold is taboo.

The front of the buttress between Scorpion and The Mantelshelf has
been claimed as **Frontier** (E1 5b). Blinkers and imagination are
essential.

24   The Mantelshelf   6m   VS   P1
5a The centre of the face with a mantel to gain the ledge and a less steep finish.

25   Austin's Pullover   6m   VS   P1
5a The left arete is more difficult than it looks. Gaining the ledge from the left is 5b.

The right wall of the left square bay decreases in height towards the back of the bay but what it lacks in height it makes up for in quality.

26   Petite Etoile   5m   HVS   P2   ★
5b From two metres left of the arete climb straight up on positive holds after an awkward start.

27   Last Exit   5m   HVS   P2
5a Almost in the centre of the wall is a short grassy crack at the top. Start just right of this and climb straight up to an obvious curved crack which gives access to the grassy crack.

28   Je Suis Elephante   4m   MVS   P1
4b Climb the wall left of the grassy crack on good holds.

There are several problems on the left wall of the bay at a very amenable standard. The front face of this buttress has a one-metre overhang at the top with several interesting problems through it at 5b/5c. However, the right arete is easier (5a).

The edge now deteriorates into small outcrops but there is still one gem left:-

29   The Girdle   A long way in a single push.   P1
5c Climb Snoopy to the 'Handrail', move left to the arete of Joe Cool. Hand traverse across the wall using upper crack to Gollyberry. Continue mid-height across the left wall and the slabs across the V-bay to the gully at the back. A tricky move is needed to get established on the left wall then traverse left, at roughly two thirds height, to the arete of Hammill's Horror. Another awkward move round this and using the ledge for the hands gains the right arete of the left square bay. Follow the second crack to the back of the bay and continue across the easy left wall. Finally hand-traverse the overhang on the front of the last buttress.

Now run back to the car park before the gates are locked!

PENYGHENT

SITUATION AND CHARACTER The crag is on the very exposed westerly slopes of Penyghent at the edge of the summit plateau at the mercy of bad weather and strong winds. This gives it one advantage; it is mainly quick drying, although a few of the crack lines take seepage. The climbs have that 'big route' feeling about them, being at an altitude of 600 metres with the ground falling away steeply below. The main buttress is mainly of sound, well-weathered gritstone but the crag becomes broken and grassy at its boundaries.

APPROACHES AND ACCESS Although high up, the climbs can be reached in 45 minutes from Dale Head on the Stainforth to Halton Gill road. Follow the Pennine Way footpath to the summit, then walk back and scramble down to the west (right looking down) of the crag. From Horton-in-Ribblesdale the crag is reached in about an hour by taking the footpath from Brackenbottom to join the previous route at the boundary wall on the right-hand side of the crag below the ridge. The farmer has asked that climbers avoid making a direct approach to the crag up the steep hillside below and this includes contouring across from the main paths on either side of the summit plateau. **No dogs, litter, camping or fires. Climbers are also requested not to go in groups of more than eight and to avoid busy bank holiday weekends.** Do not disturb nesting birds and if found on the crag in Spring report details via BMC access officer.

THE CLIMBS These are described from left to right from the descent route just left of the main buttress.

1 Meddler's Crack 10m D P1
The prominent left-hand corner crack 5 metres left and 7 metres higher than the corner crack of Red Pencil, above the right-hand side of a ledge. Climb the short crack until an awkward move on to the overhanging corner block can be made. Now up the continuation crack above.

2 Agnostic's Arete 15m VS P1
5a The steep arete just right of the Meddler Crack. Climb the arete direct on its right-hand side. Difficult to start.
The arete can be climbed on the right wall, avoiding the crux, at Severe.

3 Red Pencil 28m S P1   ★★★
A superb gritstone outing. The original route of the crag taking the
obvious right-angled corner crack. Climb the crack until the
overhang forces a traverse left for 4 metres. Enter a chimney which
is followed to the top.

4 Red Pencil Direct 28m HS P1   ★★★
Follow the original route to the overhang, move out right and climb
the wall between the overhangs.

5 Gladiator 26m VS P1   ★★★
4b A fine direct line which tackles the overhangs avoided by Red
Pencil. Follow Red Pencil to the roof which is climbed on good
holds. Strenuous.

6 Damocles Groove 28m HS P1   ★
4b In the middle of the wall 4 metres right of Red Pencil is a groove
at 10 metres. Climb cracks to a platform below the groove. Climb
the short wall above to enter the groove which is followed to a
perched block. By-pass this on the left and finish up the final wall of
Red Pencil Direct.
Alternatively by-pass the perched block on the right and climb the
wall above at the same grade.

7 Brass Monkey 28m HVS P1   ★
5a A fine climb. Right of Damocles Groove, a wide groove leads to
a steep thin crack. Climb the wall to the thin crack and enter it by
way of a tricky step right. Climb the crack strenuously to a ledge.
Follow the broken groove above to the overhang, which is turned on
the right in a fine position, and follow the final groove to the top.

8 Christian's Crux 27m HVS P2
5a Just right of Brass Monkey is a large curving overhang. Climb the
wall to the overhang where a difficult move right is made to the roof.
Pull directly over the roof and continue to the top past jammed blocks.

9 Pagan's Purgatory 28m VS P2
4c Two metres right of the last route is a V-shaped niche beneath a
block. Climb this direct to the overhang of Christian's Crux. Move
out right and climb to the top, just right of the overhanging corner to
the left of the bulge.

10 Bilberry Wall 27m VS P1
4c Follow Pagan's Purgatory until a step right can be made to a
thin crack. Climb the crack and wall above to a groove which is
followed to the overhangs. Step left and up to finish.

11 Main Buttress Girdle 75m MVS P2
1. 25m 4a Climb Meddler's Crack to the overhanging block,

traverse right to the foot of the chimney of Red Pencil. Traverse
beneath the overhang into the corner and on to the ledge on the
right. Belay.
2. 25m 4b Continue the traverse to Damocles Groove, descend
past the perched block to gain the long ledge and traverse right for
8 metres to reach a grass gully. Belay.
3. 25m 4b Move left and climb the groove to the overhang which is
turned on the right. The rock on the final pitch should be treated
with care.

12 Bale Out 25m S P?
The wall left of Pitchfork Crack is climbed via a flake and lichenous
breaks leading to a direct exit over the top tower.

13 Pitchfork Crack 25m HVS P1 ★
5b Another good climb. Ten metres right of the main buttress is a
wall with an obvious crack in the centre which forks at the top.
Climb easy, but loose ground, for 7 metres to a ledge. Climb the
crack in the overhang on the good jams and follow it to the top.
Strenuous.

14 Red And Green 26m VS P?
4c Twelve metres left of Shepherd's Chimney climb the left edge of
a small face to a grass ledge and then move up left under big
blocks to an easy but dirty finish.

15 Gardeners Question Time 26m HVS P?
5a The wall immediately left of Shepherd's Chimney is climbed to a
grassy mantelshelf. Follow the crack and wall above moving right to
the top of the chimney.

16 Shepherd's Chimney 27m D P1
The corner chimney left of Flying Buttress leads to a ledge and
thread belay. Climb the wall above direct on good holds.

17 Flying Buttress 27m HS P2
4b The obvious steep buttress approximately 40 metres right of the
Main Buttress. Climb the front of the buttress to a ledge and
optional thread belay. Up the wall above as for Shepherd's
Chimney.

18 Nose Cracks 18m VD P1
At the extreme right end of the crag, about 50 metres right of
Shepherd's Chimney, a series of cracks go up the nose of the fell
starting at a ridge directly below the prominent overhang. Climb the
arete and a large flake to the overhang. This is turned on the right
where a short crack leads to a platform below the final wall. Follow
cracks in the wall above to the top.

ROBIN HOOD ROCKS

SITUATION AND CHARACTER   The rocks are comprised of two distinct edges overlooking Cragg Vale, near Mytholmroyd. The left edge is compact; the right one longer and more broken. The rock is of the best-quality gritstone in very pleasant surrounding. It has a sunny aspect facing west which makes it especially pleasant on warm summer evenings (or even winter afternoons). The left edge, particularly, can be green in the early months of the year. The grades are mainly in the Diff to HVS range with little to attract the extreme climber. On many climbs protection is sparse.

APPROACHES AND ACCESS   From the traffic lights in Mytholmroyd take the B6138 to Cragg Vale. Robin Hood Rocks can be seen high on the left about 2 kilometres up the road. Shortly after the Cragg Vale sign park at a row of terraced houses (Mid Birks and Twist Clough). Take the small road between them, after the second terrace take the path left. For the right edge (right hand side) go immediately right after the gate and, in the next field, follow a track left leading to another gate and a signposted track right leading obviously to the crag. For the left edge go a little further into the woods where the uppermost of two footpaths leads between the two edges. When the top is reached go left for about 100 metres. The crag is below a seat. From here to reach the right edge it is best to keep on top until the obvious nose is reached (200 metres right of the path) dropping down immediately past it to arrive at the last route in the guide.

THE CLIMBS   These are described from left to right.

Left Edge
The main buttress of the left edge can just be seen from the path. The first routes are about 50 metres left of the main buttress.

1   Broken Buttress   9m   D   P1
Start at the lowest point and climb direct.

2   Solo Route   8m   D   P1
Just right is a narrow slab. Up this to easier ground.

The next few routes are on a buttress just in front and left of the main buttress. It is characterised by a narrowing crack on the left climbed by Haigh's Route.

3 Haigh's Route 9m VD P2
Climb the narrowing crack above the triangular cave, taking the arete above.

4 Double Trip 8m E1 P1
5c Reach the break with difficulty using broken underclings. Climb the wall above with some reachy moves.

5 Single Trip 8m VS P2   ★
4c Climb the blunt arete on the right of the buttress stepping left slightly to gain a ledge and then mantelshelf to the top.

6 Silly Route 10m MVS P1   ★
4b Swing out left from the recessed corner and up the wall above.

Right, and behind, is the main buttress.

7 Tinker 6m HVS P2
5c Climb the blunt arete on small holds just left of the scoop.

8 Tailor 6m HVS P2
5b Gain the obvious scoop at 3 metres and finish straight up.

9 Soldier 6m HVS P2
5b Three metres right is a hanging flake above an undercut start. Gain the flake via a good pinch grip, trending right to finish.

To the right are two cracks with tricky starts.

10 King Swing 8m VS P1
4c The left-hand crack (now heather filled).

11 Mini Swing 8m VS P1
4c The right-hand crack.

12 Technic 8m HVS P2
5b Start just right of Mini Swing and climb direct to the finish of Meander.

13 Meander 8m S P2
Start up the rib at the right-hand end of the wall to a ledge. Mantelshelf right on to a higher ledge. Step left using two side pulls and finish direct.

14 Trender 8m S P2
As for Meander but following the right arete direct if you can be bothered.

15 Freemason 11m S P2
As for Meander up to the two side pulls but instead of finishing direct traverse left past the Swings to finish up a nose. Not worth picking.

Right Edge
The routes on this edge are easiest worked out backwards!
Allegedly the start can be hard to find as it grows out of the jumble
of rocks and trees. It lies above a large slab (traditionally used for
playing tig!).

16 Haphazard 6m D P2
Up the easy short slab and sharp arete.

Right is a holly bush with a slab to its left.

17 Lecker Lecker Eisbonbons 9m E1 P1
5c Mantelshelf the slab directly from the middle of the wall and take
the overhang directly.

18 Holly Bush Arete 9m S P(rickly - very!)
4a Up the arete left of the bush on to a slab. Over the roof on the right.

Right is a walk-through chimney. To reach it defy the holly and
broken glass. In the back wall is a subsidiary chimney.

19 Hidden Chimney 8m S P3 (P1 if you've no objection to
severe lacerations)
Bridge the entrance to the chimney.

20 Pothole Direct 8m D P1
Climb the subsidiary chimney.

21 The Mole 8m S P1
Climb the main chimney at the narrowest point.

22 Fallout 8m VS P3
4c Take the outer left arete which makes the entrance of the
chimney. An awkward layaway mantelshelf enables the top to be
reached.

23 Ledgeway 8m D P2
The centre of the buttress and right arete.

On the outer side of the through-chimney is a roof.

24 Summersault 8m E3 P2
6a Climb the roof with difficulty and then up the arete to finish. This
route was an old VS until crucial jugs fell off

25 Ye Gods 8m VS P2
5a Two metres left of Titan's Wall (at the right-hand end of the roof)
climb to a horizontal break via an undercut in a slot at 3 metres.
Finish direct.

26 Titan's Wall 8m MVS P2   ★★
4b Start in the middle of the wall and trend leftwards. Step right at

the break and exit up the steep wall above on good holds.

27 Enterprise 10m MVS P2
4b As for Titan's Wall to the break. Hand traverse strenuously left to the arete and up.

28 Thor 9m MVS P2
4b As for Titan's Wall to the break. Hand traverse right.

29 Thor's Hammer 7m HVS P2
5b Climb direct up the wall and arete right of Titan's Wall.

30 Gully Flake 6m VD P1   ★
The obvious flake on the right wall of the gully.

31 The Scoop 8m HS P1   ★
4a Start in the corner and trend awkwardly left, then right to gain the scoop. It is usual to use protection in Gully Flake. The move left from immediately under the overhang is 4c.

32 Wing Nut 8m HVS P2
5a Move right from the corner (or climb the first few metres of Kneemonia) before launching over the overhang to the left and up the steep wall.

33 Kneemonia 8m MVS P1   ★
4b Right is a short crack about 3 metres above the ground. Climb this and the groove above.

34 Duckunder 7m HS P2
4a Hunch leftward under the roof and awkwardly stand up to continue up the arete.

35 Fowl Up 7m HVS P2
5b Climb the roof above Duckunder and finish direct.

After the break comes

36 The Grunter 6m HVS P1
5a Climb to the left of the holly bush and over the overhang with difficulty.

37 Cantilever 10m VS P1
4c Ascend sloping ledges right of the holly bush and surmount the jutting roof direct.

38 Trepidation 6m HS P2   ★
4a Take the obvious scoop on the right.

39 Breakout 6m D P1
The right arete by easiest way.

ROBIN HOOD ROCKS – GRADED LIST

E3
Summersault (6a)

E1
Lecker Lecker
Eisbonbons (5c)
Double Trip (5c)

HVS
Wingnut (5a)
Thor's Hammer (5b)
Tinker (5c)
Tailor (5b)
Soldier (5b)
Technic (5b)
Fowl Up (5b)
The Grunter (5a)

VS
Ye Gods (5a)
Mini Swing (4c)
Single Trip (4c)
King Swing (4c)
Cantilever (4c)
Fallout (4c)

MVS
Kneemonia (4b)
Silly Route (4b)
Enterprise (4b)
Titans Wall (4b)
Thor (4b)

HS
The Scoop (4a)
Duckunder (4a)
Trepidation (4a)

S
Holly Bush Arete (4a)
The Mole
Hidden Chimney
Freemason
Meander
Trender

VD
Haigh's Route
Gully Flake

D
Breakout
Haphazard
Pothole Direct
Ledgeway
Solo Route
Broken Buttress

ROLLING GATE

SITUATION AND CHARACTER The crag lies on the edge of Barden Moor, some one and a half miles east of Cracoe village. It is one mile north along the moor edge from the prominent Cracoe Memorial, which is itself one mile north of Rylstone Cross. The buttresses are varied, some pleasantly slabby and others severely undercut. The coarse gritstone is lichenous and dirty in several places, due to the north-westerly aspect, but there are exceptions, notably the impressive Rolling Gate Buttress. The crag has little to entice the rock athlete, but there is plenty of interest for the average climber, particularly on a fine dry day when a walk along the moor edge to or from Rylstone, picking off the boulders, adds much to the enjoyment. On a summer's evening, Rolling Gate can be an attractive, sunny spot with magnificent views up the Wharfe valley.

APPROACHES AND ACCESS The crag is reached by following the Skipton to Grassington road (B6265) as far as Cracoe. Take the moor lane just past the Devonshire Arms (possible parking at the start of the lane, no vehicles further on) for half a mile. The crag is visible on the left skyline. On reaching the moor strike diagonally leftwards - there is no definite track. Allow 45 minutes. The crag can also be reached along the moor edge from Rylstone in about 30 minutes. **The crag is within the Barden Moor Access area so please refer to special notes on page 10.**

THE CLIMBS These are described from left to right.

At the extreme left of the crag, to the right of a shallow gully, is a slab with a wrinkled wall above it.

1 Lichen Slab 14m D P2
Ascend the centre of the slab and continue rightwards up the wrinkled wall.

2 Jeepster 16m MVS P?
4c Start on the left wall of The Pillar at a crack-line . Strenuous moves lead up until it is possible to move right onto the slab. Finish up to the left of the twin cracks.

3 The Pillar 15m HVD P1
A rib coming down from the right-hand side of Lichen Slab is ascended on its right edge to a stance. Climb the top wall using the pocket and obvious twin cracks.

Round the corner is a bay with three prominent cracks and at short undercut nose at the bottom left, which can be climbed on the left or right at about V.Diff.

4 Six Metre Wall 6m! D P2
This is the short, wrinkled wall on the left of the bay.

5 Veteran's Flake 15m D P1
Start 2 metres left of the first crack and climb a water-worn slab to a flake. Step off the flake and climb the wall to the top.

6 Moss Crack 9m D P1
The left-hand crack.

7 Choss Crack 9m M P1
The aptly named central chimney crack.

8 Long Crack 17m D P1   ★
Climb the right-hand crack to the left of the large buttress. Enjoyable climbing finishing up the left side of the slab.

9 Rolling Gate Buttress 21m MS P1   ★★★
The classic of the crag. Climb the front of the buttress on its right edge. Move out left at the overlap and ascend the slab trending rightwards. Worth the walk-in.

10 Wilkinson's Wall 18m VS P1   ★
5a At the top end of the grade. Takes the right-hand wall of Rolling Gate Buttress. Climb the cracked wall, then make a hard move right to an alcove. Step left to the rib and finish on the slabs above. It is possible to finish straight up the rib of the buttress, avoiding the step right, at 4b.

11 Great Chimney 18m M P1
The obvious chimney crack.

12 The Outsider 15m S P2   ★
A good climb. The slab right of Great Chimney is followed to the overlap which can be ascended in its centre or the right-hand edge.

Fifty metres further right is a large block guarded by two smaller boulders.

13 Under A Winter's Coat 10m MS P?
A green slab beneath a large roof, above and to the left of Yorkshire Wobble is climbed from bottom right to top left followed by a pull over the roof.

14 The Yorkshire Wobble 15m MVS P3
4b (a.k.a. The Nelson Touch) Start at the lowest point below the two boulders. Climb up between the boulders and step off the right

one to ascend the centre of the wall above via a pocket to a mantelshelf finish (crux). A variation finish to the left of the pocket on the upper wall is HVS 4c, a further variation described as moving left from the halfway ledge to the arete and up on slopers is HVS 5a.

15 Lady Hamilton 10m E2 P?
5c The right arete of the Yorkshire Wobble block, starting from the right-hand side of the right-hand boulder. Climb strenuously to shallow scoops and eventually a good ledge.

16 Upstairs at Alice's 8m E1 P?
5b The cleaned wall to the right of Lady Hamilton.

17 In The Footsteps Of Anon 8m S P1 ★
The obvious and excellent flake on the right hand side of the buttress containing The Yorkshire Wobble.

The back of the 'Wobble' block and the nearby boulders contain various problems including **Hardy** (6a), on the back of the block.

18 Lazyitis 10m E1 P2
5b The right arete of the smooth slab to the right of Yorkshire Wobble. Start on the front and continue past a large pocket.

19 On The Verge Of The Red Eye 6m D P?
A green lichenous slab right of a short crack, 7 metres or so right of The Yorkshire Wobble block.

The next buttress, a few metres to the right, is identified by a slab capped with a large overhang.

20 Crossover 15m S P1
Climb the right-angled corner, moving left at the top, to the left edge of a slab. Traverse rightwards and finish up the middle.

21 Looking to the Future 15m HVS P2 ★
5a Start on a spiked flake 3 metres right of the corner. Hand traverse rightwards to an awkward pull on to a slab. Up this to join Crossover. Nice climbing.

22 Escape 15m VD P1
Climb the slab to the overhang, traverse out left and make an awkward pull to join Crossover, finishing up this.

23 Colditz 14m VS P1
5a Start a few metres to the right of Escape. Climb the corner crack to the roof. Now escape rightwards then up the crack.

24 Colditz Direct 13m VS P?
4c Climb the cracks just around the arete from Colditz to join that route on the corner and continue up it for a few feet before moving

out left to finish up the arete.

25 Smiler   9m   HS   P2
4c Ascend the off-width crack right of Colditz Direct with a problematical start.

26 The Handrail   15m   MVS   P1
4b A promising line which doesn't live up to expectations. Start 2 metres left of Crossover. Climb the short rib to the slab and up this to the obvious big traverse line. Follow this rightwards all the way to an awkward finish up the bulge at the end.

The last buttress before the stone wall has a short wall at its base with a lichenous pocket in the middle. The next route starts up the boulder to its left.

27 A Walk Too Fur   10m   VD   P3
Pull onto the boulder and climb the arete of the slab above to a furry finish.

On the boulder with the pocket is:-

28 Learning To Dance   10m   HS   P3
4b Using the pocket mantelshelf awkwardly onto the ledge and follow the slab above to a hard pull to reach easy ground.

On the other side of the dry-stone wall are a number of impressive undercut buttresses with soaring prows. To the left of the first prow is a nice little buttress with a dog-leg crack.

29 Contortionist's Crack   10m   VS   P2
4c Climb the first crack, step (or squirm) left and climb the second crack to a ledge. Finish up the blunt rib by way of a scary mantel.

30 V Groove   8m   VD   P1
Climb the horrible, green groove just to the right.

31 One   10m   D   P?
Traverse right from the start of V Groove, along the lip, to the edge of the buttress. Follow this up with care.

31 To Pluck A Crow   10m   VS   P?
5a Start 5 metres right, on the other side of the lip in the back of the gully. Make a short awkward traverse left to a difficult pull onto the front and follow this easily to the top.

Just right is a gap in the overhang and an obvious projecting foothold.

32 Dirk's Philosophy   10m   S   P?
Step up on the foothold and pull through with care on jammed

boulders. Step left and ascend to a flake on the right-hand side near the top.

33 Orang Outang 8m VS P?
5a Opposite the traverse of Cruising Altitude is a similar break but with the footholds high up. Crouch across this from the gully until it is possible to move up a short groove.

34 Cruising Altitude 12m VD P1   ★
Spectacular positions at a surprisingly reasonable standard. Start up the gully between the prows and traverse right up the parallel diagonal cracks to reach the edge of the void. Finish up the rib with one awkward step. Large Friends.

35 Ceiling Crack 9m VS P1   ★
4c Climb the overhanging crack in the second prow. A hand-searing Austin special.

36 Jeff's Route 9m VS P1   ★
4c Further right is a capped chimney. Ascend the buttress on the right over two small overhangs. Good value.

37 The Magpie Wave 10m MS P?
Start to the right of, and below, Jeff's Route in a small alcove with some dubious rock. Climb up this and mantelshelf onto a large ledge. Gain and climb the easy curved arete above.

38 The Brink 9m VD P1
Climb the last buttress on its right-hand edge on rounded, precarious holds.

39 The Greengrocer 6m VS P?
5b Left of The Brink, under the overhang, is a small green groove with good holds. Climb this and exit right.

Half way between Rolling Gate and the Cracoe Memorial, a few hundred metres in from the moor wall, are a couple of isolated outcrops which offer splendid bouldering and several micro-routes in the Diff to Severe standard.

One of the outcrops is quarried and has an obvious square-cut chimney. The other is a couple of hundred metres nearer the memorial and this contains 3 climbs, including a pleasant Severe up the highest face and a Diff corner round to the right. Well worth taking in on the walk between Rylstone and Rolling Gate.

RYLSTONE

SITUATION AND CHARACTER   The crag runs along the north-western edge of Barden Moor above Rylstone village and is clearly visible from the Skipton-Grassington road as a number of separate outcrops and pinnacles, bounded on the left by the obelisk of Cracoe War Memorial and on the right by Rylstone Cross. The Warm-up Buttress is a little further right of the cross at a point shown as Sun Moor Hill on the O/S map. The crag appears broken from the road but closer inspection reveals a series of large, and sometimes quite extensive, buttresses.

The rock is mainly rough moorland grit and offers a variety of climbing styles including technical walls, classic slabs and brutal rounded cracks. An abundance of boulders provide potential for hundreds of problems though few have been formally documented here yet. From spring to autumn the crag basks - if you're lucky - in the afternoon and evening sun. Some faces, and particularly the boulders in the Far Group, benefit from the morning sun as well. But it must be remembered that the crag is at an altitude of 450 metres and often exposed to strong winds; the rocks do dry quickly after rain, however.

The best routes here are in the grade range of Diff to E3 but modern developments have added a handful of very high standard test-pieces, all of which can be sampled in a peaceful, scenic setting away from the crowds associated with the more popular crags. The only audience here is likely to be the occasional rabbit, red grouse or ring ouzel.

APPROACHES AND ACCESS   Follow the Skipton - Grassington road (B6265) for 5 miles towards Rylstone village. There is a small lay-by (room for 4 cars) on the right just before the Rylstone village sign. A couple of cars can be squeezed in on the left in front of the sign itself. More extensive parking is available in the village. From the lay-by, double back along the road for 100 metres to a gate and walled track on the left and follow this for 600 metres, bearing round a right-hand bend past a small stream to a gate on the left. The official public access point on to the moor lies 100 metres further up the hill, but the track from the gate is soon re-joined and leads up the hillside passing an isolated conifer plantation. It is best to continue up the track directly to the moor edge and from here the small, but obvious, Warm-up Buttress is soon reached. Follow the well-marked track leftwards to the cross (25 minutes to the moor edge - if you're fit!).

The crag can be approached by longer routes by climbers who like to incorporate a good walk into their day. The moor-edge paths from Crookrise or Rolling Gate provide excellent outings. The bridle path across the centre of the moor from Halton Heights is also pleasant and worthwhile and takes about an hour and a quarter. **The crag is within the Barden Moor Access area. See access notes on page 10.**

THE CLIMBS are described from right to left.

The Warm Up Buttress
This small, but aptly named, quarried buttress is 250 metres right of Rylstone Cross. The climbs are short but clean and get the sun earlier than most of the main crag.

1   Yellow Badge of Faith   8m   HVS   P3   1988   ★
5a Start below the obvious convex slab, just right of the arete. Pull up and mantelshelf with difficulty onto a small ledge at the foot of the slab, then step right and climb its smoothest part.

2   Rib of Gold   7m   HS   P2   1988
4a Climb the first couple of metres of the broken left edge of the slab and make an awkward step up right to the ledge using small pockets. Then climb the slab via its left edge or, slightly harder, just right of the edge.

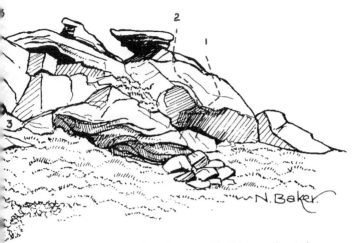

Climbing the scratched and easily escapable flakes on the on the left wall of the slab and pulling on to it half way up is unsatisfactory and **Cheating** (VD).

3 High Bark Crack 6m HS P1 1988
4b The hanging crack in the right wall of the prow. A long reach gains good finishing holds.

4 Full Frontal 6m HVS P2 1988
5b The hanging, square prow is climbed direct.

5 Beginner's Bulge 6m VD P1 1988
Climb the slab to below the broken yellow bulge and pull over on good holds and jams.

6 High Flying Adored 8m E1 P3 1988   ★
5b Climb the left edge of the slab and then hand traverse left along the lip of the overhang to a spectacular aerobatic finish via a hidden pocket at the highest point. Bold but satisfying.

7 Undercarriage 7m HVS P2 1988
5c Climb the right-hand side of the concave wall and make precarious moves left to gain, and progress along, the glacis beneath the prow.

8 Sunhill Slab 6m D P1 1988
Traverse the obvious quarried slab left of the gully to finish up the groove right of the arete.

Just to the left is **One-Eyed Wall**, a nice problem with or without the eye. (4a/4b).

Between the Warm-Up Buttress and the Cross Group is a jumble of large boulders scattered down the hillside to the left of the wall. The next climb takes the largest of these and it is best approached by descending from the path for about 20 metres.

9   No Man's Land   6m   VS   P2   1988/98
5a   The steep undercut wall above a short slab is gained from the left by a long step on to the ledge. Pull up on small holds and finish direct. A shorter, but more direct variant, **Trespasser** (S 4a) climbs straight up the wall on the left via shallow corners.

The Cross Group
An extensive and complex collection of rocks. The cross sits atop the buttress containing Monument Crack but down to the right is a large rambling buttress which is divided into three tiers. The lowest tier is the smallest and contains climbs of only problem length; the second tier, however, contains the following two climbs which are good in their own right but can also be combined with routes on the more extensive upper crag.

10   Full Nelson   9m   E1   P1   1988
5c   Start from a short crack on the right and contort up and left on to the protruding nose. Then, falls, knockouts and submissions permitting, the upper slab is gained and climbed.

11   Half Nelson   9m   S   P1   1988   ★
From the top of the ramp above the lower tier climb up and then right to gain a short traverse leading to a standing position on the protruding nose. Step up and follow the upper slab as for the preceding route.

12   Grouseland   10m   HS   P2   1988
4b   A short corner bounds the steep south wall of the upper tier. Climb the corner and cracks above on the left to below the final tower. This is crossed to the left in an exposed position to good finishing holds. Harder for the short.

13   End of the Line   10m   E2   P2   1989
6a   Climb the wall immediately left of the short corner of Grouseland. Finish direct to the final holds on that route .

14   Terminus   7m   HVS   P2   1972   ★
5b   Take the centre of the steep, clean south wall via an obvious slot (if you can reach it) and belay on the big ledge. Climb the slanting crack up left as on the original route or, more logically, traverse off right.

15 England Expects 7m E1 P2 1988 ★
5c The prominent arete is gained by a swing left from the boulder below Terminus. Bold and quite technical but very satisfying. (A direct start is 6a)

16 Highlord 10m MVS P2 1988 ★
4b The first obvious break 5 metres left of the arete is climbed on to the slab just left of the heather. Continue rightwards up to the diagonal crack in the bulge above and pull through awkwardly to the easy top slab. A good extension to Half Nelson.

17 Kiss Me Hardy 10m E2 P2 1988 ★
5b Takes a central line over the upper bulge via a shallow depression and short flake. Start from the ramp and move easily up right to arrange crucial Friend protection in the rusty horizontal intrusion. Pull up and left on to the upper slab via a blunt rib.

18 Crossover 10m VS P1 Pre 1969
4c Start at the top of the terrace, but below and right of the largest overhang. Scramble up to a short wall which leads to a prominent rightward-slanting crack. Gain and climb this to an awkward exit on to the upper slab finishing via a rib on the left.

N. Baker.

19 Lower Traverse 20m VD P1 Pre 1950
A wandering, old-fashioned climb, but with some nice finishing
moves. It starts to the right of Crossover and takes the easiest line
rightwards across the slabs. From the top right-hand edge (best
belay here), move up and round the corner and ascend the
rightward cracks.

20 Midget Gem 6m E3 P1 C.1977
6b The large overhang at the left of the upper tier. It is climbed by
way of a strenuous pull and long reach to gain jams in the roof. Pull
up left into the wider crack above. Not the most aptly named route!

The Cross Buttress itself lies across the gully and contains some of
the best climbs on the crag. At the right end of the gully wall is a
short prominent chimney.

21 Beginner's Chimney 7m M P1 1988
After an awkward start, the difficulties soon ease, as does the
angle.

22 Anonymous Cross 8m S P1 1988
Start just left of Beginners Chimney below a small overhang. Pull over on to a bulge and step up and left on to the steep slab. Continue via a tiny overlap to the easier slab above.

23 Double Crack 8m S P1 1980
The line is obvious, just left again. Start in a short corner below and left of the large boulder. Move up to the twin cracks and climb them with an awkward exit.

24 Arm Jam 12m HS P1 Pre 1969 ★
4b The prominent, short handjam crack in the centre of the wall. Start below it and slightly left. The wider continuation crack leading directly to the cross provides a fitting conclusion.

25 The Eyes Have It 8m VS P2 1989
4c Climb up to and past the two obvious shallow depressions left of the short crack on Arm Jam.

26 Pocket Battleship 10m E3 P2 1988 ★
6a The compelling line of shallow horizontal slots in the bulging wall leading to the final moves of Monument Crack. Start up a short crack and gain a ledge below the pockets. Arrange protection here and launch up left with all guns blazing to a final slap for the break. Low in the grade.

27 Sword Dance 20m E1 P2 1970 ★★
An excellent route with two contrasting pitches. Start at the short crack, as for Pocket Battleship.
1. 11m 5b Climb the short crack then move delicately left to gain the vertical section of Monument Crack. Continue, descending slightly left on superb, but hand-rasping jams, to a difficult exit round the corner on to the big ledge.
2. 9m 5b A bold pitch. Climb straight up to gain the arete and grope over the top to find a good pocket. Pull on to the slab and climb the edge to the break below the final bulge. Good holds up and right provide the finish.

28 Monument Crack 15m E1 P2 1965 ★★★
5b A superb, strenuous and, without 'heavy metal' protection, intimidating route. Start on the slab at the lowest point of the buttress. Climb up to the roof and pull over to gain the rightward-leading diagonal crack. Follow the crack past a semi-resting position to the wide section across the steepening wall. A difficult pull at the end gains good jams and the easier upper slab.

29 Catwalk 18m VS P2 Pre1923 ★
Start as for Monument Crack at the lowest point of the buttress.

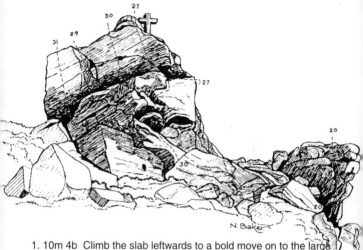

N. Baker

1. 10m 4b Climb the slab leftwards to a bold move on to the large sloping shelf. Belay.
2. 8m 4c Step left and climb the obvious ramp line precariously to the top.

30 Puss-Puss 7m HVS P1 1972
5b A good line which climbs the steep wall right of the Catwalk ramp via pockets and a long reach. A contrived start can be made up the dirty wall below the big ledge.

31 Whiskers 6m E2 P1 1977
6a The clean steep wall left of the Catwalk ramp with a very technical rock-over move and long reach rightwards to finish.

Two problems to the left of Whiskers are **Mr Mistopheles** (5b), the arete; and **Tiger** (5c) the wall just left again.

32 The Full Monty 6m VS P1 1998
5a The wall across the gully opposite Whiskers. Start a few metres right of the lowest point and make some good reachy moves to finish just left of a short vertical crack.

33 Artist's Impression 6m HVS P2 1988
5b Start at the lowest point and gain the short ramp above the overhang with difficulty. Move right and climb the steep wall with a mantelshelf finish.

Just left of Artist's Impression is **Short And Sweet** (4c) a worthwhile exercise with good moves through the bulging fault.

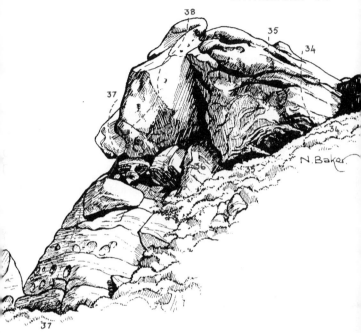

The next named route lies about 50 metres left on a buttress with an arched, overhanging corner.

34 Sandy Gully 8m D P2 Pre 1923
A pleasant route and misnamed. It does, in fact, take the clean slabby wall to the left of the dirty gully about 6 metres right of the overhanging corner. Trend right towards the top.

35 Impending Gloom 8m HVS P1 1988
5c Just right of the hanging corner is a steep fingery wall. Step off a flat block and make a couple of hard pulls on small holds to reach a protruding horn on the ledge. Take one step right and climb the top wall delicately to a rounded finish.

36 The Grunt 8m HVS P1 1965
5b An infamous Rylstone test piece. Well named!
Climb into the hanging corner and move right on to, and up behind, the Damoclean flake with ease but trepidation. Exit above, usually with great difficulty and rarely with style. The grade is nominal.

37 Sandy Buttress 16m VD P3 Pre 1923   ★
A pleasant climb with scant protection on pitch 2.
1. 8m From the lowest part of the slab just left of The Grunt ascend
via rounded pockets and a vertical crack to a belay.
2. 8m Step right on to the smooth upper slab and climb delicately
up to, and over, the small overlap to the top.

38 Yet Another Hillside Attraction 9m HS P2 1988
4b Start as for pitch 2 of Sandy Buttress. Step up right and
continue traversing across the fine exposed slab to the right edge.
Climb up to, and over, the overlap on shallow pockets to better
finishing holds. A good, though usually green, pitch.

39 Lower Slab 11m HD P2 Pre 1923   ★
The front of a huge slabby boulder directly below Sandy Buttress.
Pull on from the right and climb delicately up just right of centre.

40 Old Pals 9m S P2 1988
Start on the left-hand side of the slab at a short dirty crack. Step
right and move delicately up to the crest of the rib which is followed
direct to the top.

The Main Buttress
Some 300 metres left of the cross the edge provides the most
extensive area of climbs. The first few rocks offer short problems
and then a small, but attractive, rusty slab is reached. This slab is
concave at its right-hand side with a short shallow crack leading up
to a blunt arete towards the centre.

41 Nobular Structure 8m E1 P2 1986   ★
6a An intricate and technical problem. Start below the centre of the
concave section and climb straight up on rusty excrescences to the
horizontal break. Step right and finish up a short crack.

42 Angry Woman 7m VS P1 1988
5b An interesting start leads to a pleasant finish. Gain the shallow
crack with difficulty and continue up the blunt cracked rib stepping
right to finish.

43 Bad Boys 7m VS P1 1988
4c Start just left of the arete and gain the slab and flake above by a
long reach. Continue direct to a thought-provoking finale over the
bulge.

44 Monkey Corner 9m VD P1 Pre 1923
Start just right of the dirty corner and make a difficult step up on to
the slab which is crossed by a diagonal line to finish round the
corner as for Angry Woman. A direct finish up the wide crack on the
left is more logical.

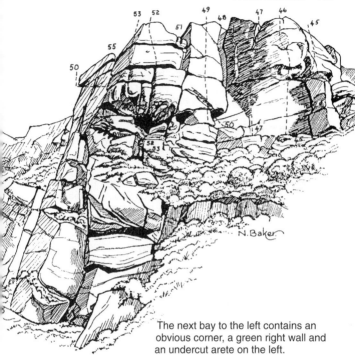

The next bay to the left contains an obvious corner, a green right wall and an undercut arete on the left.

45 The Artful Dodger 8m E2 P3 1988
5b Start in a short corner on the right of the bay and pull up below the steep arete. Step right and climb boldly up the rib on the slabby side.

46 Tasslehoff Burrfoot 8m E2 P1 1988 ★
5c Climb the steep pocketed wall just left of the previous route to a sloping shelf. Move up left on to this with difficulty and finish direct. Strenuous.

47 Pickpocket 8m HVS P1 1979
5a Climb the green wall just right of the main corner by a thin crack and useful pockets. Easier than it looks and worth a dabble.

48 Twin Cracks 8m S P1 Pre 1923
The obvious corner which forms two distinct cracks from half height. Pleasant enough when dry.

49 Sundowner 9m HVS P2 1988   ★
5a The slim clean wall just left of the corner via a tricky move using a shallow round pocket at half height. Using the left edge is cheating.

50 Senator's Saunter 20m VD P1 1988   ★★
An obvious rising traverse line from the foot of Twin Cracks to the top of Dead Kennedys. It gives some good moves in fine, exposed positions.

51 Falcon Crack 10m VD P1 1935   ★
The prominent wide crack just left of the corner provides a clean and attractive route. Once established, pleasant jamming leads to the top.

52 Frankie Comes To Rylstone 10m E1 P2 1988   ★
5b A direct line up the wall between Falcon Crack and the arete. Good jams in the hanging crack up the bulge lead - if you can stand the pain - to nice moves up the wall with the crux right at the top, just right of the arete. Worth taping your hands for.

53 Hanging Cracks 11m VS P2 1970   ★★
5a Start, as the last route, up the painful hanging cracks, but then move left round the arete and climb the bold, slabby edge in a superb position.

54 Misty Moo 18m S P1 1991   ★
A worthwhile hybrid. Climb the left hand side of the detached slab below and right of President's Slab. Step left across the gap and move up right. Join Presidents slab for a couple of moves then move right to climb the left side of the arete in a fine position in common with the finish of Hanging Cracks.

55 President's Slab 18m HD P1 1922   ★★★
A Rylstone classic. One of the best diffs on grit. Start at the lowest point of the slabs. Climb directly up the well-scratched slab to the halfway ledge and possible belay. Continue up slightly rightwards taking the easiest line to cracks leading back left to the top. Superb.

56 The Hot Line 16m E1 P2 1988   ★★
5b The most direct line possible on President's Slab, via a thin flake line between the original and Dead Kennedys. A bold move is required to reach a pocket just below the top horizontals. The final block is then climbed direct. An indirect but independent start, at a similar standard, is **President's Prologue** which climbs the steep slab to the right of Misty Moo before moving left across the gap onto the main slab.

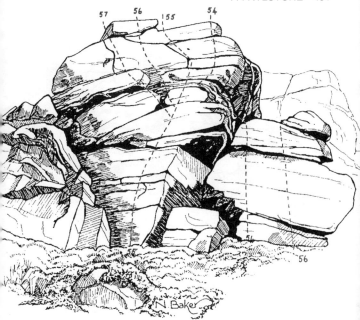

57 Dead Kennedys 16m VS P2 1979   ★
5a Start as for President's Slab but, at half height, trend left up the shallow, bottomless crack with a useful pocket on the left. An indistinct variation to the left has also been recorded possibly using the pocket, without the crack.

The next section of crag starts about 50 metres to the left, but amongst the jumble of boulders on the hillside below President's Slab is a distinct cave with a short clean wall above it.

58 Cave Face 7m VD P1 Pre 1950
Climb the right rib of the cave and the wall above.

Back on the main edge the next feature is an undercut rectangular slab. Climbing the right-hand side of this is,

59 Little Gem 7m E2 P2 1996
5c From a convenient pointed block below the overhang gain good holds and protection on the lip. Pull awkwardly onto the wall using pebbles and then step up and right to exit. Walk off, or climb the easier slab above just right of the arete.

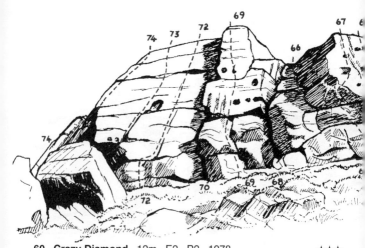

60 Crazy Diamond 12m E2 P2 1978 ★★★
5b A gem of a climb, low in the grade but with a rather serious start.
Pull on to the steep slab left of centre, and climb it delicately to
reach the break. Move up to the short diagonal crack and climb it
and the wall above, via a long reach and small pocket, to a
'sparkling' finish.

61 Lichen Chimney 11m M P1 Pre 1923
The easy chimney left of the broad slab leads to a ledge and short
wall.

62 The Glass Slipper 11m E2 P3 1991 ★
5b Take a direct line up the slab just left of Lichen Chimney to the
ledge. Step across onto the short steep rib above and pad coolly to
the top.

63 Chimney Slabs Route One 11m S P1 Pre 1950
4b The slab just left of the chimney is climbed, trending left at first,
to an awkward step up before a wide ledge is reached. Finish up
the short back wall round to the left.

64 Lichen Crack 11m VD P1 Pre 1923
The dirty line which climbs the chimney and crack above the small
cave.

65 Chimney Slabs Route Two 10m S P3 Pre 1950 ★
A good bold pitch up the pocketed slab above and left of the small
cave.

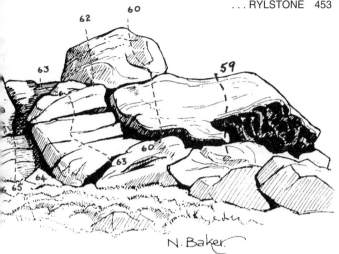

N. Baker

66 Trowel Face 14m HS P1 1955
4b A leftward-slanting flake crack line starts 4 metres up above a
bulge. Pull on to the bulging slab just right of centre and move
across left to the foot of the crack. Enter this awkwardly and follow it
to the top. A problem start (5c) takes the dirty, undercut crack on the
left and moves right across the slab to gain the original route at the
foot of the flake.

67 How Fast Dad 14m E1 P2 1997
5b Start between the two starts of Trowel Face and climb up to the
flake. Move up and right on crimps and a shallow pocket, through
the bulge, and rock over onto the right side of the slabby arete.
Follow the arete left of Chimney Slabs Route Two, finishing past a
good pocket.

68 Chockstone Chimney 14m VD P1 Pre 1923 ★
A rather strenuous chimney, hard to start direct, but the wall to the
left gives a more pleasant alternative to the first few moves. The
chockstones have been there a long time but move alarmingly.
Handle with care.

69 Persistence 15m VS P2 1955 ★
4c The narrow buttress between the two chimneys. A good climb.
Go through the bulge using the obvious crack then continue up the
broken slab to a ledge. The final tower gives an exhilarating, reachy
move up the left edge.

70 V Chimney 14m VD P2 Pre 1923
The right-bounding chimney of Dental Slab. Protection is sparse in the middle but the hardest moves are lower down.

The next four climbs lie on the best piece of rock at Rylstone, Dental Slab. They are all best protected by a selection of Friends.

71 False Teeth 20m VS P2 1988 ★
4c An 'artificial' line, but giving good moves on clean rock. Start at the foot of V Chimney and bridge up left to gain the slab proper. Move diagonally left, crossing Extraction to stand in the 'eyes' of Dental Slab then step left again and climb straight up 2 metres right of the left arete.

72 Extraction 17m HVS P2 1971 ★★
5b An excellent line up the right-hand side of the slab. The problematic start can be avoided by using the start of the previous route. Start just right of centre and make a hard pull up to reach a horizontal slot then step right and climb the vertical crack and blank section above it to a nice finish on some flutings.

73 Dental Slab 20m S P1 1935 ★★★
The best severe on Yorkshire grit. A brilliant pitch. Start at the left-hand side of the slab and traverse right until it is possible to pull up via the obvious 'eyes' above the bulge and step right again to a ledge (this point can be reached more easily by continuing the original traverse line for a few feet and then moving up and left to the ledge). Continue, taking the easiest line, with a step left to gain a narrow ramp leading back to the centre. Grit your teeth and make an airy mantelshelf to gain the top.

74 Laughing Gas 17m HVS P2 1979 ★
4c Climb the edge of the slab from a start in the crack just left. Bridge up it until it is possible to step right on to the arete and climb it direct. The upper section is quite bold and no laughing matter. A more difficult variation start, **Incisor**, has been reported pulling over the bulge from the traverse of Dental Slab.

75 Matterhorn Ridge 10m S P3 Pre 1950
The prominent pointed boulder below Dental Slab is climbed from its lowest point. Remember what happened to Whymper's party as you contemplate your descent!

Immediately left of Dental Slab is a heathery groove system and left of this is a slab bounded by a hanging flake chimney. Use the belay stake at the top of Dental Slab for climbs in this section.

76 Forgotten 13m D P1 1980
Climb the shallow crack in the centre of the slab until a large block on the right can be gained. Step up from this to reach the top.

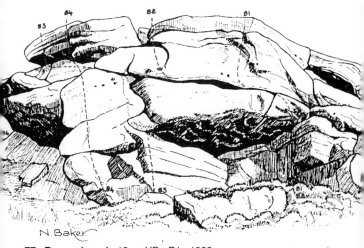

N. Baker

77 Remembered 12m VD P1 1988   ★
A direct continuation of the previous line up the thin crack. Pleasant.

78 Moorland Memories 11m MVS P2 1988
4b The slab and pocketed upper wall just right of the chimney flake.
A thin step-up on the green slab leads to holds in the cracks above
and right. Climb straight up the nicely-positioned pockets to the top.

79 Flake Chimney 10m VD P1 Pre 1950
Layback, thrutch or jam - or all three - up this innocuous-looking
little climb.

Left again and at a lower level is the **Overhang Buttress** which
comprises three stepped tiers, the top tier not immediately obvious
from below. The next three climbs, utilise only the lower tier but
Castrol climbs all three and is the longest route on the crag.

80 February Climb 10m S P1 1998   ★
Start to the right-hand side of the roof and climb easy ledges to a
crack. Climb this with interest to the shelf (and an easy escape to
the right). Traverse the horizontal crack or cross the fine slab
above, leftwards for 3 metres, finishing over the overlap.

81 The Marine Who Had No Friends 12m E4 P2 1986   ★
6b Start below the right-hand side of the roof and climb up to a
good slot. Move left using the hanging crack to make a difficult pull
up on to the upper wall. Climb this via long reaches to good
pockets, but a rounded finish.

82 After Eight 14m E4 P2 1973   ★
6a An extremely strenuous traverse from right to left across the
buttress. Protection is good but difficult to place. Originally soloed
and graded HVS! Start as for the previous route but continue the
traverse until a long reach gains a short, bottomless curving crack
to finish.

83 Castrol 30m VS P1 1950/58   ★★
The longest route at Rylstone with an excellent first pitch which can
be done in its own right. The upper pitches tend to get dirty but are
not without interest and the whole route is varied and worthwhile.
1. 11m 4c The clean vertical crack is gained awkwardly and then
followed to a line of good jams leading left to a ledge and thread belay.
2. 11m 4c Climb above the thread and traverse left for 4 metres to
climb the bulging break above to another ledge.
3. 8m 5a Make a precarious step up to gain the green slab which is
climbed with trepidation or delight dependent upon the amount of
lichen present at the time. This pitch can be avoided by a traverse
off to the right.

84 G.T.X. 20m HVS P1 1981   ★★
The clean, attractive wall left of Castrol and a bulging crack above
make this an excellent route.
1. 10m 4c Climb the improbable looking wall past good slots to the
finishing move of Castrol's first pitch. A delight.
10m 5a Climb up above the thread, step left, then straight up the
bulging crack. Not a delight!

85 Pipeline 7m VD P1   1988
The dank, green corner just left of the arete provides the slimiest
route on the crag. Award yourself a large black spot.

86 O'il Be Hanged 10m E2 P1 1996
6b The huge roof below the left-hand side of The Overhang
Buttress can be breached via a thin undercut flake, reached from
slopers below the lip. Climb to a big ledge and then the left side of
the rib above gains the belay below the last pitch of Castrol.

87 Secretary's Slab 12m VS P2 1952
4b The prominent isolated slab up and left of the Overhang
Buttress is often green. Start below the centre of the slab and move
up right below the bulge until a bold step left gains the upper slab.
Follow the diagonal crack to finish at the top left-hand corner.

Rylstone Wall Area
Down and to the left again is a steep clean buttress which contains
a variety of good-quality climbs.

88 Baldrick 6m VD P2 1988
The 'acned' slab on the right is climbed from bottom right to top left
with an awkward step at half height.

89 I Have A Cunning Plan 6m HS P2 1988
4b A 'brainwave' from Baldrick, climbing direct over the bulge from
the centre of the slab via a prominent pocket. Up right to finish.

90 Balance Crack 9m VD P1 Pre 1950   ★
The obvious chimney with peculiar knobs on its left wall. The initial
bulge is stubborn but the climb is good for its grade. Finish over or
through the final chockstone.

91 The Last Days Of May 9m E1 P1 1997
5c Start in the centre of the wall just left of Balance Crack and
move up past the break to reach the 'peculiar knobs'. Follow these
to the next break and rock over left onto the slab above. Bridging
out right is not allowed.

92 Off Balance 13m S P1 1965
Take the first bulge of Balance Crack then move left to the ledge on
the arete. Step up and move steeply left to finish in the niche.

93 Beached Whale 12m E2 P2 1988   ★
5b An exciting eliminate up the overhanging arete. Good holds on
the right of and beneath the arete lead to a belly-flop onto the ledge
of Off Balance. Follow this for a few moves, then step back right on
to the pebbly nose to finish.

94 Rylstone Wall Direct 14m HVS P2 1965   ★★
5a Not really any more direct than the parent route but a very good
climb nonetheless. Start below the overhanging arete and traverse
left until a long reach (crux) gains a short vertical crack and nut
protection. Continue straight up with a step right round the final
bulge to finish.

95 Freebooter 15m HVS P2 1971   ★
5a Start under the overhang in the centre of the buttress and move
right below it to gain the short crack on Rylstone Wall Direct. Climb
this, but when the final bulge is reached kick off left along the rising
traverse line and layback up into the niche to finish.

96 Rylstone Wall 14m VS P1 1952   ★★
4c An interesting and sustained route, much better than it looks.
Start just right of the ramp leading into the chimney crack. Pull up
steeply right past a hole to gain good holds and jams leading right
into a horizontal crack on the front of the buttress. A reachy move
up and right gains further horizontals leading to the bulge which is
avoided by a final rightwards step.

97 Rylstone Crack 12m MVS P1 Pre 1923 ★★
4b The obvious wide crack left of the overhangs. A classic for traditionally-trained and clad gritstoners, but not recommended for those with delicate skin, especially if wearing shorts. Climb gracefully (?) to the capping block and bridge round it until it is possible to step right into the niche.

98 Wall of the Evening Plight 12m E1 P1 1988 ★★
5c A fine direct line up the wall between Rylstone Crack and Bowler's Chimney, passing an obvious letterbox on its left (crux) to finish up the hanging flake. Friends essential.

99 Orbital Highway 20m E1 P2 1988
5c A rising traverse of the buttress with little new climbing but some of the best moves. Start as for Rylstone Wall Direct, but after the short vertical crack traverse horizontally left into Rylstone Crack. Step left on to Wall of the Evening Plight at its crux letterbox and up this to the top.

100 Bowler's Chimney 14m D P1 1935
The green chimney in the corner contains some nice moves when dry.

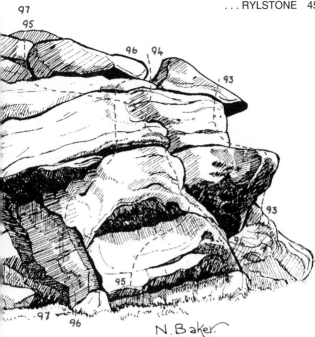

N. Baker

101 Keep Left 13m HS P1 1970
4b The wall just left of the green chimney. Start up a diagonal line
leading to a prominent flake on the edge of the chimney. Reach up
to a pocket then left into the counter-diagonal leading back across
to the arete up which the climb finishes.

102 Never Climb With Guidebook Writers 12m E1 P1 1988 ★
5b Start in the centre of the steep wall and climb direct to a
horizontal break at 4 metres. Make a hard move up to gain the next
break. Step right and up again crossing the ramp of Keep Left to
gain a ledge in the bay above. Pull out on to the left arete to finish.

103 Loiner 14m VS P1 1965 ★
4c Start as for the last route, but at the break at 4 metres traverse
left to the arete. Continue easily up the rib to finish on good holds
over the bulge just right of the short crack.

104 Up And Over 10m VD P1 Pre 1950
An obvious short crack is climbed with difficulty to the slab just left
of the arete. Finish up the wide crack at the top.

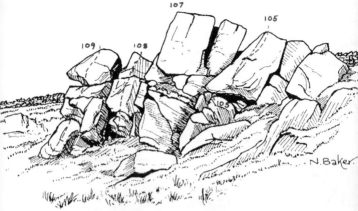

N. Baker

The edge now degenerates until after about 100 metres a series of
buttresses containing a prominent undercut arete is reached. The
next two routes utilise a clean slab to the right of this.

105 Veteran 8m E3 P3 1994   ★★
5c Start from the ledge at the foot of the main slab and step up to
the good foothold on the right. Climb boldly and directly to the
overlap and pad up the right-hand side of the arete to finish. A
runner can be placed round to the left to protect the top section.

106 Face Savour 12m HVS P2 1988   ★
5b Start well down, below the slab at the foot of a short, prominent
rib. Climb this awkwardly on its left-hand side, move right across
ledges and step up to good footholds at the bottom of the main
slab. Traverse delicately leftwards, then move up to finish up the left
side of the overlap.

107 Heart Beat City 8m E8 P3 1989   ★★
6c To the left is a frighteningly undercut and blank right-hand arete.
Approach from the right and rock on to the left-hand side of the
arete. Cool your way direct to the top.

The next climb is round to the left of the prow up a narrow slabby
buttress.

108 Forgotten Friends 10m HVS P1 Pre 1969
5a The narrow buttress is climbed direct, slightly right of centre, to
a difficult finish up the right arete.

The large buttress, visually reminiscent of Brimham's Dancing Bear,
is the next major feature. It contains two routes.

109 Bare Faced Streak 13m E4 P2 1989 ★★
6a A bold route despite good Friend protection in the break. Climb the lower section of the buttress on the right and from the horizontal break step up and over the overlap making precarious moves to gain a sloping ledge. Step up left more easily onto the scooped slab to finish.

110 Three Step Buttress 13m HS P2 Pre 1950 ★
1. 8m 4c Start on the right and take the easiest line up to the obvious break to a bulge and surmount this with difficulty moving left along the diagonal crack to a belay.
2. 5m 4b Step boldly up right on to the rounded rib and climb it delicately in a nice position to the top.

The Far Group
This group comprises all the rest of the isolated buttresses and pinnacles spread across the moor to the Cracoe Memorial. There are few major climbs in this area but dozens of short ones and innumerable problems, many of high quality and worth seeking out. The following is but a small sample of what's on offer. The first named climbs are situated 300 metres left of Three Step Buttress to the left of easy slabs which bear a number of short problems.

111 Rainbow Sunset 6m HS P2 1988
4b Just left of the easy-angled slabs is a steeper buttress with a smooth front face and a series of short, disjointed flakes up the right edge. Climb the line of flakes steeply to the top.

112 Starlight Express 6m VS P2 1988
5a Takes the rib on the left of the buttress via pockets to the smoother section above. Continue up the centre.

113 Little Horror 5m VS P2 1998
5a The shallow flake in the right wall of the narrow gully to the left of Starlight Express

114 Pancake Slab 8m S P3 1988 ★
The obvious slanting slab is climbed from left to right using the rusty brown pancakes as handholds. A harder but less satisfying variation start is possible from the gully on the right, **Maple Syrup** (5b).

Round to the left of a large boulder, the front of which contains a nice problem **Rusty** (4c), is a bay, containing a clean steep wall.

115 Slip Slidin' Away 8m E3 P2 1989 ★
6a Climb the steep slab and rib to the right side of this wall with a precarious move to gain the break. Move left over the bulge to finish.

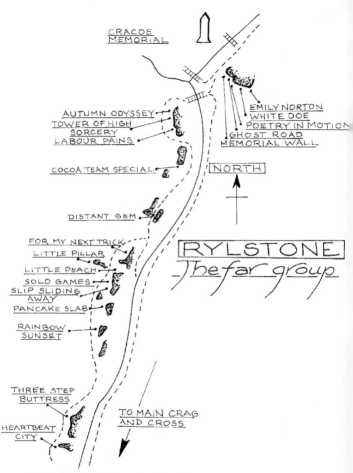

CRACOE MEMORIAL

AUTUMN ODYSSEY
TOWER OF HIGH SORCERY
LABOUR PAINS

COCOA TEAM SPECIAL

EMILY NORTON
WHITE DOE
POETRY IN MOTION
GHOST ROAD
MEMORIAL WALL

NORTH

DISTANT GEM

FOR MY NEXT TRICK
LITTLE PILLAR
LITTLE PEACH
SOLO GAMES
SLIP SLIDING AWAY
PANCAKE SLAB
RAINBOW SUNSET

RYLSTONE
The far group

THREE STEP BUTTRESS
HEARTBEAT CITY

TO MAIN CRAG AND CROSS

116 Poke And Hope 6m E4 P2 1993
6a The steep slab squeezed in between Slip Slidin' Away and Solo Games utilises a 'monodoigt' for the precarious finish.

117 Solo Games 6m E1 P2 1988   ★
5b The left side of the wall is climbed direct past a pear-shaped pocket to finish with interest just right of the arete. Nice!

118   V Crack   8m   HS   P2   Pre 1950
The prominent buttress just left contains two obvious cracks. This is the right-hand one.

119   Bird's Nest Crack   8m   HVD   P1   Pre 1950   ★
The left-hand crack, just right of the arete, gives a good climb.

120   Little Peach   6m   E3   P3   1988   ★
5c A steep slab just left of the arete of Bird's Nest Crack. Nice technical moves and a choice of finishes, but the lack of protection and worrying landing make for somewhat stimulating climbing. The arete on the right is out of bounds.

121   The Niche   8m   HVS   P3   Pre 1950   ★
5b Across the gully to the left is an undercut crag with two obvious large pockets. Traverse in from the right to gain the left-hand pocket, step up right and make a reachy, rounded exit.
(The original niche problem described in the 1930s may have been the similar, but shorter, pocketed wall to the right 5a).

122   For My Next Trick   6m   HVS   P2   1988
5b Another good problem which climbs the overhanging flake to the left of the arete and then continues straight up with a bold mantelshelf to finish.

The broken buttresses just left provide good problems as do a small cluster of rocks about seventy metres lower down the moor where the next route is found, a short attractive rib.

123   Little Pillar   6m   HS   P2   1988
4b Start on the right and move delicately up and left to good finishing holds.

About 50 metres left again a larger collection of boulders contains more problems and two which attain route status.

124   Surfer's Paradise   6m   E2   P1   1988
6b The steep slabby central rib is difficult to start and then follows flaky lay-away holds up the left edge.

125   Bondi Bitch   6m   HVS   P1   1988
5b The left-hand arete. A difficult rock-over start leads to a dirty horizontal and a slightly easier finish.

Straight back up the moor is an isolated block split by a short shallow chimney. The wall just left of the chimney contains :-

126   Distant Gem   6m   HVS   P1   1965
5b A steep shallow crack slanting slightly left up the front of the buttress is climbed by an intricate series of balancey layaway moves.

Left again, beyond more isolated boulders and good problems, is a larger tilted block not far from the wall. It presents an imposing overhanging face with a bottomless crack starting high up which for many years was only overcome with the aid of a human pyramid,.

127   The Cocoa Team Special   6m   E5   P1   1995   ★★
7a The lower wall to gain the crack is highly problematical, staying with it once you reach it is not so easy either!

128   The Definitive Gritstone Chimney   6m   VS   P1   1970
Unprotected and technically ungradeable but once wedged in you are unlikely to fall out. Masochistic tendencies and expertise in the infamous 'udge' are all that's required.

Left again and round at a slightly lower level is a hidden wall of more continuous rock.

129   Impending Arrival   8m   VS   P1   1965
4c The first steep crack towards the right of the wall. Strenuous jamming is required to surmount the bulge.

130   Labour Pains   6m   VS   P1   1965
4c The easier looking crack 2 metres left. don't be deceived by appearances.

131   Living On A Tarot Reading   10m   E4   P2   1993   ★
6a Start just right of Tower Of High Sorcery below a small overlap at 3 metres. Climb up to and over this, step right and make a long reach for the break. Step up and using undercuts make another long reach to a rounded edge on the right. A difficult pull on slopers gains a good break and a flake, step left and finish up the centre to a rounded finish.

132   The Tower Of High Sorcery   10m   HVS   P2   1988   ★
5b Climb the centre of the obvious steep wall passing a large round pocket to make a bold move up and left to reach the short vertical crack. Climb the rib above (crux) and move right to finish.

133   Autumn Odyssey   12m   E1   P2   1988
5b Start across the gully. From the slab below the bulge traverse right along a diagonal crack on the gully wall until it is possible to move back left along the wider, rounded break above. The next bulge is surmounted by moves back right to gain a short prominent flake in yet another bulge. The final moves up this are the crux.

134   The Final Fling   8m   S   P1   1988
4b Climb the overhanging crack in the left end of the lower bulge to gain a large ledge. The wider continuation crack above is problematical but fun.

There are more problems to the left but the next named climbs are on the last boulders of substance before the memorial is reached. Cross the wall and follow the path for about 100 metres to a steep clean block with a sunny southerly aspect (except when the mist swirls in and the ghostly origins of some of the route names take on a special significance).

135   Emily Norton   6m   E1   P2   1988   ★
5b The clean right arete is laybacked from a start on the detached boulder.

136   The Verge of Tranquillity   7m   E5   P3   1992/6   ★★
6b The steep slab between Emily Norton and The White Doe is a test of smearability. Start just left of Emily Norton and make a high step up. Move precariously left to gain a poor hold in the base of the high right-hand depression. Mantel boldly into this or take the easier original finish stepping left into the lower scoop on White Doe (E4 6a)

137   The White Doe   7m   E2   P3   1988   ★★
5c The centre of the clean slab is climbed delicately on small holds and pebbles to a good hold in the base of the lowest scoop. Step up into this to finish. Superb, but quite bold.

The next two lines are based on the prominent central arete.

138   Wordsworth Fail Me   7m   E3   P2   1996   ★★
6a The arete is climbed on the right. Slightly harder and more sustained than the next route but an escape left to the easier finish on that climb is possible for the timid.

139   Poetry in Motion   7m   E2   P1   1988   ★★★
6a The arete is climbed on the left. The crux is low down and the landing good. The name says it all.

140   Ghost Road   6m   E3   P2   1996   ★
6b The left wall of the block. Start in the centre and use small pockets and the edge of the diagonal slash on the left to gain the rounded scoop at the top.

141   Moorland Apparition   6m   HVS   P1   1988
5c The rib immediately right of a chimney in a corner left of the central arete. Climb the front of the rib with difficulty and some assistance from the diagonal slash on the right to reach the small ledge. Continue steeply, but on better holds, to the top.

The rib just left of the chimney is **Ghostbuster**, a short problem at 5b, no bridging allowed!

142 Memorial Wall 6m   VS   P2   1988
5a A pleasant slabby wall to the left with a reachy semi-mantel at the top.

The remaining rocks up to and over the wall opposite the monument provide numerous short problems, many of high quality on clean rock.

RYLSTONE – GRADED LIST OF CLIMBS

E8
Heartbeat City (6c)

E5
Cocoa Team
Special (7a)
The Verge Of
Tranquillity (6b)

E4
The Marine Who Had No
Friends (6b)
After Eight (6a)
Bare Faced Streak (6a)
Poke And Hope (6a)
Living On A Tarot
Reading (6a)

E3
Ghost Road (6b)
Midget Gem (6b)
Wordsworth Fail Me (6a)
Slip Slidin' Away (6a)
Pocket Battleship (6a)
Veteran (5c)
Little Peach (5c)

E2
Surfer's Paradise (6b)
End Of The Line (6a)
Oil Be Hanged (6b)
Whiskers (6a)
Poetry in Motion (6a)
Tasslehoff Burrfoot (5c)
The White Doe (5c)
Little Gem (5c)
Kiss Me Hardy (5b)
The Artful Dodger (5b)
The Glass Slipper (5b)

Crazy Diamond (5b)
Beached Whale (5b)

E1
England Expects (5c)
Nobular Structure (5c)
Full Nelson (5c)
Orbital Highway (5c)
Wall of the Evening
Plight (5c)
The Last Days Of May
(5c)
High Flying Adored (5b)
Solo Games (5b)
Autumn Odyssey (5b)
Emily Norton (5b)
Sword Dance (5b)
Never Climb With
  Guidebook Writers
(5b)
Monument Crack (5b)
Frankie Comes to
Rylstone (5b)
The Hot Line (5b)

HVS
Moorland Apparition (5c)
The Grunt (5b)
Impending Gloom (5c)
Undercarriage (5c)
Tower of High Sorcery
(5b)
President's Prologue (5b)
Face Savour (5b)
Bondi Bitch (5b)
Terminus (5b)
Puss Puss (5b)
Extraction (5b)
Distant Gem (5b)

For My Next Trick (5b)
Full Frontal (5b)
Artist's Impression (5b)
Pickpocket (5b)
The Niche (5a)
Forgotten Friends (5a)
Yellow Badge of Faith
(5a)
Sundowner (5a)
G.T.X. (5a)
Freebooter (5a)
Rylstone Wall Direct (5a)
Laughing Gas (4c)

VS
Angry Woman (5b)
No Man's Land (5a)
Hanging Cracks (5a)
Starlight Express (5a)
The Full Monty (5a)
Memorial Wall (5a)
Labour Pains (4c)
Impending Arrival (4c)
Rylstone Wall (4c)
Cat Walk (4c)
Castrol (4c)
False Teeth (4c)
Persistence
Loiner (4c)
Short And Sweet (4c)
Dead Kennedys (4c)
False Teeth (4c)
Persistence (4c)
Crossover (4c)
Bad Boys (4c)
Secretary's Slab (4b)
The Definitive Gritstone
  Chimney

MVS
Rylstone Crack (4b)
Moorland Memories (4b)
Highlord (4b)

HS
Grouseland (4b)
Trowel Face (4b)
I Have A Cunning Plan
(4b)
Keep Left (4b)
Arm Jam (4b)
Little Pillar (4b)
V Crack (4b)
Rainbow Sunset (4b)
Yet Another Hillside
   Attraction (4b)
Three Step Buttress (4b)
High Bark Crack (4b)
Rib Of Gold (4a)

S
The Final Fling
Pancake Slab
February Climb
Dental Slab
Matterhorn Ridge
Chimney Slabs Route 2
Chimney Slabs Route 1
Half Nelson
Anonymous Cross
Misty Moo
Double Crack
Twin Cracks
Old Pals

VD
Birds Nest Crack
Balance Crack
Up And Over
Sandy Buttress
Flake Chimney
Remembered
Pipeline
Monkey Corner
Falcon Crack
Baldrick
V Chimney
Chockstone Chimney
Beginners Bulge
Senators Saunter
Lichen Crack
Lower Traverse

D
Lower Slab
President's Slab
Bowler's Chimney
Forgotten
Sandy Gully
Sunhill Slab

M
Lichen Chimney
Beginners Chimney

SHIPLEY GLEN

SITUATION AND CHARACTER   The Glen is situated just north of and above Shipley and faces roughly westwards. Sound rock, high technical standards, strenuous climbs and generally safe landings make the Glen a superb training ground. Due to its popularity as a picnic area, the hazards of broken glass (and other less damaging but more obnoxious objects) are occasionally encountered.

The rocks can be divided into three fairly distinct areas. The first, directly opposite Bracken Hall Countryside Centre, is on the edge of a small wood and tends to be rather green, taking time to dry after heavy rain. The most continuous section lies about 200 metres further north directly below a fairly extensive car parking area. It has clean rock, better landings and a more open aspect, drying fairly quickly after rain. The final section is made up of a series of separate buttresses extending towards Eldwick, ending where the road bends away from the edge of the Glen.

The special character of this soloing Mecca has decreed the use of technical grades only. Visitors should note that this system in no way indicates the seriousness of the climbs. This is particularly true for the longer routes on the main buttresses and those with bad landings. If in doubt use a rope but remember that decent belay points at the top of the buttresses are few and far between and cars are often essential to provide the necessary 'hitching post'! It will be noted that some natural routes have already been ruined by chipping holds. There is no licence for this technique at the Glen.

In recent years bouldering here has become even more specialised and dozens of micro-problems involving sitting starts, one-move wonders and bum-scraping traverses have been developed. It has been decided, for the sake of consistency and clarity, to leave these modern desperates to the specialist bouldering guides. If you don't possess one just use your imagination and try everything - but don't venture more than 2 metres above the ground. There are only two grades for these new problems DI (done it) and CDI (can't do it). Essential equipment seems to be a mattress and an old rag.

APPROACHES AND ACCESS   From Shipley take the Otley road (A6038) until, after half a mile, the left-hand fork to Baildon is followed. Once in Baildon turn left at the roundabout and continue until the Old Glen House pub and tea shop are reached. Both are highly recommended. The rocks extend intermittently north-westwards for about 1 kilometre. Cars can be parked at the top of the rocks. The Glen may also be reached by bus and train to Saltaire and then a short walk.

THE CLIMBS   The routes are described from south to north (RIGHT to LEFT) beginning with a concentrated series of buttresses which start about 150 metres from the Old Glen House and directly opposite Bracken Hall Countryside Centre. They are easily recognised by the iron stakes on top and the trees below. The extreme right of these buttresses is a steep slabby wall with a narrow chimney on its right-hand side and on its left side a green overhanging arete with an oak tree at its foot. On the extreme right of this wall are many problems, including a boulder with a large roof.

1   Easy Route   3c   The right wall of the chimney.

2   Easy Wall   4a   The wall left of the chimney avoiding the chipped holds.

3   Diagonal   4a   Start just right of the thin groove towards the left-hand side of the wall and follow the obvious rightward diagonal line finishing up Easy Wall.

4   Easy Groove   4a   The groove to the left and wall above.

5   Green Rib   4a   The left arete which relents after an initial difficult pull-up.

6   Mouse Wall   5c   The overhanging wall on the left side of the arete.

7   Shoddy Wall   4a   A steep crack on the gully wall with an awkward finish.

8   Tiger Wall   5b   The short steep wall left of Shoddy Wall.

9   Flake Crack   2c   The easy crack on the left side of the gully.

10   Woolman ★   5a   The front of the tall prow beside the crack finishing round to the left.

11   Pirouette   5a   (4c if you can reach the finishing hold!)   Two metres left of the prow using the faint rib.

12   K.C.Arete   3a   The arete in the middle of the gully.

13   Paddy's Saunter   3a   From the right-hand end of the green scoop on the buttress to the left climb straight up the slab to finish just left of the wide crack.

14   Scoop   4a   The green scoop followed diagonally.

SHIPLEY GLEN

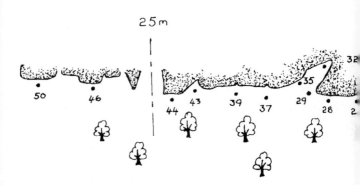

25m

50   46   44   43   39   37   29   28   2   35   32

15   Scoop Direct   5a   Chiselled holds lead directly to a junction with the Scoop. Finish direct. Quite thin.

16   Scoop Arete   5b   The bold, blunt arete in the centre of the buttress directly through the initial overhang.

17   Pillar Rock   5b   The obvious chipped holds up the front of the buttress starting at the chipped name 'Pillar Rock'. Very bold.

18   Pillar Rib ★   5a   The arete to the left finishing up the scoop with a bold move.

19   Deep Chimney   3a   Obvious.

20   Dreadnought   6c   Take the overhang just left of Deep Chimney with a desperate move to gain the ledge and finish up the centre of the wall above.

21   Fearnought ★★   5a   The bulges to the left of the chimney. Good.

22   Nought To Fear   5b   The arete of Fearnought. Use of the ledge and holds round to the left is cheating!

There are some shorter problems in the broken bay. To the left of

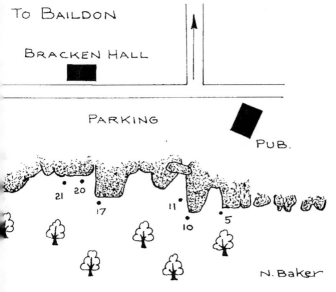

To Baildon

Bracken Hall

Parking

Pub.

N. Baker

the bay is a large buttress with a slanting undercut handjam crack on its right side.

23 Autumn Traverse 4a Start from the boulder choke in the gully and move up to the break below the overhang via a faint rib. Traverse left along the break to finish up Jamcrack.

24 Nobbler 6a The steep wall just right of the crack on pebbles. This has become harder with the demise of several crucial pebbles. A direct finish through the capping overhang has been claimed at the same grade (6a).

25 Jamcrack 5a The hanging crack.

26 Good Golly 6a Start 1 metre left of Jamcrack and take the overhang direct to a chipped hold on the face above and a finish up Jamcrack.

27 Austin's Hangover ★ 5b Over the wide overhang and up the arete moving left to gain the break. Move right to the obvious ledge on Jamcrack.

28 Hammill's Horror ★★ 6a Pull through the initial overhang then boldly up the front of the large buttress.

29   Glen's Mantle ★   4c The left arete of the buttress via a ledge and thin rightward-trending crack.

30   Go-Between   5b Climb the blunt rib just right of the wide crack, crossing a short slab to a steep finish. The crack is strictly out of bounds at this grade.

31   Classic Rock ★   3b The wide polished crack in the right wall of the gully.

32   Vee Pod   5b The deep vee cleft.

33   Old Peter ★   5b The chiselled wall route left of Vee Pod through the depression and just left of the shallow arete. There is a bold, long reach at the top.

34   Brush Off ★   6a Takes the thin discontinuous cracks just right of the blunt arete to a thin, rounded finish.

35   Kia Ora Wall ★★   5b The excellent blunt arete via the first of the discontinuous cracks and the small ledge on the left.

36   Echinococcus   6a The bulge and wall just left of Kia Ora Wall.

37   Original Route   4a The first wide, undercut crack to the left.

38   Interstellar Overdrive ★★   6a The wall between the two cracks.

39   Old Crack   4a The thinner, left-hand crack.

40   Step Up ★   5a Start up the steep stepped gangway just to the left and follow it to finish up the right arete.

41   Step Down   5b The thin discontinuous crack above the start of Step Up.

42   Next Arete   5a The arete to the left with a bold move from the little ledge.

43   Don't Bother   4a The chimney crack.

44   Green Death ★   5c Follow the thin cracks up the small buttress to the left.

45   Shipley Promenade ★★★   5c A stroll. From Green Death traversing back right at about half height until the rock runs out.

About 25 metres to the left is a square buttress, undercut at its base (The Wall of Horrors).

46   Saplink   5b The overhang and slanting narrow gangway left of the sapling growing from the face.

47 Phantom Crack 4a The deep chimney crack. Subtle bridging allows the worst excesses of the crack to be avoided.

48 Phantom 3c The middle of the short wall left of the corner from the block propped against the face.

49 Phantom Rib ★ 5b The right arete of the buttress.

50 Phantom Wall ★ 5c The buttress front direct. Bold if taken direct at the finish.

51 Phantom of The Opera 4c Start off the block below the left arete, move up to gain the horizontal break and traverse right along it to finish up Phantom Rib.

About 25 metres leftwards out of the wood is a wall with a horizontal crease and overhung base.

52 Wood's Wall 5a The wall right of the roof via a shallow curving groove.

53 Wood's Arete 5a The right arete of the roof tackled from its right-hand side.

54 Raspberry ★ 5a The roof direct. Good, but beware the rattling flake in the roof.

55 Wood's Crack 3a At the left side of the roof.

56 Manson's Must ★ 5c The scary arete on the left above the ominous boulder.

57 Al's Arete ★★ 5b The innocuous-looking left arete of the block.

About 50 metres to the left and at the same level are two small isolated buttresses which are most easily found from above. Looking out from the obelisk holding the quotation from Psalm 68 verse 4 these buttresses lie 30 metres or so down to the right. The first has a fairly square front face and no real features; the second is somewhat higher, similarly shaped but with two distinctive angular cracks, one low and one at the top.

58 Paddy 4b Directly up the wall 2 metres right of the lower crack.

59 Rupert Bear 4b Start just right of the lower crack and move up using it to gain the upper crack and the top.

60 Sam 4b The left arete to a rather rounded finish.

About 150 metres to the left and across a small stream is the next buttress. It has an undercut arete with a scoop on its right.

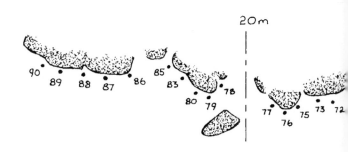

20m

WOODS WALL TO KENS ARETE

61   The Dobby   3c The shallow rib above the start of the gangway.

62   The Gangway   2c Follow the scoop.

63   Simian Traverse   5b Hand traverse the gangway.

64   Red Baron ★★★   6b The hanging arete direct. From a sitting start it is 7a.

65   By-Pass   5b The crack/groove left of the arete.

66   Amalgam   5b By-Pass and Red Baron linked.

67   Undercracker   5c The wall between the two cracks.

68   Straight Crack   4b The straight crack left again.

Over the gully on the left is a buttress with a corner containing a tree. Just left of the gully is a small overhang close to the ground.

69   Three Moves Wall   4a Directly up through the overhang.

70   Smear ★   5c The thin groove right of the arete.

71   Vim ★★★   5c The arete right of the tree.

72   Phil's Wall ★★   6b Directly up the wall just right of centre. Bold and hard.

ROAD

PARKING

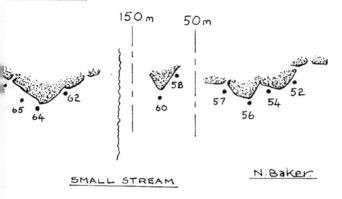

150 m   50 m

SMALL STREAM

N. Baker.

73 Manson's Wall ★★ 6b Very thin climbing up the wall right of the tree stump.

74 Stump Crack 2a Obvious.

75 Off Stump 4c The wall between Stump Crack and the arete to the left.

76 Daz 6a The arete left of Stump Crack.

77 Omo 6a The wall left of Daz.

The next buttress has a nose-like profile and a large pointed boulder a little below it. The boulder has several easy slabby problems on its front face.

78 Short Side 4b The right-hand side of the buttress via the hole.

79 Nosey 5b The nose direct on side pulls.

80 Parker 6b The left arete of the cutaway to the scoop.

81 Why Crack 4b The obvious crack climbed direct.

82 Right-hand Variant 5b Reach the scoop on the right via the curving crack starting up Why Crack.

ROAD

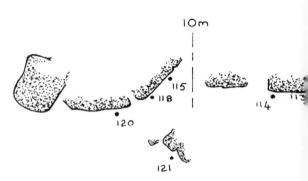

10m

115
118

120

114   113

121

BANANA FLAKE TO HIDDEN GEM

83 Adieu Les Patisseries 5b The wall between Why Crack and Right-hand Variant can be climbed direct from the ground via the overhang and two horizontal breaks.

84 Side Pull 4b The narrow wall between Why Crack and the hillside.

85 Layback 5a Use the flake rib to make a long reach to the top, mantel to finish.

86 Green Arete 4b The right arete of the wall with another long reach at the top.

87 Green Wall 4c The wall between the arete and the tree.

88 Tree Crack 2a The crack passing the large tree.

89 Mike's Mantel ★ 5c Directly up the wall left of the tree.

90 Ken's Arete ★ 5c Over the roof and directly up the arete. Easier moving right after the initial pull-up or by starting off the block.

91 Funnymove ★ 5a A problem just left of the arete moving right, or straight up (harder). The wall just left again is 5c.

Across a broad gully is a small buttress with an obvious 'banana' flake.

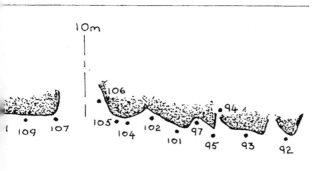

N. Baker

92 Banana Flake 4b Up through the cutaway using the flake.

The next section is undercut to a rounded arete with horizontal pancakes of rock.

93 Original Route 3a Move right across the pancakes to gain the ledge and then the top.

94 Easy Chimney 2c The right wall of the chimney to the right of the undercut prow.

95 Prow 5b The sharp undercut prow in the recess. Use of Easy Chimney is not permitted at this grade.

96 Hairline 4c The faint rib just left of the Prow.

97 Open Book 4b The corner just left.

98 Flake Wall 5a Directly up the wall left of Open Book.

99 Cracked Rib 5a The right arete of the flat reddish wall.

100 Lurch 5b The wall left of the arete via the hole. Easier if jumped (or could be a dyno).

101 Red Wall 5b The wall between Cracked Rib and Lurch via small holds in the breaks.

102 Lurcher 5b Via the left-most hole in the wall.

103   Red Wall Traverse ★   5c Start up Lurch and traverse the horizontal break to finish up Lurcher. Devotees will start up the Prow and traverse left at half height for a good pump.

104   Last Addition   5b Climb the deep crack behind the boulder below the wall on the left at right angles to Red Wall. Move right through the overhang to gain the deep horizontal break. Finish direct.

105   Don't Fall Off   5b Pull up below the crack in the front face of the tower to the left of Red Wall. Move right to the arete and pull up again to the ledge. Use of the pointed boulder for anything other than breaking one's back is prohibited!

106   Nicely ★   4b The left face of the tower via the shallow arete.

Across the wide gully is a very steep, blank wall with undercut aretes. All the routes on this wall can be highly recommended, with the proviso that none has any worthwhile protection.

107   Blitzen ★★★   5b The right arete.

108   Sleighride ★★   6a Low on the wall and just left of the arete is a small but obvious undercut hole. Move directly through this then climb the wall above to finish near the arete.

109   Millstone Grit ★★   6c Start just left of the undercut and climb the wall directly up the middle. Bold and hard.

110   Millstone Grip ★★   6b The left arete of the wall finishes at an obvious ledge. The route takes a direct line up the wall finishing about 1 metre right of this ledge.

111   Donner ★★   5b
The left arete via a large notch.

112   'B' Team Traverse ★   5b
Traverse of the wall with hands on the horizontal break at half height.

113   Adolph ★   5c
The innocuous arete across the easy chimney.

114   Bonny's Wall   4a
Between the right arete and the gully on the left is a ledge at half height. Straight up using this. (5b up the faint arete without the ledge).

Left again past a tree growing out of the rock is a slabby wall facing south. It is bounded on its left by an easy crack.

115   Crank   5b The right-hand side of the wall starting from a block in the gully.

116 Stewpot 4b Directly up the centre of the wall via the obvious hole.

117 Barbecue Rib 4c Takes the obvious rounded miniature rib left of the hole.

118 Spare Rib 4b The wall just right of the chimney.

119 Squeeze Chimney 4a The obvious chimney. Quite awkward.

120 Chalkwall 4a The undercut wall left of the arete to the left of Squeeze Chimney.

Below the slabby wall and facing slightly left (facing out) is a large block with a very steep crack rising from a small cave.

121 Hidden Gem ★ 5b The crack direct. Try it from a sitting start!

Left again past a little cave to a large slabby boulder with good problems up the front and a traverse across the overhanging back wall (5c without sitting on the ground). The section up to the slabby boulder has an arm-pumping traverse along the horizontal break (5b). Up to the left above the slab is a small, severely undercut buttress.

122 Lemur 5a The roof at its right side.

123 Leeper 5a The roof direct at its widest point.

124 Jug For a Thug 4c Just left is a small ledge with a jug to its right. Up using both these.

125 Lemming 4c The undercut wall and bulge a few feet to the left.

To the left is a broad recess, at the back of which is a twisted tree growing from the rock.

126 John 4c The obvious mantelshelf right of the tree above the chipped name 'John'. Hard for the short.

127 Gensing 3a The crack/arete just right of the tree.

128 Kate's Horror 3a The slabby arete left of the tree.

To the left there is a short wall facing south , the left arete of which contains a shallow groove.

129 Reach For The Sky 5a The centre of the wall.

130 Grooved Arete ★ 3c The groove in the arete.

131 Stretch 4c Directly up the wall just left of the arete.

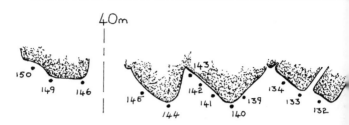

ROAD

40m

150
149   146

143
142
146   141   139   134
144   140   133   132

LEMUR TO ONE HAND ONE HOLD

Directly below the arete is a large block with an excellent traverse just above the ground (6a). Across the wide gully is a small buttress with a deep gully/chimney separating it from a wall containing a shallow cave at half height. At the left of this is a gully and then a south-facing wall. Beyond this is a corner with a tree in front of it. The rocks then gradually fade into the hillside.

132   Golden Oldie   4b   The front face of the separate buttress.

133   Chart Topper   5a   The right arete of the wall with the shallow cave.

134   The Hole   4c   Directly up through the shallow cave.

135   Left Edge   5a   The short wall above the overhang just left of the shallow cave.

At the right-hand end of the south-facing wall is a small overhang at half height.

136   Jimmy Jump   4c   Mantelshelf on to the ledge then through the overhang to a rounded finish.

137   Faint Heart   5a   The shallow arete just left of the small overhang has an awkward finish.

138   Groovy   4b   The centre of the wall to finish at a chipped hold.

139   YMC Wall   4c   The left side of the wall via a thin groove and past a pocket to finish at the chipped hold again.

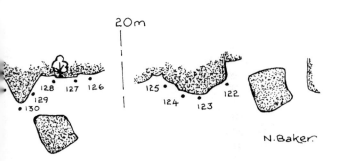

20m

128 127 126
129
130

125
124 123 122

N. Baker

140   The Glen Arete ★★★ 4c The superb rib to the left.

141   Mike's Wall ★ 5a
The fine wall climb round to the left above the tree using the obvious layaway.

142   Lancashire Hot Pot 6a The wall immediately above the tree is undercut. Start from here and move up on the thin rounded breaks to finish just left of Mike's Wall.

143   Fair Lady 6a The wall just right of the corner using the thin horizontal breaks.

144   Revived 45 5a The prow which forms the arete left of the corner.

145   Last Line 4a Takes the face above the rock step just before the rocks fade into the hillside.

Broken rocks for about 40 metres lead to a distinctive square-topped buttress set at a lower level.

146   Lay-Away 5a The sharp right-hand arete. Harder if holds on the arete alone are used.

147   Square Face 5b The face just left of the arete.

148   Central Route 4c Straight up from the highest point of the ledge via an obvious nose.

149   Side-step 4c Move left from Central Route to the ledge on

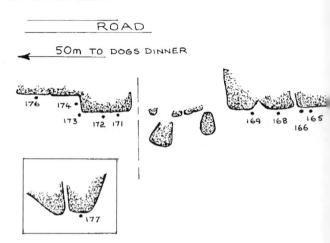

ROAD

← 50m TO DOGS DINNER

FOOLS MIRROR TO DOGS DINNER

the left. It is possible to climb straight up using an obvious undercut (5a).

150 One Hand One Hold 4c The overhang of the ledge taken direct.

To the left is a buttress.

151 Fool's Mirror 3a The right-hand arete.

152 Reflection 4b Straight up the middle of the front face via rounded breaks.

153 Flute Route ★ 3b Up passing the sapling and flutes.

154 Oboe 4b Directly up between the crack and right arete.

155 Image 4b The left arete.

156 Pickpocket 3c The left wall past a large hole.
Below and slightly left is a pinnacle consisting of an easy-angled section topped by a rounded overhang. There is a large tree growing out of the right-hand side.

157 Tweedledee 5c Climb the front face just left of the right arete.

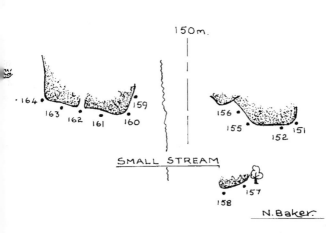

N.Baker.

158   Tweedledum   5c   The left arete.

About 150 metres to the left and across a small stream is a buttress with a wide kinky crack up it.

159   Wooden Wedge   5b   The south-facing wall via undercuts and the overhang direct.

160   Snoopy   5b   The overhang and arete direct from a reclining position on the ground!

161   Lucy   4c   An eliminate up the wall twixt crack and arete.

162   Woodstock   3a   The crack.

163   Linus   4c   Wall left of Woodstock.

164   Rerun   4b   The left arete of the buttress.

Going left again is a wide gully with a slabby boulder at the bottom. On the left of this is a wall with a break at two-thirds height. It is split by a deep crack and then, after another vertical crack, it becomes severely overhung.

165   Good Evans   5b   The centre of the slab direct via a faint groove.

166 Evans Above   5c An eliminate line just left.

167 Leaper   4a The arete right of the sickle-shaped crack.

168 Hammer   4a Climbs the sickle-shaped crack in the central buttress directly.

169 Wall and Roof   5c The shallow right arete of the overhanging wall to a difficult finish. This can be avoided by stepping right at the horizontal break (4b).

170 Gosh   5a A traverse at mid-height across all the walls.

To the left again, past a slab which has good problems, is the last major buttress.

171 Christine's Horror   3b Has the name chipped on the rock.

172 Higher Terra   4b Start just to the left and follow the crack above.

173 Fowler   5a The left arete.

174 Kestrel Crack ★   4c The fine hanging crack on the left.

175 Falcon   5a The wall just left of the crack.

To the left is a short wall with a diagonal crack.

176 Sparrowhawk   4a Takes the wall just left of the crack direct.

The rocks now fall away to reappear as an isolated buttress about 50 metres further left. Here lies one of the best of the easier routes in the Glen.

177 Dog's Dinner ★★   4a Straight up the front face of the buttress.

To the left are many minor problems and then the path down to the bridge over the stream is met. A few metres down this is an obvious natural boulder. The south face is easy angled with several interesting problems, while the arete above the path gives a good 4b route. The small overhanging face on the left has a recent rock scar towards the left-hand top corner. This is gained using the horizontal break and leads to an awkward finish, well worth 5a.

As the path bends left towards the stream, the track on the right leads to the final rocks (at last!). These are the remains of an old quarry which has only recently been developed and the routes are still somewhat dirty.

SHIPLEY GLEN – GRADED LIST

7a
Red Baron's Roof

6c
Dreadnought
Millstone Grit

6b
Red Baron
Phil's Wall
Millstone Grip
Parker
Manson's Wall

6a
Sleighride
Brush Off
Daz
Omo
Interstellar Overdrive
Good Golly
Hammill's Horror
Nobbler
Lancashire Hot Pot
Fair Lady
Echinococcus

5c
Manson's Must
Smear
Adolph
Red Wall Traverse
Green Death
Evans Above
Vim

Undercracker
Ken's Arete
Shipley Promenade
Wall and Roof
Phantom Wall
Mouse Wall
Mike's Mantel
Tweedledee
Tweedledum

5b
Nought to Fear
Saplink
Simian Traverse
Crank
Tiger Wall
Square Face
Snoopy
Hidden Gem
By-pass
Al's Arete
Nosey
Right-hand Variant
Don't Fall Off
Lurch
'B' Team Traverse
Go-Between
Adieu Les Patisseries
Blitzen
Wooden Wedge
Step Down
Red Wall
Lurcher
Scoop Arete
Donner
Last Addition

Good Evans
Pillar Rock
Phantom Rib
Austin's Hangover
Kia Ora Wall
Old Peter

5a
Left Edge
Pirouette
Chart Topper
Layback
Step-up
Faint Heart
Reach for the Sky
Gosh
Woolman
Wood's Arete
Cracked Rib
Leeper
Lemur
Flake Wall
Prow
Jamcrack
Falcon
Fearnought
Lay-away
Wood's Wall
Next Arete
Mike's Wall
Raspberry
Fowler
Funnymove
Revived 45
Pillar Rib

SIMON'S SEAT

SITUATION AND CHARACTER   Simon's Seat is the obvious rocky fortress topping the north-eastern rim of Barden Fell at a height of approximately 500 metres. The rock is good quality gritstone, rough in texture, rising to a height of 20 metres. The crag is split into two distinct areas; the well-weathered south-west-facing crag, which dries quickly and catches a lot of sun, and the main edge which lies below the summit trig point and faces north-east overlooking Appletreewick and the Wharfe valley. Unfortunately this exposed main edge catches little sun, making it rather slow drying. Simon's Seat has never been as popular as the more accessible gritstone crags, but in some ways this adds to its charm. Solitude and some excellent routes await the climber who makes the effort to strike out from the valley.

APPROACHES AND ACCESS   The quickest approach is from Howgill Farm. This is reached by taking the B6160 Bolton Abbey-Grassington road to Barden Tower where the more turn off to the right is signposted Appletreewick. Follow this road down and over Barden Bridge and then for a further mile until a gravel track on the right leads to Howgill Farm. There is limited parking by a stream and the gate leading up on to the moor. Take the track through the gate and follow it, ever upwards, through the woods to the open moor. The track continues leftwards and the craggy summit reached in 35 to 40 minutes from the valley. A longer but much more scenic, and less strenuous, approach is from Bolton Abbey's Cavendish Pavilion and through the Valley Of Desolation. Highly recommended if time permits. (About an hour and a quarter). **The crag is within the Barden Moor Access area so refer to special access notes on page 10.**

THE CLIMBS   These are described from left to right. When approaching from Howgill, the well-weathered south-western outcrop is reached first. It is situated to the left of the path before the trig point. At the left end of the crag is a prominent split buttress.

1   Corner Crack   7m   VD   P1
The steep open-book corner on the left of the buttress.

2   And She Was   8m   E3   P2   ★★
6a   The superb left arete of the steep pillar, on its right-hand side.

3 I'll Bet She Does 8m E3 P3   ★★★
6a The steep clean wall between And She Was and Straight Crack.
A problematic start leads to a bold but easier finish.

4 Straight Crack 8m VS P1   ★
4c The prominent split crack is climbed using chicken heads and
classic jams.

5 Inaccessible Crack 8m VS P1
5a The bottomless crack on the right of the buttress proves to be
misnamed when gained by a hard move from the right.

Twenty metres of shorter, broken rocks lead to a wall with radiating
cracks and more chicken heads. These provide excellent short
climbs including :-

6 Left-Hand Arete 6m HVS P2
5a Guess where this goes.

7 Out With The Old 7m E1 P2
5b Start just right of Left Hand Arete and climb the middle of the
wall until a step right reaches 3 large 'chicken heads'. Step back
left to finish.

8 Central Cracks 7m S P1   ★
4b Obvious and worthwhile.

9 Right-Hand Crack 7m S P1   ★
4b More knobbly fun!

10 Chunky Chicken 7m E1 P1
5b The wall and rib just right of Right-Hand Crack.

From here more broken rocks lead to the right end of the outcrop,
where 'hidden' climbs start behind a huge boulder.

11 Hidden Chimney 10m VD P1
The obvious crack, not a chimney at all, is climbed direct.

12 Hidden Crack 10m S P2
4a The crack just left of Hidden Chimney is taken to a short corner.
Step left, mantelshelf, then up the slab to the top.

13 Open Face 10m HVS P2   ★
5b A good route. Reach and climb the flute on the arete right of
Hidden Chimney. Step left and go boldly up the open face on yet
more chicken heads.

14 The Egg, Of Course 10m E2 P2   ★
5b The bulging rib to the right of the upper section of Open Face,
starting as for that route. A direct start is 5c.

15   Blinkers Rib   8m   HVS
5c The rib immediately right of the easy gully around on the east face is climbed direct. Protectable but escapable.

16   Grumpy's Crack   7m   HS
4b The steep crack just right of Blinkers Rib.

From here to the trig point are many excellent boulder problems and micro-routes. Towards the left, almost above the end of the main edge is a large block with a prominent chimney-crack containing a subsidiary flake. Photographic evidence indicates this was soloed in 1895!

17   Victorian Climb   6m   HVS   P1   ★
5a Gain entry with difficulty, then realise you're facing the wrong way. Struggle to turn round in the pod and then contemplate the steep and awkward exit. Don't snag the pockets on your tweed jacket!

18   A Life Less Ordinary   7m   E6   P3   ★
6b A very bold and thoroughly modern companion to Victorian Climb is the arete to the left started from the ledge but climbed on 'crimps' to a pocket and hideously rounded finish.

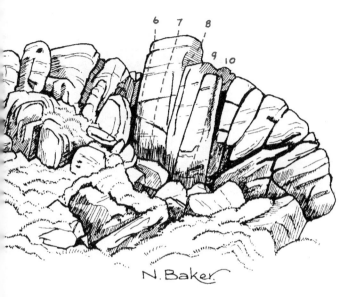

N. Baker

THE MAIN EDGE

This lies directly below the trig point. The descents are by either flank. The routes are described from left to right.

19 Layback Crack 10m VD P1
Climb the wide crack, high up, on the extreme left of the crag.

20 North Gully Buttress 20m VS P1
5a Starts lower down the hillside and takes a line up the slab left of the gully. Surmount the overlap with difficulty, then climb leftwards to a ledge on the edge. Continue up the short bulging wall and crack to finish.

21 North Gully 22m D P1
Ascend the gully to the left of the obvious arete.

22 Flake Climb 16m VD P1   ★
Climb North Gully for 6 metres and then move out right on to the wall. Continue via a large flake and finish either direct or by moving right and up the arete.

23 High Nose Traverse 23m S P1
Start up North Gully for 3 metres and traverse right with feet in the

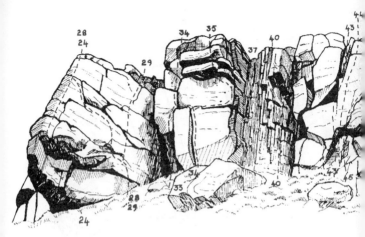

first horizontal break to the arete. Move up a metre or so and then
follow the traverse line across the face finishing at the chimney.

24 Arete Direct   20m   VS   P1   ★★★
4c The obvious arete. A very fine climb in a superb position. Start a
couple of metres up the hillside to the right, below an overhang.
Traverse leftwards under the overhang to gain the arete which is
followed direct, with a thin move near the top.

25 Dog Lead   17m   HVS   P1   ★
5a Start as for Arete Direct, under the overhang but after a couple
of metres of the traverse climb through the bulge using the obvious
crack. Move up to the thick flake and step onto it and then climb the
slab above, helped by small pockets, until you reach the crack of
Arete Wall. Continue above with the aid of a small pocket out right
to reach a thin shallow crack. Climb the crack direct using a long
reach or a poor smear (5b for the short) to good jams and flutings.

The following two routes were only recorded at the 'eleventh' hour
of the guides production. Their positions and independence relevant
to adjoining routes has not been checked.

26 Hair Of The Dog   18m   VS   P1
5a Start one metre left of Dog Lead and climb through the bulge on
undercuts to a sloping ledge and then a pocket. Rock over left to a
big ledge and follow a slanting crack to join Arete Wall. Finish up the
crack of Arete Wall or, slightly harder, the slab direct.

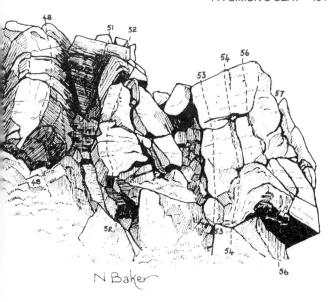

N Baker

27 Posh Spice and the Bend in Beckham's Set Piece 22m
VS P1
5a Gain the arete of Arete Direct from a boulder directly below and
climb it for two metres before moving right into a crack system.
Follow this rightwards to finish, eventually, up the final crack of Y
Front.

28 Arete Wall 16m S P1   ★
A few metres up the slope again. A high step in the centre of the
wall enables wide cracks to be reached. Follow these leftwards to
the arete and make exposed moves to the top.

29 Y Front 12m S P1   ★
Start as for Arete Wall but then move up and rightwards to finish up
the right-hand of the Y-shaped cracks.

30 Gentleman's Support 12m E1
5b A variation finish to Y Front, climbing the wall to the left of the
left hand crack.

31 Chimney Wall 12m S P1
At the right-hand end of the wall, just left of the chimney, are some
cracks. Jam up these passing a pod at 3 metres.

32 Window Chimney   13m   D   P1
An 18-carrot route! Wander into the dark depths of the chimney, then head upwards to the patch of light. Later, with luck and determination, it may be possible to squeeze through the window to perch on the chockstone. Either traverse the left wall or finish direct.

33 Clappers Crack   10m   E1   P1
5b A thug route to the Turret Crack belay. Climb up to the roof just right of the chimney and with grim determination, jam round it and take a breather and belay, on Turret Crack.

34 Turret Crack   20m   VS   P1   ★★
An excellent route up the obvious leaning crack on Turret Buttress. High in its grade.
1. 10m 5a Strenuously layback the very steep crack to the belay ledge.
2. 10m 4b Jam the continuing crack to the top.

35 Outside Finish   20m   HVS   P1   ★★
5a A very good bold variation finish to Turret Crack. Follow Turret Crack to the belay ledge and hand traverse rightwards along the crack to the edge. Climb up a metre or so, then back left under the overhang. Pull over this on big holds for an exciting finale.

36 The Gunner   20m   E1   P1
5c On the right arete of Turret Buttress is a short, steep and usually dirty ramp. Gain this strenuously and climb straight up to meet Outside Finish. Traverse right and finish via a sloping ledge and short corner.

37 Square Chimney   17m   VD   P1
This is the wide chimney which can be climbed by various ways to the top.

38 Baggin's Variation   17m   VS   P2
4c Start 3 metres up Square Chimney and climb diagonally rightwards into a groove line (Azimuth). Finish steeply on large, but insecure, blocks.

39 Azimuth   16m   E3   P2
5b Climb a shallow corner a metre right of Square Chimney to an overhang. Move slightly right, pull over the overhang then ascend the steep cracks and insecure blocks. Not recommended, unless addicted to loose rock.

40 Finesse   16m   E4   P2   ★★
6a Climb the overhanging fin of rock 1 metre right of Azimuth - and just keep on truckin'. Very enjoyable to say the least.

41   Pothole Chimney   20m   VD   P1
Start immediately right of the overhanging prow. Another through trip, allowing you to ferret about in the gloom behind the chockstone.

42   Blind Alley   18m   HVS   P1
5b   Start as Pothole Chimney but instead of the caving trip, break out and climb the hanging groove to a ledge. Move right to finish up a crack.

43   Chockstone Chimney   20m   VS   P1   ★
4c   Good climbing up the shallow chimney line to the right of the blank slabs. Climb the crack and pull out with difficulty to gain the large niche. Ascend the fissure above by bridging, chimneying, semi-laybacking and anything else you'd care to throw in.

44   Shush Popeye   20m   E3   P3   ★★
5c   A good route up the left arete of Question Of Balance. Quite bold.

45   A Question of Balance   20m   E2   P2   ★★★
5b   The imposing pillar in the centre of the crag, to the right of Chockstone Chimney, gives one of the best routes in the area. Climb the crack awkwardly through the bulge to good runners and a small ledge on the right. Commit yourself to the slab above and climb it with the aid of the right edge to the horizontal crack and a rounded finish.

46   Griffith's Chimney   20m   D   P1
This is the next chimney and is usually green and lichenous. You have been warned.

47   Winter Finish   23m   VD   P1
Climb Griffith's Chimney to about half height, then take off rightwards along the obvious ledge to the arete. Climb the slab on the right which leads to a diagonal crack in the slab above.

48   Another Question   18m   E2   P2
5b   Climbs the blunt arete of the next buttress. Follow the leftward-slanting cracks at the foot of the buttress to the left of the arete. A couple of very thin moves are necessary to gain a ledge, then climb directly and more easily to the top.

49   And Others   18m   HVS   P1
5a   Start just left of Real Chimney. Up the finger cracks and wall to the second of two horizontal breaks. Follow this leftwards (crux) and finish up Winter Finish.

50   Real Chimney   15m   D   P2
The deep cleft chimney. Either ascend the inside until near the top or its outer limits throughout in traditional style. Gulp!

51 Slant 10m VS P1
5a From the base of Real Chimney climb the green lichenous ramp on the right and the shorter wall above.

52 Simple Simon 23m S P1   ★★
4b An entertaining expedition. Start lower down the hillside at a short slab. Climb its left edge then move right to the deep crack. Follow this to a big ledge (possible bivouac). Pull over the tiny roof and climb a short slab and a final steep crack.

53 Paws For Thought 8m HVS P2   ★
5b The blunt left-hand arete 3 metres left of Beaky is gained by a tricky move from a boulder. Mantel on to slopers and reach horizontal breaks and then 'Paws' before making a committing step into a small pocket on the left. Another slopey mantel then gains easier ground.

54 Beaky 10m HVS P1
5a Start a few metres up from the lowest point of the crag below an obvious oozing green nostril at half height. Climb direct, using the nostril and curving crack above.

55 Low Nose Traverse 17m VS P1   ★
4c Start as for Beaky below the green nostril. Traverse right round the nose and continue with a delicate move (crux) on the front of the buttress to gain a deep crack up which the climb finishes.

56 Gymkhana 18m E1 P2   ★★
5b A classic. On the front of Low Nose Buttress is an overhang with a good crack at its centre. Climb this, then move up and left around the corner. Up the right-hand side of the slabby wall above on pockets. Quite bold.

57 Low Nose Crack 18m VS P1
5a The obvious crack on the right of the buttress is climbed strenuously on jams. Difficulties rapidly ease.

58 Flirtin' Cos I'm Hurtin' 10m E4 P2   ★★★
6a Superb climbing up the clean wall 2 metres right of Low Nose Crack. From a ledge at 3 metres gain the large shallow pocket in the wall. Move left to gain a ramp then up to another shallow ramp and use this to gain the left arete (thread runner). Follow the arete to the top.

59 Amen 12m HVS P1
5b Twenty metres right of the main crag is a buttress split by a prominent green overhanging crack. Slither up this and then strenuously jam leftwards to a short finishing crack. Award yourself a medal.

Further right again, and slightly lower down the hillside, is a large isolated boulder with a superb clean arete.

60 The Naked Edge 7m E3   P3   ★★★
6a The technical and sustained left arete provides a brilliant series of moves. No runners, but the crux is low down. Once established you shouldn't fall off!?

61 Dino-Mania 7m E5   P3   ★
6b The wall right of Naked Edge. Make a gymnastic move to gain the base of the scoop and move up easily to a large pocket. Traverse left from this to climb the upper wall via a tiny pocket to a worrying finish.

The scoop in the right hand side of the slab, gained from the boulder, offers a good 5b problem in its own right - or a technically easier start to Dino-Mania. The left wall is now **A Fall From Grace**, E6 6c (see Afterthoughts page 688).

From the summit trig point, a further outcrop can be seen 500 metres to the north-east. This is Lords Seat. The Isolated buttress seen across the moor to the left when returning along the Howgill track is Earl Seat, both contain immaculate micro-routes and boulder problems and are now both described in detail in the Connoisseurs Crags section.

SIMON'S SEAT – GRADED LIST

E6
A Fall From Grace (6c)
A Life Less Ordinary (6b)

E5
Dino-Mania (6b)

E4
Flirtin' Cos I'm Hurtin' (6a)
Finesse (6a)

E3
I'll Bet She Does (6a)
And She Was (6a)
The Naked Edge (6a)
Shush Popeye (5c)
Azimuth (5b)

E2
Question of Balance (5b)
Another Question (5b)
The Egg, Of Course (5b)

E1
The Gunner (5c)
Gymkhana (5b)
Clappers Crack (5b)
Out With The Old (5b)
Gentlemen's Support (5b)
Chunky Chicken (5b)

HVS
Amen (5b)
Open Face (5b)
Blinkers Rib (5c)
Blind Alley (5b)
Pause For Thought (5b)
Outside Finish (5a)
And Others (5a)
Beaky (5a)
Left Hand Arete (5a)
Dog Lead (5a)
Victorian Climb (5a)

SLIPSTONES

SITUATION AND CHARACTER A delightful edge of clean, good quality gritstone, facing South West across the pleasant valley of Colsterdale, 6 miles west of Masham. The rocks comprise a series of buttresses which seldom exceed seven metres in height yet offer a multitude of superb short climbs and problems, to tease and torment the most capable. The geology of the rock is particularly suited to those climbers possessing 'steel fingers' and good technique, as much of the climbing is slightly overhanging, on small holds. Despite its altitude and moorland solitude this crag is a winter sun-trap, often at its best on a bright, crisp, February afternoon.

APPROACHES AND ACCESS From Masham pass through the villages of Fearby and Healey. Take the second right turn after Healey at a fork in the road. Follow this road for almost 2 miles to an obvious parking place on the right just beyond some hairpin bends on the bank. Please park carefully, allowing room for others.

From the parking area, walk a little further along the lane until a track leads north-west and follow this until it turns north through a dry-stone wall. Leave the track and, keeping the dry-stone wall on your right, follow it for about 350 metres to a gate. Pass through the gate and follow the main track across the moor with the crag in full view on the right. Continue until almost at the left end of the crag where a small path leads to the rocks. Time : Car to crag - 15/20 minutes.

THE CLIMBS are described from left to right.

BUTTRESS 1
This is the isolated buttress 25 metres left of the main edge.

1 Extremities 5m E1 P2 1982
5c Climb the centre of the wall left of the steep arete on small holds. Nasty landing.

2 Paul's Arete 6m E1 P2 1982   ★★★
5b Climb the right side of the arete. Superb. The left edge is also good but 6a.

3 Steve's Wall 6m E1 P2 1982   ★★
5b The wall is climbed direct by some awkward moves. An excellent climb.

4 Heather Crack 5m D P1 1957
The obvious crack.

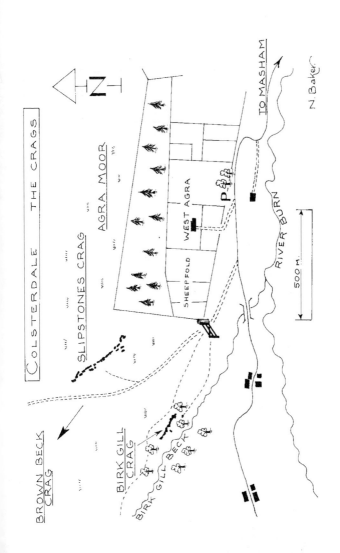

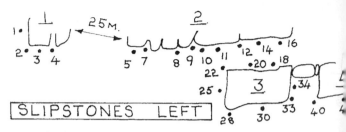

SLIPSTONES   LEFT

BUTTRESS 2
Provides the start of the main edge.

5 Roofed Corner   4m   D   P1   1957
Climb the left-hand corner of the obvious shallow recess.

6 Little Corner   4m   D   P1   Circa 1958
The right-hand corner.

7 Overhanging Crack   5m   VD   P1   Circa 1958
Takes the wide crack direct.

8 Undercut Double Crack   6m   S   P1   1964   ★
The short leaning crack is gained by an awkward start. Strenuous.

9 Not So Tight Chimney   5m   VD   P1   1960
A good climb of its type. Ascend the cleft facing left.

9a Breakwind Arete   8m   HVS   P2   1995   ★
5c Climb the arete, on its right, to the right of Not So Tight Chimney
and to the left of Space Trucking.

10 Space Truckin'   8m   E1   PI   1982
5b The blunt arete via a fragile looking flake - sustained.

11 Escalator   8m   HVS   P1   1964   ★★
5a Climb the centre of the wall to a long reach finish. High in its
grade.

The next route lies at the entrance to a wide gully formed by the
massive block of Buttress 3.

12 Mantelshelf Crack   6m   VD   P1   1960
The crack leads into a recess and choice of finishes.

13 Staircase   6m   M   P1   1957
Follow the stepped gangway leftwards into the recess.

14 Mantelshelf Wall   5m   HS   P1   1964
4b Start just right of Staircase climb. Gain the ledge by an awkward
move then escape right up the ramp.

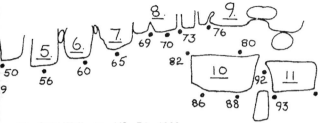

15 Cold Wall 4m VS P2 1968
4c The wall 2m right of the last climb.

16 Hole In The Wall 4m VS P2 1965
4c Past the hole to a flake and awkward finish.

BUTTRESS 3

The highest block on the crag with climbing on all four faces. The routes on the overhanging front (south) face are particularly fine. The climbs described begin at the rear of the block, (north side) at the top of the gully.

17 Left Edge 3m D Pl 1958
The short slab just left of the shallow corner.

18 Old Corner 4m VD P1 1960
The delicate right facing corner is worth doing.

19 Petch's Groove 5m S P2 1960
Follow the shallow curving groove above the cave.

20 Twenty Foot Crack 6m VD P1 1964
Climb the fault line to a choice of short cracks to finish.

21 North Wall 6m HVS P2 1977
5b The delicate wall on the right is climbed direct.

22 Tranmire Arete 6m MS P2 1964 ★★★
The superb right hand edge of the wall.

WEST FACE

23 Tranmire Crack 6m VS P1 1980
4c Climb the thin crack just right of the arete, starting from the block. A direct start without the block is 5b.

24 High Level Traverse 50m E1 P1 1982
5b A strenuous climb crossing Buttresses 3 & 4. Start up Tranmire Crack, gain the horizontal breaks and follow these rightwards

around both buttresses to finish at the top of Wisecrack.

25   Jenny Binks Wall   7m   VS   P1   Circa 1968   ★
5a Climb the centre of the steep wall on well spaced horizontal breaks with the longest reach to finish.

26   Easy Pickings   7m   VS   P1   1980   ★★
4c The wall to the right of Jenny Binks. Start from a sloping block and make delicate moves up rightwards to a slot. Step left and finish direct.

27   West Face Eliminate   8m   E2   P1   1986
6a Starting from the lowest point climb the left side of the blunt arete to finish steeply over the final projections.

SOUTH FACE (FRONT FACE)

28   Beldin Direct   8m   E1   P1   1975   ★
5b Climb the right side of the blunt arete to finish up the final short crack.

29   Variation Start   8m   E2   P2   1981
5c To the right of the direct is a shallow groove. Follow this leftwards to finish up the short crack.

30   Beldin   10m   HVS   P1   1968   ★★
5b Gain the gangway and follow it leftwards to escape up a short crack. Good climbing.

31   Original Route   8m   HVS   P1   1964   ★★
5a Gain the gangway then make an awkward pull right to reach the obvious flake crack and a strenuous finish.

32   Gollinglith   8m   E1   P1   1969   ★
5b Climb the strenuous thin crack to the break. Pull left to finish up Original Route or right to join Zoom.

Around the corner of the Buttress is a square cut alcove separating Buttresses 3 and 4.

33   Zoom   7m   HVS   P1   1966   ★★★
5b Start just right of the arete. Gain the flake and trend left to the final short crack. Simply superb.

34   Atomic   7m   E3   P1   1982   ★★★
6a Climbs the centre of the left wall of the alcove. Climb to the break, step left then up (crux). A very fine problem.

35   Atomic Right Hand   7m   E3   P1   1995   ★
6b From the break on Atomic, move out right then up.

36 Barnley Crack 6m S P1 Circa 1960   ★
Take the left hand corner crack. Awkward.

37 Barnley Wall 6m HS P1 1966
4b Climb the centre of the back wall.

38 Ulfers Crack 6m VD P1 Circa 1960   ★
The right-hand corner crack.

Forming the right wall of the alcove is:-

BUTTRESS 4

39 Forever Onward 6m E1 P2 1988
5c Climb the centre of the right wall of the alcove. The finish requires a long, long reach!

40 Timeless Divide 7m E2 P2 1983
6a Climb directly up the nose of the arete to finish on the spectacular fin.

41 Variation Start 4m E2 P2 1996
6c Climb the right side of the arete to the ledge. A difficult problem.

42 Agrete 7m HVS P2 1965/1980   ★
5c Ascends the problematic wall one metre right of the arete. Climb the wall and black flake to gain the ledge. Finish up the left arete.

43 Agra Direct Start 7m HVS P2 1981   ★
5c Climb the wall 3 metres right of the arete to the ledge. Finish over the roof of Agra.

44 Agra 8m HVS P2 1965   ★★★
5b Start at the foot of the slab. Trend leftward across the slab to a ledge under the roof. Surmount the roof at its weakness. Superb climbing.

45 Agra Right Hand 8m HVS P2 1980
5b Start as for Agra but climb straight up past a small spike to the break, move right and pull over the roof.

46 Narrow Margin 8m E2 P2 1992
6a Start just right of Agra below a small overlap. Pull up right to gain a line of poor pockets. Cross the rock scar to finish over the roof.

47 Wisecrack 6m HVS P2 1982   ★★★
5c Gain the hanging crack by a difficult move from the right.

48 Direct Start 1997
6b For those with sticky fingers and talent the crack can be gained direct on sloping holds. A hard problem.

49 Alan's Arete 6m VS P2 1980
4c/5b The arete can be climbed on its left side at 5b or, by the right side at 4c.

50 Shine On 5m VD 1958
Layback the crack in the recess.

51 Mantle On 4m S 1964
4b A problematic start gains the hanging groove.

52 Groove On 4m HD 1964
The shallow groove at the right end of the wall.

Across the descent gully is a large undercut block with an obvious hole in its front face this is:

BUTTRESS 5

53 Wall Climb 4m D 1960
Climb the centre of the left wall of the Buttress.

54 Block Arete 5m HS P2 1967
4b Climb the wall just left of the arete.

55 Beta Blocker 6m E1 P2 1982
5b The right side of the arete directly above the 'man eating' flake.

56 Impregnable 8m E2 P2 1982   ★★
6a Climb the centre of the face past the large hole.

57 Get Nervous 8m E2 P2 1982
5c The undercut arete right of Impregnable. Keep your cool and avoid escaping into the chimney.

58 Chockstone Overhang 7m HS P1 1960
4b The undercut chimney provides good, strenuous exercise.

BUTTRESS 6

59 Squawk's Arete 8m HVS P2 1980
5b Climb the left arete of the buttress with increasing difficulty.

60 Undercut Flake 8m HS P2 1964   ★★
4b Follow the layback flake until a step left allows the final corner to be gained. An excellent route.

61 Direct Start 8m HS P2 1964
4b Climb the wall direct into the final corner.

62 Tilt 8m HVS P2 1979
5a Climb the crack of Undercut Flake then continue up the arete above.

62a Flakeout Arete 8m HVS P2 1995 ★
5a Climbs wall and arete right of Undercut Flake and left of Dark
Cleft without touching the flake on the arete. A thin start and a
reachy finish.

63 Dark Cleft 5m VD 1958
The chimney in the recess.

63a Face To Face 6m VS P2 1998
4b Climb the wide entrance chimney to Dark Cleft and finish over
the capstone.

BUTTRESS 7

64 Forever Young 7m E2 P2 1983 ★★
6a Follows the vague crack-line up the wall to the right of Dark
Cleft with a nasty finish.

65 Seven Up 7m E2 P2 1981 ★★
5c Climb the imposing front face by launching off from the left arete
to finish on a suspect flake to the right. A **Direct Finish** (E3 6a)
moves left from the slot, with even more difficulty to another flake.

66 Variation Start's 1983
6a Directly up the front or, by a rock over, from under the roof on
the right.

67 Fuser 4m VD P1 1960
The layback corner crack.

68 Tony's Torment 4m HVS P2 1983
6a Climb the centre of the wall without the use of either crack. An
awkward little problem.

69 Wedge Down Crack 4m HS P2 1964
4b The awkward wide crack.

BUTTRESS 8

70 Dennis in Darlo 6m E1 P2 1981 ★
5c Straight up the centre of the wall to finish up a shallow corner.
Harder than it looks!

71 Low Level Traverse 100m Arduous 1984 ★★★
6b For the connoisseur of 'pumpy problems'. Start from Dennis in
Darlo and traverse leftwards to finish at Tranmire Arete or the
reverse. This is an excellent problem containing numerous 6a/6b
moves just above the ground, and is particularly useful for winter
training.

72 Barren Waste 6m E2 P2 1984
5c Climb the right side of the wall with a long reach to finish.

73 Easy Groove 5m D 1957
The cracked groove at the right edge of the buttress.

74 Edge Route 5m M 1957
Climb the stepped blocks forming the right end of the buttress.

BUTTRESS 9

This is the short wall behind the large detached block forming Buttress 10.

75 Little Arete 4m VD 1996
Ascend the front face of the arete left of the chimney.

76 Roofed Chimney 3m M 1957
Climb the chimney.

77 Awkward Finish 3m D 1957
The wall just right of the chimney.

78 Staircase Mantle 4m D 1957
Climb the wall via a pocket hold.

Note: Other harder problems can be worked out on this wall, including a low level traverse (5c)

BUTTRESS 10

This is the large detached block separated from the main edge by a wide gully. The climbs start in the gully at the left end of the rear face and are described from left to right.

79 Left Arete 4m VD 1958
Climb the left arete of the slab.

80 Frank's Wall 4m D 1997
Step off the block and climb the wall at its centre.

81 Scratch And Go 4m VD 1997
Pull over the undercut just right of the curving overlap, trending leftwards to finish.

82 Right Arete 4m VD 1958
Climb the undercut right edge of the wall. This is also the usual descent from the block.

83 Problem Wall 5m HVS P2 1982 ★
5b Climb the wall using the short horizontal slot to start and tiny edges to finish.

84 Left Wall 5m VD P2 1960   ★★
Climb the shallow curving groove. An excellent little route.

85 Sowden Left Hand 6m E1 P2 1982
5b Start at the front face and climb the wall finishing up the blunt
arete.

86 Sowden 6m HVS P2 1964   ★★
5a Climb the obvious flake crack. Requires a bold approach.

87 Sinbad 6m E3 P2 1983   ★★
6b Start just right of Sowden at a short corner. Climb the flakes to a
pocket, pull right to escape.

88 Space Plucks 6m E3 P2 1983   ★★
6a Climb the weakness 3 metres right of Sowden past a slot to a
good finishing pocket.

89 Dixon's Dilemma 5m VS P2 1984
4c Start in the gully by a large block. Climb the wall on angled
holds without bridging from the boulder.

90 Witton Wall 5m HS P1 1964
4b The flake crack in the left wall of the gully. Distinctly awkward.

Across the gully to the right is:

BUTTRESS 11

91 Halfway Chockstone 4m D 1958
Starts at the top of the gully on the right. Climb the chimney to exit
left around the capstone.

92 Central Bay Route 4m HD 1958
Climb the stepped groove.

92a Psyche 4m HVS P2 1998
5c Start in the gully just left of Leany Meany and use the pocket to
climb the shallow groove direct.

93 Leany Meany 8m E1 P2 1980   ★
5c Start at the left arete, pull onto the wall and climb to the obvious
slot, finish straight up.

94 Killer 8m E3 P2 1983
6b At the right end of the wall is a shallow corner. Use the corner to
gain pockets on the wall on the left, follow these to the top. A
difficult climb with a technical start and bold finish.

95 Ripper 8m E1 P2 1980   ★★★
5c Climb the grooved arete by a variety of precarious manoeuvres.
Simply brilliant.

SLIPSTONES   CENTRAL

96   Ripper Traverse   12m   E1   P2   1983
5c   Start at Leany Meany.   Follow the horizontal break rightwards to finish up Ripper.   Failure to join Ripper reduces the grade to 5a.

BUTTRESS 12
The sheltered wall split by a wide crack.

97   Picnic Wall   4m   D   1957
The blocky chimney to the left of the main face.

98   Cummin's Route   5m   HVS   P2   1982
5c   Climb the wall to the left of the wide crack.

99   Christopher Robin   6m   HS   P2   1960   ★
4b   Climb the awkward wide crack.

100   Right Wall   6m   HVS   P2   1983
5c   The fingery wall just right of the crack.

101   Marr's Route   6m   VS   P1   1964   ★
5a   Climb the wall and overhang direct 3m right of the Christopher Robin.

102   DA's Route   6m   VS   P2   1995
5a   Climb a faint groove between Marr's Route and the chimney on the right, finishing over the roof.

103   Moderator   4m   M   1958
The chimney on the right of the buttress.

104   Little Gully   3m   M   1958
The short gully on the right of the small buttress.

A poor route (VD) can be climbed up the block buttress left of Little Gully.

BUTTRESS 13 (The Siamese Blocks)
Comprising two large boulders separated by the chimney of Siamese Bridge.   The first two climbs are sadly much harder than before due to the demise of a good flake hold.

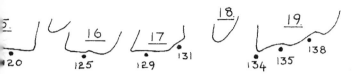

105 Friday 13th 4m HVS P2 1982
6a Climb the left arete on its left side via a snapped hold.

106 Sunday 20th 5m HVS P2 1983
6a Climb the left arete on its right side.

107 Siamese Bridge 5m D Circa 1958
The chimney between the two buttresses.

108 Right-Hand Twin 5m HVS P2 1980   ★
5b Climb the problematic arete right of the chimney on its left side.

109 Leaning Wall 5m HVS P2 1980
5c Climb the right side of the arete of Right-Hand Twin.

110 Strictly Personal 5m E1 P2 1983   ★
6a The arete to the right of Leaning Wall is climbed mainly on its
left side. A difficult problem.

111 Brush Up 4m HVS P2 1983
5b Climb the wall right of the arete.

BUTTRESS 14

112 Pothole Chimney 3m D 1958
The scrappy chimney on the left of the buttress.

113 String Vest 6m HVS P2 1982   ★
6a Ascend the shallow groove on the left side of the face. Very
delicate!

114 Withering Heights 6m HVS P2 1982
5c Start 2 metres right of the left arete. Climb the wall direct with a
long reach to finish.

115 Aces High 6m VS P2 Early 1970's   ★★
4c Climb the wall right of centre to a sloping ledge then either step
right to finish on the arete or exit direct by way of a long reach. A
popular route with some delicate moves.

116 Trumps 6m VS P2 1968   ★
4b Climb the right arete via a slanting finger slot to join the finish to
Aces High.

116a Trumps Right-hand 5m HS P2 1968
4b Climb the wall just right of the arete to finish up the black stain.

BUTTRESS 15

Comprising a steep wall split by a horizontal crack at 2 metres.

117 Heather Wall 4m D 1958
The stepped wall on the left of the buttress.

118 Pinnacle Chimney 4m D 1958
The short chimney.

119 Yaud Wall 5m VS P1 1960
5a Climb the awkward hanging corner on the left side of the face.

120 Ellingstring 5m VS P1 1978   ★★
4c Start below the centre of the wall. Climb up to the overlap, step up right then pull left to a pocket hold and finish. Not as difficult as it looks.

121 Diagonal 6m VS P1 1966   ★
4b Start just right of Ellingstring and follow the overlap rightwards to a strenuous pull to finish.

122 Gymnast 5m VS P1 1980
5a Take the undercut right arete direct.

123 Fiddlesticks 4m VS P2 1997
5b Climb the wall just right of the arete on flat holds. Looks easy doesn't it!

A poor climb Girgle (VD 1960) traverses the buttress via the horizontal break.

BUTTRESS 16

Identified by a series of small overhangs at its right side.

124 Fearby 6m VS P1 1960
4b Climb the left hand side of the front of the buttress starting from a block.

125 Stainthorpe's Wall 6m E1 P2 1980   ★★
5b Start just right of Fearby. Pull up right to the break and finish up the centre of the wall.

126 Variation Start 4m HVS 1965   ★★
5c Start at the right end of the overhangs. Pull up then go leftwards to gain the slot on Stainthorpe's wall, finish as for that climb.

127   Fascinationby   6m   E2   P2   1983
5c   Climb the hanging groove starting at the rock scar.

BUTTRESS 17
This buttress is split by a horizontal crack, and has a shallow groove on the right.

128   Jug Handle Pull Up   5m   VD   1960
The left arete of the buttress.

129   Wall Centre   5m   HS   1961
4b   Climb the centre of the buttress to an awkward exit.

130   Happy Daze   5m   HS   1979
4b   Climb the wall just left of the right arete.

131   Double Mantelshelf   6m   VD   1960
The stepped groove at the right of the buttress.

132   Right Edge   3m   VS   1980
5b   The short right arete.

A few metres further right is a small block with two minor climbs, this is:

BUTTRESS 18
An **Easy Mantelshelf** (Diff) Climbs the front face. Whilst the **Right Arete** is 4b. A short distance to the right is:

BUTTRESS 19
133   Hand Traverse   6m   D   1960
Start low down on the left of the buttress. Follow a crack rightwards to finish just before the arete.

134   Lay-by Arete   6m   E2   P2   1985   ★★★
6c   Start on the right side of the arete but finish on the left. Superb technical climbing.

135   Lay-by   5m   HVS   P2   1976   ★★
6a   Climb the flake crack. Another excellent problem.

136   Little Baldy   5m   HVS   P2   Circa 1985
6c   Climb the wall just right of Lay-by (without using the flake), finish via the 'rock scar' on Rock On left-hand variant.

137   Rock On Left-hand Variation   5m   HVS   P1   1981   ★
5c   Gain the slot in the wall right of Lay-by. Hand traverse the slot leftwards until it is possible to reach the 'rock scar' and exit.

138   Rock On   4m   HVS   P1   1980   ★
5c   Climb directly up the wall using the slot.

139   Rock Off   4m   HVS   P1   1980
5b   Climb the blunt arete to the right.

140   All Off   3m   HVS   P1   1980
5b   The short wall on the right provides a poor climb.

BUTTRESS 20

141   Ten Foot Moderate   3m   M   P1   1958
The crack on the left.

142   Twenty Something   4m   VS   P1   1994
4c   Climb the centre of the left wall.

143   Overhanging Arete   5m   VS   P1   1966   ★
5a   The gymnastic leaning arete.

144   Flaky Wall   5m   HS   P1   1970
4b   The awkward right wall is climbed in its centre. Surprisingly
strenuous.

145   Problem Traverse   6m   HVS   P1   1980
5c   Start at Twenty Something, swing around the arete, cross the
fingery wall to finish up Flaky Wall.

146   Left Wall   4m   VD   P1   1960
The arete just left of the wide crack.

147   Two Chockstones   4m   D   P1   1958
The wide crack.

148   Right Overhang   4m   D   P1   1958
A poor route up the wall right of the crack.

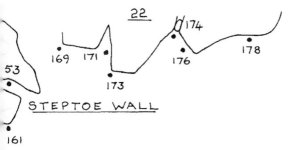

STEPTOE WALL

LOWER

BUTTRESS 21
This is the collective name for the jumble of large blocks which step down the hillside in three tiers. The path tends to weave naturally between the middle and lowest tiers, but requires the easy descent of a small slab en route. The first climbs commence in the 'crevasse' formed between the upper and middle tiers, and start from the left.

UPPER TIER

149 Stomach Traverse 8m Easy Circa 1958
Included for its novelty factor - crawl along the shelf under the overhang. The kid's love it!

150 Bratt Pack 3m VS P2 Mid 1970s
4c Climb the centre of the wall, left of the main arete.

151 Play-A-Long 4m HVS P2 Mid 1970s
5b The main arete can be climbed on either side.

152 Wild Thing 3m VS P2 Mid 1970s
4b Climb the centre of the wall right of the arete.

The crevasse narrows between two blocks and forms a chimney which can be climbed at D. The chimney opens again forming a blank looking corner on the left, this is:-

153 Micro Corner 4m HVS P1 1982 ★★
6b Climb the blank looking corner. A brilliant problem.

154 Problem Arete 4m VS P1 1982
4c Ascend the left side of the arete to the right of Micro Corner.

A poor route, **Slab and Mantelshelf** M (1957) climbs the small block and right side of the arete.

155 Shorty's Dilemma 3m VS P1 1997
5b Climb the wall directly opposite Micro Corner by stepping into the slot from the left.

MIDDLE TIER
Consists of two large blocks. The left block is known as **The Son**, the right block is **Steptoe**. Starting on The Son is:-

156 Son Of A Bitch 7m HVS P1 1995
5c A strenuous left to right traverse of the block. Start from boulders below the left arete, continue across the wall under the capstone to finish at the top of Curving Crack. Good for removing hard skin!

157 Curving Crack 3m S P1 Circa 1960
Climb the crack just left of the gap between the two blocks.

STEPTOE WALL

158 Bert Wells 3m HVS P1 1983
5b Climb the thin flake on the wall just to the right of the corner.

159 Centre Left 4m HVS P1 1983   ★
5c Start 2 metres right of the corner. Climb the overlap using a finger slot.

160 Steptoe 5m HVS P2 1982   ★★
6a Start 4 metres right of Curving Crack. Levitate up the delicate wall with increasing difficulty.

161 Tiptoe 5m VS P2 1965   ★★
5a Climb the fine right arete by some delicate moves. An excellent climb and high in its grade.

LOWER TIER
Comprising an immaculate concave slab with a vertical side wall on the left end.

162 Welcome Wall 5m VS P2 1982
4b Climb the centre of the left wall.

163 Stereo Android 6m VS P2 1982
4c Climb the right arete by its left wall throughout.

164 Tommy's Dilemma 6m VD P2 Circa 1960   ★
Ascend the pleasant narrow slab by the left arete.

165   Gypsy Wham   5m   HD   P1   Circa 1960
The centre of the slab via the obvious large ledge.

166   Tea Party Slab   4m   VS   P1   1965
5a   Climb the bulge and slab right of Gypsy Wham without using the ledge of that climb.

167   Question of Balance   4m   VS   P1   1965   ★
5c   Climb the slab just to the left of the obvious pocket.

168   Right Edge   4m   VS   P1   1965
5b   Climb the slab just to the right of the pocket. Other easier variations are possible to the right.

To the right of Tip-toe and left of Buttress 22 is an isolated block.

168a   Simple Sally   5m   E4   P2   1994   ★
6c   Reach into the middle of the wall from the left arete (feet on adjacent block to start) to very small horizontal finger holds. Continue direct via slaps and lurches up the centre of the wall.

BUTTRESS 22
This comprises the final group of blocks which form the main edge. The next climbs are to be found on the small wall set back into the hillside above and right of Tiptoe.

169   Left Arete   3m   D   P1   1980
Climb the left arete of the short wall.

170   Goblin's Ear   3m   VD   P1   1980
Climb the small curving flake crack.

Across the corner chimney is a short slab.

171   3.3 Metre Slab   3.3m   HS   P2   Mid 1990s
4b   Ascend the slab/wall just left of the faint crack.

172   Ten Foot Slab   3m   D   P1   Circa 1958
Climb the slab and arete to the right of the faint crack.

The next route starts at a lower level by the left arete.

173   Davies Ramp   6m   E2   P2   Mid 1980s
6a   Climb the arete until the ramp line can be followed rightwards.

Around the arete to the right is an overhanging wall ending at a short corner, which is:-

174   Chockstone Pull Up   3m   D   P1   Circa 1958
Do as the name implies!

175 All The Two's   10m   E2   P2   1995
6a A sustained right to left hand traverse of the overhanging wall.
Start at the chockstone, pull up and finish up Ten Foot Slab.

176 Supple Wall   3m   HVS   P1   1985   ★
6b Climb the short wall to the left of the arete.

177 Sulky Little Boys   4m   HVS   P1   1985   ★
6c The short arete on its right side. A difficult problem.

178 Slanting Flake   4m   HS   P1   1959   ★★
4b Climb the curving flake on the right end of the wall. An excellent
route which can be started and finished by a variety of ways.

GRADED LIST – SLIPSTONES

E4
Simple Sally (6c)

E3
Atomic Right Hand (6b)
Killer (6b)
Sinbad (6a)
Atomic (6a)
Space Plucks(6a)
Seven Up Direct Finish
(6a)

E2
Lay-by Arete (6c)
Timeless Divide Var.
Start(6c)
Davies Ramp(6a)
Forever Young(6a)
Impregnable(6a)
Timeless Divide(6a)
Seven Up Var. Starts(6a)
West Face Eliminate(6a)
All The Two's(6a)
Narrow Margin(6a)
Fascionationby(5c)
Barren Waste(5c)
Get Nervous(5c)
Seven Up(5c)
Beldin Var. Start(5c)

E1
Strictly Personal(6a)
Paul's Arete (Left)(6a)
Ripper (5c)
Ripper Traverse (5c)
Extremities(5c)
Forever Onward(5c)
Dennis in Darlo(5c)
Leany Meany(5c)
Beldin Direct(5b)
Paul's Arete (Right)(5b)
Steve's Wall(5b)
Space Truckin(5b)
High Level Trav.(5b)
Gollinglith(5b)
Beta Blocker(5b)
Sowden Left Hand(5b)

HVS
Sulky Little Boy's (6c)
Low Level Traverse (6b)
Little Baldy (6b)
Wisecrack Dir. Start (6b)
Micro Corner (6b)
Supple Wall (6b)
Steptoe(6a)
Lay-by(6a)
String Vest(6a)
Tony's Torment(6a)
Friday 13th(6a)
Sunday 20th(6a)
Wisecrack(5c)
Agra Direct Start(5c)

Cummin's Route(5c)
Right Wall(5c)
Agrete(5c)
Rock On(5c)
Rock On-Left Hand(5c)
Centre Left(5c)
Stainthorpe's Wall
Var.(5c)
Withering Heights(5c)
Leaning Wall(5c)
Son of a Bitch(5c)
Problem Traverse(5c)
Agra Right Hand(5b)
Agra(5b)
Squawks Arete(5b)
Right-hand Twin(5b)
Bert Wells(5b)
Problem Wall(5b)
Zoom(5b)
Beldin(5b)
North Wall(5b)
Rock Off(5b)
All Off(5b)
Play-A-Long(5b)
Escalator(5a)
Sowden(5a)
Original Route(5a)
Tilt(5a)

VS

Alan's Arete Left Side(5b)
Jenny Binks Wall(5a)
Marr's Route(5a)
DA's Route(5a)
Yaud Wall(5a)
Gymnast(5a)
Fiddlesticks(5b)
Shorty's Dilemma(5b)
Tiptoe(5a)
Overhanging Arete(5a)
Right Edge(5b)
Question of Balance(5c)
Tea Party Slab5a)
Alan's Arete Right Side(4c)
Ellingstring(4c)
Diagonal(4b)
Stereo Android(4c)
Bratt Pack(4c)
Problem Arete(4c)
Wild Thing(4b)
Cold Wall(4c)
Twenty Something(4c)
Aces High(4c)
Dixon's Dilemma(4c)
Easy Pickings(4c)
Tranmire Crack(4c)
Hole in the Wall(4c)
Welcome Wall(4b)
Fearby(4b)

HS

Wedge Down Crack(4b)
Undercut Flake(4b)
Chockstone
Overhang(4b)
Barnley Wall(4b)
Undercut Flake Dir. Start(4b)
Christopher Robin(4b)
Slanting Flake(4b)
Trumps Right Hand(4b)
Mantelshelf Wall(4b)
Witton Wall(4b)
Block Arete(4b)
Flaky Wall(4b)
Happy Daze(4b)
Wall Centre(4b)
3.3 Metre Slab(4b)

S

Mantle On
Barnley Crack
Undercut Double Crack
Petch's Groove
Tranmire Arete
Curving Crack

VD

Not So Tight Chimney
Ulfers Crack
Fuser
Twenty Foot Crack
Dark Cleft
Shine On
Little Arete
Left Wall
Right Edge
Scratch and Go
Mantelshelf Crack
Jug Handle Pull Up
Left Wall
Tommy's Dilemma
Goblin's Ear
Double Mantelshelf
Left Arete
Overhanging Crack
Girgle

SPOFFORTH PINNACLES

SITUATION AND CHARACTER   Spofforth Pinnacles are pleasantly situated in an unspoiled meadow just off the A661, Harrogate,
Wetherby Road, close to the River Crimple. The rock is a sandy
gritstone, generally soft and weathered which results in ball-
bearing covered holds and some friable flakes. None of the
pinnacles exceed 7.5 metres in height, in reality few of the routes
actually attain it.

The landings are generally good and ropes superfluous. Only the
very best routes have been given stars but most are worthwhile if
you like this sort of thing.

APPROACHES AND ACCESS   The majority of the climbing is on
the rocks between Braham Hall and Crosper Farm. There is parking
for two cars at the corner of the plantation, on the left when
approaching from Wetherby. From the parking space go over the
stile and walk along the side of the field to a second stile, cross this
into the meadow where the following outcrops and pinnacles are to
be found. The Twins, Scoop Block, Tower Block and Isolated Block.

THE ROUTES are described from north to south and are easily
located by reference to the plan.

THE TWINS. The first rocks seen as you enter the field.

1   Birds Lavatory
4a The limed scoop on the south face finishing either left or right.

2   Hang Up
4c Climb directly up and over the overhang on the south west
corner of the block.

3   Jamline
4c Climb the bulge on the south west face at a notch.

4   The Slab
3b Climb the slabby steps on the west face of the left twin.

5   South Face Crack
4b Climb the crack on the right-hand twin.

5a   Tricky Dicky
4a The south westerly point of the Right Twin

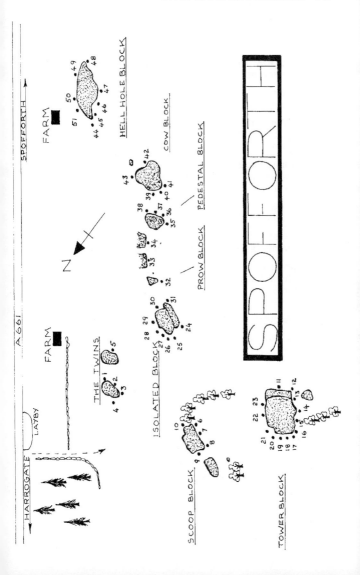

5b The Whale
4a The north west face direct

SCOOP BLOCK This rock has a shell scarred appearance and is rather more friable.

6 The Arete
Climb the stepped arete on the left edge of the south face.

7 Shell Shocked
5a Start just left of the hole in the crag. Climb the nasty bulge just left of The Arete.

8 Crumbling Edge
5a The twin of Shell Shocked and equally nasty . Takes the right side of the north west arete.

9 Green Wall
4c Climb directly up the centre of the north face.

10 Limboist
5a The overhang, just right of the south east arete, direct.

11 South Face
The South Face can be climbed anywhere and is the easiest way up or down.

TOWER BLOCK The largest block, and furthest west.

12 South West Corner
4c Climb the overhung nose to exit through the branches up a crack.

13 Stone Me
5c Start by a hole left of South West Corner and climb straight up the wall to finish at the end of a slanting crack.

14 Western Edges
5c Surmount the initial bulge before moving up and right over the top overhang to a slanting crack.

15 West Face ★
4b Climb the short steep central rift to finish over bulges.

16 Sandman ★
6a Climb the crumbly wall between the arete and Western Edges.

17 North West Arete
4a Climb the arete bordering the West and North faces starting just left of the undercut.

18 North Face
5b Climb directly up the wall. Easier variants meander from the true line.

19 Left Side Story
5c Climb the centre of the wall via a 'wee' hole.

20 North East Corner ★★
5a Climbs the fine arete on its left side. Move right at the top to finish up a slanting crack.

21 Curlew
5b Start near North East Corner by a crack. Climb the wall to a horizontal break and move left to a pocket then up and left over a bulge to more bird limed holes. Finish up and over the final overhang which, alarmingly, is detached. Alternatively climb direct up the wall to the pockets.

22 East South East Route
5b Climb a shallow groove to a good hole and exit left across the slab. Alternatively, from the hole move right to a pinch grip finish up and right just to the left of Curlew.

23 Rock Around The Block ★★★
6a One of the best problems here. Start on a ledge on the South Face, traverse the block at mid level.

ISOLATED BLOCK Situated about 200 metres right of Tower Block

24 Sideline
4b Start on the big ledge on the west face and climb the short wall on the right.

25 North Face Groove
Climb the open groove right of the bulging north wall.

26 Isolation Ward
6a Climb the bulging wall on dubious holds.

27 Side-show
4b Takes the left edge of the bulging north face finishing on grassy holds.

28 Isolated Wall
5b Climb boldly up the wall on the shady side of the crag using always green, and sometimes friable, holds.

29 Isolated Crack
5b Takes the short hanging crack near the west arete of the block.

30 Pockets Wall
6a Climb the steep wall right of the graffiti using the obvious pockets.

31 Graffiti Arete
5a The leaning arete just right of the arete.

PROW BLOCKS : These are small overhung blocks south of Isolated Block.

32 The Prow
5a Climb the overhanging west nose.

33 Pot Scoop
The central scoop left of the chimney.

34 Set Square
4c Front face right of the chimney.

PEDESTAL BLOCK: The round block supported by the pedestal.

35 Pedestal Arete
4c Climb the blunt arete directly above the pedestal.

36 The Scoop
5b The scoop on the south face exiting to the left.

37 Exclusive
4a Climb the series of shallow scoops left of Lime Hole.

38 Lime Hole
4a Climb directly up and past the limed hole.

COW BLOCK: This lies 400 metres south of Pedestal Block.

39 Green Lining
5b Climb directly up from the short vertical crack onto the ledge. Exit awkwardly via a niche in the roof.

40 Bull Nose
5a The blunt arete left of Heifers Cleft, finish easily up ledges.

41 Heifers Cleft
4b The obvious short, wide crack.

42 The Inquisitive Bullock
Climbs the cleft on the south face, exiting either left or right. Easier variation: climb the slabby arete right of the cleft.

43 The Gathering
4a Takes the wall and overhang on the east face.

HELL HOLE BLOCK: So called due to the large hole through the buttress. This block lies in the grounds of Crosper Farm some 800 metres south west of The Tower Block

44   The Nose
6a Mantel the nose at the north end of the block with difficulty.

45   Hell's Bells
5a Climb the overhanging crack right of the nose, finish delicately up the wall above.

46   Wee Nick
5b Takes the wall right of Hell's Bells to a scoop hold in the wall above.

47   Devil Make Care
5a The wall on the right is climbed via undercuts, finish boldly up the wall or sneak into the hole on the right.

48   The Trunk
4c Climb the 'trunk' on the south face and finish up the shallow crack.

49   Leftward Ho!
5a This line is on the north east face, left of the crack. It climbs the bulge to an escape along the grassy finish as for Hell Crack.

50   Hell Crack
5b A brutal crack with a grassy finish.

51   Poisson Rouge
4c The crack right of Hell Crack finishing up and right.

SYPELAND CRAG

SITUATION AND CHARACTER A series of small crags and isolated boulders about a mile south west of Ash Head Crag on the moors above Upper Nidderdale. The rock is good quality well weathered grit and dries quickly, but the area is exposed and somewhat remote. The climbing is similar in character to The Bridestones with around one hundred and twenty micro-routes and named problems. As bouldering in its pure form is beyond the scope of this guide only the longest and most significant climbs have been described. Virtually all have been soloed, the landings are generally good, but a rope may be found useful on first acquaintance by some.

APPROACHES AND ACCESS Approach as for Ash Head Crag along the moorland track which is followed for just over a mile, through two gates, to park by a shooting lodge on the right. From a gate by the lodge follow a line of grouse butts passing between the 3rd and 4th towards the twin pinnacles known as Jenny Twig and her daughter Tib. The edge extends from here for about half a mile facing west to the final, and possibly the best, boulder now named Tib's Tent. **NOTE: The area is a private grouse moor and there is no official access. It would be advisable to avoid the nesting and shooting season and leave dogs at home.**
STOP PRESS : Following publication of the Wild Bouldering guide in the spring of 1998 the landowners issued a ban on climbing and negotiations were under-way via the BMC as this guide went to press.

THE CLIMBS are described from left to right.

The first rocks are **Jenny Twig and her daughter Tib.** There are 5 named problems on these pinnacles between 4a and 5a. The steep west face of 'Jenny' is, however, still virgin?

The next large buttress close to the fence about 150 metres to the south is named **The Towel Horse** and is approached by skirting around the Woozle Wam,a large marshy area.

1 All Pull Together 6m S P1
4a Climb a short slab to the left of the main overhang and then ascend the side wall direct.

2 Round In Circles 10m VS P2
5a From the short slab step out right and gain the ledge between the overhangs. Move across and climb the top roof via a nick on the right.

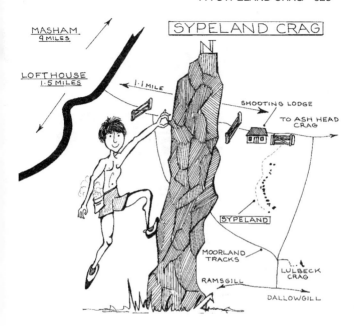

3 What Happens Now? 7m E3 P2   ★
6b Climb direct over the first roof - and then ask the question!

Thirty metres right is a prominent and clean buttress known as
Tracking Tor.

4 Foolish And Deluded 6m HVS P1   ★
5b The small groove on the left is awkward. Finish at the crease.

5 Hot And Anxious 6m HVS P2   ★★
5b Tackle the short flake on the right and sweat it out up the ripples
above.

Ten metres to the right is the severely undercut **Rabbit Rock** with a
5c problem on the left side. In the centre is :-

6 Bother 6m VS P1
5a The central recess is climbed trending left past a dodgy flake.

7 Henry Rush 6m HVS P2
5a From a difficult start on the nose above the enormous thread
traverse left to a bold finish.

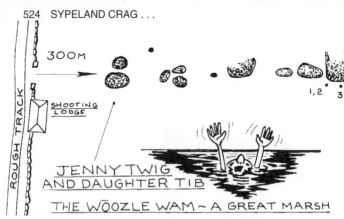

300M

SHOOTING LODGE

ROUGH TRACK

1, 2 3

JENNY TWIG
AND DAUGHTER TIB

THE WOOZLE WAM ~ A GREAT MARSH

The overhang on the right side has been climbed at 5b.

The next few boulders contain minor problems until a larger block is reached. This pinnacle often has an in-situ pool below its southern bulges.

8 One Hundred Inches Long 7m E1 P2
5c Start up the steep scoop on the back of the block and traverse left over the water to finish at the upper weakness.

There are 3 other short problems on this boulder but the next challenge is on the back of the slabby block a few metres further right.

9 Malt Extract 5b The short overhanging crack and the upper face to its left.

10 Bounces 6m E1 P1   ★
6a Adjacent to Malt Extract on the back of a larger block is a green slanting scoop gained and climbed with difficulty from an undercut start.

11 Boughed 6m HVS P1
5c A high step from the grassy ledge left of the arete gains a technical wall and a steep finish.

12 Peaceful Smile 6m HVS P1
5b A slanting scoop leads to a bulging finish on the right.

There are three shorter problems around 5b on the west face but more significant is an obvious crack-line on the boulder behind.

13 Stones Too Much 6m VS P2
4b The crack, or the wall just to the right, leads to a bulging finish.

14 Droopy Drawers 5m MVS P1
4b The nose of the more isolated pinnacle a few metres south has good holds but the customary rounded finish.

The next collection of rocks, known as the **Piglet Pinnacle Area**, is more extensive and contains the longest routes and some fine problems. The first boulder reached has a 5b problem up the left arete whilst the central arete is tempting, but still unclimbed. Starting from an adjacent boulder is:-

15 A Very Grand Thing 7m HVS P1   ★
5b From the smaller block on the right gain the short sharp crack on the larger rock and top out with interest.

Heffalump Tor is the large buttress to the right with a compelling, but still virgin, main wall. On the left of it close to an easy chimney is;-

16 On The Other Hand 7m VS P1
5a The thin crack is climbed to a ledge with an exit leftwards.

17 Twiggy 8m E1 P2   ★★
5b The prominent layback crack leads to an exciting finish directly over the rounded bulge. Proficiency at the Western Roll may be an advantage.

18 Lumping Along 10m VS P2   ★
5a Climb a short slab to its apex and then make a difficult mantel onto the wide ledge above. Traverse right and climb the easier chimney.

19 Cracking Up 8m HVD P1   ★
Climb the short, but stubborn, crack to gain a more direct entry to the upper chimney.

20 Long Time Coming 7m E1 P1   ★
6a The short, problematic rib at the entrance to the gully. Move left to the chimney to finish.

21   A Deep Pit   8m   HVS   P2
5a   From the far end of the gully traverse left on the back wall of Heffalump Tor, along a blind crease, to finish through the roof.

22   Got Any String   5m   VS   P1
5a   The rib and bulge above the start of Deep Pit.

A Sinking Feeling 5b is the green rounded rib opposite Got Any String. To the right at the lower entrance to the gully once again is:-

23   A Cunning Trap   6m   E3   P3
5c   The rounded roof from the top of the slab above the right end of the shelf.

24   Like Nothing   5m   E1   P2
5b   The shorter wall and bulge to the right has two small eyes; climb straight over between them.

In front of Heffalump Tor is a smaller, flat topped, block known as **The Tablecloth.** It has at least seven excellent problems the best of which is, **Agroan** up the centre of the west wall from a small low ledge at 6a -ish?

Thirty metres right of Heffalump Tor is **Woozle Tor,** one of the very best buttresses on the moor. It has a wide north wall above a slabby gully and a fine overhung west face.

25   Thoughtful Way   5m   HVS   P2
5b   The left edge of the north wall above a dodgy landing.

26   Tracking Something   6m   HVS   P2   ★★
The centre of the wall via the 'eye'.

27   Funnything Accidents   7m   E1   P2   ★
5c   The short and shallow right facing corner 2 metres right.

28   Breaking Out   7m   E3   P2   ★★
6b   The arete up its left-hand side.

SYPELAND

29 Caught In An Eddy 8m E2 P1   ★★★
6a Start on the arete and swing right on slopers heading for an escape up the obvious bulging weakness to a ledge and an easier finish above.

30 Lacking In Smack 7m E2 P1   ★★
6b Start below and right of the rib and climb direct through the bulge of Caught In An Eddy.

31 Eeyore 8m E2 P1   ★★
6a Start in the shallow corner and move up and right to the handrail. Swing back left to finish as for Eddy.

32 Horse Gone Wonky 9m E2 P1   ★★★
6a From the centre of the west wall climb up to the handrail and traverse left all the way round into ..Eddy.

33 Trained Bloodhound 9m HVS P1   ★
5b From the centre of the wall climb to the handrail but escape rightwards around the roof but then move back left to finish above the centre.

34 Drop The Dead Donkey 11m E3 P1   ★
6c A technical low level traverse R to L across the west wall finishing up Eeyore.

There are some lesser problems on the next two blocks and then a 5 metre pinnacle **Tigger's Tor** stands forward of the line of the edge

35 Bounced 5m HVS P1   ★
5a The pleasant slabby north face of Tigger's Tor is good value.

36 Tigger's Can Fly 5m E1 P1   ★★
6a The bulging western nose of Tigger's Tor may give you a flying lesson!

Behind Tigger's Tor is a block containing **A Little Something** 5b over the bulge whilst just to the right is a larger undercut boulder called **Pooh Profile.**

37   Pooh Sticks   6m   S   P1
4a The left-hand side-wall of Pooh Profile

38   A little Anxious   7m   E1   P2   ★
5b Gain the shelf from the left, traverse right and then 'anxiously' up the centre.

The two boulders to the right are small and then a larger square block **The Honey Pot** gives:-

39   Twitchy Sort Of Way   6m   HVS   P2   ★★
5b A good wall climb just left of centre to the highest point on the north wall.

40   Adulterated Bliss   6m   VS   P1   ★
5a The scoop at the right-hand side of the north wall.

41   Gales   6m   E1   P2
5c Up the north west arete from the right but swing around left near the top avoiding the real challenge.

42   A Little Trouble   6m   E2   P1   ★★★
6a The leaning wall is climbed to the break, and runners if you've brought them. Reach up and right to a rounded finish. Straight over is possibly 6b.

43   Heap Of Everybody   5m   HVS   P1
5c The undercut wall a few metres right of the Honey Pot. Pull over and move left.

The next block, **The Honey Comb** has three short routes

44   The Jagular   5m   VS   P1
4b The steep scoop and slabby wall on the left.

45   Sparkling Along   5m   HVS   P1   ★
5b A frontal attack on the nose moving right into a crack.

46   What If   5m   VS   P1
4c The slabby right wall is harder than it looks.

The last two boulders on the edge provide some of the best routes and problems. The large triangular block reminiscent of Caley's Sugarloaf is known as **Tib's Tent** whilst the smaller, rounder and very undercut block 50 metres away is **Puff Pastry**.

TIB'S TENT

The routes and problems are described Clockwise from the chipped descent in the centre of the slab.

47 Tentacle 8m VS P2 ★
4c Start just left of the left edge on the slab and pull up and right from an embedded block. Climb the slab without recourse to the edge or the chipped holds.

48 Testicle 8m VS P2 ★
5a Gain the slab just left of Tentacle, using a flake. Climb the left edge to the top.

49 No Loitering 6m E2 P2
5c The blind, slanting crack just right of the arete.

50 Burglary Within Tent 7m E2 P3 ★
5c The right-hand side of the overhung face to a committing finish.

51 Under The Awning 7m E3 P3 ★
6a The centre of the overhung face with a difficult and committing finish.

52 Flying Colours 7m HVS P2 ★★
5b The left side of the overhung face to good holds on flutings.

53 Striding Edge 7m E1 P2 ★★★
5b The left side of the arete gives a tricky start on pockets then excellent moves to a fluted finish

54 Swirral Edge 9m E3 P1 ★★
6b A hard boulder problem start on the undercut right arete of the slab leads to easy padding up the edge.

55 Itchy Chin 9m E3 P1 ★
6c Another desperate start between Swirrel Edge and the chipped descent leads to an easier finish.

56 Just Pad Dad 10m S P3 ★
Gain the slab using the first chips of the descent route then move 2 metres right and pad smoothly to the top.

Puff Pastry , the last boulder on the moor, is the undercut block 50 metres south. It has ten named problems in the 5b/c range, all with harder, optional, sitting starts. If you've any skin left on your fingers by now there is always **Lulbeck Crag** visible about 1 kilometre of heather tramping further south. See Connoisseurs Crags for an easier approach.

WIDDOP

"The gods are good! At times, they blinded the eyes of the greedy pioneers. At least one good thing escaped their grasping maw. The result is, in this year of grace 1929, I have to announce, miribile dictu, the discovery of a new climbing ground. The whereabouts of this precious find will be announced in due course. Of course, those can climb it who can find it. In the meantime, there are three cragsmen who know where it is, and I am also in the secret. The discoverer's personal view is that 'If it leaks out, blighters (i.e., tigers) like A.S. Piggott and Morley Wood - others could be named - will go and mop up everything before anyone else gets a look in.' So for the present I propose to designate the main crag Mystery Buttress."

A.E.Chisman, Rucksack Club Journal, Vol 6. 1929.

SITUATION AND CHARACTER   The rocks are found in a superb setting high on the moors overlooking Widdop reservoir on the Yorkshire/Lancashire border. The gritstone is of good quality but parts of it tend to look green as the crag is mainly north facing. However, in dry weather Widdop offers fine, often bold climbing away from the crowds. The boulders are particularly good, often in condition when the main edge is not.

APPROACHES AND ACCESS   Widdop reservoir is approximately 6 miles equidistant between Hebden Bridge and Nelson. From Hebden Bridge, negotiate the turning circle just west of the town centre on the A646 and head up the hill towards Heptonstall. Avoid the village itself and continue until the road forks. Take the right fork, signposted Widdop, and park just before the reservoir after 3 miles. If approaching from Lancashire, you have our sympathies, but rumour has it that tarmacadam actually winds its way up from Nelson and Burnley to Widdop reservoir. The crags lie on the far side of the reservoir and can be reached in a few minutes by crossing the dam wall. Camping and bivvying is not tolerated as this is a water catchment area.

THE CLIMBS   These are described from left to right.

The largest buttress at Widdop is Mystery Buttress, which lies on the hillside directly above the dam wall. However, the first routes are to be found on Cave Buttress some thirty metres to the left.

CAVE BUTTRESS

1 Dessert 10m E2 P2
5b On the left wall of the buttress, climb easily to a pedestal. Finish up the shallow groove above uneasily.

2 A Trifle Sweet 11m E2 P2
5c The arete left of the Curving Crack is climbed using holds on either side until a mantelshelf gains the first ledge. With protection on the right use pebbles and small holds to make the crux moves to a rounded edge and then move right to a flake and another ledge. Using a pocket above make a final mantelshelf onto the top.

2 Curving Crack 15m VS P1
5a The obvious crack either leads to the cave, or moves left then back right before finishing direct.

3 Cave Crack 14m VS P1 ★
4c This excellent climb follows the corner crack, past the cave in the middle of the buttress.
A 5c variant climbs the arete between Curving and Cave Crack to the cave.

4 Cave Arete 14m E2 P2
5c The steep arete right of the Cave Crack to the break. Move around the arete and climb the right wall to the top.

5 Wickerwork Crack 7m HVS P1
5b The vertical crack in the buttress just right of Cave Arete might be easier if it ever dried out.

6 Wickerwork Wall 7m MVS P1
4b The wall to the right (facing Mystery Buttress) from bottom left to top right.

MYSTERY BUTTRESS

Generally short pitches between good ledges characterise climbing on Mystery Buttress. Many of the routes are delicate and quite bold and pitches can be interspersed at will to provide many long and enjoyable expeditions.

7 Neptune 9m E2 P2
5c On the left flank of the buttress is a hanging crack above a small overlap. Climb the blank-looking lower wall on minute crimps then the crack to a ledge. May be easier for the tall, wearing a full wet suit.

On the ledge where Neptune finishes, the next short route begins.

Mystery
Buttress

8 Scratch 'n' Sniff 6m E3 P2
5c Climb a short crack to a break, then the very shallow scoop above, with a long reach for the top.

9 The Links Climb 17m HVS P3 ★
5a Links three short but bold pitches, with little useful protection. Start with a high step off the large block on the left-hand side of the buttress to gain the undercut rib and first ledge. A scoop on the left leads to Demon Corner, a short arete, after which a crack on the right leads to the top, and relief.

10 The Nature Reserve 28m E2 P2
6a A series of variations, the first of which climbs a shallow groove left of the start of Links Climb. The second climbs the wall to the right of Demon Corner and right of a crack (side runner). Move diagonally right to a ledge. Above is an obvious flake on the

headwall and just to the right is a small groove in the arete. Climb this to a rounded finish.

11   Ordinary Route   30m   VD   P1   ★
Good varied climbing starting from the foot of the buttress, just right of a cave. Straight up to the first ledge, then a tricky move to gain the second ledge. Move right, then up an easy slab to the third ledge. From here a stomach traverse right followed by an awkward move up past the "Bull's Horns" gains the fourth ledge. From the right-hand corner of the ledge step up and traverse right to an easy finishing chimney. It is apparently also possible for those of well above average height to reach the top from the step up.

12   Ordinary Route Variation Start   VD   P1   ★
Just right of the original, a small corner then crack leads to the second ledge.

13   Birtwhistle's Crack   9m   VS   P1
4c   The steep vertical crack above the second ledge moving left to join the top crack of The Links Climb.

14   The Three Cs   30m   VS   P3   ★★
4c   Fine situations make this a most enjoyable route. It is also quite

bold. Begin just right of Ordinary Route's Variation Start. The Centipede; climb to a bulge above where delicate moves enable the second ledge to be reached. Keeping low traverse right under a nose to the centre of Cascara Wall, which is climbed on small holds. Move back left to belay on the third ledge. A ramp rises to the left; climb this to gain the Corbel. Awkward moves left lead to an easy finishing corner.

15   The Flake Direct   E1   P2   ★★
5b   From the third ledge, climb directly, and boldly, to the flake and so to the top.

16   Krypton Route   25m   M S   P2   ★
On the right-hand side of the buttress is a prominent overhang at 3 metres. Pull over this into the shallow corner, climb this to a ledge then a slab on the left to the third ledge. The short wall behind leaves you on the ledge with three finishes available:-
The Layback   5m   VS   P1
4c   The overhanging corner, though short, is very strenuous.
The Flake   6m   MVS   P1   ★★
4b   From the ledge move left to climb the flake. Exposed.
The finish of the Ordinary Route (VD).

17   Krypton Eliminate   19m   E1   P3   ★★
5b   Bold climbing up the right edge of the buttress. From the right-hand end of the buttress climb the edge until half a metre from Krypton Route make a hard move onto the slab and then back right to regain the edge. Alternatively, the original way traversed left from the foot of the gully (missing the first hard move) and climbed up direct to a break. The blunt rib leads to a delicate and bold step to the "Bull's Horns" on Ordinary Route. Finish up this or more in keeping:-

18   The Krypton Factor   6m   E1   P2
5c   The wall just left of the Bulls Horns provides a harder direct finish to the Eliminate.

19   The Gully   17m   D   P1
The chimney separating Mystery Buttress from Wrinkle Wall offers pleasant climbing.

THE WRINKLED WALL ROUTES

Just to the right of the gully a wide crack leads to a ledge.

20   Wrinkley Arete   15m   HVS   P3
5a   From the left-hand end of the ledge climb the blunt rib, about one metre right of the gully.

21 Wrinkled Wall Direct 15m VS P3 ★
4b Climb up from the centre of the ledge to a smaller one before moving right to finish up a small groove.

22 Wrinkled Wall 15m HVD P1 ★
Step up from the right-hand end of the ledge and climb slightly left passing a smaller ledge before reaching the top.

23 Oblique Crack 15m D P1
This is the wide crack slanting to the right from the foot of Wrinkled Wall.

Across the wide descent gully is a steep wall 9 metres high.

24 Fever 9m E1 P1
5c Climb the obvious groove with hard moves to the break. Finish up the wide crack above.

25 Brinkley Arete 9m E3 P2
6a The right arete of the groove, climbed on the right-hand side.

Just to the right are several excellent short problems.

OVERHANG BUTTRESS

The Overhang Buttresses are to be found 50 metres to the right. The first route here is:-

26 The Zig-Zag 9m VD P1
At the left-hand end of the buttress is a narrow rib. Climb this to the roof then use a good hold to traverse right and gain a platform where several escapes are possible. A poor climb.

27 Canine Fruitbat 15m E5 P2 ★★
6b Starting below the left side of the main overhang the steep wall is climbed on good holds to gain a standing position left of the bulging headwall. Reach up right to a pocket and gain the break followed by a difficult crux mantelshelf.

28 Felicity 9m HVS P2
5a This takes the short , but wide and very overhanging crack in the middle of the buttress. A classic thrutch - If you like that sort of thing!

The large overhang to the right of Felicity has two crack lines, both classic test pieces of their respective eras:-

29 Ceiling Crack 15m E2 P2 ★★
5c With some trepidation gain the left-hand crack, from the left, using what's left of the decaying flakes in the roof. An awkward but

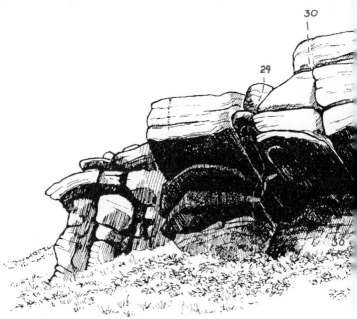

exhilarating move at the lip, on much better rock, is followed by easier climbing to the top.

30 Thirty Seconds Over Winterland 15m E5 P1 ★★★
6b A fine and memorable roof crack, one of the longest on Grit. Start directly below the crack and climb it gymnastically and athletically to gain perfect jams for the final pull into the upper niche. Originally started by swing from the chimney on the right to gain the good jams at E4 6a

31 Slime Chimney 15m VD P1
Climb the corner of the slab and finish up the shallow chimney at the right-hand end of the overhang.

32 Slime Chimney Direct Start HVS P2
5b Totally out of character with the original. Swing ape-like up the overhanging prow to land on a ledge on the original route.

In the recess to the right are two wide cracks, the left-hand crack is graded Very Difficult, P1, and the right-hand crack in the corner is **Easy Chimney** 12m Moderate, P1.

N. Baker.

Immediately right of Easy Chimney is Celebrity Buttress. Three metres from the left edge a shallow groove slants rightwards. The following routes start here.

33 Stage Fright 12m E3 P2
6a From the groove gain a jug then a break. Move up on to the left arete and follow it on rounded holds to the top.

34 Celebrity Buttress 12m VS P1   ★★
5a Follow Stage Fright to the break then move up and gain a vertical crack to finish. Variations; A hand or a foot traverse from the left is also possible, as is the ascent of wide crack slanting up left (the original way). All are similar in grade but different in character.

35 Libel 13m VS P2
5a Reach the break by any of the previous starts or alternatively, the undercut right arete (5c) and traverse right, round the corner. Finish up the small corner on the right wall.

36 Limpet HVS P2
5b The right wall of the buttress has a ledge. An awkward move gains it and another leaves it.

Mid-way between Limpet and the Purgatory Buttress is a small block with a prominant overhanging crack known as **Hargreaves' Route** (4b). At the right-hand end of the escarpment is a tall buttress with a peculiar block perched on top. This is The Guinea Pig or Purgatory Buttress. Piton Wall is just to its left and contains a couple of problems (see Afterthoughts page 688) on the left before:-

37 Piton Crack 10m E1 P1   ★
5b The longer crack, containing tempting pockets, once followed provides a tricky last move.

38 Mantel Madness 10m E3 P2
6a Starting at the same point as Piton Crack, climb delicately to a shallow scoop. Hard moves above this bring the crack on the right within reach, but a direct finish provides more hard moves.

PURGATORY BUTTRESS

This buttress offers some high-class routes and most are bold propositions. On the left wall of the buttress and starting just right of a chimney is:-

39 Alibi 12m HVS P2
5b A ledge at 3 metres has a huge chockstone leaning against it. Gain the ledge from the left before moving right, and round the corner, to join the finish of Artificial Route.

40 Retribution 20m E4 P2
6a Climb the centre of the left wall of Purgatory Buttress via an awkward mantel and leftward reach to gain a flake. Move right to the arete and round it to arrange protection. Step back down and climb the left side of the arete then move further left to finish up the centre of the wall.

41 Pulp Friction 20m E3 P2   ★★
6a The left-hand arete of Purgatory Buttress taken direct. Finish over the bulge on Artificial Route.

42 Afternoon Delight 20m E4 P2   ★
6a Start at a small flake 3 metres from the left edge of the buttress. Climb direct to a good runner placement on Artificial Route. Above, the rock becomes steep, so traverse right, past two old bolts, and step off at the top of the chimney.

43 Swift and Sure 20m E5 P2   ★★★
6b Superb climbing. Start 2 metres left of the chipped holds and climb direct to the good runner on Artificial Route. Move diagonally right on to the rib which leads to a break and a diagonal crack. Move left and over the bulge to finish.

N.Baker

44 Artificial Route 21m VS P3 ★★★
4c A popular climb 'created' before climbers knew better. Follow the chipped holds to good runners where the slab steepens. Move left and climb to a break below the roof. Traverse awkwardly left round the corner and finish on more 'good' holds.

45 Purgatory Problem 18m E5 P3 ★★
6a Just right of Artificial Route, a line of bolt holes leads, above a nasty landing, to two old bolts. Off to the right is the usual finish. However, a bold direct finale up the arete is also possible.

46 Argon and the Final Step E3 P2 ★
6a Start right of and below Alibi. Traverse the slab rightwards to join Artificial Route. Follow this to below the roof, then traverse right and finish as for the direct finish of Purgatory Problem.

47 Purgatory Chimney 16m VD P1
The obvious chimney formed by the edge of the buttress and the block on the right.

The next two routes are amongst the hardest on Gritstone. The last wall on the edge, facing west, provides perfect rock, invariably clean and dry.

48 Reservoir Dogs 13m E8 P3   ★★★
7a The stunning arete is bold and technical to halfway and then steep, harder and more technical above. Rather marginal protection at the top.

49 Widdop Wall 12m E9 P3   ★★
7a Climb the steep technical wall right of Reservoir Dogs boldly to runner placements in slots at half height . Climb the centre of the upper wall on tiny crimps trending right to a desperate finish.

THE BOULDERS

There are many unrecorded boulder problems on the scattered rocks above and behind Mystery Buttress and on the boulders between the overhanging group and Purgatory Buttress. However by far the best of the boulders at Widdop are undoubtedly the eight superb blocks that temptingly catch the sun below Purgatory Buttress. Unlike most of the rest of the crag they can be found in good condition in any season offering a variety of splendid problems, though mainly technical and slabby rather than severely overhanging. Some are long enough to be classed as micro-routes, usually soloed, above generally flat landings. The following is a summary, and selection, of the longest of these mini gems.
P.S. If you don't like the names - feel free to ignore them!

The blocks are numbered 1 to 8 ascending the hillside.

Block One. A 3 to 4 metre square boulder with about 10 pleasant problems mainly in the range of 5a to 5c.

Block Two. A larger block with around 15 identifiable problems up to 6c. Four on the west face are just long enough to qualify as micro routes.

1 Fight On Black 6c ★★ The blunt south west arete.

2 The Runnel 6b ★ The wall just right of the arete with a feint runnel below a hole.

3 The Shelf 5c ★★ A short broken crack leads to a deceptively difficult move to gain the shelving ramp.

4 The Traverse 6a ★ Gain the shelf from the crack and swing left on slopers to a testing move up to the final moves of Fight On Black.

Block Three. A large clean block with a steep west face and a pleasantly slabby south wall.

5 The Big Top 10m HVS P3   ★★
5b Start up the short crack on the north west arete and then hand traverse the rounded top edge of the west face all the way to the apex. Throwing the left leg over reduces the grade but forsaking the edge at the notch halfway to use only the pockets and blind crack to reach the right arete dramatically increases it (to 6b!).

6 Pick-Pockets Wall 6a ★★ The evenly spaced pockets make perfect finger holes for those with small digits. What you do with your feet is another matter!

7 Pick-Pockets Crack 5c ★★★ Similar pockets lead to the short high crack and, theoretically, an easier finish.

8 Fagin's Ridge 5a ★ The right arete of the west face on the steep side.

The slabby south wall, known by some as **Boozer's Slab** has two obvious left slanting grooves, **Mild and Bitter** a Diff and a Severe, but the whole slab can be climbed anywhere at a range of grades - up to 5c if you avoid all obvious holds. The best line is probably;

9 Stout 5b ★★ Pad up the slab, using (or better avoiding) tiny chipped holds, slightly right of the blunt rib in the centre.

Blocks Four and Five together contain about 20 shorter problems including a classy 5b arete **Four Square**, on the western tip of block four and **The Red Edge**, the northern tip of block Five (5c on the left and 6a on the right).

Block Six is the largest boulder with about a dozen lines and some contrived traverses. The 2 obvious cracks are considered by many as real routes with real protection. The arete between them is an absolute classic.

10 The North Face 6m E1 P2   ★
5b The steep slab just right of the crack is harder and steeper than it looks.

11 The Big Crack 6m S P1   ★★
4a Climb the crack - its a classic.

12 Umpleby's Arete 7m HVS P3   ★★★
5a Probably the best 'route' amongst the boulders. The huge arete on the eastern tip has a committing high step - quite high up!

13 The Offwidth 6m HS P1   ★
4a The wide crack on the south east face is a good pitch, but spoils itself by having holds which let you off from the sort of struggle this type of feature usually provides.

A couple of very hard problems climb the wall to the left of the crack and the big easy angled slab on the back of the boulder provides a descent route and potentially long easy lines around V Diff, depending on the line chosen.

Block Seven has around 7 short routes and a couple of traverses, predominantly on the north east face. They include

14 The Seventh Wave 6b ★ The very rounded arete at the lowest point of the boulder.

15 Seven Steps to Heaven 5a ★★ A compelling line from right to left with the hardest move at the start to get established.

16 Seventh Heaven 5b ★★ A high and committing step above the start of the traverse is very satisfying if it works, painful if it doesn't, but more often frustrating as you bottle out.

17 Seven Deadly Sins 6m E2 P3   ★
5c The wall and shallow scoop just right of the pocket.

The flakes below the left end of the boulder provide amusing variations and the low-level traverse is 6b.

Block Eight is a large but easy angled slab, ideal for tiny-tots and absolute beginners to gain confidence in their boots and practice technique. It can be climbed anywhere and is never harder than severe.

WIDDOP DRUMS
Also known as Widdop West these rocks are at the far end of the reservoir, almost on the Lancashire border and probably best approached from the top of the pass. They have been said to resemble a massive jazz drum kit. From the bottom rocks upwards:

The Tom Toms - the two lowest small rocks have a few short moderate/diff problems.

The Bass Drum - the main outcrop.

1 Baby 12m D P1
The lower rocks leading to the obvious wide crack on the bottom face.

2 Gene 12m D P1
A traverse of the same face to either the second crack or the end.

3 Shelley 9m E1 P1   ★
5b The obvious arete.

4 Big Sid 9m VS P1   ★★
4c The crack system just left.

5 Jo Jones 8m E2 P2   ★
5c The centre of the wall starting on chicken heads and moving a
little right at the break, into a crack.

6 Philly Jo Jones 8m E2 P2
5c A direct finish to Jo Jones.

WIDDOP - GRADED LIST

E9
Widdop Wall (7a)

E8
Reservoir Dogs (7a)

E5
Swift and Sure (6b)
Purgatory Problem (6a)
30 Seconds Over
  Winterland (6b)
Canine Fruitbat (6b)

E4
30 Seconds Over
  Winterland (6a)
Afternoon Delight (6a)
Retribution (6a)

E3
Mantel Madness (6a)
Argon and the Final Step
(6a)
Brinkley Arete (6a)
Pulp Friction (6a)
Scratch 'n' Sniff (5c)
Stage Fright (6a)

E2
Ceiling Crack (5c)
The Nature Reserve (6a)
A Trifle Sweet (5c)
Cave Arete (5c)
Dessert (5b)
Seven Deadly Sins (5c)
Neptune (5c)

E1
Fever (5c)
The Krypton Factor 5c
Piton Crack (5b)
The Flake Direct (5b)
The North Face (5b)
Krypton Eliminate (5b)

HVS
Alibi (5b)
Slime Chimney Direct
Start (5b)
Wrinkley Arete (5a)
Limpet 5b
The Big Top (5b)
Wickerwork Crack (5b)
Felicity (5a)
Umpleby's Arete (5a)
The Links Climb (4c)

VS
Curving Crack (5a)
Libel (5a)
Celebrity Buttress (5a)
The Layback (4c)
Artificial Route (4c)
Three Cs (4c)
Birtwhistle's Crack (4c)
Cave Crack (4c)
Wrinkled Wall Direct (4b)

MVS
The Flake (4b)
Wickerwork Wall (4b)

HS
The Offwidth (4b)

S
The Big Crack

MS
Krypton Route

HVD
Wrinkled Wall

VD
Zig Zag
Ordinary Route
Slime Chimney
Purgatory Chimney

D
The Gully
Oblique crack

WOODHOUSE SCAR

SITUATION AND CHARACTER Woodhouse Scar, known locally as 'The Rocks', is located a mile south-west of Halifax town centre just below The Albert Promenade. Situated on the northern edge of the Calder valley it affords interesting views of the local industrial heritage. The outcrop extends for 250 metres, attaining a maximum height of 12 metres. The scar is millstone grit and is essentially sound. Being south-west facing, the crag has a sunny aspect and is fairly sheltered from the elements. However, the trees along the base mean that at times parts of the crag may become green. Delicate slabs contrast with powerful overhangs, whilst the smaller buttresses offer numerous and varied boulder problems. Although all the climbs are fairly short the variety and easy access makes it well worth a visit.

APPROACHES AND ACCESS The scar is best approached from the A646 Skircoat Moor Road. On reaching the open expanse of Savile Park turn down the appropriately named Rocks Road. The rocks are situated below Albert Promenade. Wainhouse Tower, which lies a few hundred metres to the north-west, provides a fine landmark. Ample parking exists along the road. From the town centre A 25-minute walk leads south down Skircoat Road, turn right past the Infirmary and cross Savile Park.

THE CLIMBS The climbs are described from left to right. The seating bays in the wall on Albert Promenade make reference markers to help locate the buttresses. The first climbs, on Cave Buttress, lie directly below the third bay (counting from the Wainhouse Tower end). The flat top of the last, and largest buttress, Spire Rock, is clearly seen between the fifth and sixth bays. Thirty metres to the left of Cave Buttress is a short steep 'warm-up' slab with a corner at its left-hand end. Numerous problems, 4a to 5c give a taste of things to come. Moving along to the real thing, we have:

CAVE BUTTRESS

1 First Chance 11m HS P1
4b Delicately climb the front of the short left arete passing a mantelshelf at half height and finishing up the arete.

2 The Stretch 8m E1 P2 ★
6b The obvious concave wall to the left of Basin Cracks can be climbed, but usually only by giants.

A popular problem just left of Basin Cracks is **Metal Micky** (5c)★.

3   Basin Cracks   11m   VD   P1   ★
The green corner crack leads directly into 'the basin'. Pull out leftwards up the crack and follow easier ground to the top.

4   Chryophorous   11m   VS   P1
5a   The blunt, undercut arete has a hard start until the halfway ledge is reached. Move right and continue up the centre of the wall. The wall just right of the arete is **Johnny One Time** (5c), climbing direct to the ledge via a one finger pocket.

5   Centipede   11m   S   P1
4b   The face just right of centre provides fingery climbing via slots to the ledge. Finish up the right-hand edge of the upper wall.

6   Original Route   11m   VD   P1
Climb the edge of the slab on chipped holds. Move leftwards along the ledge to finish above the basin via a worn crack and wall.

7   Black Wall   8m   VS   P1
4c   The left side of the chimney contains a niche which is passed with difficulty. The steep wall is followed on good holds, avoiding the temptation to bridge out for a rest.

PEBBLE BUTTRESS is recognised by the large detached block 5 metres right of the last climb.

8   Salvage   8m   E1   P2
5c   Just right of the chimney is a short smooth wall which is undercut. Climb directly to the wall and, using a pinch on the arete make a precarious move to gain the ledge. Step right and finish up the upper arete, or the wall to its left.

9   Jetsam   9m   VD   P1   ★
The obvious corner crack gains the top of the block. Traverse boldly left on large holds and climb the arete.

10   Flotsam   9m   VS   P1   ★
4c   Climb the front of the block. Step off the top and pull positively over the bulge to a hold set well back..

11   Cave Crack   10m   VD   P1
The crack system at the right end of the wall is followed to the top. The short wall to the right can be climbed at the same grade.

12   Cave Crack Direct   6m   VS   P1
5c   Two metres to the left is a small pocket. Slap up then follow better holds leftwards to the top.

THE OVERHANG GROUP   This is a large buttress 10 metres to the right of the last climb and is, surprisingly, recognised by a continuous overhang at half height. The first few routes all start from a short prominent crack below the left end of the overhang.

13   The Corner   10m   D   P1
Easily gain the ledge and climb the green corner.

14   Corner Arete   9m   D   P1
Climb to the ledge. Traverse right onto the arete and climb it on positive holds all the way.

15   Pinch   10m   E3   P2   ★
6a Tiptoe up the wall, right of the short crack, and move leftwards to the small cave. Deep breath. Boldly pull straight over and up the middle of the wall.

16   The Lip   10m   VS   P1   ★
4c Climb the worn groove to a small recess. Good underclings allow better holds to be gained above the roof. Pull into the crack and continue to the top.

17   Bisto   10m   HVS   P2   ★★
5a Start 3 metres right at the foot of a layback crack. Move leftwards across the wall. Undercut the roof to reach better holds. Mantelshelf on to the ledge and follow the short crack. A harder variant **Chicken Route** (5b) is alleged to maintain independence just to the right.

18   The Layback   10m   VD   P1
Skate up the corner crack to the roof. Traverse right on big holds. Pull on to the wall and so to the top. A direct start up the blunt arete is **Foster's Arete** 6b.

19   Collie's Crack   7m   S   P1
4b The short, strenuous, green crack rises from the cave and may be thugged by either laybacking or jamming.

20   Perseverance   9m   HVS   P2
5b The undercut nose to the right has a hard, gymnastic start to gain the ledge. Step right and follow the steep face via a pocket and rock-over (committing) trending left towards the top. Several micro-variants are possible.

21   Ogion The Silent   9m   HVS   P2
5c The smooth wall immediately right proves frustrating, with no recourse to holds on the right. From the ledge move right and pull boldly into the scoop and quickly to the top.

The leaning **Gym Boy Wall** to the right can be climbed by any combination of holds, with or without the use of feet.

PITON BUTTRESS is easily distinguished by a steep thin crack on the left side and a large cave at the front.

22 Piton Crack 6m E2 P1   ★★
6b An old classic. The fierce finger crack in the left wall is very difficult to enter but, thankfully, short-lived.

23 Fandango 7m E1 P2   ★
5b Climb the short wall then skip up the leaning arete on rounded pockets.

24 Fairy Steps 8m HVS P2   ★
5b Step off the platform and climb the left arete to a good hold at the break. Intricate moves past a finger pocket lead delicately, and boldly, to the top.

25 Woodhouse Eliminate 10m E1 P2   ★
5b Start above the cave at the right-hand side of the buttress. Sneak along the lip to a large pocket and up to the break. Mantelshelf to the next ledge and climb directly up the wall.

26 The Wobbler 9m E2 P3
5c A much bolder variation of the Eliminate is to climb the wall directly above the first move with a committing mantelshelf to reach the top.

Above the finish of Woodhouse Eliminate is a short, juggy arete above a snappy landing (5a).

27 Piton Ring 13m E2 P1
6b Follow Woodhouse Eliminate to the break. Traverse left, round the arete, to the base of Piton Crack which provides a fitting finale. **The Woodhouse Way** (E3 6b) is a more sustained variant which keeps lower on poor pockets.

28 Close To The Edge E2 P3
6b Start below the right end of the slab. Climb onto it, and finish with a mantle. Hard and technical.

A modern classic roof problem, **Houdini** (7a), attempts to escape from the centre of the cave moving left, and up to a sloper on the slab.

GASHED BUTTRESS   This is 15 metres further right and contains an obvious flake chimney near the left-hand end and a short, thin crack in the centre.

29 Kriss 9m VD P1
The steep wall left of the flake chimney is climbed directly, passing

a scoop at two-thirds height on good holds.

30 Slanting Cleft   10m   S   P1
Starting at the small cave climb up and leftwards. an awkward move at half height gains better holds on the edge of the rib. Squirm stylishly to the top.

31 Ardus Direct   10m   HVS   P3   ★
5b Right of the cave is a blunt arete. Gymnastic moves to the break. Move up slightly right via a chipped hold to join the final moves of Ardus.

32 Ardus   10m   VS   P1   ★★
4c Start just left of Kryton Crack and climb straight to the ledge. Climb up to the roof and traverse left on good jams to where it thins to allow a mantel to the top. Or finish directly over the widest part of the roof at 5a.

33 Kryton Crack   8m   S   P1
Step up and climb the short, thin crack on good finger jams. Finish easily up the corner.

34 The Woolly Jumper Route   8m   HVS
5c The wall between Kryton Crack and Curving Crack from a large slot to a sloper and a difficult pull-up. Easier above.

35 Curving Crack   8m   S   P1
4b The left-hand flake chimney has a hard start but soon eases.

36 Diminishing Crack   8m   S   P1
The short chimney and wall are climbed on good holds.

37 Alpha   8m   VD   P1
The short wall to the right is climbed past a break at half height.

38 Gully Buttress   6m   VD   P1
The squat buttress, separated on either side by a gully, is climbed on its front face.

PYRAMID BUTTRESS is immediately to the right of the last climb and contains a large, scooped cave at two-thirds height and a wide hanging chimney to the right.

39 Afternoon Wall   9m   HVS   P1   ★
5b Start 2 metres left of the arete. Sloping holds lead to a large break at 4 metres. Pull convincingly over the bulge and follow the arete on poor holds.

40 Eagle's Nest Direct   9m   VS   P1   ★★
5a The steep arete provides an interesting start followed by

acrobatic moves leftwards to gain a ledge. Move right on to the edge of the face and climb to the top.

41 Pyramid Wall 10m VS P1   ★
5a Follow the thin crack 2 metres right of the arete to its end. Stretch out left and up to the break to finish directly up the wall.

42 Spread-eagle 11m VS P1   ★★
4b A good climb taking the central line of the buttress. Follow the crack of Pyramid Wall until moves right allow access to the upper crack. Bridging leads to the ledge and a close encounter with a gorse bush. Vacate the ledge by the wide crack.

43 Barker's Wall 11m E1 P1
5b Start 2 metres right of Spread-eagle at an obvious arete. Climb this and the overhang above, moving slightly right.

44 Heavy Duty 11m HVS P2
5b Climb up to the ledge with a difficult rock-over move at half height, then steeply and boldly to the top via a pocket.

45 Destra 10m HVS P1   ★
5b The wide undercut chimney is attained by a series of pulls on widely-spaced holds. Once established in the crack difficulties relent and the top is easily reached.

46 Minotaur 10m E3 P2   ★
6a Climb easily to the overhang using holds on the right wall. Swing out left on to the arete and make a series of committing pulls to gain the ledge with relief. Easy climbing remains to the top

A varied low-level traverse can be constructed between Minotaur and Afternoon Wall. And it stays dry in the rain!

47 Innominate Crack 9m S P1
Climb the obvious thin crack on the right wall until a long reach gives access to the wall above. This is climbed direct past a small tree.

48 Tower Face 10m VD P2
Across the gully is a narrow tower. Climb worn holds on a slab to a ledge. Continue past a small pocket moving leftwards on to the arete for the final moves.

The broken rocks to the right provide a varied excursion at about Difficult standard.

The next section provides fine boulder problems, the first being located behind a small tree is **Mantelpiece** (5b) following the wall to pull over the bulge with difficulty.

Up and right is a delightful smooth wall and upon this is; **Frontis-piece** (4c) Climbed directly on good holds one metre right of the corner. **Sticky Micky** (6c), just to the right provides a technical problem of tenuous cohesion.

Ten metres further right is an undercut nose. **Left-side** (4b) starts on the left to pull over the bulge and finish up the short flake crack. **Undercarriage** (5b) is the front of the buttress, yielding to a hard rock-over followed by nimble moves to the top. **Right-side** (3c) is the recess face direct.

Further along is a prominent arete. **Sinister** (5a) is the left face of the arete on small holds. **L'arete** (5a) is the arete direct. **Droit** (5a) is the wall right of arete trending leftwards. **Tee-Hee** (5b) is the middle of the wall to the right of arete (direct).

Five metres to the right is an undercut mini-buttress with a large oval recess. The next two problems start below this. **The Oval** (5a) Climbs to the ledge via dimples then up and left to the top. **Lords** (5a) Climbs to the right hand end of the recess and finishes direct.

Below the last problem, starting by a vague path, is a short wall and blocky arete which gives a Difficult excursion. There are numerous other shorter problems in this area.

SPIRE ROCK   This is the last of the high buttresses and contains a number of excellent climbs.

49   Monkey Business   7m   HVS   P2
5b   From the ledge on the left side of the great overhang pull up and move leftwards up the wall.

50   Jacob's Ladder   7m   VS   P2
5a   Exciting! Start up the gully on the left of the large roof. Step right and make unprotected moves, above a disproportionate drop, to gain a short break. Finish easily.

51   To Boldly Go   12m   E3   P2
6a   Start just below Jacob's Ladder and cross the roof with difficulty left to right. Pull round on to the face on the right of the arete and climb directly to the top.

52   Clingen   12m   E2   P1   ★★★
5c   A fine climb. Start in the centre of the scooped alcove. Pull directly to a break then ape leftwards along flakes until a stiff pull gains the upper wall. Whilst strength remains sprint the final wall.
Although the flake will take Friends, the brittle nature of the rock means that it is probably better to either top rope or solo the route, otherwise the route could be ruined for those more thoughtful or able.

53   Baboon   11m   HVS   P2   ★

5b The overhung arete right of Clingen is climbed until a difficult move gains a ledge. Trend leftwards on rounded holds.

54   Interface   10m   E2   P2   ★

6a Start 1 metre right of Baboon. Difficult moves are needed to reach the break then climb directly to the top bisecting Baboon and Twin Cracks. Excellent fingery climbing. Protection can be arranged in Twin Cracks.

55   Twin Cracks   10m   VS   P1   ★★

4b Climb the wall on chipped holds to the base of the crack. Good jams lead to a traverse left and the final crack.

56   Parete   10m   HVS   P1   ★★

5b Boulder out the wall to the left of the arete. From the ledge climb directly up the rippled wall. Friends in the breaks give piece of mind.

57   Spigolo   10m   HVS   P2   ★★

5a The steep right arete is climbed in its entirety passing a delicate move at half height.

58   Nervous Shakedown   8m   E4   P2/3   ★

6b Climb the technical, and poorly protected wall between Spigolo and Bull's Delight. The good gear only arrives near the top, well after the crux. Deviations to the arete reduce the grade.

59   Bull's Delight   8m   VS   P1

5a Start 3 metres up the gully. Step on to the wall and climb up and rightwards to gain a thin crack which leads to the top.

Ten metres right is a small buttress. **Greenie's Grunt** (5a) starts at the left end and traverses right to pull round the arete and up the wall. **Headbanger** (6b) pulls directly over the middle of the overhang.

GREEN BUTTRESS   This is 60 metres further along by the side of the main path.

60   Beginner's Crack   8m   D   P1

The prominent chimney is climbed to the top.

61   Green Wall   8m   VS   P1

5c Start in the centre of the wall to the left of the chimney. Pull rightwards over the bulge then step back left and climb delicately up the wall.

62   Beginner's Wall   7m   D   P1

Wander up the broken wall to the right of the chimney.

WOODHOUSE SCAR - GRADED LIST

E4
Nervous Shakedown (6b)

E3
To Boldly Go (6a)
Minotaur (6a)
Pinch (6a)

E2
Clingen (5c)
Close To The Edge (6b)
Piton Ring (6b)
Piton Crack (6b)
The Wobbler (5c)
Interface (6a)

E1
The Stretch (6b)
Fandango (5b)
Barker's Wall (5b)
Woodhouse Eliminate (5b)
Salvage (5c)

HVS
Heavy Duty (5b)
Parete (5b)
Destra (5b)
Baboon (5b)
Fairy Steps (5b)
Ogion The Silent (5b)
Afternoon Wall (5b)
Perseverance (5b)
Monkey Business (5b)
Ardus Direct (5b)
Woolly Jumper Route (5b)
Bistro (5a)
Spigolo (5a)

CONNOISSEUR CRAGS

ADEL CRAG

A boulder in Adel Woods close to the car park on Stairfoot Lane. It
is approximately 5 metres high and provides a limited variety of
both easy and technical problems and of course some traversing.
The first legible ascent of the pinnacles was recorded in 1866 with a
hammer and chisel, subsequent ascents by L.U.F.C. and F★★★.
Team are somewhat less pleasing to the eye. The crag is of
interest for two reasons, firstly is its inclusion in the book Where To
Climb In England by Pyatt in 1960, and secondly the crag is
supposed to have been the inspiration for several Henry Moore
sculptures. *Having lived within a couple of miles of it for some 20
years it never inspired me to put my rock boots on! (Ed.)*

AIR SCAR CRAG

The obvious outcrop visible on the right when driving out of Burnsall
towards Bolton Abbey. It faces North-west and is probably only worth
visiting on mid-summer Evenings. There is one main buttress,
various jumbled boulders, and a hidden crevasse-cum-gully. The
routes are relatively short and no more than mediocre in quality, and
the bouldering is generally disappointing with poor landings. It is
apparent that the gully has been explored and climbed in from the
earliest times judging by the nail scratches but no one thought it
worth recording until Tony Barley and then Tony Simpson made
separate visits in the 1990s and named the following climbs. Park in
a lay-by near the entrance to the woods and follow a footpath up to
the open moor. Turn right and follow the wall for 400 metres then
scramble up rough ground to the crag. About 15minutes from the car.

1 Sack Race 7m S P1
The right-hand wall of the main face between the two obvious crack
lines.

2 Fell Race 8m S P1
The wide crack with a wedge shaped chockstone on the main face
is gained from directly below.

3 In Cahoots 9m VS P1
5a The thin diagonal crack-line is gained from an undercut start
and followed out leftwards to the upper part of the arete to finish.

4 Thick As Thieves 10m E1 P2
5b Start under the nose of the buttress at a loose projection. Climb

steeply up rightwards to gain the face and then move across left under the overlap and step down to gain the nose. Climb the rib on its slabby left side to the top.

5 Bag End 10m E5 P3
6a The arete via the lower bulges. But where does it start?

6 Burnsall Sports 6m E2 P3
5c Start on the left of the nose at a projection and step across right onto the steep face. Move up and reach right to gain the upper slab to finish.

In a bay up and left of the arete are some short scrappy problems but left again and through a crevasse is an obvious overhanging wall.

7 Burnsall Ham 5m E3 P3
5c The centre of the roof is climbed into the scoop above. With a better landing this would make a superb boulder problem.

8 The Greasy Pole 5m E1 P2
5b The lesser overhang and steep fingery wall just right of the hanging rib.

Moving back behind the main buttress is a deep crevasse with walls generally about 6 metres high but only about a metre apart for most of its length. Six routes up to E6 were claimed in here by Tony Simpson but, as at any point it is possible to bridge or chimney, the major difficulty would seem to be to avoid the opposite wall. This area is best suited to climbers looking for safe and unusual Diffs and V.Diffs. which can be contrived at almost any point.

BIRK CRAG   N.G.R. SE 278547

Birk Crag is a series of gritstone buttresses situated approximately 4 kilometres from the centre of Harrogate near Harlow Carr Gardens. The crag faces generally North West and even in summer gets very little sunshine because of the thick woodland setting. The buttresses vary in height from 6 to 15 metres and are of generally good quality gritstone but are, unfortunately, heavily vegetated and will require constant traffic or regular cleaning to keep them in a climbable condition. **The Interflora Slabs area, however, with a little effort could become a useful training ground for school and beginners groups**. The only routes really worth the attention of serious climbers are Ilex Wall Direct and Armpit. The majority of climbs were recorded by Greg Tough, R. Kinnaird and C. Stuttard in 1972 and there is little scope for further development.

From Harrogate take the B6162 Harrogate-Beckwithshaw road

turning right on a minor road towards Harlow Carr Gardens, park in the car park on the left at the end of the road. Approach the crag by following the footpath sign-posted "Birk Crag", at the end of the main path is Crag House and the main 'House Buttress' area is directly below here. Interflora Slabs can be found by following the path to the right (eastwards) along the fence line for about 250 metres whilst Woodpecker Crag lies in the jungle 500 metres left and upstream of Crag House on the opposite bank. Possibly the best time to visit is late spring before the woodland canopy becomes all enveloping.

The climbs are described from left to right when facing the rock.

Interflora Slab

An easy angled, quarried slab suitable for novices. Tree belays or top ropes can be arranged.

1 Wendy 7m VD
Start on the ledge 6 metres above the base of the crag on the left adjacent to a small Silver Birch. Climb straight up to a small overhang which is overcome by a mantelshelf.

2 Fiona 12m D
Start on the ledge above and left of the toe of the buttress. Climb the slab direct.

3 Moira 17m M
Start at the toe of the slab, climb directly to the Birch Tree at 10 metres, finish up the upper slab to the rowan tree.

4 Hilary 12m VD
Start at the narrow gangway 6 metres up and right of the toe of the buttress, straight up for 3 metres move left to mantelshelf by a twin tree. Continue directly up to finish just right of the rowan.

5 Tom 12m VD
Start 6 metres left of Hilary below a short groove. Climb up obvious holds to a heather ledge (the heather now almost reaches the ground) and trend left on good holds to finish right of the rowan.

6 Jerry 12m D
As for Tom to the ledge, step left and go up just right of the overgrown rib.

House Buttress Area

The first four routes climbed the easy angled, but now very vegetated slabs, to the left of the prominent slender pinnacle of Ilex Wall. They would require a mammoth cleaning effort to restore them to their former glory. For the record they were, **Fox Trot** 18m M; **Reptile** 6m VD; **Grapolite** 9m VD; and **Trilobite** 9m VD.

To the right of the slabs, on the right -hand side of the slender pinnacle is the best and cleanest line on the crag;-

7   Ilex Wall Direct   8m   HS   ★
4b Start behind the large holly and climb the slabby rib on the left on good clean rock.

8   Ilex Wall   8m   VD
Climb the wall behind the holly tree finishing with a mantelshelf at the top.

A few metres further right is a buttress directly below Crag House, split into a steep and slabby section by a gully.

9   Rosla   15m   S
The obvious crack just left of the eastern most rib. Ascend the crack and mantelshelf left at 3 metres. Pull into the crack above and ascend this moving left to finish with an interesting move up the front of the left hand pinnacle.

10   Armpit   11m   HVS   ★
5a/b A fine route if the bulge above the overhang is kept clean. It takes the front of the buttress just right of Rosla. Move up to reach undercut holds beneath an inverted rock finger. Layback up to the right and with difficulty attain a bridging position beneath the overhang. Surmount this strenuously with the aid of two pocket holes. Go directly up the front of the remaining wall to the top of the pinnacle.

11   Birk Crack   9m   S
The next crack to the right. Ascend by a chimney to a ledge at 5 metres. Continue up the crack to a dirty finish.

12   Surprise Crack   10m   S
The crack 3 metres right of Birk Crack. Climb up just left of the rib below the crack to a large ledge at 3 metres. Ascend the crack to a heathery finish.

13   Lilac Crack   12m   HS
4a Across the easy gully, on the left wall of the right section of the buttress is an obvious diagonal crack. Climb this to the ledge at 10 metres. Move with difficulty into a wide crack slanting up leftwards and finish by mantelshelfing.

14   Lilac Slab   12m   MS
Start just right of the rib to the right of Lilac Crack. Surmount the wall directly to the undercut. Climb slabs above a to a ledge below

the final crack of Lilac Crack. Finish up just right of this.

15 Girdle Traverse 31m MS

When clean this was described as an extremely enjoyable route. It started 5 metres right of the start of Lilac Slabs and finished by crossing Armpit above the crux bulge to reach the final moves of Rosla. If you can find any rock in between consider it a bonus!

Further to the right, next to the path are the easy House Slabs, very suitable for absolute beginners. Below these and to the left is a slab which has at its base a peculiar spider-like tree. This is:-

16 Joan's Climb 8m VD

Ascend this slab (without the help of the tree) which eases towards the top.

17 Epilobium 8m HD

This is a similar slab about 10 metres to the right of Joan's Climb. The route goes up the centre of the slab by obvious holds.

Right of Epilobium, and on a level with House Slabs, is a large loaf-shaped boulder. The next climbs start below this.

18 Generalissimo 10m S

Climb up the centre of the long low slab below the boulder, then take the layback crack up the right hand side of the boulder.

19 Trotter 8m M

Lies 10 metres below and to the left of the base of Generalissimo. Climb along a narrow slab to finish with a move up onto a sharp horizontal arete.

Woodpecker Crag

This is a steep buttress heavily disguised as a mound of moss, half a kilometre further right and on the other side of Oak Beck.

20 Woody Woodpecker 10m S

Ascend about 2 metres left of the right hand rib. The hard move is on the steep section 3 metres below the top.

21 Woodpecker Crack 10m VD

This is the obvious crack in the centre of the buttress.

22 Firefly 10m D

Ascend the obvious holds approximately 1 metre left of Wood-pecker Crack.

23 Brush-Off 8m D

This lies on an isolated buttress 18 metres to the left of Firefly. The way is obvious (if you Brush it Off again!)

BLAKE DEAN PINNACLE   N.G.R. SD 958314

A large split block in the valley quite close to the Scout Hut at Blake Dean. It can be seen from the road when approaching Widdop from Heptonstall. From the parking place near the hut walk down the hill, through the metal gate and cross the stream via the bridge. Turn upstream and the crag comes into view again on the right after 200 metres. The pinnacle has a sheltered sunny aspect and offers ten short but pleasant routes and some problems. All the lines were soloed and named by Malcolm Townsley in November 1994 but he acknowledges that most if not all may have been climbed before. They are described from left to right starting from the northern end.

1   North Face   VD
The wall on the north face.

2   Blocked Nose   VD
The undercut nose on the north-west corner is gained from the adjacent block and climbed trending left.

3   Nose and Slab   VS
5a The nose is gained from the ground and the slab above climbed direct.

4   Gang Of Four   E1
5b The crack cutting through the overhang at the left side of the main face. Start from the block, or better at the back underneath.

5   Squeaking Wall   E1
5c The wall to the right of Gang Of Four trending slightly right at the top. Try not disturb the resident bats!

6   Old Chimney Variant   VS
4c The wall left of the central chimney then into the upper chimney to finish.

7   Old Chimney   S
4b The main chimney.

The overhanging wall to the right is unclimbed.

8   Guano Corner   HVS
5b The obvious slabby corner at the right end of the main face to a ledge, then the slabby wall above.

9   Nose And Arete   VS
5a The awkward nose then the easier arete at the south end of the crag, started from the stream side.

10   Hanging Arete   MVS
4b The back wall and arete around right from Nose and Arete.

There are several problems on the back wall and a good low-level traverse leftwards from Squeaking Wall. A smaller block down stream also offers a couple of easier routes and more problems.

BURLEY WOODHEAD QUARRY   N.G.R. SE 145452

The quarry lies on the moor above Burley Woodhead a few hundred metres above the moor road to the Cow and Calf. There is parking for cars on the left before the hairpin bends, from here follow the track up onto the moor and into the quarry, if you must. Initial development took place in the early seventies when several routes were climbed by John Harwood and John Syrett. These were recorded in the 1973 L.U.C.C. Journal, and are described below, however part of the line of Chicken Finger has become one of the latest in a long line of horizontal classics. The remaining lines have been repeatedly claimed since the dawn of time, the names of Paul Dawson , Andy Bowman and Mark Radtke standing out as the most persistent.

The climbs are described from left to right.

1 Fragility   12m   VS
4c The loose groove bounding the smooth and highest point of the left wall.

2 Slanting Arete   12m   VS
Start on the wall right of Fragility and move up to diagonal ledges leading back to the arete. Unprotected. The direct start is 5b. Climb the arete direct to the ledges.

3 Fish Fingers   12m   E3
6a Climb the thin crack left of where Chicken Finger used to be.

4 Chicken Finger   12m   HVS
5a Climb the obvious crack in the open right facing corner, it is now possible to climb the top part first.

5 Disappointment   12m   HVS
5a Climb the obvious line between the corner at the back of the bay and Chicken Finger.

6 Cod Piece   8m   E3
5c Climb the thin flake and the crack in the right wall, approximately 5 metres right of the corner.

7 Soul Food   8m   HVS
5b Climb broken cracks in the wall right of Cod Piece.

8   Hermits Hole   8m   HVS
5a Start right of Cod Piece and climb direct out of the prominent
hole and then up the slab trending left.

9   The Greaser   12m   E2
5b Takes the right arete of the right wall via a slab and thin crack
with more slab climbing on the upper arete. Sustained, badly
protected, but escapable at half height.

10   Green Streak   5m   HVS
5c Climb the light green streak on the short right wing terrace.

11   Two Ten Job   6m   E1   P3
5b The shallow groove 2 metres right of Green Streak.

BRUNTHWAITE   N.G.R. SE 059463

Overlooking Silsden on the end of Addingham High Moorside is
Brunthwaite Crag, approach from Ilkley along the A65, Ilkley -
Skipton road, turn left up Cocking Lane, at the second cross-roads
turn left up Light Bank Lane follow the road until it drops down
towards Silsden, park halfway down the hill on the right where a
footpath leads off through a gate on the right. Go through the gate
and then almost immediately through a second gate on the right,
continue diagonally across the hillside to the crag. The crag
comprises a broken natural edge which leads into a slabby quarry
at its left end. The quarry has several easy angled aretes and
corners and a flat grassy base, it is about 8 metres high and the
cracks are a little overgrown. The natural edge is about 6 metres
high and broken, but provides some easy routes and scrambling for
novices along with a few technical problems. Below the natural
edge at the right-hand side is an extremely weathered buttress with
a classic Hard Severe up its front face.

CALVERLEY QUARRY   N.G.R SE 201377

The quarry is situated in Calverley Wood about one and a half
kilometres north-east of Greengates. After passing through Calverley
Village, when approaching from Leeds along the A657 an avenue
leads off on the right where cars can be parked. After walking down
the avenue you pass under a bridge to enter a steep sided ravine
offering some dirty traversing, from the end of the ravine follow a
track rightwards through the wood to the main quarry. The quarry,
normally dirty due to drainage from above, is generally slabby though
there are steep corners, cracks and roofs, none of which could be
described as redeeming features. The large roof has been climbed

and claimed several times by Uncle Tom Cobley and all. The quarry attains a height of 15 metres and an easy gully behind the main buttress is useful as a descent. Originally a haunt of the whack and dangle brigade and recently used by various graffiti artists, the crag is presently home to a few old copies of Playboy, several used condoms and an old washing machine.

DRUIDS ALTAR   N.G.R. SE 093399

Situated on Harden Moor with spectacular views over the Aire Valley, the name fires the Imagination but the eyes behold the reality. Approach from Bingley along the B6429 towards Harden, after 200 metres a track on the right (Altar Lane), marked "Unsuitable for vehicles" leads after 1.5 kilometres onto the top of the moor where several tracks meet. The top of the crag lies just across the field to the right. The rock is fairly clean gritstone and is an apparently quarried edge which varies between eight and ten metres high. The left side is split by numerous cracks and chimneys. At the extreme right hand side is a large cubic block offering some highly technical face climbing problems.

EARL SEAT   N.G.R. SE 071584

This is the crag you've all seen, and wondered about, during the walk back down from Simon's Seat towards Howgill. There is no clear path to it and the best approach seems to be straight up (south-east) after emerging from the woods at the top of the steepest part of the Howgill track. The rock is clean and rough - and possibilities still exist!

1   Jams To The Slaughter 7m   HVS   P1   ★★★
5b A classic crack climb based on the left side of the left arete of the largest buttress.

2   Crack With A View 7m   S   P1
The central crack-cum-chimney feature provides one interesting move but possibly the best belay view in the Yorkshire Dales.

3   Entrance Exam 5m   E1   P1   ★
6a The bottomless crack in the right wall of the gully provides a good test of tenuous jamming.

4   Pebble Pincher 6m   E2   P2   ★★
6b The left arete of the right-hand buttress climbed mainly on the left. Treat the pebbles with care - they are all crucial - as is a long reach!

An excellent problem **Knobbles In Toyland** (5c) climbs the right wall on rusty excrescences.

ELDWICK   N.G.R. SE 124423

A small outcrop and quarry on the south side of Ilkley Moor just
above Dick Hudson's. It boasts a handful of problems and micro
routes together with a couple of short traverses. None are worth
travelling far for.

GORPLE   N.G.R. SD 931315

A well spread collection of boulders and escarpments above and
beyond Widdop on Shuttleworth Moor overlooking Gorple reservoirs. The rock is good rough gritstone and, due to its constant
exposure to the lashing westerly gales, is usually clean. The largest
crag is situated about one mile south - west of Widdop and the best
approach is from there. Cars can be parked by the dam, cross the
dam and walk along the far shore to the end of the plantation, from
here a track leads up onto the moor and eventually to a sign post
where two tracks meet. The most prominent crag can then be seen
on the left. There are several good problems and micro-routes but
the only 3 known to be named and deserving full route status are;

1 Eternal   10m E7 P2   ★★★
6b The striking and very overhanging arete on the most prominent
buttress is climbed from the right.

2 Carmen Picasso   10m E9 P3   ★★★
6c The same arete but climbed more directly on its left side is
harder, and the protection even more dubious.

3 Louise   6m E4 P3   ★
6a The shorter wall around to the left of the arete is still a bold
proposition.

The best bit of the crag for bouldering and some good micro-solo-
classics is a little lower down midway between the two Gorple
Reservoirs. This area can be reached directly from the track which
leaves the road about half a mile south of the Widdop car park and
skirts the northern edge of the Lower reservoir. It is however in full
view of two shooting boxes so it may be sensible to avoid the
shooting season.

GREETLAND QUARRY - WEST VALE   N.G.R. SE 094215

A locally popular and excellent training ground, well worth visiting to
test the digits on its technical traverses. If the low level tendon
tearers prove too testing there's usually an easier solution, the only
penalty being that it will be to the top of the crag. A considerable

number of vertical routes have been climbed but they are little
more than serious boulder problems. Most are identified in the
specialist bouldering guides. The crag is a long clean cut quarried
wall of good quality gritstone, rising from a pleasant grassy bay.
Approach the crag from West Vale and at the traffic lights take the
Rochdale Road. After 350 metres turn right up Road End, cars can
be parked opposite The Star public house, continue up the hill and
right along Dean End bearing left up into the Quarry. Don't let the
graffiti put you off - its part of the traditional charm of the place!

HAVARAH PARK   N.G.R. SE 250534

A small outcrop and associated boulders close to Ten Acre
Reservoir in Haverah Park near Beckwithshaw. Approach by a 20
minute walk along a pleasant track from directly opposite the cricket
ground in Beckwithshaw village towards Springhill Farm. There are
small boulders close to the path but the main attraction is a larger
block towards the left of the dam easily approached along a
subsidiary path. Several boulder problems and a handful of micro
routes are on offer and the picnic possibilities are good for family
outings.

HIGH CRAG (Stump Cross)   N.G.R. SE 090627

A low west-facing edge overlooking Stump Cross Caverns. There
are around 40 low to medium grade problems and short routes
suitable for beginners but little scope for anything harder. The
aspect is pleasant and the rock clean. Documented by Malcolm
Townsley in 1994

HOLMFIRTH - THE CLIFF   N.G.R SE 148086

SITUATION AND CHARACTER
High above the small town of Holmfirth hides a shy little crag known
as 'Cliff'. Cliff features many technical aretes and face climbs
usually approached as extended boulder problems. It is, allegedly,
home to over one hundred and seventy seven short routes,
problems and traverses . In places 'Cliff' rises to over 6m high and
faces north west, well worth an evenings visit if in the area. The
rock is generally good quality quarried grit with a friable top layer,
but don't be put off by this, with a bit of practice this can soon be
mastered, or avoided.

The Cliff is split up into four areas: The main crag which comprises two equal sections and consists of a series of bays separated by a number of sharp aretes. This peters out into lower walls suitable for bouldering. The left half is known as The Lost World which is slightly overgrown and un-cared for (which will hopefully change one day), and The New World is the right hand half which is the most popular part of the crag. On the far right past the end of the main crag lies Ix. This is a small bouldering area just below the top footpath. Endor lies at the far left side of Cliff past the main crag and on the top footpath. It consists of a few small outcrops which are suitable for bouldering.

The rocks have been known to locals and climbed on for over 30 years but never before considered worthy of detailed description. The following notes come courtesy of Daimon Beail who devoted a year of his life to the place in 1997 and collated names from several sources for a comprehensive bouldering type guide. The sample below should get you started.

APPROACHES AND ACCESS
Take Dunford Road out of Holmfirth and turn immediately left up South Lane. Drive up the hill and take the second turning left up New Laithe Lane to the top. In front and to the left is a track. Park here and walk along the track to the crag. Access has never been a problem but please give consideration to the local residents, whose houses are overlooked by the crag and please respect their parking facilities.

The Main Crag
Right in the centre of the crag on the extreme left of the New World is a small easy angled face with an obvious crack running just left of centre. This is known as the Baby Face and is a useful reference for locating the routes, which are described from left to right.

The Lost World
The routes described are on the two buttresses left of the Baby Face.

1 Pob 6m E1
5b This is on the left-hand buttress and is easily identified by the two obvious pockets half way up the face. Climb the centre of the face to the two pockets and gain the ledge. Move up and right for a sloping hold and climb direct to the top.

2 Miles Apart 6m E1
5b The centre of the right-hand buttress. Climb the obvious line with interesting balancey moves.

The New World
The first routes are on the Baby Face.

3   I.F. 4a Left of the crack.

4   Nora's Batty 4a The crack.

5   Bumbachum 4c Right of the crack.

6   Baloo 4a Just right of Bumbachum.

Right of the Baby Face is an arete. The right-hand side of this is
Candlestick Arete 6a.

The right face of the next buttress gives three good problems.

7   Silent Running ★★ (5c) The bulge on chipped holds.

8   Grand Central ★ (6c) The centre of the wall.

9   Moois The Moo 4c The obvious crack on the right.

To the right of the corner is a face with a crack running through it.
This is:

10   Newton's Law ★★ 5b The dogleg crack. Move right to finish.

11   King Razz ★★ 5c Climb the arete using two holds on the left
wall. Traverse left at the top.

12   At Your Own Risk 5b Just right of the arete climb the small
ramp and then move directly up to a jug. Climb to the roof and cross
it with extreme care and respect on the right, NOT the left. The
direct start goes at 5c. This route, although good, has not had that
many ascents and is a bit loose, so climb it at your own risk.

13   Shades Of Orion 8m   E1   ★★
5b A classic route which climbs via small flat holds on the right of
the wall to the sandy basin. Move up and slightly left to reach a hold
on the corner under the roof. Move right to a juggy ledge and climb
directly to the top passing a peg on your left.

Away and to the right is an obvious arete that looks like a witch's
nose. This is **Uncle Lubin** (5a). Start on the right side with an
overhanging start and so to the top.

The next buttress gives an interesting route on the right face:

14   Seeking Sanctuary 5b Climb the right-hand crack to the
upper wall. Climb this using good holds on the left.

To the right is an area which drops down to give a longer wall and
some extreme routes.

15   The Postman   10m   E2
5c Climb the juggy flake crack to reach undercuts under the roof.
Reach for the letterbox hold right of the rusty peg and climb straight
up taking care at the top.

A little way right is an overhanging bouldering area with some
excellent problems, of which Daimon recommends:

16   Yendor ★★ (5c) This is a fantastic traverse which starts in
the right corner and moves left using pockets above the upper
overlap. Move down past the arete and under the roof, finishing up
the nose at the end.

The last section of the crag is at the far right hand end. The little
overhanging section contains:

17   Sinbad ★ (6a) Climb the centre of the wall with difficulty via
two flat holds. Go over the first little roof to a large chalked hole,
then make some tricky moves over the second roof to finish.

18   Trance Atlantic ★★ (5c to 6b) The aim of this adventure is to
traverse the entire crag in one go, in either direction. In certain
sections it becomes disjointed but please persevere. It takes an
hour or two to complete and there are several variations. The
principle aim is to avoid touching the top or the ground. Good Luck1

HONLEY QUARRY   N.G.R. SE 126121

Honley village is midway between Huddersfield and Holmfirth. If
approaching from Huddersfield turn right into the village centre and
after a quarter mile turn right down the lane below the library
trending right again at the first fork. Continue down hill passing an
old mill complex and fork left up a wooded lane to a lay-by 150
metres further on. Follow a path up through the trees on the left.
The quarry is box shaped with a subsidiary bay on the left. The
harder routes, on the right wall, are well established and most have
been repeated. They are generally cleaner than the easier routes,
which are described here for the first time and may not have been
repeated. All are described anti-clockwise around the bays from the
'tower' at the right end of the impressive right wall. With a little
effort, a good brush and a pruning saw, the area could provide a
reasonably varied venue. The rock quality is good but a lack of
traffic has resulted in rapid re-generation of vegetation. There is
plenty of scope for further development.

1   My Brain is In The Cupboard   9m   E3   ★★
5c The right arete of 'The Tower' to a grassy ledge. Start on the
right and finish on the left.

2 Undilutable Slang Truth 16m E6 ★★
6c The centre of the obvious tower to the right of the leaning wall. Start up the zigzag finger crack and finish up a short crack utilising a small tree to gain the final break.

A few metres to the left the face stands proud and overhangs. The right hand end of this face, just right of the arete, contains:-

3 Joker Hysterical Face 13m E4 ★★
6b The slabby looking wall immediately right of the arete. Attain a standing position on the sloping ledge and make technical and intricate moves right to gain a break. Lean out and finish by a tree.

4 Jesus Loves America 15m E3 ★★
6a Climb the hanging nose and bulging arete from the right, starting up a fragile flake, then a crack to a pocket on the left. Finish more easily.

5 Millions of Dead Christians 15m E4 ★★
6c The wall 3 metres right of the central crack. A depressingly difficult start up a thin finger-crack may eventually lead you to the break. A pull up to a jug and then easier moves rightwards lead to the arete and the top.

6 The Dogs Biscuits 15m E4 ★★
5c The stunning central crack line. Allegedly a major classic. The name has been changed to protect our younger readers.

7 Straight Outta Cleckheaton 15m E5 ★★
6b The wall left of the central crack trending right to the crack of the previous route near the top.

8 My God Rides A Skateboard 13m E4 ★★
5c The left arete of the leaning right wall, climbed somewhat strenuously on the right.

9 Triple Bad Acid 13m E2 ★
5c The arete, climbed more directly from inside the chimney. Hand traverse out and swing round to the right, then make a difficult move up left to a break. Finish, via a small cave, to a tree.

10 Shedpoojsize 13m E2 ★
5b The blunt flake line left of the arete in the centre of the back wall of the quarry. Finish between the saplings.

The following route descriptions were provided without technical grades or star ratings. Some of the lines look worthwhile but grades should not be taken at face value.

11 Sue's Chimney 15m HVD
A tight squeeze up the back left corner.

12 Jammer 15m HVD
Working left across the left wall the first feature is a jamming crack.

13 What Tree 15m HS
The next crack to the left is followed to loose ground. Trend right to finish.

14 Elasta Plast 16m HVS
The crack in the centre of the left wall is followed leftwards to the top.

15 Bottle Neck 15m MS
The narrowing chimney has a good finish on the left.

16 Tress Pass 15m MVS
Follow crack to first tree. Trend right to crack below second tree and follow this to finish.

17 Arete's Revenge 15m VS
Follow arete keeping right.

18 Arete Edge 15m MVS
The left side of the arete.

The climbs now continue in the same direction around the subsidiary bay on the left.

19 Birch Climb 14m MVS
Start in front of the Birch, just left of the arete, and follow cracks and a flake to the top.

20 Sticky Bun 15m E1
Start at the mid point of this wall following a small crack before trending right on the flake.

21 Sore Fingers 15m E1
As for Sticky Bun but climb the continuation of the crack and the upper flake on the left.

22 Watch Yer Back 15m E1
Start at the bottom left side of this wall, beneath an overhang, and follow flakes and breaks to the top.

The back wall of the subsidiary bay provides generally well protected routes with good belay stakes sunk well back.

23 Smoking Slab 13m E1
The exception as far as protectability. Start on the right and climb direct to a stout birch..

24 Escape Route 10m VD
Climb the short chimney and continue to the right of the 'bricked-up' cleft above.

25 White Crack   13m   MVS
Start left of the chimney at a square pocket. Step right and follow a crack to the top, left of a small tree.

26 Zig And Zag   12m   MVS
Follow the zigzag crack on good holds (just left of white paint). Good protection.

27 Square Head Phil   12m   MVS
The crack just right of the corner chimney.

28 Joe's Chimney   D
Back and Foot the chimney. Exit left.

29 Ladders   8m   VD
A direct line on the wall just left of the Chimney.

30 The Devil's Steps   10m   MVS
From the foot of Ladders climb diagonally left following the 'steps' in the rock.

31 Phil's Traverse   15m   HVS
Start on the left, near the entrance to the bay, and below a small overhang. Traverse right and up, following beneath small square pockets to exit at the top of Ladders.

HUGENCROFT   N.G.R. SD 924275

This small, clean, pleasant gritstone outcrop is situated on Stansfield Moor just off the Hebden Bridge-Burnley Road about 400 metres past the Sportsman's Inn. Climbing on the crag has been banned for some considerable time and due to the close proximity to the crag of the landowner's home attempts to climb usually end in confrontation.

LINDLEY MOOR QUARRY   N.G.R. SE 102188

The crag lies in the lee of the M62 motorway between junctions 23 and 24, below the cricket ground, and overlooking Elland. When travelling west leave the motorway at junction 24 and drive towards Rochdale on the A643, turn right down the minor road just after the Wappy Spring public house. Park just on the right after passing under the motorway. The crag starts just round the left hand bend and comprises two large quarried bays linked by a short wall, after the second bay the crag continues as an intermittent natural edge offering some short boulder problems. The peg scarred cracks remain as a testament to the enthusiastic efforts of previous generations not to mention the numbers painted at regular intervals along the bottom of the crag. The quarries attain a height of about ten metres and the routes are obvious though no one, to my knowledge, has ever bothered to write them up.

LITTLE ALMSCLIFF   N.G.R. SE 232523

Though relatively close to its larger namesake, Little Almscliff is disappointing from a climbing point of view . There is one steep block of about 5 metres and a few of lesser height. It is however a scenic and popular picnic spot where limited bouldering can be enjoyed whilst children can play and scramble in relative safety. The best approach is by a two minute walk from a lay-by on the Beckwithshaw to Norwood Road, though a one mile walk through the woods from the top of Norwood Edge on the Washburn Valley side is also quite enjoyable.

LONGWOOD EDGE   N.G.R. SE 104174

Situated on the North West side of Huddersfield just off the M62 motorway. When travelling West leave the motorway at junction 23 and drive along the A640 towards Huddersfield, turn right after 1.0 kilometre down Longwood Edge Road, straight on for about 1.5 kilometres and the crag can be seen on the left. All but the ardent connoisseur would at this point proceed to the nearest pub, however, boldly going where few have been before, press on through the undergrowth armed with a machete. The crag is shielded by trees growing close to its base, it is about 11 metres high and offers a variety of climbing. Anybody keen enough to climb here should also note the other esoteric gem, back up the hill and below the road is another quarry that attains even greater height and even greater anonymity. Its only redeeming feature is, at its left end, adjacent to the footpath is a short clean buttress with six good problems.

LORD'S SEAT   N.G.R. SE 085599

This crag, 500 metres north-west of Simon's Seat, has been mentioned in every Yorkshire Gritstone guide since 1957 but its routes and problems have never previously been documented. The rock is excellent and clean giving a variety of enjoyable routes and problems. The routes recorded below are all between five and ten metres in height but most were soloed during 'eleventh-hour' checking for this guide, hence the absence of P grades. Protection placements appeared sparse but the landings are invariably good. The crag catches any available sunshine and the venue is an ideal picnic spot.

Only the most obvious lines have been described. They are listed from left to right, first along the upper tier and then along the lower level. Finally the separate buttress beyond the boundary wall completes the collection.

1 Slab and Crack VD
Climb the slab, trending left to finish up cracks.

2 Slab and Overlap MVS
4b The slab and the crack in the bulge above it.

Set back in a left facing bay is.

3 Harvey S
Climb the wall left of the crack on satisfying holds.

4 The Crack S
Follow the most obvious crack.

5 Wallbanger VS
4c The wall right of The Crack to a steep finish.

6 The Slab VS
4b The delicate slab to the right. Starting direct is 5c.

Back on the line of the main edge is

7 Overhang Direct HVS   ★
5c The prominent overhang provides several variants and a swinging traverse.

8 Hanging Groove S
Climb leftwards out of the cave then the groove above it.

9 Gritstone Special HVS   ★
5a Traverse rightwards out of the cave to the obvious hanging, prickly, crack. The name is most appropriate. **Tranquility** (5b) climbs through the roof direct.

Just right of a large boulder is a pleasant wall.

10 Flake And Wall VS   ★
Climb the flake to the ledge. Then the wall above.

11 Mantel Fantastic HVS   ★★★
5a Climb directly up the arete, just right of Flake And Wall, via a mantelshelf move. Finish boldly above.

12 Grit Crack S   ★
The excellent crack just to the right.

13 Bulging Wall HVS   ★★
5b The wall just right again. Climb directly over the large bulge and

finish to the right of the crack.

Further right and slightly forward of the edge is an obvious arete, corner and slab. Right again and set back is a pocketed wall.

14   Three Pocket Wall   VS
4c Climb the wall using five ? pockets.

The final prow on the right gives a good 5a problem.

At the left -hand end of the lower level is a large cave.

15   Traverse And Arete   S
Traverse awkwardly rightwards out of the cave then follow the arete.

16   Ripple Wall   VS
4b Climb the rippled wall just right of the arete.

The arete just right again gives an excellent problem at 5b and the short crack is 4c. Sixty metres right of Ripple Wall is a buttress with a wide smooth overhang.

16a   Serenity   E1
5c Start on the left of the buttress and hand traverse right to make an awkward move to reach a large, soil filled pocket. Climb the slab above to finish. The pocket can also be reached from the right by bridging.

17 Pebble Wall VS
4c Start just right of a hanging nose at 3 metres. Climb awkwardly on pebbles to a shelf and finish easily.

18 Layback Left VS
4c The obvious lay-back crack finishes by traversing left to the shelf. This clearly avoids more macho rightward possibilities!

19 Larkin's Right E1 ★★
5b Start as for Layback Left but, using jams and the shelf above, gain the ledge on the right. (Check for skin on the back of hands!) Move right and finish via a large hole on top. An alternative finish **No Larkin About** pulls back left onto the nose to a more exposed finale but still the same grade.

20 Pocket Wall VS ★
4c The large boulder to the right has an obvious pocket. Step into this, then straight up to finish.

21 Pocket, Traverse And Arete HVS ★★
5a Step into the pocket then traverse right to a smaller pocket at the same level. Finish up the arete.

21a Solitaire HVS ★★★
5c Climb directly through the 'Pocket Traverse' and use a large pebble to reach the top. Brilliant

Wall Buttress is the collection of rocks beyond the boundary wall to the north described from left to right.

22 Lay-Away MVS ★
4b The compelling crack yields to…. the clues in the name.

23 Jammed Sandwich S ★★
A classic. 'Jam' the initial crack and get 'sandwiched' in the chimney above.

24 Pump Friction E2 ★★
6a The hanging slab is gained by the short wall. A Friend 4 protects the precarious moves to stand on the slab. An easier step gains the top. An easier variant skirts the roof on the right of VS 5a.

The next buttress, set a little further back contains:

25 Nice Mover VS ★
5a Starting from a small ledge move up on small edges trending right.

26 Pure Gold E1 ★★★
5c The undercut cracks are gained by strenuous lay-backing followed by steep jamming.

27   Steppin' Out   E1   ★★
5b   Start just right of the arete and use surprisingly good holds to 'step out' onto the arete proper. Rock over with confidence and climb more easily to the top.

28   Steppin' Up   S
Pleasant moves up the line of flakes.

28a   Groovy Baby   S
The short groove in the corner.

29   Fascinating Pockets   HVS   ★
5c   The boulder furthest back lures the unsuspecting by its 'fascinating pockets. Gaining them is easy - leaving them (upwards) is not!

LULBECK CRAG   N.G.R. SE 139727

A remote outpost facing west on Fountains Earth Moor above Ramsgill in Upper Nidderdale. The best approach is as for Sypeland and Ash Head Crags, following the moorland track from the road and turning right at the second junction. Follow this track for about a mile and park just before second gate. The crag is then a ten minute walk up to the left. There are eleven short routes and problems here from 4a to 5c on good rock. The best are **Lullaby** (5b) which takes the bulging crack from the left, **Ready Brek** (5b) Via a pocket over the first bulge finishing leftwards and **Beckon** (5a) The bulging rib and top arete on the right-hand side. All are the work of Tony Barley in 1993 and 1995.

MIXENDEN   N.G.R. SE 070272

A series of crags and quarries, facing west, above Crag Lane in Mixenden near Halifax. About 50 routes and several problems adorn this urban landscape as do several old mattresses, bike frames and other assorted rubbish. The best time to visit is probably during school hours in term time to avoid the cheery? attention of small children?? Its a shame really, the climbing is quite good.

MYTHOLM STEEP QUARRY   N.G.R. SD 979277

Mytholm Steep lies in the trees, almost facing Heptonstall Quarry across the valley. It is a steep cliff of good solid gritstone and as the road is only a 20 metre 'hike' away, it is easily accessible should you wish to drop in, if only to do the minor-crag classic; Revolution. Access is open. The crag is reached from Church Lane on the main Todmorden - Hebden Bridge road. Church Lane is 400 metres on the 'Tod' side of the Heptonstall road in Hebden. A kilometre of steep hill leads to a hairpin bend left and the quarry is on the right. Most of the lines are the work of Bob Whittaker and friends; the classic Revolution in 1966 and the best of the harder routes, Edge of Extinction in 1981.

The climbs are described from right to left.

1 Spider Crack 14m S
Climb the arete for a metre or so, then move diagonally right to a thin crack. At the top swing left and finish direct.

2 Tree Groove 14m VD
Start as Spider Crack, but continue up a groove to finish left of a tree.

3 Prospector 15m HVD
Climb the corner on the left to a small roof, then move right and finish as Tree Groove.

4 Swastika 15m S   ★
The crack on the left leads to another crack on the left and then a ledge. Follow the right curving crack above to a short corner, and finish up this.

5 The Edge of Extinction 17m E2   ★★
5b Start in the same place as Swastika and hand traverse left to gain a good ledge on the arete. Make a hard mantel onto a break, then climb a steep wall to a large ledge which crosses the centre of the face. Climb the arete above, moving right for the last 2 moves to finish at a small tree. N.B. On the first ascent a very high runner was placed in Swastika for the top section of the climb. On the second ascent a situ PR was placed on the arete.

Around on the front to the left is an obvious wide chimney.

6 The Rift 20m VS
4c Climb the chimney to the ledge which crosses the face, then move up and left to cracks running through an overhang, and finish up these.

7 Revolution 24m HVS   ★★
5a The large corner on the left. Awkward to start and finish, with the crux being surmounting an overhang 3 metres below the top.

Around the arete to the left is a wide overhanging crack a metre or so off the floor, this gives:-

8 Turncoat 26m VS
Climb the crack to a slabby niche on the left. Up this and then move right into a grassy chimney. Follow this to the top.

In the centre of the quarry behind the rowan tree, easily spotted by the ship's bow shaped rock lies;

9   Keel Haul   19m   S   P1
Climb the blocks to the bow and with an awkward step move left and up to the first ledge. Continue up to a second ledge where a hidden hold makes topping out a pleasure.

10   The Bender   12m   HVS
5a   The obvious slanting layback crack on the left-hand buttress is much harder than it looks.

MYTHOLM EDGE   N.G.R SD 980279

This collection of edges line the rim of the valley opposite Heptonstall Quarry. They are of solid gritstone, some being slabby whilst others are steep with stiff wall and crack climbs. Access and approach are as for Mytholm Steep Quarry, from the quarry follow paths below and to its right, contouring round to the buttresses. There are many problems and short routes, the most notable being on the largest buttress. A slab on its left gives V Diff to VS climbing according to line whilst the overhanging corner roughly central to the buttress gives a stiff HVS 5b. A line left of this via a corner then a long traverse left gives another HVS.

NORLAND EDGE   N.G.R. SE 058218

An edge of small quarries and isolated boulders just above Shaw Lane between the villages of Norland and Barkisland, high above Sowerby Bridge on the southern rim of the Calder Valley. Though north-west facing it is a pleasant spot on open moorland providing some quality bouldering and a number of short solos up to 7 metres high. Park near the Moorcock Inn. Access is unrestricted.

NORTH NAB   N.G.R. SE 080565

The outcrop which overlooks the Valley Of Desolation on the scenic route from Bolton Abbey to Simon's Seat. It faces west, the rock quality is good and all the routes are between 6 and 8 metres long and easily protectable. The crag is within the Barden Fell Access Land area so the usual restrictions as on page 10 apply. The routes were recorded at the 'eleventh hour' of guidebook production in September 1998 by Stuart and Karen King and Simon Reed. They have not been checked.

The first climbs are on the overhang buttress, the largest part of the outcrop.

1 Twisted Chick S
4a Up the left wall to a ledge. Traverse right to a thin crack and a rounded finish.

2 Jojo La Perouque M
The corner crack to the ledge then an easier crack to the top.

3 Mangenon Groove HVS ★
5a The steep clean groove at the right end of the overhang buttress. Strenuous but with several helpful pockets.

The broken slab to the right of overhang buttress is;

4 Frogslegs slab S
4b Easily to a ledge then with more difficulty up the wall.

5 Timewaster M
The wide crack-line is quite straightforward.

The outcrop below Overhang Buttress is Desolation Pinnacle.

6 Peggy Babcock HD
From the green cave on the left ascend diagonally right below the overhang to climb the wide central crack and perched block.

7 Formic Crack D
Up the lower arete to finish as for Peggy Babcock

8 Desolation S
Ascend a delicate slab on the right-hand side of the buttress to a heather ledge. Finish up the right edge of the perched block.

9 Inertia Arete D
The juggy arete behind Desolation.

10 Stop Grousing S
4b Tenuous moves on the rounded bulge lead to a pleasant finish up the slab.

PANORAMA CRAG   N.G.R. SE 162654

The crag overlooks the B6165 Pateley Bridge to Summer Bridge road. Approach from Pateley Bridge, after about 1km turn left up Panorama Way, which leads up to some cottages and a church. Park near the church. From here walk along a narrow road rightwards to an iron gate on the right which gives access to a fenced viewing platform. Down the left side is a narrow stair from the base of which a track leads leftwards (east) to the rocks. The crag takes the form of a part-quarried, part-natural edge generally quite small but, facing south-west, it dries quickly and is an excellent sheltered venue for a short winter's afternoon. The first buttress is a large block about 11 metres high with an overhang at its base, not well-endowed with runners.

1 News Night 11m E1 P2 ★
5b Start from the block below the right arete. Climb the arete on its left side to a rounded finish.

2 Yesterday's News 10m E2 ★
5b The original line which starts below the right arete of News Night trending left to the top of World In Action.

3 Panorama 11m E3 P2 ★
5b Takes a line up the centre of the front face. Surmount the roof and pull into the niche just over the lip. Move up and right to a large hole. Climb straight up the wall above to finish.

4 World in Action 11m E4 P2 ★
6a Pull into the niche as for Panorama, but move left to the arete, teeter up the arete on layaways to a good ledge. Finish more easily.

5 No News Is Good News 11m E5 P2
6b Takes a line up the left wall of the buttress. Start just left of the overhang, move up and right to a pocket (poor runners). Make an awkward move to stand in the pocket (another poor runner) then more difficult moves lead rightwards to good holds just left of the arete. Finish straight up.

100 metres to the right is a smaller undercut wall of best quality gritstone containing the following routes, described from left to right:-

6 Pateley Show 7m HVS
5c Start with difficulty over the bulge on the left-hand side of the buttress and finish up the slab and left arete.

7 Glasshouse Groove 7m VS ★
4c An awkward pull over the initial bulge gains a crack and thin flake which leads, with a step left, into a short finishing groove.

8 Nidderdale Wall 8m S ★★
4a Gain a ledge in the centre of the crag where the guardian bulge is smallest and trend left into a scoop which leads to a large roof. Step left below the roof to join the final move of Glasshouse Groove

9 Not The Nine O'clock News 8m E3 P2 ★★
6a From the scoop below the roof on Nidderdale Wall arrange just enough small wires to give confidence for a thin step right followed by a difficult move up over the overlap.

10 Dimbleby's Crack 7m HVS   ★
5b The compulsive off-width crack with a stubborn but interesting start.

11 Power Pull 6m HVS
5c A difficult start just right of the crack leads to easier but pleasant climbing near the top.

12 Padded Arete 7m HVS
5c The arete formed by the left side of the chimney with the Elder Tree, one metre right of Powerpull, is climbed on the left side.

The Chimney containing the elder tree and the crack to the right are both Diff, but hardly worthwhile.

13 Ripley Bank 7m VD
The undercut right rib is gained from the crack and climbed to the top.

The slabby walls and ribs further right provide mild problems whilst **Rob Wood 1827** is a steep and juggy 5a bulge at the extreme right.

There are 5a/5b problems on the right wall of the main buttress and on the back arete. Further left are a series of short walls and broken ridges of various lengths from Diff to VS.

PLOMPTON ROCKS   N.G.R. SE 356537

A collection of often steep, usually rough and always green buttresses dotted around the ornamental lake of the Plompton Hall Estate located just off the A661 Harrogate-Wetherby road about 3 miles south east of Harrogate. Access is restricted to paying visitors on weekend afternoons and bank-holiday Mondays and climbing is currently discouraged. A list of routes climbed during 1981 by John Mackenzie and friends was published in the 1994 supplement but, due to the current situation, it seems pointless to reproduce it here. Other references can be found in the YMC journal of 1962.

REIN ROAD QUARRY (MORLEY)   N.G.R. SE 269265

A truly esoteric spot, Rein Road Quarry is disused and full of water but has one clean wall which rises 10 metres above the usual water line. In 1995 the following description appeared in the Centresport new routes book accompanied by map and confirmatory photographs compliments of Mike Hibbert and Keith Tilley

Splash Dance 10m HVS
5a Below a hawthorn bush on top of the North East Wall abseil in to the water line. Take a hanging belay and climb back out again up a widening crack. Step left to a mantel at the top.

SCOUT CRAG

Situated on the opposite side of the valley from Widdop this extensive edge offers some excellent climbing and bouldering. The most prominent feature of the crag is a vertical wall towards the left end of the edge, this is Simian Wall. The rocks are well weathered and split by numerous cracks and faces all of which are alleged to have been climbed. Many during the 1940s and 50s.

The access situation here has, historically, been tenuous and No Climbing signs used to be in place. The signs however have long since fallen into disrepair and recent visitors report no challenge. The land is still private, however, and it would be unwise to wander far onto the well-managed grouse moor above the crag. A recent written request for a formal access agreement, had not, 9 months later, received the courtesy of a reply. The best approach is probably along the line of the edge from the Widdop car park. The routes, however, are described from left to right starting with **Cave Buttress** at the far end.

1 Route One 7m VD P1
The left nose.

2 Route Two 8m VD P1
To the ledge from the left, then up leftwards.

3 Route Three 9m D P1
Onto the block - then to the ledge - then straight up.

4 Route Four 9m HS P1
4a The thin groove just right.

5 Route Five 6m D P1
Into the cave from the right, then the big crack via the block.

6 Route Six 6m HS P1
4b The hanging crack.

7 Route Seven 6m VD P1
The nose on the right of the cave.

A little way right is a large square block.

8 The Shelves 6m HVS P2
5b A succession of sloping shelves across the face.

A short juggy wall then offers strenuous problems before another large block provides:

9 The Block 8m VD P1
The face of the block delicately, followed by the corner.

Further right is **The Grey Buttress** and a large crack with an unusual 'gargoyle' worthy of any cathedral for the first hold.

10   Gargoyle Chimney 6m   D   P1
Ascend with delight.

11   Grey Buttress Chimney 7m   D   P1
The chimney crack immediately left of the biggest buttress.

12   Grey Buttress Route 9m   HVS   P2   ★
5a The smooth lower wall is climbed on the right to finger-holds in the break. Traverse left and up to the sloping ledge in the centre. Delicate moves gain better holds above.

13   Pulpit Route 7m   D   P1
The crack on the right to the 'Pulpit' then an awkward mantel leads to an exit through a gap.

14   Amphitheatre Rib 8m   VD   P1
A right-hand variant to the finish of Pulpit Route.

Simian Wall is the steepest and probably best part of the crag though it does suffer from some seepage.

15   The Big Crack 7m   D   P1
The first crack.

The wall to the right looks E2 - has it been led?

16   J & K 7m   HVS   P1
5a The next crack.

17   Bold Wall 7m   HVS   P2
The wall right again.

18   Twin Cracks 7m   HVS   P1   ★★
5a The double crack system is really nice.

19   Twin Cracks Eliminate 7m   HVS   P2
5b The broken wall without recourse to the cracks.

20   Wide Cracks 7m   HVS   P1
5a One big and one small, half a metre right.

21   J & K Wall 7m   HVS   P1
5a The next crack, trending left at the top. Direct variants are possible, but harder.

22   Sixth Crack 7m   HVS   P1
5a The thin crack with a small hole at 3 metres.

23   The Waterfall 7m   HVS   P1
The last crack is rarely dry but is good when it is.

24 The River 6m D P1
The final chimney is also often damp!

SCOUT HUT CRAG   N.G.R. SD 957124

A relatively new collection of micro routes situated on four large
boulders 200 metres from the Hebden Bridge to Widdop Road, to
the north of the stream that runs out of Lower Gorple Reservoir at
Blake Dean. The aspect is south facing and sheltered, the rock
generally clean and sound. When approaching from Hebden
Bridge the rocks are to the left of the steep hill and Z bends, about
half a mile short of The Pack Horse Inn. Limited parking is available
on the left, opposite the Scout Hut, which is on the right. Refer to
the diagram for the relative positions of each route..

Big Block Buttress This is the furthest of the four from the scout hut.

1 Nite Howl 5m HVS P1
5b The short arete on the left-hand side is climbed on the right.

2 Too Eye Lite 6m HVS P2
5c The blind crack to a hard finish.

3 Moon Dance 7m HVS P2   ★
5a From the small ramp, climb direct up the centre of the wall.

4 Arenaceous 8m E2 P1
5c Pull through the roof to ledge and finish more easily.

5 Loogabarooga 8m E3 P2   ★★★
6a The central line through the roof and into the groove. Excellent
and even harder if you're tall!

6 Swinny's Bottle 8m E2 P2
5c Gain the arete from below and avoid the escape route right.

Bottom Block Buttress   This is the block nearest the stream. It
has a cave at one end.

7 Coppice Moon 5m HVS P1   ★
5c Steep climbing up the breaks. The traverse left below the top
can also be followed.

8 Rock Shock 6m HVS P1
5a Gain the ledge and follow the diagonal crack to finish as for
Coppice Moon.

9 Slippery People 6m E2 P1   ★
6b The short crack and then the steep wall with a long reach.

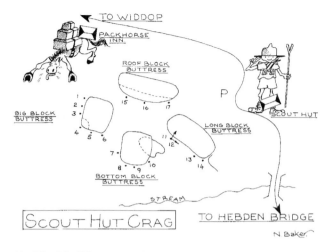

TO WIDDOP

PACKHORSE INN

ROOF BLOCK BUTTRESS

BIG BLOCK BUTTRESS

P

SCOUT HUT

LONG BLOCK BUTTRESS

BOTTOM BLOCK BUTTRESS

STREAM

SCOUT HUT CRAG

TO HEBDEN BRIDGE

N Baker

10 Dib, Dib, Dib 6m HVS P1
5b The stepped arete on its right.

Long Block Buttress The nearest buttress to the Scout Hut.

11 Glam Rock 9m E1 P2
5b Start at a small ledge near the left-hand end of the buttress and aim for the short hanging crack in the top roof. Finish direct past this.

12 Colour Scene 10m E1 P2
5b Start as for Glam Rock but traverse ledges rightwards under the roof until it is possible to pull through a shallow scoop to finish.

13 Strone Road 7m E4 P2   ★
6b The obvious pocket above the roofs left of Needle of Dreams.

14 Needle Of Dreams 7m E4 P2   ★★★
6b A superb route climbing the blunt nose above the initial roofs. Unprotected but the landing is reasonable.

15 High Moon 7m E3 P2
5c Gain the hanging ledge then swing right onto the rib to finish.

Roof Block Buttress The buttress above all the others.

16 Health, Fitness, and Beauty 5m HVS P1
5b Pull through the roof just right of the left edge of the buttress.

17 Lie Down Dave 5m E3 P1   ★★
6b Attack the centre of the buttress protected by friends, to a hideous body roll finish.

18 Nezzz... 5m HVS P2
5a Swing up onto the right edge of the buttress and finish direct. A little friable with a worrying landing.

SHARP HAW AND FLASBY FELL   N.G.R. SD 957551

A series of small natural gritstone buttresses and boulders overlooking the A65 between Skipton and Gargrave. Although a little spread out the crags offer some interesting bouldering and a few short but pleasant routes. The main edge faces south west, providing clean rock and fine views over Airedale whilst the isolated boulders further back on Flasby Fell are greener and rougher but worth a visit in good weather for those who prefer a little solitude.

The history of climbing here is vague and never previously documented however the rocks have certainly been visited and scrambled on since at least the 1930s when Sydney Waterfall and friends explored the area. The first recorded ascent was Fall Off Like A Grape by Robin Fuller in 1990 and then various parties including The Musgrove's in 1995, Mark Radtke and Dave Barton in February 1997 and Brian Swales later the same year, brought the chronicle up to date.

From the A65 or Skipton take the B6265 Grassington road and take the first turn left after the Craven Heifer pub. Follow the lane for about 300 metres to a sharp bend and park here. An obvious track then leads off towards a plantation and just before reaching it go through a gate on the right and head towards the wall. Follow the wall round to the right to a gateway giving access to the open fell-side and after a few hundred metres the first small boulders and problems on either side of the lower end of the ridge.

The first noticeable boulders face east above and to the right of an oak tree but better is a short steep wall about 4 metres high facing west overlooking the valley. This wall provides several excellent and clean problems between 4b and 5c. The first sizeable outcrop is Sycamore Buttress, characterised by a slab on the right and roofy section on its left. Twenty metres right, at the start of the edge, is an undercut slab with a small niche in it. The climbs are described from right to left.

1 Estafonit 5m MS P2
Climb direct past the small undercut niche on rounded holds.

One and a half metres left is;

2 Gerronweeit 5m MS P2
Pull onto the undercut slab and continue more easily to the top.

The undercut rib and slab to the left of the cleft provides an interesting problem at 4c/5a.

To the right of the tree is

3 Gerrodonit 5m MS P2   ★
Climb up easily to the undercut wall, pull up to the chimney and continue up the slab.

4 Sycamore Slab 7m Diff P1
Climb the slab just left of the Tree.

5 Slab Direct 7m MS P2
Start 2 metres left and climb the slab direct.

6 Central Scramble 7m Diff P1
The obvious ridge between the slab and the roof.

7 Showin' Fagin 7m VS P1
4c Start 4 metres left and climb a corner to the roof. Swing right and up the slabby wall above.

8 Fagin's Id 7m MS P1
As for Showin' Fagin to the roof but then left and finish up the easier wall.

The wall just left of Fagin's Id has a couple of easier problems. One hundred metres to the left is a short red slab and higher broken rocks to its left providing several good problems. Up the middle of the first slab is:-

9 Pendle's Nipper 5m MVS P2
4b start just left of the undercut slab and climb direct to the top.

Several hundred metres further north-west another sizeable buttress **Tarn Crag,** can be found overlooking a pool. It is separated from the previous routes by a dry-stone wall which is best avoided by a short scramble around its left hand end. A low fence can then be stepped over giving easy access to the crag.

10 Right-hand Crack 8m V.Diff P1
The narrowing crack and blocky rib on the right-hand side of the buttress.

11 Green Groove 8m S P1
4a The awkward slabby groove between the blocky rib and the clean cracked wall.

12 Fall Off Like A Grape 9m HVS P1   ★
5a The clean cracked wall to the right of the sharp arete starting from a hollow sounding flake. Climb cracks to a horizontal break and finish direct, or traverse left and finish more easily up the arete.

13 Embryonic Womb Walk 9m E1 P2
5c Climbs the obvious arete on its right-hand side.

14 Linear Negra 7m VS P1
5a Climbs the arete on its left-hand side starting off the obvious block.

15 Problem Wall 8m E1 P1
6c Climbs the wall to the left of the arete with some testing moves at the start.

16 Cave Chimney 6m HS P1
4b Bridge up the deep chimney to an awkward finish; or, for extra fun, squeeze out right above Problem Wall to finish up the arete - the grade apparently depends on your girth!.

17 Getting The Horn 6m HVS P1
6a Start left of the chimney. Make a dynamic move to gain the horn and climb the easier wall above.

A number of easier routes can be found on the buttresses below the pool at the edge of the wood, Fifty metres past the wall is a detached pinnacle with 3 routes.

18 Valley Side 9m D P2
Climb the valley side.

19 Scoop 6m MVS P2
The left face with a circular scoop

20 Wall Side 5m D P1
The right hand face, by the wall.

Forty five metres further on is another pinnacle opposite the pool.

21 Central Rib 7m D P2
The line is obvious

22 Left Face 6m MS P2
The left side of the rib.

To the right it can be climbed in a couple of places at the same grade.

Seventy Five metres further on, past a few smaller problems is:-

23 The Bulging Slab 7m MS P2
Climb the slab direct over the small bulge half way.

The best problems are on an egg-shaped boulder a hundred metres or so west of the pool just above the top of the steep wooded bank.

24 Aye-n-ard Crack 7m E2 P1   ★★
6b Gain the break at the left-hand side and hand traverse right to reach the bulging bottomless crack. Climb this with an awkward final pull onto the upper slab. A bold solo but protectable if you've brought a rope.

25 Young Dave's Nose 6m E1 P1   ★
6b From the foot of Dave's Slab swing right to the rounded rib and climb it on shallow pockets and slopers.

26 Dave's Slab 5m HVS P1   ★
6a Climbs the slabby west face of the boulder with a difficult pull to gain a thin crack system.

27 The Pocket Problem 4m VS P1
5b The left rib with two shallow round pockets near the top.

No doubt a few more problems could be unearthed in the forest edge below but if you fancy the walk over the top of Sharp Haw the three rounded tops of Flasby Fell to the North-west are littered with large boulders which are reminiscent of some of the rough isolated blocks on nearby Rylstone. The highest of the tops, known as Rough Haw has a craglet on its northern slope containing a pinnacle. The easy side is a worthwhile scramble but a wire brush and tape for your fingers might provide greater rewards in this vicinity!

SHEPHERD'S CRAG - OLD COTE MOOR   N.G.R. NY 931741

The crag is situated high on the Littondale flank of Old Cote Moor about one kilometre south east of the summit cairn and will only appeal to climbers who are happy to walk a long way in search of esoteric mediocrity. The crag comprises a series of short quarried walls, ribs and corners up to nine metres in height. The aretes and walls are generally clean but the cracks and corners are somewhat overgrown. All the finishes require care. The routes detailed below were named and recorded in January 1989, however all bore signs of being climbed before, no doubt by Earnest Shepherd and Jack Wilson who claim to have discovered, cleaned and climbed several lines here in the 1960s. There are about twelve climbable lines between Diff and Very Severe, the best being :-

1 Old Cote Rib 8m S P1
4a The leftmost of three prominent aretes in a bay behind the detached pinnacle.

2   Offset Arete   8m   HS   P1
4b The right-hand of the three aretes, requiring a couple of subtle side-steps to avoid pointless extra difficulties.

3   Pinnacle Wall   6m   VD   P1
The cracked wall left of the overhang, behind the pinnacle.

4   Slabby Wall   6m   VD   P1
The clean line up the steep slab to the right of the pinnacle.

5   Diagonal Crack   6m   D   P1
An obvious, leftward slanting line, starting about 30 metres right of the pinnacle.

6   Arncliffe Arete   7m   MVS   P2
4b A prominent arete at the right-hand end of the main section providing the best line on the crag.

STAINLAND QUARRY   N.G.R. SE 076200

This north facing quarry is situated, some 6 miles from Halifax. It stands prominently over the A6025 Elland to Rochdale road and can be seen high up on the left half a mile or so after crossing the B6112 from Halifax to Holywell Green. Follow the B6112 south from Halifax through Holywell Green and into the narrow streets of Stainland. There is a public car park just to the right (North), off the main road, in the village centre. A footpath leads into playing fields. A gate at the left hand end of the last of these leads directly to a track down into the right hand part of the quarry. The rock is good but finishes are loose and belays difficult to arrange. Protection is generally well spaced. (P grades were not given).

1   Chrisening   7m   HVS
5b A short climb which starts at the extreme left hand end of the quarry at the foot of a grass bank by some broken blocks. Thin technical moves start the wall which is climbed directly. A Friend 0 in a blind pocket to the left of the start and RPs in the thin short crack at half height help.

2   Chris's Crack   9 m   VS
5a Surprisingly pleasant. This is 5 metres right of Chrisening below an obvious crack starting 3metres from the ground. Reachy moves take you to the crack and a sapling. Continue directly to finish.
To the right of this is a west facing wall. The next three routes are all on this.

3   Aracus   12 m   VS
4c Climb to the crack and then up it.

4 The Dane 12 m VS
5a The wider crack beyond the wide chimney, trending left to right.

5 Slave To The Dane 12 m HVS
5c Above the cave is a fingery crack. Climb it.

This part of the quarry offers a number of low level boulder problems, but the location of these is best left for individuals to re-discover them.

Moving across to the right-hand section, the first climb takes a prominent flake on the left.

6 Old and Bold 7m E1
5b Bold but short. The obvious fin/flake is gained easily to the break - then layback the flake.

7 The Beginning 10m S
4a The chimney to the right of and behind Old and Bold

8 Tennis Ball 12m VS
4c Climb the bulging crack to the right of The Beginning to the ledge then traverse right and up the wall.

The next route is some 20 metres to the right.

9 Rock Lob 12m HVS
5b Start under and left of the vertical crack in the upper block. Climb to this and up it. Traverse right to finish up the next crack. There is a direct finish above the vertical crack at E1 5C

10 Lucky Luke 10m S
4c The chimney 10 metres further right is climbed direct.

11 Cabbage 10m HVS
5b Up the sandy crack over the break. Finish up the short crack on the left of the wall.

12 Fairy Steps 10m VS
5a Start in the corner right of the painted keyhole. Move up to half height and either lay away up to the right or go left up the corner crack.

13 Hard Start 10m HVS
5b Start at the lowest point then climb with difficulty to the thin crack. Follow this to its finish.

14 Jakes Flake 10m VS
4c Start in the middle of the sandy slab. Climb up to the undercut and follow this to the right and up the wall.

15   Pigeon Corner   10m   D
4a   The corner 2 metres right is climbed direct.

16   Left Route   10m   E1
6a   The obvious roof starting in the small corner 5 metres right

17   Twin Cracks Right Route   10m   VS
4c   Start one metre right of the painted yellow flower. Climb the
crack into the groove and finish up it.

18   Nee   7m   E1
6b   The desperate and very fine, thin right-hand crack starting a few
feet up succumbs best to a knee bar!

19   Retreat   7m   HS
4a   At the right hand end of the long wall is a deep crack behind a
large flake. The route follows the crack to the ledges and an
interesting scramble to the top - or a retreat by the timid!

20   One Point   11m   VS
4c   The crack system left of the back corner in the bay to the right.
Follow the crack to the first break and finish straight up to a sloping,
loose, heathery finish.

THRUSCROSS   N.G.R.   SE 157574

Situated upon a wooded hillside, facing west, just below the dam of
Thruscross reservoir, this collection of boulders and craglets offers
short routes and problems on generally sound rock. The tree cover
and prolific bracken growth, however, makes moving around hard
work in summer and promotes the rapid re-growth of lichen on
many boulders. Visits are bests reserved for dry and sunny
afternoons from late autumn through to mid spring. Over 100 lines
have been recorded here by Tony Barley and friends but the
majority are short problems and only those which can be classed as
mini-routes are detailed here. The routes described all stay
reasonably clean but a stiff brush in you pack may be a sensible
accessory Access has never previously been challenged but the
recent erection of a new, high deer fence suggests care should be
taken on your choice of approach. It is probably best to scramble up
the quarried walls at the end of the dam and follow the moorland
side of the fence for about 400 metres to the second gate. The
Thruscross Boulder and Washburn Walls are just below and to the
left of here. These are the prominent blocks which can be clearly
seen from the road on the opposite side of the valley. The climbs
are described, generally, right to left from these more obvious
landmarks.

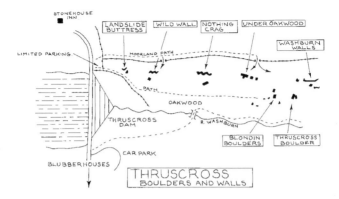

The Washburn Walls

At the extreme right-hand end of the crag is a mini edge with several short lines. The most obvious is a viciously overhanging off-width crack.

1 Laughter Lines 6m E3 P1

6b Climb the crack.

2 Capelshaw Beck 6m HVS P1

5a The stepped corner to the left is steep but more reasonable.

3 Ratlin' Row 6m E3 P2   ★★

5c Below the bulges left of the corner is a thin crack. Climb this and swing right to reach a good hold over the lip. The finish is short but strenuous.

4 High Lair 6m E1 P2   ★

5b Climb the cracked wall below the large perched boulder. Move right and up, and then back left to finish on top of the boulder.

5 Green Syke 6m HVS P2

5b Climb the wall below the boulder moving left to finish up a scoop in its left side.

There are a couple of shorter problems on the next block to the left and several more to the right of, and below, those described above.

The Thruscross Boulder

The very best that Thruscross has to offer is on and around the obloid block a few metres down and to the left of the Washburn Walls.

6 Holy Trinity 8m HVS P1   ★★
5b A good line up the sharp edged, truncated arete to the right of the main boulder. The technical crux is at the start but even with a wire in the slot the upper edge feels quite precarious. Easier starts can be made from either side.

Winkling Wall 6a ★ is a good but serious problem up the horizontal creases in the upper wall of the main block left of Holy Trinity. **Cracklin' Crease** 6b ★★★ is the very slim groove starting from a ledge on the right wall. It is perhaps the very best problem at Thruscross but does 4 metres of hard climbing with the chance of an 8 metre fall make it a route? You decide - it looks full E4 to me.

7 Cotton Reel 8m E2 P2   ★★
5c Make maximum use of the front face of the block by gaining the right arete and traversing precariously left. Climb the front of the left arete to better holds and a step right to finish over the top centre.

8 Yarn Spinner 6m E2 P2   ★
6a/b A highly problematic start allows the left arete to be climbed direct.

There are two problems which make use of the horizontal slot on the left side of the block. **Flax Trade** (5b) on the left and **Right Eye** (5c) on the right.

The Blondin Boulders
Twenty metres or so further left are a collection of rocks with about 20 named problems the best of which feels like a route and is worth seeking out.

9 Walk The Blondin 10m HVS P3   ★
5a The large trapezoid boulder is gained from the left and the crest is ascended with some delicacy. Try it no hands for the full tick.!

Several problems gain the ridge from the slab on the right at 5a/b.

Under Oakwood
This area is about another 50 metres to the left and its centrepiece is a vertical wall, green and slabby on the left but with a fine clean arete on the right, just behind a stout tree.

Barking Up The Wrong Tree 5a A pleasant ramp with a tricky finish in the gully just right of the tree. **Heycorn** 5b ★ is the arete on the right side. **Heart Of Oak** 6a ★★ climbs the superb arete on the left, just behind the tree. Whilst **Strong As An Oak** 6b ★ is a left to right traverse of the break at 2 metres.

10 Rising Of The Sap 7m E3 P2 ★★
5c A diagonal rising traverse from the green slab to the green flakes to a green rounded finish. Brilliant and rather committing moves despite the colour!

Eighty metres further left **Nothing Rocks** and **Flatfish Slab** provide a dozen short problems up to 5c whilst another 100metres of jungle bashing left at the same level finds the **Wild Walls** and **Cuckoo Slab** with another 15 problems up to 6b.

Landslide Buttress
This is the last buttress 80 metres left of Wild Walls and quite close to the new fence near the end of the dam. The right wall of the upper buttress provides several problems 5a to 5c based around a thin undercut crack.

11 Stenislag 9m S P2 ★
A fun route which climbs a lower subsidiary slab followed by a hand traverse across the left edge of the next block before transferring to the rib of the main buttress for an airy finish.

Compulsory Purchase 5b climbs the lower blocks to the right of Stenislag and **Dambuster** 5b climbs the left side of the middle block.

12 Dam It All 6m E2 P3 ★
5c Climbs the front face of the undercut upper buttress with a precarious step.

13 Holland, Hannen and Cubbitts 6m E1 P2
5b The same wall started further left but trending right above the overhang.

On the opposite side of the valley is a large buttress of immaculate rock quality, alas it is heavily camouflaged and gets little sunshine. It contains three routes at present but could however provide one of the best 'last great problems' Yorkshire has seen for many years! Are you tempted? - Well go find it!

UPPER HULLER STONES (Skell Gill)   N.G.R SE 197687
Yet another esoteric gem courtesy of Tony Barley. This crag lies on the eastern bank of Skell Beck about a mile downstream of the Pateley Bridge to Kirby Malzeard Road which crosses the stream. It is a pleasant sunny spot but unfortunately with less than ideal landings. **Access permission is required of the gamekeeper, Mr Guy on 01765 658295 but dogs are not allowed.** The crag is best

approached from a parking area about 400 metres north of Skell Beck, walking South East across the moor. Drop down into the valley and across the stream. The main buttresses can then be clearly seen on the other side. Twenty five climbs, most of which are no more than boulder problems, have been recorded here but only the most significant are included in this guide to give a taste. They are described from right to left starting on the craglet to the right of the highest buttress.

Fountains Buttress   There are seven recorded problems up to 5c on this block the best is,

1 Wonderbar   5m   HVS   5b   P2   ★
The wall on the right of the twin aretes is climbed on superb holds after a reachy start.

Skell Buttress   This is the largest buttress with 4 fine routes.

2 By The Birch   7m   S   P1
4a Climb the right wall past the tree and up cracks above

3 Too Gnarly For Barley   9m   E3   P2   ★★
6a The right arete provides the best line on the crag with a reachy start and intimidating finish.

4 Solitude   10m   E3   P2   ★★
6a The centre of the wall is gained by moving left on good holds then up via a pocket to the break. A move right leads to a hard and committing move up to gain small but positive holds on the upper wall. Excellent climbing

5 Peace   9m   VS   P1   ★
5a Start as for Solitude but continue left to the ledge on the arete. Climb delicately up the scooped rib and finish just on the right, or slightly more easily round to the left.

Immediately left of Skell Buttress is a short wall with a couple of 4c problems but ten metres left is the greatly undercut block of **Rievaulx Buttress** with two easy problems on the right wall and two more challenging lines.

6 Chalice   5m   HVS   P2
5b Start below the right side of the roof, pull up and move round to good holds on the side wall. Swing back left onto the rib to finish.

7 Student Games   6m   E2   P2   ★★
6a Tackle the huge roof from the back, directly in the centre using the obvious but worrying flakes. From the lip a move up and left gains good finishing holds.

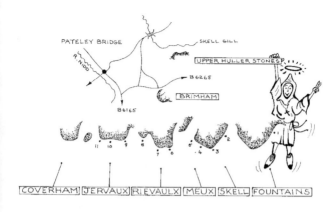

UPPER HULLER STONES

8 Mitre 5m VS P2
5a Left of the roof is a pointed nose and a leaning slab climb this.

Jervaux Buttress
Left again is another undercut buttress with a smaller roof and 5 lines the best are:-

9 Mother Superior 5m HVS P2
5b The right rib direct, with a spectacular move over the bulge.

10 Henry The Eighth 4m E1 P2
5c Climb the overhang direct to a jug and continue to the top. A move right reduces the difficulty but avoids the main challenge.

11 Cardinal Wolesly 4m HVS P2
5a Climb the overhang via a hold on the lip at the left-hand end. Move back right and finish direct.

Left again is the final buttress, a smaller one with a slab leaning against the right wall and two 5a problems.

Half a mile to the north-east can be seen another cluster of boulders known as **Lower Hullah Stones**. About 70 problems have been recorded here and all are identified in a privately produced pamphlet guide called Wild Bouldering in Yorkshire. The Stones can be approached from Upper Hullah Crag or from the Brimham road where it meets the Ripon to Pateley Bridge road.

WHINS WOOD
N.G.R. SE 053382

A steep, sandy, quarried gritstone face around 15 metres high. The crag is situated alongside the A629 Keighley - Halifax Road in Whins Wood Recreation Ground. Approach along the A629 from Keighley and park on the left immediately after the sign for "Cross Roads With Lees". Part of the crag overlooks the bowling green, this section is overgrown.

WHITE CRAG
N.G.R. SE 064467

Situated on the edge of what was White Crag Plantation this short clean gritstone outcrop has a westerly aspect and even in winter collects any afternoon sun available. Approach from Ilkley along the A65 Ilkley - Skipton Road, turn left up Cocking Lane, at the second cross-roads turn left up Light Bank Lane. Park at the large parking space / alfresco rubbish dump on the right. The crag can be seen on the hillside to the left. Go through the stile in the wall and follow the footpath up the hill. The first buttress is just over the wall on the right, whilst the second section of the crag is 100 metres further along. The crag comprises a number of clean, rough buttresses and although it is never more than 6 metres high it provides some excellent bouldering a little off the beaten track. Some of the problems are quite technical and a well padded mattress may be useful for the generally uneven landings

WINDGATE NICK
N.G.R. SE 072472

A pleasant series of buttresses sitting high on Addingham Moor in the heart of the Leeds/Bradford commuter belt. The crag faces roughly north and is surrounded by a plentiful supply of bilberries which are sometimes fiercely guarded by equally plentiful midges. From Ilkley follow the A65 westwards for 3 kilometres where a left turn leads up Cocking Lane. A further 3 kilometres up this is a cross-road. Turn left here into Straight Lane until parking places below the crag are reached. As the chairlift is out of action, the final ascent is arduous. A longer but more pleasant approach can be made by walking along the moor edge from Ilkley in about 40 minutes.

The climbs are described from right to left. The first buttress has an obvious cleft which splits it.

1   Snowdrop   15m   HVS   P2
5b The pebbled wall right of the cleft starting up the narrow ramp.

Climb up to the breaks and finish up the sandy crack in the headwall.

2 Windgate Crack 15m HS P1   ★★
4a Climb the cleft and then the crack by pleasant thrutching.

3 Tell Mick Ryan Nowt! 15m E4 P2   ★
6b The problematic lower wall is gained from two chipped footholds just left of Windgate Crack. Climb the chicken heads to a faint rib and then to the break. Finish anywhere up the wall above.

4 Old Nick 12m E2 P2
6a Three metres left of Windgate Crack is a small triangular cave. Bridge up this and climb out of it on its right, up the rib to the break. Finish up the lichenous wall above.

Fifty metres left and over the wall is a sharp-nosed buttress.

5 Plandit 10m E3 P2   ★★
5c Climb the series of flakes first right of the arete.

6 Pans Meadow 10m E5   ★
6b The main arete of Plandit Buttress, and just left of the route Plandit. Start left of the arete and move round to the right at half height.

7 Dinka people 8m E2
6a The steep square wall to the left of Pans Meadow.

Ten metres left again is a buttress split by twin cracks which contain a hanging block which would probably not be there if someone had climbed up the cracks. A good unclimbed arete is to the left. This buttress is compact, of perfect gritstone and bounded on its right by a dirty chimney.

6 Revival 10m HVS P1
5b The green groove and wall left of the chimney. Trend left to finish.

7 Gled's 8m HVS P2
5b Climb the left wall of the buttress below the perched block. Start at the chipped-looking hold.

8 Fireman's Helmet 6m HVS P?
5c On a buttress 100 metres left of Gled's. Start at the lowest point just right of the small cave and left of the green chimney. Climb the blunt arete to the break then obvious holds left of arete to a sandy, rounded finish.

WOOLLEY EDGE QUARRY

N.G.R. SE 307137

Situated close to a picnic area approximately 4 kilometres from junction 38 on the M1 Motorway. Leave the motorway at junction 38 and drive towards the village of Woolley, at the first cross-road after the village turn left, at the next turn right. The first crag is situated in the picnic area on the right. The crag does not exceed 5 metres in height and, due to drainage, is usually green. The cleanest section of rock lies at the right hand side offering some short problems and traverses, but even here graffiti and rubbish generally deter most visitors. The second section of the crag lies, from the left end of the picnic area, about 100 metres down the road on the opposite side. Were it not for its continued use as an unofficial rubbish dump this indeed would be a pleasant place to climb. The main feature is a 10 metre high easy angled buttress with some potentially pleasant routes.

YORKSHIRE GRITSTONE - THE DEFINITIVE HISTORY

The 19th Century and the birth of The Yorkshire Ramblers Club

As we reach the end of the millennium it is a good time to reflect on the history of gritstone climbing in Yorkshire. In a little over one hundred years the sport has come a long way from very humble beginnings.

The early history is vague and very poorly documented but the consensus seems to be that Cecil Slingsby from Skipton was the first alpine mountaineer to use gritstone outcrops both as training for climbing big mountains and, apparently, as an end in itself. Whether he actually climbed the eponymously named chimney on Crookrise is not clear but it is documented that he regularly climbed on the edges of Barden Moor and Fell near his home from as early as 1864. He climbed several chimneys at Almscliff in 1870 and was invited to be the first president of the Yorkshire Ramblers club on its formation in 1892.

The Yorkshire Ramblers were indeed the first locally based climbing club and the earliest records of specific climbs done by them are to be found in a pencil written guide by Thomas Gray dated 1894 listing 10 climbs at Almscliff. Gray's partners around this time were Herbert Ingle, Edward Calvert and C.T. Dent and it appears that they climbed regularly at Almscliff and undoubtedly pioneered many more climbs there and elsewhere but, alas, records were either not kept or have since disappeared.

The next clue that rock climbing in Yorkshire was alive and well before the turn of the century was unearthed in a small paperback book written around 1900 by Edmund Bogg which contained a photograph dated 1895 of a climber, un-named, in nailed boots soloing a crack on one of the large boulders on Simon's Seat. This crack has never previously been recorded as a route but 100 years later, armed with the photograph it was re-discovered, climbed and considered a good 5a, and quite bold. This suggests that perhaps our Victorian ancestors were far more advanced than we have previously believed.

The Turn Of The Century - Articles, Almscliff and Ilkley

In 1906 Claude Benson wrote an article for Fry's Outdoor Magazine which described in detail, accompanied by photographs, some of the more popular climbs at Almscliff and Ilkley. These included Birds Nest Crack, then known as The Beehive at Almscliff, and

Flake Climb and Blasphemy Crack at Ilkley. By this time it is known that the Botterill brothers, Fred and Matthew were active, cycling regularly from their home in Leeds to climb at The Cow and Calf. Fred Botterill in particular was also said to have been keen on bouldering at Almscliff and by 1913 John Laycock's guidebook suggested that there were some 170 climbs there. Someone must have been keeping records but unfortunately Laycock only recorded twenty six of the most significant. Benson said, in his article, of Almscliff, *"One meets nail marks everywhere. I should think that almost every yard of cliff and boulder has been tried at one time or another"*. (Pete Brown please note!)

For almost 30 years the Yorkshire Ramblers Club was the only known climbing club in the area. Its membership increased and annual journals were meticulously compiled chronicling the daring deeds of club members around the world. Unfortunately the journals rarely mentioned local gritstone climbing until, in 1911, an article by Walter Greenwood listed 22 climbs at Ilkley but gave no details of first ascents. It was forty years before Ilkley next appeared in a guide but it was known to be one of the most accessible and popular of crags in the area.

It is strongly suspected that the Y.R.C. visited most of the gritstone outcrops in the county around the turn of the century and another article by Benson featured the relatively innocuous Spofforth Pinnacles in some detail. Can it be true that this group never climbed on the nationally famous Brimham Rocks? No record of such can, however, be found.

Between the Wars - Frankland, The Gritstone Club, Widdop, 'Waterfalls' and Winston.

In 1922 The Gritstone Club was formed in Bradford and its members, headed by Cecil Wood, made the first records of climbs in the Skipton area for a guidebook entitled Recent Developments published by Fergus Graham the following year. Rylstone, Crookrise and Simon's Seat were documented for the first time and soon became popular. Almscliff was updated for this guide by Claude Dean Frankland and his ascent of The Green Crack stood out as the major test-piece of the era. Frankland was regarded as one of the best rock climbers of his generation. A letter from Geoffrey Winthrop Young states *"I wish to be allowed to thank you for giving me one more - and that perhaps the best - demonstration of how beautiful climbing movements on difficult rock can be"*.

Frankland was killed in 1927, on the relatively simple Chantry Buttress on Great Gable, and his untimely death left a void. There

were few significant developments in terms of increases of technical difficulty for over a decade. There were, however, several groups of activists working away during the 1930s in their local areas, notably the Craven Pothole Club led by its best known member Sydney Waterfall, his brother Arnold and friend Bill Bowler. This group were responsible for continued development of the Barden Moor and Barden Fell crags with their most notable find being the 'unearthing', apparently literally, of Dental Slab at Rylstone in 1933. They also visited the Great Wolfrey and climbed extensively at Sharphaw but recorded nothing at either.

Widdop was discovered and first developed during the early 1930s by A.E. Chisman, Herbert Hartley and Maurice Linnell. Several routes were recorded but the crag was named 'Mystery Buttress' and its location wasn't revealed. The secret was soon out, however, and development was progressed by Manchester University Mountaineering Club members, in particular Arthur Birtwhistle (who also made the first lead of the Drainpipe Crack of Vember on Cloggy) and Allan Allsop. This pair's best effort at Widdop was Celebrity Buttress but they also prospected further afield. Allsop opened up Caley climbing Pedestal Wall in 1938 and moved on to complete the first ascents of S Crack and Ferdinand at Ilkley in 1939. Birtwhistle became enamoured with Guisecliff for a while claiming, amongst others, the eye-catching feature of Roc's Nest Chimney.

The early 1930s also witnessed the rise of another Ilkley team led by Winston Farrar. Farrar climbed extensively in Rocky Valley only vaguely aware of the previous efforts of the Yorkshire Ramblers. He gave most of the earlier climbs their now-accepted names and, in fact, believed that many were first ascents. He also began the 'Napoleonic' trend with his ascent of Josephine in the quarry. He was initially accompanied by Reg Cooper and Percy Bryson and, around 1935, introduced a young Charlie Salisbury to the crag. Salisbury and Farrar added a number of important lines together, the best of which was undoubtedly Illegitimate Crack. By 1937 Farrar had given up climbing due to illness and Salisbury took over the pioneering role with new friends, who later became inaugural members of The Yorkshire Mountaineering Club. He continued to be involved in the production of new routes for the next twenty five years. Walewska, Napoleon and Blucher were three of his early classics all climbed before the Second World War.

The first record of routes at Brimham date from the 1930s with Cubic Corner, Notice Board Crack and Lovers Leap Chimney being mentioned by Sydney Thompson. He witnessed some indications of previous activity but considered the crag relatively unexplored. This is surprising given the area's geological interest unless, because of this, climbing was actively discouraged? Sydney Thompson also, around this time, made a significant contribution at Almscliff with his technical and bold traverse of the South West Face.

As the 1930s ended Denys Fisher became an influential figure at Almscliff and Caley. He led Pothole Direct, Jacob's Ladder and his eponymous Traverse and Stride and became an early mentor and close friend of the next great Yorkshire pioneer Arthur Dolphin.

The 1940s and the dominance of Dolphin

Like Frankland, Dolphin met a tragic end when he slipped during the descent of the Dent du Geant in 1953. He was 28. But the Dolphin era, from 1940 until his death, produced some of the all-time classics of British outcrop climbing. Virtually every climb he created is of true simplicity of line. He even top-roped The Wall of Horrors, years ahead of its time, and but for his untimely death, may well have led it. Indeed the ethics and attitude of the day involving new routes were simple. According to Dolphin's friend, John Cook, the sequence was top rope in rubbers, top rope in boots, and then lead in rubbers. The climb was only considered fully developed after a lead in nailed boots! Demon Wall, Z Climb, Overhanging Groove, Black Wall, Birdlime Traverse and the superb Great Western were all the products of Dolphin's craftsmanship. His crossing of the North-West Girdle, with John Cook and John 'Pug' Ball, is regarded as a remarkable exploit, particularly as Ball, totally unprotected as the last man, had not an inkling as to where he was being taken.

Rivalry and competition has doubtless always been a feature of climbing and it is worthy of note that Cook remembers the team holding perhaps the first-ever speed climbing competition at Almscliff (just for fun, mind you). Cook could do Bird's Nest Variation in 16 seconds, he recalls.

In Yorkshire Dolphin is perhaps best remembered for his Almscliff routes but he climbed extensively throughout the county meticulously recording new climbs at Ilkley, Earl Crag, Caley and Widdop. His diaries and his friends also recall visits to Brimham, Simon's Seat, Shipley Glen, Spofforth Pinnacles and Hetchell. He evidently considered some of the smaller crags as mere training because specific routes are not named. At Ilkley he was probably the first to 'peg' Wellington Crack.

Several of Dolphin's friends were pioneers in their own right and in particular John Cook and John Ball made significant contributions themselves at Ilkley in 1943. Cherry Valley Rib, Pebble Groove and

Arthur Dolphin at Almscliff Circa 1950

(photo by Dennis Gray)

Bald Pate were their creations, the latter without the benefit of the chipped holds on Doris which appeared much later. Most of the chipping at Ilkley and Caley is now believed to have been done by David Gibbons but, surprisingly, it doesn't seem to have met with the condemnation it would today.

Other independent activists during the 1940s were relatively few, due no doubt to the war, and it wasn't until the end of the decade that things got moving again. One of the first new groups to emerge was an informal team known as The Bradford Lads. An anarchic collection of individuals who generally spurned the ideals of established clubs they nevertheless toured the local outcrops adding important routes to several crags. Tom Cranfield's leads of Viscounts Route and Perch Wall at Earl and the main pitch of Castrol at Rylstone, along with Dennis Gray's Eraser Slab at Earl and Neville Drasdo's Alibi at Widdop were all significant. They probably pioneered much more but recorded nothing at the time. It has been left, in the main to Dennis Gray to stake retrospective claims on behalf of 'The Lads' for ascents he witnessed or was involved in.

Several of this group merged with Arthur Dolphin's team in the early '50s including John Lockwood and Don Hopkin who accompanied Arthur on the Flake Direct at Widdop, and Peter Greenwood, Jack Bloor, John Ramsden and Alfie Beanland who continued developments with him at Almscliff and Caley. After Dolphin's death in 1953 the group seems to have split and gone separate ways with only Dennis Gray retaining spasmodic pioneering interest in Yorkshire Grit with his new friends, members of a newly formed club, The Rock and Ice.

The 1950s -The advent of Austin
Brian Evans and friends from the newly formed Yorkshire Mountaineering Club took up the reins after Dolphin's death and began a systematic charting of several edges including Brimham, Hebden Ghyll, Earl Crag, Crookrise and Ilkley. The most active club members as 'new routers' in these early days were Ronnie Hields, who added Comet Wall to Guisecliff, and the desperate Gremlins Wall (has something come off this? If not it was the hardest route on grit for many years!) in Rocky Valley. Charlie Salisbury, Ron Hirst, and Harold Barraclough concentrated on Hebden Ghyll but picked off several lines elsewhere. Evans himself developed the outlying Brandrith and Great Wolfrey, before teaming up with the area's new star, Allan Austin, in 1955.

Allan Austin typifies the classic Yorkshire stereotype, stubborn, determined, rooted in the county's woollen district heritage and,

Allan Austin bouldering below Jacob's ladder, Almscliff circa 1960
(photo by Dennis Gray)

allegedly, not too keen on 'wasting' money. He had a reputation for always wearing several layers of jumpers and insisting in climbing in all weathers. It was under his leadership that the YMC guidebook style took shape and he, perhaps more than any other, kept meticulous records of new climbs. In the mid-fifties the Austin / Evans partnership was the dominant force in new route development in the area. Classics at Brimham such as Rough Wall, Allan's Crack, Lancet Crack and Frensis Direct amongst a host of lesser lines at last established this crag as major climbing venue. At Ilkley Transparent Wall, Sylveste and High Street nudged standards up another notch whilst amongst several good additions at Crookrise The Shelf was outstanding.

Austin's team didn't have it all their own way during the 1950s, however, as Dennis Gray kept importing the Rock And Ice stars to snatch several plums. The best of these were Joe Brown's Hovis and Small Brown at Crookrise and Charming Crack and White Wash at Brimham. Brown almost succeeded on Gigglin' Crack at this time, slithering back down from close to the top in a fit of hysterics brought about by the jocular comments of his companions. This route today merits E6 - it is interesting to speculate what Brown would have given it had he succeeded.

Other early '50s activists were Craven Pothole Club members Brian Hartley, John Gott, Andy Anderson and John Wilson who kept plugging away on the Barden Moor and Fell Crags. They recorded little but are believed to have been responsible for most of the development sub-HVS, on Rylstone, Rolling Gate, Crookrise and Deer Gallows.

Widdop remained the premier crag in the western Pennines during the 1950s but ancillary development was taking place at The Scout, and Woodhouse Scar at this time. Once again record keeping was not high on the list of priorities for the pioneers but Jack Umpleby, John Wilson, Albert Ashworth and Don Whillans were regular contributors to the moorland crags whilst John Gaukroger, Edwin Leggett, and Derek Bull began to climb at Woodhouse. Gaukroger's early routes included Parete and Destra and he has continued to take an active interest in the crag for over 40 years, organising clean-ups and badgering the council to prune invasive trees etc. By the end of the decade Chris Ambler produced a pirate guide listing over fifty routes at the Scar.

Don Whillans' only notable big route in the '50s was Ceiling Crack at Widdop but he is known to have been a Bridestones devotee during this period and was responsible for many of the now classic problems including The Duck, The Villain, and The Whillans Jam.

His most famous Yorkshire route came early in the next decade at Heptonstall. 'Heppy's' development only started in the late 1950s when John Hartley, Leggett and Bull first realised its potential. Fairy Steps, Sunstroke Slab and the magnificent Bull's Crack were outstanding early achievements followed up when Peter Grindley joined the team by Triplex, Pulpit Route and Grindley's Grunt. None of the regulars, however, could make any real impression on 'the big crack' until Don Whillans was invited to visit.

The following Thursday evening Don arrived at the crag, a top-rope was set up and the line was attempted. The same happened a week later, Don trying the crack again, this time looking more comfortable (!) on it. It was on the third Thursday visit that Don abseiled the line, placed a wooden wedge in the first 'zig' of the crack and proceeded to lead it, the wedge providing the only protection on the route.. There was no doubt that Forked Lightning Crack was one of the most difficult climbs in the area. Hartley commented: *"It must be hard, it took him two fags"*.

Meanwhile back at Almscliff comparable advances were being made by Allan Austin. In the late 1950s Austin was undisputedly the leading climber of his generation in Yorkshire. He was to dominate the local scene for over a decade. His Western Front, climbed in 1958 after a miraculous escape from a ground fall on the first attempt, brought a new standard of difficulty to the crag which could only be bettered by his lead of Wall of Horrors three years later. Both routes must have been horrendous undertakings without the assurance of modern protection. Wall of Horrors, although surpassed by many of the modern routes in terms of technical difficulty, is still the finest sustained hard route on the crag but its early reputation ensured very few repeats until wired nuts and Friends became available in the 1970s.

During the 1960s Austin became less prolific on grit but still continued to produce a steady stream of hard climbs on most of the county's crags. Typical examples were Noonday Ridge at Caley, The Waster on Chevin Buttress, Monument Crack at Rylstone, Fishladder at Earl, Bell at Hetchell and Pillar Front at Eastby. Though non surpassed the big two at Almscliff for steepness and sheer technical difficulty they were all bold and the hardest routes on their respective crags at the time. Pillar Front must have given Austin a particular fright because he told friends at the time he thought it the most serious first ascent he had ever done. All these routes now rate 3 stars and, though trade routes by today's standards, still command respect.

The Swinging Sixties - Nidderdale, Slipstones and Hetchell.
When Austin's attention wandered to the newly developing
playground of limestone two young brothers from Summerbridge
emerged as the fresh dominant force on the grit. Initially Robin and
Tony Barley concentrated their attentions on the Nidderdale crags
closest to their home where they completely revitalised Guisecliff
adding around 50 routes together during the decade. Routes such
as Creation and Dingbat stand out as the most significant of the
period on this crag but at the same time they were scouring
Brimham adding another 30 or so there, including the famous test-
piece Beatnik on the Cubic Block. The brothers were still teenagers
during this period and were equally prolific on limestone writing the
Malham section for the first Yorkshire Limestone guide during 1967.

The Barleys opened up new crags as well during the 1960s being
the first to report routes at Ash Head, Panorama, and Cat Crag.
They climbed some fine lines, including the futuristic and gymnastic
Swinging Free, on the bigger buttresses at Eavestone (though
these did not receive the publicity they deserved till much later).
They added fewer but no less important routes on other crags and
in particular Tony's Black Wall Eliminate, and Yellow Wall at Almscliff
have stood the test of time.

Another pioneering team came from the rejuvenated Gritstone Club
in the shape of Roger Sutcliffe and Chris Ambler who, following their
guide writing efforts at Woodhouse Scar, made Horsehold Scout their
own. They also climbed a series of new routes at Ash Head during
1962 predating the Barley's claims by 3 years.

In the same vicinity as Ash Head, Slipstones was becoming a
popular venue for Tees-side based climbers. It had been used as an
outdoor activity location by local schools and, in particular,
Pollington borstal during the 1950s. Geoff Milburn and Peter Martin
added a dozen routes in 1959 but serious development only
commenced in the mid 60s when, with route descriptions provided
by Peter Martin, a visit by the Cleveland Mountaineering Club in
1964 introduced Eric and Tony Marr to the crag. The brothers soon
worked through all the established routes and noted the gaps. A
few weeks later they returned for Tony to lead the then unprotected
Escalator and the strenuous Original Route. They ended their visit
with Eric adding Marr's Route. Returning in 1965 the brothers
worked on solving the slab start to Buttress 4 and eventually
produced the excellent Agra, along with a variation start to the left
which eventually became Agrete. The following year, accompanied
by Ken Jackson, Tony took the lead and won the first ascent of the
superb Zoom.

Tony Barley - first ascent of Black Wall Eliminate (E2), Almscliff 1967
(photo by Dennis Gray)

Hetchell, or Pompey Caley as it used to be known, had probably been frequented by locals for many years and indeed recent correspondence from John Temple recalls that he climbed there in 1955 and was introduced to the crag by his Scoutmaster J.A. (Rex) Fairbrother who had climbed there in early war years with Arthur Dolphin and Bill Brigham. Most of the cracks and chimneys had been ascended by then, and the line now taken by Bell was pegged. No specific records of ascents from this era can, however, be found.

In 1962 John Johnson and Bill Todd climbed and named seven of the most obvious crack and chimney lines including the excellent and still popular Centurion and Pompeii Chimney. They then introduced other friends, including Brian Evans, to the crag. Evans added a few harder climbs including the superb Cassius Crawl with his wife Aileen. However, the hardest climb of the year, The Corbel, required the importation of the club's 'top gun', Allan Austin, to ensure success.

These early routes were written up in a supplement of the 1965 YMC journal and the crag became instantly popular. By the end of the decade Dave Musgrove had led (or soloed) several new routes including Wailing Wall, Crutch and, with Bob Knapton, added a girdle (with a ground fall from the second pitch when a hold broke). Allan Austin returned with Chris Mitchell climbing Mitchell's Wall and the previously pegged Bell.

The 1970s - Leeds University, Livesey and Fawcett.
The late 1960s saw a general lull in major developments on grit throughout the area as most of the established activists concentrated on the 'Golden Age' of limestone development. It wasn't until 1970 when things got a real kick start from a group of highly talented students from the Leeds University Union Climbing Club who soon found that, with a little effort and healthy competition on their latest piece of campus sports equipment - 'The Wall'- they could easily compete on the crag with the best of the local gurus.

John Syrett became the best known star but with co-stars like Allan Manson, Pete Kitson, Geoff Hankinson, Brian Hall, Tim Jepson, Mike Hammill, Steve Bancroft and John Stainforth, and a full supporting cast including journal writer, log keeper and bouldering king Bernard Newman their place in climbing folk lore soon became assured. The club was not an exclusive group and several non-university members became almost indistinguishable from the students because of associations struck up on The Wall. Ken Wood and Andy Wild fell into this category. The University Club had had an active climbing team throughout the 1960s with the likes of Dave Nicoll, John Moss and Mike Mortimer being particularly active on the limestone. Their influence inspired the 70s group into a gritstone revolution of spectacular proportions. The first new route was Ken Wood's True Grit at Brimham in June 1970 then in November 1970 John Syrett opened his account on The Brutaliser at the same crag. The following day he made what was then thought to be the second ascent of Wall Of Horrors at Almscliff.

Over the next four years routes such as Big Greenie, Encore, Rectum Rift, The Virgin and The Gypsy at Almscliff; Jokers Wall, Picnic, and Red Tape at Brimham; Fingernacker Crack and Dypso at Caley; Gronff and Backslider on the Chevin; Earl Buttress and Early Riser at Earl Crag, After Eight at Rylstone; Guillotine at Guisecliff; Brown Sugar and Heatwave at Heptonstall, Augustus and Livia at Hetchell and Propeller Wall at Ilkley was as impressive a list of important new routes as any comparable group had achieved in previous generations including Dolphin's in the forties and Austin's in the late fifties and early sixties. In the LUUCC log book, where most of this record of achievement is chronicled, descriptions are recorded in a modest and matter-of-fact way with most of these climbs graded either VS or HVS! The boys just didn't appreciate how good they were and a typical example was Propeller Wall at Ilkley which Syrett soloed and graded VS! It was repeated in similar fashion by several of the group and although someone added an H to the grade it didn't seem to occur to anyone that it was significantly harder and bolder than most of what had gone before. It now rates E5 and sees very few on-sight repeats!

Syrett's dominance faded in the mid 70s following a seriously severed tendon but the momentum was maintained by Mike Hammill and Al Manson. High Noon was a route typical of this pair and born out of a friendly but serious rivalry. Manson won in this case but some of Hammill's later efforts such as Opus, The Ems Telegram and Yellow Peril at Almscliff; Swan Arcade and Left Wall at Brimham and Quark at Caley put him firmly in the 'top flight' of contemporary pioneers. Al Manson continued developments throughout the Seventies and Eighties concentrating most on Almscliff, Caley, Brimham and Hetchell. At Brimham Grit Expectations was an outstanding lead and an inspired, and inspiring, route name. Adrenaline Rush at Caley was another memorable achievement. Manson, who never truly grasped the concepts of the grading system, nevertheless felt that this was by far the hardest route he had ever climbed and gave it Hard Extremely Severe (7b) in the 1982 guide. He went on to even greater things at Caley during the eighties, but more about that later. Manson's long 'affair' with

Hetchell started in 1974 and during the next few years his persistence here produced such technical gems as Lurcio's Lip, Up Pompeii, and Reach For A Peach. At Brandrith, Battlecat climbed with Andy Wild remains the hardest route on the crag even today.

The Leeds University boys didn't have it all their own way during the mid seventies. A new wave was rapidly developing in the form of Pete Livesey, quickly followed by his apprentice Ron Fawcett. The Livesey/Fawcett partnership became instantly famous, not least because of monthly publicity in a news hungry new magazine called Crags. A full page advertising picture of Fawcett soloing Western Front at Almscliff was particularly memorable, and highly inspiring.

Pete Livesey had been around the Yorkshire scene for several years and initially became notorious for his futuristic (but not necessarily ethically pure) free ascents of several limestone peg routes but in 1974 his first free ascent of Wellington Crack hit the gritstone headlines. He followed this up with the bold arete of Guillotine and the technical Beyond the Fringe also at Ilkley before teaming up with Al Manson for the strenuous All Quiet across the most impressive wall at Almscliff. With Fawcett in tow he made the first complete lead of 'Arries 'Ook although Hammill and Manson had climbed the upper crux a few days earlier. At Crookrise he led the very serious Walkover and at Heptonstall joined forces with Al Manson again on Hard Line.

Ron Fawcett grew up at Embsay and in his youth soloed almost all the existing routes on the crags in the Skipton district adding numerous new ones in the process. He submitted descriptions of many only to have most rejected by the guidebook committee of the day as minor boulder problems (how things have changed). Those that did impress the committee however, have impressed many of us since. Slip And Slide at Crookrise was probably the area's first E6 and routes like Cheshire Cat at Eastby and Kipper at Earl still see few repeats. He provided a companion route to Adrenaline Rush at Caley with Psycho but it was at Ilkley that he really pushed standards up another notch. His early routes here included the pumpy Hand Jive, Diamond Dogs and the Sunburst Finish, followed in 1977 by Slide Zone and another rarely repeated E6, Shock Horror. Milky Way climbed in 1978 is arguably his best known Yorkshire grit route but Desperate Dan, climbed the following year is now acknowledged as probably the first true E7.

Though the Leeds University teams along with Livesey and Fawcett dominated the decade in terms of standard advancement the 1970s saw considerable consolidation on most crags from several other teams. Tony Barley continued his passion for green and vegetated

Guisecliff producing two of its best climbs yet, Aftermath and Mastermind amid a host of less memorable excavations. At Brimham he 'imported' Jerry Peel to triumph where Brown had failed 20 years earlier on Gigglin' Crack. Jerry was also beginning to make his mark at Widdop by the end of the decade adding Piton Crack and the bold Afternoon Delight. His Naked Edge climbed in 1978 at Simon's Seat is one of the finest 'micro-routes' on Yorkshire grit.

Ian Edwards and Bill Turner began a very systematic and thorough campaign to climb every available line on the neglected Baildon Bank and added around 80 new routes between 1973 and 1979. They also played a supporting role to Fawcett at Ilkley but their routes there, though technically difficult were less significant.

John Eastham produced three classics in 1978 his Thumper at Eastby is bold and was previously an undergraded frightener. It is nevertheless a fine piece of climbing. Crazy Diamond at Rylstone and A Question Of Balance at Simon's Seat are more amenable but delightful E2s.

In the Calderdale area the Johns Barraclough, Barker and Sheard together with Steve Foster took over the development at Woodhouse Scar, with occasional visits from Livesey and Fawcett. Sheard's Clingen was an early breakthrough followed later by routes such as the bold Pinch soloed by Foster in 1977. Bob Whittaker and his Lancashire raiders were beginning to gain prominence developing Robin Hood's Rocks and adding several routes at Heptonstall. Charlie and Sheila Vigano also crossed the border from Blackburn to initiate the exploration of Halton Heights Quarry. Charlie, an ex-member of the 1950s Creagh Dhu and Rock And Ice clubs, became in later years a true connoisseur of quarried esoterica.

Martin and Bob Berzins added some climbs to Brimham, notably Martin's leap for posterity to clinch Vam, and Bob's fine arete, Rotifer. They even ventured into the jungle at Guisecliff and came out Nice 'n' Sleazy. Bob retired from climbing soon after but Martin continued his campaign well into the next decade with, most notably, several hard extended boulder problems on the Virgin boulder at Almscliff.

The Eighties and the rise of John Dunne.
The early 1980s saw new teams emerge at Almscliff and first off the mark were Charles Cook and up and coming guidebook editor Graham Desroy who produced three hard climbs including the intimidating but very fine Grand Illusion. Even harder, however, and

not repeated for many years were Rob Gawthorpe's China Syndrome and Forgotten Wall. China Syndrome containing probably the first 7a move above bouldering height on Yorkshire Grit. Al Manson and Pete Kitson re-formed their old partnership to celebrate All Our Yesterdays on the crag that made them famous a decade earlier. Gawthorpe also climbed several last great problems at Baildon and Hetchell during this period including Scar Arete and Intrepid at the former and Hunchback at the latter.

Mike Hammill continued as he'd left off in the seventies with several new routes at Brimham and did a sterling job in collating over 100 routes and problems at Shipley Glen for the 1982 guidebook. Many of the Glen's longer and most serious problems are Mike's work from this era. Ilkley was fairly quiet in the early eighties but Paul Craven's Voyage To The Outer Limits over the roof on the Cow was impressive and Andy Brown's Super Direct start to Bald Pate gave the locals something to work on for a while (some are still trying!). Andy Brown came to prominence during the seventies excelling on several serious extended boulder problems at Caley. His best known there being the wall left of The Great Flake but he vied with Manson for the first ascents of several others.

Bob Whittaker and Ralph Pickering appeared to have the development of many of the Calder Valley crags to themselves during 1981 adding virtually every route of any consequence to Horsehold Scout and Robin Hood's Rocks. During the winter of 1982, however, Bruce Goodwin led another team of Lancashire raiders to develop what, by Yorkshire standards, is the highly esoteric Crow's Nest Wood Quarry. The dank north facing walls here provided stars such as Mark Leach, Greg Rimmer, Mick Ryan and Tony Nicholls several days of pleasure and routes up to E3 in standard. They may be good by 'red rose' standards but haven't tempted many 'Tykes' to take up the challenge and continue the task. Goodwin and Gordon Mason then almost single handedly brought Darby Delph into the climbing limelight before, fortunately, a pair of nesting peregrines gave the rest of us an excuse to avoid the place for most of the year.

At Slipstones Ron Kenyon and Stew Wilson recorded the first ascent of the excellent Ellingstring while checking descriptions for the North of England Guide. Unfortunately even before that guide appeared in 1980 it was rendered out of date due to the exploits of a strong team from Teesside. Paul Ingham, Ian (Squawk) Dunn, Steve Brown and Dave Paul were introduced to the crag by Tony Marr and Alan Taylor early that year. Over several consecutive weekends Taylor added Alan's Arete and Easy Pickings, Ingham climbed Agra Right Hand, Leany Meany, Rock On and the superb

Ripper, whilst Marr added Agrete and Right Hand Twin. Squawk's Arete was the work of Ian Dunn and finally Dave Stainthorpe climbed 'his' wall to end a very productive years work.

Returning early in 1982 Ingham produced the bold, Paul's Arete and the testing Impregnable, and later added two popular test pieces - Wisecrack and Micro Corner. The highlight of the year came from Ian Dunn with his three star gem Atomic. In February 1983 an article a new magazine, Rock Action One, updated the developments at Slipstones and one of Yorkshire's best kept secrets was finally open to all. The crag became increasingly popular but it was the Tees-side regulars who maintained the developmental momentum until 1985, after which exploration waned for a while.

Visitors to Great Wolfrey were infrequent until, in the mid seventies, Ken Wood climbed Walter's Rib, the prominent arete above the plaque and John Eastham recorded Werewolf in 1980. The crag became relatively popular for a time with regular forays by John Mackenzie who on one of his visits made the unfortunate mistake of letting go, the penalty was a slow and painful retreat. Martin Berzins, Chris Sowden and Tony Burnell visited the crag in 1988 and climbed several routes including, Little Red Riding Hood, A Company of Wolves and Sheep's Clothing. Since then the fences have got higher and the 'Private' notices more prominent and relatively few pioneers have taken up the challenge.

During the mid eighties activity on the mainstream crags involved several parties of both old and new pioneers. Caley witnessed some early breakthroughs in 1984 with the ascent of two last great problems. The Great Flake by Craig Smith was closely followed by Allan Manson's bold push on Marrowbone Jelly creating the county's second true E7. At Chevin Quarry in 1983 a young Don Barr beat the opposition to the major line of Jenny Tulls but fate cruelly robbed us of an outstanding young climber later the same year when he was killed by lightning in the Verdon Gorge.

At Crookrise Paul Greenland, Brian Swales and Richard Davies pushed development forward for a while but Derek Hargreaves' contributions here, at Eastby, Widdop, Earl and Simon's Seat were more significant and have continued sporadically until the present day. He first came to notice at Earl, with ascents such as Jump To The Beat and Captain Gap, followed in 1984 by Grape Nut. He championed developments at Halton Heights the same year adding nine routes, mostly solo and then returned to Crookrise to complete the bold Pen Sketches and had A Lifetime's Dream on Walker's Slab. In 1988 And She Was and Finesse gave him the two hardest routes at Simon's Seat.

Jerry Peel was active throughout the eighties at Widdop where the superb Swift and Sure brought a new boldness to the area but it was at Earl that amongst several hard but lesser lines his Desert Island Arete took pride of place and for 10 years repelled most, if not all, repeat attempts. Jerry picked off minor plums at Almscliff and at Ilkley made two significant contributions to the right side of The Cow with Galaxy and The Marine Who Slept In. These latter routes were major lines but overshadowed somewhat by the dramatic achievements of the area's newest rising star, John Dunne.

John started his climbing career at Ilkley and within a few years the teenager from Bradford repeated almost everything on the crag and made it his own. In 1986, at age seventeen, he produced the first of a series of hard new routes with Late Fever, Peach Melba, Desperate Dredd, Deathwatch and Superb Too Right. An impressive first solo ascent of Wellington Crack was followed by the serious Snap Decision in the quarry and an incredible solo ascent (it is unprotected) to create Yorkshire's first E8, Countdown to Disaster in Rocky Valley.

1987 was the second of the two big years for Dunne and Ilkley. He added two very hard micro-routes to the Calf, Super Set and Three More Reps. Then in October, after months of rehearsal and psychological preparation, he led the right arete of the Cow to create the truly magnificent New Statesman, the major prize of the decade. It had repelled all previous top rope attempts and is undoubtedly one of the finest pieces of gritstone climbing anywhere. It waited 9 years for a repeat and by the time this book went to press had only just received its third ascent, and a starring role in two films!

Dunne also made significant contributions at Baildon where Cool Trickster was probably his best addition, and at Caley he proved Nothing's Safe when he completed the very difficult arete right of Great Flake. It should be remembered that he was also breaking new ground at Malham Cove during this period before going on to astound the Peak regulars climbing Parthian Shot at Burbage, the first gritstone E9 in 1989.

The 1989 Guide inspires fresh impetus
1988 was an important year throughout the region as work on the last edition of this guide began. Almost all the crags received a thorough review and several, such as Rylstone, Hebden Ghyll, and Great Wolfrey a complete overhaul to bring them up to date following periods of developmental decline. Brandrith and Eavestone were written up in detail for the first time by Kim Buck

and Tony Barley respectively though in the case of Eavestone the guidebook deadline came just too soon. Brown Beck crag was discovered in Colsterdale and gave the committee a dilemma, as to include this new find without Slipstones seemed illogical and there was some uncertainty whether a new North of England guide would be produced or not. In the event both were included written up by Tony Burnell who also visited and documented several other new minor crags.

At Rylstone Dave Musgrove and Frank Wilkinson with an assorted supporting cast more than doubled the number of recorded routes from 51 to 121 in less than 12 months and the popularity of this erstwhile moorland outpost soared. An important contribution had been made in 1986 by Greg Rimmer but his Marine Who Had No Friends was found to be vastly undergraded, and extremely strenuous. Musgrove's Pocket Battleship, Beached Whale and Full Nelson are memorable along with several excellent micro-routes recorded for the first time but which may well date back to Fawcett's youth in the 1970s. Of these, High Flying Adored, England Expects, Slip Slidin' Away and the White Doe are particularly satisfying. Wilkinson's highlights were the topically named Frankie Comes To Rylstone, Orbital Highway, Solo Games and the sweet but serious, Little Peach. Paul Greenland joined in later on and added the delightful Poetry In Motion and tricky Surfer's Paradise. At the eleventh hour of guidebook production Graham Desroy was imported to push it out up the Bear Faced Streak.

At Brimham a similar frenzy of activity was on-going under the 'captaincy' of Steve Rhodes. His team, including Martin Berzins, Chris Sowden, and local guru Al Manson accounted for around 30 hard new climbs almost all in the E2 to E5 category. Rhodes led Steady VS Arete and Berzins Michael Michael Superman. Berzins and Manson inspired each other to some excellent finds, the best being Sow's That and Reach for the Stye and Berzins got Rat Arsed with the help of Nic Kidd. The old notice boards and their bolts were put to use on a unique trio of routes, Cocoa Club Board Meeting, Take No Notice and Board to Tears by Rhodes who then shared leads with Greg Rimmer on Mae West's Rib and House Points Tomorrow. John Allen stole a march on the locals in September by sneaking in armed with rope and wire brush and sneaking out with a Morose Mongoose.

1988 was also another important year at Caley. Following John Dunne's ascent of Nothing's Safe Al Manson got worried that his long term projects on the far left of the Roadside Group may be under threat so he pulled out the stops to finalise matters on Death

Drop 2000 and To Be Is Not To Bolt. Quark at last got its scientific bedfellows when Graham Desroy added Charm and Steve Rhodes led Strangeness. All four have merited up-grading in this edition in the light of subsequent experience!

Eastby was not left out of the guidebook up-date with Alan Taylor and Kevin Barrett joining Derek Hargreaves in bringing the crag to maturity. Defective Direct and Genuflex being particularly notable from this period. At Hebden Ghyll a young Y.M.C. team including Adam Wainwright, Fraser Hardie and John Paul Hotham almost doubled the number of routes in this 'sleepy' valley.

One other new name came to the fore in 1989 producing a series of very bold lines which rivalled the test-pieces of John Dunne at Ilkley. In August that year Dave Pegg began a short but intensive campaign at Earl Crag with an E5, an E6 and then the E7 Mind Bomb before moving on to Rylstone where he soloed the much eyed Heartbeat City. The unthinkable landing below this stunning E8 arete makes it as serious as anything in the county and it remains unrepeated 10 years on. He added Resurrection and The Bottom Line, another E7, to Brimham and finally a short bold arete, Dead Babies to Eastby before sensible maturity dawned and he discovered bolted limestone at Kilnsey satisfied his new routing urge in a less stressful environment.

Towards E9 - The 1990s
It almost seems impossible to imagine that such a relatively small and continuously popular crag as Almscliff could go on producing a steady flow of new routes through yet another decade but the 1990s saw no change in the pace of development. Admittedly many of the additions have been extended boulder problems like Oliver Wright's super pumpy Jess's Roof and Tony Simpson's desperate start to Magnum Opus. A number of others have found worthwhile variants such as the bold finish to Retribution Rib from John Paul Hotham. Duncan Drake's Penny Pip and Tony Marr's No Man's Land, which provides an interesting extension to either Great Western or Western Front were also significant.

The title of 'Almscliff Obsessive of the Decade', however, must go to Pete Brown from York who, over the last eight years has produced over a dozen new climbs or variations as well as repeats of every existing route, including the second ascent of China Syndrome. His first ascents include a new direct finish to Opus, a hard eliminate and a new traverse on Whisky Wall and Microscopic Wall a direct finish up the bold blank rib above Z Climb. Brown's final contribution of 1997, and perhaps his most impressive is Megadoom, the direct finish up the headwall that Impending Doom avoided. Undoubtedly this is the most exposed series of 6b moves on the crag. Three final additions in 1998 were only upstaged in August by Paul Clarke who found a gap between Traditional Climb and Forgotten Wall and squeezed in Remembrance Some Day - how did Pete miss that!

Developments continued apace elsewhere and at Brimham Nick Dixon broke into E8 territory in 1990 but almost also broke some bones during a ground fall from Tender Homecoming. This fine arete lost a crucial pebble soon afterwards and has resisted all repeat attempts since. Nick's Pig Slip Cow Punk on the same crag is also a bold and very serious little number. In 1994 Dave Slater made Friends And Enemies whilst a bold and bulging micro-route on Kangaroo Wall gave Tony Simpson a Road Rage Experience in 1996. The following year Hedge Up and Senior Service were provided by Mick Johnson, and Nigel Baker found a Stone Age Reveller in the gully close to Lancet Crack.

Since the last 'bumper fun book' was published, however, Tony Marr and his friends from Tees-side, notably Mike Tooke, Frank Fitzgerald, Peter and Pam Shawcross have taken over the most prolific route development role. Few major climbs have been added by this most enthusiastic team but around 50 very worthwhile variants and fillers in have been found. These include Wise Crack, an excellent traverse on the Cubic Block; Spring Steal, a delightful E1 on the Anvil; Stepped Buttress, the Lovebug variants and the arete finish to Who Needs Friends in the Lovers Leap area; Crackeroo, Walleroo and several others in the vicinity of Kangaroo Wall. They also added ten routes on the previously undeveloped Hare's Head rocks in the north eastern corner of the estate.

Tony Marr's team also completely re-wrote Slipstones and Brown Beck Crag for this edition having been disappointed with the historical and grading inaccuracies in all the previous guides. Several new routes were added to Brown Beck during this process and Frank Fitzgerald wandered off into the hidden valley below to stumble across another completely virgin crag, Birk Gill in 1993. Inevitably it didn't stay virgin for long and of 20 routes pioneered over the next two years Class Action by Marr and Tooke is undoubtedly the best.

Returning to the Brimham area, the outlying crags were receiving quiet attention from several teams. John Henderson and Paul Carling added six routes to these crags including the bold Amadeus and Salieri to Crow Crag and State Of The Union in the Plantation. Around the same time Luke Dow and Rob Liddle took time off from a substantial re-development at Rolling Gate to find Salubrious

Navaho Indians and a Curious Motion down amongst several other new climbs in the trees of the Plantation Crack area. In 1997 Phillipe Osborne sorted out the descriptive confusion on these crags adding several variants of his own but his best effort was the fine looking Riddler on the main prow of Bat Buttress.

Phil Osborne was also active at Crookrise in 1997 where his eliminate Mighty White formed a thin 'sandwich' between Hovis and Small Brown. Others active at Crookrise since the last guide include Jerry Peel who soloed the bold and serious groove of Duck 'n' Dive, Julian Lines who squeezed a couple of bold eliminates onto Walkers Slab and Derek Hargreaves whose Massive Attack on the rib above Small Brown looks a rather serious proposition. As with Tony Marr at Brimham the local guru here, Brian Swales, set about a thorough review of unclimbed, and previously unclaimed, lines and recorded around twenty that hadn't appeared in print before. Best of this bunch were the well placed Lyndhurst, Moonshadow and the Mindbender trio. He provided the same service at Eastby cleaning up the left-hand slabs and several variants on the main cliff.

At Brandrith, Kim Buck's evocative write up for the 1989 guide provoked a short flurry of renewed interest the following year when Jeff Appleyard and Mike Gale forced The Torso Twins whilst Dave Musgrove and a new bristle brush combined to create the techni-cally frustrating New Broom Sweeps Green. Developments lapsed again until 1995 when David Burnett girdled the West Buttress and claimed the very pleasant Summertime Solo. The obvious eliminate line of Intruding Fool saw three claims in two years, Stuart King pipping two others (one of whom was Bob Larkin) to the post in 1996. Two late claims (one from Stuart King) for the even better line just right of Antler's Route had to be discarded however when it was discovered Bob Larkin had recorded Eastern Arete in 1989. Finally David Burnett and friends from the Craven Club then mopped up several micro-routes and a few eliminates during a very thorough re-appraisal for this guide.

For many years, Bridestones had its own last great problem. The Obscene Cleft was top roped by Mark Leach in the early eighties, but he was chastised by onlookers for actually bringing a rope on to the edge and he never returned to lead it. Neither did anyone else until John Dunne broke with tradition in 1996 just beating various other hopefuls to the prize of this grotesque and amazing feature. Since the last edition many new micro problems and one move wonders have been added and, no doubt, will continue to be added by new generations. Many will have been done before but not recorded, though they may be equally worthy to many in this guide.

Since Dave Pegg's onslaught at Earl in 1989 only Martin Wood's Abstract Attitude in 1991 has been really notable. In 1995 Andy Cave thought he detected female pheromones rather than something fishy in the vicinity of The Kipper and Scent Of A Woman became the result. A year later Derek Hargreaves ventured into the quarry for a couple of micro routes and various others claimed, and reclaimed, odds and ends and variants but little else of historical importance has emerged.

Late in 1989 Tony Barley co-opted Dave Musgrove to try a couple of Lines at Eavestone and though on his first two visits Dave wasn't too impressed the ascent of Eavestone Crack in August got him hooked on the place. Three years, two pruning saws and several wire brushes later the pair emerged with a fully developed crag containing around 160 routes. Dave's best efforts included The Alamo, Battlement, Touching The Void, Here There Be Dragons and the crag's first two E5s, Genesis and Dragonslayer, whilst amongst Tony's leads Crazy Paver, Treasure Island, Little Gem, Canada Dry, Cream and Over The Looking Glass were outstanding.

Several others became enchanted with this idyllic location for a while, but few were prepared to put in the required technical cleaning time. Kim Greenald led Strange Attractor and the highly technical Pebbledash before making the first free ascent of Eavestone Wall. Steve Webster made a comeback to lead Don't Worry I'm A Nurse, and Going Catatonic whilst David Musgrove Jnr. snatched Fat Chance from under dad's nose. The hardest route, only completed after two ground falls, was Life Begins At Forty, an E6 'birthday present' for Bob Smith.

Guisecliff had slipped from popularity during the eighties but In 1990 Paul Jenkinson and Steve Earnshaw climbed the striking arete of On the Edge to provide a superb and committing adventure which, at E6, is currently the crag's hardest route. Mark Radtke made an early repeat and on this visit made a mental note of several other possibilities. In 1997 keen for something new he discovered the high quality Scrying on Comet Buttress and Over The Top on the North Buttress Block. Both were climbed with Dave Barton, although Dave had to be enticed onto the sharp end on the latter. Also on the North Buttress Block Radtke and Greg Rimmer added the unusual but fine, Cutting the Cord, whilst on Slot Buttress Radtke and Jerry Peel both led the superb Warriors of Hunaman which ascends an improbable but irresistible feature. Also at this time Greg Rimmer and friends developed the boulders near the folly and produced about fifteen good problems although it was Andy Cave who

Mark Radtke - modern activist on the first ascent of The Skryking (E5),
Guisecliff 1997   *(photo by Greg Rimmer)*

pulled out the stops and climbed the obvious bold overhanging nose.

The same team, captained and motivated by Mark Radtke also championed the revival of Hawkcliffe near Steeton. Brian Emmison who published a guide to the crag in Climber magazine in 1965 documented over twenty routes in the Moderate to Severe grades and at the end of his article enticingly indicated that *"After the publication of this guide the number of climbs will be doubled within a month"*. Unfortunately no documented evidence of the anticipated activity appears to exist.

Whilst it is likely that most of the obvious easier lines were climbed by Emmison and friends during this period other developments remain unclear. It is believed that Jimmy Fullalove and John Sheard climbed Squirrel Crack during the late 1960s and Dave Cunningham together with Jack and Alan Firth also made visits around this time. Access then became restricted and only sporadic, clandestine raids occurred during the 70s and 80s and no records can be found.

Paul Jenkinson and Mick Ryan explored the crag in the early 90's but climbed only the bold Woodland Ecology. In 1995, extensive logging of the wood exposed some of the buttresses to the elements even making them visible from the Keighley bypass. The following spring, intrigued by the sight of the newly exposed outcrops Mark Radtke visited the crag and seeing the potential set about enthusing an able bodied but sometimes lethargic new routing team. After realising the potential their lethargy evaporated and over the next few weeks a batch of hard and excellent new routes were climbed. Radtke was accountable for Ginny Greenteeth, Stepmother Jag, The Dawning and The Crack of Dawn. Jerry Peel delighted in the discovery of more unclimbed aretes and added the superb The Blood on The Shamrock and Flame Arete, whilst Dave Barton climbed Babes in the Boneyard, Creaking Joints and Walk By. Not to be outdone Mick Johnstone added the excellent and technical Driveby and later that year Terry Holmes and Neil Herbert added Freedom, whilst Alan Firth and Ian Fenton climbed What No Boc No.

Early in 1998 Mark Radtke introduced Andy Cave to the crag and pointed him at Hawkcliff's last? great plumb. The obvious and impressive line on Tower Buttress had been cleaned and prepared by Dave Barton and Jerry Peel three years previously but despite their considerable efforts it did not succumb. Cave completed his ascent in fading spring light accompanied by a delightful chorus from the local inhabitants and compared

Birdsong with the likes of Beau Geste and Janus in terms of feel and difficulty. A month later Radtke shared leads with Dave Barton on Bubba and Call Of The Curlew, two more technical aretes. The following day Andy Watts climbed the reachy Abandon Hope, and finally in May Dave Musgrove got a slice of the action adding Black Forest Gateaux.

Mark Radtke and Ian Cooksey had put in an equal effort at Heptonstall in 1987 to conquer the headwall above Pulpit Route creating A Step in the Light Green. Three years later Radtke was back with Jerry Peel, combining talents to add a companion route, Orange Crush to the same piece of wall. In 1995, this time with the able assistance of Dave Barton they traversed the same section on The Blue Bus. The mid 1990's saw minor additions to the right hand outcrop and then Derek Hargreaves traversed out of Haboob at a high level creating Climb And Tick Conditions at a 'reachy' E3. A more significant addition on this wall came in 1997, however, when Matt Troilett and Steve Smith gathered Vertical Speed and the crag's first E7!

After the tremendous developments of the 1980s at Ilkley it is perhaps not surprising that the last decade of the millennium has been one of consolidation here. In 1991 Sean Miles 'red-pointed' the bold and difficult Rodney Mullen whilst Mark Radtke and Jerry Peel traversed the front of the Cow on one of their Black And White Days the following year. Several lesser routes and variants were added by various parties over the next 5 years but intense bouldering development seemed to satisfy the urges of the most able potential new routers during this time and it was 1997 before serious route development restarted. First came Big Buels from Dave Kells on the wall to the right of Guillotine then John Dunne returned to the fray with what is described as a 'safe' E8 - if that isn't a contradiction in terms - the pendulum potential of Loaded, however , should give the day trippers some excitement from the auditorium in the quarry. John also added the bold Baby Spice and the desperate Fast Forward whilst his friend and newcomer Jason Pickles got 'In A Pickle', a scary E6 extended problem to the right of the Cow.

In the late 1980s at Hetchell Justin Voglar attacked the direct finish to Tiberius to produce The Fall of the Roman Empire and then Kim Buck added the more independent and very fine Dead Angst. Since then little of major significance has been added. Buck squeezed in Arc en Ceil and Adamant whilst Dave Musgrove filled a few more gaps with When In Rome, The Empire Strikes Back and Caligula but during the last few years the regulars have concentrated on

ever more desperate boulder problems with pride of place going to Kim Buck and Dave Sarkar for the traverse Preparation H. Surely there now can't be a single hold left unfondled here, - except perhaps...?

The early 1990s at Rylstone were years of consolidation. The 1989 guide had made the crag popular once again but, for a while, little new of real importance was found. Julian Lines filled some gaps on the boulders and Frank Booth straightened out the finish of Face Savour with Veteran. The next breakthrough came in 1995 when Tim Clifford cracked the oft tried technical problem of The Cocoa Team Special to give the hardest (but probably safest) move on the crag. Since then several more fillers and variants have been claimed by the Musgroves, Nigel Baker, and Tony Marr but the long awaited ascents of the regularly brushed walls to the left of Heartbeat City and the right of Bare Faced Streak have failed to materialise. This crag is still far from full maturity!

At Simon's Seat the 1993 film Jurassic Park inspired a significant addition, the short but serious Dino-Mania by Dave Musgrove (Jnr.). He returned in 1995, with dad and Julian Cooper in tow, to clean up the unrecorded lines on the south-west buttress, though many of these had probably been done before. In 1997 Johnny (The Dog) Cutliffe climbed Dog Lead, and Pause For Thought, two longer but easier lines on the main crag. In 1998 Derek Hargreaves returned with Matt Troilett and led Flirtin Cos I'm Hurtin, a fine clean E4 before Matt soloed the crag's first E6 the bold arete he named A Life Less Ordinary.

Across at the nearby Lords and Earls Seats the brilliant micro-routing and bouldering potential of clean and weather beaten, but long neglected gritstone boulders and small buttresses was at last documented by Bob Larkin in 1998 providing a spur for follow-up visits and consolidation by Nigel Baker, Dave Musgrove and Andy Watts. Over 30 short routes were named and though many may have been done in the past it is hard to believe that routes of such quality have never been recorded before.

The 1990s at Widdop have witnessed some dramatic develop-ments. The decade started conventionally enough with a couple of new lines added to the left side of Purgatory Buttress, and whilst Mark Radtke breached the overhang to the left of Felicity, Jerry Peel snatched the direct start to 30 seconds over Winterland 'Just In Time' to beat off a raid by 'outsiders'. John Belbin and Friends John Cramphorne and David Challenger added some fillers to the main crag and started work on the neglected Widdop West or The Drums as they are now known.

These climbs were all eclipsed, however, in 1995 when Robin Barker led a raiding party from The Peak to make off with the major prize of Reservoir Dogs, one of the hardest, and finest, lines on Yorkshire Grit. John Dunne however, regained local pride early in 1997 when he climbed Savage Earth to give the county its first Grit E9. Not satisfied that this started from Reservoir Dogs he gave it an independent start early the following year to make it even more sustained. He also renamed it Widdop Wall. John was also active on the dramatic prow at nearby Gorple where his 1995 E7, Eternal was upstaged 3 years later after much preparation by his Carmen Picasso, another wild E9.

The Bouldering Revolution

Bouldering has always been an integral part of gritstone climbing particularly in the winter when keeping moving to keep warm was not conducive to sitting belaying in the wind or fiddling with cold karabiners, nuts and Friends. It was always a part of the Summer evening scene too as a sociable and competetive element of crag behaviour but its rising profile in the climbing 'media' in recent years seemed to indicate that a significant and radical change in climbing attitudes was taking place. This is not necessarily true but one difference during the mid 1980s and early '90s was a push towards increasingly technical and powerful sport climbs on the limestone requiring intensive training to strengthen fingers, shoulders and stomach muscles. Low level traverses, sitting starts and low-slung gritstone roofs provided an ideal and relatively safe outdoor gymnasium without the sterility of indoor walls, cellar boards and weight rooms. As climbers generally trained in groups so, inevitably, competition ensued and many new problems were worked out and became yardsticks on which to measure ones progress towards some ultimate goal. For many, bouldering on grit did become an end in itself and as hundreds of new problems proliferated so the demand for a specialised bouldering guide grew.

Steve Rhodes obliged us in 1993 when his Bouldering on Yorkshire Grit was published providing details of several hundred problems on selected crags and it gave us a taste of a new grading system as well. The main activists in developing the new power problems are recorded in that guide and rumour has it that an updated version should be published around the same time as this one. Tony Barley produced a guide in 1997 to Wild Bouldering in Yorkshire which concentrates on the less frequented Nidderdale crags. As it was decided that bouldering in its new refined form could not be fully included in this guide I do not propose to include a definitive history here but some of the most noteworthy breakthroughs are credited within the first ascent lists which follow.

The Future

The impressive efforts of John Dunne and Dave Pegg in the eighties which culminated in the creation of the three E8s recorded in the last guide led to a period of stability and consolidation during the early nineties. As the decade and indeed the millennium draws to a close it is now clear that several brilliant young climbers are jockeying for position to move the game to new levels in, or even before, the 21st Century. Dunne is still the undisputed leader having pushed on at last to E9, but by the time the cool of Autumn creates those days of perfect friction and this book hits the bookshelves I suspect it will be time to start work on the supplement!

FIRST ASCENTS

ALMSCLIFF CRAG

Circa 1870   **Three Chockstones Chimney, South Chimney, The Leaf Climb, Low Man Easy Way, Tight Chimney**   William Cecil Slingsby and friends

Circa 1891   **Cup and Saucer**   Herbert Ingle, Thomas Gray
This was the first climb attempted by the pair who may also have been accompanied by Edward Calvert and C.T. Dent, all of whom were among the founder members of the Yorkshire Ramblers' Club.

1893   **The Great Chimney**   Herbert Ingle, Thomas Gray
Also known in the early days as Sixty Foot Chimney and nowadays as Long Chimney.

Pre-1894   **The Pulpit**   Thos. Gray and friends
The party climbed up the Easy Way and descended via Fat Man's Misery, calling the climb The Needle.

Pre-1894   **V Chimney and Traverse**   Herbert Ingle, C.T. Dent, Thos. Gray
Gray thought the hardest climb on the crag and Calvert said, in 1894, it was as hard as anything on the North Climb on Pillar Rock.

Pre-1894   **Stomach Traverse**   Herbert Ingle, C.T. Dent, Thos. Gray
The climb originally started up what is now Central Crack. The direct start was added later, but before 1913.

Pre-1894   **The Goblin**   Edward Calvert
Then known as Calvert's Stomach Traverse.

Pre-1900   **The Pothole, Stewpot, Square Chimney**   Ingle, Dent, Gray, Calvert

Pre-1900   **Fluted Columns**   Ingle, Dent, Gray, Calvert
The climb at that time incorporated part of the crack to the left and was known as Fluted Pillars.

Pre-1900   **Bird's Nest Crack**   Herbert Ingle, Edward Calvert
Calvert tried first but fell off! The climb was also known as the Beehive by some of the early pioneers.

Circa 1900   **Parsons' Chimney**   William Parsons
This was for many years, the hardest climb at Almscliff.

Pre-1912   **Whisky Crack**   Fred Botterill.
It was said of Fred Botterill in his obituary that "he never felt lonely until he'd run out a hundred feet of rope". However, other references and photographs from the period suggest he worked out many of the crag's boulder problems and may well have been the instigator of some, or all, of the following climbs which were recorded in Laycock's 1913 guide but not credited to anyone in particular.

Pre 1912   **The Virgin Climb, North Face, Crack and Wall, Pinnacle Flake, Zig Zag** (and the Direct),**The Niche**
According to John Laycock The Niche was "Almost the hardest problem at Almscliff". - It still is to some!

Pre-1912   **The Nose**
Also known as the 'Elbow Climb' in the early days. It was described as "fancy gymnastics" by the Yorkshire Ramblers' President, Claude Benson.

Pre-1912   **South Face Climb**
Originally named South Face Traverse.
Many of these, and other problems, were described by Benson in an article dated March 1906 in which he stated: "One meets nail marks everywhere. I should think that almost every yard of cliff and boulder has been tried at one time or another".

1919   **Frankland's Green Crack**   Claude Dean Frankland
A major achievement. The first description states: "The leader can be played

from the top of The Pulpit" indicating that side runners were allowed! However, both written and photographic evidence shows that Frankland made frequent solo ascents of this climb in the 1920s.

Pre-1923 **Central Climb** Claude Dean Frankland
Variation finish (now incorporated in Z Climb Eliminate) Dolphin and Fisher 1.8.43

Pre-1923 **Pigott's Stride** Claude Dean Frankland, Fred Pigott

Pre-1923 **South Wall Traverse** Claude Frankland
Originally named South Face Climb but the description including a difficult variation given by Frankland and the relatively-modest grade of severe led to confusion. Dolphin re-named and re-described the route in 1950.

Pre-1927 **Pulpit Corner** Claude Frankland
This was the first pitch only. Frankland thought it unjustifiable and did not record it. The second pitch was added by Austin and Evans in 1956.

1931 **Kiernan's Traverse and Rough Crack** Leonard Kiernan (solo)

Circa 1934 **Thompson's Traverse** Sydney Thompson
A technical exercise by a very fine climber which must have been quite a test piece at the time.

1938 **Pothole Direct, Fisher's Traverse, Fisher's Stride** Denys Fisher

1940 **Demon Wall** Arthur Rhodes Dolphin
The emergence of a man who, over the next 13 years, was to increase the standard of climbing in Yorkshire and the Lake District.

1940 **Z Climb** Arthur Dolphin
The first half had been done pre-1906 as a variation start to Cup and Saucer.

3.5.41 **Overhanging Groove** Arthur Dolphin, Robert Heap
Another bold effort and a typically-fine ARD line.

24.8.41 **Black Wall** Arthur Dolphin and Robert Heap
Direct finish by Mike Hammill, Stephen Williams, Mike Raine and Simon Collins in 1980.

30.8.41 **Crack of Doom** Arthur Dolphin, Robert Heap

29.11.42 **V Crack Direct** Arthur Dolphin, David Varley, John Cook
This may, in fact, have been V Chimney Direct which Dolphin referred to in letters in 1948 but which was not recorded in his diaries.

C. 1943 **Jacob's Ladder** Denys Fisher

19.9.43 **Great Western** Arthur Dolphin, Robert Heap
Dolphin was apprehensive, but was spurred on by the crowd that had gathered to watch. It was an outstandingly-bold ascent of, perhaps, Almscliff's best route. ARD led the alternative finish some time later.

14.5.44 **The North West Girdle** Arthur Dolphin, John Cook and John (Pug) Ball
Dolphin had inspected the line before. Ball, however, was an "Ilkley man" who joined the team at the last moment with no prior knowledge of the route and climbed it in style as last man on the rope. A magnificent achievement.

18.3.45 **Retribution Rib** Arthur Dolphin, David Varley
Short, but as bold as anything at the crag at this time.

23.4.46 **Z Climb Eliminate** Arthur Dolphin, John Cook
Superdirect start by Paul Dawson, Dave Musgrove, Andy Wild 19.6.82

18.8.46 **Birdlime Traverse** Arthur Dolphin, John Cook
Dolphin recorded the first descent of Overhanging Groove the same day.

25.4.48 **Teaspoon Variation** Arthur Dolphin, Des Birch
The culmination of Dolphin's remarkable Almscliff years.

Circa 1956 **Morrell's Wall** Mike Drysdale, Dennis Gray
Tom Morrell had found it but couldn't do it!

28.4.57 **Finale Slab** Allan Austin, Brian Evans
Des Birch had climbed the line some years earlier with a peg for aid.

30.11.57 **High Level Traverse** Allan Austin (solo)

22.4.58 **Shuffle Crack** Allan Austin, Brian Evans
This was the first recorded ascent. It is documented that Dolphin top-roped the line in April 1942 and called it Crack of Apollo. There are also strong

suggestions that he led the route in 1952/53 shortly before his death. The route still hadn't appeared in print by 1967 when Ed Drummond had the audacity to claim it and name it The Two Ton Sardine, and he used a peg!

9.7.58   **Western Front**   Allan Austin (solo)
A major breakthrough. Austin had failed on a top rope and then took a solo fall, luckily threading the boulder, before he eventually succeeded.

28.6.61   **The Wall of Horrors**   Allan Austin (solo)
Another major achievement. The line had been top-roped by Dolphin in 1944 and Austin practised the climb thoroughly on a rope before making his ascent. Even then, combined tactics were necessary for the problematic start. The variation on the left was added by Charles Cook and Andy Swann in 1980

1966   **Barley Mow**   Tony Barley (solo)
A serious, and rarely repeated boulder problem.

June 1966   **Yellow Wall, Black Wall Eliminate**   Tony Barley, Chas Hird
Two typically bold and strenuous efforts from Tony Barley.

May 1967   **Green Gully Wall**   Tony Barley, Tony Roche

May 1967   **The Complete Crag Girdle**   Tony Barley (solo)

Oct 1969   **Oubliette, Clematis**   Eric Lillie, Ian Brimrose

Pre 1969   **Rift Crack, Constipation Crack**   unknown
Often confused with each other

4.6.72   **Syrett's Roof**   John Syrett
A new dimension in bouldering!

June 1972   **Pram Pusher's Paradise**   Al Manson, Pete Kitson
The new Leeds University team cut their teeth on "The Crag" after discovering, exploiting and setting the trend for indoor wall training.

Aug 1972   **Rectum Rift**   Al Manson, Pete Kitson

Mar 1973   **Yorkshire Puddin'**   Al Manson, Pete Kitson

24.4.73   **Whisky Wall**   John Syrett, Al Manson

28.4.73   **Acetabulum**   Al Manson, Geoff Hankinson, Pete Kitson

28.4.73   **Gypsy**   Pete Kitson (solo)

1.5.73   **Big Greeny**   John Syrett, Al Manson
A long-standing problem. It was named after the No. 56 bus which served the university in Leeds.

1.5.73   **Encore**   John Syrett, Al Manson, Ken Wood
Previously led by Eric Lillie using a hand-placed piton for protection. The strict ethics of the day dictated that the ascent was not valid.

4.5.73   **First Night**   John Syrett, Al Manson

12.7.73   **Twelfth Night**   Pete Kitson, Al Manson

15.7.73   **Virgin**   Pete Kitson (solo)

1973   **Kitson Did it First**   Pete Kitson
In less than two years Syrett, Manson and Kitson had raised the technical standards by two full grades to ensure that Almscliff retained its position at the forefront of British outcrop climbing.

29.7.73   **Orchrist**   Hank Pasquill
A major blow to Yorkshire pride. The Machiavellian mind of Steve Bancroft designed the protection.

Circa 1973   **Bancroft's Roof**   Steve Bancroft

27.6.74   **All Quiet**   Pete Livesey, Al Manson
A descent was made down Western Front to rest. Nevertheless a bold lead.

2.2.75   **Torpedo**   Mike Hammill, James Mackinley

1975   **Blackpool Promenade**   Dave Musgrove, Mike Butler

1975   **'Arries 'Ook**   Pete Livesey, Ron Fawcett
A devious solution to a long-standing problem. The name arises from the fact that Harry Mammal (Mike Hammill) had been trying the more direct line and had, it is rumoured, considered using a skyhook. Hammill and Manson did, in fact, climb the direct finish in April 1975, before the lower wall was solved.

5.4.75   **Opus**   Mike Hammill (solo)
The variation finishes added by Pete Brown 29.6.97

Circa 1976 **Dolphinian**   Al Manson

Circa 1976 **Why Climb**   Al Manson, Ray Conlon

Circa 1976 **WASC**   Al Manson, Ray Conlon
Standing for What a Silly Climb and Manson gave it a silly grade too -HVS 5b!

Circa 1977 **Depth Charger,**   Al Manson
Possibly pre-dated by Mike Hammill.

Circa 1977 **The Ems Telegram**   Mike Hammill

Circa 1979 **Chastity, Up Periscope**   Dave Musgrove (solo)
both possibly done before

1979   **The True Two Ton Sardine**   Martin and Bob Berzins
*Named in honour of Drummond's ascent of Shuffle Crack. Chris Addy
straightened out the finish a little.*

1979   **Grand Illusion**   Charles Cook

1980   **Impending Doom**   Graham Desroy, Paul Dawson

1980   **Fungus the Bogeyman**   Graham Desroy, Charles Cook, Paul Dawson

1980   **Forgotten Wall**   Rob Gawthorpe, Pete Jackson

1980   **Yellow Peril**   Mike Hammill, Mike Raine

1980   **China Syndrome**   Rob Gawthorpe
The technical master raising standards again. A climb years ahead of its time.

Pre-1982 **Fence Buttress**   Unknown
Possibly Syrett, Manson or Kitson during the early 1970's.

Jan 1982 **Gypus**   Martin Berzins

24.7.82   **All Our Yesterdays**   Al Manson, Pete Kitson
So named to commemorate the comeback of a famous partnership.

1.4.83   **Hobgoblin**   Andy Wild, Dave Musgrove

4.9.84   **Merlin**   Mark Furniss

8.6.85   **Daisy Chain**   Pete Kitson (solo)

Sept 1985 **Roast Beef**   Jerry Peel (solo)

Sept 1985 **The Tramp**   Jerry Peel (solo)

13.11.85 **The Lady**   Ron Cowells (solo)

Autumn 1987 **Everyman Has His Niche**   Paul Greenland, A. Burnell, C. Sowden

Spring1988   **Al says 6a**   Jerry and Gill Peel

2.6.88   **Exit Stage Left**   Martin Berzins, Al Manson
*Extending the traverse named Grand Finale by Dave Humberstone and Kevin
Hunt on 28.6.85*

21.8.88   **Magnum Opus**   Martin Berzins, Al Manson
Direct Start by Tony Simpson on 7.9.94

29.8.88   **Jack on Fire**   Al Manson, Martin Berzins

1988   **South Wall Direct**   Martin Berzins, Al Manson
Probably climbed before.

24.4.90   **The Bitch**   Graham Desroy (solo)

24.4.90   **Blackhead**   Graham Desroy, John Paul Hotham
*Via the now filled in bolt hole. The route has, however, been repeated by a
very tall chappie called Doug Shepherd.*

1.9.91   **No Man's Land**   Tony Marr, Mike Tooke
*Also claimed as **Over The Top** but climbed as a finish to Western Front by
Pete Brown and Steve Turner 25.6.92.*

25.9.91   **Retribution Rib Direct**   John Paul Hotham, Guy Maddox
Almscliff's boldest lead.

1992   **The Nelly Moser Finish**   Pete Brown, Steve Turner, Dave Garner

22.6.92   **A Step In The Right Direction**   Adam Goulder, Mathew Collins (FRA)
Almost certainly done before

18.8.92   **Microscopic Wall**   Pete Brown, Matthew Ramsden
*This was the top rib only. Repeated as described, incorporating the direct start
to Z Climb Eliminate by Brown and Andy Turner 9.9.97*

29.5.94   **Jess's Roof**   Oliver Wright
If its a route it could be Almscliff's hardest!

14.8.94   **Wharfedale Wall**   Pete Brown, Dave Garner

18.8.94	**Trident** Pete Brown, Steve Turner	
22.7.95	**Penny Pip** Duncan Drake (solo)	
25.9.95	**Stepoffable** Pete Brown (solo)	
29.10.95	**Toad's Nose** Pete Brown (unseconded)	

The start is a Mike Hammill '70s problem.

Spring 1997   **Pinnacle Direct, The Final Finale**   Dave Musgrove & The Almscliff All Stars.

Probably both done in 1897!

17.6.97	**Suppository Wall** Pete Brown, (solo)
29.6.97	**Supo Direct** Pete Brown

The variation finish to Opus.

15.7.97	**Envy Of Angels** Steve Bollen (solo)
29.7.97	**Green Gully Rib** Pete Brown (solo)

Summer 1997   **West Chimney Rib**   Pete Brown (FRA)

5.8.97	**Spirit Level** Pete Brown
11.10.97	**Megadoom** Pete Brown, Andy Turner, Stuart Purvis

Autumn 97   **Angelic Upstart**   Pete Brown (solo)

1.2.98   **Something's Cooking**   Dave Musgrove (jnr.) (solo)

ASH HEAD CRAG

Early 1950s   **Windy Wall**   Jack Wilson

May 1962   **"A" Climb, Fluted Rib, Easy Ridge, Gangren**e**, Rhombic Girdle**   Roger Sutcliffe, Chris Ambler, Ernie Hodgson

27.9.65	**The Horn, Headstand, The Result** Robin and Tony Barley
27.9.65	**Thunder Crack, Lightning Variation, Barnstorm, The Tea Party, Finale** Tony and Robin Barley

Thunder Crack Top-roped in 1962 by Sutcliffe, Ambler and Hodgson.

27.9.65   **Rhythm**   Tony Barley (solo)

27.9.65   **Actress & Rhyme, Wanderlust, Up and Under**   The Barley Brothers

First recorded ascents but probably climbed earlier. Most of these climbs were included in an interim guide published in various journals.

18.7.72	**Last Rites** Greg Tough, R. Kinnaird
13.7.74	**Dust Off** Tony Barley, Ken Wood
13.7.74	**Flake Crack** Tony Barley (solo)
25.6.76	**The True Knobbler** Al Manson, Ken Wood
30.11.88	**Tip Off** Martin Hannan (solo)

BAILDON BANK

Circa 1950   **HMS Amethyst**   Arthur Dolphin

1950-56   *Ian Clough and Geoff Grandison systematically worked their way along the crag climbing some 60 routes up to VS.*

Pre 1956   **Solomon's Crack**   Eric Metcalfe

1960s   **Ian's Bolt Route, Eternal Peace**   Ian Clough

Early 1970s   **Push Off, Depegomania, The Arch ,Time, Wet Wall, Hidden Corner, Saw Off, Sometime, Flake Wall, Fingers, South Wall, Overtime Wall, Spider, Drop Out , Cream Legs, Ulley Right & Left , The Fin, Agame**   Iain Edwards

1972   **Scar, No Top, Curving Cracks, Pillar, Stubby Legs**   Iain Edwards

1972   **Born Free**   Bill Turner

1972   **Clean Stone Crack**   S. Artis

1973   **Stretch, La Cathedralle, Nude Groove, Toss Off, Leeway, Solomon's Diedre, Moria, Last Day, Jumper Ramp, Do Knot, Monkey Puzzle, Split 'Em, Up and Over**   Iain Edwards

1973   **Bamboozle Bottom**   Iain Edwards, Bill Turner

1973	**Karen, Agoa, Half Crack, Dan Dan the Fighting Man** Bill Turner
1973	**Joanna** Bill Turner, Iain Edwards
3.4.74	**Syrett's Crack** John Syrett, Al Manson
1974	**Ram, Stretcher, Big Curver, Green Arete, Pullover, Rampant Arete, Fly Groove, Triang, Matey's Crack** Iain Edwards
1974	**Scar Direct Finish, Red Wall, Jeanette, Beesting, Cleanstone Wall** Bill Turner
1975	**Gold Rings Alternative** Bill Turner
1975	**Future Times** Bill Turner, Iain Edwards
1975	**Quietus, Chipper** Roger Whitehead
1975	**Dave's Crack** Dave Salter
1975	**The Flakes, Satire, Mandy Fly Me, Futurama, Carnival Carousel, Bipod** Iain Edwards
1976	**Going for Oneness** Dave Salter
1976	**Dave's Crack Direct** Bill Turner
1976	**Hemispheres, Hergest Ridge, Playtex, Last Edge, Scoop, Desperado, Lightning, Anne of Cleaves** Iain Edwards
1978	**Scar Wall** Andy Brown
1980	**Intrepid, Scar Arete, Gesticulation** Rob Gawthorpe, Bill Turner
1980	**Fizzicle Fizzle** Craig Smith
1981	**The Sunday Lunch Mob** Bill Turner
1982	**Geeta Nob Out** Craig Smith
1982	**Heave Too, Swingover Wobbling Wall** Iain Edwards
1983	**Smear Fear** Paul Craven
1983	**Van Wrinkle** Iain Edwards
17.9.83	**Armageddon (outahere)** Iain Edwards, Bill Turner
August 1984	**Camera Shake** Jason Myers
1984	**Fear the Buzz** Bill Turner
1984	**Closing Time** John Dunne
1984	**Enterprise** Iain Edwards
1985	**Van Wrinkle Direct Start** Bill Turner
1985	**Timex, Cool Trickster** John Dunne
5.2.86	**Rawhide** Andy Jack, Jason Myers
March '86	**Yob Society** Damian Tolon
March '86	**Gentle Persuasion** Jason Myers
26.7.86	**Anniversary Arete** Damian Tolon
26.7.86	**Scythe Man** Iain Edwards
26.7.86	**Van Wrinkle Direct Start** John Dunne
1987	**To a Reckless Flash** Bill Turner
1987	**Iain's Swansong** Iain Edwards
1988	**Jess** Bill Turner
13.1.89	**Adam's Apple** Adam Collinge, Matt Bateson
16.5.90	**No Pegs Please We're British** Adrian Gill (solo)
2.6.90	**Steel Monkey** Adrian Gill, Graham Kinsley
7.6.90	**Theakstone Man** Adam Collinge, Andy Brown
7.6.90	**Turk In The Hole** Adam Collinge, Matt Bateson
3.7.90	**Adamski** Adam Collinge (solo)
9.5.93	**A Path For An Evil Soul** Chas Ward (shunt then solo)

BIRK GILL CRAG

13.3.94	**Cat Walk, Birk Gill Crack** Tony Marr, Mike Tooke, Frank Fitzgerald
13.3.94	**Downbeat** Frank Fitzgerald, Mike Tooke
13.3.94	**Mary Archer** Mike Tooke, Frank Fitzgerald
13.3.94	**Bygones** Tony Marr (solo)
20.3.94	**Black Groove** Tony Marr, Mike Tooke, Frank Fitzgerald, Peter Shawcross
20.3.94	**Narrow Margin** Tony Marr, Mike Tooke

20.3.94	**Little Wonder** Tony Marr, Mike Tooke, Peter Shawcross
20.3.94	**Sorrento, Frank's Slab** Frank Fitzgerald, Peter Shawcross
18.9.94	**Quantum Leap, Class Action, Party Piece, Tough Enough** Tony Marr, Mike Tooke
9.10.94	**Class Action Left Hand** Tony Marr, Mike Tooke
9.10.94	**Heart Beat** Frank Fitzgerald, Tony Marr, Mike Tooke,
9.10.94	**Facade** Tony Marr, Mike Tooke, Frank Fitzgerald
9.10.94	**Cutting Edge** Tony Marr (solo)
5.2.95	**Fast Track** Tony Marr, Mike Took, Frank Fitzgerald
5.2.95	**Corvus** Frank Fitzgerald, Tony Marr, Mike Tooke,

BRANDRITH

A crag with a confused history. Several interim guides were produced in journals and magazines before the crag was fully described in the 1989 definitive guidebook.

1952	**Cave Crack** The Yorkshire Ramblers Club
	The earliest known record. This, the best of the obvious easy lines, may have been done before.
1953	**Indian's Fin, Leader's Lament, Slab & Crack, Antler's Route Nameless Chimney, Western Crack** Brian Evans
	Also many more easy, unclaimed lines, almost certainly done before (many now overgrown).
Nov-53	**Harmony** Brian Evans
	Originally named Brandrith Buttress and though a piton was used it was a superb and still bold effort for the time.
1955	**Evening Ambler** Brian Evans
	Had been mentioned as a "fine vertical Very Severe crack" by Evans in his guide in that years YMC journal. Subsequently claimed by Robin Barley as "The Twist" in 1961, and by Allan Austin in 1964.
1975	*Ken Wood rediscovers crag and solos 16'new' routes. No doubt some of the above and probably some later claimed by Mackenzie and Fowler*
July 1984	**Battlecat** Al Manson, Andy Wild (both led).
	Far and away the crag's hardest route – recorded at HVS 5c!
17.6.85	**Butterfingers, Problem Child, Going Bald, Sod's Law, Verdi Grease Finger Dancer** John Mackenzie, Mick Fowler (both solo)
	Going Bald and Sod's Law were dug-out from the heather! Direct finish to Finger Dancer by Kim Buck 1989
20.6.85	**Flummox Crack, Edge Biter, Discord** Mick Fowler, John Mackenzie (both solo)
	Discord then using the finish now adopted by New Broom.
2.2.89	**Butterfingers Left-hand, Finger Dancer Direct, Flummox** Kim Buck (solo)
26.7.89	**Eastern Arete** Bob Larkin (solo)
	Claimed at least 3 times since.
23.7.90	**The Torso Twins, Leaders Lament Direct** Jeff Appleyard, Mike Gale
28.9.90	**New Broom Sweeps Green** Dave Musgrove (solo)
9.8.95	**Block Crack, Bag Of Snot, Rocky Slab, Summertime Solo, Why Not (Do A Girdle)** David Burnett (solo)
Sept 1996	**Intruding Fool** Stuart King
22.9.96	**Western Bulge** Paul Clough, Karl Zientek
29.7.97	**Diwaly, Sharks Fin Crack, The Hoper, Filthy Grovels, Upset Crack** David Burnett
9.8.97	**The Opportunist** Paul Kitchingman
14.8.97	**Sunset Staircase** Fiona Burnett
7.9.97	**The Haven** John Ward

BRIMHAM ROCKS

Pre-1937	**Lover's Leap Chimney, Cubic Corner, Notice Board Crack** Sidney Thompson	
Circa 1950	**Right-hand Crack, Jabberwok** Probably A. Marsden and the East Yorkshire M.C.	
20.3.55	**Birch Tree Wall** Brian Evans, Allan Austin	

20.3.55   Birch Tree Wall   Brian Evans, Allan Austin
There was evidence of earlier traffic.

1955   President's Progress   Harry Stembridge, Donald McKelvie *and other members of the Yorkshire Ramblers' Club.*

1955   Allan's Crack   Allan Austin, Brian Evans, Doug Verity, Brian Fuller.
The first contribution from a team which was to dominate development for the next few years. The Slab start was added by Austin in 1958 and the direct finish by Les Brown and Tony Marr in 1967.

22.1.56   Hatter's Groove   Allan Austin, Brian Evans, Ron Tyler
Combined tactics and a peg for aid were necessary. Led free in April, 1958, by Joe 'Morty' Smith, Joe Brown and Dennis Gray.

1955/56   Lichen Chimney, Graft Crack, Duggie's Dilemma, Last Crack, Slippery Crack, Brief Crack, Constrictor Chimney, Fag Slab, Pig Traverse, Corner Crack, Little Funnel   Allan Austin, Brian Evans, Doug Verity, Brian Fuller, Jennifer Ruffe *(Various leads and combinations).*

Jan 1956   Fag Slab Variant   Brian Evans (solo)

1956   Parallel Cracks   Allan Austin, Brian Evans
Keeper Crack.

1956   Cake Walk   Allan Austin, Brian Evans, Jennifer Ruffe

1956   Picnic Variation   Allan Austin, Brian Evans, Jennifer Ruffe
A fine climb, pushing up the standards.

1956   Hourglass Chimney   Brian Evans, Allan Austin, Brian Fuller, Doug Verity

1956   Frensis   Allan Austin, Doug Verity
One of the hardest leads on the crag at that time. It has since been soloed in wellies!

Pre 1957   Old Corner, Heather Wall, Great Slab, Problem Wall, Cleft Buttress & Pinnacle, Cracked Corner, Lichen Slab, Nameless Chimney, Difficult Crack, Tight Chimney, Grit Corner, Indian's Turban Route, Indian's Turban West, The Chimney, Maloja, Birch Climb, Cannon Route, Roadside Crack, Desperation Crack, Central Crack.
All these problems were recorded in the 1957 guide or the 1957 Y.R.C. Journal. Some were obviously long established judging by the depth of nail scratches. The East Yorkshire M.C. is probably responsible for many, but its records are no longer traceable. Birch Tree Wall and Maloja were originally credited to Johnny Lees but he categorically disowns them. Any claimants?

14.4.57   Frensis Direct   Allan Austin, Brian Evans, Brian Fuller
The crag's first extreme

14.4.57   Long Funnel   Brian Evans (solo)

6.10.57   Rough Wall, Crossover   Allan Austin, Brian Evans, Jennifer Ruffe

6.10.57   Lilo, Cracked Rib   Brian Evans, Allan Austin, Jennifer Ruffe

26.10.57   Minion's Way   Allan Austin, Brian Fuller
A controversial climb. Did Austin really stand on his second's shoulders? Dennis Gray led the climb the same day but the crux had, in fact, been worked out the week before by Brian Evans.

1957   Right Wall   Dennis Gray, Joe Smith

1957   Three Tree's Crack   Allan Austin, Brian Evans

1957   Mantelshelf Corner   Allan Austin, Brian Evans, Doug Verity, Brian Fuller, Jennifer Ruffe

2.2.58   Mirky Crack   Allan Austin (solo)

24.4.58   Chinese Crack   Allan Austin, Brian Evans

24.4.58   Lancet Crack   Allan Austin, Brian Evans
A good find, much better – and easier – than it looked.

Apr 58	**Moss Side** Joe Smith, Dennis Gray	
1958	**Charming Crack, Go Jo** Joe Brown	
1.2.59	**Rat Bag Closet Crack Jackabu** Pete Hindle, George Steele	

The top section of Jackabu was added later.

Apr 59	**Hawk Traverse** Brian Evans
1959	**Fag End** Harold Barraclough

Later spoiled by chipped holds.

Late 50's	**White Rose** Flake Don Whillans
Circa 1960	**Dogleg** Crack Des Hadlum, Dennis Gray

The top pitch was climbed first.

1.1.60	**Choked Chimney** Brian and Aileen Evans
1961	**The Snuffer** Baz Ingle, Hugh Banner, Alan Clarke

A raiding party from the Alpha Club snatch an obvious, but intimidating, line.

1961	**Half-Crown Corner** Des Hadlum, Dennis Gray

The finishing hold was scooped out by Nat Allen using a coin. (The forerunner of the wire brush).

1962	**Felicity** Dennis Gray, Eric Beard
1962	**Indian's Arete** Tony and Robin Barley

An insignificant climb, but it marked the emergence of two young brothers who were to take over, and dominate, the crag's development throughout the 1960s.

1962	**Boa Cracks** Robin Barley.
1963	**Mole Hole** Robin and Tony Barley
1963	**Britt** Tony Barley (solo)
1963	**Bog Crack, Thin Line** Tony and Robin Barley
1963	**George II** Tony and Robin Barley

A peg for aid was required. It was climbed free by George Broadhead and Bob Metcalfe in 1974, hence the name.

Aug 1963	**Beatnik** Robin and Tony Barley

An important addition, for many years considered the hardest climb at Brimham.

Spring 1964	**Hoover** Roger and Graham Mackintosh
1964	**Moss Lane** Tony and Robin Barley
1964	**Moss Alley** Tony Barley
Sept 1964	**Square Root** Tony Barley
1965	**Blind's Crack, Cantilever Pinnacle, Fall Out, Flake Out** Tony Barley
Circa 1965	**Merle Peerless** Ernie Shepherd, Jack Wilson
1965	**R.P.T., K.P.T Layback Crack**. Ken Tilford

Possibly climbed before.

Aug 1966	**The Black Chipper** Tony Barley, Chas Hird
1966	**Straddle, Alcove Wall** Ken Jackson, Tony Marr
1966	**Grit Bit** Tony Barley
1966	**The Hattery** Tony and Robin Barley

Rediscovered in 1973 by George Broadhead who climbed a variation finish.

Mid 1960s	**Wedge Crack** J. Fullalove
Pre-1970	**Hanging Flake** Tony Barley
Pre-1970	**Appiewand** Jeff Appleyard
Pre-1970	**The Belfry, Druid's Chimney, Gnome's Arete, Cave Chimney, Kangaroo Wall, Narrowing Chimney, Detour, Harry's Crack** Unknown.

All these routes were first Recorded in the1969 guide. The section writer was Jeff Appleyard who presumably climbed them at or around this time, but some may well be of greater antiquity.

18.6.70	**True Grit** Ken Wood, Mike Mortimer

A finger crack of the highest calibre and difficulty marked the start of a new wave of development.

8.8.70	**Lovebug** Tony Barley, Tony Roache
4.11.70	**Brutalizer** John Syrett

The first 'first' from a young rising star who graded it HVS. "F***ing impossible, *but only just. A pitch to delight the connoiseur"- Bernard Newman's comment in L.U.C.C. logbook.*

10.1.71	**Double Back**	Ken Jackson, Tony & Eric Marr
18.3.71	**Viper**	Ken Jackson, Tony Marr, Ken Austin
15.4.71	**Red Tape**	John Syrett

An easier variant had been climbed by Ken Tilford in the mid 1960s.

17.4.71 **Joker's Wall** John Syrett

Another major step forward. It climbed the line of the bogusly-claimed Lecher's Wall and became 'the route to do' at Brimham during the 1970s. Even Syrett took several falls before the successful ascent.

15.5.71 **Excursion, Mumbo Jumbo** Tony Barley, Tony Roache
16.10.71 **Enigma** Ken Wood, M. Biden, Mike Mortimer

The groove finish was led by Tony Barley the following day. Variation start by Tony Barley and Tony Roache 30.4.72.

17.10.71 **Rainy Day** Jeff Appleyard, Frank Wilkinson, Mike Bebbington

The only dry bit of rock on the crag.

30.4.72 **Rat Trap** Tony Barley, Tony Roache
24.7.72 **Chicane, Deep Chimney, Way Out, Playout** Tony Barley, Mike Mortimer
13.8.72 **No Doubt, Gully Arete, Mad Hatter** Tony Barley
3.9.72 **Top Dead Centre, Right-hand Bias, Left-hand Bias** Tony Barley, Robert Kinnear
1.10.72 **The Mantelshelf** Tony Barley
15.10.72 **In Retrospect** Bob Larkin (solo)
1972 **Backbreaker, Legover, Charming Chimney** Tony Barley
Apr 1973 **Ambidexter** Tony Barley, Robin Brown
May 1973 **Black Tower Face** Tony Barley, Robin Brown
7.6.73 **Picnic** John Syrett, Geoff Hankinson, Pete Kitson

It certainly isn't! Direct start by Syrett 20.1.74.

10.6.73 **The Hattery Arete** George Broadhead
12.5.74 **Mons Meg** Dave Musgrove, Jim Worthington

The Rock & Ice return to put a big gun on Cannon Rock.

13.5.74 **Stone Wall** Tony Barley
1974 **Classic Bagger** Chris Hamper, Nick Hallam
Circa 1974 **The Arch** Ken Wood
Circa 1974 **Joker's Wall Arete** Hank Pasquill
1975 **Natural Grit** Jerry Peel, Tony Barley

The intended line of Black Chipper.

1975 **Grit Expectations** Al Manson

A new boldness reaches Brimham. The groove used to have a grass sod in it – a test of manhood was to pull on this. Steve Webster pulled too hard!

3.8.75 **Smoke Ring** Tony Barley
Pre 1976 **Lithos Direct** Al Manson
1976 **White Wash** Martin Berzins, Chris Sowden

This is the first recorded ascent but it was believed that Joe Brown climbed a similar line in 1958.

1976 **Heather Wall Direct** Tony Marr
1976 **Hanging Groove** Mike Hammill
1976 **Lithos** Mike Hammill or Al Manson
1976 **Gigglin' Crack** Jerry Peel, Gill Peel

An absolute monster. Named after a fit of hysterics which brought about Joe Brown's failure from close to the top in 1958.

1976 **Leap Frog** Jerry Peel, Dave Hollows, Tony Barley
1976 **Swan Arcade** Mike Hammill, Mark Clark, Tony Barley.

The start had been climbed before.

16.10.76 **Syrett's Rib** John Syrett
16.10.76 **Gordon's Wall** Martin and Bob Berzins, Gordon Higginson, John Syrett
16.10.76 **Cleft Arete** Gordon Higginson, Martin Berzins
1977 **Spare Rib, Rotifer** Bob Berzins

1977	**Close to the Hedge, Gwyneth** Al Manson	
1977	**Vam** Martin Berzins	
1977	**Botany Bay** Andy Wild, Al Manson	
Sept 1977	**Left Wall** Mike Hammill, Al Manson	

Sept 1977 **Left Wall** Mike Hammill, Al Manson
A well-rehearsed, but brilliant and bold ascent. As hard as anything on grit in Derbyshire at this time.

1978 **Birch Tree Wall Direct Start, The Shootist** Al Manson
1978 **Green Prioress** Ron Kenyon, D. Bowers
1978 **Happy Days** Chris Hamper
Pre-1980 **Tube Break** John Syrett
Pre-1980 **For Pete's Sake** Steve Webster
22.8.80 **Woodbine** Duncan Drake
1980 **Idle Slabs Arete** Tony Marr
1980 **Buena Ventura, Acme Wall, Acme Wall Traverse** Mike Hammill
1980 **Pathos** Al Manson
1980 **Who needs Friends** Mike Hammill, J. M. Hammill
1980 **Ugly** Mike Hammill, Mike Raine
Circa 1980 **Ritornal** Bob Berzins
Probably done before.
1980 **Bilge Crack** Al Manson
Unlikely ever to be done again.
Jan 1981 **Left Wall Girdle** Mike Hammill, Paul Craven (alt.)
29.7.81 **Charlie's Dilemma** Iain Edwards, Tim Riley
Circa 1981 **Filter Tip** Derek Hargreaves, Lianne Jay
1981 **Black Bob** Rob Everett
1981 **Acme Error, Gordon's Proffer** Ken Tilford, Gordon Russell
1981 **Right-hand Arete, Lunatic Rib** Ken Tilford
The above four routes were named and recorded for the 1982 guide but were old problems probably first climbed in the 1950s.
1981 **Notice Board Wall** Mike Raine, Mike Hammill
Pre 1982 **Easy Exit** Unknown
1982 **Lichen Wall** Nick Dixon, Paul Ingham
A similar line on this wall had been climbed much earlier by Tony Barley.
1982 **Mantelshelf Blues, High Steppa** John Mackenzie, G. Corner
1982 **For Crying Out Loud** Ian Dunn, George Haydon, Nick Dixon
1982 **Dennis the Menace, Brown's Crack** Steve Brown, Paul Ingham
1982 **Fook Nose** Paul Ingham, Nick Dixon
23.4.84 **Silk Cut** Paul Clarke
Top-roped first.
6.5.85 **Forever Man** R. Allen, M. James
19.3.86 **Successor State** Richard Davies
Pre-1987 **Druid's Reality** Alec Burns
Tony Barley climbed a route, Dingo, on this wall in 1975.
Mar 1988 **Eyes Right** Steve Rhodes
Mar 1988 **Eyes Left** Nic Kidd
27.3.88 **Rat Arsed** Martin Berzins, Nic Kidd
27.3.88 **Michael Michael Superman** Martin Berzins, Nic Kidd, Steve Rhodes
Done in bits previously, Mike Hammill (bottom), Jerry Peel (top).
5.4.88 **Womb with a View** G. Milner, D. Fitt
17.4.88 **Pig's Ear** Steve Rhodes (solo)
17.4.88 **Reach for the Stye** Martin Berzins, Craig Smith, Al Manson
19.4.88 **Sow's That** Al Manson, Martin Berzins
Apr 1988 **Rattler, Ratfink, Ratatwoee** Martin Berzins, Al Manson
5.5.88 **Bare Back Side** Steve Rhodes, Martin Berzins
5.5.88 **Cocoa Club Board Meeting** Steve Rhodes, Martin Berzins
The board held Martin's weight; it should hold yours.
6.5.88 **Fat Belly Gut Bucket** Greg Rimmer, Steve Rhodes
A self portrait.

2.6.88	**Take No Notice**	Steve Rhodes, Rona Ryan
10.6.88	**Mae West's Rib, Don't Step Back Crack**	Steve Rhodes, Greg Rimmer
10.6.88	**House Points Tomorrow**	Greg Rimmer, Steve Rhodes
12.6.88	**Chox Away**	Tony Burnell, Mick Ryan, Ed Douglas
12.6.88	**Board to Tears**	Steve Rhodes, Nic Kidd, Mick Ryan, Ed Douglas
22.6.88	**Running in the Red**	Steve Rhodes, Al Manson
July 1988	**Halcyon Daze, Sir Les, A Sign for the Dynosaurs**	Al Manson (solo)
July 1988	**Dame Edna**	Pete Kitson (solo)

In a pair of "Streaky" re-soled trainers.

27.7.88	**Rataonee**	Steve Rhodes, Nic Kidd, Al Manson, Martin Berzins
1.8.88	**Layback and Think**	Steve Rhodes, Nic Kidd, Jack (A mate from the States).
8.8.88	**Steady VS Arete**	Steve Rhodes, Alec Burns, Justin Vogler
8.8.88	**Peekabu**	Steve Rhodes (solo)
21.8.88	**Bilberry Jam**	Mick Ryan, Steve Rhodes, Alec Burns
Sept 88	**Morose Mongoose**	John Allen
23.9.88	**Grit Attack**	Ron Kenyon (unseconded)

Believed to have been climbed before

1988	**Shorty's Dilemma**	Tony Marr, Mike Took, Frank Fitzgerald
20.5.89	**Rough Stuff, Rough Neck**	Tony Barley
10.8.89	**Resurrection**	Dave Pegg (solo after top rope)
17.9.89	**Jelly Baby Wall**	Nic Kidd, Steve Rhodes
26.11.89	**The Bottom Line**	Dave Pegg
10.12.89	**Frost In The Shadows**	Terry Holmes (solo)
C. 1989	**R.P.T. Extension**	G. Tailby
25.3.90	**Hard Hat**	Tony Marr, Frank Fitzgerald
1.4.90	**Pig Slip Cow Punk**	Nick Dixon, A. Mclean , A. Taylor
7.4.90	**Tender Homecoming**	Nick Dixon (solo)

The crag's first E8.

19.5.90	**Bellyporker's Progress**	Nick Dixon, Andy Popp. (Allegedly climbed before

by Andy Bowman)

15.7 90	**Pebbledash**	Tony Marr, Alan Taylor, Peter Shawcross
14.10.90	**Point Blank**	Tony Marr, Mike Tooke, Peter Shawcross
17.11.90	**Goof Aydee and The Mango**	Dean Bradley
1.12.90	**White Flag**	Dave Musgrove (solo)
28.3.92	**Spring Steal**	Tony Marr
15.7.92	**Mohole Direct**	Tony Marr, Mike Tooke
4.7.93	**Wisecrack**	Tony Marr, Mike Tooke
1.8.93	**Walleroo**	Tony Marr, Mike Took, Peter Shawcross
5.9.93	**Tube Break Direct Start**	Tony Marr, Mike Tooke
17.10.93	**Bilberry Groove**	Tony Marr, Mike Tooke, Peter Shawcross
31.10.93	**Grit Escape**	Tony Marr, Mike Tooke
20.2.94	**Knobbly Wall**	Marr, Took, Shawcross, Fitzgerald
3.4.94	**Stone Cold**	Tony Marr, Mike Tooke
10.4.94	**Emerald Eye**	Tony Marr
10.4.94	**Zakely Syndrome**	Tony Marr, Mike Took, Peter Shawcross, Frank Fitzgerald
10.4.94	**Zakely Right-hand**	Peter Shawcross
17.4.94	**Hare's Head Crack**	Tony Marr, Mike Tooke

The original finish traverses left to join the finish of forced entry at the same grade. Marr & Tooke 10.4.94

17.4.94	**Homefront**	Tony Marr, Mike Tooke
28.4.94	**Forced Entry**	Tony Marr
1.5.94	**Love Bug Variation Start**	Tony Marr, Mike Tooke
1.5.94	**Acme End**	Tony Marr, Mike Tooke, Frank Fitzgerald
2.5.94	**Love Bug Direct Start**	Tony Marr
9.5.94	**Little Wonder, Inside Out**	Tony Marr, Mike Tooke, Peter Shawcross
20.6.94	**Games with the Nephfesch**	Steve Parker (unseconded)
20.6.94	**Here Be Dragons**	Steve Parker, Gill Kirk
July 1994	**Friends And Enemies**	Dave Slater, Andrew Simon

8.6.94	**Stretching Hekate** Steve Parker, Gill Kirk	
7.8.94	**Hyde And Seek, Finders Keepers** Tony Marr, Mike Tooke, Frank Fitzgerald	
28.8.94	**Allan's Crack Right-hand** Tony Marr, Mike Took	
1995	**Boc No Hero** Alan Firth, Roy Healy	
16.4.95	**Who Needs Friends - Arete Finish** Tony Marr, Mike Tooke	
29.5.95	**Concave Slab** Tony Marr, Frank Fitzgerald, Mike Took	
2.6.95	**Castle Crack** Tony Marr, Mike Tooke	
4.6.95	**Crackaroo, Gluon** Mike Tooke, F. Fitzgerald, T. Marr, P&P Shawcross	
4.6.95	**The Flue** Frank Fitzgerald, Mike Tooke, Pam Shawcross	
27.8.95	**Serendipity** Tony Marr, Mike Tooke	
8.10.95	**Kneewrecker** Tony Marr, Mike Tooke Frank Fitzgerald, Pam & Peter Shawcross	
1996	**The Road Rage Experience** Tony Simpson	
	A short but serious addition to Kangaroo Wall	
14.6.96	**Stepped Buttress** Tony Marr, Mike Took	
22.9.96	**West Indian's Turban Route** Tony Marr, Mike Took	
22.9.96	**Zero Option** Tony Marr, Mike Took, Peter Shawcross	
15.12.96	**Keystone Chimney** Tony Marr, Mike Tooke	
Pre 1997	**Vax, Dyson, Tilt, Wilt** Tony Marr	
	Old problems named for this edition	
9.2.97	**Love Bite** Tony Marr, Mike Took, Peter Shawcross	
2.3.97	**Castle Corner, Squeeze Crack** Tony Marr, Mike Tooke	
16.3.97	**Little Corner, Green Crack** Tony Marr	
24.6.97	**North West Arete** Andy Wild	
July 1997	**Senior Service** Mick Johnson, Dick Tonge	
19.7.97	**Max Crax** Dave Musgrove, Nigel Baker (FRA)	
22.7.97	**Mild Steel** Dave Musgrove (solo)	
22.7.97	**Stone Age Reveller** Nigel Baker (unseconded)	
2.10.97	**Hedgeup** Mick Johnson, Dick Tonge	
	This may have been climbed before, Dave Slater remembers keeping right of the arete in 1991 thinking this was the original way on Close To The Hedge.	
15.8.98	**Kangaroo Wall Variation Finish** Tony & Linda Marr	

BRIMHAM OUTLYING CRAGS

1955	**Trio Wall** George Dale, Allan Austin	
	Direct finish 1955 by Allan Austin, George Dale, Brian Fuller.	
	The first route here by this prolific team.	
1956	**End Slab** Allan Austin, Brian Evans, Jennifer Ruffe, Brian Fuller	
1956	**Owl Chimney** Allan Austin, Brian Evans, Jennifer Ruffe, Brian Fuller	
	Variation finish by Malcolm Lomas, Austin and Evans on 23/11/58.	
1956	**Grasshopper** Allan Austin, Brian Evans, Jennifer Ruffe, Brian Fuller	
Pre-1957	**Bat Buttress, Crack and Chimney, Holly Tree Climb, Yo-Yo** Unknown	
14.4.57	**Corkscrew** Allan Austin, Brian Evans, Jennifer Ruffe	
	Crow Crag's plum line. An Extreme but they didn't know it!	
23.11.58	**Spoiler** Allan Austin, Brian Evans, Malcolm Lomas	
Circa 1960	**Plantation Crack** Dennis Gray, Des Hadlum	
	The first, most obvious and best route on this crag. Probably also the only route that Dennis has claimed without anyone questioning the validity of the ascent.	
1961	**Staircase Chimney, Narrow Buttress Chimney, Lost Crack, Monawin, Bracken Crack, Deception, The Prow, Evergreen Cracks, Easter Egg Crack** Tony Barley, Robin Barley	
8.9.61	**Strongbow** Tony Barley, Robin Barley	
May 1962	**Vomer** Dennis Gray, H. Harrison	
	Direct start Allan Austin 1965.	
Aug 1963	**Bat Buttress Direct** Robin Barley, Tony Barley – 1pt of aid	

Allan Austin and Dennis Gray both claimed the first free ascent a short while later.

1969	**Dragnet, Escape Route, Easy Way, Oak Tree Crack, Hearts of Oak, A-Corner** Jeff Appleyard	
1969	**Greenfingers** Jeff Appleyard, J. Ellis	
31.3.71	**Fiddlesticks** Andy Wild	
16.9.71	**Batman** Ken Wood	

Thankfully wet most of the time.

2.10.71   **Abrasion** Tony Barley, Ken Wood

Short and mean – the route or the climbers? Originally named The Mangler!

18.3.72   **Side Track** Tony Barley, Tony Roach
25.7.72   **Easter Edge Ridge** Greg Tough
25.7.72   **Left-hand Ridge** Greg Tough
25.7.72   **Overhung Buttress** Greg Tough

Climbed by Nic Kidd on 24.9.88 thinking it was a new modern test piece!

25.9.88   **Armed, Dangerous and off Medication** Nic Kidd (solo)

Climbed using the frog? technique.

25.9.88   **Intreegued** Nic Kidd, Alec Burns
12.4.92   **Southern Belle** John Henderson, Paul Carling
12.4.92   **Yankie Beau** Paul Carling (unseconded)
12.4.92   **State of the Union** Paul Carling, John Henderson
6.3.93   **View From The Hill, Summer Dreams** Luke Dow, Rob Liddle
6.3.93   **Curious Motion** Luke Dow, Rob Liddle

Alt finish - James Brooke, Phillipe Osborne 7.3.97

7.3.93   **Sameness** Luke Dow (solo)
27.3.93   **Passing Strangers** Luke Dow (solo)
31.4.93   **Amadeus** Paul Carling, John Henderson
31.4.93   **Salieri** John Henderson, Paul Carling
7.5.93   **Horizontal Memories, Six Inch Stare** Rob Liddle, Luke Dow
8.5.93   **Salubrious Navaho Indians** Luke Dow (solo)
Circa 1994   **Sparrow Wall** Dan Duxbury
30.5.95   **Virtual Reality, Corkage** John Henderson, Paul Carling
2.11.96   **The Riddler** Phillipe Osborne, Tim Habour
3.11.96   **Grotto Wall, Caped Crack** Phillipe Osborne (solo)
23.9.97   **Vomit** Phillipe Osborne, James Brooke

BROWN BECK CRAG

1983   **Big Boss, Top Man, Holly Hover, Wichita Linesman, Escape, Transcendence, Phenomenology, Pella, Let The Children Play, Child's Play, Dealer, Bahia, Brown Boots, Big Boots, Dawn, Eric, High Adventure, Go Within** Dave Paul, Steve Brown.

A very productive start to the crag's development by these Teesside Activists

Jan - Apr 1988   **Holly Hover, Nuttal's Mintoe, Cadbury's Flake, Mouth to Mouth, Browned Off, The Wobbler, The Other Arete, Chimney Wall, Clean Sweep, Pussy Cat, Owl Wall**

Crag is "re-discovered" by Paul Clark, Nick Dalzel and independently by Tony Burnell and Chris Sowden.

June/July 1988   **Ingham's Route, Den, L'unacy, Last Gasp, Clueless, Undun, Slant, Bedlam** Paul Ingham, Tony Marr

June/July 1988   **South Face Route, Off Beat, Curving Chimney** Tony Marr
Aug 1988   **Hanging Crack, Bandido, Hombre** Tony Marr, Geoff Vaughan
May 1989   **Next of Kin, Big Easy, Drop Zone, Cutting Edge** Tony Marr, Geoff Vaughan
May 1989   **Problemania** Geoff Vaughan
11.6.94   **Bryan's Rib** Bryan Mitchell
1997   **Tyto** Tony Marr

23.2.97	**Cheap Trick, Gideon Up, Rugrats, Cave Chimney, Square Chimney, Heartbeat, Fire Brigade** Tony Marr
9.3.97	**The Watchman** Frank Fitzgerald, Tony Marr
9.3.97	**Little Wall, Staircase** Tony Marr
9.3.97	**Gully Wall, Talespin, Dab Hand, Owl Corner, Butt End, Butt Head** Tony Marr, Mike Tooke, Peter Shawcross
9.3.97	**Ledge End** Mike Tooke

CALEY CRAG

Pre-1938	**Flue Crack, Holly Tree Scoop, Square Chimney, V Chimney** Unknown
Circa 1938	**Pedestal Wall** Allan Allsop, Denys Fisher
Circa 1938	**Boot Crack** Denys Fisher
Circa 1944	**Plantation Ridge** Nancy Heron, Denys Fisher
Circa 1950	**Block Chimney** Johnny Lees
	Possibly climbed earlier by Arthur Dolphin.
21.6.50	**Little Cenotaph, Rabbit's Paw Wall** Arthur Dolphin
	Recorded by Dolphin as Inverted Crack and Overhanging Wall, but believed to be these two climbs from the vague descriptions provided. The climbs were named and accurately recorded in 1958 following ascents by Allan Austin.
1952	**Lad's Corner** Arthur Dolphin, Peter Greenwood
	This was the first recorded lead although an entry in Dolphin's diary dated 1941 seems to indicate this climb.
1952	**Compulsion Crack** Peter Greenwood
1953	**Unfinished Crack** Alfie Beanland, Dennis Gray
Pre-1953	**Angel's Wall** Arthur Dolphin
Pre-1953	**The Scoop** Arthur Dolphin
	Reputedly sometime in the early 1940s and said to be "the hardest climb in Wharfedale".
Pre-1953	**Zig-Zag, Morris Crack, Roof Layback, Rib and Slab, Central Climb, Double Ridge** Unknown
26.8.58	**Tippling Crack** Allan Austin, Doug Verity
17.9.58	**Hanging Groove** Allan Austin, Doug Verity
May 1964	**Permutation Ridge** Terry Burnell, Dennis Gray
	Originally called The Clinger. Direct Start by Mike Hammill (1977).
3.10.64	**Noonday Ridge** Allan Austin (unseconded)
	Though no more technical than its predecessors, this climb was much bolder in concept.
Pre-1969	**Routes 1 & 2** Unknown
Pre-1969	**The Sentry Box** Unknown
	These three routes probably very old problems.
5.4.71	**Tipster** John Syrett, Ken Wood
6.4.72	**Fingerknacker Crack** Ken Wood, John Syrett
	Climbed with aid in 1964 by D. Cronan.
19.8.72	**Black Jumper** Greg Tough, Mike Dransfield
	Indirect Start by Neil Carson in 1991
5.4.73	**Dypso** John Syrett, Andy Wild, John Porter
16.4.73	**Redundancy Rib** Al Manson, Pete Kitson
25.5.73	**I Can't Believe It's A Girdle, Girdle** Pete Kitson, Al Manson
20.4.75	**High Noon** Al Manson, Mike Hammill
	"My hoots of derision, and ironic enquiries as to whether it would go, were mere camouflage for my true fears, which were that he might actually succeed and so deprive me of all the glory". (Al Manson speaking of his feelings when catching Hammill inspecting the line on a top rope a week before the successful ascent).
29.6.75	**Otley Wall** Dave Musgrove, Mike Butler
	The direct start was added a couple of years later.

26.8.75 **Forecourt Crawler** John Allen, Steve Bancroft
Direct finish by Ron Fawcett a few weeks later.

1975 **Morris Dance** Al Manson

21.6.76 **Dusk** Dave Musgrove, Tim Leach (both solo)

1976 **The Can, Tip Off, Rip Off** Mike Hammill (solo)

1976 **Gary Cooper** Steve Bancroft
The forerunner to Fred Zinnerman, considered redundant when that route was climbed. Resurrected for the last guide by popular request.

C. April 1977 **Harry's Heap** Mike Hammill

May 1977 **Adrenaline Rush** Al Manson
"But fear, as well as being the best laxative known to man, is the key to many Last Great Problems. I didn't want to fall. Furthermore reverse gear was impossible to engage and, most of all, I was afraid of someone else stealing the line. If the rubber could have been tapped from my legs it would have kept Goodyear in business for years". Al Manson's account of the first ascent from Extreme Rock 1987.

Circa 1977 **Psycho** Ron Fawcett, Iain Edwards
By the popular start swinging in from the left. The direct start by John Dunne 1988.

Oct 1977 **Quark** Mike Hammill
Soloed after much practice and cleaning.

1977 **Ephedrine** Tim Clifford, Dennis Gray
Mistakenly called What Climb in the last guide

1977 **Fred Zinnerman** Al Manson

1978 **Frank Miller** Ron Fawcett

10.9.78 **Rising More Slowly** Dave Musgrove (solo)

Circa 1980 **The True Pebble Wall** Al Manson

Early 80s **I Can't Remember** Tony Burnell

12.5.82 **Quark Walk** Dave Musgrove, Andy Wild

7.4.84 **The Great Flake** Craig Smith
Another Last Great Problem!

16.4.84 **Thin Slab Direct** Dave Musgrove (solo)

29.6.84 **The Knobbler Traverse** Dave Musgrove (solo)

29.6.84 **Marrow Bone Jelly** Al Manson
The very last 'really' great problem.

17.6.86 **Amazing Grace** John Allen

4.6.88 **Storm In A Teacup** J. Thorpe

1988 **Nothing's Safe** John Dunne

1988 **Charm** Graham Desroy

1988 **Death Drop 2000, To Be Is Not To Bolt** Al Manson

1988 **Strangeness** Steve Rhodes, Martin Berzins
A very bold effort. Surprisingly there is rarely a queue.

1.9.89 **One Man And His Dogmas** Al Manson (solo)

23.6.90 **Terry** Andy Swan (solo)

24.8.95 **Waite** Andy Swan (solo)
Climbed by Christian Durkin around the same time.

26.4.96 **Welcome To The Neighbourhood** Nigel Baker, George Pieniazek

1.10.97 **Indecent Postures** Nigel Baker, Andy Watts

12.3.98 **Compulsive Viewing** Nigel Baker
A hybrid of sections of three less popular climbs creating a more balanced line. It may in fact be identical to Compulsion Crack Variation recorded by John Syrett in 1973.

CHEVIN BUTTRESS AND QUARRY

Circa 1950 **Central Route, Vampire's Ledge** Johnny Lees

Circa 1956 **Weasel** John Ramsden, Dennis Gray

> *This was a free ascent, but the route was subsequently pegged by unknown parties, hence the scars.*

Circa 1956 **Max Wall**   Dennis Gray

> *At least this was an ascent of the approximate line of this route, the later removal of grass has probably destroyed every handhold Dennis pulled up on.*

7.1.57   **Chevin Buttress**   Brian Evans, Rick Horner

1957   **Central Route Direct**   Dennis Gray, Doug Verity

Circa 1958 **Leech's Wall**   Rod Leech

23.6.60   **The Girdle Traverse**   Allan Austin, Brian Evans, Eric Metcalf

> *Another route that upset the farmer - resulting in the team being escorted from the crag.*

11.5.65   **The Waster**   Allan Austin (solo)

> *Originally the route moved left to finish. The direct finish, as described, was soloed by Al Manson in the mid 1970s.*

11.5.65   **Straight Crack, Twin Cracks**   Allan Austin (solo)

4.4.71   **Rampant Hippo**   Dave Musgrove, Bob Knapton

> *An obvious line which surely must have been done before. A sling was required at the top to exit up a loose wall of collapsing earth. Climbed free, July 1971, by Frank Wilkinson and Allan Austin.*

11.4.71   **Ladder Climb**   Dave Musgrove, Bob Knapton

> *Probably done before.. Though grassy, the line showed signs of previous traffic.*

14.4.71   **Backslider**   John Syrett, John Lupton

12.4.73   **Gronff**   Ken Wood, John Harwood

> *The noise made by Boot, the Perisher's dog, when eating sausages!*

13.4.75   **Gronff Left Hand**   Mike Hammill, Al Manson

Summer 1977 **Smokey Joe's Last Freakout**   Peter Brown (age 10!)

Summer 1977 **Freestyle**   Tim and Andy Wilkinson

1977   **Deception**   Alec Burns, Andy Brown

Circa 1977 **Solo Slab, Sand Crab & Layback Corner**   Unknown

> *Named by Burns, Brown and Wilkinson but probably done earlier.*

8.4.78   **No Prisoners**   Alec Burns, Andy Brown

25.9.80   **Magic Rabbit**   Alec Burns, Andy Brown

Circa 1980 **Porno Crack, The Thin Crack**   Alec Burns, Andy Brown

Circa 1980 **Pooh Sticks**   Andy Brown, Tim Wilkinson

1981   **Visual Deception, Rear Entry**   Mike Hammill, Mike Raine

> *Hammill considered the routes to be insignificant variations and didn't claim them at the time. The names were given by Simon Howley and Tony Burnell respectively when they re-discovered the climbs in 1985.*

Pre-1982 **Slide Back**   Unknown

4.6.83   **The Inmate**   Damian Tolan, J.Boggiano

1983   **Jenny Tulls**   Don Barr, Brian Lockett, G. Watson.

> *The Chevin's hardest route and the scene of some impressive earlier attempts. The upper section had been reached previously by B. Woodley by a traverse from Freestyle and Alec Burns had surmounted the lower roof only to be deposited on his back on the ground by a loose flake which followed him down and knocked him unconscious. Don Barr was killed later the same year by a freak lightning strike in the Verdon Gorge*

21.6.84   **Last Regret**   Richard Davies (solo)

28.6.84   **Bellow**   P. Cole, S. Ringrose

Apr 1985 **Slide In**   S. Ringrose, T. Valley

1985   **Dennis The Dilapidated Pensioner**   Simon Howley (solo)

1985   **Midget Digit**   Simon Howley, Duncan Swarbrick

1985   **Blunt Nose, Groovy, Two Foot Tumbler, Sweet and Sour, Done But Not Dusted, Slape, Short and Sweet, Fossil Groove, Done and Dusted, Nine Foot Crack, Another Deception**. Tony Burnell (solo)

1985   **Split Ends, Layaway   Tony Burnell** , Mark Spreadborough

June 1985 **Give-away**   Chris Sowden, Tony Burnell

24.4.88	**Revision Revolt** Adam Wainwright, Simon Franks	
April 1990	**Raynman, Time After Time** Andy Watts (solo)	
21.9.91	**Obstinacy** Chris Wentworth	
1992	**Cool For Cats** Darren Hawkins, Carol Mossop	
17.5.92	**Ladder Climb Direct** Nigel Scarth, Chris Wentworth	
4.11.95	**Growler** Paul Clough, Karl Zientek	
10.6.97	**Lindsay, Lindsay** Peter Sissons, Robert Addey	

CROOKRISE

Pre-1900   **Route 1, Chockstone Crack, Descent Gully, Slingsby's Chimney**
Unknown
It has been suggested that Puttrell and Baker made the first ascents of these routes in the 1890s but research confirmed that Cecil Slingsby and friends climbed here from the 1860s. No definitive records can be found.

Pre-1923   **Griffiths' Chimney** E. Griffiths

Pre-1923   **Moulson's Climb** David Moulson

Pre-1923   **Problem Buttress, Crack Climb, Diagonal Crack Twin Cracks, Slab and Nose, Long Climb, Open Chimney, Chockstone Chimney, Narrow Crack, Crooked Chimney, Green Crack, High Step Climb, Flake, Chimney Buttress, Face Arete and Wall Climb**
All these climbs were recorded around 1922 by the newly-formed and very active Gritstone Club. They were included in the 1923 guide Recent Developments though some of the names have changed over the years they are identifiable to any interested researcher. Many had probably been done earlier by the Yorkshire Ramblers' Club.

1930s   **Route 2** Arnold and Sidney Waterfall, Bill Bowler
This was an exceptional lead for the time, being both delicate and bold it showed a move away from the traditional style of route.

1930s   **Bilberry Crack** Arnold and Sidney Waterfall, Bill Bowler

1930s   **Craven Crack** Arnold and Sidney Waterfall, Bill Bowler

1937   **West Wall Climb** Arthur Birtwhistle, Allan Allsop

Pre 1949   **Route 2.5, Route 3, Traverse and Crack, Crookrise Crack, Easter Crack, Straight Crack** Craven Pothole Club

Pre-1949   **Leaf Crack and Slab** Craven Pothole Club
The route was originally recorded as just Leaf Crack. The upper slab pitch was added in 1950.

1950   **Arsenic Slab** Craven Pothole Club

1951   **Flake Wall, Tiger Rag** John Wilson, Brian Hartley
Tiger Rag was originally recorded as Traverse Wall Buttress.

1952   **Walker's Wall** George Walker
Footloose Finish by Phillipe Osborne 13.12.96 - by mistake!

1952   **Crease, Cat's Whiskers, Walker's Farewell** George Walker
Walker left for Australia shortly after completing these routes.

1952   **Old Lace** Charlie Salisbury, Ron Hirst

April 1954   **Bull's Horns** Brian Evans, Charlie Salisbury, Trevor Jones

Oct 1955   **Knuckle-duster** Allan Austin, Brian Evans, Ashley Petts

1955   **Knuckle Crack** Brian Evans, Allan Austin, Ashley Petts

1955   **Right-hand Route** Allan Austin, Brian Evans, Ashley Petts

1956   **Slab & Nose Alt. Finish** Allan Austin, Brian Evans

1956   **The Sole** Allan Austin, Brian Evans
A superb route which offered no protection at the time and called for a new degree of strength and agility.

1956   **Embsay Buttress Fat Man's Agony Fern Crack Grassy Gully, Woodside Wall, Woodside Buttress** John Wilson, Brian Hartley

16.9.56   **The Shelf** Allan Austin
The route was soloed with Brian Evans holding a sling over the top – just in

case.
An outstanding achievement for its time remaining a test piece for 10 years.

Pre-1957	**Left-hand Route, Chimney Variation, Octopus, Buster, Edge, Central Route** Unknown	
1957	**Crease Direct** Allan Austin	
2.3.58	**Winter Traverse** Allan Austin, Brian Evans, Ron Tyler, K. Stewart	
Aug 1958	**Hovis, Small Brown** Joe Brown	

Exceptionally difficult routes for the time, the ascent of Small Brown involved tension from Slingsby's Chimney to overcome the initial moves. The route was soloed free on 25/7/73 by a young Ron Fawcett.

1960   **Thin Air** Des Hadlum, Dennis Gray
Ventures into the boulder field were made while the smoke was still rising from the embers of a huge forest fire.

24.5.60   **Ledge Buttress** Allan Austin, Eric 'Matey' Metcalfe, D.G. Roberts

2.10.60   **The Scoop** Allan Austin, Jennifer Austin, D.G. Roberts

2.10.60   **The Ruffian** Allan Austin, Jennifer Austin

16.4.61   **Slingsby's Girdle** Allan Austin, Brian Fuller
Much of this was described in Recent Developments in 1923

22.5.62   **Wonderloaf** Allan Austin, Eric Metcalfe
The top pitch only as a variation finish to Walker's Farewell. The climb was named by Tony Barley when he added the bottom pitch in 1971.

22.2.63   **Long Day** Allan Austin, Dave Duffield

1966   **Sunstroke** Dave Berry
The awkward direct start was added at a later date.

1966   **Seres, Wallflower, Route 4, Rushlight, Evasion, Agag** Norman Elliott

1966   **The Urchin** Bob Enwright

C. Early '70s   **Diet-Pepsi, Left Arete, Left Centre, Right Centre, Right Arete, Right-hand Crack, Sunshine Slab Right-hand Sunshine Slab Left-hand Right-hand End, Offwidth Crack, Central Roof, Hanging Flake** Unknown, though many the work of Ron Fawcett, Chris Gibb, Brian Swales and Paul Greenland

C1974   **Ron's Crack (I), Ron's Crack (II)** Ron Fawcett

1974   **Left-hand Rib** Unknown

1974   **Longlurch, Pitou, Elm Tree Wall** Ron Fawcett

Oct 1974   **Cave Crack** Geoffrey Newsholm, J. Hale
The route was originally recorded as Mosquito Crack, but had probably been climbed before this date.

1976   **Slip "n" Slide** Ron Fawcett, R. Cox
A major test-piece of the time; it still receives few on-sight leads.

Aug 1976   **Mother's Little Helper** Steve Bancroft, Choe Brookes, Bernard Newman

Sept 1976   **Shelter Stone** Paul Greenland, Frank Crossley

1977   **Walkover** Pete Livesey

April 1977   **Family Matters** Paul Greenland, Martin Atkinson
Originally thought by the first ascentionists to be the line of Mother's Little Helper.

Aug 1977   **Buster Direct, Wallflower** Paul Greenland

Oct 1977   **Bilberry Wall** Brian Swales

1978   **Leaning Wall** Brian Swales

1979   **Fly** Ron Fawcett
The pebbles on the route have been slowly disappearing since the first ascent but the climb is still possible!

1981   **Jug Wall** Brian Swales, Ian Dobson (both solo)

1981   **Horny Matter, Layback Crack** Brian Swales

1981   **Sole Direct** Paul Craven

Mar 1984   **Lonesome Pine** Paul Greenland

19.2.85   **Frost Animals, Spellbinder, Breaking Out** Richard Davies (FRAs)
The first 2 had certainly been done before Circa 1971.

8.6.85   **Indirect Little Crack** Richard Davies (FRA)

8.6.85   **Magic Tricks** Richard Davies

15.6.86	**A Lifetime's Dream** Derek Hargreaves (solo after practice)	
28.7.86	**Avoidance** Andy Say	
	Wrongly named Invasion in the previous guide.	
Mar 1987	**Footprint Arete Left-hand** Steve Clegg	
18.10.87	**Pen Sketches** Derek Hargreaves (solo)	
30.12.87	**Winter Rain** Bob Larkin, Terry Holmes (both solo)	
April 1988	**Green Velvet, Greenland** Chris Sowden, Tony Burnell	
April 1988	**Wailing Wall** Tony Burnell, Chris Sowden	
April 1988	**Evasion** Chris Sowden	
June 1988	**Footprint Slab** Brian Swales	
June 1988	**Footprint Arete Right-hand** Brian Swales	
Summer 1988	**Artful Dodger** Kevin Barrett, Alan Taylor	
Aug. 1988	**Fitou** Tony Burnell, Paul Greenland, Tim Leech	
Oct. 1988	**Streaky Re-Sole, Streaklet** Graham Desroy	
Oct. 1988	**Rampant Bilberry** Steve Rhodes	
Nov. 1988	**Elephant Trods** Paul Greenland	
26.11.88	**Midget Morsel** Dave Musgrove	
Pre 1989	**Octopus Direct** Unknown	
May 1989	**Malcolm's Route** Malcolm Stork, Bill Stubbs	
July 1990	**Duck 'n' Dive** Jerry Peel	
	Soloed after practice and then used as a top-rope problem during an illicit but highly popular outdoor bouldering competition.	
June 1991	**Side Salad, Malicious Cut Of Grapefruit, Vicious slice of Mango, Overhead Projection** David Williams	
1992	**Pebble-dash Yer Toilet** David Williams, L. Pickering Robb Wilks.	
12.12.92	**Gambling With Crystals, Ice Fall** Julian Lines (solo)	
1992	**Mother's Milk, East of the River** David Williams (solo)	
April 1994	**Friction Slab, Hidden Wall** Brian Swales (solo)	
13.8.94	**Gibb's Rib** Chris Gibb, Dave Barton	
18.8.94	**Dewhurst Mill** Brian Swales (solo)	
25.8.94	**Lyndhurst** Brian Swales	
29.8.94	**Quashqui** Brian Swales (solo)	
30.8.94	**Stepping Out ,The Forager, Basic Training, Grovelhog** Brian & Sue Swales	
30.8.94	**Born Again** Sue & Brian Swales,	
	Brian only just squeezed through!	
1994	**Moon Shadow** Brian Swales (certainly climbed before**)**	
2.7.95	**Bull's Eye** Tony Marr, Mike Tooke	
2.4.96	**Mindbender, Mindless** Brian Swales (solo)	
2.5.96	**All In The Mind** Brian Swales (solo)	
24.6.96	**Massive Attack, Fear No Evil** Derek Hargreaves (solo)	
1996	**Jason's Roof** Jason Myers	
	An outrageous roof problem, possible the hardest on grit.	
May 1997	**Wholemeal** Mick Johnson (solo)	
May 1997	**A Reach Too Far** Mick Johnson, Dick Tong	
May 1997	**Gromit** B. Swales, T Birk. (FRA)	
23.7.97	**Perplexity** Tony Marr, Mike Tooke	
9.8.97	**Premium White** Bob Larkin (solo)	
10.9.97	**Matador** Brian Swales solo	
21.10.97	**Mighty White** Phillipe Osborne (solo)	
	Believed to have been done in the 1980s by Paul Greenland.	
3.11.97	**Nasty** Phillipe Osborne	
1997	**Crease Arete** Phillipe Osbourne	
	The lower part is an old problem.	
1997	**Wallace** Terry Holmes (FRA)	
30.1.98	**Knuckle-duster Direct, Facade, Trivial Pursuit, Dirty Tackle** Tony Marr (solo)	

CROW'S NEST WOOD QUARRY

February 1982 **Icy Start** Bruce Goodwin
March 1982 **The Bow, Wet Wednesday, Reversed Image** Tony Nichols
     Reversed Image was so named because of its resemblance to Atherton Brothers Climb at Shining Clough.
March 1982 **BG And His Brush** Mark Leach
March 1982 **Crow's Nest Wall** Bruce Goodwin
March 1982 **Floss** Ian Conway
March 1982 **Calcis** Clive Morton
     Clive's first route after a serious accident the year before
April 1982 **Crache, Diagonal** Bruce Goodwin
April 1982 **Nic's Route, Himalayan Balsam** Ian Conway
June 1982 **Mantelpiece** John Vose
June 1982 **Afterthought** Bruce Goodwin
1983 **The Big Wind Up** Gregg Rimmer, Mick Ryan
1983 **Hot Temper** Mick Ryan (solo)
1984 **Stainless Steel Screw** Bruce Goodwin, Clive Morton, John Vose
1984 **Birch Wall Fritters** Bruce Goodwin, Gordon Mason, Tony Nichols
1984 **Ring Pull** Bruce Goodwin, Clive Morton, Tony Nichols
? **Travelling Right** Tony Nichols, Bruce Goodwin

DEER GALLOWS

Pre 1930s **Deer Gallows Chimney, Deer Gallows Original, Fist Crack (bottom section), Staircase Rib, Pinnacle Wall, Layman's Arete, Right-hand &Left-hand Route**
     First ascents unknown, but most were climbed by the Waterfall brothers, Sidney and Arnold, and their friends in the 1930s. They believed they had been climbed much earlier.
Circa 1950 **Balance** John Wilson
1953 **Cave Crack** Ron Hields
     A fine plum for a gifted climber
April 1963 **Fist Crack** Dennis Gray, Ian Howell
     Bottom section obviously climbed before - and, perhaps, the top, too, for all anyone knows!
25.10.64 **The Cringe** Frank Wilkinson, Bob Enwright
     A climb which caused a ripple at the time, but which proved to be not as hard as first thought.
25.10.64 **Zig Zag** Mike Bebbington
1964/65 **Cave Crack Alternative** Frank Wilkinson, Mike Bebbington, Dave Berry
     No-one can remember who was first.
1965 **The Nose** Dave Berry
June 1970 **The Skinner, Deer Gallows Wall, The Wreath** Mike Hammill
1971 **Knows, The Pocket, Pebble Promenade** John Syrett
     Technical masterpieces from the technical master.
Early 1970s **Hangman's Wall Rock Bottom Brown Dancer** Ron Fawcett
     The teenage Fawcett flexing his muscles.
Pre-1982 **Slide, Slip** Unknown
Pre1989 **Gallows Pole** Unknown
1983 **Rift Arete** T. Heaton
2.11.88 **Slither** Dave Musgrove
11.3.89 **Pochette Surprise** Kim Buck (solo)

DERBY DELPH

1983	**Watch It, Catch It, Crack It, Moon Tiger, Gnatty, Chironimid, Bloodsucker, Wusac, White Streak, Green Streak, Pool Wall, Flank Attack, Question Mark, White Tower, Right Arete, Plugged, Grey Man, Cave Wall, Masgor, Sloper Variations, Booth Dean Arete, Swapped** Bruce Goodwin, Gordon Mason
1983	**Longer, Just In Line** Gordon Mason, Bruce Goodwin
1983	**Correction, Organe, Rogane, Nogare** Bruce Goodwin, Gordon Mason, G Thomas
1983	**Completion, Illusion** Bruce Goodwin, Gordon Mason, John Lord
1983	**Sloper** Bruce Goodwin, John Lord
1983	**Deliverance** Clive Morton, Bruce Goodwin
1983	**Whitegree** Bruce Goodwin, Tony Nichols
1983	**Digger, Little One** Bruce Goodwin (solo)
1983	**Half Done** Gordon Mason (solo)
1983/4	**Windy** Gordon Mason, Bruce Goodwin
1984	**Munch It** Bruce Goodwin, Gordon Mason
1984	**Shaky Start, Caractarcus** Gordon Mason, Bruce Goodwin

DOVESTONES

March 1960	**Pellet Climb** Brian & Aileen Evans
17.12.61	**The Fogger** Allan Austin
1962	**Mist Crack, Fingers** Tony & Robin Barley
Pre 1969	**Finale** Unknown
29.7.72	**Raven's Peak Wall** Greg Tough & Miss A. Tough
22.5.74	**Faithful Wall** Ken Wood, Gwyn Evans
Spring 1980	**The Great Santini** Mike Hammill, Paul Craven
21.7.83	**A Coin For A Beggar** John Mackenzie
	Also climbed around this time by Paul Craven as August Arete
Pre 1989	Almost everything else! *Presumably by Tony Burnell who wrote up the crag for the last guide but claimed nothing specific.*
August 1997	**Waltzing Matilda, Class Warrior** Jon Aylward

EARL CRAG

16.7.43	**Demon Traverse** Arthur Dolphin, John Cook
	Possibly one of the Tiger Traverse lines.
1947-48	**Little Buttress, Indicator Crack** Allan Allsopp
27.3.49	**Earl Crack** Arthur Dolphin, Mick Dwyer
Mar 1949	**Tiger Wall** Arthur Dolphin
1949	**Viscount's Route** Tom Cranfield, Alfie Beanland
1950	**Perch Wall** Tom Cranfield, Peter Greenwood
1952	**Erasor Slab** Dennis Gray, Alfie Beanland
29.3.58	**The Hand Traverse, Mantelshelf Slab** Allan Austin (solo)
29.3.58	**Awkward Crack** Allan Austin, Miss Jennifer Ruffe
23.4.58	**Pedestal Rib, Flake Crack** Allan Austin, Miss Jennifer Ruffe
23.4.58	**Cave Wall** Allan Austin (solo)
8.5.58	**Mousehole Slab, Shothole Ridge** Allan Austin, Miss Jennifer Ruffe
	The numerous variants of Shothole Ridge have been claimed and counter-claimed almost every year since.
5.6.58	**Boundary Wall, Butterfly Crack** Allan Austin (solo)
1958-59	**Overhanging Wall** Neville Drasdo

29.6.60	**Fishladder** Allan Austin, Derek Farley, D. Roberts	
	Previously climbed with and by Neville Drasdo and friends, 1954.	
7.4.71	**Problem Rib** John Syrett, John and Gordon Stainforth, Ken Wood	
21.4.71	**Earl Buttress** John Syrett, Ken Wood	
21.4.71	**Hatchet Crack** Ken Wood, John Syrett	
4.5.71	**Green Rib** Ken Wood (solo)	
1972	**Erasor Slab Direct** John Syrett, Ken Wood	
22.8.72	**Moonlight Saunter** Greg Tough, H. Walker	
	Climbed in the dark after an evenings bouldering.	
28.4.73	**Cave Traverse** Ken Wood, Max Biden	
11.9.73	**Little Greeny** John Syrett (solo)	
17.6.74	**Early Riser** Al Manson (solo)	
11.4.75	**Rat Juggling** Al Manson (solo)	
11.4.75	**Rat Au Vin, Sour Grapes** Mike Hammill (solo)	
12.6.75	**Trite Rib** Ken Wood, Charles Dracup	
26.6.75	**Blade** Ken Wood (solo)	
31.7.75	**Evasion** Ken Wood, Mike Mortimer	
31.7.75	**Trifle** Ken Wood, Charles Dracup	
1976	**The Kipper** Ron Fawcett (solo)	
1979	**Pitch at Will** Derek Hargreaves	
1980	**Pee Pod** Mike Hammill (solo)	
Sept 1980	**Stall** T. Pollard, D. Snowden	
1980	**Tick-Tock Man** Mike Hammill (solo)	
1981	**Jump to the Beat, Overhanging Wall Direct, Captain Gap** Derek Hargreaves, Mark Hudson	
May 1982	**Flight** T. Pollard, D. Snowden, A. Say	
1982	**Cut Throat** Ron Fawcett	
1983	**Prowler** Phil Garlick	
	One of the few he was allowed out of many doubted claims.	
Apr 1984	**Sweet Apples** Jerry Peel (solo)	
May 1984	**Butterfly Wall** Gary Healey (solo)	
May 1984	**Mantel Maniac, Green Rib Right-hand** Jerry Peel (solo)	
May 1984	**Grape Nut** Derek Hargreaves (solo)	
1984	**Valentine's Frog** Derek Hargreaves, Martin Atkinson	
1984	**Liz's Wall** Martin Atkinson, C. Pickles	
May 1986	**Desert Island Arete** Jerry Peel (solo)	
Nov 1986	**Edge of Darkness** Jerry Peel (solo)	
Aug 1987	**Trite Rib Direct** Jerry Peel (solo)	
Apr 1988	**The Ribber** Roger Hindle (solo)	
Apr 1988	**Pedestal Wall, The Twister** Jerry Peel (solo)	
17.8.89	**Mind Bomb** Dave Pegg	
	The crags first E7!	
26.8.89	**Aliens Stole My Bolt Kit** Dave Pegg	
3.9.89	**Distant Early Warning** Dave Pegg	
27.9.91	**Abstract Attitude** Martin Wood	
10.8.93	**Jock Jones** Neil Herbert, Lee Downham (FRA)	
	Almost certainly climbed before.	
6.9.93	**Cosmic Baby** Danny Reinsch (solo)	
1995	**The Scent Of A Woman** Andy Cave, Mark Radtke	
May 1996	**Sicca, Riddance, Run A Mock** Derek Hargreaves	
8.6.96	**Straight Shot** Ian Farnworth, Paul Wheeler	
5.8.97	**Cave Direct** Phillipe Osbourne, Chris Barker	
19.8.97	**A Stretcher Case** Phillipe Osbourne (unseconded)	

EARL SEAT

27.7.98	**Jams To The Slaughter**	Nigel Baker, Dave Musgrove
27.7.98	**Pebble Pincher**	Dave Musgrove, Nigel Baker
27.7.98	**Crack With A View, Knobbles In Toyland**	Dave Musgrove (solo)
28.7.98	**Entrance Exam**	Nigel Baker, Paul Kitchingman

All now reclaimed by Paul Clarke and friends c.1990.

EASTBY CRAG

1930s **Eastby Buttress, Waterfall Chimney, Broken Arete, Nose Climb, Waterfall's Crack** Sidney Waterfall and friends

1930s **Mantelshelves** Unknown

1960s **Corner Crack, Corner Groove, Eastby Groove, Traverse and Chimney, Slab and Chimney, The Flake, Holly Bush Groove, Original Route, Birch Tree Crack** Unknown

23.4.60 **Whaup Edge, Scoop and Crack, Knuckle Slab, Block Buttress** Allan Austin, Jennifer Austin

28.8.60 **Mist Slab** Allan Austin (solo)

22.10.60 **Stepover** Allan Austin, D.G. Roberts, Jennifer Austin

4.11.61 **Recess Crack** Allan Austin (solo)

1.9.62 **Pillar Front, Swastika** Allan Austin, Brian Evans

6.9.64 **Thrutch** Frank Wilkinson (solo)

17.5.65 **Pillar Rib** Frank Wilkinson, Dave Barnett

1965 **The Padder** Keith Roberts, J., A. Firth
Direct Start by Ian Dobson 1970s

Circa 1965 **The Struggler, Knuckle Slab Arete, Index Variation** Unknown

June 1970 **Mist Slab Direct, Struggler Direct** Mike Hammill

1977 **Thumper** John Eastham, Geoff and John Myers

1977 **Cheshire Cat** Ron Fawcett

26.4.80 **The Boldness Of Youth** Bob Larkin (solo)

Pre 1982 **Lobe** Unknown

1984 **Mistaken Identity** Paul Craven

19.2.85 **Crossing The Line** Richard Davies

1986 **Hangs** Derek Hargreaves

21.2.88 **Easy Touch, Defective Too Early** Derek Hargreaves (unseconded)

28.2.88 **Action Traction** Alan Taylor, Kevin Barrett

April 1988 **Thumper Direct, Genuflex, Defective Direct, Blinkered Variation** Alan Taylor, Kevin Barrett

April 1988 **The Hatchback Forager** Brian Swales

April 1988 **Impetus** Kevin Barrett

April 1988 **Aretus** Derek Hargreaves

Pre 1988 **Pullover** Unknown

25.3.90 **Dead Babies** Dave Pegg
Direct Start by Dave Musgrove (jnr) March 1988.

Spring 1990 **Accidental Baby** Paul Jenkinson

Circa 1990 **Aperitif L&R** Brian Swales (solo)

1990 **Heather Flake** John Belbin
Claimed by various parties

1991 **Rock and Roll** Tim Pollard, Andy Thackray

Sept 1992 **Lucy** Tim Pollard, Pete Mellor, John Belbin

Aug 94 **Blue Max** Tim Pollard, Rob Hanson, Andy Thackray

2.9.95 **The Mason's Arms** Brian Swales (unseconded)

2.9.95 **The Cavendish, Early Doors** Brian & Sue Swales
Early Doors is an old problem

Summer 1996 **Eastby Buttress Alt. Finish** Brian Swales (solo)

30.8.97 **Mr. Grumpy, After Hours, Opening Time** Brian Swales (solo)

3.9.97 **Jaywalk** Brian Swales (solo)

4.9.97 **Last Orders** Brian Swales (solo)

EAVESTONE

Virtually all routes here were cleaned to some extent before the first ascent. Almost all the solo first ascents were completed only after top rope inspection and/or practice.

Jan 62 **Central Chimney, Narrow Slab, Chequers Crack, Tiptoe** Peter Checkland
The routes, but not the location, were tantalisingly revealed in a magazine article.

21.4.65 **Ripples, Wedgewood** Tony Barley, Robin Barley

21.4.65 **The Heel** Robin Barley, Tony Barley

21.5.65 **Galleon Tower** Tony Barley, Robin Barley
Pitch 2 only - Pitch 1 added by Tony 15.3.90

29.7.65 **Watery Grave** Tony Barley, Robin Barley

27.8.65 **Swinging Free, Microchip** Tony Barley, Robin Barley

27.8.65 **The Keep** Tony Barley

27.8.65 **Wet Landing, Checkmate** Robin Barley, Tony Barley

7.2.66 **Gorilla** Tony Barley, Robin Barley, Dennis Gray

April 1967 **Oubliette, Hallmark** Tony Barley, Chas Hird

April 1967 **Eavesdropper, Stonerag, Evenso, Taper** Tony Darley, John William

6.8.67 **Alleycat, Tin, Pan** Tony Barley, K. Robson

6.8.71 **Castellan, Battlement** Tony Barley, Anthony Roche
The modern crux of Battlement was avoided by gaining the rib high up from Castellan.

6.8.88 **Mystery Man** Tony Barley, Steve Jenkins

10.5.89 **Stonechat** Dave Musgrove, Tony Barley, Dave Musgrove (jnr)
"Well, now I've seen the place I won't be in a hurry to come back" Dave Musgrove after his first visit! - By 1992 he had been back 57 times. "First impressions can be deceptive!"

10.5.89 **Upper Sail** Tony Barley

10.5.89 **Lower Sail** Tony Barley

20.5.89 **Eavestone Wall** Tony Barley
started from the left and a sling was used for aid

6.8.89 **Prowler, Alleycracker** Tony Barley, Dave Musgrove

6.8.89 **Chiminalley** Dave Musgrove (solo)

10.8.89 **Spinnaker** Tony Barley, Dave Musgrove

10.8.89 **Bowsprit** Dave Musgrove, Tony Barley

12.8.89 **Eavestone Crack** Dave Musgrove, Tony Barley
It took 4 visits but was the real catalyst to the new route frenzy that followed.

19.8.89 **Pitching Wedge** Dave Musgrove, Tony Barley

19.8.89 **Bunkered** Tony Barley, Dave Musgrove

10.9.89 **Gangplank** Tony and Nina Barley.

13.9.89 **Trapeze, Keelhaul** Tony Barley, Steve Jenkins

23.9.89 **Eavestone Wall (Direct Start)** Tony Barley (solo)
A sling was still needed above.

24.9.89 **Still Water, Sun Bird, Sun-Up, Sunstroke, Sundown, Sundial, Little Gem, Flaw, Yardarm** Tony Barley (solo)

28.9.89 **Troubled Water** Tony Barley (solo)

28.9.89 **Rough Water** Dave Musgrove (solo)

28.9.89 **Crazy Paver** Tony Barley, Dave Musgrove (both led)

30.9.89 **Rampart** Dave Musgrove (unseconded)

5.10.89 **King Of The Castle** Dave Musgrove, Tony Barley

5.10.89 **Dirty Rascal** Tony Barley, Dave Musgrove

8.10.89 **Dungeon, Stockade, Crenellation, Machicolation, Arrow Slit** Tony Barley (solo)

15.10.89 **Portcullis** Tony Barley (solo)

15.10.89 **The Alamo** Dave Musgrove, Tony Barley

15.10.89 **Excalibur** Tony Barley, Dave Musgrove

19.11.89 **Starboard Crack, Glacier Apron, Leaving The Bergshrund** Tony Barley (solo)

26.11.89	**Thin Ice, Murky Water** Tony Barley (solo)	
29.12.89	**Beech Peach** Tony Barley (solo)	
12.3.90	**Reflections** Dave Musgrove (solo)	
12.3.90	**Pushing The Boat Out** Dave Musgrove, Tony Barley.	
15.3.90	**Strange Attractor, Pebbledash** Kim Greenald	

Kim soloed them both whilst Dave and Tony were cleaning the top!

20.3.90	**Heave Ho, Rough Cut, Bauble** Tony Barley (solo)
20.3.90	**Spanish Main** Tony Barley

This was the 1st pitch only - Pitch 2 had been led by Dave Musgrove (jnr) on 10.5.89

6.4.90	**Little Sparkler, Pyrites** Tony Barley (solo)
8.4.90	**Hanging Serac** Tony Barley (solo)
13.4.90	**Good Friday** Dave Musgrove (solo)
16.4.90	**Captain Pugwash** Tony Barley, Barry Groves
16.4.90	**Under The Eaves, Battlement, Casement Crack** Dave Musgrove (solo)
17.4.90	**Sea Of Tranquillity** Dave Musgrove, Andy Wild, Tony Barley
17.4.90	**Don't Pay The Ferryman** Tony Barley, Dave Musgrove (alt leads)
18.4.90	**For Keepsake** Dave Musgrove, Tony Barley
18.4.90	**Fat Chance** Dave (jnr.) & Dave Musgrove.
24.4.90	**Touching The Void** Dave Musgrove, Tony Barley

An apt name, if you've read the book.

28.4.90	**Eavestone Wall** Kim Greenald, Paul Dawson

First completely free ascent.

1.5.90	**Apache** Dave Musgrove, Tony Barley
1.5.90	**Treasure Island** Tony Barley, Dave Musgrove

A mammoth cleaning job revealed this superb line - alas it will need repeating regularly to keep it in condition.

12.5.90	**Merlon** Robin & Tony Barley
14.5.90	**Stonechat Ramp** Robin and Tony Barley
31.5.90	**Jolly Roger** Tony Barley, Dave & David Musgrove
31.5.90	**Atlantic Voyager** Dave Musgrove, Tony Barley
31.5.90	**Flawless** Dave Musgrove (solo)
31.5.90	**Canada Dry** Tony Barley

A solid 6b problem from the man who claims he can't climb 6a!

8.6.90	**Genesis** Dave Musgrove, Tony Barley

A major prize - climbed at 6.30 am before work on a Friday to beat an imagined weekend raid by an interested On The Edge team.

8.6.90	**Over The Looking Glass** Tony Barley (solo)
13.6.90	**Mhlabatini, Tonquani, Umkomeni** Tony Barley (solo)
13.6.90	**African Skies, Sekorora** Dave Musgrove (solo)
16.6.90	**Shiver Me Timbers, Cannon Fodder, Ready For Action, Armada, Finish The Bowls** Tony Barley (solo)
23.6.90	**Chainmail** Tony Barley (solo)
28.6.90	**Scalp, Portal Rib, Sangatte, See The Light** Tony Barley (solo)
5.7.90	**Rearguard, Dance On White Horses** Tony Barley (solo)
14.9.90	**Spitfire, Hurricane** Dave Musgrove (solo)

Climbed on the 50th anniversary of the Battle of Britain.

19.1.91	**Winter Sunshine** Dave Musgrove (solo)
21.3.91	**Whistling In The Dark** Dave Musgrove (solo)
3.4.91	**Officer Dibble** Dave Musgrove, Steve Webster
3.4.91	**Going Catatonic** Steve Webster, Dave Musgrove
4.4.91	**Director, Savage** Tony Barley (solo)
11.4.91	**The Pirates Ear** Tony Barley, Dave Musgrove
11.4.91	**Swashbuckler** Dave Musgrove (solo)
14.4.91	**Banana Boat** Tony Barley (solo)
20.4.91	**Brave New World** Tony & Tim Barley
27.4.91	**Don't Worry I'm A Nurse** Steve Webster, Pete Lawson
27.4.91	**Life Begins At Forty** Bob Smith (unseconded)

The hardest route on the crag, completed only after 2 ground falls.

30.4.91	**Long John Sliver** Tony Barley (solo)	
7.5.91	**Here There Be Dragons** Dave Musgrove (solo)	
8.5.91	**Cracked Ice** Tony Barley (solo)	
11.5.91	**Glissade** Tony Barley (solo)	
18.5.91	**Ice Dance, Iced Diamond** Tony & Robin Barley	
29.5.91	**French Connection** Tony Barley 29.5.91	
30.5.91	**Cream** Tony Barley (solo)	
30.5.91	**Garden Of Eden, Forbidden Fruit, Eavestone Eliminate, Rib Tickler, Treebeard** Dave Musgrove (solo)	
5.6.91	**The Fissure Barley** Tony Barley (solo)	
15.6.91	**Oakey Kokey** Dave Musgrove (solo)	
15.6.91	**Puff** Tony Barley, Dave Musgrove	
15.6.91	**Dragonfly, Ride The Magic Dragon** Tony Barley (solo)	
18.6.91	**Wellington Crack II**, Dave Musgrove (solo - in wellies!)	
18.6.91	**The Meaning Of Life** Dave Musgrove, Tony Barley	
23.6.91	**Ditch** Tony Barley (solo)	
23.6.91	**The Gatekeeper** Dave Musgrove, Nigel Baker, Steve Webster, Rupert Wyard	
27.6.91	**Jumping Jack** Tony Barley (solo)	
27.6.91	**Secret Obsession** Dave Musgrove (solo)	
10.7.91	**Purely Esoteric** Dave Musgrove (solo)	
4.8.91	**Dragonslayer** Dave Musgrove, Nigel Baker (both led)	

After several days of cleaning and one ground fall!

20.9.91	**Top Cat, The Ginnel** Dave Musgrove (solo)
1992	**Roses Of Picardy** Steve Findlay, Chris Shorter
25.7.93	**Too Much Too Young** Tony Simpson (solo)
6.8.94	**Sun Bingo** Noel Curtis, Darren Wade, Jason Lister (all solo)
19.4.97	**The Plunge, Sea Dog** J ohnny Cutliffe, Mick Darfield
August 1997	**Alligator, Crocodile** Andy Moss (unseconded)

GILSTEAD

Gilstead crags have been frequented for many years but first ascents are lost in the mists of time. All the listed routes and problems were recently collated, named and described by two local teams working independently Rick Hardicre and P. D. Benn in one group and Chas Ward, Adrian Jebb, Matt Booth and Richard 'Wally' Walshaw in another during the late 1980s and early 1990s. Only the following are claimed as definite firsts.

28.5.93	**Cream Dream** Chas Ward, Wally Walshaw
1997	**Photo Finish** Matt Booth
1997	**Euphoria** Adrian Jebb
15.3.98	**Ninja Darkness** Chas Ward (unseconded)

GORPLE

This crag has been frequented and bouldered upon by Widdop activists for over well over 50 years. The first named routes were only formally recorded recently.

Winter 1995	**Louise** Andy Long, John Dunne
Winter 1995	**Eternal** John Dunne, Andy Long
Summer 1998	**Carmen Picasso** John Dunne

GREAT WOLFREY

Circa 1950	Several cracks and chimneys climbed by Jim Walton, Brian Smith and Ed Thackeray
1952	**Chockstone Crack, North Chimney, Hangover Crack & Chimney, Arete Chimney, Loyalty Crack, Wolfrey Crack Indirect, Great Wolfrey Buttress,**

Hollybush Crack, Heather Groove, West Face, Corner & Traverse   Brian Evans, Phillip Leese

November 1955	**Deception** Brian Evans, Allan Austin, Ashley Petts, Ernie Shepherd.	
17. 6.75	**Walter's Rib** Ken Wood, Charles Dracup	
27.9.80	**Werewolf** John Eastham, Geoff & John Myers	
	Mistakenly called What You Like in the last edition	
1983	**Cowell's Rib** Ashley Cowell	
Pre 1985	**Shades Of Green** John Mackenzie, Norman Hitch	
23.10.85	**Autumn Gold, Alternative Arete** Glen Gorner, John Mackenzie	
23.10.85	**Holly Tree Hover** John Mackenzie, Glen Gorner	
16.5.86	**Wolf At The Door** Mike Hammil, John Yates	
6.11.88	**Teacake Wall, Good Friends, Grand Defiance** John Mackenzie, Rik Weld	
6.11.88	**Lipstick Wall** Rik Weld, John Mackenzie	
6.11.88	**Slapstick Slab** Rik Weld (solo)	
23.6.91	**Limited Company, Foxy** Bob Larkin (solo)	
30.12.93	**Huff-Puff Chimney** Dave and David Musgrove (solo)	
	Undoubtedly done before!	
29.10.95	**Recess Arete, Flow Arete, Summer Of '76** Malcolm Townsley (solo)	
19.6.96	**The Duke, Rock 'n' Roll** Dave Musgrove (jnr) (solo).	

GUISECLIFF

1910-1930	**Climbs Unknown** Eric Addyman, Eric Roberts
1933-1950	**Letterbox Climb, Shelter Climb** Harry Stembridge, Fred Stembridge
	Plus others now forgotten.
1937	**Roc's Nest Chimney** Arthur Birtwistle, Heywood, Pearson
1937	**Ledge and Crack** Arthur Birtwistle, Heywood, Pearson
1937	**Arbor Crack** Arthur Birtwistle, Heywood, Pearson
	Ascended with a sapling at 10ft and gained from the left to "circumvent the underfoot of the crack" plus a "hanging twisted tree and loose chockstones essential to progress - 70ft severe"
	Thin Man's Delight Arthur Birtwistle, Heywood, Pearson
	These are the earliest routes, published in the MUMC Journal 1937-38.
Pre 1954	**Milroy's Climb** Milroy and Party
Pre 1954	**Pulpit Chimney, Right-hand Wall, Buttress Route, Shoulder Gully, Boundary Chimney, Apparition, Scissors, Aiguille de Mouton, Intestine, Fireplace Chimney, The Chimney, North Buttress Pinnacle** Yorkshire Ramblers Club members and Royal Engineers Climbing Club members.
	Geoff Scovell recorded these routes in "Climbs on Guisecliff" YRC Journal 1955.
1954-1957	**Postman's Crack, Tree Cracks, Oak Wall, Little Something, The Slot, Hook Route** Yorkshire Mountaineering Club
May 1954	**Forgotten Chimney** Ashley Petts, Mrs Petts, Brian Evans
1954	**Brian's Climb** Brian Hields, Ronnie Hields
	A fine effort by two young brothers on this very steep buttress.
1954	**Phillipa's Ridge** Ronnie Hields, Brian Hields
	The girlfriend got the route name.
1955	**KOYLI** Ronnie Hields, J. Eastwood
	Ronnie was serving with the King's Own Yorkshire Light Infantry. Variation Start: John Eastham, Geoff Myers 1969.
1957	**Comet Wall** Ron Hields, Vince Murphy
	A major edition to the crag although some aid (pegs still in situ) were necessary to avoid the flake crack. FFA: Tony and Robin Barley, July 1963.
1958	**The Bastion** Ron Hields, Derek Marshall
	A mixed free/peg climb starting at Agrippa and finishing up the overhanging crack/chimney of Nice 'n' Sleazy.

26.4.58	**Double Top** Allan Austin, Brian Evans
26.4.58	**North Buttress Crack** Allan Austin, Brian Evans
29.10.58	**North Buttress Ordinary** Bill Todd, John Johnson

Bill Todd insisted his future wife accompany him on his first ascent only for her to part company with a tree branch and be lowered off with a cracked rib.

Circa 1959	**Boundary Chimney Direct** Jack Wilson
Jan 1960	**Daniel** Allan Austin, Brian Evans
Jan 1960	**Tarzan** Allan Austin, Brian Evans

A vegetated route left of Forgotten Chimney.

| 30.4.60 | **Holly Grooves**   Allan Austin, Dave Roberts |
| 30.4.60 | **Cuckoo**   Allan Austin, Dave Roberts |

A vegetated route right of Hawk Slab.

| 24.7.60 | **Hawk Slab**   Allan Austin, Eric "Matey" Metcalfe |
| 1960 | **Beard Route**   Allan Austin and Party |

A vegetated route left of Shoulder Gully.

Autumn 1960	**Nippem** Harold Barraclough, Ron Tyler, Hilda Tyler, Charlie Salisbury, Bill Todd
Autumn 1960	**Root Crack** Harold Barraclough, Ron Tyler, Hilda Tyler, Charlie Salisbury
Autumn 1960	**Barracuda** Harold Barraclough, Ron Tyler
Autumn 1960	**Sling Wall** Harold Barraclough, Ron Tyler

Left of Barracuda a wall with a peg and sling.

| 1960/61 | **Sprog Stigma Dhobi Illusion Rhino Cretin's Crack**   Frank Spence, Lynn Noble, M. Sanderson |

During his two-year period of climbing Frank Spence made a notable addition to the crag with some steep corners, cracks and grooves. Stationed at RAF Topcliffe, he also opened routes at Sutton Bank.

Feb 1961	**Kandahar Groove** Robin Barley, Tony Barley
Mar 1961	**Ryvoan Crack** Tony Barley, Robin Barley
1961	**The By-Pass** Tony Barley, Robin Barley
1961	**Jezebel** Tony Barley, Robin Barley (Alt)
1961	**Arbor Crack – Cordite Start** Tony Barley, Robin Barley

Direct Start up the undercut crack to gain a sapling at 10ft. Birtwhistle's "loose" chockstone impacted with cordite smoke.

| 1961 | **North Buttress Direct**   Tony Barley, Robin Barley (Alt) |

An exposed addition to the North Buttress, but with a tree in the bulging crack.

| 1961 | **Take Five**   Robin Barley, Tony Barley |

Five aid pegs, practising for Kilnsey. FFA 1965.

29.10.61	**Ruminant** Brian Evans, Tony Barley, Robin Barley
Nov 1962	**Overhanging Groove** Robin Barley, Tony Barley
Nov 1962	**The Kraken** Robin Barley, Tony Barley
Mar 1963	**April Rib** Tony Barley, Robin Barley

Now the start of Midsummer Night's Dream.

| Mar 1963 | **Drum Crack**   Robin Barley, Tony Barley |
| Aug 1963 | **North Wall Eliminate**   Robin Barley, Tony Barley |

Immortalised in a magazine article by Dennis Gray in 1968, as one of 'The 10 best climbs on Gritstone'.

| Sept 1963 | **Pinnacle Face**   Tony Barley, Robin Barley |
| Sept 1963 | **The Peeler**   Robin Barley, Tony Barley |

For peeling skin!

1964	**Lectern Chimney** Robin Barley, Tony Barley
1964	**Footpatter** Robin Barley, Tony Barley
June 1964	**Pendulum** Robin Barley, Dennis Gray, Tony Barley

A swing on dubious holds.

| June 1964 | **Stretcher**   Robin Barley, Dennis Gray, Tony Barley |

Direct start by Tony Barley in 1965.

| Aug 1964 | **Agrippa**   Robin Barley, Tony Barley |
| Sept 1964 | **Magnificat**   Tony Barley, Robin Barley |

Acquired the name after attendance of the compulsory school service!

28.3.65	**Number Five Buttress Girdle** Robin Barley, Tony Barley (Alt)	
	Became the central section of Jaywalk.	
22.5.65	**Creation** Tony Barley, Robin Barley	
	Climbed after a morning ascent of Forked Lightning Crack at Heptonstall. Considered harder and, with only token protection, one of the hardest routes in Yorkshire at that time.	
29.8.65	**Crack of Roots, Speedway** Tony Barley, Robin Barley	
1965	**Careful Crack, Coyote Wall** Tony Barley, Robin Barley	
12.3.66	**Wafer Crack** Robin Barley, Tony Barley	
18.6.66	**Winklepicker** Robin Barley, Tony Barley	
2.7.66	**Dingbat, The Verger** Tony Barley, Robin Barley	
	Cleaning on route resulted in exhaustion on the final move from the corner and a long fall. Finally it was climbed with two aid points. FFA: John Syrett and Al Manson 1973. A very impressive feat.	
10.7.66	**Energy** Tony Barley, Robin Barley	
13.7.66	**The Belfry** Tony Barley, John Williams	
13.7.66	**Curate's Crack Pulpit Steps** Tony Barley, John Williams	
16.7.66	**Ruscator** Tony Barley, Robin Barley	
	Originally with an aid peg but later FFA by same party.	
16.7.66	**Microcrack** Robin Barley, Tony Barley	
17.7.66	**Bold John** Robin Barley, Tony Barley, John Williams	
	An unlikely line; start added later by Tony Barley	
4.9.66	**Autobahn** Tony Barley, John Williams	
1966	**Hotrod, Ringway** Tony Barley, Chas Hird	
27.7.68	**Right-hand Wall New Finish** Allan Austin, Ken Wood	
5.10.69	**Hook Route** Eric Lillee, A. Hogburn	
	First ascent in its present form after block fell out. Was originally Hard Severe.	
9.8.70	**Sideshow** Tony Barley, Tony Roche	
13.9.70	**Tombstone** Tony Barley, Robin Barley	
13.9.70	**Skyjacker** Tony Barley, Robin Barley	
	Beginning of a cleaning spell on the impressive Comet Buttress. First pitch with 2 pegs. FFA: Peter Short, Alan Towse 7.7.84.	
20.9.70	**Comet Wall Left-hand Finish** Tony Barley, Robin Barley	
4.4.71	**Shindig** Tony Barley	
	A sling was used for aid at the roof. FFA: Ken Wood, John Harwood 11.7.72.	
14.5.71	**Synchromesh** Tony Barley, Tony Roche	
22. 9.71	**Aggrippina** Tony Barley, Robin Brown	
3.10.71	**Jaywalk** Tony Barley, Ken Wood (Alt)	
	A complete 400ft girdle of No. 5 Buttress starting on Comet Buttress. Completed with final pitch added (14.11.71 – Tony Barley, Tony Roche)	
16.4.72	**The Catacomb, The Cleavage** Tony Barley	
16.4.72	**Nobutjust** Tony Barley, Robin Brown	
	Also direct start added.	
29.4.72	**Spring Fever** Tony Barley, Tony Roche	
27.5.72	**Gossamer** Tony Barley, Tony Roche	
27.5.72	**Campanile** Tony Barley, Joe Tasker	
	A fine finishing pitch up the final tower after gardening.	
21.6.72	**Midsummer Night's Dream** Tony Barley, Robin Brown	
13.8.72	**Fairway** Tony Barley, Howard Walker	
	Ascended earlier on sods – probably as it exists now!	
25.6.72	**Voortrek** Tony Barley, Howard Walker	
	North Buttress Girdle.	
7.7.72	**The Right Rib** Tony Barley	
7.5.73	**Guillotine** John Syrett	
	Previously called Stingo, with two aid points by Tony Barley 1.6.71	
Mar 1973	**Aftermath** Tony Barley, Chas Hird	
	One point of aid. FFA: Jerry Peel, Tony Barley 27.10.74.	
10.6.73	**Barleycorn** Gordon "Speedy" Smith, John Midgley	

The Right Eliminate of Guisecliffe snatched by the Rock and Ice under the nose of the local experts.

24.2.74	**Clodhopper**	Tony Barley, Martin Jones, Gwyn Evans
14.4.74	**Mantelshelfman**	Tony Barley, Martin Jones, R. Brown
14.4.74	**Haberdashery**	Tony Barley

One aid point on first ascent.

5.7.75   **Mastermind**   Tony Barley, R. Brown
A new advance in difficulty possibly Tony's hardest lead. A peg was used on the damp first pitch. FFA: Peter Short, A. Towse 7.7.84.

1.9.78   **Nice "n" Sleazy**   Martin Berzins, Bob Berzins
A free ascent of an old peg route (Bastion) through a large overhang.

1.6.85   **Savage Sentence**   Andy Wild, Dave Musgrove
12.5.87   **Campanile Alternative**   Colin Tee, Paul Dearlove
18.5.87   **Albatross**   Colin Tee, Paul Dearlove
21.5.87   **Crystal Dance**   Colin Tee, S. Cook
24.9.88   **Humus**   John Eastham, Geoff Myers
Good rock revealed after gardening on the Long Wall.

11.3.89   **Offspring**   Tony Barley, Tim Barley
11.3.89   **Arbor Crack Direct**   Tony Barley
Route much harder with departure of Birtwhistle's sapling and twisted tree (HVS).

June 1989   **Foreign Bodies**   Robin Barley, Nick Barley
June 1990   **On The Edge**   Paul Jenkinson, Steve Earnshaw
The crag's first E6 which was supposed herald a new gold rush of hard routes - I wonder why it took 7 years!

May 1997   **The Skrying**   Mark Radtke, Dave Barton
May 1997   **Cutting the Cord**   Mark Radtke and Greg Rimmer
May 1997   **Over the Top**   Dave Barton and Mark Radtke
June 1997   **Warriors of Hunaman**   Mark Radtke, Jerry Peel

HALTON HEIGHTS

Circa 1950   **Easter Island, Left Crack, Right Crack**
Members of the Craven Pothole Club, including Sidney Waterfall, made the first forays and climbed what are now thought to be these routes.

Pre-1974   **Crack Line One**   Unknown
Charlie Vigano climbed it in 1974 on old pegs already in place.

1974   **The Fingerstone**   Charlie and Sheila Vigano
   Wombling Upwards   Charlie and Sheila Vigano
   The Arete   Charlie and Sheila Vigano
Believed to have been done before.

1974   **Small Wall, Censored, Tobermory, Black Wall Arete**   Charlie and Sheila Vigano
Some old pegs were in evidence.

1976   **Shortcake**   Paul Greenland, Martin Atkinson
Circa 1976   **The Quantum Leap**   Brian Swales
1984   **Greenham Cruisers, In Your Mind, In the Flat Field, Both Ends Burning**
   Derek Hargreaves (solo)
1984   **Empires and Dance**   Derek Hargreaves, Norman Wilkinson
1984   **Chip Chop**   Derek Hargreaves
1984   **The Wild Wild Goose Chase**   Derek Hargreaves, Chris Pickles
1984   **The Pretenders**   Chris Pickles, Derek Hargreaves
14.6.85   **Get Nervous**   Richard Davies (solo)
14.6.85   **Crack Line Two**   Richard Davies (solo)
This was the first known free ascent of this previously-pegged line. Loose flakes were removed in 1988 making it a safer proposition.

16.2.88	**Coma Toes** Paul Clarke (solo)	
16.2.88	**Chip Chop Direct** Paul Clarke (solo)	
	Finish possibly done before.	
21.2.88	**Fission Chips** Paul Clarke, Nick Dalzell	
1988	**Nick's Arete Nuclear Winter** Paul Clarke, Nick Dalzell	
	Both named by these two but obviously done before.	
May 1991	**The Ugsome Thing** Dave Platt	
16.5.91	**The Invisible Worm** Dave Platt, Bob Larkin	
4.6.91	**Urizen** Bob Larkin, Dave Platt	

HAWKCLIFFE

C 1965	**Inspiration, Gyro, Preference, Skylight Chimney, Gully Exit, Crack and Flutings, First Steps, Central Buttress** Brian Emmison
	" An obvious through chimney leads into the Great Rift, an awesome sight when viewed for the first time" Brian Emmison describing his ascent of Skylight Chimney in 1965.
C 1965	**Dirty Chimney, Acorn, Dammit, Ramp Cracks, Suicide Corner, Dinkums Delight, White Wall Chimney** Brian Emmison
	The above 7 climbs were recorded in Climber Magazine in 1965 described as left of Cavern Tower Rift and graded Moderate to V.Diff It is now difficult to accurately identify them.
Late 1960s	**Squirrel Crack** Jimmy Fullalove, John Sheard
	A very bold lead without Friends!
C 1969 ?	**R.I.P.** Jack Firth, Dave Cunningham, Alan Firth
Early 1970's	**Syrett's Slit** John Syrett
	It is assumed this was Syrett's route but it could well be that he climbed the Great Crack as well.
1990	**Woodland Ecology** Paul Jenkinson, Mick Ryan
Pre 1995	**Brian's Crack, Right-hand Arete, Emmis' 'Orror** unknown
	Obviously climbed before - named in honour of Brian Emmison's pioneering work.
Mar 1996	**Ginny Greenteeth** Mark Radtke, Jerry Peel
Mar 1996	**The Blood On The Shamrock** Jerry Peel, Mark Radtke
Mar 1996	**Stepmother Jag, The Crack of Dawn** Mark Radtke, Greg Rimmer
Apr 1996	**Walk By** Dave Barton, Jerry Peel.
Apr 1996	**Flame Arete** Jerry Peel, Dave Barton
Apr 1996	**Babes in the Boneyard** Dave Barton, Jerry Peel
Apr 1996	**Creaking Joints** Jerry Peel, Dave Barton
Apr 1996	**The Dawning** Mark Radtke, Jerry Peel, Dave Barton
Apr 1996	**Driveby** Mick Johnstone
12.5.96	**Babylon** Dave Platt, Bob Larkin
Jun 1996	**Freedom** Terry Holmes, Neil Herbert
Jun 1996	**What No Boc No** Alan Firth, Ian Fenton
Mar 1998	**Birdsong** Andy Cave
	A route cleaned, prepared and abandoned by Jerry Peel, and Dave Barton. Rad couldn't second it! Does this give a clue to its difficulty?
Mar 1998	**Zyo Kruk Klik** Mark Radtke, Andy Cave
18.4.98	**Bubba** Dave Barton, Mark Radtke
18.4.98	**The Call Of The Curlew** Mark Radtke Dave Barton
19.4.98	**Abandon Hope** Andrew Watts, Dave Musgrove
19.4.98	**Back To Basics** Dave Musgrove, Andrew Watts
	This may have been climbed by Jimmy Fullalove in the 1960's
20.5.98	**Black Forest Gateaux** Dave Musgrove, Chris Gooder, Nigel Baker
July 1998	**Blull Gum Sloggitt, Constriction Chimney** Mark Radtke, Jerry Peel
July 1998	**Lauren's Wall** Mark Radtke (solo)

HEBDEN GHYLL

Circa 1939	**Tree Climb**	Unknown. *(Believed to be a local farm boy).*
23.3.46	**Friction, Jerry Wall**	*A 60ft VS and an 80ft V.Diff recorded by Ron Hirst and J. Greaves respectively (possibly the original versions of Right of Way and Wall and Nose)*
Circa 1957	**The Layback, Innominate, Twin Cracks, Wall & Nose**	Various Y.M.C. Members
	Thin Crack	Charlie Salisbury
	Fat Crack	Bill Todd
	Right of Way, Jerry and Ben	Harold Barraclough

Three other routes were mentioned in the 1957 guide on what is believed to be Copper Nob Buttress, one of them named Ripple Rib (possibly the climb now known as Hieronymouse)

1964	**The Way**	Tony Barley, Robin Barley
1964	**Prosecutor**	Dave Berry (second unknown)
19.7.80	**Midway**	Chris Sowden, Tony Burnell
31.7.80	**Magnificrack**	Chris Sowden, Tony Burnell, Gordon Higginson
	Climbing by Runners	Gordon Higginson, Tony Burnell, Chris Sowden
	Crevasse Wall	Chris Sowden, Tony Burnell, Gordon Higginson

A fine day's work on a bold piece of rock.

8.5.88	**Fun With Friends**	Adam Wainwright, Glyn Appleyard

Done before.

	Friendly Fun	Glyn Appleyard, Adam Wainwright
24.6.88	**Fat Man's Slab**	Ian Renshaw
24.6.88	**Do or Diet**	John Paul Hotham

A reference to 'Fat Renny'.

24.6.88	**The Mutant Midge**	Adam Wainwright

Soloed on sight.

24.6.88	**Dan Dare**	John Paul Hotham
29.6.88	**What!!!**	Fraser Hardie, Martin Perry, Simon Franks, Adam Wainwright
29.6.88	**The Unpaid Chauffeur**	Fraser Hardie, Adam Wainwright
29.6.88	**Hieronymouse**	Fraser Hardie
29.6.88	**Bisexual Bratwurst, Shed Ahoy**	Simon Franks
29.6.88	**Adamante, Tall Man in the Bidet**	Adam Wainwright

Several of these routes had possibly been done before. Reference to climbs on Copper Nob Buttress appeared in the 1957 guide.

17.7.88	**The Buneater**	John Paul Hotham, Adam Wainwright
17.8.88	**French Fancy, Wacko Saco, Dead Man's Crankshaft**	John Paul Hotham
3.5.93	**Tigga The Bagpipe Dog**	Kate Turner, Luke Dow
3.5.93	**The Crag, The Climber, His Girl and her Dog**	Luke Dow, Kate Turner
3.5.93	**Comeuppance**	Luke Dow (unsecended)
1.6.96	**Diethard, Slim With Avengence**	Jason Lister (solo)

Graded E1 5b! At least one subsequent ascentionist thought it might be worth E5.

19.6.96	**Saunter**	Mike Bebbington (solo)
22.2.98	**Lardies Route**	Dave Musgrove (solo)

HEPTONSTALL

1957	**Red Wall Direct**	John Hartley, Rob Brown

Aided on the first visit to the quarry since superseded by Brown Sugar (John Syrett, 1973).

1958	**Fairy Steps**	John Hartley, Edwin Leggett

There was evidence of an earlier ascent and local rumour suggested that the line had been climbed by Johnny Parker, pre 1957.

1958	**Drainpipe Groove**	Edwin Leggett, John Hartley

Several pegs. The aid was reduced by Bob Whittaker (1967) and freed by Al Manson.

1958	**Scorpion** John Hartley, Edwin Leggett, Derek Bull

1958   **Scorpion**   John Hartley, Edwin Leggett, Derek Bull
The crag's first totally-free first ascent. The line was straightened somewhat by Leggett at a later date.

1959   **Sunstroke Slab**   John Hartley, Derek Bull, Edwin Leggett
Done in the wet with two pegs for aid. First free ascent Bob Whittaker and Bill Hardacre 1961.

1959   **Bull's Crack**   Derek Bull, John Hartley, Edwin Leggett
Top-roped first.

1959   **Fraternity**   Edwin Leggett (and his brother!)

1959   **Interlude**   John Hartley (solo)

1960   **Main Line**   John Hartley, Edwin Leggett
1 peg. First free ascent claimed by many.

1960   **Haboob**   John Hartley, Edwin Leggett

1960   **Triplex**   Derek Bull, Pete Grindley, John Hartley
Each led a pitch on separate days and Leggett was in on it, too. The aid was reduced by Bob Whittaker (1967). Freed by Jerry Peel circa 1979.

1960   **Trespasser**   John Hartley, Edwin Leggett
Freed by Jerry Peel and Tony Barley 1975.

1960   **Hesperus**   John Hartley, Rob Brown
"A wreck of a route".

1961   **Pulpit Route**   John Hartley, Edwin Leggett

1961   **Senility**   Pete Grindley, John Hartley, Edwin Leggett
Led by the oldest member of the team, the younger members struggled to follow.

1961   **Grindley's Grunt**   Pete Grindley, John Hartley, Edwin Leggett
1 peg for aid. First free ascent Bob Whittaker, Carl Fletcher, Dec. 1965.

1961   **Curving Crack**   Don Whillans, Albert Ashworth

1961   **Forked Lightning Crack**   Don Whillans
It must have been 'ard for it took two fags! In fact for the next 15 years it was considered one of the most formidable leads on gritstone.

1961   **Cup and Lip**   Edwin Leggett, John Hartley
Some aid.

1961   **The Girdle Traverse**   John Hartley, Derek Bull, Edwin Leggett
A massive undertaking done in various stages and involving some aid. The original line went from right to left across the whole quarry, but was flawed by much grass, some easy scrambling and an abseil. The modern free line from left to right was forced by Barry Rawlinson and Dave Barton in 1977.

1961   **Sue**   John Barraclough

1962   **Trepidation, Dress Circle**   M. Day, John Oddie
Dress Circle is another obsolete aid extravaganza. It traversed left from the rabbit ledge to Fairy Steps at a high level.

1965   **Monkey Puzzle**   John Barron, Edwin Leggett
A very bold lead before much protection.

1965   **The Corner, Sentinel Crack, The Left Arete**   Bob Whittaker, Carl Fletcher

1967   **Mitre, The Chimney, Pocket Wall, Main Buttress**   Bob Whittaker Carl Fletcher

1967   **Columbus, Nameless, Kassi**   Bob Whittaker, Geoff Smith, Carl Fletcher
The last ten climbs may well have been climbed by Hartley, Leggett and Co. They certainly believed to have explored the outlying crags, unfortunately they recorded nothing.

Summer 1967   **Trespass Not, Fairy Steps Direct**   Bob Whittaker, Carl Fletcher

July 1967   **Sacrifice**   Bob Whittaker, Carl Fletcher, Geoff Smith
1 point of aid on each pitch. Freed by Jerry Peel and Tony Barley 1975.

Aug 1967   **Man of God**   Bob Whittaker, Carl Fletcher

Aug 1967   **Triplex Direct**   Bob Whittaker, Geoff Smith
Top pitch totally free by the same pair in 1968.

Sept 1967   **Wasp Wall**   Bob Whittaker, Geoff Smith, Mike Redfearn

Winter 1967   **Thin Red Line**   Mike Quinn, Paul Horan

> *One nut for aid. The route had, however, been top roped the week before by Whittaker and Smith. First free ascent by Barry Rawlinson and Jerry Peel (1972).*

1967	**Diagonal Route** Bob Whittaker, Geoff Smith	
1968	**Sentinel Wall** Bob Whittaker, Geoff Smith	
1972	**Lumber Vertebra** Mike Bebbington, Allan Austin	
1972	**Cream** Barry Rawlinson, Jerry Peel	

> *A very bold effort!*

1972   **Strange Brew** Barry Rawlinson, Jerry Peel (AL).
24.6.73   **Brown Sugar** John Syrett
1.8.73   **Earthshrinker** Bob Whittaker, Gordon Mason, Brian Middleton

> *One point of aid. Climbed free by Jerry Peel and Paul Farrish in 1979.*

1.10.73   **Heatwave** Al Manson
1973   **Scarab, Windsong** Bob Whittaker, Ralph Pickering
1973   **Hunchback** Bob Whittaker, Sid Siddiqui
11.6.74   **Hardline** Pete Livesey, Al Manson
Circa 1975 **Demerara** Ron Fawcett, Jerry Peel
June 1979 **Skullduggery** Steve Bancroft, Tim Rhodes
1979   **Poundstretcher** Jerry Peel, Ray Conlon
Pre-1982 **Fallout, Pulpit Route Direct Start** Unknown
Aug 1983 **Badlands** Jerry Peel
1985   **Boo Boo's Roof** Simon Howley
Aug 1985 **Big Ben, Discoloured Pitch** J. Hirst, N. McFarlane
Aug 1985 **Midnight Lightning** Jerry Peel, Barry Rawlinson
Apr 1987 **A Step in the Light Green** Mark Radtke, Ian Cooksey. (Varied leads)
9.4.89   **Short Back and Sides** Dave Musgrove, Kim Greenald, Mike Butler
9.4.89   **Peepod, Mille Feuille** Dave Musgrove, Mike Butler
9.4.89   **Dog With Two Tails** Dave Musgrove, Mike Butler, Christine Walker
9.4.89   **Coat of Arms Chimney, Badge Climb** Dave Musgrove (solo)

> *The last five climbs had undoubtedly been done before.*

Spring 1990 **Orange Crush** Mark Radtke, Jerry Peel
Autumn 1995 **The Blue Bus** Jerry Peel, Dave Barton, Mark Radtke
May 1994 **Miss Rags - Tantric Mistress of Mazland** Jim Heelam
1995   **Climb and Tick Conditions** Derek Hargreaves, Marcel ?
23.4.96   **Nutian Jamb** Tony Beard, Ian Walker
16.10.96 **Afro With A Chin Strap** R. Moss (solo)
18.9.97   **Vertical Speed** Matt Troilett, Steve Smith
27.9.97   **Out On A Limb** Phil Brown, Terry Holmes (Alt leads)

HETCHELL CRAG

The recorded history is as follows though it is now accepted that climbing activity goes back at least to the 1940s

27.1.62   **Oak Scoop** John Johnson, Bill Todd

> *The first treeless ascent - after the demise of the 'oak' tree to Dutch Elm Disease! - Craig Hannah 2.2.90.*

27.1.62   **Roman Crack** Harold Barraclough, Ron Tyler, Bill Todd
27.1.62   **Narrow Chimney, Centurion, Pompey Chimney** Bill Todd, John Johnson
27.1.62   **Zig Zag** Bill Todd, John Johnson

> *Then known as Cassius chimney with a start from the left.*

11.2.62   **Twin Cracks, Hanging Chimney** Harold Barraclough, Ron Tyler, Bill Todd
1962   **The Wall** Brian Evans
1962   **Cassius Crawl** Brian and Aileen Evans

> *Still one of the best routes on the crag.*

1962   **The Corbel** Allan Austin
1962   **End Wall** Probably Evans or Austin

1962	**Beckside Buttress** Probably Evans	

All the above were first recorded in the 1965 YMC Journal Supplement. It is certain that some of the more obvious lines had been climbed before.

Easter 1966   **Cassius Direct**   Dave Musgrove, Bob Thornton

Chipped holds on the top suggest the route had been climbed earlier.

Easter 1966   **Tarquin's Terrace**   Dave Musgrove, Bob Thornton

The first foray on to the bolder walls.

July 1966   **Wailing Wall**   Dave Musgrove (solo)

Climbed around the same time by Paul Exley, who named the route for the 1969 guide.

5.11.66   **Crutch**   Dave Musgrove (solo)

Climbed around this time by Paul Exley. Both remember that the name was already chipped below the start.

5.11.66   **The Main Wall Girdle**   Dave Musgrove, Bob Knapton (Alt)

5.11.66   **Bob's Traverse**   Bob Knapton (solo)

17.4.68   **Bell**   Allan Austin, Chris Mitchell

The route had been pegged in the 1940s and the phantom chipper had named the line Bell long before Austin's ascent. The direct finish was added by Rob Gawthorpe in 1980.

17.4.68   **Mitchell's Wall**   Chris Mitchell, Allan Austin

1968   **Jim's Wall**   Jim Worthington (solo)

Pre 1969   **Ripple Arete**   Not known, possibly Paul Exley

28.3.72   **Augustus, Livia**   John Syrett (solo)

1972   **Tiberius**   John Syrett (solo)

7.8.73   **Bell Left Hand**   Dave Musgrove, Mike Butler

Possibly done before.

1974   **Bell End**   John Harwood

A climb that resisted all-comers until holds miraculously appeared on the previously-rounded ledge at the time of the first ascent.

May 1974   **Rainbow**   Pete Kitson, Al Manson

1974   **Lurcio's Lip, Up Pompey**   Al Manson (solo)

These two climbs marked a significant rise in technical standards on the crag.

1974/5   **Tear Across The Dotted Line**   Al Manson (solo)

1974/5   **Bronco**   Al Manson (solo)

1975   **Crutch Direct**   Al Manson (solo)

This is the earliest known ascent, but Manson believes the climb was long established.

1975   **Dutch Elm**   Dave Musgrove , Mike Butler

July 1975   **Daniel's Den**   Mike Butler (solo)

Possibly done before. All the other problems around the descent gully were worked out around this time by Musgrove and Butler, though they could well have been pre-dated the other regular activists.

Circa 1975   **Veni Veci Oblivisci**   Dave Musgrove, Mike Butler

1976   **Superturd Traverse**   Al Manson (solo)

The two other unpleasantly-named routes on this buttress were also climbed by Manson at this time, but he disassociates himself from the names, which were already chiselled on the rock, as were the finishing holds at the top of the direct.

1977   **Lend Me Your Ears**   Al Manson (solo)

Wandered across by Manson whilst prospecting the line of Reach for a Peach.

Spring 1978   **Newton John**   Al Manson (solo)

Summer 1978   **Reach for a Peach**   Al Manson (solo)

Named after a problem in Tuolumne Meadows in the US (where Al went to train for Hetchell).

Sept 1978   **Corbel Variation**   Al Manson, Stuart Lindsey

1979   **Hunchback**   Rob Gawthorpe, Pete Jackson

Oct 1979   **Grease**   Al Manson

1979 Summer   **Peach Wall Low Traverse**   Al Manson, Rob Gawthorpe

1983   **Hadrian's Wall**   Al Manson (solo)

June 1984 **S for B** Al Manson (solo)
Spring 1988   **The Fall of The Roman Empire** Justin Vogler (solo)
10.7.88   **Dead Angst** Kim Buck (solo)
  New faces brought a fresh, bold approach to succeed on these last two lines
  which, though not as technical as previous climbs, are on the highest and most
  serious part of the crag.
4.3.89   **Adamant** Kim Buck (solo)
6.3.89   **Arc en Ceil** Kim Buck (solo)
21.8.89   **The Empire Strikes Back** Dave Musgrove (solo)
October 1989   **Lunging For Melons** Kim Buck (solo)
3.4.90   **Caligula** Dave Musgrove (solo)
1.11.90   **When In Rome** Dave Musgrove (solo)
23.11.90   **Smokeless Zone** Dave Musgrove (solo)
1997   **Preparation H** Kim Buck, Dave Sarkar
19.2.98   **Et Tu Brute** Nigel Baker (solo)

HONLEY QUARRY

1988   **Funky Nose** Paul Hardwick
  This route is now believed to Arete Edge or Birch Climb
April 1990 **Jesus Loves America** Simon Panton, Nigel Fawcett
April 1990 **Shedpoojsize** Simon Panton, Mark Blagborough
May 1990 **My Brain is In The Cupboard** Robert Spares, Simon Panton
May 1990 **My God Rides A Skateboard** Simon Panton, Robert Spares
May 1990 **Triple Bad Acid** Simon Panton, Nigel Fawcett
June 1990 **Millions of Dead Christians** Simon Panton (unseconded)
June 1990 **The Dogs Biscuits** Steve Honeyman, Simon Panton
Aug 1990 **Undilutable Slang Truth** Simon Panton (unseconded)
Aug 1990 **Joker Hysterical Face** Simon Panton, Steve Honeyman
Aug 1990 **Straight Outta Cleakheaton** Simon Panton, Steve Honeyman
1994/5   All the easier routes climbed, collated and named by Philip Statham and
  Joseph Downey

HORSEHOLD SCOUT

1962/3   **Greensleeves, The Long Climb, Charleston Wall, Homer's Flight Odyssey,**
  The Bit, Original Route, Kestrel Cracks, Guano Grooves, Pigeon Loft
  All the above were climbed and first recorded by Chris Ambler, Roger Sutcliffe
  and friends from The Gritstone Club though it seemed apparent at the time
  that some, if not all, had been at least attempted before. John Hartley wrote up
  the climbs for the 1969 guide and mentioned other shorter climbs to the right of
  these but did not specifically identify them. No doubt they are amongst the
  following.
18.4.81   **Birthday Crack, Birthday Wall, Trio** Bob Whittaker, Ralph Pickering
5.7.81   **Long Corner, The Pod** Ralph Pickering, Bob Whittaker
5.7.81   **Tap Dance, Overhanging Corner** Bob Whittaker, Ralph Pickering
5.7.81   **The Groove** Les Hardman, Geoff Haigh
5.7.81   **Pocked Groove** Geoff Haigh, Les Hardman
10.1.88   **Gracelands, Hartleys, Tumbril, Firelighter** Bob Whittaker, Ralph Pickering
Phil Latcham
10.1.88   **The Sizzler, Bigfoot** Ralph Pickering, Bob Whittaker Phil Latcham
10.1.88   **Phil's Route** Phil Latcham, Ralph Pickering Bob Whittaker
14.2.88   **Pocked Wall** Bob, Robert and Alec Whittaker (father and sons)
14.2.88   **Harriet** Bob Whittaker, Ralph Pickering
21.2.88   **Portrait** Brian Middleton, Gordon Mason
21.2.88   **Blue Watch** Gordon Mason, Brian Middleton

ILKLEY

Pre-1902 **A Climb, The Sentinel** Unknown
The above climbs were mentioned in correspondence from W. Parsons dated 1902. His letter inferred that other climbs existed at Ilkley by then.

Pre-1906 **Flake Climb, Blasphemy Crack** Unknown
Blasphemy Crack was known by the Yorkshire Rambler's Club as Crooked Crack and mentioned in an article in 1906 by Claude Benson as "one of the stiffest little bits in broad Yorkshire, most destructive to clothes and cuticle"

Pre-1911 **Sentry Box** Unknown
"A climb of the nightmare type". Y.R.C. Journal 1911. The direct start was led by Winston Farrar in 1931.

Pre-1911 **Kestrel**
It seems that the climb had only been top-roped by this date as the 1911 description stated "No.13 begins in a small cave. A wide deep crack leads upwards along an airy path to the stance of No.12 (Sentry Box). It must be sheer ill luck that this airy path has not yet been traversed for its foot has often been reached, but each time the sight of it has made the leader feel suddenly faint and he has thought it wiser to descend". The first known leader who didn't feel faint was Winston Farrar who gave the climb its name in 1931.

Pre-1911 **Gutsie**
Earlier research suggested that there was evidence that Fred Botterill led this climb in 1904.

Pre-1911 **Little A Climb, Stiction, Stiction Chimney, The Strid, Fly Paper, Black Chimney, The Flake Climb, Oak Tree Slab, Twin Cracks, Throstle's Nest Climb, Long Chimney The Chute Stump Chimney Arrowhead Lady Mabel Route Matchbox Overhanging Chockstone Crack Double Chockstone Crack Holly Tree Route Spread-eagle** Unknown
All the above were recorded in the Y.R.C. Journal 1911 in an article written by Walter Greenwood, who claimed to have led all but Sentry Box, Kestrel and Throstle's Nest by that time. It is also documented that Fred and Matthew Botterill cycled regularly to the crag from as early as 1901 and were, perhaps, responsible for the first ascents of many of the above climbs. Most of the climbs were un-named in the first guide, identifiable only by numbers. The modern names were mainly added in the 1930s by Winston Farrar and his friends who were unaware of the existence of the earlier descriptions.

Pre-1931 **Botterill's Crack** Matthew Botterill?
The climb was not recorded in the 1911 Y.R.C. guide and Fred gave up serious climbing in 1909 (he died in 1920). Matthew, Fred's brother, lived in Ben Rhydding from 1917 and continued to host Ramblers climbing meets from his home for many years. It is likely, therefore, that he was involved in the first ascent of this famous route, probably during the early 1920s. It was certainly an established test piece by the time Winston Farrar began his associations with the rocks in 1931.

6.5.31 **Cooper's Slab** Reg Cooper, Winston Farrar, Gorden Daley
Farrar remembered the date because it was his 22nd birthday.

1931/32 **Josephine** Winston Farrar, Percy Bryson
Bryson rushed into the quarry late, in rather a sweat, just as Farrar was about to start climbing and, on being invited to join the rope, uttered those immortal words "Not tonight Josephine", so starting a tradition of route names that continued for 50 years.

1931/32 **Josephine Traverse** Winston Farrar, Reg Cooper

1931/32 **Josephine Direct** Winston Farrar

Circa 1935 **Three Slabs Route** Winston Farrar

Circa 1935 **Fairy Steps** Charlie Salisbury, Winston Farrar

Circa 1935 **Illegitimate Crack** Winston Farrar, Charlie Salisbury

Circa 1935 **Bogey Wall** Charlie Salisbury
At least two sources say Charlie called it "Bugger it Wall", but guidebook

censors disapproved.

Circa1936/7 **Sound Box**   Charlie Salisbury

Circa 1938 **Walewska Napoleon, Blucher**   Charlie Salisbury (second unknown)
On the first ascent of Walewska the mantelshelf ledge was grass-covered. The direct start was added by John Ball and Jack Greenwood about three years later.

1939   **S Crack Ferdinand**   Allan Allsop
The hand traverse variant was added in 1962 by Alan Swithenbank and George Broadhead using Lignum Vitae chocks as protection.

Circa 1941 **Cow Rib Highfield Corner**   John (Pug) Ball, Jack (Grenner) Greenwood

4.9.41   **Josephine Superdirect**   Arthur Dolphin

11.4.43   **Pebble Groove**   John Cook, John Ball, Arthur Dolphin
Dennis Gray did it from the left in 1956.

20.8.43   **Herbaceous Border Variation**   Arthur Dolphin, Robert Heap

21.9.43   **Overhanging Blocks**   Arthur Dolphin

Circa 1943 **Bald Pate**   John Ball, John Cook
No chiselled holds then. A piton belay was used on the traverse to split the pitch and maintain sanity. A solo ascent, in boots, was recorded by Peter Harding in 1946.

7.5.44   **Cherry Valley Rib**   John Ball, John Cook
Both led the pitch the same evening. The name is a corruption of Greek and Latin for farewell; Ball was leaving to join the Army the next day. The direct start was added 12.7.60 by George Steele, M. Doughtie, M. Wainwright.

30.3.45   **Evening Wall**   Arthur Dolphin, Robert Heap, John Lockwood, David Varley

2.6.46   **Central Wall, Central Rib**   Arthur Dolphin, John Cook, John Lockwood, Michael Parkin

15.6.47   **Somersault**   Arthur Dolphin (solo)
Dolphin in his prime climbing two of Ilkley's finest natural lines.

28.9.47   **Curving Cracks, Curving Corner** Arthur Dolphin and "Jack"
(possibly Jack Bloor or John Lockwood). The Corner was one of Dolphin's boldest leads, rarely repeated until the advent of nut protection.

29.2.48   **Little B Route**   Arthur Dolphin, John Lockwood

1948   **Beeline**   Arthur Dolphin (solo)

1949   **Hades**   Ron Hirst

16.4.50   **Catapult Crack**   Arthur Dolphin, Peter Greenwood, Jack Bloor

Pre-1951 **Chiseller Gibbon's Wall**   David Gibbons
The chiseller, probably responsible for all the chipped routes at Ilkley. He was believed to be active during the late 1940s and early 1950s.

Pre-1951 **Little Kaiser**   Unknown
Surely dating from First World War times with such a name?

Pre-1951 **V Groove**   Unknown
The groove right of Flypaper. In 1911 Greenwood identified it and said -"We have not heard that it has yet been climbed. It is offered to those of our readers who hanker after a 'bonne bouche'. Surely such a challenge can't have been resisted for long.

Pre-1951 **Olicana Crack, Patience, Cow Crack, Ladybird, Flake Crack, Spider Wall, Earwig Rib, V Chimney, Old Crack, Letter Box, Wellington Chimney, Stomach Traverse, Sand Chimney, Nailbite, Sinister Cracks, Brush Crack, Oak Tree Crack, Windy Buttress, The Ogre**   Unknown
Most of these "pre-1951 routes must date from the earliest days of climbing at Ilkley. No records can be found.

4.7.51   **Little John**   Peter Tuke

Circa 1952 **Walker's Hangover**   Ron Hirst, Charlie Salisbury, George Walker

1952   **Short Circuit**   Peter Greenwood
The climb had previously been top-roped but on this occasion it was led with a piton for protection. Allan Austin straightened out the finish in 1956 and led it without the peg on 30.4.58.

1952   **The Gnome**   Peter Greenwood

Greenwood had been trying it for months and other teams had made top-rope attempts. The second ascent was not recorded until Mike Hammill gave the climb its name in 1970.

Summer 1953 **Gremlin's Wall** Ron Hields

A very significant lead. Hields was 16 at the time and spent most of the summer bivouacking in Rocky Valley and quickly became the local expert. This climb was the hardest at Ilkley (and probably the hardest on gritstone anywhere) at the time and the validity of the ascent was questioned for many years by subsequent aspirants who failed to repeat the route. It was omitted from the 1969 guidebook and the second ascent wasn't recorded until 1977 when Al Manson re-discovered the climb.

November 1954 **Smog Wall** George Walker, Brian Evans

1955/56 **Tremor Wall Finish** Allan Austin, Doug Verity, Brian Fuller, Dennis Gray

Mar 1956 **Piton Wall** Allan Austin, Brian Evans

Previously with 2 pegs for aid, which were retained as runners for a while.

28.1.56 **Sylveste** Brian Evans, Allan Austin

Previously pegged by Ron Hirst.

17.6 56 **High Street** Allan Austin, Brian Evans

A short climb but one which retained a big reputation for many years.

Summer 1956 **A Climb, Alt. Finish** Allan Austin, Brian Fuller

27.10.56 **Gym Crack** Allan Austin, Brian Evans, Brian Fuller, Ernie Marshall, Ron Tyler, Ashley Petts

16.4.57 **Transparent Wall** Brian Evans, Allan Austin, Brian Fuller

13.10.57 **Bald Pate Direct Start** Neville Drasdo (solo)

10.11.57 **Nordwand** Brian Evans

Previously pegged.

Pre-1958 **Cow Udder, Doris's Route, Lost Boots** Unknown

These three routes all rely on artificially manufactured holds and are believed to be the work of David Gibbons the notorious chiseller.

Pre-1958 **Dot's Crack Scoop and Hole, Crack and Wall, S Route** Unknown

Pre-1958 **The Link** Unknown, probably Ron Hirst

Pre-1958 **Tombstone Crack** Charlie Salisbury, Trevor James

Pre-1958 **Dale's Delight** George Dale

Pre-1958 **Taj Mahal** Charlie Salisbury, George Dale

5.4.59 **Sinister Rib** George Steele, Malcolm Wainwright

A new advance in boldness. Given the nominal Yorkshire HVS tag at the time.

July 1961 **Beetroot** Ronnie Hall, Ernie Goodyear, Tony Lee, D. Swales

Circa 1962 **Corner and Scoop Peg Crack** Alan Swithenbank, George Broadhead

Circa 1962 **Spiral, Old Spice** Charlie Salisbury

Charlie was getting on a bit but still climbing well and as enthusiastic as ever.

Mid-1960s **Green Chimney, Nightshade, Too Far, Quarry Girdle** Alan Swithenbank

All the last 4 were recorded in the 1969 guide but probably done before.

Pre 1970 **Butch Crack, Cassidy's Crawl** Unknown

19.1.70 **Tufted Crack** Allan Austin, Angela Faller (Soper)

The line had been previously climbed on wooden wedges, by George Walker in 1954. Austin and Evans top-roped the line in 1957.

24.2.72 **Propeller Wall** John Syrett (solo)

Graded VS when first written up in the LUCC log book!

Summer1972 **Veste** Pete Kitson, Al Manson

3.6.73 **Sylvia** Pete Kitson, John Syrett

1973 **Waterloo** Pete Livesey, John Sheard

First climbed by starting up Spider Wall and then moving left. The start was straightened out to go direct at 6a by Andy Brown in 1974.

1973 **Blind Valley** Pete Livesey (solo)

Previously aided and called Thor's Wall.

April 1973 **Wellington Crack** Pete Livesey, John Sheard

A major advance. The line had been pegged by Dolphin in 1948. Livesey needed one point of aid for resting on the first attempt. He led it free on a

		subsequent ascent a few months later while posing for photos.
1974	**Serendipity**	Iain Edwards, Eriks Zvaignze
1974	**Hand Jive**	Ron Fawcett, Chris Gibb
		An early start beat an irate Iain Edwards.
1974	**Bald Eagle**	Pete Livesey (solo)
Oct 74	**Facet Wall**	Mike Hammill (solo)
		graded mild severe!?
1975	**Guillotine**	Pete Livesey, Jill Lawrence
		A controversial ascent, vigorous cleaning appeared to have uncovered holds not previously noticed by other aspirants. Nevertheless, a bold lead.
1975	**Beyond the Fringe**	Pete Livesey, Jill Lawrence
		With a runner in Beeline.
1975	**Sticky Fingers**	Iain Edwards, Bill Turner
18.5.75	**Hipgnosis**	Iain Edwards, Tim Riley
Late 1975	**Berserker**	Mike Hammill
1976	**Sunburst Finish**	Ron Fawcett (solo)
1976	**Diamond Dogs**	Ron Fawcett
Circa 1976	**Peg Wall**	Ron Fawcett
		May have been done before. The upper wall was added in 1984 by D. Lloyd.
1977	**Carrie, Slide Zone, Shock Horror**	Ron Fawcett
1977	**Mad Dogs**	Ron Fawcett, Iain Edwards
1977	**Ruby Parrot**	Al Manson
1978	**Milky Way**	Ron Fawcett
		It is rumoured that Ron was so pumped he couldn't even crawl to the belay or untie his rope. The line was first pegged by Brian Evans and Allan Austin on 14.1.56.
1978	**Blackball**	Chris Bray, Huw Jones
1978	**Mini Grip, Tricyclist**	Ron Fawcett (solo)
1979	**Desperate Dan**	Ron Fawcett (solo)
		Though not acclaimed at the time this was probably one of the first true gritstone E7s in the country.
Circa 1979	**Fairy Wall**	Iain Edwards, Bill Turner
		Believed to be an old problem, probably done before.
Circa 1980	**Bald Pate Super Direct**	Andy Brown
21.4.80	**Voyage to the Outer Limits**	Paul Craven, Huw Jones.
21.7.80	**Bird of Prey**	John Reeve, Bob Larkin
25.7.81	**Not Tonight Josephine**	Huw Jones, D. Lloyd
24.6.83	**Fear of a Failed Race**	Nigel and Graham Pedley
1984	**Doing the Business**	Roger Lambert, David Lloyd
1984	**Blue Meanies Tea Party**	Roger Lambert, Andrew Spink
1984	**Spreading the Disease**	John Dunne
1985	**Smog Monster, Cyclist**	John Dunne
July 1985	**Bernie the Bolt**	Rob Gawthorpe
1986	**Late Fever, Peach Melba**	John Dunne
19.3.86	**Desperate Dredd**	John Dunne
20.3.86	**Deathwatch**	John Dunne
June 1986	**Countdown To Disaster, Snap Decision**	John Dunne
		Two very bold and significant ascents.
9.9.86	**Superb Too Right**	John Dunne
1987	**Galaxy, The Marine Who Slept In**	Jerry Peel
Aug 1987	**Three More Reps, Super Set**	John Dunne
		Desperate training problems which set John up for the route of the decade -
Aug 1987	**The New Statesman**	John Dunne
		Probably the hardest route on grit at the time - still only 2 repeats by 1998.
4.9.89	**Where The Blue Tits Dare**	Justin Vogler
9.8.89	**Jiggery Not Pokery**	Charlie Ward (solo) - Certainly done before
23.6.90	**Captain B.O.'s Kiss Of Death**	D. Greenall, C. Idle, J. Lowther
March 1991	**Rodney Mullen**	Sean Miles

Originally graded F8a but with pre-placed protection, and a hanging rope, just in case! Still not led in 'pure' style.

17.7.92	**Cow Flap**	David Williams, Clement Pickering
1992	**Shadowlands**	David Williams (solo)

An old problem never previously recorded.

Autumn 1992	**The Black And White Days**	Mark Radtke, Jerry Peel
14.8.94	**Vital Spark**	Adam Collinge, Gareth Kinsley
27.6.96	**Am I Brown**	Karl Bronslow, Mandy Robertson

Probably done before

30.10.96	**String Vest**	Nigel Baker
17.9.97	**Grand As 'Owt**	Adi Gill (solo)
9.9.97	**Magic Pie**	Adam Collinge, Graham Kinsley
12.4.97	**Big Buels**	Dave Kells
April 1997	**Loaded**	John Dunne
1997	**Baby Spice, Doris Direct**	John Dunne

Classic micro-routes or big modern boulder problems?

May 1998	**Fast Forward**	John Dunne
May 1998	**In A Pickle**	Jason Pickles, John Dunne

LORD'S SEAT

Most , if not all the climbs here may have been climbed in the past however nothing has ever been previously recorded and, except on the easiest cracks and corners there was little sign of earlier traffic. All recorded routes with the following exceptions, were soloed and named by Bob Larkin in July 1998.

17.7.98	**Larkin's Right, No Larkin About**	Nigel Baker, Dave Musgrove
18.7.98	**Overhang Direct, Pump Friction, Lay-Away, Jammed Sandwich, Pure Gold, Stepping Out, Fascinating Pockets**	Nigel Baker, Andy Watts (varied leads and solos)
11.8.98	**Solitaire** Bob Larkin (solo)	
15.8.98	**Tranquility, Serenity** Bob Larkin (solo)	

MYTHEM STEEP QUARRY

1964	**The Rift**	Bob Whittaker, Geoff Smith
1966	**Revolution**	Bob Whittaker, Geoff Smith
Sept 1981	**Spider Crack, Tree Groove, Prospector, Swastika**	Bob Whittaker, Gordon Mason
October 1981	**The Edge Of Extinction, Turncoat**	Bob Whittaker, Ralph Pickering
28.9.90	**The Bender**	Gee Gibson, I. Oates
20.5.96	**Keel Haul**	Tony Beard, Paul Nicholson

OGDEN CLOUGH

Mid 1950s	Most of the easier routes climbed by Harold Drasdo and friends	
1955-1960	**Snoopy**	Allan Austin

Finished with a step left to avoid the final bulge. Route as described probably Mike Hammill in the early 70s .

1955-1960	**Joe Cool, Austin's Pullover**	Allan Austin
1955-1960	**The Reach**	Allan Austin

After top rope inspection. Without Friends, this was effectively a solo with very hard moves at the top.

1965-1972	**Mike's Meander, Linus**	Mike Hammill
Pre 1980	**Erosion**	David Brown
Circa 1980	**Steve's Stroll**	Stephen Coates

| 24.7.81 | **Frontier** David Brown |
| 25.9.81 | **Surplomb** David Brown |

PANORAMA CRAG

Easter 1963	**Yesterday's News, Glasshouse Groove, Nidderdale Wall, Dimbleby's Crack, Power Pull** Robin and Tony Barley
April 1983	**Patley Show** Tony Barley (solo)
1988	**Newsnight, No News is Good News** Chris Sowden, Tony Burnell
1988	**Panorama, World In Action** Tony Burnell, Chris Sowden
10.6.94	**Not The Nine O'Clock News** Julian Cooper, Dave Musgrove
20.9.94	**Padded Arete** Malcolm Townsley (solo)

PENYGHENT

6.5.53	**Red Pencil** Tony Greenbank (solo)
	What a plum! One of the best, and longest, Severes on gritstone.
17.5.53	**Meddler's Crack** Tony Greenbank, J.C. Greenbank
9.7.54	**Red Pencil Direct** Tony Greenbank, J.C. Greenbank
19.8.55	**Damocles Groove** Tony Greenbank, B. Greenbank
19.8.55	**Pagan's Purgatory** Tony Greenbank, J.C. Greenbank
22.4.60	**Christian's Crux** Tony Greenbank, J.C. Greenbank
29.4.61	**Flying Buttress** Ian Clough, R. Wilkinson
25.6.61	**Agnostic's Arete** Ian Clough, Geoff Grandison
8.10.61	**Main Buttress Girdle** Geoff Grandison, Ian Clough
8.10.61	**Shepherd's Chimney** Ian Clough
29.4.62	**Gladiator** Ian Clough, R. Wilkinson
5.10.65	**Pitchfork Crack, Bilberry Wall** Allan Austin, Alan Swithenbank
	Brass Monkey A. Swithenbank, Allan Austin
Pre 1969	**Nose Cracks** Unknown
Pre 1982	**Damocles Groove (Direct Finish)** Unknown
27.7.90	**Bale Out** Matt Podd (solo)
14.8.93	**Gardeners Question Time** Rob Liddle, Luke Dow
14.8.93	**Red And Green** Luke Dow, Rob Liddle

ROBIN HOOD ROCKS

March 1978	**Cantilever, The Scoop, Trender, Meander, Double Trip, King Swing, Mini Swing** Bob Whittaker, Ralph Pickering
March 1978	**Silly Route** Bob Whittaker (solo)
10.4.78	**Duckunder, The Grunter** Ralph Pickering, Bob Whittaker
16.4.78	**Single Trip** Harry Taylor, Bob Whittaker, Ralph Pickering
16.4.78	**Titan's Wall** Bob Whittaker, Ralph Pickering, Sid Sidiqui
16.4.78	**Trepidation** Les Hardman, Geoff Haigh, Ron Blunt
16.4.78	**Breakout** Bob Whittaker (solo)
16.4.78	**Haigh's Route** Geoff Haigh, Harry Taylor
Summer 1978	**Hidden Chimney** Bob Whittaker (solo)
Summer 1978	**Kneemonia** Bob Whittaker, Ralph Pickering
	Whittaker was suffering from a bad cold and then got his knee stuck in the crack.
Summer 1978	**Ledgeway** Les Hardman (solo)
Summer 1981	**Broken Buttress** Harry Taylor, Geoff Haigh
Summer 1981	**Haphazard, Solo Route, Fallout, Gully Flake** Bob Whittaker (solo)
Summer 1981	**Freemason** Bob Whittaker, Ralph Pickering, Gordon Mason
Summer 1981	**Holly Bush Arete** Harry Taylor, Bob Whittaker
Summer 1981	**Enterprise** Les Hardman, Bob Whittaker

Summer 1981	**Thor** Harry Taylor
Summer 1981	**Wingnut** Unknown
Spring 1982	**Tailor, Soldier** Tony Nichols
October 1983	**Technic** Bob Whittaker, Ralph Pickering, Mike Duffy
October 1983	**Thor's Hammer** Bob Whittaker, Gordon Mason
July 1988	**Tinker, Pothole Direct, The Mole** Eddie Martinez (solo)
July 1988	**Lecker Lecker Eisbonbons** Eddie Martinez, Amanda Green
3.9.89	**Fowl Up, Somersault** Graham Desroy (solo)
	Somersault had been climbed much earlier at VS but had been un-repeated for some time after crucial jugs fell off.
31.3.96	**Ye Gods** Jason Lister

ROLLING GATE

Pre 1964	**Rolling Gate Buttress, Lichen Slab, Moss Crack, Choss Crack, Great Chimney, Long Crack, Crossover, Escape, Smiler, The Outsider**
	First ascents unknown. Many of them 1930s vintage and before. All named and recorded by Frank Wilkinson and John Young in 1964.
30.3.58	**Ceiling Crack** Allan Austin, Brian Evans
31.10.71	**Jeff's Route** Jeff Appleyard, Frank Wilkinson, Mike Bebbington
15.12.74	**Wilkinson's Wall** Frank Wilkinson, Allan Austin, Steve Wood
	Left Unnamed - Chris Sowden added the Appellation.
	Colditz Allan Austin, Frank Wilkinson, Steve Wood
Pre 1982	**The Pillar, V Groove, The Brink**
	First ascents unknown. Recorded sometime between 1969 and the 1982 guide.
3.10.87	**The Yorkshire Wobble** John Mackenzie (solo)
	Called The Nelson Touch in the last guide, following Chris Nelson's ascent in 1988. Get your descriptions in on time, John!
Apr 1988	**Veteran's Flake** Graham Mackintosh, Chris Nelson
	Possibly done before.
Apr 1988	**Looking to the Future** Chris Nelson, Graham Mackintosh
19.6.88	**Six Metre Wall** Frank Wilkinson
	The Handrail Frank Wilkinson, Andrew Mackintosh, Graham Mackintosh
16.11.88	**Cruising Altitude, Contortionist's Crack** Dave Musgrove, Frank Wilkinson
April 1990	**Lasyitis** Andy Watts (solo)
Summer 1991	**One** Mike Draper & Luke Dow
8.6.92	**Under A Winter's Coat, A Walk Too Fur, Learning To Dance, Dirk's Philosophy** Luke Dow , Rob Liddle
8.6.92	**To Pluck A Crow, The Magpie Wave** Rob Liddle, Luke Dow
20.6.92	**Lady Hamilton** Rob Liddle (solo)
20.6.92	**Upstairs at Alice's** Luke Dow (solo)
20.6.92	**In The Footsteps Of Anon, On The Verge of the Red Eye** Luke Dow, Rob Liddle
8.5.93	**Jeepster, Orang Outang** Luke Dow, Rob Liddle
8.5.93	**The Greengrocer** Rob Liddle, Luke Dow
10.10.95	**Colditz Direct** Mike Bebbington, Jeff Appleyard

RYLSTONE CRAG

| 1922 | **President's Slab**   E.A. Porter, Eric Griffiths and Cecil Wood |
| | *"The first president (of The Gritstone Club) was E.A. Porter, one of the Chess Club contingent. He took to the rocks with the zest of a man half his age, which must have been near fifty. On ten foot severes his prowess was remarkable. He showed us the way up the tallest little buttress on Rylstone Fell, known to us thereafter as the President's slab. At the time, a gale was blowing and in the* |

moment of triumph, the presidential hat took off, like a rocketing grouse, across the moor and was never seen again." (E. Griffiths, Gritstone Journal 1963)

Pre 1923	**Catwalk (pitch 2), Sandy Gully, Sandy Buttress Lower Slab**
	"Keep to the right where the holds attain the requisite standard of diminutiveness" - Cecil Wood 1923
	Twin Cracks,Lichen Crack ,Lichen Chimney, Chockstone Chimney
	"Some chockstones are 'deceivers ever'. This one belongs to that unfaithful species, and should be left alone." - Cecil Wood 1923
	Rylstone Crack
	Originally called Long Chimney
	All the above first ascents unknown but all recorded in Recent Developments on Gritstone by Fergus Graham published in 1923. The section writer for Rylstone and the Skipton area was Cecil Wood who presumably did the climbs about this time, with other founder members of the Gritstone Club.
Circa 1935	**Bowler's Chimney** Bill Bowler, Sidney and Arnold Waterfall.
	A green V chimney mentioned in Recent Developments could well have been this climb.
1935	**Dental Slab** Bill Bowler, Sidney and Arnold Waterfall.
	A potholing ladder and trenching tools were used for cleaning.
1935	**Falcon Crack** Sidney and Arnold Waterfall, Bill Bowler.
Pre 1950	**Lower Traverse, Balance Crack** Unknown
	Monkey Corner, Cave Face, Chimney Slabs Rt. 1 & 2, Matterhorn Ridge, Flake Chimney, Up And Over, V Crack, Bird's Nest Crack, The Niche, Three Step Buttress Unknown
	Probably all of the above were the work of the Craven Pothole Club, some by Bill Bowler and the Waterfall brothers between 1933 and 1939 and the remainder were probably by Brian Hartley, John Gott, Andy Anderson and John Wilson between 1945 and 1949.
1950	**Castrol (pitch 1)** Tom Cranfield, Alfie Beanland
1952	**Secretary's Slab** Dennis Gray, Robert Sowden
18.8.52	**Rylstone Wall** Barry Cliff, Jim Rennie
June 1955	**Trowel Face** Allan Austin, Brian Evans, Doug Verity
11.12.55	**Persistence** Allan Austin, Brian Evans, Doug Verity
30.3.58	**Castrol (pitches 2&3)** Allan Austin, Brian Evans
30.3.58	**Trowel Face (alt start)** Allan Austin
13.3.65	**Monument Crack** Allan Austin, Jimmy Fullalove
20.3.65	**The Grunt** Dave Berry (unseconded)
20.3.65	**Loiner** Dave Berry, Colin Ellis
20.3.65	**Catwalk (pitch 1)** Frank Wilkinson
20.3.65	**Off Balance, Rylstone Wall Direct, Impending Arrival, Labour Pains**
	The above 7 routes were done by a YMC team comprising Dave Berry, Frank Wilkinson, Colin Ellis, Dave Barnett, Graham and Roger Mackintosh, John Young, Tony Norton (Uncle Tom Cobley and all). Unfortunately they kept no detailed records. The last two only being named and written up in 1988.
C. 1965	**Distant Gem** Tony Barley (solo)
Pre 1969	**Crossover, Forgotten Friends** Unknown
17.5.70	**Hanging Cracks** Frank Wilkinson, Dave Bradley
17.5.70	**Keep Left** Frank Wilkinson, Steve Wood
Summer 1970	**Sword Dance** Pete Heys, Dennis Bullcock
5.12.70	**The Definitive Gritstone Chimney** Joe Brown
	An obvious problem, undoubtedly done before. However, on this wet and wintry occasion, a large Rock & Ice Dinner team all failed to follow.
1.8.71	**Extraction, Freebooter** Tony Barley, Tony Roche, Robin Brown
20.7.72	**Puss Puss** Greg Tough
22.8.72	**Terminus** Ken Wood, John Harwood
18.8.73	**After Eight** Pete Kitson, John Syrett
	Both solo! The pair slept below the Overhang Buttress and climbed the route when they awoke, just "after eight" a.m.

Circa 1977	**Whiskers, Midget Gem** Ron Fawcett	

Circa 1977   **Whiskers, Midget Gem**   Ron Fawcett

10.5.78   **Crazy Diamond**   John Eastham, Geoff and John Myers

5.8.79   **Laughing Gas**   Bob Larkin, John Reeve (both solo)
This may have been pre-dated slightly by Brian Swales and Ian Dobson who used a more direct start, and the name Incisor.

5.8.79   **Dead Kennedys**   Bob Larkin, John Reeve (both solo)
Two variation finishes soloed by Brian Swales on May 11th 1981, both allegedly to the left of the original?

5.8.79   **Pickpocket**   Bob Larkin, John Reeve
as Stiff Little Fingers - The wrong name and credits have mistakenly appeared in the last two guides. The name has been retained - the credit rectified.

Summer 1980   **Double Crack, Forgotten**   Martin Ryder, Roger Macintosh, Mike Gill

12.5.81   **G.T.X.**   Brian Swales, Ian Welsh

Summer 1986   **Nobular Structure, Marine Who Has No Friends**   Greg Rimmer, Chris Riley

6.4.88   **England Expects, Half Nelson**   Dave and David Musgrove
Grouseland, Highlord   Dave and Dave Musgrove

11.4.88   **False Teeth, Beginner's Chimney, Anonymous Cross**   Dave Musgrove (solo)

11.4.88   **Remembered**   David and Dave Musgrove

11.4.88   **Moorland Memories**   Dave and David Musgrove

13.4.88   **Yellow Badge of Faith, Rib of Gold**   Bob Larkin, Mike Haffner
Undoubtedly done before.

17.4.88   **Frankie Comes To Rylstone**   Frank Wilkinson, Dave Musgrove
Wilkinson returned after a gap of 18 years to renew his acquaintance with the crag and straighten out Hanging Cracks which he pioneered in 1970.

17.4.88   **Bad Boys, Sundowner**   Dave Musgrove, Frank Wilkinson

17.4.88   **Angry Woman**   Frank Wilkinson, Dave Musgrove
After a cold windy day, a calm sunny evening tempted the team to linger and get into hot water from an angry wife stranded in Skipton.

20.4.88   **High Flying Adored Undercarriage High Bark Crack Beginner's Bulge, Sunhill Slab**   Dave Musgrove (solo)
Most of these probably done before. Sidney Waterfall remembered climbing on this outcrop during the 1930s.

20.4.88   **Wall of the Evening Plight**   Frank Wilkinson, Dave Musgrove
A similar line was climbed by G. Edwards in 1985 and called Styleron Wall.

20.4.88   **The Artful Dodger**   Dave Musgrove, Frank Wilkinson
An escape from what later became Tasslehof Burrfoot.

22.4.88   **England Expects (Direct Start)**   Dave Musgrove

5.5.88   **Tasslehof Burrfoot**   Dave Musgrove, Frank Wilkinson

5.5.88   **Pocket Battleship**   Dave Musgrove, Frank Wilkinson
Only completed at dusk - after two falls - with a last-ditch "slap in the dark".

15.5.88   **Full Nelson**   Dave Musgrove, Mike Butler

15.5.88   **Kiss Me Hardy**   Dave Musgrove, Mike Butler, Christine Walker, Keith Bostrom.

18.5.88   **Baldrick**   Dave Musgrove, Dick Dodgson

18.5.88   **I Have A Cunning Plan, Beached Whale**   Dave Musgrove, Graham Arthur

18.5.88   **Never Climb With Guidebook Writers**   Graham Arthur, Dave Musgrove

2.6.88   **Pipeline**   Dave Musgrove (solo)

11.6.88   **Full Frontal**   Dave Musgrove (solo)

11.6.88   **Orbital Highway**   Frank Wilkinson, David Musgrove, Tony Barley

11.6.88   **Solo Games**   Frank Wilkinson (solo)

26.6.88   **Face Savour**   Dave Musgrove, Frank Wilkinson

26.6.88   **For My Next Trick**   Dave Musgrove (solo)

9.7.88   **The White Doe, Tower Of High Sorcery**   Dave Musgrove, Keith Bostrom

9.7.88   **Moorland Apparition, Memorial Wall**   Dave Musgrove (solo)

13.7.88   **Pancake Slab, Rainbow Sunset, Starlight Express**   Dave Musgrove (solo)
Pancake Slab probably done before.

27.8.88	**Impending Gloom** Frank Wilkinson, Dave Musgrove	

27.8.88   **Impending Gloom**   Frank Wilkinson, Dave Musgrove
Musgrove had bouldered out the lower wall on a previous visit.

27.8.88   **The Hot Line**   Dave Musgrove, Frank Wilkinson
This was climbed by Bob Larkin in April 1988 using high side runners, but may in fact have been climbed in 1981 by Brian Swales who soloed 2 variation finishes to Dead Kennedys but described them both as being to the left of the thin crack - he's not so sure now!

27.8.88   **Senator's Saunter, Little Peach**   Frank Wilkinson, Dave Musgrove

3.9.88   **No Man's Land**   Dave Musgrove, Jim Worthington, Eric Winfield

         Old Pals   Jim Worthington, Dave Musgrove, Eric Winfield

18.9.88   **Artist's Impression**   Dave Musgrove, Eric Rhodes
Eric drew all the diagrams for the 1989 guide

18.9.88   **Yet Another Hillside Attraction**   Dave Musgrove, Eric Rhodes

16.11.88   **Autumn Odyssey**   Frank Wilkinson, Dave Musgrove

16.11.88   **Final Fling, Little Pillar**   Dave Musgrove, Frank Wilkinson
Theses had almost certainly been done before

27.11.88   **Emily Norton, Poetry in Motion, Bondi Bitch, Surfer's Paradise**   Paul Greenland

27.5.89   **End of the Line, The Eyes Have It**   Graham Desroy (solo)

27.5.89   **Bare Faced Streak**   Graham Desroy, Dave Musgrove

27.5.89   **Slip Slidin' Away**   Dave Musgrove (solo)

14.9.89   **Heart Beat City**   Dave Pegg (solo)
One of the most serious gritstone climbs in the country.

11.5.91   **The Glass Slipper**   Dave (Snr. & Jnr.) Musgrove
This was young Dave's 111th route of the day as part of a sponsored marathon.

1991   **Misty Moo**   Peter Keen, Alan Boardman

4.10.92   **The Verge Of Tranquillity**   Julian Lines
Direct finish, Dave Musgrove Jnr. 5.10.96

9.5.93   **Living On A Tarot Reading**   Julian Lines (solo)

Sept 1993   **Poke And Hope**   Julian Lines (solo)

3.7.94   **Veteran**   Frank Booth, Sid Hall

Autumn 1995   **The Cocoa Team Special**   Tim Clifford (solo)
A long sought after problem, on this occasion Robin Barker cracked the crux sequence first but fell from the jamming crack above! Climbed in 1984 with the aid of a human pyramid.

16.6.96   **Little Gem**   Tony Marr, Mike Tooke, Peter Shawcross

14.9.96   **O'il Be Hanged**   Nigel Baker, Dave Musgrove

5.10.96   **Ghost Road, Wordsworth Fail Me**   Dave Musgrove Jnr. (solo)

3.6.97   **How Fast Dad**   Paul Wheeler, David Normanshire

3.6.97   **The Last Days Of May**   Paul Wheeler (unseconded)

August 1997   **Maple Syrup**   Andrew Watts (solo)

22.2.98   **February Climb**   Tony Marr, Frank Fitzgerald, Mike Tooke

22.2.98   **Little Horror**   Tony Marr (solo)

22.3.98   **The Full Monty, Short And Sweet**   Tony Marr, Mike Tooke

3.5.98   **Trespasser**   Tony Marr (solo)

3.8.98   **President's Prologue**   Tony Marr (solo)

SCOUT SCAR

Climbing here dates back well over 50 years and many of the early Widdop pioneers climbed the most obvious lines. The Grey Buttress Route had been led by 1969 but no records can be traced. The only recent claims came in 1985 from John Belbin, John Ward and Keith Greenwood who believed their ascents of **J & K** and **J & K Wall** to be new.

SCOUT HUT CRAG

All first ascents by combinations of Neil Herbert, Terry Holmes, Keith McGregor, Roy Healey and Derek Hargreaves during May 1996

SHARPHAW

Climbed on since the 1930s by Jim Walton and Sydney Waterfall and no doubt before, and many times after, by others but nothing was recorded until 1990.

11.11.90	**Fall Off Like A Grape** Robin Fuller (solo)	
24.3.96	**Right Hand Crack, Green Groove, Cave Chimney** Dave Musgrove (snr.) (solo)	
24.3.96	**Dave's Wall** Dave and David Musgrove (solo)	
	Later claimed and named Dave's Wall by Dave Barton. Though it had probably been done years before the name now seems appropriate.	
24.3.96	**Young Dave's Wall** Dave Musgrove (jnr.) (solo)	
Feb 97	**Showin Fagin, Embryonic Womb Walk, Problem Wall** Dave Barton (solo)	
Feb 97	**Linear Negra, Getting The Horn** Mark Radtke (solo)	
Feb 97	**Aye-n-ard Crack** Mark Radtke, Dave Barton	
	The pair also soloed and named several other easier routes that day	
1.11.97	**Pendle's Nipper, Scoop** Brian Swales (solo)	
	Plus several Diffs and Mild Severes all believed to have been climbed before.	

SHIPLEY GLEN

The history of climbing at the Glen is poorly documented, problems have tended to develop over the years by a process of elimination rather than a single push by a particular person. Only a few first ascent claims are documented, often these are outdated or of dubious validity. The author offers the following to stimulate discussion rather than as a definitive history.

Circa 1922	Eric Griffiths recalled that the founder members of The Gritstone Club trained here.
Pre-1940	A long lost guide published by the Theakston brothers in the late forties listed about thirty routes and probably covered many of the problems up to 4a/4b.
1940-1950	**Fearnought, Jamcrack, Step-up, Right-hand Variant, Prow** and **Kestrel Crack** Arthur Dolphin and friends.
	Details are vague and many more were probably climbed by this team.
1950-1960	**Tiger Wall, Austin's Hangover, Green Death, Phantom Rib, By-pass, Lurch, Blitzen** Allan Austin,
1952	**Kia Ora Wall** Dennis Gray
	*Later pegged by Ian Clough and renamed **Piton Rib**.*
Late 1950s	Gray, Clough and Ken Wood were very active at Shipley during the late 50s and early 60s and probably accounted for many first ascents which were never recorded.
Circa 1960	**Nobbler** and **Ken's Arete** Ken Wood
The 1970s	**Good Golly, Manson's Must & Wall, Daz, Omo, Millstone Grip** Al Manson
1975	**Mike's Mantel** Mike Hammill
1976	**Amalgam, Echinococcus, Hammill's Horror, Red Baron** Mike Hammill
	The roof start to Red Baron by Jason Myers 1996.
1980	**Brush Off, Nobbler Direct, Sleighride** Mike Hammill
1982	The 1982 guide book at last identified 103 individual routes and problems named and collated by Mike Hammill
1983	**Phil's Wall** Phil Davidson
	An on-sight solo of a route locals had been trying for weeks.

Mar 1984   **Millstone Grit**   Pete Gomersall - another on-sight solo.
1985   **Tweedledee**   Chris Sowden, Tony Burnell
1985   **Tweedledum**   Tony Burnell, Chris Sowden
1986   **Dreadnought**   Bill Turner

SIMON'S SEAT

Circa 1895   **Victorian Climb**   Unknown
Pre-1920   **Hidden Chimney, Real Chimney, Pothole Chimney, Square Chimney, North Gully**   Unknown
Mid-1930s   **Straight Crack, Corner Crack, Arete Wall, Flake Crack, Layback Crack, Chockstone Chimney**   Arnold and Sidney Waterfall, Bill Bowler (varied leads)
7.8.43   **Beelzebub Crack** and several other routes   Arthur Dolphin, John Cook
Sadly, it is impossible to pinpoint these climbs.
1949   **Chimney Wall**   Sidney Waterfall, W.J. Anderson
High Nose Traverse   Sidney Waterfall, W.J. Anderson
1.3.58   **Winter Finish**   Allan Austin, Miss Jennifer Ruffe, Miss Wilby Newton.
Inaccessible Crack   Allan Austin
30.8.58   **Turret Crack**   Allan Austin, Frank Spence, Brian Evans
Originally called Antimacassar. Frank Spence fell down the hillside from the top of the crack while attempting the first ascent. He survived to lead the top pitch after Austin mastered the crack.
Clappers Crack   Allan Austin
Arete Direct   Allan Austin, Brian Evans, Frank Spence
This arete had been top-roped from pre-1923, but from a much higher traverse line. Originally known as Traverse and Arete.
Low Nose Crack   Allan Austin, Brian Evans, Frank Spence
Low Nose Traverse   Brian Evans, Allan Austin, Frank Spence
Top-roped in 1949 by Sidney Waterfall.
1958   **Simple Simon**   Frank Spence
17.7.60   **Y Front**   Brian Evans, A. Evans
23.7.60   **Outside Finish**   Allan Austin
July 1961   **North Gully Buttress**   Brian Evans, L. Howarth
18.9.71   **Slant**   Tony Barley, Tony Roche
Gymkhana   Tony Barley, Tony Roche
Open Face   Tony Barley, Tony Roche
April 1973   **Amen**   Tony Barley, Robin Barley
June 1975   **Baggin's Variation**   Tony Barley, Robin Barley
Azimuth   Tony Barley, Robin Barley
A nut was used for aid to climb the overhang.
7.5.78   **A Question of Balance**   John Eastham, Geoff Myers, J. Myers
Beaky   John Eastham, Geoff Myers, J. Myers
Autumn 78   **The Naked Edge**   Jerry Peel
17.6.84   **Blind Alley**   Tony Marr, K. Jackson, Paul Ingham
26.4.87   **Another Question**   John Eastham, Geoff Myers
And Others   John Eastham, Geoff Myers
15.5.88   **The Gunner**   John Eastham, Geoff Myers, R. Pendleton
July 1988   **Gentleman's Support**   John Byrne, Peter Pozman
9.8.88   **Finesse**   Derek Hargreaves, Andrew Lindley
9.8.88   **And She Was**   Derek Hargreaves (solo)
31.12.89   **Out With The Old**   Andy Say (solo)
1.8.93   **Dino-Mania**   Dave Musgrove (Jnr)
(soloed after top-rope practice)
23.9.95   **I'll Bet She Does, Chunky Chicken**   Dave Musgrove (jnr) (solo)
23.9.95   **The Egg, of Course**   Julian Cooper, Dave and Dave Musgrove
23.9.95   **Blinkers Rib**   Dave (Snr) & Dave (jnr) Musgrove
23.9.95   **Grumpy's Crack**   Dave Musgrove (Snr) (solo)

20.4.97	**Dog Lead**	Johnny 'the dog' Cutliffe, Mick Darfield
Sept 1997	**Paws For Thought**	Johnny Cutliffe
June 1998	**Flirtin' Cos I'm Hurtin'**	Derek Hargreaves, Matt Troillet
27.6.98	**Hair Of The Dog**	John Cutliffe, Mick Darfield, John Phoden
27.6.98	**Posh Spice etc.**	John Phoden, Mick Darfield and John Cutliffe
July 1998	**A life Less Ordinary**	Matt Troillett (solo)
July 1998	**Shush Popeye**	Derek Hargreaves, Ian Farnsworth

SLIPSTONES

1957 **Heather Crack, Roofed Corner, Staircase, Easy Groove, Edge Route, Roofed Chimney, Awkward Finish, Staircase Mantle, Picnic Wall.**

1958 **Little Corner, Overhanging Crack, Left Edge, Shine On, Dark Cleft, Left Arete, Right Arete, Halfway Chockstone, Central Bay Route, Moderator, Little Gully, Siamese Bridge, Pothole Chimney, Heather Wall, Pinnacle Chimney, Ten Foot Moderate, Two Chockstones, Right Overhang, Stomach Traverse, Ten Foot Slab, Chockstone Pull Up, Wedge Down Crack (down climbed only)**
Attributed to Martyn Berry with lads from Pollington Borstal

July 1959 **Slanting Flake** Geoff Milburn

Oct 1960 **Not So Tight Chimney, Mantelshelf Crack, Old Corner, Petch's Groove, Barnley Crack, Ulfers Crack, Wall Climb, Chockstone Overhang, Fuser, Left Wall, Christopher Robin, Yaud Wall, Girgle, Fearby, Jug Handle Pull Up, Double Mantelshelf, Hand Traverse, Left Wall, Curving Crack, Tommy's Dilemma, Gypsy Wham** Geoff Milburn, Peter Martin

April 1964 **Undercut Double Crack, Mantelshelf Wall, Twenty Foot Crack, Tranmire Arete, Mantle On, Groove On, Undercut Flake & Direct Start**
The above 6 routes were climbed by various members of the Cleveland Mountaineering Club during a weekend meet.
~~**Sowden, Witton Wall** Mike Railton (solo)~~

July 1964 **Escalator** Tony Marr, Eric Marr
Tony had just started an apprenticeship with a lift manufacturer, hence the name.
Original Route Tony Marr, Eric Marr
Marr's Route Eric Marr

Easter 1965 **Hole in the Wall, Agrete, Agra** Tony Marr, Eric Marr
Only the first wall was climbed at this time.
Stainthorpe's Wall Variation Start Tony Marr
Climbed as a problem before the "wall" was ascended in 1980.

May 1965 **Tiptoe, Tea Party Slab, Question of Balance, Right Edge** Tony Marr, Eric Marr, Ken Jackson

June 1966 **Zoom, Barnley Wall, Diagonal, Overhanging Arete** Steve Wilson

1967 **Block Arete** Steve Wilson

1968 **Cold Wall, Beldin** Ken Jackson, Tony Marr
Jenny Binks Wall Unknown - Many Claims
Trumps, Trumps Right-hand Ken Jackson, Tony Marr

1969 **Gollinglith** Steve Wilson (solo)
A typical "Wilson" problem, steep and strenuous. Unfortunately we will never know how talented Steve would be as an abseiling accident a few months later cruelly ended his climbing career.

1970 **Flaky Wall** Tony Marr

Early 1970's **Aces High** Unknown, many claims

Mid 1970's **Bratt Pack, Play-A-Long, Wild Thing** Andrew Webb

April 1975 **Beldin Direct** Alan Taylor, Tony Marr, Ken Jackson

July 1976 **Layby** Alan Taylor
Taylor produces the hardest problem on the crag at that time.

Spring 1977 **North Wall** Alan Taylor

1978	**Ellingstring** Ron Kenyon, Stewart Wilson
	Climbed whilst checking routes for Wilson's 1980 North of England Guide.
23.04.79	**Tilt** Tony Marr, Ken Jackson, Alan Taylor
06.05.79	**Happy Daze** Alan Taylor
07.09.80	**Tranmire Crack** Tony Marr
	Easy Pickings Alan Taylor, Tony Marr, Paul Ingham
	Agra Right Hand Paul Ingham, Tony Marr, Alan Taylor

Paul Ingham's first visit to the crag was unplanned; because of rain at Brimham. The team detoured to Slipstones on the way home. Ingham was not impressed as the crag came into view, "poxy little thing" he said, but on closer inspection and a guided tour his views were changed. In fact it was difficult to get him to leave, and the team returned on several consecutive weekends. The crag would never be the same again.

07.09.80	**Alan's Arete** Alan Taylor (solo)
	Squark's Arete, Right Arete Ian Dunn (solo)
	Right Arete, Goblin's Arete Tony Marr
04.10.80	**Leany Meany** Paul Ingham, Tony MacLean
05.10.80	**Agrete** Tony Marr, Paul Ingham, M Davison
	Marr adds an independent finish to his 1965 start.
	Rock On, Rock Off, All Off Paul Ingham
	Problem Traverse Tony Marr
12.10.80	**Ripper** Paul Ingham (solo)
	Taylor solved the start but Ingham claimed the prize!
	Right-Hand Twin Tony Marr (solo)
	Leaning Wall Alan Taylor (solo)
	Gymnast Tony Marr, Alan Taylor
	Stainthorpe's Wall Dave Stainthorpe (solo)
	For variation start see Easter 1965
15.03.81	**Beldin Variation Start** Paul Ingham (solo)
	Agra Direct Start Tony Marr
	Seven Up Paul Ingham, Tony Marr, Steve Brown
	Dennis in Darlo Steve Brown (solo)
	Rock On Left-hand Var Paul Ingham
07.02.82	**Friday 13th** Steve Brown (solo)
14.02.82	**Extremeties** Tony Marr (solo)
	Paul's Arete, Beta Blocker Paul Ingham (solo)
	Steve's Wall Steve Brown (solo)
	Space Truckin Ian Dunn, Steve Brown, Paul Ingham
	Impregnable Paul Ingham, Ian Dunn, Tony Marr, Steve Brown
	Get Nervous Ian Dunn, Paul Ingham
	High Level Traverse Paul Ingham, Ian Dunn (both solo)
17.04.82	**Atomic** Ian Dunn, Paul Ingham
	A bold and difficult climb, setting the standard for others to match
05.08.82	**Problem Wall** Paul Ingham, Alan Taylor
	Sowden Left Hand, Cummin's Route Paul Ingham (solo)
Sept 1982	**String Vest, Withering Heights, Steptoe** Steve Brown (solo)
	Steptoe, a much attempted problem finally succumbs
Oct 1982	**Welcome Wall, Stereo Android** Paul Ingham
28.11.82	**Micro Corner** Paul Ingham
	Another 'impossible' problem solved
	Problem Arete Tony Marr
4.12.82	**Wisecrack** Paul Ingham (solo)
	The hanging crack eventually falls
23.01.83	**Seven Up Variation Starts, Ripper Traverse** Paul Ingham (solo)
	Right Wall Tony Marr (solo)
June 1983	**Forever Young** Steve Brown, Dave Paul
	Sinbad, Killer Dave Paul (solo)
	Paul's two plums

13.11.83	**Brush Up** Paul Ingham	
	Centre Left Tony Marr	
20.11.83	**Sunday 20th, Strictly Personal, Bert Wells, Fascinationby, TimelessDivide**	
	Space Plucks Paul Ingham	
	Tony's Torment Tony Marr	
May 1984	**Barren Waste** Steve Brown	
	Dixon's Dilemma Nick Dixon	
28.06.84	**Low Level Traverse** Paul Ingham	

Started life as a winter training problem, but grew into a excellent technical exercise. Ingham's original grade - "quite hard 5c".

1985	**Layby Arete** Paul Ingham	

Ingham shows his mastery of levitation

	Davies Ramp Richard Davies	
	Little Baldy, Supple Wall, Sulky Little Boys Ian Cummins	

Supple Wall and Sulky Little Boys being two very difficult problems by Mr 'Steel Fingers'

1986	**West Face Eliminate** Steve Brown, Dave Paul	
1988	**Forever Onwards** Paul Ingham	
26.06.92	**Narrow Margin** Tony Marr, Linda Marr	
1994	**Twenty Something, DA's Route, Son of a Bitch** Steve Crow	
	Atomic Right Hand Hugh Harris, Ian Cummins	
28.08.94	**Simple Sally** Dave Slater	
15.1.95	**Flakeout Arete** Phillipe Osbourne	
	Breakwind Arete Phillipe Osbourne, David Maudsley	
26.03.95	**3.3 Meter Slab** Steve Crowe	
23.04 95	**All the Twos** Steve Crowe	

Another arm stretching addition

Spring 1996	**Little Arete** Tony Marr	
	Timeless Divide Variation Start Mick Gardiner	
19.01.97	**Shorty's Dilemma** Tony Marr	
26.01.97	**Frank's Wall** Frank Fitzgerald, Mike Tookes	
	Scratch and Go Tony Marr, Frank Fitzgerald, Mike Tooke	
02.02.97	**Wisecrack Direct Start** Mick Gardiner	

A much attempted problem succumbs

06.04.97	**Fiddlesticks** Tony Marr	
08.04.97	**Seven Up Direct Finish** Tony Marr	
25.01.98	**Face to Face** Tony Marr, Mike Tooke, Frank Fitzgerald, Peter Shawcross	
	Psyche Tony Marr	

STAINLAND QUARRY

18.7.97	**Chrisening, Chris's Crack** Chris Hall	
2.8.97	**Retreat** Andy Chapman (solo)	
8.3.98	**Old and Bold** David France (solo)	
18.4.98	**Nee** Tom Lawrence (unseconded)	
18.4.98	**One Point** Nathan Lawrence, Alex Lawrence	
19.6.98	**The Beginning** Mark Sturman	
19.6.98	**Tennis Ball** Jens McCartney	
23.6.98	**Rock Lob** Martyn Hirst	

and the direct finish

26.6.98	**Twin Cracks R.H.** Jens McCartney	
10.7.98	**Aracus** Martyn Hirst	
July 1998	**The Dane** Jens McCartney	
14.7.98	**Slave To The Dane** Martyn Hirst	
17.7.98	**Pigeon Corner** Jens McCartney	
17.7.98	**Hard Start, Left Route** Martyn Hirst	
21.7.98	**Jakes Flake** Mark Sturman	

24.7.98   **Cabbage**   Martyn Hirst
24.7.98   **Fairy Steps**   Jens McCartney

SYPELAND CRAGS

All named routes and problems soloed by Tony Barley between 1988 and 1996 except those below.

26.5.91   **Under The Awning**   Robin Barley
8.6.91   **Burglary With Intent**   Dave Musgrove (solo)
8.6.91   **Twiggy**   Tony Barley, Dave Musgrove
1996   **Swirrel Edge, What Happens Now**   Jerry Peel (solo)
1.6.96   **Agroan, Testicle, Tentacle, Gales**   Dave Musgrove (solo)
31.7.96   **Eeyore, Breaking Out, Drop The Dead Donkey, Itchy Chin**   Dave Musgrove (jnr.) (solo)

THRUSCROSS

July 1965   **Holland, Hannen &Cubitts; Compulsory Purchase, Stenislag, Flax Trade, Yarn Spinner**   Tony Barley (solo)
June 1973   **Cotton Reel**   Tony Barley (solo)
8.5.93   **Green Syke, High Lair**   Tony Barley (solo)
13.5.93   **Rattlin' Row, Capelshaw Beck**   Tony Barley
26.3.94   **Holy Trinity, Walk The Blondin**   Tony Barley (solo)
17.4.94   **Barking Up The Wrong Tree**   Tim Barley
28.4.94   **Heart Of Oak**   Tony Barley (solo)
27.5.94   **Dambuster**   Dave Musgrove (solo)
7.6.94   **Dam It All**   Tony Barley (solo)
7.6.94   **Strong As An Oak, Heycorn, Cracklin' Crease, Laughter Lines**   Jerry Peel (solo)
11.6.94   **Right Eye**   Mark Radtke (solo)
1.6.95   **Rising Of The Sap**   Tony Barley (solo)

In all around 100 problems have been developed here by Tony Barley in the last 30 years.

UPPER HULLAH STONES

17.6.70   **Peace**   Tony Barley, Anthony Roche
27.6.91   **By The Birch**   Tony Barley (solo)
28.6.91   **Solitude**   Tony Barley (Unseconded)
28.6.91   **Mother Superior, Henry The Eighth**   Tony Barley (solo)
28.6.91   **Cardinal Wolesly**   Tim &Tony Barley
28.6.91   **Wonderbar**   Tony & Tim Barley
15.7.91   **Mitre**   Tony Barley (solo)
27.7.91   **Chalice**   Tony Barley (solo)
28.6.93   **Too Gnarly For Barley**   Dave (jnr) & Dave Musgrove & Tony Barley
          After years of failure Tony offered the lead of the best line on the crag to young Dave - He was pleased with the route but not so sure about the name!
28.6.93   **Student Games**   Dave Musgrove (jnr) (solo)

WIDDOP

Circa 1928   **Cave Crack**   Maurice Linnel, Herbert Hartley
Circa 1928   **Purgatory Chimney**   Maurice Linnel, Herbert Hartley
          "The first few feet are particularly strenuous and many people will need to remove as much clothing as possible. It is the lean man's privilege." - A.E.

Chisman 1929.

Circa 1929 **The Original Route**   Herbert Hartley, Maurice Linnel
On an early attempt the party were perplexed by the choice of finishes and resorted to abseil.

Circa 1929 **Krypton Route, The Corbel**   Herbert Hartley, Maurice Linnel

Circa 1936 **Wrinkled Wall, Slime Chimney**   Allan Allsop, Arthur Birtwistle
The direct start to the latter, a very hard problem, was added later but certainly prior to 1951.

Circa 1936 **Birtwistle's Crack, Celebrity Buttress**   Arthur Birtwistle, Allan Allsop

Circa 1939 **Libel**   David Jackson

Circa 1939 **Centipede**   Frank and Hartley Simpson
This was added to the Corbel to create two of the Three Cs. The origin of the third, Cascara Wall, remains unknown.

1946   **Demon Corner**   Allan Allsop
The final link of The Links Climb.

1947   **Felicity**   J. Greaves

1948   **Krypton Eliminate**   Allan Allsop

28.6.48   **The Flake Direct**   Arthur Dolphin, John Lockwood, Don Hopkins
The crag's first extreme - but apparently nothing out of the ordinary for this new team of hard men. John Lockwood said in 1989 "I don't remember it, we just followed Arthur but he didn't always tell us we were doing a new route. It wasn't important to most of us, but Arthur logged everything. If his diary says I was there, it'll be right."

Circa 1948 **The Artificial Route**
Also known as the Guinea Pig Direct and falsely credited to Jack Umpleby for many years, the true culprit has only recently been revealed.

Pre-1951 **Curving Crack**   Unknown

Pre-1951 **Wrinkled Wall Direct**   Unknown

Pre-1951 **Oblique Crack**   Unknown

Pre-1951 **Zig-Zag**   Unknown

Pre-1951 **Limpet**   Unknown
Possibly all of the above were the work of Allsop and the Manchester University M.C. in the pre-war years.

Circa 1952 **Alibi**   Neville Drasdo
Thought to be the first lead. The route was reported as a regular top-rope course in the 1951 guide.

Circa 1955 **Ceiling Crack**   Don Whillans, Albert (The Muscle) Ashworth
A spectacular roof typical of the early Whillans on grit. The grade was also typical - VS!

Pre 1957 **Umpleby's Arete**   Jack Umpleby
*Several other boulder problems were recorded in the guides during the 1950s - **Hargreaves Crack** presumably being credited to A.B. Hargreaves.*

14.5.74   **Fever, Neptune, Argon**   Allan Austin, Rod Valentine
Almost 20 years had elapsed since the last new route at Widdop and then Austin added three in one evening!

Circa 1974 **30 Seconds Over Winterland**   Mike Hammill, Allan Austin, Rod Valentine
This was from the right-hand start. Probably done the same evening as the previous routes. Hammill thought the route was only HVS, in fact he failed on Flake Direct the same evening. The direct start, as now described, by Jerry Peel in 1996

1977   **Piton Crack, Afternoon Delight**   Jerry Peel, Paul Hartley

May 1983 **Purgatory Problem**   Martin Atkinson , Derek Hargreaves
Direct finish by Dougie Hall 1988.

Apr 1984 **Swift and Sure**   Jerry Peel, Terry Birks

May 1984 **Cave Arete, Dessert, Brinkley Arete**   Jerry Peel

1985   **The Final Step**   Don Eastham
Added to Austin's Argon to provide a logical line.

1986	**The Nature Reserve, Wrinkley Arete** Derek Hargreaves
1986	**Stage Fright** Roy Healey
Sept 1988	**Scratch 'n' Sniff** Derek Hargreaves
1990	**Baby, Gene, Big Sid** John Belbin
1991	**Jo Jones** John Belbin
Spring 1995	**Reservoir Dogs** Robin Barker
31.5.95	**Pulp Friction** P. Dudgeon
11.9.95	**Retribution** Mark Halstead, Mick Forrest
1996	**Canine Fruitbat** Mark Radtke
Spring 1997	**Savage Earth** John Dunne
	*This became **Widdop Wall**, when John linked in a direct and totally*
	independent start early in 1998.
9.8.97	**The Krypton Factor** David Challenger, John Cramphorn
24.10.97	**Wickerwork Wall** John Belbin (solo)
1997	**A Trifle Sweet** David Challenger, John Cramphorn
17.5.98	**Shelley** David Challenger, John Cramphorn
24.5.98	**Philly Jo Jones** David Challenger, John Cramphorn

WINDGATE NICK

4.5.75	**Old Nick, Revival** Ken Wood (solo)
4.5.75	**Plaudit** Ken Wood (unseconded)
17.5.75	**Snowdrop** Ken Wood, A Gledhill
	Because there's <u>no</u> drop!
17.5.75	**Gled's Wall** A. Gledhill, Ken Wood
Pre 1989	**Tell Mick Ryan Nowt!** Chris Sowden
27.1.90	**Dinka people** Jon Biddle (solo)
6.2.90	**Pans Meadow** Jon Biddle
July 1996	**Fireman's Helmet** Malcolm Townsley

WOODHOUSE SCAR

Most of the climbs below 5a can be attributed to the first known explorers, Neville Sykes, John Hollins, David Kemp, John Shackleton, Miles Ruckledge and John Gaukroger.

Pre-1956	**Parete, Destra Fairy, Steps** John Gaukroger
	Ogion the Silent
	Spigolo
Pre-1960	**Piton Crack** Edwin Leggett
	(Before the flake came off; it was then 5b).
	Fandango, Woodhouse Eliminate, Baboon, **Bistro** Edwin Leggett
1971	**Clingen** John Sheard
1977	**To Boldly Go** Pete Livesey
	Minotaur Alan Stevenson
	Pinch Steve Foster
1978	**Nervous Shakedown** Ron Fawcett
1988	**Interface** Dave Cobly
23.5.90	**The Woolly Jumper Route** David Hanner

THE CLASSICS TICK LIST - The Three-Star Way To
Yorkshire's Gritstone Heaven (plus all routes E7 and above)

E9
Widdop Wall
Carmen Picasso

E8
Countdown To Disaster
The New Statesman
Loaded
Reservoir Dogs
Heartbeat City
Tender Homecoming

E7
Marrow Bone Jelly
Mind Bomb
Deathwatch
Strangeness
Birdsong
Snap Decision
Bottom Line
Vertical Speed
Eternal

E6
Life Begins At Forty
Fast Forward
Wasted Years
Armageddon
Desert Island Arete
The Great Flake
Gigglin' Crack
Milky Way
Slip 'n' Slide
A Step In The Light
   Green
On The Edge
The Blood On The
   Shamrock
Driveby

E5
Psycho
Adrenaline Rush
Ginny Greenteeth
Genesis
Swift And Sure

Dragonslayer
Left Wall
The Warriors Of
   Hunaman
Last Edge
30 Seconds Over
   Winterland
The Skryking

E4
High Noon
Quark
Stepmother Jag
Wellington Crack
Flirtin' Cos I'm Hurtin'
Grit Expectations
Grand Illusion
Thumper
Small Brown
The Dawning
Eavestone Crack
Werewolf
Wombling Wall
Mastermind
Needle Of Dreams

E3
The Big Greeny
Blind Valley
Wall Of Horrors
Eavestone Wall
Atomic
Western Front
I'll Bet She Does
Jesus Loves America
The Naked Edge
Loogabarooga
Ron's Reach
Swingover
Forked Lightning Crack

E2
Layby Arete
Horse Gone Wonky
Scar
Gronff

The Creation
A Little Trouble
Joe Cool
Clingen
Caught In An Eddy
Black Wall Eliminate
Earl Buttress
Swinging Free
The Shelf
Pillar Front
A Question Of Balance
Black Chipper
Crazy Diamond
The Alamo
Poetry In Motion
Satire
Class Action

E1
Ripper
Frensis Direct
North West Girdle
Noon Day Ridge
The Thin Red Line
Squirrel Crack
Hovis
Pure Gold
Paul's Arete
Z Climb Eliminate
The Waster
Permutation Rib
Monument Crack
Finger Dancer
Striding Edge

HVS
Solitaire
Rabbit's Paw Wall
Demon Wall
Great Western
Birdlime Traverse
Wisecrack (Slipstones)
Minions Way
Transparent Wall
Agra

Jams To The Slaughter
The Sole
Pebble Groove
Wailing Wall
Zoom
Wedgwood
Beeline
Comet Wall
Bull's Crack
The Girdle (Hetchell)
North Wall Eliminate
Overhanging Groove
Angel's Wall
Umpleby's Arete
Mantel Fantastic

VS
Rough Wall
Artificial Route
Hatter's Groove
Frankland's Green
  Crack
Walewska
Thunder Crack

S Crack
Arete Direct
Joanna
Allan's Crack
Chevin Buttress
Hades (Baildon)
Birch Tree Wall
Pillar Rib
Illegitimate Crack
Earl Crack
Right-Hand Crack
Gladiator

MVS
Tiger Wall
Square Chimney &
  Whisky Crack
Long Climb

HS
Parsons' Chimney
Josephine
Red Pencil Direct
Epitaph

S
Spinnaker
Dental Slab
'A' Climb
Nose Climb
Red Pencil
Greensleeves
The Flake Climb

MS
Rolling Gate Buttress
Tranmire Arete
Cave Crack (Brandrith)

HVD
Long Chimney (Almscliff)

VD
Fluted Columns
Eastby Buttress

D
President's Slab
Long Chimney (Ilkley)

AFTERTHOUGHTS

ALMSCLIFF

49a Left Cheek 10m E3 P2
6a The upper bulge between Acetabulum and Rectum Rift from good pockets to poor slopers.
31.5.98 Pete Brown, James Allum

57a Remembrance Some Day 10m E4 P2
6b A left-hand variant to Forgotten Wall. From the break on Thompsons Traverse step left and climb up with difficulty just right of Traditional Climb. The upper section, via a large pocket, is easier but worthwhile.
August 1998 Paul Clarke.

78a Brown's Roof 8m E4 P2
6c The huge roof to the left of The Nose is climbed with great difficulty to a belly-bouncing, leg dangling finish. Two belayers help stop the swing.
18.10.98 Pete Brown, Stuart Purvis, Julian Simmons, Ritchie Allen, Phil Osborne

99a Pulpit Friction 8m E2 P2
5c The left edge of the front face of the Pulpit.
7.6.98 Pete Brown, Mike Green, Stuart Purvis

109a Tortoises And Hares 14m E3/4 P2
6a Climb the direct start to WASC to the niche, traverse right a few feet and ascend the wall above with a big move to gain two 2 obvious flutings and the break. Move left and up the wall with a tricky move, just right of the vertical finishing crack on WASC, and finish rightwards.
11.6.98 Pete Brown, Andy Turner, Dave Garner.

BRIMHAM ROCKS

103a Wasted Years 10m E6 P2
6c The wall and bulge between Minion's Way and Jokers Wall Crack via a blind flake to a hideously sloping finish.
14.9.98 Jerry Peel, Dave Barton

104a No Way Out 10m E3 P2
6a From the top of the first crack on Minion's Way step right to a thread and then make difficult moves up the arete to a slopey finish just right of the top corner.
17.7.98 Nigel Baker, Paul Clarke, Andy Kassyk

149a Tensile Strength 10m E1 P2
5b Climb Mild Steel to the ledge. Step left and slot yourself into the break below the arete. Attempt to stand up then climb the flake to good finishing holds.
17.7.98 Dave Musgrove, Nigel Baker, Paul Clarke

CROOKRISE

61a Slideshow 10m VS P2
4b From 3 metres left of Moulson's Climb pull onto a wide ledge and trend right across the wedged boulder. Cross Moulson's Climb to finish up a steep headwall.
May 1998 Brian Swales (solo)

64a Eggsplorer 8m VS P1
4c Climb the wall between Easter Crack and Crack Climb direct to a steep finish then under the capping boulder.
20.6.98 Brian Swales (solo)

85a Prints of Swales 10m E1 P2
6a The wall left of Buster Direct using both the arete and crimps on the face. At the ledge step right and climb up past a 'letterbox', trending left to finish.
22.7.98 Phillipe Osborne, Andy Gudgeon.

EARL CRAG

3a Sobieski's Winged Hussars 13m E4 P1   ★★
6a The most obvious arete in the quarry is climbed direct past 2 peg runners.
31.8.98 Mark Radtke (unseconded)

78a Cheeted 8m E6 P3
6b Climb directly through the lefthand side of the roof to join Tiger Traverse and finish direct.
29.9.98 Jerry Peel, Mark Radtke

A large slab at the bottom right (when looking north) of the boulder field, not far from a gate. It is not clearly visible from the more popular problems but its northern face provides 5 routes all around 9 metres long . The left arete is Hard V. Diff and then four lines to the right are all around MVS 4b but bold and unprotected. From left to right they are, **Nothing Arete, Molly, Big Time Sensuality, Survival Car and Leave The Biker** (the latter is a diagonal traverse from right to left).
May 1998 David Roberts (solo)

EASTBY CRAG

2a Apache 6m VS P2
4c Fifty metres left of Blue Max is an undercut block which looks like a face. Start below a thin hanging groove which is gained awkwardly The finish is somewhat easier.
8.7.98 Brian Swales (solo)

2b Renegade 7m MS P2
Twenty metres right of Apache is a slab capped by a 'sculpted boulder'. Climb this feature to a pocket over the top.
8.7.98 Brian Swales (solo)

9a The Experience Of Age 35m HVS   ★
A high level traverse of The Pillar Front and Padder Buttresses.
1. 15m Start to the left of Eastby Grooves and climb pleasant slabs diagonally rightwards to a point just below the top of Eastby Grooves.
2. 10m Climb down Eastby Grooves for 3 metres and traverse the wall rightwards under the overhang. Belay round the rib at the foot of a heather groove. Or, as a variant, hand traverse right direct from the belay.
3. 10m Climb the heathery groove and put a sling on a tree. Step down and traverse the upper Padder Slab in its middle, on pebbles, to finish up Whaup Edge.
2.7.98 Bob Larkin, Gill Peel

HEPTONSTALL QUARRY

68a Dogged Arete 12m E1 P2   ★★
5b Step off the block below Dog With Two Tails and climb the pleasant arete to the break, finishing at the notch.
Sept 1998 Tom Lawrence

69a Stranger In The Woods 11m   HVS   P2   ★
5a Start as for Pocket Wall but move left into the niche, thewn
move up diagonally leftwards to finish.
Sept 1998 Nathan Lawrence

70a Heather Wall 10m   VS
4c A line parallel to Pocket Wall but just to its right.
Sept 1998 Nathan Lawrence (possibly done before)

71a Scarab Direct 10m   HVS
5a Essentially a straighter version of Scarab finishing left of the
arete.
Sept 1998 Nathan Lawrence (possibly done before)

SIMON'S SEAT

59a Fall From Grace 7m   E6   P3
6c The compelling wall to the left of Naked Edge provides a serious
and technical exercise.
Sept 1998 Matt Troilett, Roy Healey

WIDDOP

33a Gallon Drunk 10m   HVS
5b Climb directly up the left wall of Celebrity Buttress to finish at
the top of Stage Fright.
June 1998 Derek Hargreaves (solo)

36a Scuppered 6m   HVS
5b A short line of previously pegged pockets left of, and parallel to,
Piton Crack
July 1998 Derek Hargreaves (solo)

36b Forty Calorie Cocoa 8m   E3
6a A more serious line from the foot of Scuppered to the rounded
runnel just left of the finish of Piton Crack.
10.8.98 Derek Hargreaves (solo)

NEW ROUTES

All new route descriptions should be forwarded to the editor.

Dave Musgrove, 1 Lindley Farm Cottages, Cinder Lane,
Lindley, Nr. Otley LS21 2QN.

NEW ROUTES

NEW ROUTES

NEW ROUTES

NEW ROUTES

NEW ROUTES

NOTES

NOTES